Our Story

Our Story

Vivian L. Beeler

To order additional copies of this book, contact:
Xlibris Corporation
1-888-795-4274
www.Xlibris.com
Orders@Xlibris.com
102990

CONTENTS

Summer 2011

I dedicate this journal (book) to all the members of my family with *lots* and *lots* of *love* . . .

I've put off, walked around, made excuses for not putting these writings together for much too *long!* They were getting piled up and taking up far too much space. I kept saying, "I need an agent," to help me organize and put these writings together. I think the task scared me, and I really didn't know how to organize them so that they would make sense to those who read them. *Anyway,* it was really bothering me, and I think I finally realized that an agent was not going to walk through my front door. So one day, I just started laying the papers out all over the couch and chairs in my living room, trying to create some order with dates and decades. They are not in perfect order, but this is what I came up with. I've told you before these are memories and what I remember and of course time travel back and forth from my feelings and writings today to those of days gone by.

I do hope you will enjoy reading this, and perhaps it will make a little of history come alive for you. Perhaps I have opened my heart to much in some areas, but since I have lost my partner, with whom I could talk to about anything, I wrote it out on paper. I love every one of you so much and remember . . . I will always be a part of your DNA and in your heart!

Introduction to *the Story of Our Lives*

Vivian Louise Tallman Beeler: 1921—
William Joseph Beeler: 1919-2000

I'm going to start this "story" with some words and quotes. I love words, and I'm sure you will realize this by the time you finish reading *Our Story*.

Words are the voice of the heart. (—Yang)

I have opened my heart in a lot of these writings, hoping you will know me as a real person, also hoping you will feel I have left something worthwhile behind.

> Every one of us has his or her story. We think our lives are dull uninteresting, white bread bland, but it doesn't take much looking back to realize we all have a rich, weird, engaging past, peopled with heroes and eccentrics, encompassing moments of tragedy and moments of delight. There are times we need to plumb the past to make sense of the future. (*Writing to Heal the Soul*)

> Ancestors are citizens of the earth. They offer strength and guidance, wisdom and understanding to those who call them. They send messages and comfort. They are the keepers of all of the wisdom and knowledge that came before you. The underground universe of ancestors can ground and center you. (Dorothy Randall Gray)

I don't remember where I got this explanation of DNA, but it intrigued me:

> DNA . . . Traits, Habits, Looks of the people we are descended from. The unseeable made seen, in our children and our children's children. The connecting line that defines the constellation of family. Consistency . . . Continuity . . . Continuation.

To be a writer, you must remain a child in some areas and not grow up, you have to keep your imagination open. (Fannie Flagg)

Reminiscing helps us to put our lives in perspective. As we get older, we can see how each stage, every memory, fits into the grander scheme of things . . . My life has included sorrow as well as happiness. And all those emotions, all those bittersweet memories have created what I like to think of as a bright, colorful, firmly woven tapestry. (Barbara Johnson)

I have read somewhere.

That words woven together like the heft and warp of yarn can show the highs and lows of our lives and make a stunning tapestry.

I hope these words woven together over time and reminiscing will prove that we really did exist, felt all the human emotions, of love, happiness, and sadness *and* that we contributed something to this planet of ours. To all my family and friends reading this, remember life is a circle and we are all connected to one another. While we are all different and individual in our own way, we still have a connection to the past. Always keep your mind open to new ideas . . . keep learning. To my family, I cherish our love and support for one another. To my friends, I really care about you. Live every day and count your blessings Take care of one another and always be able to look in the mirror and say, "I did my best."

Enjoy *Our Story.*

EARLY YEARS

Our Story: For Our Kids and Grandkids

A *bit of history, genealogy, our lives and feelings through the years to* try and let you know . . . we were *real people.* We laughed, loved, cried, and experienced a lot of the same emotions you feel. Remember you have our genes! Hope you got the *good* ones!

Vivian Louise Tallman-Beeler was born on September 30, 1921, to Eva Violetta Manley-Tallman (b. May 16, 1899; d. June 13, 1991) and Ackerson Nickerson Tallman (b. November 18, 1894; d. January 1938).

Ackerson was born in the Tiffin, Ohio, area to Richard B. Tallman (b. March 24, 1860; d. January 15, 1915) and Phoebe Ann Fields (b. May 7, 1864; d. November 6, 1918). His dad died of heart problems and his mother during the flu epidemic in 1918. Ackerson was named after a favorite neighbor of his folks. When he was a small child, his parents moved to Michigan around the Howell, Williamsburg, area where his dad rented an 191 acre farm, His folks were farmers. His younger sister, Fanny, was born there. Later they moved to the Jackson, Michigan, area. He served in the army in France during World War I. From records that my cousin Clair (Bud) Tallman found in his genealogy search, my father joined the service and was sent to Fort Custer, Michigan, September 18, 1917. He was transferred overseas on February 16, 1918, and was there fighting in France until October 20, 1918. During that time, he survived a poison gas attack. But it did affect his later life (more on that later). He was discharged from the service in October 1919. He met Eva through mutual friends after his discharge. He had two brothers. One of them was our Uncle Clair, who was married to our Aunt Elma. They had two children: our cousin Bud (Clair) who I mentioned did this army research and his sister Jean. Uncle Clair and his family were very important in our lives, and I am still in contact with Bud and Jean. Uncle Clair was a policeman in Jackson. My dad's other brother, Uncle Henry, was always sort of considered the "black sheep" of the family. He took off for parts unknown, and we did not know him. In those days, Fanny was a popular name for girls, but as our aunt was growing up, she grew to hate that name and later had it legally changed to Frances. Aunt Fran was a wonderful aunt and very important in our lives also. More about her later. Ackerson was trained as an electrical technician.

He was a very popular person and well liked. He had lots of friends, loved to have fun, was a hard worker, and loved his family. He was a great dad.

Eva was one of eight children of Martha Ann Reed-Manley (b. December 7, 1869; d. January 4, 1963) and William Henry Manley (b. May 1, 1865; d. 1904). She was born in Canada as her parents were farmers there. Not to far from the Windsor area., her father, Henry, as he was called, was killed in a forest fire. I wish I had more information, but when people were alive to tell me, I wasn't thinking about how someday that information would be interesting and important in telling our story. Eva was very young at the time, so didn't remember much about it. All I know is that Grandma Manley came to the Big Rapids, Michigan, area shortly after as she had relatives in the area. I heard stories about her taking in washings and cleaning for other people just to keep her family together. She had lost one child when it was an infant, so there were seven children then. My mother, Eva, was number six. Aunt Leona and Uncle Henry were after her. As I am writing this in 1999, Aunt Leona is still living in Jackson, Michigan, and is ninety-six years old and still mentally all there. They seemed to do all right; everyone went to work as soon as they were old enough. I remember my mother talking about going to Ferris before it became a university and taking business courses. Now Erik is just finishing his four years there and graduating in criminal justice. He said he thought about walking around where his great-grandma had walked.

Grandma Manley lived with us when I was growing up. She was a lovely person and taught me so many, many things: sewing, cooking, housekeeping skills. My dad and she got along great, and he told her that she would always have a home with him. She thought the world of him too. More about her later as she was very important in my life.

Eva had a business education. Somehow over the years, they moved to the Jackson area, and she met my dad through mutual friends. They fell in love and married. Shortly after I was born in Foote Hospital in Jackson, they moved to Park Street in Dearborn, Michigan, and my dad started work for Ford Motor Company as an electrician. My sister, Evelyn, was born in May 1923.

As I remember, my childhood was a happy one. Again, we didn't have a lot of material things, but I don't remember missing anything. We always had food to eat. And like I was telling about Bill's family, family get-togethers were a big part of our lives. Radio programs were important: *One's Man's Family, Fibber McGee and Molly, The Lone Ranger, Jack Benny*. We would sit around the radio, like people watch TV today, and listen together. On special nights, we would have a dish of ice cream or bowl of popcorn. Again . . . simple pleasures. Bill and my childhood days were similar. Sunday school and Church were important too. One difference was that my family were Baptist and didn't drink, except when my dad's brother came to visit. My dad and Uncle Clair always found a bottle in the back of the cupboard (for medicinal purposes?) and they had a drink or two. In Bill's family, with a Swiss German background, beer and wine were very common. Bill's dad made them. So Bill taught me my bad habits. Ha!

William Henry Manley
11-23-1887
B. 5-1-1865
D. 1904

Martha Reed
B. 12-7-1869
D. JAN 1963

Phoebe Ann Fields
B. 4-7-1864
D. 11-6-1918

Richard Tallman
B. 3-24-1860
D. 11-15-1915

Eva violeta Manley
B. 5-16-1899
D. 6-13-1990

Ackerson Nickerson Tallman
B. // 1894
D. / 1938

Vivian Louise Tallman
B. 9-30-21

Alice Louise Beeler
B. 5-20-1951

Kathy Jean Beeler
B. 5-25-1947
D. 6-8-2000

Joseph Marus Beeler
B. Oct 16, 1865
D. Sept 22, 1904

Agnes Kaelin
B. Jan 1,1872
D. Oct 4,1899

9-8-97

William Sebastian Wirtz
B. Jan 29, 1874
D. Jan 14, 1964

Charlotte Louise Hartwick
B. Oct 25, 1878
D. Sept 15, 1942

Joseph Beeler
B. Feb 23, 1892
D. Oct 26, 1976

5-14-18

Marguerette Louise Wirtz
B. Mar 13, 1900
D. Apr 17, 1980

8-30-41

William Joseph Beeler
B. 10-20-1919
D. 4-14-2000

Susan Louise Beeler
B. 11-30-1942
D. 4-13-1943

Carol Ann Beeler
B. 4-18-1944

Barbara Sue Beeler
B. 5-20-1951
D. 10-15-2005

William Joseph Beeler Jr.
B. 7-1-1965

It's been so many years since my childhood it's hard to remember. A lot of water has gone over the dam. But as I said, my childhood was happy. I was always a quiet person. I didn't like arguments and was more of a loner. Ever since I can remember, I have liked to read. Give me a good story and a quiet corner and I was happy. I still am! I was a good student and liked school. I always took things too seriously and probably missed some fun out of life. Bill was much more outgoing and helped me with that to a degree. My sister Evelyn also was a more outgoing person and had more friends. Friends that I did have, I kept.

My mother worked at J. L. Hudson Co for years to help out. Remember, I was growing up during the Depression years. This is one reason why though that I became very close to my grandma Manley. As I said before, she taught me so many things. My dad liked to cook too. And between the two of them, they made cooking a fun thing for me. Evelyn could have cared less—same parents, but completely different personalities. We got along with one another though and I think, looking back, learned from one another. Having our grandmother living with us, we had a lot of company on weekends. Mother's sisters, husbands, and children would come over, and we had big family dinners with Aunt Freda and Uncle Lyle, Mona and Edward, Aunt Bea and Uncle Wilbur, Dorothy, and Pete and Harold. Uncle Henry married Arline when we were grown up enough to go to their wedding. Then Uncle Clair and Aunt Elma with Bud and Jean from Jackson would come down for a weekend, or we would go to Jackson. That was a *big* trip in those days. There were lots of summertime picnics at Cass Benton park. Also Aunt Freda and Uncle Lyle owned a lot at Woodland Beach on Lake Erie, and that was a full and fun day there.

When I was sixteen, my father died. That was a difficult time. I mentioned that he had been gassed in France during World War I. That caused Hodgkin's disease, and then he had a brain aneurysm. He was only forty-three. I remember some of the things about that day quite well. We were staying with my aunt Freda and uncle Lyle, as Mother was spending most of her time at the hospital. My aunt and uncle got the call that my dad was gone and told us. It really didn't seem real. It was a beautiful January day and the sun was setting. My aunt and uncle and cousins tried to be so nice to us, but the next few days seem to be foggy. Mother did not know how to drive, and we had to depend on our uncles for transportation. Getting a bit ahead of my story, soon after that my uncle Wilbur taught me to drive. I was sixteen, and you were not required to take driver's training, etc. So I was the chauffeur in our family for quite a while until my mother learned how to drive. But just between us, she never was a very good driver; she just did not have any confidence. I never liked to let any of my children go in the car with her. She was a wonderful grandma in every other way. I had planned on going to college. I wanted to be a teacher, but that changed everything. I had my senior year of high school yet and changed to a business course. I did graduate with honors in January 1939. I was seventeen. No one would hire me. "Come back when you are eighteen" was the story I heard everywhere. We live in a different world today. I finally got a job as a receptionist in a real estate office for $5.00 a week. Can you believe that? I gave my mother $2.50 and kept $2.50. You would be surprised on how far that went in those days. Remember, there were no fast-food restaurants in those days. How did we live? I can hear you asking.

Anyway, it was a lucky job for me because that's where I met Bill!

He came into the real estate office with his mother as they were looking for another house. While his mother was talking with the realtor, Bill was talking to me. We found out that we had both graduated from Fordson High, he in 1937. We had never met one another in school. We also found out that we both had been born in Jackson. Anyway, I told him I was going to night school for business courses, and he asked if he could walk me there. That's how it all started, and it has lasted for fifty-eight years so far.

Break in my story and break in my heart. I lost Bill on April 14, 2000, and seven weeks later we lost our daughter, Kathy, on June 8, 2000, My whole world has been turned upside down and inside out. I feel like I'm in a black hole spinning around and am going to break into a million pieces. Everyone tells me I'm strong, but I don't feel strong inside. I have to force myself to do things, and nothing seems to have any purpose or reason anymore. I'm trying to take Kathy's advice, "one day at a time," but sometimes it just seems to be too much. Nothing is "fun" anymore. The family says I'm important to them, and I do appreciate that, but . . .

July 9, 2000

I have been re-reading Leo Buscaglia's book *Love*. What life is all about! I came to a part that really connected with me at that time in my life. Norman Cousins wrote, "Hope is the beginning of plans. It gives men a destination, a sense of direction for getting there, and the energy to get started. It enlarges sensitivities. It gives proper values to feelings as well as to facts." His hope involves "a rekindling of human imagination—about life as a man might like it; about the full use of his intelligence to bring sanity and sensitivity to his world and to his art; about the importance of the individual; about his capacity for creating new institutions, discovering new approaches, sensing new possibilities."

Certainly, all this is true.

> *But love goes beyond hope. Hope is a beginning. Love is forever.*
> —*Love*

In a way that kind of explains to me how I feel. I've lost "hope," my sense of direction, a rudderless ship spinning around, going nowhere, and the energy to do something about it. I "hope" time will help me find myself . . . again. I do know I was loved, and I have wonderful memories of that, but right now I hurt.

August 25, 2000

Bear with me while I try to get my thoughts and memories together to continue our story. Remember, 1939 and 1940 were still Depression times, so Bill and my dating times were dependent on whether he could borrow his parents' car and how much things would cost. I do remember very vividly how we were falling in love and how much we wanted to be together. We spent a lot of time walking and at one another's houses. Also big bands were becoming very popular: Glenn Miller, Tommy Dorsey, Sammy Kaye, Artie Shaw, Freddy Martin, Charlie Barnett, Lawrence Welk (laugh if you want, but he played wonderful music to dance too). We went to the Graystone Ballroom in Detroit, and Walled Lake had a wonderful dance pavilion. We had some great times and always liked to dance. Also we went to the show once in a while. Like I said earlier, we did a lot of family things together and got to know one another's families. Bill proposed to me on Valentine's Day in 1941, and we planned an August wedding. He had got hired by Ford Motor Company, and I was working for Michigan Bell as an operator. In those days, you picked up the phone and asked the customer for the number you wanted, so I said "number please" and connected you to the party you wanted at a switchboard. Can you believe that? With the technology that we have in today's world most young people seem to have cell phones growing out of their ears. Our parents thought we were a bit young but went along with our plans. I got my wedding dress at Hudson's for $125.00 with my mother working there; her discount helped, but we still thought that was a lot of money. It was moiré taffeta, sweetheart neckline, and had detachable long sleeves, leaving a puffed short sleeve. I thought it was beautiful. It turned out that August 30 was one of the hottest days we had had that summer, and I about died in that heavy taffeta, but it was in style!

Because Bill was much more involved and active in his church than I was in mine, we were married in the Lutheran Church. My mother was a little upset at first but went along with it. My sister, Evelyn, was maid of honor, and my cousin Mona was a bridesmaid. Our reception was back at our house on Orchard Street in Dearborn. We had a wedding cake and punch. Remember, my mother was widowed and we had no extra money. Bill's folks invited everyone to come to their house afterwards and had sandwiches and *beer!*

Then I changed into a brown crepe two-piece dress my grandmother had made for me, and I really thought I looked very grown-up. We spent our wedding night at the Book Cadillac Hotel in Detroit. It was "the hotel" at the time. Well, I'm not going into any graphic details as I don't think our children and grandchildren want to think about Grandma and Grandpa having "sex." I just would like you all to know that love and sex were not invented just in your generation. We had all the same feelings and emotions that are displayed so publicly in today's world. Let's just say that we did not get much sleep on our wedding night. It's probably hard to believe, but we grew up in an era where "good young people" did not have sex before marriage. That rule had been instilled in both of us. I have to admit it was difficult to follow; while there was some heavy petting, we did not follow through until we were married. Anyway, I think you will all agree that the physical side of "love" was an important part of Grandpa's and my marriage. along with respect for one another's opinions. We just had a three-day honeymoon, and hey, it worked. We went up to Traverse City and over by Lake Michigan and had a wonderful time. We had rented an upper flat on Pinehurst in Dearborn and came back to that. What fun! We thought we had the world by the tail and no one had ever been so much in love.

Bill was doing well in his apprenticeship in the tool room at Ford's, and I kept my job at the telephone company. There was good public transportation in those days, and we thought nothing of catching a bus or a streetcar to get to work. Then the middle of October, I started to hemorrhage, and Bill rushed me to the doctor's office. I was having a miscarriage and had a D and C. We grew up quite fast for a couple of young innocents and learned some lessons in birth control. I stayed with Grandma and Grandpa Beeler for a few days while I was recuperating. Grandma Beeler told her relatives that I had the flu. Just in case if she told them the truth, they would think we had had sex before we were married. That kind of ended my job at the telephone company. To be very honest, I loved being a homemaker. I loved practicing my cooking skills. Bill was on shift work, so that way I was always there when he came home. I had a sewing machine and was making things, curtains, and some of my own clothes. We had a group of friends our age, also newly married, and we got together with them for evenings of card games, etc. Also we were still going to dances and shows when we had the money. Eating meals out was a rare occasion. People did not spend money on eating in restaurants very often. It's so different in today's world.

I have mentioned how much I liked to read and how it has always been an important part of my life. Just before I met Bill, *Gone With the Wind* by Margaret Mitchell came out. I had never read a book that enthralled me and kept my interest like it did. I lived with those characters. Since then I have reread it three times over the years and each time have learned something more from it. The movie later on was enjoyable, but I don't think it had the same impact on me as the book. I have read hundreds of good stories since, but that one still sticks in my mind, I suppose partly because I was at a very impressionable age. I felt badly when Margaret Mitchell was killed by a car in downtown Atlanta a few years later. I wanted to read more from her.

Eva V. Manley-Tallman-Miller

On This Day in History: Tuesday, May 16, 1899

Top News Headlines This Week

> May 17: Victoria and Albert Museum foundation laid in England. May 18: World Goodwill Day, twenty-six nations meet in First Hague Peace Conference. May 24: First auto repair shop opens (Boston). May 25: 33rd Belmont Stakes, R. Clawson aboard Jean Beraud wins in 2:23. May 30: 24th Preakness: R. Clawson aboard half time wins in 1:47. May 31-June 5: Conference of Bloemfontein fails.

Top Songs for 1899

"O Sole Mio"
"Always"
"My Wild Irish Rose"
"Where the Sweet Magnolias Grow"
"Absent"
"The Girl I Loved in Sunny Tennessee"
"Heart of My Heart"
"She'll Be Comin' Round the Mountain"

1899 Prices

Bread:	$0.03/loaf
Milk:	$0.28/gal
House:	$4,200
Avg Income:	$635/yr
DOWAvg:	66

U.S. President: William McKinley
U.S. Vice President: Garrett A. Hobart

People Born on May 16

1928: Billy Martin baseball second baseman/manager (New York Yankees, Oakland A's)
1955: Debra Winger, Columbus, Ohio, actress (*An Officer and a Gentleman*)
1952: Pierce Brosnan, Navan, County Meath, Ireland, actor (*Remington Steele*, James Bond, *Golden Eye*)
1919: Liberace, West Allis, Wisconsin, pianist (*Liberace Show, Evil Chandell-Batman*)

Vivian Louise Tallman Beeler

On This Day in History: Friday, September 30, 1921

Top Headlines This Quarter

Herbert Hoover presides over a national conference on unemployment. A corollary to the mass of workers without jobs is the spread of violence, led by a revitalized Ku Klux Klan. *Tarzan of the Apes* opens on Broadway with lions, apes, and other jungle animals. Ellis Island to close Sundays due to number of immigrants being detained.

Top Songs for 1921

"Kitten on the Keys" by Zes Confrey
"Dear Old Southland" by Henry Creamer
"April Showers" by Bud G. Desytva
"Coat-Black mammy" by Laddie Cliff
"Make-believe" by Benny Davis
"Learn to Smile" by Otto Harbach
"Dapper Dan" by Lew Brown
"Ain't We Got Fun" by R. A. Whiting

1921 Prices

House	$7,109.00
Car	$500.00
Milk	$0.52
Gas	$0.10
Bread	$0.10
Postage Stamp	$0.02
Avg Income	$1,215.00

U.S. President: Warren Harding
U.S. Vice President: Gavin Coolidge

People Born on September 30

    Angie Dickinson: 1932
    Johnny Mathis: 1935
    Jody Poweh: 1943
    Marilyn McCoo: 1943

Fine Arts

    Art: Max Ernst painted *The Elephant Celebes*
    Film: Charlie Chaplin stars in *The Kid*
    Music: Irving Berlin, *First Of The Music Box Revues*

1921 Sports Headlines

    Behave Yourself wins Kentucky Derby with jockey C. Thompson. Tommy Wilson wins Indianapolis 500 with an average speed of 89.6 mph. NY Giants defeat Yankees to win world series. The Ottawa Senators win hockey's Stanley Cup for the second year straight.

Early Years: William Joseph Beeler

He was the first child of Marguerette Wirtz (b. 13, 1900; d. 5, 1980) and Joseph Beeler (born. 2, 1894; d. 1976). William was born on October 20, 1919, in Jackson, Michigan (10-26-1976)

Joseph Beeler had come over from Switzerland in 1915 when war clouds were gathering in Europe. The economy was bad in his country, and an uncle had asked him to come to the United States and try his luck there. It worked out very well. Joseph was twenty-one at the time. He was trained as a mechanic. He met Marguerette Wirtz through relatives; she was only fourteen at the time. She said after meeting Joe that she was going to marry him in a few years when she was old enough. And she did! They courted and married in 1918. Joseph worked at Kelsey-Hayes Wheel in Jackson until they transferred him to their Detroit plant. The family moved to Dearborn, Michigan, in 1932.

During those years, the family grew. LeRoy was born in July 1921. Joseph Jr. was born in July 1925. Their sister Marguerette was born in December 29, 1927.

Bill remembered a happy childhood revolving around hard work, family, grandparents, aunts, uncles, and cousins. Grandpa Wirtz was a master plumber, and he took Bill along with him on some of his jobs. Bill learned a lot from him, which came in handy over the years. Bill also told stories about his mother making donuts on a Saturday morning and him taking them to the neighbors in his wagon and selling them. Remember, money was tight, the Depression was raising its ugly head, and every little bit helped. In the summer, he also sold home-grown vegetables from his wagon with his brothers. Material things were hard to come by—family get-togethers, listening to the radio together with some popcorn, or a big treat like ice cream, Saturday afternoon movies, family picnics. Attending Church and Sunday School were important.

Actually Bill and I had very similar childhoods and upbringing. Perhaps that had helped to keep us together.

After the family moved to Dearborn, Robert was born in March 1933 during a *big* snowfall. Mother Marguerette was quite ill for a while. Pop, Father Joseph, could not take time off work—no work, no money, no food. Bill as the eldest stayed home from school (he was a good student) and took care of things. He learned to cook and clean and take care of baby Robert. Boy, did I luck out over the years because of that learning and training.

William Joseph Beeler

On This Day in History: Monday, October 20, 1919

Top Headlines This Quarter

The Communist Party is formed in Chicago, Illinois. Party motto is "workers of the world unite!" First members are mostly Russian. When 1117 of Boston's 1544 policemen go on strike, Governor Calvin Coolidge promptly hires new patrolmen.

Top Songs for 1919

"The Lamplit Hour" by Thomas Burke
"My Isle of Golden Dreams" by Gus Kahn
"Peggy" by Harry Williams
"Swanee" by Irving Caesar
"Letter Song" by William Lebaron
"Ask the Stars" by Frank Stammers
"Indian Summer" by Victor Herbert
"Dardanella" by Fred Fisher

1919 Prices

House	$5,626.00	
Car	$500.00	
Milk	$0.62	
Gas	$0.09	
Bread	$0.10	-
Postage Stamp	$0.03	-
Avg Income	$1,155.00	-
		-

U.S. President: Woodrow Wilson
U.S. Vice President: Thomas Marshall

People Born on October 20

Mickey Mantle—1931
Arlene Francis—1908
Art Buckwald—1925
Grandpa Jones—1913

Fine Arts

Art: Claude Monet painted *Nympheas*.
Film: *Madame Dubarry* and *The Devil's Passkey.*
Music: Harry Tierney, *Irene in New York.*

1919 Sports Headlines

Cincinnati beats Chicago five games to three to win the world series. J. Toftus rides Sir Barton to victory in Kentucky Derby. Howard Wilcox wins Indianapolis 500 averaging 88.1 mph. Sir Barton becomes first triple crown winner. Jack Dempsey becomes new heavyweight boxing champion.

Mom Beeler

On This Day in History: Tuesday, March 13, 1900

Marguerette Beeler Wirtz

Top Headlines This Quarter

> The Social Democratic Party holds its national convention in Indianapolis, Indiana, nominating Eugene V. Debs of Indiana for president. The Gold Standard Act is ratified by Congress. By Act of Congress, Hawaii is granted territorial standing in the U.S. Buffalo Bill Cody performs at New York's Madison Square Garden.

Top Songs for 1900

> "Creole Belle" by George Sidney
> "Violets" by Julian Fane
> "Ma Blushin' Rosie" by Edgar Smith
> "The Fatal Rose of Red" by Fred Helf
> "A Bird in a Gilded Cage" by A. Lamb
> "For Old Times Sake" by C. K. "Harris
> Strike Up the Band" by A. B. Sterling
> "Midnight Fire Alarm" by H. J. Lincoln

1900 Prices

House	$4,000.00
Car	$500.00
Milk	$0.30
Gas	$0.05
Bread	$0.03
Postage Stamp	$0.02
Avg Income	$637.00

U.S. President: William McKinley
U.S. Vice President: None

People Born on March 13

Deborah Raffin—1953
Neil Sedaka—1939
Wm. Bolger—1923

Fine Arts

Art: Renoir painted *Nude In The Sun*
Film: Director Georges Melies filmed *Cinderella*
Music: In Rome, Puccini wrote the opera *Tosca*

1900 Sports Headlines

Heavyweight Champ James Jeffries ko'd James Corbett in twenty-three rounds. The baseball world series starts in three years! Lieutenant Gibson wins Kentucky Derby with Jockey Boland. The Second Modern Olympic Games is dominated by fifty-five Americans. Navy defeats the army in Annual Football Game in Philadelphia.

Joseph Beeler: Born in Switzerland

On This Day in History: Tuesday, February 23, 1892

Top News Headlines This Week:

> February 23: First college student government established, Bryn Mawr, Pennsylvania. February 25: J. Palisa discovers Asteroid #324 Bamberga. February 25: James Barrie's *Walker London* premieres in London. February 29: Britain and US sign treaty on seal hunting in Bering Sea. March 3: First cattle tuberculosis test in United States made, Villa Nova, Pennsylvania. March 4: Max Wolf discovers Asteroid #325, Heidelberg.

Top Songs for 1892

> "My Sweetheart's the Man in the Moon"
> "The Bowery"
> "The Man That Broke the Bank at Monte Carlo"
> "Waltz of the Flowers"
> "After the Ball"
> "Daddy Wouldn't Buy Me a Bow-wow"
> "Daisy Bell"
> "The Sweetest Story Ever Told"

1892 Prices

Bread:	$0.03/loaf
Milk:	$0.18/gal
House:	$5,400
Avg Income:	$635/yr

U.S. President: Benjamin Harrison
U.S. Vice President: Levi P. Morton

People Born on February 23

1940 — Peter Fonda, actor: *Easy Rider, Lilith, Wild Angels, Trip*
1883 — Victor Fleming, Pasadena, California, director: *Wizard of Oz, Gone With the Wind*

Hot New Toys in 1892

    Ouija boards
    Ship Manifest

Manifests often extend across more than one page. Your passenger may be listed in this page or a few pages forward or back. To see other pages, click "previous" or "next." Note: Each page must be saved separately to Your Ellis Island File.

Kaiserin Augusta Victoria

    Associated Passenger: Beeler, Joseph
    Date of Arrival: August 24, 1912
    Port of Departure: Hamburg
    Line #: 0021
    Page: Previous

Manifest for *Kaiserin Augusta Victoria* Sailing from Hamburg

Name	Gender	Age	Married	Ethnicity	Place of
0001. Roesner Wilhelm	M	27y	S	Germany, German	Schweidn Germany
0002. Russwurm Cenci	F	21y	M	Germany, German	Brooklyn,
0003. Russwurm, Louis	M	1y	S	U.S., American	Brooklyn,
0004. Wischnalk, Olga	F	24y	S	Germany, German	Berlin
0005. Danner, Carl	M	16y	S	U.S. citizen	Anertswe Germany
0006. Danner, Frank	M	11y	S	U.S., American	Anertswe Germany
0007 Markus, Heldegard Hedwig	F	21y	S	Germany, German	Posen, GE

0008. Hollaender, Erich	M	29y	M	Germany, German	Berlin
0009. Schkolnik, Gides	F	38y	M	Austria, Hebrew	Gartowice
0010. Schkolnik, Reile	F	15y	S	Austria, Hebrew	Gartowice
0011. Schinek, Sophie	F	20y	S	Austria, German	Brattersd
0012. Ostendorf, Gertrud	F	11y	S	Germany, German	Stelfin, G
0013. Thoma, Else	F	14y	S	Germany, German	Nurnberg
0014. Bennischke, Friedrich	M	24y	S	Austria, German	Monasee,
0015. Bennischke, Klara	F	25y	S	Austria, German	Monasee,
0016. Quidenns, Grete	F	21y	S	Austria, German	Frendentt
0017. Bierig, Fanny	F	20y	S	Germany, German	Edelfinger
0018. Koch, Jacob	M	20y	S	Germany, German	New York
0019. Jmhof, Elise	F	39y	S	Germany, German	Mainz, Ge
0020. Rottenhasns, Joel	M	37y	M	Austria, Hebrew	New York
0021. Beeler, Joseph	M	20y	S	Switzerland, German	Freienbac Switzerland
0022. Lehmann, Rosine	F	20y	S	Germany, German	Oberflatt,
0023. Goldstein, Ludwig	M	23y	S	Germany, German	Berlin, Ge
0024. Albers, Father—Herm	F	19y	S	Germany, German	Groden,
0025. Montna, Kathe	F	25y	S	Germany, German	Dahme,?
0026. Rufenacht, Hermine	F	28y	S	Switzerland, German	Bischofsz? Switzerla?
0027. Rufenacht, Hermann	M	16y	S	Switzerland, German	Bischofsz? Switzerla?
0028. Schneider, Mary	F	30y	S	Germany, German	Munsten,
0029. Bargstaller, Marie	F	28y	S	Austria, German	Dresden,
0030. Banmann, Gosef	M	52y	S	Germany, German	Ralzruhe,

Associated Passenger	Date of Arrival	Port of Departure	Line#	Page
Beeler, Joseph	August 24,1912	Hamburg	0021	previ

Kaisirin Auguste Victoria

August 1912-24

LIST OR MANIFEST OF ALIEN PASSENGERS FOR THE UNITED

Required by the regulations of the Secretary of Commerce and Labor of the United States, under Act of Congress approved February 20, 1907, to be delivered

S. S. _Kais Aug. Victoria_ *sailing from* Hamburg _16 AUG 1912_ 19

...nna	Jule	21	f	...	2-946.449	12/30/4...		
...vig	Fanny	20	f/f	"	"	"	Germany	
...sh	Jacob	20	m/o	maka	"	"	"	
...rhof	Elise	39	f/f	none	"	"	"	
...tenkains	Joel	37	m/m	butcha	"	"	Austria...	
...lor	Joseph	20	m/s	mechanic	"	"	Switzerl...	
...mann	Rosine	20	f/s	none	"	"	Germany	
...stein	Ludwig	23	f/s	morcht	"	"	"	
...os	Emma	19	f/s	none	"	"	"	

VC-973-415

Jackson relatives, 1940-41: This is a separate but connected little story of when Bill and I were going together and first married. I have mentioned how family and family doings were an important part of both our growing up years. Anyway, these are some impressions and thoughts of meeting Bill's relatives in Jackson, Michigan.

Bill's grandparents lived on Seymore Street in Jackson. When I was first introduced to them, remember I was only eighteen and trying to make a good impression, I was very impressed with their house. They had a parlor and a living room. The parlor was kept quite dark and was only used for special company. Their kitchen had a trap door with steep steps that led down to a basement with just earth floor and walls. I had never seen anything like that. Bill's grandma always made homemade noodles for chicken soup, and they served big bowls of it for meals. To me, it seemed like more noodles than soup. Everyone loved the noodles. All his life, Bill liked noodles and chicken noodle soup, and no, I never did make homemade noodles. I remember the noodles drying over a metal laundry rack in their kitchen. I know they served other foods too, but that was what really stuck in my mind. Bill's grandpa was a master plumber. In fact, according to records in the Jackson papers, William Wirtz was the first licensed master plumber in the state of Michigan. That had to be back around 1914-15. I believe Carol has the article from the papers. When Bill was growing up he spent some summers with his grandparents, and his grandpa took him with him to his jobs. He taught Bill a lot about plumbing, and boy, did that knowledge come in handy for us! Bill saved us a lot of money over the years.

Bill also liked to tell about his grandpa letting him take his car and drive back to get a special tool or something. That was before Bill had his driver's license.

I remember meeting some of his other great-aunts and great-uncles—Aunt Eva and Uncle Henry. Uncle Henry had lost an arm in a railroad accident, but he did not let that stop him from doing most anything he wanted. Again, their house seemed dark and full of things, almost like a museum. Then there were Aunt Mae and Uncle Warren. Aunt Mae always had sour cream cookies when we visited and was very pleased when I asked her for the recipe. She gave it to me, and to this very day, they are one of our family's favorite cookie recipe. I will include this recipe along with those memories. Aunt Net and Uncle Barney were farmers, and when I first met them, Uncle Barney told Bill he was going to steal me away from him. Aunt Net had a corn cob pipe she smoked, and Uncle Barney didn't have many teeth, but they so nice, welcoming, and warm. Aunt Carrie and Uncle John were also there. Uncle John was the uncle who encouraged and sponsored Bill's father to come to America from Switzerland. I wish I knew how that connection was made. Again, it didn't seem important then. Then finally there were Aunt Lizzie and Uncle Herbert. Remember, those were all great-aunts and great-uncles, so to me at eighteen to nineteen years, they seemed really *old.* The women were sisters of Bill's grandma, Charlotte Hartwick Wirtz. Now I'm that age. Where did all those years go? We always had a good time when we visited in Jackson.

You know me and my liking for books. Bill's grandparents had a rounded front glass bookcase in their living room that I was fascinated with. The books were from the turn of the century, and from what I could browse, I sort of liked what I had heard about *The Perils of Pauline*-type of story. It was a hot romance at that time.

I guess I made a good impression on all of the relatives as they were always glad to see us. They would be very warm and welcoming and wanting to feed us.

In later years, we would make trips to Jackson to visit the relatives. We were quite close with Aunt Carrie and Uncle John's daughter, Wilhelmena (Willy), and her husband, Howard (Howdy) Leach. We saw them quite a bit over the years as they came to our area for important family do too. I remember going to Aunt Carrie and Uncle John's sixtieth wedding anniversary party when our twins were around seven or eight. All the children in the families were invited to come also. They had the party in a big garage on their property. There were a lot of relatives there. That had to be in 1957 or 1958. While we were eating, Sandra, Marguerette and Wally's daughter, who was just a baby was playing with the silverware as babies do. Somehow a fork flew across the table and landed in Alice's eye. She cried of course, but it didn't seem to badly hurt. But later that evening, we ended up in Oakwood Hospital's emergency room to have it checked.

She did have a scratch on her eyeball. Thank goodness, it healed just fine. Marguerette and Wally felt terrible, but those things happen with children. Aunt Lizzie lived to be quite elderly, and Willy and Howdy would bring her with them, and we would meet at a fast-food restaurant for a quick lunch and visit when we made a quick trip to Jackson. Aunt Lizzie always, I mean always, ordered a fish sandwich. She loved them. Now why do small things like that stick in your mind?

THE 1940s

December 7, 1941

What a historic date in history, and most of you reading this will think that this happened only in your history books! We were living it!

Remember, I was a fairly new bride and as such was trying to show off my cooking abilities. December 7 was my grandma Martha Manley's birthday. Bill had that Sunday off, and we had invited my mother and grandma over for Sunday dinner and to celebrate Grandma's birthday. I had fixed a pot roast with onions and carrots, mashed potatoes, and gravy. We were eating our dinner and happened to turn the radio on as we were finishing. All of the announcers were confused and shouting that the Japanese had bombed Pearl Harbor! Of course, we had been following Hitler's takeover of the European countries, but somehow in our innocence had not thought that we would be involved. Needless to say, we were all glued to the radio for the rest of the day. No one felt like having a birthday celebration. I believe it was the next day that President Roosevelt declared that our country was at war with Germany and Japan.

When you look back over that period in our lives from a perspective of a lot of years, it makes you realize how very much World War II changed all of our history in so many different ways—the technology in aircraft design, factories and employment to clothe, feed, and supply weapons to our armed forces. Women became much more independent. I'm sure you have read or seen cartoons about "Rosy the Riveter," and their men were away fighting for our country. Women became much more than "housewives." Medicine, everything was speeded up.

During those years, in our own personal lives we were affected too. Because Bill worked in the tool room at Ford's and was married, he received several deferments for the service. He joined the Civil Defense Service and spent quite a bit of free time helping the police. He just loved being involved and he felt like he was helping. (This was just the beginning of that type of work for him. After we moved to Troy, we belonged to the Home Owners Association, and Bill went on patrol evenings as our subdivision grew.)

In late February 1942, I became pregnant, and we were very happy about it. We had rationing of sugar, meats, and fats. We saved used frying fat and turned it in. We learned to get by on less. We considered ourselves to be more fortunate than the people in England and Europe, and we were! We weren't being bombed on. We were glued to the radio newscasts but were hearing rumblings of that new television picture, which like Star Wars Trek to us. I made a lot of my own clothes and also things for our coming baby. We would get together with some of our young friends and play cards for an evening. Everyone brought their own drinks, and the hostess would usually have a snack or some kind of dessert. We also had our family get-togethers and visited our parents on Sundays if Bill was not working. He put in a lot of overtime hours with all the factories running twenty-four hours seven days a week for the war effort. Time flew by, and we were happy to be together. Life was good for us and good to us then, although as time went by, more of our family and friends were getting involved in the war. It was during this time along with Rosie the Riveter that women started to wear slacks. I remember I wore house dresses after we were married and bought our first house. The women in the neighborhood started to tease me about not wearing slacks. I started to wear them then, in1945-46 and have loved them ever since.

On June 27, 1942, my sister, Evelyn, married LeRoy Beeler, Bill's brother. They were married at Martha Mary Chapel in Greenfield Village. I was matron of honor and just a little bit pregnant. Skipping ahead a few years, their daughter, Larraine Francis, was born in May 1945. Roy was in the navy at that time and was not able to be home. I remember that I and my mother took Evelyn to the hospital.

In September 1942, Bill's grandma, Charlotte Wirtz, died of cancer. *But* no one at that time spoke the word *cancer*. We were told she died "of female problems," and because I was pregnant, the family did not want me to go to the funeral home or funeral. Strange ideas, but because I was so young and didn't like to cause waves, I went along with it. It was the older family members' beliefs and superstitions at that time.

Susan Louise Beeler was born on November 30, 1942—a healthy little girl! The doctor I had at that time was an old-fashioned type and did not believe in much of any medication. That was a pretty rough long night for me, and I remember that at that time the fathers were not allowed to be with you. I made it. *But* before my next pregnancy I checked out other doctors and changed. There were no Lamaze classes or training of any kind. At least young women today have choices. Anyway, I had to stay in the hospital for ten days. Can you imagine? Now they kick you out almost as soon as you deliver. Bill and I did think we were on top of the world. He was doing well in his work and schooling and I was reasonably healthy and bounced back quite quickly. Except for the war that seemed to be getting ever closer, our lives were full and happy.

Vivian & Bill

In April 1943, our whole world changed. We lost our beautiful happy little girl to SIDS—sudden infant death syndrome. At least that's all the doctors at that time could tell us. The day before she had been happy, healthy, and doing well. In fact, we had taken her downtown to Hudson's to have her picture taken, and everything had gone along fine. The next morning she was not acting right to me. She didn't want to eat and had not urinated. I called the doctor, and they told me to bring her in. When I got there, she was gone. It's hard to remember exactly what happened then. It all seems now like a very bad dream. I know they called Bill, and he came from work. That time and those next few days are sort of hazy for me. I know our parents, brothers, sisters, and friends were around. I know we had a funeral at MacFarland Funeral Home in East Dearborn on Schafer Road. I know we buried her at Grand Lawn Cemetery in Detroit at Grand River and Telegraph. I remember an aunt saying to me, "You're young. You will have more," and thinking that was cruel, but that whole time was sort of a painful blur. Maybe it was for the best. After all these years, it does sort of seem like a bad dream, but I don't even like writing about it now.

In the fall of 1943, I became pregnant again. I had checked around and changed doctors. I went to Dr. Edward Sieber an OB and GYN doctor. He was young and I liked him very much. He was my doctor for all of the rest of my pregnancies. He became very well known in the area. He also became very busy and had to take in a partner, Dr. Charles Pichette, who I also liked. Dr. Sieber delivered all my girls, and Dr. Pichette delivered Billy. They had a running joke about that. If I had wanted more boys, I should have had Dr. Pichette deliver. Remember, that was way back before ultrasounds, etc., so we didn't know the sex of the baby ahead of time. They were great doctors.

It was probably a good thing for Bill and me that I became pregnant so soon after losing Susan, but we were also very scared. The war was getting closer and closer and Bill's deferments were running out. He was called and inducted into the Army Air Force on March 25, 1944, and sent to Chicago for a training camp. Carol Ann was born on April 18, 1944. We had contacted the Red Cross, and Bill was given a leave to come home and see me and his new daughter. I was still in the hospital, Mt. Carmel, at 7 Mile and Outer Drive. The doctors gave me permission to go home if I stayed in bed and did not climb stairs. Grandpa Beeler carried me up and down the stairs. It's hard to believe how things have changed. *Anyway . . .*

When Bill was inducted into the service, Mom and Pop Beeler had asked me to go and stay with them. I had Bill's old room in their house on Neckle. It was a lovely big room with a huge closet, almost another little room. There was plenty of room for a crib and baby things. Mom and Pop Beeler were wonderful to me, and things worked out very well during the time I stayed there. Mom Beeler loved babies and loved having Carol there. In fact, I got a job at Peoples Outfitting Company. It was just around the corner from where they lived on Warren Avenue. I could walk there. Of course, I did have our car too. It was a furniture department store and I worked in the office. That was where I first met Betty, Elliott Scalf, and Earl Lutey. After Elliott died years later, Betty married Earl, and we have been friends to this day.

During those years, my mother, Eva Tallman, met and then married Maro or Merle Miller in 1944. We knew him as Maro, I think his legal name was Merle. He had been divorced years before and had two sons, Jimmy and Douglas, a little younger than me and my sister. It turned out to be a good marriage, and Maro was a wonderful grandpa to our children. When they were first married, Maro owned a car repair shop, and my mother did all the bookkeeping for him. Then they sold that and bought into a Dairy Queen in St. Joseph, Michigan. Carol and Kathy still remember going over there to stay and help in the store, and what fun it was! We knew his son Jimmy quite well and were at his wedding to Mary Ann. Their children, James Jr. and Michelle (Shelly), were friends with our girls, and we had a lot of family doings and fun together. (We lost Maro to a heart attack in 1959, and my mother was widowed again. She moved back to Dearborn and had a little apartment upstairs in Evelyn and Roy's home in Monroe in Dearborn.)

Bill was in the air force and was training to be both mechanic and navigator. He really liked what he was doing and had a good time in the service. I went down to Texas twice while Bill was stationed there, once on the train by myself, and just stayed a short while. That was when Bill was stationed at South Plains Army Air Field in Lubbock, Texas. Mom and Pop Beeler took care of Carol. Then when Carol was just over a year old, I took her to Texas. Bill was stationed at San Angelo just across the border from Mexico. The wife of a buddy of Bill's was going down, and we went with her in their car and shared expenses. What *fun!* Carol was a good baby but with a mind of her own even then, *and* she was healthy. I had watched her like a hawk and had taken her to the doctor's regularly for checkups after what had happened to Susan.

We rented a room with kitchen privileges from a middle-aged "born in Texas lady." At that time, I thought she was "old." She was very friendly to us and liked Carol, who was running all over by that time. That was in San Angelo. That lady, and for the life of me I can't remember her name, chewed tobacco. She had *spit cans* sitting around all over the house. Of course, those were fascinating to Carol. So I would be busy chasing Carol and trying to keep her out of the spit cans. That lady could also make the best baking powder biscuits you could ever want to taste. She tried to share her recipe with me, and I could come pretty close, but hers were better.

We had a lot of fun in Texas; we were surrounded by young people in the same boat, away from their homes., wondering what was going to happen next and determined to enjoy the moment. No one had any money to spare, but we would all gather at the PX and beer was cheap. (I still hadn't learned to like it.) We were able to do a bit of sightseeing. We took Carol to some parks and swimming pools, and she rode a goat. (She doesn't remember.) We went to Mexico one day, a little town called villa Acuna, which was just across the border from San Angelo. I took food and water for Carol, and I don't remember that we ate or drank anything either. We saw a bull fight which I could have done without. Ugh, but it was an experience. I remember how hot and dry everything was down there and the constant wind and the dust blowing in your face. You always felt "gritty." I'm talking about Texas also.

They were getting ready to send Bill's group overseas when they bombed Hiroshima, August 6, 1945, killing at least seventy-five thousand people. Three days later, the United States dropped a bomb on Nagasaki, and Japan agreed to surrender on August 14, 1945, ending World War II. We were very, very fortunate. The atomic bomb and Hiroshima was another thing that was just another story in your history books, but it had a great impact on our lives. You have probably seen movies and heard stories of Enola Gay. The horror and reality of the mass human destruction was hard to comprehend.

Bill was discharged from the Army Air Force on October 1, 1945, and we were able to get on with our lives.

Bill's job was waiting for him in the tool room at Ford Motor Company and they were also sending him to school. We found a small two-bedroom bungalow on Campbell Street in West Dearborn. Mom and Pop Beeler loaned us $500.00 for a down payment. Our house was listed at $6100.00. Can you imagine? But at that time, we were talking a lot of *money*. We were very faithful and paid back Mom and Pop Beeler for their loan and faith in us. We lived in our Campbell Street house for twenty-one years, and they were *happy* years. And what a great neighborhood it was. The girls still talk about how great their growing up years were. Phyllis and Chuck Mitchell lived next door with their two boys, Danny and David. Phyllis and Chuck are both gone now, but I still hear from Dan and David. Bob and Sophia Huebner, with Marleen, Bob Jr. Eileen, and Doris, were also there. They are also gone. There was another couple who are gone, Jane and Clyde Grizzell, with Clyde Jr. And Sue Ann, Then there were the Gerrities with Michael and Pam. My memory is not working right here. Some of the other people who were there were Raymond and Mary Cox, with their boys, Ray Jr. Donny and Frank, Helen and Marty Opavsky, with Marlene, and Jack and Hattie Baker across the street. Jack and Hattie Baker and Mary Cox came to the funeral home when Bill died. I think that's all that's left from the "Old Gang." We had some great parties and get-togethers in the neighborhood. Everyone helped one another, and our kids were great friends. It was an old-fashioned time. All the women were housewives, but our world was changing. More and more women were joining the workforce.

On May 25, 1947, Kathy Jean was born. We called her our "good luck" baby because at that same time Bill was transferred to engineering and a salaried position. All his hard work and schooling was paying off. He started out working for a man named Finkelstein, who Bill said was brilliant! He taught Bill a lot about gears and gear shifts. Then Bill got into drive shafts, all this while he was still taking classes and going to school, some through the company and some at Wayne state. Also I forgot to mention that when we first bought our house Elliott Scalf owned a mobile gas station on Warren, and Bill worked weekends there for some extra money. I kept busy sewing for myself and the girls. I loved cooking and baking, trying new recipes. I loved being a wife and mother.

Comments on World War II

Your generation is fortunate not to have lived through a war like World War II, one that threatened your own soil. We were convinced that Hitler would never make it out of Europe, but there he was bombing England! We were next. The isolationists in our country were suddenly silent. We had a common enemy now. Men enlisted because it was the honorable thing to do. Bill and Grandpa thought he was helping by working in the tool room and volunteering on the Civil Defense Program. Remember, he had a wife and a baby at home. But when he was called up, he went because he felt it was his duty. Patriotism is another thing that the new generation doesn't see the same way we did. Patriotism probably makes you think of George C. Scott as General Patten or Robert Preston in the Music Man and 76 Trombones or Mary Lou Retton winning the gold medal. To you, it's an event. To us, it was a state of mind; when we fly the flag, it's a matter of pride. Fourth of July marks a different time in our history, but they are related to what I'm talking about "here." The War of Independence gave us freedom, and we rather like it. The new generation sort of takes it for granted; we didn't. We were children of the big Depression; we may not have had the prosperity, but we wanted our freedom. That's what we fought for in World War II.

Important Dates in World War II

June 6, 1944, was the D-Day, the Battle of Normandy, terrific loss of lives, but it was the turning point and end of the Nazi hold on Europe.

On August 6, 1945, Hiroshima was bombed, which ended Japan's part, and they surrendered. End of World War II.

I hope this doesn't sound to "preachy," but that war had a huge impact on our lives.

Summer, 2011

As I re-read these papers before I send them to printers, another war has made an impact on all of our lives—the Iraq, Afghanistan wars. This summer marks ten years that we have been involved in this, which in my opinion we never should have been involved. It has cost trillions of dollars, plus we have lost way too many talented young people. That's not even counting all the wounded who will never be the same again. So many have lost limbs, and there are countless who have post-traumatic stress syndrome. This war has also contributed to the recession and problems the last few years in our government and sort of divided our country. I wish I had an answer for all of this. I just want all our young people to be home and safe. Those countries don't want us there anyway.

What's in a Sign? 1944

A lady about seven months pregnant got on a streetcar and sat across from a man. She noticed him smiling, so she changed her seat. This time his smile changed to a grin, so she changed her seat again. He seemed more amused. The fourth time she changed, he burst out laughing.

She couldn't bear it any longer, so she complained to the conductor and had him arrested. The case came up in court, and the judge asked him if he had anything to say.

"Well, Your Honor, it was like this," he replied. 'When the lady sat down, I couldn't help but notice her condition, and that she was under a sign that read 'Use Sloan's Liniment to Reduce Swelling,' and I had to smile to myself. And then she sat down under a sign that read 'The Gold Dust Twins Are Coming.' This sign made me grin. Then she placed herself under a sign which read 'William's Stick Did the Trick.' I could hardly hold myself, and when she moved the fourth time and sat under a sign 'Goodyear Rubber Would Have Prevented This Accident,' I just laughed out loud."

Case dismissed.

I found this in some of Bill's papers. He had evidently written it (copied) back when he was stationed at Lubbock, Texas. It is funny.

Vivian and Bill Beeler Married on This Day

On This Day in History: Saturday, August 30, 1941

Top Headlines This Quarter

President Roosevelt nationalizes the armed forces of the Philippines, still a United States dependency. The Revenue Act of 1941 is passed, providing sharply increased taxes in order to raise the large sums now needed for the defense effort. Judy Garland and David Rose marry in Las Vegas.

Top Songs for 1941

"Frenesi" by Artie Shaw
"Amapola" by Jimmy Dorsey
"Daddy" by Sammy Kaye
"Piano Concerto" by Freddy Martin
"I Hear a Rhapsody" by Charlie Barnet
"Dolores" by Bing Crosby
"Hut Sut Song" by Freddy Martin
"Chattanooga Choo Choo" by Glenn Miller

1941 Prices

House	$6,954.00	
Car	$925.00	
Milk	$.34	
Gas	$.15	
Bread	$.08	-
Postage Stamp	$0.03	-
Avg Income	$1,231.00	-
		-

U.S. President: Franklin Roosevelt
U.S. Vice President: Henry Wallace

People Born on August 30

Timothy Buttoms—1951
Fred Macmurray—1908
Shirley Booth—1907

Academy Award Winners

Best Picture: *How Green Was My Valley* directed by John Ford
Best Actor: Gary Cooper in *Sergeant York*
Best Actress: Joan Fontain in *Suspicion*

1941 Sports Headlines

American League beats National League 7-5 to win the All-Star Game. 2:01.2 was the winning time for Whirlaway to win the Kentucky Derby. Stanford wins 21-13 against Nebraska in the Rose Bowl. Heavyweight Champ Joe Louis beats Buddy Baer on a disqualification. New York wins 4 games to 1 over Brooklyn to win the world series.

Susan Louise Beeler

On This Day in History: Monday, November 30, 1942

Top News Headlines This Week:

> November 30-December 1: Sea battle at Tassafaronga, Guadalcanal. November 30: 109 U boats sunk this month (729,000 ton). November 30: 30 CFL Grey Cup, Toronto Hurricanes defeats Winnipeg Bombers, 8-5. November 30: Bill Terry resigns as supervisor of NY Giants minor league system. November 30: German scout ship *Altmark* explodes and sinks off Yokohama. December 1: Gasoline rationed in United States.

Top Songs for 1942

> "Jersey Bounce" by Benny Goodman
> "Moonlight Cocktail' by Glenn Miller
> "Tangerine" by Jimmy Dorsey
> "Blues in the Night" by Woody Herman
> "Kalamazoo" by Glenn Miller
> "White Christmas" by Bing Crosby
> "He Wears a Pair of Silver Wings" by Kay Kyser
> "Jingle, Jangle, Jingle" by Kay Kyser
> "Sleepy Lagoon" by Harry James
> "Somebody Else Is Taking My Place" by Benny Goodman

1942 Prices

Bread:	$0.09/loaf
Milk:	$0.60/gal
Eggs:	$0.61/doz
Car:	$1,100
Gas:	$0.20/gal

House:	$7,573
Stamp:	$0.03/ea
Avg Income:	$2,348/yr
Min Wage:	$0.30/hr
DOW Avg:	119

U.S. President: Franklin D. Roosevelt
U.S. Vice President: Henry A. Wallace

Academy Award Winners

Best Picture: *Mrs. Miniver* directed by William Wyler
Best Actor: James Cagney in *Yankee Doodle Dandy*
Best Actress: Greer Garson in *Mrs. Miniver*

People Born on November 30

1927 — Robert Guillaume, St. Louis, Missouri, actor (*Benson, Soap*)
1835 — Mark Twain (Samuel L Clemens), author (*Tom Sawyer, Huckleberry Finn*)
1874 — Winston Churchill, (C) British Prime Minister (1940-45, 1951-55, Nobel Prize winner in 1953)
1929 — Dick Clark, Mount Vernon, New York, TV host (*American Bandstand*)

Top Books in 1942

The Matchlock Gun by Walter D. Edmonds
Black Lamb and Grey Falcon by Rebecca
West West with the Night by Beryl Markham

Carol Ann Beeler Leinonen

On This Day in History: Tuesday, April 18, 1944

Top Headlines This Quarter

> With some 800 fighter planes supporting them, 660 U.S. bombers make the first United States raid on Berlin. The Allies launch a major invasion force and land in the Netherlands and New Guinea. The Japanese are caught off guard. Senator Maybank of South Carolina says the South will not open polls to blacks.

Top Songs for 1944

"I'll Get By" by Harry James
"Swingin' On a Star" by Bing Crosby
"Sesame Mucho" by Jimmy Dorsey
"Holiday for Strings" by David Rose
"I'll Walk Alone" by Dinah Shore
"My Heart Tells Me" by Glen Gray
"I Love You" by Bing Crosby
"It's Love, Love, Love" by Guy Lombardo

1944 Prices

House	$8,649.00
Car	$1,225.00
Milk	$.62
Gas	$.16
Bread	$.09
Postage Stamp	$0.03
Avg Income	$2,378.00

U.S. President: Franklin Roosevelt
U.S. Vice President: Henry Wallace

People Born on April 18

Clarence Darrow—1857
Nate Archibald—1948
Hayley Mills—1946

Academy Award Winners

Best Picture: *Going My Way* directed by Leo McCarey
Best Actor: Bing Crosby in *Going My Way*
Best Actress: Ingrid Bergman in *Gaslight*

1944 Sports Headlines

Pensive ridden by Jockey C. McCreary wins Kentucky Derby. Montreal beats Chicago to win the Stanley Cup in hockey. Cardinals defeat Browns in sixth to take world series. Green Bay Packers defeat Giants 14-7 to take football championship. Utah defeats Dartmouth in overtime to win the NCAA Championship Game.

Kathy Jean Beeler Welton

On This Day in History: Sunday, May 25, 1947

Top Headlines This Quarter

President Truman signs a bill to aid Greece and Turkey. Truman allocates $350 million in relief for foreign countries devastated by recent war. Pan American Airlines offers a round-the-world flight fare of $1700. Joan Crawford opens in "possessed." Japan regains its right to fly the rising-sun flag.

Top Songs for 1947

"Near You" by Francis Craig Orchestra
"Heartaches" by Ted Weems
"Peg O' My Heart" by Harmonicats
"Anniversary Song" by Al Jolson
"Ballerina" by Vaughn Monroe
"Mam'selle" by Art Lund
"Chi-Baba Chi-Baba" by Perry Como
"Golden Earrings" by Peggy Lee

1947 Prices

House	$12,309.00
Car	$1,500.00
Milk	$.80
Gas	$.18
Bread	$.12
Postage Stamp	$0.03
Avg Income	$2,854.00

U.S. President: Harry Truman

U.S. Vice President: None

People Born on May 25

> Beverly Sills—1929
> Ron Nessen—1934
> Karen Valentine—1947 Leslie
> Uggams—1943

Academy Award Winners

> Best Picture: *Gentleman's Agreement* directed by Elia Kazan
> Best Actor: Ronald Colman in *A Double Life*
> Best Actress: Loretta Young in *The Farmer's Daughter*

1947 Sports Headlines

> 2.06.3 was the winning time for Jet Pilot to win the Kentucky Derby. Toronto beats Montreal to win the Stanley Cup in hockey. Philadelphia beats Chicago in basketball to win the NBA title. New York Yankees win the world series in the final game against Brooklyn. Cardinals defeat Eagles 28-21 to take football title.

Edsel M. Leinonen

On This Day in History: Sunday, January 18, 1942

Top News Headlines This Week

> January 18: Nazi's arrest Frans Goedhart and Wiardi Beckman. January 19: Japanese forces invade Burma. January 19: Titus Brandsma (Carmelite priest) arrested by German occupiers for speaking out against Nazism as a "lie" and "pagan." January 20: L. Oterma discovers asteroids #1558 Jarnefelt and #1559 Kustaanheimo. January 20: On "final solution" calling for extermination of Europe's Jews. January 20: Japanese invade Burma.

Top Songs for 1942

> "Jersey Bounce" by Benny Goodman
> "Moonlight Cocktail" by Glenn Miller
> "Tangerine" by Jimmy Dorsey
> "Blues in the Night" by Woody Herman
> "Kalamazoo" by Glenn Miller
> "White Christmas" by Bing Crosby
> "He Wears a Pair of Silver Wings" by Kay Kyser
> "Jingle, Jangle, Jingle" by Kay Kyser
> "Sleepy Lagoon" by Harry James
> "Somebody Else Is Taking My Place" by Benny Goodman

1942 Prices

Bread:	$0.09/loaf
Milk:	$0.60/gal
Eggs:	$0.61/doz
Car:	$1,100

Gas:	$0.20/gal
House:	$7,573
Stamp:	$0.03/ea
Avg Income:	$2,348/yr
Min Wage:	$0.30/hr
DOWAvg:	119

U.S. President: Franklin D. Roosevelt
U.S. Vice President: Henry A. Wallace

Academy Award Winners

Best Picture: *Mrs. Miniver* directed by William Wyler
Best Actor: James Cagney in *Yankee Doodle Dandy*
Best Actress: Greer Garson in *Mrs. Miniver*

People Born on January 18

1782 — Daniel Webster, Salisbury, New Hampshire; orator/politician/lawyer
1913 — Danny Kaye, Brooklyn, New York; UNICEF/comedian/actor (*Danny Kaye Show*)
1904 — Cary Grant England, actor (*Arsenic & Old Lace, North by Northwest*)
1882 — Alan Alexander Milne, English author (*Winnie the Pooh*)

Top Books in 1942

The Matchlock Gun by Walter D. Edmonds
Black Lamb and Grey Falcon by Rebecca West
West with the Night by Beryl Markham

James N. Welton

On This Day in History: Saturday, June 02, 1945

Top News Headlines This Week

> June 4—6: Marine division occupies Orokoe Peninsula, Okinawa. June 4: USA, Russia, England, and France agree to split occupied Germany. June 5: Opera *Peter Grimes of Benjamin Britten* premieres in London. June 5: USA, UK, USSR, France declare supreme authority over Germany. June 6: *Free People* premieres in Amsterdam. June 9: *Gruesome Twosome* premieres in USA.

Top Songs for 1945

> "I Can't Begin to Tell You" by Bing Crosby
> "Till the End of Time" by Perry Como
> "My Dreams Are Getting Better All the Time" by Les Brown
> "Chickery Chick" by Sammy Kaye
> "Rum and Coca Cola" by Andrews Sisters
> "It's Been a Long, Long Time" by Harry James (also Bing Crosby)
> "Sentimental Journey" by Les Brown with Doris Day
> "On the Atchison, Topeka and the Santa Fe" by Johnny Mercer
> "There! I've Said It Again" by Vaughn Monroe
> "Ac-Cent-Tchu-Ate the Positive" by Johnny Mercer

1945 Prices

Bread:	$0.09/loaf
Milk:	$0.62/gal
Eggs:	$0.64/doz
Car:	$1,250
Gas:	$0.21/gal

House:	$10,131
Stamp:	$0.03/ea
Avg Income:	$2,807/yr
Min Wage:	$0.40/hr
DOW Avg:	193

U.S. President: Harry S Truman
U.S. Vice President: None

Academy Award Winners

Best Picture: *The Lost Weekend* directed by Billy Wilder
Best Actor: Ray Milland in *The Lost Weekend*
Best Actress: Joan Crawford: in *Mildred Pierce*

People Born on June 2

1948 — Jerry Mathers, Sioux City, Iowa, actor (*Beaver—Leave It To Beaver*)
1944 — Marvin Hamlisch, United States, composer/pianist (*The Sting, Chorus Line*)
1941 — Stacy Keach, Savannah, Giorgia, actor (*Mickey Spillane's Mike Hammer*)

Hot New Toys in 1945
Slinky Ertl Die Cast Toys

Top Books in 1945

Black Boy by Richard Wright
Rabbit Hill by Robert Lawson
Brideshead Revisited by Evelyn Waugh
Loving by Henry Green
The Age of Jackson by Arthur Schlesinger Jr.
The Open Society and Its Enemies by Karl Popper

Kenneth G. Vogt

On This Day in History: Saturday, February 28, 1948

Top News Headlines This Week

> February 29: Stern group bomb Cairo-Haifa train, twenty-seven British soldiers died. March 5: Actor Eli Wallach marries actress Anne Jackson. March 5: U.S. rocket flies record 4,800 KPH to 126k height. March 7: C. A. Wirtanen discovers asteroid #1863 Antinous. March 8: Supreme Court rules RELG instructions in pub schools unconstitutional. March 9: Provisionary Indonesian government installed in Batavia.

Top Songs for 1948

> "Woody Woodpecker" by Kay Kyser
> "Manana" by Peggy Lee
> "You Can't Be True, Dear" by Ken Griffin
> "I'm Looking Over a Four-leaf Clover" by Art Mooney
> "Twelfth Street Rag" by Pee Wee Hunt
> "Buttons and Bows" by Dinah Shore
> "A Tree in the Meadow" by Margaret Whiting
> "Nature Boy" by Nat King Cole
> "You Call Everybody Darlin'" by Al Trace
> "Love Somebody" by Doris Day with Buddy Clark

1948 Prices

Bread:	$0.14/loaf
Milk:	$0.86/gal
Eggs:	$0.67/doz
Car:	$1,550
Gas:	$0.26/gal

House:	$13,500
Stamp:	$0.03/ea
Avg Income:	$3,671/yr
Min Wage:	$0.40/hr
DOWAvg:	177

U.S. President: Harry S Truman
U.S. Vice President: None

Academy Award Winners

Best Picture: *Hamlet* produced by Universal International
Best Actor: Laurence Olivier in *Hamlet*
Best Actress: Jane Wyman in *Johnny Belinda*

People born on February 28

1940 — Mario Andretti, race car driver (1969 Indianapolis 500)
1931 — Gavin Macleod, Mount Kisco, New York, actor (*Murray-Mary Tyler Moore, Love Boat*)
1712 — Louis Joseph, de Montcalm de Saint-Vran, France, general
1945 — Charles "Bubba" Smith, Texas, NFLer (Baltimore Colts)/actor (Police Academy)
1901 — Linus Pauling, chemist/peace worker (Nobel Prize 1954, 1962)

On TV in 1948

Pantomime Quiz Time
The Ed Sullivan Show

Hot New Toys in 1948
Scrabble Cootie

Top Books in 1948

The American Political Tradition by Richard Hofstadter
The Heart of the Matter by Graham Greene
The Twenty-One Balloons by William Peme du Bois
The Naked and the Dead by Norman Mailer

THE 1950s

The 1950s were good years for Bill and me as he was advancing in his work at Ford's through classes at Wayne state and loving every minute of it.

But we were at war again in Korea, and it was not good for the 36,516 young men who died in what has been called "The Forgotten War." To give you a bit of background: Japan ruled the Korean peninsula as a colony from 1910 until World War II ended in 1945 when Korea was divided at the thirty-eighth parallel. Separate nations of North and South Korea were formed in 1948. Communists gained control of North Korea, and hostility between North and South increased as each country tried to rule a united peninsula. In June 1950, North Korean troops invaded South Korea. The United States joined the United Nations contingent pledged to repel the North. The allied forces soon drove the North Koreans to the peninsula's border with China. China intervened, slowly pushing the allies south to the thirty-eighth parallel. Negotiations resulted in a truce in July 1953. Technically, the countries are still in a state of war.

The Korean War did not affect our lives very much, as we were not personally involved and did not know many who were. Looking back, that was a sad time in our history, and I guess that is the reason it was called "The Forgotten War." The young men involved in that war who did come home did not receive the honor and acclaim that they deserved.

As I said before, the 1950s were good to us. Carol and Kathy were growing well and were generally healthy. Our parents were doing well, also my brothers and sisters. In May 1951, we had twin daughters, Alice and Barbara. Remember I told you there was no ultrasounds and other tests like that, so Dr. Edward Sieber didn't know I was having twins until I went for my regular checkup six weeks before my due date. I was complaining of how difficult it was for me to walk and how very uncomfortable I was. He examined me thoroughly and took quite a long time. Then he looked at me and said, "Vivian, I feel two heads and hear two heartbeats. You are going to have twins."

I was in shock. The doctor also said that twins usually came early. Bill had brought me to the doctor's but was waiting in the car for me rather than sit in the waiting room with a bunch of pregnant women. The husbands were not included in everything like they are today. I wish they would have been. I went out to the car, burst into tears, and said, "We're going to have twins." Bill put his arms around me and told me everything was OK. He said that he knew something was different and that he was not surprised. He said we could handle it together. I was very miserable those last six weeks, as I had gained a lot of weight, but it seemed to be all babies. I know I spent a lot of time on the couch. I could not lie in bed. I know it was twenty-nine steps to the bathroom, which I used a lot. My mother, sister, and Mom Beeler came over when they could to help out. Carol was seven and Kathy four, but they still needed attention. Bill would take over when he got home from work, and somehow we made it. But, of course, Alice and Barbara decided they were comfortable where they were, so they didn't arrive until their due date, May 2.

It was a normal delivery, and everything went quite well, except I did lose quite a bit of blood and had to have two blood transfusions. We had identical twin girls; Alice weighed 6 lb. 8 oz. and Barbara weighed 6 lb. 6 oz. That's a lot of baby to carry; no wonder I was miserable. They were healthy, and I recuperated reasonably well but did have to stay in the hospital a little longer. That was my first pregnancy where I did not have to worry about losing weight, as I had lost weight the last two months of pregnancy. I was twenty-nine and Bill thirty-one, and we were a happy family. Sounds so young looking back at those years, and they certainly were busy years. Just a little sideline, we did not have a clothes dryer as they were fairly new in the appliance field. I can still see our basement on Campbell with clotheslines strung everywhere and diapers unending. We did not have Pampers etc. in those days. In nice weather, our backyard was full of baby things plus the regular laundry. We soon managed to get a clothes dryer, and what a joy that was!

Bill was meeting vendors in his job and was being invited to a lot of sports events, golf outings, and deer and pheasant hunting camps. I was included in a lot of the dinner and sport events. What fun it was! We were both growing, learning, and expanding our horizons. Bill was constantly taking classes and going to school. We also got into square dancing with our good friends and neighbors, Phyllis and Chuck Mitchell, who lived right next door to us. We got to be very good dancers and met a lot of lovely people. Bill was even chairman of the Michigan Square Dance Convention in 1959 and 1960. During those years, Bill was also an usher and head of the finance committee at St. Paul's Lutheran Church in Dearborn. The girls went to Sunday school most Sundays, and then we all went to church. All of the girls went to Catechism classes and were confirmed at St. Paul's. I had also gone to adult classes and joined the church. One of the nice memories of those busy Sundays was when I was busy getting four little girls ready for Sunday school, plus myself, Bill was in the kitchen making French toasts for our Sunday breakfast. To this day, the girls remember Daddy's French toasts and how good it tasted.

Twin's 1ˢᵗ Birthday

We had several summer vacations up north at Burt Lake and Indian River. We rented a cottage, and Mitchells rented one right next door. David and Danny sort of grew up with our girls and are still friends. They were both at Bill and Kathy's funerals.

Thinking back over those years brings back a lot of nice memories, and I wonder now at seventy-nine years how we did it all. The years flew by. Bill's sister, Marguerette, married Walter Wagner in September, 1952, and his brother Joseph Jr. married Charlotte Kloss the following month, October 1952. They were busy, busy times growing families. Joe and Char had Christopher in 1954 and Cathy Joann in 1956. Marguerette and Wally had Sandra in 1957 and Susan in 1960. Our girls had cousins to play with at family gatherings, and we had a lot of get-togethers that all the families enjoyed. Bill during these busy years also finished off our attic and made it into a girls' dormitory. Each girl had a space marked off by rugs, chests, etc. We also added a dining room with a lot of cupboard space at one end across the back of the house. We were growing and needed more room. He also installed a toilet and a washbowl in the basement. It was in self-defense with five women using the one bathroom. There wasn't much that Bill could not do if he set his mind to it. I can't even begin to tell you the amount of money he saved us in repair bills by just knowing how to fix things. He spoiled me, and 1 loved it and him. I also did my share. I always had a nice dinner for him when he got home from work. Fast food was unheard of, and we really didn't have the money to take the children out to restaurants. In fact, in those days you didn't very often see children in restaurants. Still to this day I wonder when I see young families eating out, "How much easier it would be to feed them at home. The mother and dad don't look like they are really enjoying their meal, and how much healthier for the children to eat at home." I guess I am just "old-fashioned."

In those days, little girls wore *dresses* all the time. Material was not wash and wear, so that meant I *ironed* dresses and Bill's shirts for work. The ironing board was a fixture in our living room until we had the back room added on. I dampened the clothes and rolled them up in a basket and then ironed. The surprising part of looking back on this was that I didn't mind it. It was just part of my job as homemaker. Now I look for clothes that are wash and wear. I don't want to have to iron! I think maybe I have served my time.

During the middle 1950s, another event was taking place in our country—the beginning of the Civil Rights Movement. Our constitution says, "All men are created equal." *But* at a bus stop in Montgomery, Alabama, on December 1, 1955, Mrs. Rosa Parks refused to give up her seat to boarding whites. That brought about her arrest, conviction, and fine. The boycott began on December 5, the day of Parks's trial, as a protest by African-Americans for unequal treatment that they received on the bus line. Refusing to ride the buses, they maintained the boycott until the U.S. Supreme Court ordered integration of public transportation one year later. Dr. Martin Luther King Jr. led the boycott, the beginning of the modern Civil Rights Movement. Rosa Parks was honored in 1999 with the Congressional Medal of Honor. She also got Alabama's first medal of honor and a museum in her honor. She was eighty-seven at that time.

Another event that took place in the middle 1950s was the start of McDonald's and fast-food restaurants. That has had a very big and lasting effect on everyone in this country. Some of it not so good, causing health problems and obesity. Ray Kroc went out to California as he had heard about two brothers starting up a business of selling hamburgers and French fries with a drive-through setting and wanted to learn more about it. It ended up with him buying a franchise. He brought the idea back to his home town of Des Plains, Illinois, and started the first McDonald's restaurant. It didn't take long for the idea to spread all over. That first McDonald's is now a museum. There had been a few A&W Root Beer drive-throughs and a few independent drive throughs, but with the event of McDonald's, fast food moved into big time. Happy Meals, here we come.

Mom and Pop Beeler were very good babysitters and helped us out when Bill and I had vendor invitations, where we would be gone most of the day or very occasionally overnight. We also belonged to a babysitters club that had older women for staying with our children. As I mentioned before, those were years in our lives where we were all growing and learning a very great deal. The joys and problems of parenting, expanding social life, and meeting new people—that was a little difficult for me. Bill was always a very outgoing person. I was quiet and a little shy. I've heard that some people thought I was "stuck up," when it really was just shyness. Bill helped me a great deal in that respect, and I think I also helped him develop to think before he just jumped in, to put his ideas across with just a bit more tact. We learned and grew up together.

During the 1950s, my mother and Grandpa Merle had been over in St. Joseph, Michigan, running a Dairy Queen stand that also served hot dogs. We made several trips over there to see them and enjoy a short vacation by Lake Michigan. Carol remembers staying with them during the summer for a few weeks and helping. Kathy did a little too. All the girls participated in going to Camp Dearborn, and that was always a fun time for them. Dearborn did have a wonderful summer camp program for children. It was very reasonable, so we were able to take advantage of it. Of all the girls, I think Carol was the one who enjoyed it the most, and she went more times than the others. She helped with counseling during the last couple of summers and also worked at the Dearborn Public Pools as a lifeguard. They were busy, busy years, although I think children and parents have more activities now than we did back then—soccer moms, etc. We didn't know what that was back then.

Merle Miller died of a heart attack in November 1959. My mother had to sell the Dairy Queen business in St. Joe. She moved back to Dearborn in an apartment upstairs at Evelyn and Roy's house on Monroe in West Dearborn. She was widowed twice. I'm wondering now how she was able to cope. Looking back, I'm very proud of the way she kept going. She had her church work and helped with the Red Cross blood drives. She played bridge with her woman friends and did most of the driving for them (although, I never did think she was a very good driver, as she did not learn until she was almost forty when my dad died). Looking back, hindsight, or whatever, I thought I understood and sympathized with her. Now I know I had no idea what she was going through. Until you walk in someone's shoes, you have no idea what it is like to lose your husband and partner.

Now on into the 1960s.

Alice Louise Beeler-McCalden
Barbara Sue Beeler Vogt

On This Day in History: Sunday, May 20, 1951

Top Headlines This Quarter

U.S. Telephone and Telegraph announces that it has over one million stockholders, a first for any united states corporation. The military draft is extended to July 1, 1955. Congress lengthens military service to two years and lowers the draft age to eighteen and a half years.

Top Songs for 1951

"Too Young" by Nat King Cole
"Because of You" by Tony Bennett
"Be My Love" by Mario Lanza
"I Get Ideas" by Tony Martin
"Jezebel" by Frankie Laine
"Tennessee Waltz" by Patti Page
"Cold Cold Heart" by Tony Bennett
"Tell Me Why" by Four Aces

1951 Prices

House	$16,000.00
Car	$1,800.00
Milk	$.92
Gas	$.20
Bread	$.16
Postage Stamp	$0.03
Avg Income	$3,515.00

U.S. President: Harry Truman
U.S. Vice President: Alben Barkley

People Born on May 20

James Stewart—1908
Cher—1946
George Gobel—1919
Bronson Pinchot—1959

Academy Award Winners

Best Picture: *An American In Paris* produced by Arthur Freed
Best Actor: Humphrey Bogart in *The African Queen*
Best Actress: Vivien Leigh in *A Streetcar Named Desire*

1951 Sports Headlines

20-year-old outfielder Willie Mays joins NY Giants baseball team. 2:02.3 was the winning time for Count Turf to win the Kentucky Derby. Joe Dimaggio retires from baseball. LA Rams defeat Cleveland Browns 24-17 for football title. N.Y. (AL) beats New York (NL) 4 games to 2 to win the world series.

THE 1960s

Our Lives in the 1960s

It's hard to know where to start. So much went on in our lives and so much was happening around us. I guess the best thing to do is jump in and see where I go.

Fortune was smiling at us during the 1960s. We were very, very busy and satisfied with the direction our lives were going. Bill was ever advancing in his work at Ford's through his determination and continuing to go to school. The girls were growing and keeping us busy with their activities, although, thank goodness, children in the 1960s did not have the multitude of activities children do today, and we only had one car, which is unheard of today. Our parents were doing well and enjoying their retirement. My brothers and sisters also doing well. Life was good.

During the 1960s too, the Civil Rights Movement was growing, and there were a lot of clashes and sadness of violence, particularly in the "Deep South." I have already talked about Rosa Parks in the middle 1950s. During the 1950s and 1960s, the NAACP-sponsored legal suits and legislative lobbying were supplemented by increasing massive and militant social movement seeking a broad range of social changes. Martin Luther King emerged as a leader possessing unique conciliatory and oratorical skills; he thought non-violent tactics used by Indian Nationalist Mahatma Gandhi could be used by Southern Blacks. In the summer of 1963, King gave his famous address: "I Have a Dream." In April 1968, King was assassinated by James Earl Ray. In 1986, King's birthday became a federal holiday.

The 1960s were also a time when our space program was going full speed ahead. We were in a race for space. The Russians had launched "Sputnik" in 1957, and the United States was trying to "catch up." In 1961, Alan Shepard was the first astronaut in a fifteen-minute sub-orbital flight in the Mercury Program. In 1962, John Glenn aboard the Friendship 7 orbited the earth three times and returned safely. The NASA program was off and running. There were accidents, and in January 1967, three astronauts sacrificed their lives. Fire swept through their Apollo 1 Command Module during a pre-flight test at Pad 34 Kennedy Space Center in Florida. Their names are in our history books: Virgil "Gus" Grissom, Edward White II, and Roger Chaffee. In 1961, three weeks after winning a very narrow presidential election from Richard M. Nixon, President Kennedy told Congress, "I believe this nation should commit itself to achieving the goal, before the decade is out, of landing a man on the Moon and returning him safely to earth."

We did make that goal. On July 20, 1969, Commander Neil Armstrong, Pilot Edwin "Buzz" Aldrin, and L. M. Pilot Michael Collins landed on the moon in Apollo 11. Everyone was watching, holding their breath, on their TV screens when Neil Armstrong stepped out of the space craft and set foot on the moon. He said, "That's one small step for man and one giant leap for mankind." They spent 21.6 hours on the moon and returned home safely on July 24. It's hard to explain how excited and pleased everyone was and to be able to watch it happen. Remember, TV was still a new item for us then. Just a sideline that I thought was interesting: Armstrong's space suit was fifteen layers thick and had five hundred parts. It took him two hours just to put it on. Now it seems in today's world no one is paying much attention to the space program unless it is affecting your life in some way. People who live near the space center in Florida still love to see the rockets launched, and NASA has a lot of visitors to the center.

I mentioned President Kennedy when I was talking about the space program. I would like to also tell you that we had a very close presidential race in 1961 between John F. Kennedy and Richard M. Nixon. It was not quite as close as the one we just had last November 2000 between George W. Bush and Vice President Al Gore. John F. Kennedy was our first Catholic running for president, and that did influence a lot of people at that time.

Back to our personal lives, during that time period, Carol graduated from Edsel Ford High School on Outer Drive in Dearborn, in June 1962. We were very proud of her. She wanted to go on to college and become a teacher. Because she had not been an all A and B student, Bill and I were not sure just how serious she was. We had three other girls behind her that we had to consider too. So we said, "Go to Henry Ford Community College for two years and prove to us that you are serious about your schooling. If you do that, we will send you to Central University for your last two years." (That was where she wanted to go.) She got her Associate's degree from Henry Ford, and that was where she met Edsel Leinonen. She was taking an extra class in accounting as she was worried about her math skills; Edsel was back from two years in the military. He had been unsure what he wanted when he graduated from high school. Edsel got his business degree at Wayne State. Anyway, Carol did go on to Central University and graduated on June 11, 1966, and on June 18, one week later, she married Edsel.

Now I have to backtrack. In January 1963, we lost Grandma Martha Manley. She had been fairly well up until the last few months of her death. She was ninety-three and was "ready" to go as she said. She had lived a long and good life. That still did not stop all of us from missing her.

Also in 1963, Bill was transferred from Ford Engineering in Dearborn to the Ford Sterling Plant in Sterling Heights. It was a thirty-five-mile drive to and from work. We were used to him being five minutes away. But it was a nice promotion for him as he was made the resident engineer for Axles and Drive Shaffs.

He loved his new job, so we all adjusted to his longer hours.

On November 22, 1963, President John F. Kennedy was assassinated in a motorcade in Dallas, Texas. Lee Harvey Oswald was arrested later that evening after he was seen fleeing, and he also shot a police officer. Two days later, he was shot and killed by Jack Ruby as he was being transferred. There is still a lot of controversy about Kennedy's assassination. Did Oswald really kill him? Was Oswald a Communist, a CIA, part of a conspiracy, an angry citizen? *And* who was Ruby? A small-time hustler, a mobster, or a volatile character who shot Oswald out of righteous anger? There have been books written, movies made, and people are still debating what is the real truth. Back to the day of the assassination. The whole country was in shock that something that violent could happen in America. I know that since that time we have had so many violent things happen, but at that time, it saddened and upset the whole country. Everyone was glued to their television sets, and all of us who were old enough to remember knew where we were when we heard the shocking news. It was the first event in history with modern telecommunication that was experienced almost simultaneously by people around the globe. It had a very personal impact on everyone. I don't believe anyone will ever forget seeing Lyndon Johnson sworn in as president on Air Force One with Jackie standing by in her blood-stained pink dress and pillbox hat. Everyone in the United

States and the countries around the world that had access to television sets watched his funeral. No one will ever forget little John saluting his father's casket standing with his mother and sister, Caroline, as the procession went by. Everyone felt like we had lost a member of our family. And now sadly John Jr. is gone too, much too early in a plane he was piloting with his wife and her sister. They crashed into the sea two years ago on their way to Martha's vineyard and their home.

In the fall of 1964, Bill and I were still involved in our square dancing and still loving it. We were attending a weekend square dance convention in Lansing, Michigan. I had not been feeling very good and was fighting bouts of being sick to my stomach. Out of the blue, it dawned on me that I was *pregnant*. I was forty-three years old. Carol was twenty-one, Kathy eighteen, and the twins fourteen. I thought, "I'm too old to have a baby. My family is grown. This can't be true . . . *But* it was.". I'm trying to keep this story, memoirs, or whatever honest, so I'll have to say I seriously considered an abortion. But there was no way my conscience, brain, would let me go through with one, and to this day, I am happy that I could not. Look what we would have missed. We told the girls, and they were thrilled about it. That helped me; we told the rest of the family at our Christmas buffet. Everyone seemed excited about it, and of course that helped me too. I had a few extra doctor's appointments as they wanted to keep close tabs on me. Back then forty-three-year-olds did not have babies as a general rule. Nowadays, it seems it is quite normal. I had a fairly normal pregnancy, and the girls and Bill were very helpful and tried to make things easier for me.

Kathy graduated from Edsel Ford High in June 1965. She was very smart in math and working with figures. She had a part-time job as a bookkeeper with a couple who were running a business from their home. Kathy loved it, and they liked her very much and were paying her good money, so Kathy decided that she did not want to go to college but wanted to try her hand in the business world. I do remember going too her graduation ceremony very, very pregnant. There was no way I could climb up and sit in the bleachers, so Bill had brought a lawn chair, and I sat in it. It was a lovely evening, and at least I was able to see Kathy graduate. It was another proud evening.

On July 1, 1965, William Joseph Beeler Jr. entered the world. He weighed six and a half pounds and was a normal healthy little boy! After having four girls, I made the doctors unwrap him so I could see for myself that he was a boy. Remember, in those days you were knocked out at delivery time, so I did not see him immediately. Bill had called Carol, and she was there with him when Billy was born. Without ultrasounds like they have today, we did not know the sex ahead of time. *And* when we found out we had had a boy, I insisted that he be named after his dad. I came through with not too many complications, and things were looking good for all of us. That was one spoiled little baby though with five mothers. But they say love does not spoil, just nourishes.

The year between when Billy was born and the following year when Carol graduated from college and got married was a very busy year. In looking back, I wonder now how we did everything. We were adjusting to having a baby in the house again and planning a wedding. Also, we were talking seriously about moving to be closer to the Sterling Plant where Bill worked. Carol and Edsel were engaged and wanted to be married the week after she graduated. Edsel had got a nice job at Ford's, and Carol was planning on teaching. Bill and I liked Edsel and were happy for them. On weekends when Carol came home, we were busy shopping for bridal dresses. She wanted her sisters to be in her wedding party, so we were shopping to find something they all liked too. We were also checking halls and caterers, etc. We did decide on what used to be Roma Hall in Livonia. It is now called Burton Manor. At the same time, Bill and I were shopping and checking out different neighborhoods in Sterling Heights, Troy, and surrounding areas. It was fun, interesting, and scared us to death. The price of homes at that time scared us, and we wondered if we could make it. Being brought up during the "Big Depression" had influenced both Bill and I; we were both very cautious with money and worried about it.

Besides all of this going on, we had this baby boy who was taking up a lot of our time, but it was also giving us a lot of joy in watching him grow and develop. After the first couple of months when I had Billy in a basket next to our bed at night, we rearranged the girls' dormitory upstairs. We put his crib and dressing table in the middle of the girls' bedroom. The girls went up to bed with flashlights and tried to be very quiet, as naturally Billy went to sleep before their bedtime. Carol was away at school in the fall and winter. It was quite a deal. It was another reason for pushing us into finding a bigger house. In looking back, I wonder how we did all of that. The girls were very good about it. They loved their baby brother and were thrilled to have him. We made quite a bit of conversation in the neighborhood too with having a little boy after four girls. He got a lot of attention from all of our families too. At Christmastime that year when we were taking the family pictures in front of the tree, somehow Billy always seemed to have a little crown on his head. Back in those years, I never ever wondered what I was going to do next. There seemed to always be sixteen jobs waiting for me, but I loved my life, even if some nights I did fall into bed and was asleep before my head hit the pillow. I had a lot of help and support from Bill, which made everything worthwhile.

Middle 1960s

Carol and Edsel's wedding was beautiful. They were married at St. Paul's Lutheran Church, and Carol had her long aisle to walk down like she had dreamed of. Her three sisters were her attendants, and they looked lovely in their pale green dresses. I walked down the aisle with Billy in my arms escorted by one of Edsel's friends. A little unusual for the mother of the bride? I had a portrait shoulder yellow slub silk dress in a size 10 and matching pillbox hat. Imagine! The reception at Roma Hall was very nice, and everyone seemed to have a good time.

That summer and fall were busy ones for Bill and me. We had finally decided on a builder and lot in Emerald Lakes Village in Troy, just about eight miles from Bill's work at the Sterling Plant. We made the commitment and were very worried about being able to make it. We were also excited about building our first house and having a say in the plans. Would you believe it was for $37,000.00? At that time, that was a lot of money. It was a beautiful four-bedroom colonial, and the girls were excited about having their own rooms, . . . *but* Alice and Barbara were also very angry at us for taking them away from Edsel Ford High School and their friends. Kathy was working and driving, so it really did not bother her too much. She also had met and was going out with Jim Welton, who was going to Western in Kalamazoo. They were talking about marriage.

August 30, 1966, was Bill's and mine twenty-fifth wedding anniversary. Carol, Edsel, and the girls planned a surprise party for us at Joey's Stables. We thought we were just going out for dinner, and there was a room full of our family and friends. Joey's Stables at that time was a very popular and well-known restaurant. It was a lovely party, and it was very thoughtful of the girls to plan it for us. It was a total surprise. How many people have a twenty-fifth anniversary party and have a year-old baby at home with a sitter?

I'm sitting here at my computer on a Sunday afternoon in July 2001. It is almost ninety degrees outside, and I'm very comfortable in my apartment with the air conditioning, trying to recall, remember., and put this story in some kind of order. Some memories are like yesterday, some I'm racking my brain to remember, some are bringing back such happy times and how blessed we were, some sad as I think of so many, many people that are gone and how they influenced our lives and left footprints on our hearts, as the saying goes. Writing about our lives is sort of a two-edged sword for me. In one way, it helps to pass the time and in another way makes me realize how very lonely I am today at seventy-nine. I've had such a busy and, to me, an interesting life, and now at the tail end, I wonder. I feel blessed with my family, and I know they care about me but the daily living is so lonesome and doesn't seem to be fun anymore. Enough . . . onward and upward one day at a time.

Another Chapter, Another Day

We moved into our new home in Troy in January 1967. There was a lot of excitement and some tears on leaving Dearborn and our neighbors who had become almost family. Our home in Dearborn had not been officially sold; we were on hold for the deal to go through. It was a very anxious time money-wise. Bill developed hiccups that would not go away. That's when we met our first new doctor in Rochester. Dr. Richard Dayton was a family doctor, and he helped Bill and also took care of Billy. We all liked him very much. Back to Bill's hiccups. The doctor was almost sure they were stress related, although at that time Bill did not believe he had nerves that would betray him with body reactions. He did learn differently over the years. Anyway, the doctor tried a lot of remedies and medicines, but the hiccups sort of ran their course and lasted about ten days. It was trying for all of us and very uncomfortable for Bill. It wasn't long until we were out from under the Dearborn house and things were looking better. We had brought our Beagle dog "Corky" with us, but Bill let her out one morning and we never saw or heard anything about her again. We checked all veterinary and humane societies, but there was no dog.

That spring and summer were very busy times, getting settled in our new home, which we loved, *and* trying to keep Alice and Barbara from rebelling too much about changing schools and making new friends. I know it was difficult for them, but they had to realize we really had no choice. Their dad just could not continue to drive that distance every day. We had more school and teacher conferences and had to deal with their skipping school some days. Plus, I had a toddler running all over that I had to watch every minute. Our yard was a wasteland of clay and mud when it rained. They were building all around us, so we had to watch for dugout basements and large equipment. We were busy. The twins did make new friends and were adjusting. We had a sod-laying party one spring weekend. It was a lot of hard work. Carol, Edsel, and the girls' boyfriends helped too. It was so nice to see *green* and get rid of some of the mud.

The first neighbors we became friends with lived diagonally across the street in a house like ours—Joyce and Don Brindle with two boys, Jeff and Scott (who was just a bit older than Billy). Craig came along a little later, a little younger than Bill and I, but with us having Billy, we got along great. Then Jean and Robert Darovich built next to us, and we are still good friends to this day. Jean and Dar adopted two children, Robbe and Devene, both as small infants. Billy had other children to play with in the neighborhood. I had worried about living across the street from the lake. The lake was one reason we did not choose a lot on the lake. I worried about a small child and water. *Ha!* Billy was over at the Brindle boys and the water most of the time. Of course, Joyce and I were with them when they were small. Then we also took them to the YMCA in Royal Oak on 11 Mile Road for swim lessons, starting when they were very young. They all learned to swim like fish.

The summer of 1967 also had riots in Detroit, largely due to festering anger about police brutality, poverty, and economic oppression. The riots accelerated white flight from the city. Governor George Romney ordered in National Guard Troops to restore order. In the end, forty-three people were killed. Again, we were not affected too much by the riots being thirty miles north, but TV was starting to play a big, big part in everyone's lives with all the media coverage, another sad part of Detroit falling apart and not being the city Bill and I grew up with and knew.

How do I write about what happened next in our lives? If I had the experience and wisdom that I have at this stage in my life, I might have been more accepting and helpful. Back then, I was hurt and embarrassed about what the family would think. I was wrong, and I have regretted saying some of the hurtful things I said. Our Kathy was pregnant, and I know now that it took a lot of courage for her and Jim to tell us. I'm sure she was scared too. They loved one another and were engaged to be married. We liked Jim but were disappointed. They definitely wanted to be married and had planned to live in married housing at Western while Jim completed college. I wish I had been more understanding and helpful. Bill was more accepting than I was although I did my best at that time. I loved Kathy with all my heart and just wanted the best for her. When I look back on the wonderful marriage and the love Kathy and Jim had for one another, I would not change a thing. I hope over the years that any hurtful remarks I might have made were forgiven. Then Scotty, our first grandson, was born on July 22, 1968—a nice healthy boy. He was a joy. I know Kathy and Jim struggled and really had to count pennies, but they made it. Bill and I were so proud of both of them.

I got a little ahead of my story. Kathy and Jim did have a very nice church wedding on December 22, 1967, and all our families and friends were there. We had a great reception back at our house catered by the Danish Club. We had already talked to the Danish Club about having Kathy and Jim's wedding there before things got pushed up a bit. It all worked out; Jim graduated from Western and got a good job at Ford Motor company. It was a sad time in Jim's family though; Jim's Mother, Grace, developed cancer and died shortly after Scotty was born. Jim did not have aunts and uncles like we did in our family, so his dad, Nelson, was quite alone. He did marry again after several years to a very nice lady named Louise, who we got to know at family doings.

Bill loved his job and was very good at it. I used to tease him because he was always there early, and I said he had to let the cat out. His progress reports were always excellent. I remember some of the different companies that he did business with: Federal Screw, Dana, Whirlpool. He was invited to Spring Golf outings up near Cadillac which he always enjoyed. Also, there was a man that Bill thought a lot of—Donald Boyd (and I wish I could remember what company he worked for). He had a hunting lodge up north near Mio, and Bill was invited up there for a lot of years. Then Don Boyd developed liver cancer and was gone in three months. Bill kept in touch with his widow, Blanch, until she died several years later. Don

Boyd let our family use his hunting lodge for a fall vacation, and I think everyone still remembers what a good time we had. Also, we were given the use of a lodge at Cranberry Lake, and we had the whole family up there at one time. There are a lot of nice memories, except I should have written all of this years ago when my "memory" was sharper. We also were invited to hockey games and football games with dinner either before or after. We met lots of nice people and kept on learning and growing. We were invited for a weekend over in Benton Harbor by the Whirlpool people and a weekend at the Wagon Wheel Inn in Rockford, Illinois. I remember what lovely times we had, but I can't remember all the people's names. I wish I had kept better records. Of course, all of that took place over many years. Bill also made friends with his coworkers, and we had Friday night steak roasts at one another's houses every month or so. I was always delegated to bring a big pan of sautéed mushrooms. They liked the way I fixed them.

We lived near mushroom farms, and we would go and pick up several pounds of them very fresh. Then I would wash and slice them into a pan of butter, sautéing them with the butter, dry red wine, lemon juice, salt, and fresh ground pepper. They did taste very good with the steaks. Now the mushroom farms are gone. The land has developed into new subdivisions. The farms were near where M 59 and Dequindre cross. A lot of the people are gone now too.

You know, sometimes when I sit down here to write some more on our story, I have no idea exactly what I am going to tell you about. One memory will trigger another. I had no idea I would write about the steak roasts and mushroom farms. I haven't thought of those in years. We had a lot of good times during those years, and life was very good to us.

There is another nice memory: In May 1968, we had a fiftieth anniversary party for Mom and Pop Beeler. They were both doing well and were very pleased with the party. Their five "kids" split the cost and arranged the party at Roma Hall, where we had had Carol and Edsel's wedding. We sent out invitations to all the Jackson relatives and quite a few came. We also invited their friends from church and their senior citizen group, plus all of our families. It was a nice big party, and it was a very big success. Of course, it's a known fact that any "party" the Beeler clan throws is always *great!*

Alice and Barbara were in their senior year at Troy High School. Athens had not been built yet. Then we hit another bump in our lives. Alice had met David McCalden, a very nice young man who was going to Michigan. Both of the girls never lacked for boyfriends when we moved to Troy. Alice went to visit David at college several weekends in the fall and became . . . got pregnant. They both swore undying love for one another and wanted to get married. We met David's parents, Dave and Delorus McCalden, and they were very similar to us—same family values, nice people. We were all disappointed because Alice was only seventeen and had not graduated yet, and David had big plans for college that he would have to give up. Anyway, they did get married on November 11, 1968, with a very nice church wedding and a catered reception back at our house. Again, all our family and friends came through for us and were there. Bill was instrumental in getting David hired at the Sterling Plant. Granted it was on the assembly line (not what David had planned to do with his life}, but it gave them some income. They had a small apartment in a housing project in Sterling Heights. Alice, of course, had to drop out of school. Maybe in today's world she would still have been able to go? I will give David credit though. He insisted she get her GED, which she did.

Kelly Ann was born on May 25, 1969—a beautiful baby girl. Again, both sets of parents helped what they could, but I know those were tough years for all of them. Going ahead in my story, David did work himself up and get into a much better position and salary. He was smart and ambitious, and no way did he want to stay in assembly line work.

Barbara graduated in June 1969, and we were so proud. She was happy but also disappointed because her "twin" had not graduated with her. Barbara did not want college. She was working on a co-op program with the high school at Audette Pontiac in Troy. That was where she met Kenneth Vogt, her future husband. Ken was the tower manager at Audette and Barbara was working on the switchboard. In fact, Barbara just told me the other day that she met Ken the day he got his draft notice for Vietnam. Ken served thirteen months in Nam. He was in the finance department—payroll. He flew in helicopters with soldiers' paychecks out to the lines; to this day, this is something Ken does not want to talk about. Barbara said that Ken had terrible nightmares for several years.

The day of Barbara's high school graduation, Ken's dad, John Vogt, called us and asked us to bring Barbara over after the graduation services. We all went over to their place, and it turned out Ken had made arrangements for his dad to get an engagement ring for Barbara and to give it to her, by proxy, for Ken. It was a total surprise and quite topped the graduation day. Barbara accepted the ring, and of course, there were tears all around. Ken got back home on St. Paddy's Day, 1970, and they were married on June 27. More about this later.

Several things happened in our world in the latter part of the 1960s that I would like to touch on briefly.

Martin Luther King, who's role in the Civil Rights Movement changed the course of United States' history, was assassinated on April 4, 1968, in Memphis, Tennessee, while giving a speech. Again, the whole world was shocked. They did catch the man who shot him. James Earl Ray was a career criminal and a racist. He was sentenced to ninety-nine years in prison and did die in prison in 1998. Now we have Martin Luther King Day as a national holiday in January.

That same spring a month later, Robert F. Kennedy was assassinated in California after just completing a successful run for the California Senate. That happened in a hotel as he was leaving from a speaking engagement. June 5, 1968, was another sad day in our country's history. Kennedy was assassinated by a Palestinian Arab, Sirhan Sirhan. The Kennedys who a lot of people like to think of as "our royal family" in America may have been rich and famous, but not many wanted to trade places with them for all the sadness they had in their lives. My heart went out to Mrs. Rose Kennedy; she lost her husband, a daughter, and two sons. Money and fame cannot buy everything.

The late 1960s were when the Vietnam war was also affecting our lives and the lives of so many young people. In trying to research about it to include it in my story, there were so many conflicting reports about it that unless I went into pages and pages of details it would not make sense to you. I'm going to just briefly touch on a few things. It was a war like no other, and even our leaders in the political field were hard pressed to understand it. The Vietnam war was the first armed conflict in which political and psychological warfare were the invisible fronts that the United States has ever fought. This war between North and South Vietnam had been going on in one way or another for years. Communist propaganda was extremely sophisticated and aimed at targets all around the world, not just in Vietnam. It was very believable, and most of the ordinary people in the United States did not believe we should be involved in it. There were lots and lots of demonstrations against the war. News of terrible massacres reached us along with pictures of women and children fleeing for their lives. Kent State is one terrible example. And yet the young men and women who were drafted and felt they should serve their country (like our Ken) deserved to be honored and respected, and they were not until years later; so many did not come home. That was a war there is still a lot of debate about and the first war that United States did not win. We withdrew. It was called a sort of a stalemate in one article that I read. Enough said from me; your history books will have much more, and they will probably still be debating our involvement in it.

In January 1969, Barbara was feeling kind of low;, her twin sister was married. Ken was in service and going to be sent to Vietnam. So her dad and I decided to go to Bwanna Don's, a popular pet store on Woodward Avenue, one evening. We took Barb and Billy and were just going to look at the puppies, *just look*. Well, you know the rest. This darling three-month-old Dalmatian puppy just came right out and begged us to take her home with us. Of course, we all just fell in love with her. She rode home on Barbara's lap with Billy petting her all the way. We named her "Princess Daphney," "Daffy" for short. She was AKC registered.

When we brought Daffy home with us, the vet at the pet store had told us that most puppies have to be wormed and gave us medication. We blocked off the laundry room and made her a nice bed. I forget if it was one or two days later but sure enough there was a very gross mess all over the floor in the laundry room. I took one look and told Barbara, "You wanted the puppy, you clean it up." Yuck! Poor Barb! She did do as I asked, but I should have helped her too. I've always felt a little guilty about that. I know she will never forget that even with all the puppies they have had. Daffy was a wonderful dog, and we had her for sixteen years. All the grandchildren grew up with her, and she was so gentle with all of them. She also knew about the time that Bill was due home and would always go and watch out of the big window in the living room and run to the laundry room when she heard and saw his car pull into the drive. She was also Billy's companion for those sixteen years. Daffy was a very lovable dog and gave all of us a lot of joy over the years.

Carol and Ed were doing well and bought their home on Grandon in Livonia in 1969. Carol tells me they were scared to death, but I think that is a normal reaction for most young couples. Carol is there now and in the midst of updating and re-decorating inside and out. It takes a lot of "guts" to do those kind of things by yourself. I'm very proud of her and her dad was too, the way she has made life go on after losing Edsel. I realize now how very difficult it is.

In August 2001, Carol, Cindy, and Erik returned home from a week's vacation cruise on Alaska's Inside Passage. They had a wonderful time and will never forget it. Cindy and Erik could not thank Carol enough. Carol said she wanted to do it with them as that could be the last trip like that the three of them could take together. The helicopter ride over the glacier and walking on the glacier was one of the high points of the trip. Carol said the color of the ice, turquoise deep blue, was breathtaking, *and* the noise as pieces broke off as they sailed through parts of the glacier.

But now let's get back in time.

William Joseph Beeler Jr.

On This Day in History: Thursday, July 01, 1965

Top Headlines This Quarter

U.N. Ambassador Adlai Stevenson dies of a heart attack in London. President Johnson announces his decision to increase U.S. strength in Vietnam from 75,000 to 125,000 men. President Johnson signs the Medicare bill. A major black riot breaks out in Watts, Los Angeles. Close-up photos of Mars are sent back to U.S. by Mariner 4.

Top Songs for 1965

"Downtown" by Petula Clark
"Ticket to Ride" by Beatles—
"I Hear a Symphony" by Supremes
"My Girl" by Temptations
"Eight Days a Week" by Beatles
"Stop! In the Name of Love" by Supremes
"I Got You Babe" by Sonny and Cher
"Help Me, Rhonda" by Beach Boys

1965 Prices

House	$40,000.00
Car	$2,350.00
Milk	$1.05
Gas	$.24
Bread	$.21
Postage Stamp	$0.05
Avg Income	$6,469.00

U.S. President: Lyndon Johnson
U.S. Vice President: Hubert Humphrey

People Born on July 1

Dan Aykroyd—1952
Karen Black—1942
Jamie Farr—1934
Olivia Dehaviland—1916

Academy Award Winners

Best Picture: *The Sound Of Music* directed by Robert Wise
Best Actor: Lee Marvin in *Cat Ballou*
Best Actress: Julie Christie in *Darling*

1965 Sports Headlines

Jim Clark wins Indy 500 averaging 150.7 mph. Dodgers defeat Twins 2-0 in final game of world series. Boston beats Los Angeles in basketball to become NBA champions. The Montreal Canadians win hockey's Stanley Cup.

Scott James Welton

On This Day in History: Monday, July 22, 1968

Top News Headlines This Week:

> July 23: Fred Blasie wins Fifth Wrestling World Championship Belt. July 23: PLO's first hijacking of an El Al plane. July 23: Race riot in Cleveland, eleven including three cops killed. July 24: Hoyt Wilhelm's 907th breaks Cy Young's record for pitching appearances. July 24: L I Chernykh discovers Asteroid #7450. July 25: H Wroblewski discovers Asteroid #1993 Guacolda.

Top Songs for 1968

> "The Dock of the Bay" by Otis Redding
> "I Heard It Through the Grapevine" by Marvin Gaye
> "People Got to Be Free" by Rascals
> "Mrs. Robinson" by Simon & Garfunkel
> "Hey Jude" by Beatles
> "Love Child" by Diana Ross and the Supremes
> "Love Is Blue" by Paul Mauriat
> "Honey" by Bobby Goldsboro
> "This Guy's in Love with You" by Herb Alpert
> "Tighten Up" by Archie Bell and the Drells

1968 Prices

Bread:	$0.22/loaf
Milk:	$1.21/gal
Eggs:	$1.12/doz
Car:	$2,450
Gas:	$0.34/gal
House:	$26,600

Stamp:	$0.06/ea
Avg Income:	$9,670/yr
Min Wage:	$1.60/hr
DOWAvg:	944

U.S. President: Lyndon B. Johnson
U.S. Vice President: Hubert H. Humphrey

Academy Award Winners

Best Picture: Oliver! produced by John Wolf
Best Actor: Cliff Robertson in *Charly*
Best Actress: Katherine Hepburn/Barbara Streisand in *Lion in Winter/Funny Girl*

People Born on July 22

1908 — Amy Vanderbilt, authority on etiquette (*Complete Book of Etiquette*)
1890 — Rose Fitzgerald Kennedy, Mom of JFK, RFK, and Ted

On TV in 1968

Mission: Impossible
Star Trek
The Carol Burnett Show
Adam-12
Rowan & Martin's Laugh-In
Dragnet
Batman
Hawaii Five-0
The Monkees
The Avengers

Hot New Toys in 1968

> Battling Tops
> The Outer Space Men Colorforms
> Zeroids
> Zillion Bubble Blower
> Star Trek
> Astro-Walkie Talkies Big Sneeze
> Pop Yer Top
> Billy Blastoff
> HoppityHop

Top Books in 1968

From the Mixed-Up Files of Mrs. Basil E. Frankweiler by E. L. Konigsburg
The Double Helix by James D. Watson

Kelly Ann McCalden

dMarie Time Capsule

On This Day in History: Saturday, May 24, 1969

Top News Headlines This Week:

> May 24: Beatles "Get back" single goes No. 1 and stays No. 1 for five weeks. May 25: *Midnight Cowboy* released with an X rating. May 25: Mickey Wright wins LPGA Bluegrass Golf Invitational. May 25: Sudanese government is overthrown in a military coup. May 26: Apollo 10 astronauts returned to Earth. May 26: John and Yoko begin their second bed-in (Queen Elizabeth Hotel, Montreal).

Top Songs for 1969

"Everyday People" by Sly and the Family Stone
"In the year 2525" by Zager and Evans
"Honky Tonk Women" by Rolling Stones
"Wedding Bell Blues" by Fifth Dimension
"Aquarius/Let the Sun Shine in" by Fifth Dimension
Get Back by Beatles (with Billy Preston)
"I Can't Get Next to You" by Temptations
"Sugar, Sugar" by Archies
"Dizzy" by Tommy Roe
"Crimson and Clover" by Tommy James and the Shondells

1969 Prices

Bread:	$0.23/loaf
Milk:	$1.26/gal
Eggs:	$1.14/doz
Car:	$3,400
Gas:	$0.35/gal

House:	$27,900
Stamp:	$0.06/ea
Avg Income:	$10,577/yr
Min Wage:	$1.60/hr
DOWAvg:	800

U.S. President: Richard M. Nixon
U.S. Vice President: Spiro T. Agnew

Academy Award Winners

Best Picture: *Midnight Cowboy* directed by John Schlesinger
Best Actor: John Wayne in *True Grit*
Best Actress: Maggie Smith in *The Prime of Miss Jean Brodie*

People Born on May 24

1955 — Rosanne Cash, Memphis, Tennessee, country singer ("Runaway train," "Seven year ache," "I wonder")
1819 — Victoria Alexandrine, London, England, Queen of Great Britain (1837-1901)
1941 — Bob Dylan (Zimmerman), Duluth, Minnesota, singer/songwriter (Biowin' in wind)

On TV in 1969

Star Trek
Dragnet
Rowan & Martin's Laugh-In
Hawaii Five-0
Adam-12
The Carol Burnett Show
The Avengers
The Brady Bunch Get Smart
Mission: Impossible

Hot New Toys in 1969

Barrel of Monkeys
Silly String
Zeroids
Toss Across Nerf Ball
Upsy Downsy Babies
Easy-Bake Premier Oven
Wizzer Weebles

Top Books in 1969

Portnoy's Complaint by Philip Roth
Slaughterhouse-Five by Kurt Vonnegut
Deliverance by James Dickey
Present at the Creation by Dean Acheson
The High King by Lloyd Alexander

THE 1970s

The 1970s

I am sitting here on a cloudy Sunday afternoon in August, 2001. The temperature is in the high seventies. It is very pleasant after nine days of temperatures in the very high nineties. We still need rain badly. It all seems to go around us. Alice says they have had the wettest July in their records. The whole country seems to be mixed up. We either have too much or not any. I'm racking my brain and trying very hard to keep this story in sequence; bear with me. Remember I'm trying to write about things that happened some thirty years ago; as I said before some things come back very clearly and others. Well . . .

I believe Billy started kindergarten at Troy Union School before he was five in the fall of 1969. With just having one child in school, it gave me a chance to get involved. Over the years when Billy was in elementary and middle school, I was home room mother and many times volunteered in the libraries and as a chaperone on numerous field trips. I thoroughly enjoyed those years. I got to know a lot of the teachers, administrators, and the kids.

Barbara got an office job working for Joe Schmidt (an ex-Lion Player) and really enjoyed it. Ken was still in Vietnam, and we were all worried about him and anxiously waiting for every letter from him. The year 1970 was the scene of the Kent State incident in Ohio which made world headlines. Several people were killed in a student protest against the Vietnam war. As I mentioned before, there was a great deal of controversy over our involvement in that war, and there still was today. Our young men and women who served their country in both the Korean War and the Vietnam war did not ever get the respect and honor due to them. In these later years, a lot of people have realized that and hence the Vietnam Memorial, etc. Those were tense years in the military and political field. A peace settlement was signed in Paris in January 1973. There was not a winner. Both sides fought to an agreed stalemate. The last U.S. troops left Vietnam in March 1973. Ken got home on St. Patrick's Day in 1970, with much thankful rejoicing in all our families.

In the early 1970s, I was having some dental problems and our dentist, Dr. Charles Lewis, suggested I see a periodontal specialist, Dr. Thomas Lutomski.

Anyway, it ended up that I had periodontal surgery. They did a quarter of my mouth at a time for over several months. *Ouch!* I still remember that. I had quite a bit of cream soups and milkshakes. I was thinner than I had ever been in my adult life and was wearing size 8 and 10 dress size. But I don't recommend that as a way to lose weight—very very uncomfortable. It was for the best, though now at almost eighty years, I still have my own teeth and not too many problems. Needless to say, I have been strict with dental care over the years.

As I mentioned earlier, Ken got home from Vietnam in March 1970, and they were planning on being married on June 27 that year. We were busy. It was a beautiful wedding. Our pastor at Faith Lutheran Church was going to be on vacation which was a disappointment, but you make do. Barbara and Ken were married in a lovely Methodist church off Adams Road, and then we had their wedding reception in a lovely hall on Utica Road, and neither Barbara nor I can remember the name of it. They did something there that I have not seen since. They had a candlelight circle dance of the bride and the groom, their attendants, and their parents. It was beautiful and very moving. Billy at five was their ring bearer, and Ken's brother Fritz's little girl was a flower girl. They almost stole the show.

Barbara and Ken had been offered a free motel stay right on the ocean in Lauderdale-by-the-Sea, Florida, for their honeymoon by Barbara's boss, Joe Schmidt. They took advantage of it and came home telling us what a wonderful place it was. They went down again the following summer for a vacation. The Kon Tiki in Lauderdale-by-the-Sea played a big part in our vacations over the next eight or nine years.

Ken was back and working his way up at Audette Pontiac, which is now Audette Cadillac, and he is still there to this day as their service manager. There is so much stress in his job, I wonder at times how he keeps from blowing up. He is good with people, but it's taking its toll on him.

Now Bill and I have our four daughters married and wishing and hoping they will be as happy in their marriages as we have been. We think we have four great son-in-laws. Over the years, that has been a proven fact. Bill and I both felt that like Edsel Jim and Ken had become "sons" to us, and to this day, Jim and Ken are very important to me. David was a nice person, but he and Alice were married too young and really not mature enough to start a family. Alice has been an excellent mother, and Kelly and Davey are wonderful level-headed young people of whom I am very proud. David tried, but seemed to get lost for a while. Of course, we were only hearing one side, but saw some things that hurt. I'm so glad that Kelly and Davey seem to have a good relationship with their dad now. I do seem to get sidetracked and my mind goes off in different directions. Back to my story . . .

Now there we were, Bill, Billy, Daffy, and me in our four-bedroom colonial, with our girls all on their own. Billy really missed the girls coming and going, and it took awhile for all of us to adjust. We had a lot of family get-togethers and went to Dearborn to see Grandma and Grandpa Beeler. Grandpa was starting to show his age but was still active. They enjoyed their church and their senior citizen group. Grandma Miller was still driving, and she would come out to our place and stay with us for a few days every once in a while. Billy loved that as she always made him cookies and would play board and card games with him. I'm so glad my children got to know and be around their grandparents. They were a big part of all of our lives, and we are the richer for it. I only knew my grandma Martha Manley, but I know she was a big influence on me and taught me a great deal over the years.

In December 1970, Kathy and Jim rented a big house on Mead in Dearborn, and in January, they were offered the chance to buy it. With a little struggling and Bill co-signing a loan, they were able to get it. We trusted Jim and knew that was right for them. They started immediately to improve and remodel (the first of many).

In the spring of 1971, I had a series of what turned out to be gall bladder attacks. Dr. Dayton had me go and see Dr. Peter Duhamel, who operated on me at Crittenton Hospital in Rochester. I was there for about a week, then had six weeks recuperation at home. It was at that time that my heart started to act up. Dr. Duhamel said it had acted up during the operation, and he wanted me to see a cardiologist. That's when I started going to Dr. Constantine Cerkez. A wonderful man and doctor, Bill and I both liked him immensely. There was a strange coincidence, or at least it seemed so to us. My mother, Eva Miller, had a gall bladder surgery at the same time as I did at Oakwood Hospital in Dearborn. Neither one of us could go and see the other. Evelyn and Roy were busy taking care of Mother, and Bill was taking good care of me; even Billy tried to be helpful.

David B. McCalden, a wonderful baby boy, was born on September 13, 1971, to Alice and Dave. He was named after his grandpa McCalden and his dad; since neither of them had middle names, Davey was given the initial B. It was a lot of joy for Bill and me to see and be around those babies and to watch them grow up. Billy was so pleased to have them over. There he was just a little boy himself and was uncle to these children. They always just called him Billy, never "uncle."

It was in the summer of 1972 when we started to go to the Kon Tiki for our vacations, after hearing Barbara and Ken rave about it. We made reservations for about ten days in the later part of June and the first week of July. We were there for most July Fourths for several years. We liked it as did Ken and Barb. Nice people owned it, and we always had Room Number 18, on the second floor, looking out to the ocean. Close enough, we could hear the surf at night. Wonderful! It was an efficiency so we would have our breakfast and lunch there and usually go out for our dinner. Billy loved it there, and there were usually some other children there at the same time. Nice people seemed to go there, and it was pleasant to sit around the pool and talk. We met one couple there, Rosemary and Bruce Langford. They came at the same time we did every year. They were newly married. It was the second for both of them. We enjoyed their company, and I still keep in touch with Rosemary. Bruce has since died, and she married again and lives in Evansville, Indiana. We went to visit her and Bruce once when we were on our way to Kentucky Lakes to meet Brindles.

Those were wonderful summer vacations, and I know I have a lot of nice memories of the Kon Tiki and I'm sure Billy does too. We planned, or I should say Bill planned our trips going to and coming from Florida, which included little side trips to see all of the sights and attractions along the way. We saw Lookout Mountain, Ruby Falls, Mammoth Caves, Atlanta's Underground City, and other tourist attractions that I've forgotten. I did not care for the caves, but Bill and Billy seemed to love them. I was happy to get back on top again.

Bill and I had decided after having Billy later in our lives that we were still going to do some traveling and just take him along. Finding the Kon Tiki was so great because it was a place that Billy enjoyed also. He wasn't too happy about going out to dinner at nice restaurants in the evening, but the rest of the things he enjoyed. We saw all the nice places in Florida too that he would enjoy—Cypress Gardens, Busch Gardens, Stone Mountain in Georgia, Disney World a couple of times. We saw and did some neat things. Through Bill's contacts at work, we met Martha and Bud Rykman, who had a place on Sanibel Island. We stayed on the island one summer, and they took us out deep sea shelling. That was exciting, and Billy was thrilled to get those live shells. Then they took us back to their place and showed us how they were cleaned. They worked for the Ding Darling Environmental Park on Sanibel and were very knowledgeable about the island and the animals, fascinating to listen too. We also went to The Mucky Duck restaurant on Captiva Island, a favorite of Billy's. I think he still has a dartboard with a picture of the Mucky Duck that he painted on it. We had a lot of good times together during those summers. I've got albums and lots of pictures of those summers. Perhaps Bill will want them some day. I notice how I called him Billy when he was growing up and now I call him Bill. Of course, with two Bills in the house, it did make it easier.

On June 20, 1972, our granddaughter, Krista Ann, was born, a beautiful healthy baby girl, with just loads and loads of black hair. Barbara and Ken were very happy. Dr. Robert Johnson was the obstetrics doctor who had delivered Kelly and David also. Dr. Johnson had trained under my OB doctor, Dr. Edward Sieber. It's kind of a small world sometimes. Dr. Johnson continued his practice as gynecologist after he gave up delivering babies. That was years later, but he was a friend as well as our doctor for a lot of years. My Dr. Sieber was Kathy's doctor and delivered Scotty at Mt. Carmel Hospital in Detroit. Dr. Johnson retired several years ago and was living in the Caribbean. He was killed in a boating accident two years ago. All of us were upset when we heard. He had helped all of us in a lot of ways. He had helped me after Kathy was diagnosed with incurable cancer to accept it and do the best I could. He was so warm and understanding; things like that do make me wonder *why.* Dr. Johnson had suggested books by Dr. Bernie Siegle Cove, *Medicine & Miracles,* for me to read, and they were helpful in some ways.

Cindy Ann Leinonen arrived on March 16, 1973. Carol had to have an emergency C section. Cindy was stubborn and just wouldn't put her chin down to come out. They had us worried for awhile, but everything turned out just fine. Carol and Cindy were doing fine. Edsel was such a proud daddy. Carol had had some problems getting pregnant, and they had been starting to talk about adoption. We were all delighted when Cindy was born.

Kenneth George Martin came into all our lives on November 10, 1975. Now both our twin daughters had a girl and a boy. Barbara had quit her job at Joe Schmidt's to stay home with Krista. She and Ken had bought a house on Cummings in Royal Oak, and Barbara was taking in children for day care. She wanted to stay home with her children, and that was the way she could do it. There was good money in it, and she was good with the children, but it was a lot of hard work too. The children thrived with other children to play and learn with. Barbara always had things planned for their days. We were so proud of our girls and the way they were handling their lives. All of them were doing quite well, struggling, of course, like most young couples but making it. We were so very grateful and counting our blessings. All of our grandchildren were normal, healthy children and growing beautifully.

That was a time in our lives though when our parents were growing older and having health problems. Grandpa Beeler was over eighty and had been in and out of the Oakwood Hospital in Dearborn the last couple of years he was with us. Oakwood Hospital had just started to charge for parking, and it amounted to quite a bit for seniors on a limited budget when they went to see their mate every day. I started one of my letter writing campaigns to the management at the hospital about having reduced parking rates for seniors. It took quite a few letters and talking to different management people, *but* I'm happy to say my work did pay off and they did start a reduced rate for seniors. All that took time and didn't do Grandma Beeler much good. Grandpa Beeler died in October 1976 of congestive heart failure. He also had prostate cancer, but that did not cause his death. Because Grandpa Beeler had prostate cancer and it is a hereditary disease, all of his sons were cautioned to be checked for it and to keep a watch for it. As it turned out, each of the sons had it and were and are taking treatments for it. It was not instrumental in either Bill's or Joe's death. They had both been on hormone treatments and their PSA count was very low. So far, Robert and Roy are doing fine with treatments controlling it. But again, all the Beeler males will have to be on the lookout and keep a close check on it, starting around their forties. They are learning more all the time, and it is controllable with proper treatment.

Grandpa Beeler's death was quite a blow to our family and caused a lot of heartache. We had been very close. But again, life does go on. Grandma Beeler was an independent person, but her health was not the best, and we were all worried about her. We made a lot of trips to Dearborn for the next four years. They were willing trips because we cared. Mom Beeler and I had always gotten along good, but I think we became even closer over those years. There were daily phone calls just to check. I called it our gossip time. They were wonderful in-laws, and I thought the world of them.

During those years, Bill and I both also got involved with Boy Scouts because of Billy, and some of the friends Billy made during those years are still his good friends today and were all out in Colorado at his wedding party. Bill thoroughly enjoyed working with the Scouts, and with his church work on the council, he was a very busy man. Being busy and being helpful was one of the things that made Bill happy. He was never a person who could sit around doing nothing. He had to be busy. Sometimes I thought he was doing too much, but he thrived on it. He was also active in our Homeowners Association and volunteered for evening patrol in our subdivision as it was growing.

Meanwhile, I was busy with my volunteer work at the school, keeping up our big house and having a good meal on the table when Bill came home from work. I did love being a homemaker. I loved to cook and bake and was good at it. Also during the years just before Billy started Smith Middle School (across Rochester Road), I started another letter writing campaign. Let me explain. Since we had moved to Troy in 1967 when Rochester Road was a two-lane road, the building, subdivisions, and traffic had increased tremendously. Rochester Road had been widened, but there was no traffic light at the intersection. The school bus had to cross Rochester early in the morning to take the students to Smith Middle School. I and a lot of other parents were upset about it, but no one did anything until I started to write letters to the Road Commission Department in Lansing, Michigan. I believe the man's name was Peter Gallager. He received a lot of mail from me, begging for a traffic light to protect our kids. I also sent him signed petitions with concerned parents' signatures. It took awhile as so many political things do, *but* we finally got our traffic light! I was out there the day they were installing it and taking pictures. I was embarrassing our son to death. Now he is a parent. I bet he looks at it differently. A lot of people in the subdivision called it "Vivian's traffic light." I know I did feel good about it, and it was worth the hard work.

As I told you, my mind keeps going in different directions, and there was so much happening and going on during those years I'm not getting it all in the correct chronological order. Oh well, you will just have to accept my order as my memory goes, and who truly is going to argue with me or care?

It was sometime in 1975 that Dr. C. Cerkez my cardiologist wanted me to have a heart catheterization. He thought that perhaps I had some blockage. As it turned out, I did have a catheterization at Harper Hospital in Detroit by Dr. Emeril Espirtu. It showed that I had very, very small arteries for the blood to flow through to my heart and that was causing my spastic angina. My medication was changed (and increased), but I'm still here as this story proves. I thought that I would sure go before Bill. You sure never know. My arm was a solid black, blue green, and yellow for a while after that, but I was doing fine. It is strange for both the catheterizations that I had (another one in 1981), the doctors used my arms. Now they always seem to use the groin area!

On January 14, 1977, Erik Martin Leinonen joined our family. Carol knew that the baby would be a cesarean and planned the date. Erik was a healthy little boy, and we were all so happy with his safe arrival. Because Cindy and Erik had both been large babies, Carol was checked for diabetes, and she had a few problems. Doctors advised her that it would be wise not to have more children. Both she and Edsel were pleased with their beautiful girl and boy; that did not bother them too much. Now Bill and I had seven wonderful grandchildren. What a blessing! We had so many wonderful family parties and holidays together. We were a very lucky family.

Around this same period of time, I was taking Billy to catechism classes at our church. Our pastor at that time was Bruce Kjellburg, who all of us liked very much. Billy finished the classes and was confirmed. I know that we have the exact date in our photo albums somewhere, but at the moment, I can't pin it down. I have to tell you a embarrassing story about me, and it happened one evening as I was driving Billy to his classes at church. I was also helping with the classes. I got my first driving ticket. We had just left our subdivision street and I was taking Atkins Road short cut over to John R. I was busy talking to Billy when I saw lights flashing behind me. I was shocked and pulled over. The policeman was very nice but asked me if I knew how fast I was going. I didn't. It was a residential zone and twenty-five miles an hour, which I did know. He said I was going at about thirty-eight. I hadn't been paying attention. Anyway, I had to pay the fine. But I guess being in my fifties and it being my first ticket, I was pretty lucky. But boy, I was embarrassed about it. I did get a lot of teasing from my family about it as I have always been such a stickler for following rules. So far I have never received another, and here I am almost eighty. Lucky, I guess, which makes me wonder how long I will be a safe driver and hope I have sense enough to know when I'm not.

I found this letter tucked away in one of Bill's drawers in his chest.

August 30, 1975

To my husband on our 34th wedding anniversary—

I cannot help but love you when . . . I think of all the days . . . that we have been together in . . . so many happy ways . . . so many, many memories . . . some sad and hard to swallow . . . but always knowing our love was there. I love you for being yourself . . . your kindness to me . . . but most of all I love you for . . . *Dependability* . . . No matter what may happen, you . . . are always at my side . . . To fill my heart with solace and . . . with Confidence and *Pride* . . . I never have to worry, for . . . I know that you are there. To comfort and to kiss me and . . . keep me in your care . . . and that is why I love you, dear . . . My life belongs to you . . . My hopes, my fears, my dreams, and all of me . . . are always safe with you.

Happy Anniversary, Darling. I pray every day God will give us a lot more years together.

Thank you again for our beautiful vacation and taking me down to the ocean again, you know how I feel about it.

And thank you for this past week. As much as I love Billy . . . it is so wonderful to be alone with you for a while. It's another beautiful link in our chain of memories.

All my love always—
Vivian

I'm very *proud* and feel very *special* to be known as *Mrs.* William J. Beeler.

Wrote Aug. 26, 2001

Late 1970s

After we lost Grandpa Beeler, Bill was made executor for Mom Beeler to help her take care of their business affairs. As he was the eldest of the Beeler children and always looked up to by his brothers and sister, it was in complete agreement with all. (Marguerette made a remark the other day when she, Roy, and I were having lunch together. She was talking about moving to the Village, and with Roy and I already being here, she said, "Here we are following Bill, our big brother again" This was August 24, 2001.) I thought that was interesting. Bill and I always did get along with all his brothers and sister, and they did seem to look up to him a bit.

Anyway, this was just another job for Bill and one he was very willing to handle. He did make a few more trips to Dearborn, but we were going down anyway to check on his mother.

Around 1978, we were debating about Bill Jr. having an operation on his jaw to bring his chin forward and align his teeth better. We had been taking him to Dr. Anschultz, a well-known and respected orthodontist in Rochester. He had been wearing braces to straighten his teeth, but the doctor was now advising this operation. He sent us to see two highly respected orthodontist surgeons—Dr. Arthur Even and Dr. Bonk. We took Billy with us to hear and listen to all those consultations, as we wanted him to be a willing patient. It involved breaking his lower jaw and extending it forward. That would mean that his jaw would be wired shut for six weeks and he would be on a liquid diet. It did not sound like a lot of fun. Billy agreed and wanted the operation. We did this in the summer of 1978 or 1979. I remember it well, but not the exact year. Maybe Bill does. He came through the operation fine. It was at Crittenton Hospital, and he was in for several days. It was miserable for him, and it was a very *long* six weeks. He got very tired of milk shakes and soups;, we even tried pizza in a blender. It didn't work too well. Needless to say, his mood was not the greatest, and I can't say that I blame him. It had to be awful. It was hard on his dad and me too, just trying to live with him and keep our patience. I think Bill is glad now that he went through it. It did improve his jaw line and looks overall. It was called mandibular operation (sp). That was not our best summer but worthwhile.

In the fall of 1979, there was an advertisement in the paper by Dalton Book Store at Oakland Mall saying: "Do you like books? Do you like people? Would you like to earn some extra money for the holidays?" It just hit something in my brain that would not leave me alone. Without telling anyone, I went for an interview and was hired the same day. I had requested just part-time and day-time work. What an ego boost for me! Remember, I had not worked except as a volunteer since my early days at the phone company. *And* I was fifty-eight years old. Now I had to go home and tell Bill and Billy and the family what I had done. They were proud of me and told me to give it a try.

I was working Mondays, Tuesdays, and Thursdays from nine to three at minimum wage. I loved it. I was a cashier most of the time. When we weren't busy, I shelved books and restocked the bestseller racks, etc. When I came in the morning, I dusted floors or cleaned the bathroom, whatever had to be done. Everyone I worked with was younger, but we got along great and they seemed to like me. Being around all the books was a delight for me. Of course, we got employee discounts and I spent a lot of what I earned on books. Bill never minded the money I spent on books because I enjoyed them so much. Of course, this was after we did not have to count every penny to put food on the table and pay the bills. 1 worked at the bookstore for eight years and enjoyed every minute. I would have almost paid them to let me work there. I received several raises over the years but not any big money. I was able to help pay for our new kitchen floor and our new dinette set—Maple with captain chairs, and I'm using it and still like it today. Billy was pleased with all the science fiction books I was able to get him, and I kept my mother and Aunt Fran supplied with books. It was fun. That job filled a need for me at that time in my life. Bill was a growing teenager and didn't need me as much. Although with my hours, I was home shortly after he got home from school, which I think was a good thing. I think I also needed to feel that I was still a contributing person in our world. Like I mentioned, it was a ego boost for me. I had several bosses during my eight years there, and they all liked me and were satisfied with my work. Several times I had been asked to work more, but I really just wanted to do part time. I was very dependable, and so many of the young people weren't. I had some nice reports from the "higher ups." It was good for me.

Davey B. Mccalden

On This Day in History: Monday, September 13, 1971

Top News Headlines This Week:

> September 13: Frank Robinson hits his 500th Hr. September 13: World Hockey Association formed. September 13: Eleven guards and thirty-one prisoners die in takeover at Attica State Prison. September 13: Nikita Krushchev, Soviet premier, buried in Moscow. September 13: WIIQ TV channel 41 in Demopolis, AL (PBS) begins broadcasting. September 14: Cleve Indians and Wash Senators play 20 innings.

Top Songs for 1971

"Knock Three Times" by Dawn
"Maggie May" by Rod Stewart
"How Can You Mend a Broken Heart" by Bee Gees
"Go Away Little Girl" by Donny Osmond
"Joy to the World" by Three Dog Night
"It's Too Late" by Carole King
"Family Affair" by Sly and the Family Stone
"One Bad Apple" by Osmonds
"Brand New Key" by Melanie
"Gypsies, Tramps and Thieves" by Cher

1971 Prices

Bread:	$0.25/loaf
Milk:	$1.32/gal
Eggs:	$1.18/doz
Car:	$3,742
Gas:	$0.36/gal

House:	$28,300
Stamp:	$0.08/ea
Avg Income:	$11,583/yr
Min Wage:	$1.60/hr
DOWAvg:	890

U.S. President: Richard M. Nixon
U.S. Vice President: Spiro T. Agnew

Academy Award Winners

Best Picture: *The French Connection* directed by William Friedkin
Best Actor: Gene Hackman in *The French* Connection
Best Actress: Jane Fonda in *Klute*

People Born on September 13

1925 — Mel Torm, Chicago, Illinois, jazz singer "Velvet Fog" (Jet Set, Night Court)
1948 — Nell Carter, Birmingham, Alabama, actress (*Neii-Gimme a Break*, *Lobo*)
1944 — (Winifred) Jacqueline Bisset, England, actress (*Class*, *Deep*, *Secrets*)
1931 — Barbara Bain Chic, actress (*Cinnamon, Mission Impossible, Space 1999*)

On TV in 1971

Adam-12
Hawaii Five-0
The Odd Couple
Columbo
The Carol Burnett Show
The Mary Tyler Moore Show
The Brady Bunch Show
All in the Family
Mission: Impossible
Rowan & Martin's Laugh-In

Hot New Toys in 1971

    Mastermind
    Split-Level Aggravation
    Stay Alive
    Kicktail Skateboard

Top Books in 1971

    The Summer of the Swans by Betsy Cromer Byars
    Angle of Repose by Wallace Stegner
    A Theory of Justice by John Rawls

Krista Sue Vogt

dMarle Time Capsule

This Day in History: Tuesday, June 20, 1972

Top News Headlines This Week:

> June 22: *Man of La Mancha* opens at Beaumont Theater NYC for 140 performances. June 23: Hurricane Agnes is costliest natural disaster in American history. June 23: Nixon and Haldeman agree to use CIA to cover up Watergate. June 23: President Nixon signs act barring sex discrimination in college sports. June 24: "Troglodyte (Cave Man)" by Jimmy Castor Bunch peaks at No. 6. June 24: Wake Island becomes unincorporated territory of U.S. (U.S. Air Force).

Top Songs for 1972

> "A Horse with No Name" by America
> "Alone Again (Naturally)" by Gilbert O'Sullivan
> "I Can See Clearly Now" by Johnny Nash
> "Me and Mrs. Jones" by Billy Paul
> "The First Time Ever I Saw Your Face" by Roberta Flack
> "The Candy Man" by Sammy Davis, Jr.
> "American Pie" by Don Mclean
> "Without You" by Nilsson
> "Baby Don't Get Hooked On Me" by Mac Davis
> "Lean On Me" by Bill Withers

1972 Prices

Bread:	$0.25/loaf
Milk:	$1.33/gal
Eggs:	$1.20/doz
Car:	$3,879

Gas:	$0.36/gal
House:	$30,500
Stamp:	$0.08/ea
Avg Income:	$12,625/yr
Min Wage:	$1.60/hr
DOW Avg:	1,020

U.S. President: Richard M. Nixon
U.S. Vice President: Spiro T. Agnew

Academy Award Winners

Best Picture: *The Godfather*
Best Actor: Marlon Brando in *The Godfather*
Best Actress: Liza Minelli in *Cabaret*

People born on June 20

1924 — Chet Atkins Luttrell Tenn, guitarist (Me & My Guitar)
1945 — (Moma) Anne Murray, Springhill, Nova Scotia, Canada, singer
(Snow Bird)
1950 — Lionel Richie, singer (Commodores, Hello, Penny Lover)

On TV in 1972

The Mary Tyler Moore Show
The Bob Newhart Show
Columbo
All in the Family
The Brady Bunch
Emergency
The Waltons
M*A*S*H
Hawaii Five-0
The Odd Couple

Hot New Toys in 1972

Séance
Action Jackson
Hacky Sack
Eve/ Knievel Figures
Fashion Plates
Radio Flyer "Fireball 2000"
World's Greatest Super Heroes
Odyssey (Odyssey 100)
Pong

Top Books in 1972

The Great Bridge by David McCullough
Mrs. Frisby and the Rats of NIMH by Robert C. O'Brien

Cindy Ann Leinonon

On This Day in History: Friday, March 16, 1973

Top News Headlines This Week:

March 17: Queen Elizabeth II opens new London Bridge. March 17: St. Patrick's Day marchers carry fourteen coffins commemorating Bloody Sunday. March 18: *Seesaw* opens at Uris Theater NYC for 296 performances. March 18: Sandra Haynie wins LPGA Orange Blossom Golf Classic. March 19: Dean tells Nixon, "There is a cancer growing on the Presidency." March 20: Roberto Clemente elected to hall of fame, eleven weeks after his death.

Top Songs for 1973

"Let's Get It On" by Marvin Gaye
"Tie a Yellow Ribbon Round the Old Oak Tree" by Dawn
"Crocodile Rock" by Elton John
"Bad, Bad Leroy Brown" by Jim Croce
"My Love" by Paul McCartney and Wings
"Killing Me Softly with His Song" by Roberta Flack
"Top of the World" by Carpenters
"You're So Vain" by Carly Simon
"Keep On Truckin'" by Eddie Kendricks
"Midnight Train to Georgia" by Gladys Knight and the Pips

1973 Prices

Bread:	$0.27/loaf
Milk:	$1.36/gal
Eggs:	$1.22/doz
Car:	$4,052

Gas:	$0.39/gal
House:	$35,500
Stamp:	$0.08/ea
Avg Income:	$13,622/yr
Min Wage:	$1.60/hr
DOWAvg:	851

U.S. President: Richard M. Nixon
U.S. Vice President: Gerald R. Ford

Academy Award Winners

Best Picture: *The Sting* directed by George Roy Hill
Best Actor: Jack Lemmon in *Save The Tiger*
Best Actress: Glenda Jackson in *A Touch Of Class*

People Born on March 16

1926 — Jerry Lewis (Joseph Levitch), Newark, New Jersey, entertainer/ fund raiser (MDA), especially loved in France
1946 — Erik Estrada, New York, actor (*CHiPs, Cross & Switchblade, Lightblast*)
1912 — Patricia Nixon (Thelma Catherine), Ely, Nevada, First Lady (1969-74)
1903 — Mike Mansfield (Senator-Democrat-MT) majority whip

On TV in 1973

The Mary Tyler Moore Show
The Bob Newhart Show
The Brady Bunch
Columbo
Emergency
The Waltons
All in the Family
*M*A*S*H*
Hawaii Five-0
The Odd Couple

Hot New Toys in 1973

    Evel Knievel Stunt Cycle
    The Lone Ranger Action Figure
    Boggle
    Perfection
    Dungeons & Dragons
    Shrinky Oinks
    Fisher-Price Movie Viewer

Top Books in 1973

    Julie of the Wolves by Jean Craighead George

Kenny G. Vogt

dMarie Time Capsule

On This Day in History: Monday, November 10, 1975

Top News Headlines This Week:

November 10: Ore ship *Edmund Fitzgerald* and crew of twenty-one lost in storm on Lake Superior. November 10: PLO leader Yasser Arafat addresses UN in NYC. November 10: UN General Assembly approves resolution equating Zionism with racism. November 10: Royals release slugger Harmon Killebrew, ending his twenty-two-year career. November 11: Angola gains independence from Portugal (National Day). November 11: Australian PM removed by crown (first elected PM removed in two hundred years).

Top Songs for 1975

"Rhinestone Cowboy" by Glen Campbell
"Fly, Robin, Fly" by Silver Convention
"Bad Blood" by Neil Sedaka
"That's the Way (I Like It)" by KC & the Sunshine Band
"Island Girl" by Elton John
"Love Will Keep Us Together" by Captain & Tennille
"Jive Talkin'" by Bee Gees
"He Don't Love You" by Tony Orlando & Dawn
"Philadelphia Freedom" by Elton John
"Fame" by David Bowie

1975 Prices

Bread:	$0.28/loaf
Milk:	$1.40/gal
Eggs:	$1.26/doz

Car:	$4,950
Gas:	$0.57/gal
House:	$42,600
Stamp:	$0.10/ea
Avg Income:	$15,546/yr
Min Wage:	$2.1 0/hr
DOWAvg:	852

U.S. President: Gerald R. Ford
U.S. Vice President: Nelson A. Rockefeller

Academy Award Winners

Best Picture: *One Flew Over The Cuckoo's Nest* directed by Milos Forman
Best Actor: Jack Nicholson in *One Flew Over The Cuckoo's Nest*
Best Actress: Louise Fletcher in *One Flew Over The Cuckoo's Nest*

People born on November 10

1483 — Martin Luther, Eisleben Germany, founded Protestantism
       1925—Richard Burton, South Wales, actor (Cleopatra, Virginia Woolf)
1959 — MacKenzie Phillips Alexandria VA, actress (Julie-one Day at a Time)
1935 — Roy Scheider Orange NJ, actor (All That Jazz, Jaws)

On TV in 1975

The Waltons
The Bob Newhart Show
The Rockford Files
Happy Days
All in the Family
Little House on the Prairie
*M*A*S*H*
Barney Miller
Columbo
Emergency

Hot New Toys in 1975

Evel Knievel Chopper
The Green Machine
Hello Kitty
Payday
The Archies
Holly Hobbie Oven
Evel Knievel Road and Trail Adventure Set
Hugo: Man of a Thousand Faces
Space: 1999 figures

Top Books in 1975

The Great War and Modern Memory by Paul Fussell
A Dance to the Music of Time by Anthony Powell
M. C. Higgins, the Great by Virginia Hamilton
Ragtime by E. L. Doctorow

Shannon Marie Pack-Beeler

On This Day in History: Monday, December 29, 1975

Top News Headlines This Week:

December 29: Eleven killed, seventy-five hurt by terrorist bomb at LaGuardia Airport in New York, NY. December 30: Constitution of Democratic Republic of Madagascar comes into force. December 30: "Boccaccio" closes at Edison Theater NYC after seven performances. December 31: 42 Sugar Bowl: Alabama 13 beats Penn State 6. December 31: Felix Aguilar Observatory discovers Asteroid #4725. January 1: NBC replaces the peacock logo.

Top Songs for 1975

"Rhinestone Cowboy" by Glen Campbell
"Bad Blood" by Neil Sedaka
"Fly, Robin, Fly" by Silver Convention
"That's the Way (I Like It)" by KC & the Sunshine Band
"Love Will Keep Us Together" by Captain & Tennille
"Jive Talkin'" by Bee Gees
"Island Girl" by Elton John
"He Don't Love You by Tony Orlando & Dawn
"Philadelphia Freedom" by Elton John
"Fame" by David Bowie

1975 Prices

Bread: $	0.28/loaf
Milk:	$1.40/gal
Eggs:	$1.26/doz
Car:	$4,950

Gas:	$0.57/gal
House:	$42,600
Stamp:	$0.10/ea
Avg Income:	$15,546/yr
Min Wage:	$2.1 0/hr
DOWAvg:	852

U.S. President: Gerald R. Ford
U.S. Vice President: Nelson A. Rockefeller

Academy Award Winners

Best Picture: *One Flew Over The Cuckoo's Nest* directed by Milos Forman
Best Actor: Jack Nicholson in *One Flew Over The Cuckoo's Nest*
Best Actress: Louise Fletcher in *One Flew Over The Cuckoo's Nest*

People Born on December 29

1947 — Ted Danson, San Diego, California, actor (*Sam Malone-Cheers, 3 Men & a Baby*)
1938 — Jon Voight Yonkers, New York, actor (*Deliverance, Midnight Cowboy*)
1876 — Pablo Casals Vendrell, Catalonia, Spain, cellist/conductor/ composer

On TV in 1975

The Waltons
The Bob Newhart Show
The Rockford Files
Happy Days
Little House on the Prairie
*M*A*S*H*
All in the Family
Barney Miller
Columbo
Emergency

Hot New Toys in 1975

Evel Knievel Chopper
The Green Machine
The Archies
Hello Kitty
Payday
Holly Hobbie Oven
Evel Knievel Road and Trail Adventure Set
Hugo: Man of a Thousand Faces
Space: 1999 figures

Top Books in 1975

The Great War and Modem Memory by Paul Fussell
A Dance to the Music of Time by Anthony Powell
Ragtime by E. L. Doctorow
M. C. Higgins, the Great by Virginia Hamilton

Erik Martin Leinonon

On This Day in History: Friday, January 14, 1977

Top News Headlines This Week:

> January 15: Coneheads debut on *Saturday Night Live*. January 15: Jane Blalock wins LPGA Colgate Triple Crown Golf Tournament. January 16: Cap's H Monahan scored on second penalty shot against Islanders. January 17: 7th AFC-NFC pro bowl, AFC wins 24-14. January 17: Zaire President Mobutu visits Belgium. January 17: KC releases Tommy Davis, ends an eighteen-year career with ten teams.

Top Songs for 1977

"Sir Duke" by Stevie Wonder
"Best of My Love" by Emotions
"Evergreen (from 'A Star Is Born')" by Barbara Streisand
"Rich Girl" by Daryl Hall and John Oates
"I Just Want to Be Your Everything" by Andy Gibb
"You light Up My Life" by Debby Boone
"Star Wars Theme" Cantina Band by Meco
"How Deep Is Your Love" by Bee Gees
"Tom Between Two Lovers" by Mary MacGregor
"Got to Give It Up" by Marvin Gaye

1977 Prices

Bread:	$0.32/loaf
Milk:	$1.44/gal
Eggs:	$1.30/doz
Car:	$5,814
Gas:	$0.64/gal
House:	$54,200

Stamp:	$0.13/ea
Avg Income:	$18,264/yr
Min Wage:	$2.30/hr
DOWAvg:	831

U.S. President: Gerald R. Ford
U.S. Vice President: Nelson A. Rockefeller

Academy Award Winners

   Best Picture: *Annie Hall* directed by Woody Allen
   Best Actor: Richard Dreyfuss in *The Good-bye Girl*
   Best Actress: Diane Keaton in *Annie Hall*

People Born on January 14

1919 — Andy Rooney Albany, New York, CBS news correspondent (*Sixty Minutes*)
1906 — William Bendix, New York City, New York, actor (*Lifeboat, Babe Ruth Story, Life of Riley*)
1941 — (Dorothy) Faye Dunaway, Bascom, Florida, actress (*Chinatown, Bonnie & Clyde*)
1892 — Hal Roach, early film director/producer (*1 Million BC*)

On TV in 1977

   Mork & Mindy
   Alice
   Soap
   Laverne & Shirley
   Three's Company
   Happy Days
   CHiPs
   Little House on the Prairie
   Charlie's Angels
   Barney Miller

Hot New Toys in 1977

Pro Foto-Football
Mr. Machine (Re-issue)
Pulsar
The Fembot
Star Wars Action Figures
Evel Knievel Strata Cycle
Battling Spaceships
Fisher-Price Movie Theater
Mr. Microphone

Top Books in 1977

Samuel Johnson by Walter Jackson Bate
Roll of Thunder, Hear My Cry by Mildred D. Taylor

THE 1980s

March 17, 2002
The 1980s

Here it is almost Halloween in 2001. It's taken me awhile to get back to writing. I've had a trip out to Colorado for Sydney's first birthday and of course a date in history that all of you will not forget—September 11, 2001: the terrorist attack on the World Trade Center, the Pentagon and the plane crash in Pennsylvania, the loss of over five thousand lives. It's hard to comprehend or to make any sense out of it. Now we are at war "again." I've lived through too many it seems. This is a different "war." We are fighting an enemy that we can't find, an "evil" that we can't see and don't know where they will strike next—a biochemical anthrax attack in our postal system. In one way, it has united this country like never before, *but* it has also created a feeling of fear and uneasiness. We don't feel "safe" anywhere anymore.

Then in our own family, our own world turned upside down again with the news of Barbara's breast cancer. It did not show up in her mammogram. It was swollen and inflamed, and she thought that perhaps she had injured it in some way. Biopsies proved cancer. After losing our Kathy to ovarian cancer the previous year, that did not seem fair. I can't help but wonder why I have to see two daughters of mine go through that very rough road. We are all very positive and we know for a fact that there are a lot more breast cancer survivors than ovarian cancer survivors. We know Barb is going to make it. But that still doesn't answer the question of "why?" Barb has had two chemo treatments so far and is due for her third one on November 1. The doctors are talking of four treatments, three weeks apart, then surgery. Of course, she has lost her hair, and that is very, very hard for any woman. My heart aches for her. Why couldn't it be me? As a mother, I can't help but ask that question and especially at my age. I've lived my life. I would give anything to trade places with her. I also realize that is not possible. Barbara has a wonderful attitude. Ken is with her all the way; with her family and her many friends, she will get through this. I'm very proud of her.

I also turned the big eighty since I was last writing *Our Story*. I wrote about some of my feelings and that day in "Reflections on Turning Eighty" in a paper I will include with these.

I do have to tell you a little about our trip to Colorado, which was a sort of a "Comedy of Errors." I am very grateful we were able to go and to see Shannon, Bill, and Sydney on her first birthday, but I really wondered for a while if we were supposed to go. Carol had offered to go with me, and I was relieved. I have never traveled by myself, and I'm not sure if I would have gone alone. Anyway, Carol was going to help me make the trip. Then at one o'clock on the morning of the day we are leaving Carol ran into a chair leg with her bare foot and broke a bone just behind her toes on her left foot. Putting ice on it and hoping she had just injured it, she waited awhile. It was very painful; Erik was sleeping (he was staying there waiting to sign closing papers on the house he had bought). Carol woke him, and he took her to ER. Sure enough, it was broken. They taped it and gave her a special shoe and a crutch and said, "Good luck." There was no sleep for her that night. Eve and Carol picked me up at 10:00 a.m. as arranged.

There was Carol in the back seat with her leg stretched out on the seat and looking a little pale. She said, "Mom, we are going" I'll make it." We got through security and checked in without too much trouble. Carol was in a wheelchair, and I was hurrying those long concourses to keep up. Carol was telling the attendants to slow down for me. We got to the proper place and tried to get Carol's leg propped and comfortable. Even with pain pills, she "hurt." Of course we were there the two hours ahead of time they had suggested. Then our plane had a two-hour mechanical delay The flight itself was uneventful. We did not get into Denver until almost evening. We were supposed to be there at 1:00 p.m. their time. Shannon was waiting and was shocked to see Carol in a wheelchair with her leg propped up.

Anyway, we got to Bill and Shannon's and were very grateful. Both Carol and I were so tired because of the long delay and flight. Carol was in pain and had no sleep. We weren't the best company that evening, and both went to bed much earlier than we usually do. Of course, there was a two-hour time change also. Bill had wanted to take us out for a nice dinner, but Carol did not want to move and neither did I. We suggested pizza, and that worked out fine. Sydney was such a little doll, but of course, we were strangers to her, so we just watched. She seemed so little to be toddling all over, such a sweet smile and so proud of herself. What a joy! It was fun to be there for her birthday party and seeing Shannon's family again and their friends. I think there were ten little children at Sydney's party. I had not been around those many little ones in years. I just watched in awe! They were all good too. What energy! Oh, I would like some. I wish it would come bottled. Carol had to sit in Bill's La-Z-Boy in the comer and just watch too. I know she would have preferred to participate. She is so good with children.

We had a lovely time the few days that we were there. Bill was becoming quite a chef. He fixed us steamed shrimp and steamed asparagus one night and grilled filets and steamed broccoli another night. They both had taken time off to be with us, and we enjoyed every minute. Bill was staying up half the nights to study and do papers as finals were that week too, talk about things piling up. He got A's in both classes, so it was worth it. His dad would be very proud of him. 1 know I am. He is such a good husband *and* daddy. He and Shannon seem very happy. It was so much fun to see him taking care of Sydney. I watched him give her bath one day. She loved it. Even when he poured big cups of water over her head, she laughed. It was fun. The last couple of days we were there, Sydney was raising her arms for me to pick her up and smiling just for me. It melted my heart; too bad we lived so far apart. We went to Cherry Creek Mall the last day as Bill wanted me to visit "The Tattered Cover" bookstore as I had mentioned reading about it in one of my book papers. It was quite a place to see. We spent most of the time in the children's section watching Sydney; she loved books. I hope it will continue. I found out about the program of *Bear, In The Big Blue House* and books to go with it. It was delightful! There were wonderful memories to take home, *and* I was glad to be home. I think I'm getting a little old for traveling. It does seem to wear me out.

Now that I've written what's been going on in the present time, I guess it's time to go back to the 1980s where I left off in our story. Got to get my "remembering" cap on.

The 1980s were mostly good years for us and of course very busy ones. I do have to start on a sad note though. We lost Mom Beeler in April 1980. She had just turned eighty (my age) in March. She had been in ill health ever since "Pop" had died in 1976. She had a rare form of anemia, and her blood count kept going lower and lower. It caused her to "black out" and fall several times. It was not leukemia, but doctors were puzzled. She was in the hospital a couple of times for blood transfusions. We would down to Dearborn very often as we were concerned about her. At one time, she stayed with us for a short period of time, but she wanted to go back to her "own" place. My own personal feeling is that besides her blood problem, she just gave up; she missed her partner so much. We did have an autopsy as doctors were so puzzled by her blood condition. We thought it might be genetic. It turned out they really could not discover anything to help us. I missed her terribly. She had turned out to be a good friend to me and a wonderful mother-in-law. We had become even closer with our daily phone calls; we called it our "gossip time," but she knew I was checking on her too. Bill was very busy trying to settle all the business affairs, and we had to get the house cleaned out to sell. His brothers and sister, wives and husband pitched in to help, and everything seemed to move along quite smoothly. It was a big job though and made all of us say, "We have to go home and start cleaning out our own homes." *But* like most good intentions, not many of us did it.

I was still working at the bookstore and loving it, but in early 1981, my angina started to act up again. Dr. Cerkez had gone into teaching back in Greece and had turned me over to Dr. Pierre Atallah, a younger doctor with a very good reputation. Dr. Atallah wanted me to have another heart catheterization, which I had at Crittenton Hospital in Rochester. I was in the hospital for several days. They seemed to keep you longer then and not ship you out so fast. They adjusted and changed some of my medications. Again the results of the cath were very narrow veins and arteries but no blockages, which was good news. Bill had been so worried and was there at the hospital before he went to work in the morning and again in the evening. It was a bit of a scare, but I came through it fine. It was because I had been having some heart problems for years that I always thought I would go first, not Bill. He was always my "rock of Gibraltar" and always took care of me. Strange, I went back to work and on with our lives.

40th Anniversary Party

August 30, 1981, was our fortieth wedding anniversary. Our family had a wonderful party for us at Dula Party Hall on Grand River in Detroit. I think everyone we knew was there—friends, neighbors past and present, family and cousins from Jackson, etc. It was a wonderful party. They had a professional photographer there, and we got an album of pictures to treasure. This was before video and digital cameras. There were lots of food, drinks, dancing—wonderful, wonderful memories.

Another memory is coming back. Alice and David were divorced in 1981. It was a sad time for all involved. They had just been way too young to handle all the problems of marriage and being parents. I think both felt that they had missed out on a lot of things in their life. (This is just my opinion.) I'm sure there were a lot of reasons. Alice was a very good mother. David, well, he lost out on some of the wonderful times of seeing his beautiful children grow up, *but* the main thing is they all have a good relationship now.

Before that, in the spring of 1980, Alice developed a blood clot in her lung and was in the hospital in Cincinnati. That was a scare for all of us. We went down, of course, and so did her sisters, but there was not much any of us could do. She had good doctors; thank goodness, she did recover from that!

In February 1982, Bill and I went on a dream vacation to celebrate our fortieth anniversary. We took a two-week cruise on the *Nordic Prince* of the Royal Caribbean Line. It was absolutely fantastic! We had so much fun we were not ready to get off the ship when it was over. It was like living in a "fantasy" world. Our real world seemed a million miles away—the company we met, the food, the islands we visited, the shows, the weather, and the seas. Looking back at it, it was a beautiful dream, with memories to cherish. I made a lovely album of our cruise too. We had left Bill Jr. in charge of the house and Daffy (with a few misgivings), but we came home to a clean house. We think he really worked hard the last two days before we came home. We had told him he could have his friends over, and I think they pitched in to help him too. Those same friends are still his friends today, and I think that is very special and remarkable.

In June 1983, Billy graduated from Athens High School, and of course, we had a party at our house. The weather cooperated, so we were able to have it inside and out. Steve Williams, Bill's good friend, lived down a few houses and our backyards were not far apart. They were back and forth at one another's houses for their parties. What a relief for Bill and me! There we had been wondering when I was pregnant with Billy at forty-three if we would be around to see him graduate from high school, *and* there we were in not too bad a shape. Bill Jr. had been accepted at Lake Superior State in Saute Saint Marie up north and was very happy about it.

That fall we loaded our car and took our "baby" to start his college education. I had strange feelings leaving him there and heading back home. It was different than when Carol went to Central, perhaps because Carol had had two years at Junior College first and was a little older. Also I still had children at home. Now it was back to just Bill and me. We had both looked forward to that day. That same summer we had lost Daffy; she was sixteen years old, and we had been lucky to have her that long. Bill and Billy took her to the vets, and it was very difficult for all of us. That same fall, Bill and I took a two-week trip through Pennsylvania, New York, and the New England states. It was wonderful. We saw history—the Liberty Bell, Independence Hall, the Boston Tea Party, Paul Revere's Ride, Acadia National Park in Maine. The fall colors were spectacular. Bill got his fill of lobsters. There were so many places along the side of the roads you could just pull off, and they had those huge barrels of boiling water waiting for you to throw in a lobster for you to eat right there with paper plates and plastic silverware, but who cared? Lobster's OK, but perhaps because I don't like butter, I would rather have something else. It was a lot of fun though. We had high tea and scones at Jordan Pond in Acadia National Park. The scenery was gorgeous and also tea delicious. On our way to Hartford, Connecticut, we were almost run over by "Gloria" the hurricane. We were also most run off the road by the winds. Wind was fierce with tree limbs flying around. We tried to stop, but no one had any power. Bill kept driving carefully, and slowly we made our way into Hartford. It was eerie—no lights, no traffic. We made it to the hotel, and they were surprised we had got through. We both said that was an experience we would just as soon not go through again. All in all, it was a wonderful trip. We sent some live lobsters to Bill Jr. at school, and we heard later that the fellows had a race with them before they cooked and ate them.

Bill was seriously thinking of retiring. He had been working for Ford Motor for almost forty-five years. He still loved his job, but things were changing, and he thought perhaps that was enough.

On February 1, 1984, Bill retired from Ford Motor Company. His friends and coworkers had a party for him at a hall over on Van Dyke. All of our family, Bill's brothers and sister, were able to come. Our daughters and son got up in front of the mike and did quite a little comedy sketch of their lives growing up as the "Bill Beeler kids." It got a lot of laughs. There were several other nice speeches about Bill's dedication and hard work ethics. It was a lovely evening and a great send-off for Bill into a new phase of life.

I decided to keep my little job for a while until we saw how things would work out. It was nice. On the days I worked, Bill would have dinner started when I got home from work. I only worked three days a week. I think Bill enjoyed having the house to himself when I was gone. That March, we took a trip down south, Nashville, where for the first time we heard the beautiful song, "Wind Beneath Your Wings." This was at a nightclub in Nashville and performed by a male quartet. We thought it was beautiful then and still do. Then we moved on to New Orleans—the French Quarter, Cafe Du Monde, a city tour, and the strange above the ground graveyards because of the high water level. We saw Al Hirt in a show at one of the big hotels there. He was great. Then we moved on through Alabama and the Pan Handle of Florida. Those were all the places we had never seen before, and it was a joy traveling together and seeing new things. Bill and I always got along very well and seemed to enjoy doing a lot of the same things. We visited Joe and Charlotte in Leesburg and saw their beautiful home there for the first time. They made us feel very welcome and we had a fun filled couple of days with them. We came on home through the Carolinas.

That trip was so different for us in the sense that we had never traveled before at that time of year. We actually had *two* springs that year. We saw early spring down South and then had a nice repeat when we got back home. We saw the beautiful Azalea Gardens in Alabama. I believe they were called the Bellingham Gardens. We also saw a lot of different foliage and flowers driving through the Carolinas. We stopped in Ashville, North Carolina, to see that famous Biltmore Estate. Here I go off on another tangent of history or trivia or whatever.

The Biltmore Estate was built by George Washington Vanderbilt, grandson of Cornelius Vanderbilt. Cornelius Vanderbilt was the famous New York financial baron into shipping and railroads. I'm sure most of you have read about him in your history books. He was one of the "robber barons" along with John D. Rockefeller, J. P. Morgan, Andrew Carnegie, and Jay Gould. They controlled the financial "State of the Union" in the late 1800s and early 1900s. They were the cream of New York society. But they were hated by a lot of lesser mortals because of their ruthless ways of taking over everything. George Vanderbilt, grandson of Cornelius, was into agriculture and forestry; he did quite a bit of good with his experiments in those areas. He decided to built that mansion to rival the great manor homes of Europe. He picked North Carolina for the property and wooded area. The home took six years to build. It was started in 1895. It had 250 rooms, 34 master bedrooms, 43 bathrooms, and 65 fireplaces. It was filled with priceless works of art. In 1898, George married New York socialite, Edith Stuyvesant Dresser, in Paris. After their honeymoon in Europe, they returned to live in Biltmore Manor. They had only one daughter, Cornelia, who was born and grew up there. As I remember it, it seemed rather cold to me with a lot of cement walls. But from what I have read, the family was comfortable there, and it was used and lived in. Now I understand that there is quite a vineyard being developed that is becoming famous. Bill was getting interested in old estates as he had just joined the Squires Men's group that volunteered and helped with the upkeep of our own Meadow Brook Hall, the Dodge-Wilson Estate in Rochester, Michigan, which I will tell a little about a bit later. We came home through Hershey, Pennsylvania, and of course went through the chocolate factory. Yum!

It was another wonderful trip, and writing about it brings back a lot of very nice memories. Although to be very honest, memories are wonderful, but they don't take away the loneliness when you have lost your partner. As I sit here writing on this cold afternoon on the last day of February 2002, I can't help but be distracted by what is happening in our own family lives right now. Barbara is scheduled for her surgery (a mastectomy) Monday morning on March 4. Alice is driving up from Cincinnati today to be there to help Barb get through this weekend. We are all jittery. I know things will be fine, but it has and is breaking my heart watching another daughter go through the ravages of cancer treatment. At least Barbara does not have all the other health problems that our Kathy had, so that is in her favor.

Carol has been in Florida visiting her friend Nancy Michaelson and will be flying home on Monday. Cindy has been out to Longview, Washington, for an interview paid for by the company that wants to hire her. She has decided to accept their offer. She liked what she saw out there, and they offered her quite a bit more money and would pay all moving expenses. It was an opportunity she couldn't turn down. She has been very depressed with her job here at Bi-County Hospital. Hey, who knows, maybe she will even meet "Mr. Right" out there. From what Cindy can determine, social workers are very scarce out there, and in this area, we are overloaded. I selfishly hated to see her move so far away, *but* it sounds like a wonderful opportunity. Cindy does have a good girlfriend who will only be an hour away. Then again, all my granddaughters will be far away—Krista in Arizona, Kelly in Cincinnati, Ohio, Sydney in Denver, Colorado, and now Cindy in Washington. I'm feeling sorry for myself. I know they have to spread their wings and *fly*. Our circle expands, but we all are still linked together.

Cindy is coming to have dinner with me this Saturday evening, and I will hear more about it. Barb, Ken, and Alice are coming down on Sunday and having brunch with me. I'm very, very grateful for my family. In a way, perhaps I am an anchor for them. I like to think so.

Wednesday, March 6, 2002: The last few days I feel like I have been on an emotional roller coaster. I'm so tired today, and I know it's stress and emotions. Barbara had her mastectomy surgery at 10:30 a.m. on Monday, March 4, at Troy Beaumont Hospital by Dr. Ruark. Ken and Alice were there, and they kept me posted. Alice called me at 12:55 p.m. that Barb was in the first recovery room, and the surgeon said she had come through fine and things looked good. I got hold of Carol just before Nancy took her to the airport to fly home. She was very relieved. Then 1 made a lot of calls to friends that Barb had given me a list to take care of for her. (They wanted to keep me busy, which was good.) It had been very difficult for Ken too. He was with Barb all the way and would do anything to help make her feel better. Truthfully, it'd been very hard on all of us. It wasn't that long ago that we had lost Daddy and Kathy. Seeing Barbara go through some of the same things that Kathy did was heartbreaking. The treatments have been brutal. All of us are very hopeful and know Barb is going to beat that, but getting through it is *rough*. Carol picked me up at 3:45 p.m. yesterday, and we went to see Barb. She had been discharged from the hospital around noon. It just seems amazing that for an operation that serious they only keep you for one night.

Barbara looked pretty good, and she showed us her incision. It is difficult to realize her breast is gone. There will be a mourning period, which everyone says is normal. I don't know what I expected, but the incision goes from her right armpit straight across her chest and doesn't look too bad. It is truly wonderful what the doctors can do today. We all shed some tears, but then we had some laughs too which is normal for our family. No one was very hungry, and they decided to just to get something from Wendy's, which Carol and I went to pick up. Alice, Barb, Carol, and myself had salads and Ken had a hamburger with frosties of course They have some new salads and they were quite good. We were home again around seven. We knew Barb would relax and rest better with fewer people. They were all exhausted. No one had been sleeping well, and Alice had got herself a good case of bronchitis too which was not helpful. Now the healing, then what's next?

Sunday, March 17, 2002, St Patrick's day: I think you folks are going to have to regard this story as a time travel one. It seems like I have to write about what is happening right now and then get back to the past.

Barbara is improving, but she still has one drainage tube in that is really bugging her. She says, "Here I am cut all across my chest, and it's this damn tube that really hurts." Hopefully, it will come out Wednesday. Alice went home last Tuesday and is hoping her house will sell soon so she can get back up here. She says she has to be here with Barb and help her get through this. I do know it does help Barb also to have her there. Ken is grateful also because of the long, long hours he works. He worries about Barb being alone too much and *thinking*. It's very difficult for everyone. Like Barb says, she has been on both sides of the fence, and she knows what it is like for the family too. The girls think I should be protected, and perhaps I don't realize how serious Barb's cancer is. But I told Alice and Carol that I knew IBC inflammatory breast cancer was a very aggressive type of cancer. 1 knew from the way Barbara's treatments were that this was not just ordinary breast cancer. If you can call any cancer ordinary I have to know the truth! But it does seem as if my life has been on an emotional roller coaster the last few years, *and* it *hurts*.

Well, back to the past in 1984.

That summer and fall, Bill was invited to join the Squires Men's Club at Meadow Brook Hall. They did volunteer work: maintenance, helping with tours, the big money maker, "the Christmas walk," the car show every August, Concours d'Elegance. Bill loved all of it, whether he was dressed up in a dark suit and tie for the social activities and money makers or dressed in his work clothes gluing down the stair treads that were constantly coming loose. He liked the people—the men in the Squires group, the women docents and caretakers, the office staff. He loved the social activities of the Squires group too, where the wives were invited. We had several lovely dinners at the hall and played "Whist" afterwards, a card game where you kept changing partners. I'm not big on cards but managed to hold my own. Bill received his ten-year Tudor Rose pin and just missed his fifteen-year pin. The first year after we moved here, Bill went for the Christmas Walk and the Concours. But then in 1999, he had to give it up because his back was giving him problems. It almost broke his heart. He didn't like what age was doing to him. There were times to be perfectly honest that I was a little jealous of Meadow Brook Hall. Now for another side track into "history."

In the very early 1900s, John and Horace Dodge were running a small foundry and machine shop started by their father and doing quite well. Henry Ford approached them about re-tooling and helping him build the Model T. They worked out a satisfactory arrangement and the rest is "history." In a couple of years, the Dodge brothers sold their Ford stock and started their own car company. John Dodge had married Ivy Hawkins in 1892 and had three children with her. She died in 1901. John married again in 1903 to Isabelle Smith. They were divorced in 1907. In the meantime a young twenty-year-old, Matilda Rausch, started work as secretary to John in 1903. In the middle of a lot of gossip, Matilda and John were married that same year he was divorced in 1907. You are probably saying to yourselves, "OK, what does this have to do with Meadow Brook Hall?" Bear with me.

John Dodge bought the property, 320 acres, in 1908 on which Meadow Brook Hall is built, as a farm and retreat for his family. John and Matilda had three children: Francis Matilda born in 1914, Daniel George born in 1917, and Anna Margaret born in 1919. Francis and Danny have rooms named after them at Meadow Brook. Anna died of measles at the age of five in 1924. Before that, though, John Dodge died of influenza in New York in 1920. His brother Horace was with him and was so heartbroken by his brother's death that he died a few months later. Even the very rich have problems and heartaches. I knew quite a bit about this history from Bill learning about it at Meadow Brook. But it was interesting to refresh my memory by using the Internet and looking up those people and places. Technology . . . it's truly amazing! Matilda married a lumber broker, Alfred George Wilson, in 1925. They started to build Meadow Brook Hall in 1926. It was a hundred-room Tudor revival style. Matilda went to Europe to buy furniture to furnish the mansion. Some people say her taste was not the greatest and some of her collections were a bit tacky. Gossip? I do know the woodwork and the beautiful carvings cannot be duplicated today. No one teaches that craft anymore or perhaps it is just too expensive. It is a beautiful place and was lived in and used.

Listen to this. I found it interesting. The Wilsons had more than one and a half acres in garden and would store up vegetables for household use and for horses in winter. They grew a lot of carrots for their horses as well as potatoes, apples, cherries, peaches, pears, strawberries, and raspberries. They used to make cider and wonderful fresh ice cream. From the gate house on Adams Road, they would sell the surplus produce. They grew about three hundred to four hundred bushels of peaches, five hundred bushels of pears, three thousand bushels of apples, and picked over thirty-five crates of cherries.

Matilda and Alfred Wilson adopted Richard in 1930 and Barbara in 1931, and they grew up in Meadow Brook Hall. Alfred Wilson died in 1962 and Matilda in 1967. Her will donated the estate to Oakland University. It was opened to the public in 1971.

Bill arranged for our family who lived around there to have Mother's Day dinner there one year. It was a lovely day, and Bill was so proud showing off Meadow Brook Hall. If you have not seen it, try and make a special trip to go through it. It was a very special place for Bill and well worth seeing in its own right.

> *Our family is a circle of strength and love. With every birth and every union, the circle grows. Every joy shared adds more love. Every crisis faced together makes the circle stronger.*
> —Regina Walters

THE 1990S

The 1990s

I am sitting here at the computer on a warm and sunny day in September 2002 and trying to think back to our lives at that time. I wonder how many tricks my mind is playing on me. Hopefully this will all make sense to those reading about us now.

Continuing in the 1990s

I was getting more and more involved with my artwork. I was finding that I did have a little talent and I just loved learning and doing more. I had two great teachers—Jo Chiapelli and Joan Cox. I started taking classes from both of them at Niles School on Square Lake Road just a mile from our house. I started to turn out some decent work and had a lot of fun doing it. Bill and my family were very encouraging. It was in those years that I started to make my own Christmas cards. Each year, my list kept growing as more and more people wanted my cards. Last year (2001) I sent over 110 cards. I had added our doctors and staff there at the Village. They all have been very appreciative. Of course, it was a big ego boost for me.

Bill was more and more involved with his part-time job as a rep for Tawas Plating. Gene Jensen was turning more work over to Bill as he was having health problems. Bill was also busy and involved with his volunteer work at Meadow Brook Hall. Both of our lives seemed full and satisfying, and that was a very nice feeling.

One worry at that time in our lives was my mother. She had a very bad case of shingles in the late 1980s and never totally recovered from them. One quarter of the left side of her skull was affected, which included her left eye. I never in my life have seen anything like them. She ended up at Oakwood Hospital out of her mind with the pain. She did come through that session, but things were never the same. It affected a nerve in her eye and caused severe pain off and on at times. Her eyesight deteriorated, and she was not able to do her beautiful needlework that she loved to do. We tried to help her to do easier plastic work and projects, but it was not the same. She had done such beautiful work before that it was disappointing for her. It affected her reading also. Whenever anyone mentions having shingles, I cringe. I hope and pray that I never have to experience anything like them. Mother died in her sleep on June 13, 1990. She was ninety-one years old. It was a shock and in another way a blessing. The family had just celebrated Mother's Day and her birthday on May 16, a month before, with her. What a wonderful way to go! Then we had the job of cleaning out her apartment and dividing her things. With all the grandchildren, it went quite easily.

In January 1991, Billy had talked his dad and me into getting another dog. After eight years since "Daffy," we were all ready, I guess. We checked pet stores and newspaper ads for breeders. We had all decided on trying to get a black Lab. We happened on a Flint breeder who had ten-week old puppies for sale. The three of us took a ride up to Flint to check them out. We immediately fell in love with a little black puppy, whom the breeder called "Ruby." She came running to us and captured our hearts. Needless to say, we brought her home with us. Our pockets were $400.00 lighter, but we had this bundle of black fur and joy. All of us decided to call her "Katy" rather than Ruby. We also decided to crate train her, which we had not done with Daffy. We were all happy with that puppy, though we had forgotten how much work and training a puppy required. So we were busy, but she was a joy, and all of us loved her. We took her to puppy training classes and were all trained. One of the things that brings back memories was "hanging her out to dry." They taught us that when the puppy got to rambunctious or did things she shouldn't, we were to pick her up under her front legs and hold her up off the floor, so she just sort of hangs there and can't do anything. It seemed to work. Of course, that was with a puppy who didn't weigh too much. With a grown Lab, it doesn't work.

Those memories are "bittersweet" as Billy and Shannon just had to have our "Katy" put down a month ago. When Bill and I moved here to the Village in January 1998, we shipped Katy out to Bill and Shannon in Denver, Colorado. Now they have "Roxy," a little yellow Lab puppy, as they could not stand not having a dog in the house. All of them missed Katy too much, and Sydney was too young to understand what had happened to Katy. Roxy is keeping them very busy again. Katy gave all of us so much love, and when Billy moved out to Denver in 1993, she was Bill Senior's companion and buddy through his knee and hip operations. The pain of losing an animal is almost like losing a member of your family, and it *hurts*.

There was another milestone in August 1991. We celebrated our fiftieth wedding Anniversary, *and.* Carol and Edsel were celebrating their twenty-fifth wedding anniversary. The family had a wonderful combination party for us on a beautiful day in August at Kathy and Jim's place in Milford, with family and friends attending. It was a very special day to be celebrating together.

We were also celebrating Billy's graduation from Walsh College with a business administration degree. It had taken awhile with his working also, but he made it!

During that same time frame, age, wear, and tear on Bill's knees was taking its toll. All of his walking all over the automotive plants all his working life added up. He had to have both knees replaced. The first one was in March 1993, the second one in September of that same year. They were both done at Crittenton Hospital by Dr. Jeffrey DeClair. They were both very successful. But recuperation and therapy take *time.* I was doing well during that time and was able to help him and also drive him to his therapy sessions. I'm grateful for that.

Also in 1993, Bill Jr. decided he was not making any headway or going anywhere with his business administration degree. His good friend Kevin had moved to Denver, and he talked Bill into coming out there. He said that he would help Kevin pay for his condo and try his luck out in Denver. Besides, the snowboarding was *great* in that area. In August 1993, Billy left for Denver. After all those years, Bill and I were alone again. Strange, it took some getting used to, but we did enjoy it. Both Bill and I had worried about Bill Jr. and that he did not get what he seemed to want from life. He was always a hard worker and did well in the jobs that he did have. He just couldn't seem to find his "field." In one way, we hated to see him move so far away, but in another way I think we encouraged it, thinking perhaps things would break for him out there. Looking back at that time, it did work out well for him, although it did take awhile. He got into the computer field and met Shannon, whom the whole family loves. Now they have Sydney who will be two years old this October 12. She is a little doll. It seems so strange to have another little granddaughter when my other grandchildren are all grown-up. But it's so much fun and joy.

In July 1994, our family and world took another blow. Our Kathy was diagnosed with incurable ovarian cancer. She was forty-seven years old. We were all heartsick. In some ways, it brought our family even closer together. That started six years of horrible, terrible treatments for Kathy. The whole family got involved with support groups and took her for treatments. She was so brave and put up such a *fight*. The doctors had told Bill and I that she had probably eighteen months to two years. She proved all of them wrong. She fought that battle for six years and had some good times and some travel between all those treatments. Jim and Scott were with her every step of the way. It was an up and down time for all of us. Carol and Barbara were very involved and became even closer to Kathy. Jim was still working up until the last year, and Carol and Barb were able and willing to be with Kathy and take her for doctor appointments and treatments. Bill and I pitched in when we could. We went to quite a few different support groups with Kathy and Jim and joined Gilda's Club. It was helpful for all of us.

During those years too, Bill had taught himself needlepoint. In between his Tawas job, his volunteering at Meadow Brook Hall, his woodworking hobby, his knee operations, he still had some time on his hands. Bill was not the type of person who could just sit and stare at TV or do nothing. He said, "If your mother and Aunt Fran can do it, I can too." He started with a small cardinal kit from Frank's Nursery and Crafts Store and did well and enjoyed it. He decided to take lessons from Jacobson's Department Store, which had a wonderful needlework department in their Birmingham store. He took classes from several different teachers over those years. It was so sad when they phased that department out, *and* of course now there are no more Jacobson stores. Bill was a fast learner and did beautiful work. Jacobson's displayed some of his work in one of their exhibits. All the girls and Bill Jr. have pictures, pillows, and also Christmas stockings as a result of his work. I also have several lovely pieces hanging here in our apartment. It was a hobby that was satisfying and helped Bill through some difficult times when he was not physically able to do what he was used too. He missed his golf leagues but didn't complain. Bill was never a complainer; with all the pain and operations he went through, he kept a bright outlook and always kept busy.

Those were the years when personal computers were becoming more and more popular. Kathy and Jim talked and talked about us getting one. They said it would help keep Bill busy when he wasn't able to get out a lot because of his knee surgeries. They ended up getting us one, installing it, and giving Bill lessons. Of course, we were agreeable and paid for it. We both enjoyed the e-mail, and Bill also enjoyed playing different games on it. I learned the e-mail and loved learning to use Microsoft Word to write letters on. I still love that part of it. I just wish I had paid more attention and learned how to file things correctly. Maybe someday I'll learn. In the summer of 2001, Billy talked me into getting a new Dell and an HP photo smart printer; the one we had was acting up and was not dependable. That one will print out pictures of Sydney, Sage, and Ché (when I learn how to do it correctly). It is helping me write this story, which I hope my family will enjoy.

July 2003: Here I am time traveling again. I hope by dating these writings it will help the people reading this now to make some sense out of my story. I have to be in the mood to write, and there are times when I would much rather be doing something else. Anyway . . .

Bill, Shannon, and Sydney were just here for a ten-day visit. What a joy it was to see them! They all looked so good and Sydney . . . what a beautiful little doll! She is a sweetheart. Shannon had got an unexpected bonus, and they decided to spend the money to come and see the family. Then to make things really exciting and wonderful, Bill got word when they got here that he had been hired by Dictaphone Company. He had been going for a lot of interviews but was not counting on anything as he had been disappointed several times before. It had been almost a year since Bill had been let go by IBM. The economy and the tech business had been terrible for several years now. Everyone was complaining and hurting. We all were so pleased. It was cause for *celebration!*

They got in on Friday evening, July 11. Carol picked them up from the airport and brought them here. We all had pizza together and talked and played with Sydney. She was so good and was so lovable. She loved books and people reading to her. Then she would read the books back to you. For two and a half years, she seemed very, very smart. On Saturday, Bill worked on my computer; he spent some time troubleshooting with Dell and then decided the monitor was bad and that I was to call ViewSonic Monday morning. We had lunch down at Windows, and Marguerette met us to see the family; it worked out well. In the afternoon, they went to Mike and Maria's in Rochester Hills for a barbecue with all of Bill's Michigan friends there. It is so nice that they still stay in touch and enjoy being together. They were all in school, band, and Boy Scouts together.

It was midnight when they got home, and Sydney was overtired and just wanted to sleep with her mommy. It was kind of difficult for Shannon on the couch, but she managed. Bill didn't want to open the sofa bed. He prefers the floor. Carol had loaned them some nice comfy comforters. On Sunday morning it took awhile for everyone to shower and get organized. They were packing up to go to Barb and Ken's cottage too. Sydney was so good through it; it was a joy to have her around. On Friday night she slept with Grandma, and she loved when I read books and played an alphabet board game with her. On Sunday, we went down and had brunch in Great Lakes dining room, and they left for the cottage about at 1:30 p.m. I hiked over to the care center to see one of my friends who was there. I met some of her family and found out how she was doing. When I got back to my apartment at about 3 p.m., I put on my robe and just vegetated the rest of the afternoon and evening. It makes me very unhappy that I get so tired. Walking distances bothers me and it also worries me. What is happening to my body? I don't want to lose my independence. Going to the care center didn't help either. It's depressing. Getting *old* is scary.

On Tuesday at 10:00 a.m., Carol picked me up to go to the lake. In the van were Erik, Eve, Scooby, Parker, and Erik and Eve's new little Welsh Corgi, "Bella," who was six weeks old. What fun! We stopped at Chicken Shack in New Baltimore for chicken and coleslaw, and on our way for noon ferry there was so much road construction that we just about made it to the ferry, too close for comfort. Jim and Hannah were already there. We had a beautiful day. Sydney was so much fun to watch. She was so full of energy and was busy every single minute. She is a very lovable child, smiling and happy most of the time. Everyone enjoyed being around her. We had a rain shower for a couple of hours in the afternoon, but it really didn't bother us too much. We took the six o'clock ferry back to mainland and stopped for a Subway for me to eat in the car and take pills. Carol saved hers for later, and Erik and Eve weren't hungry. We reached home about 7:45 p.m. We were worn out but had a wonderful day.

I talked to family every day so I felt included in everything. On Wednesday I rested and just had an entertainment committee meeting at two in the afternoon. They were always interesting. I came home and got a robe on again. I had got a hamburger for lunch at Windows, so just had a snack in the evening and rested. On Thursday, Carol picked me up again about 10:15 a.m., and we made the trip to the cottage again. Carol is so good about that, and she loves being with Bill, Shannon, and Sydney too. Sydney loves her and runs right to her when she sees her coming. We got the noon ferry again. Steve Williams and his girlfriend Julie were there also. He was again a long-time school friend of Bill's and also one of Sydney's godparents. It was always nice to see him, and it was another beautiful day with more sunshine that day as I watched Sydney in the water. She had no fear. She just loved it. Julia and Danielle, the girls in the cottage behind Barb and Ken's, and their little brother, Nino, were there playing with her too. They were eleven, nine, and five I think—very nice family. Carol and I got the 6:00 p.m. ferry again. There was another quick rain shower, but we were able to get a Dairy Queen first. I had a hot fudge sundae, Carol had a Boston cooler, and Scooby had a "pup cup." It was fun; In two days I had had a Subway sandwich and a Dairy Queen, something I had not had in several years. I enjoyed both. Again, I was home about 7:45 p.m., tired out. I did not do a lot on Friday.

On Saturday, Bill, Shannon, and Sydney got back here about noon. I made French toast for Sydney, and Bill and Shannon had got Subways. They had planned on going out to Joel and Melissa's in Milford but decided it was too long a drive, so instead did wash. Bill was printing pictures and teaching me how to do them also. A little after four we went to Rio Bravo Restaurant for supper. It was interesting; the only time I'd go to a Mexican place was when they were in town. I do like Tacos and the chips. It was fun to watch Sydney eat a Bean Burrito. She loved them. I just read to Sydney, and we all talked and watched some comedy programs on TV. It was a very nice evening. Time had gone by too fast. Sydney slept with me again Saturday night. What a doll! Five o'clock came much too soon. I was packing last minute things. Carol was here at 5:45 a.m. She came in and said, "It's a good thing I love you. This is not a good time to go anywhere." I hated saying good-bye. It was hard; I couldn't go back to bed then, so I washed my hair, read the paper, and got ready to go for brunch. Shannon called in the afternoon, and they were home safe and sound. Why do the good times go by so fast? I have some beautiful pictures and memories, so I will have to be satisfied with those.

Sunday, August 24, 2003

Here I am getting back to "normal" after our blackout last week. I wrote about that in a separate article, which will be included in this story. It certainly is a experience I hope I never have to go through again. I can remember that back when we had power outages before they were kind of a "campout" experience. But I was younger, more active, and I had Bill with me. It made a lot of difference. This one was not *fun* in any sense of the word. Anyway, about family news, Cindy has been going with a young man named Joe Rivet, who works at the hospital where she does. He is twenty-five and has been married before. Joe has 50/50 custody of their little son, Corbin. Corbin will be three in September. It is getting very serious. Joe says the five-year age difference does not matter and really it does not. They are already talking of wanting to get married. Joe has sent Carol and me e-mails and pictures of him and Corbin—nice! They are coming in October for Cindy's friend Ann's wedding, and we will meet Joe and Corbin then. I'm hoping it works out for Cindy. It's time. She is such a wonderful young lady and deserves to be happy, and she loves children.

What Else Was New?

AMA Journal announced Sister Kenny's treatment for polio. Grand coulee Dam opened. Cheerios marketed. Underwater photography began. National Gallery of Art opened in Washington, DC. Four freedoms speech by FDR, freedom of speech and worship and freedom from fear and want. Penicillin treatment introduced. Liberty ships.

Those Were the Days

1941—Bill and Vivian Got Married
Japan bombed pearl Harbor. Greta Garbo retired. Norman Rockwell created "Willie Gillis" for Sat. *Evening Post* covers. Superman rated 4-F because of X-ray vision. *Citizen Kane* movie Cookie began in *blondie*. Woody Guthrie wrote *Roll on Columbia*. *Red Skeleton* began on radio: "God bless."

1951—Bill and Vivian's Tenth Anniversary

Dennis the Menace comic strip began. Drive-ins, convertibles, crew cuts, and strapless gowns. Dean Martin & Jerry Lewis were popular. *I Love Lucy* and *See It Now* with Edward R. Murrow new on TV. Mickey Mantle joined Yankees. General MacArthur's farewell speech: "Old soldiers never die; they just fade away."

1966—Bill and Vivian's Twenty-Fifth Anniversary
Jim Ryan ran world record mile. *Mame* with Angela Lansbury and *Cabaret* on Broadway. Granny glasses, go-go boots, dark eye makeup. Beatles last Live concert. Simon & Garfunkel and the Mamas & the Papas introduced soft rock. Bob Hope won Emmy Christmas special: "Thanks for the memories."

I have put off, walked around, done everything I can to avoid writing about the later 1990s. It seems like too many bad things happened in our family, and I just don't want to relive those memories. I'll try, but bear with me. Some things may not make a lot of sense.

Monday, March 14, 2005
The sun is shining and the temperature is trying to make it up to thirty degrees—heat wave! It has been a very long and very snowy cold winter. Everyone is ready for *spring*. But this is Michigan, so we know we still have a couple of months of uncertain weather. I had to go to another funeral this morning, one of my friends here at the Village. While it was a blessing for her, as she had a lot of health problems, it still hurts the family and friends who are left. But it also made me stop and think. I've been trying to get this story put together and organized—sorting all my papers and getting the different years put together. When I came to the 1990s, I realized again I had not finished them.

In May 1995, Cindy graduated from Central Michigan University, the first of our granddaughters to graduate from college. We were able to attend her graduation ceremony in Mt. Pleasant, and that was a very happy occasion. It's nice to write about happy things.

I've already mentioned Kathy's battle with ovarian cancer. Then we lost Edsel to suicide on February 28, 1997. That is still unbelievable. Edsel had diabetes and he had had a small stroke the previous June at his nephew Mark's wedding. Since that time, Edsel had not really been his regular self. Plus, he had taken care of his mother's business and health care and watched her go downhill with dementia in a nursing home. She had just died during Thanksgiving time. Edsel was also worrying about retiring as the company was doing buyouts for those who had worked for thirty years. The stress of everything was just too much. We truly believe that he had another stroke and could not face the fact of life as an invalid. We knew he was ill, but none of us realized how ill. He was such a loveable guy and was a "son" to Bill and me. We know he was happy with his marriage and loved Carol; plus he was so proud of (with good reason) Cindy and Erik. It's very hard for us to understand and difficult to write about. It affected all of us deeply.

You learn to live with things like that, accept and go on, but you never really "get over it." Those were difficult times.

Bill was having more health problems. Food got stuck in his throat, which led to endoscopy and then stretching the esophagus, Carpel Tunnel operations on both hands—all as an outpatient. Then the Turps operation on his prostate followed with continuous follow-ups with Dr. Badalament. It seemed like the doctor visits were never-ending. Poor guy, he did very little complaining, and between all of those things, we had some nice times. Thank goodness, my health was not causing too many problems during those years. I was busy taking care of him, and we were both worrying about our Kathy. We were hurting for Carol also; it was a very rough time for her, Cindy, and Erik. At that time, we had decided that it was time for us to move to Henry Ford Retirement Village. With all of both our health problems, we just could not keep up our home the way we wanted to. When we hired people to do the jobs that Bill had always done they just did not measure up to his standards and they were *expensive*. We were on the waiting list, and after Bill had his hip replacement surgery in May 1997, we decided *now* is the time. Our house went on the market in August, which we learned later the hard way that family homes don't sell well in the fall. Most families had made their moves in spring and summer so that their children were set for the fall school sessions. Anyway . . .

Kathy and Jim came and helped us organize things. They were so good at things like that. We had lived in that house for thirty-one years and of course had collected and collected. Don't do that . . . *simplify!* I know, I know. It's easy to say. We had a big garage and estate sale that the whole family helped us with. No way could we have done it by ourselves. Bill and I had picked out a corner apartment called the Stafford floor plan. We just loved it at first sight and didn't even look any further. It had lots of windows and light—two bedrooms, one of which we knew was going to be just a computer or extra room. Who knew that it would eventually became my garage, my attic, my basement. Whenever I didn't know what to do with something, in that room it went. That all changed this last November when Alice and Barb came down and reorganized me with shelves; plus I got rid of my big exercise bike that was too high for me to get on safely, also some other junk I had just been storing. I had opened my mouth about having the family Christmas party there and I knew I had to get that room cleaned out. The girls did a fantastic job in just one long day.

Back to selling our house . . . I got so tired of always having to have it ready for inspection by our real estate agent who would bring strangers by, making sure Katy was in her crate, etc. A lot of people liked it, but there were no good offers until early December. A nice couple in their second marriage with couple of college age kids came and fell in love with it. Everything fell into place, and we closed another chapter in our lives and moved to the Village in January 1998. It was difficult for us to leave Sandshores. There were so many nice memories. Jean and Dar Darovich were our good neighbors and friends. But it was time.

The year 1998 was a pretty good year for us. We were making adjustments and making new friends, getting involved in life in the Village. We both realized that that had been a very wise move on our part and were grateful that things were working out for us. Of course, our Kathy was a constant worry, but there were a lot of good times in between her bad times. We tried very hard to appreciate them.

I would like to read a poem that Kathy had written about Aunt Fran for her ninety-fifth birthday last year.

I have amended it to be appropriate for today.

She had help with some of the history by Cindy Ann Leinonen, who did an interview with Aunt Fran for a class project.

Then I will share a couple of my memories with you.

My Poem About Aunt Fran

A ninety-six-year-old lady lived in Westland town
Presbyterian Village on Cherry Hill bound

She was born near Owosso on a farm in 1901
Running barefoot in summer for sheer pleasure and fun

Moving near Howell, living on two other farms
Riding her first automobile was a real charm

At age eleven, moving to Jackson, Michigan
Trading country for city life was a challenge again

Now this ninety-six-year-old lady was a spoiled child
The only girl—a little wild

Being the youngest with three older brothers
She had to be the envy of many others

At an early age she lost her parents
Making her responsible and independent

Having to make money and work her own way
Saving so Business School she could pay

Advancing in jobs from many different companies
As secretary or bookkeeper—just being at ease

Being the comptroller or working on income tax
This lady was one who was never lax

Sharing rooms and living at the YMCA
Till she got her own apartment one day

Mr. William Redmond five years she did date
A marriage in 1944 they became mates

This ninety-six-year-old lady did try to retire
But staying at home she did not require

Another bookkeeping job was found in the ads
Setting her own hours was not the fad

But working only three weeks out of four
Till final retirement kept her from bore (dom)

With the loss of her spouse and best friend
In 1977 she wouldn't let this be her end

She traveled and toured the world with abandon
To Europe, Holy Lands, British Isles, and Scotland

To keep busy when she did not punch a time clock
She would needlepoint many wonderful blocks

Pictures and pillows were made from her labor
That family and friends are lucky to savor

Seeing the advancements in radio
Telephone, television and audio

Automobiles and traffic lights
Remembering the Wright Brothers first flight

While having no children of her own labor
Her love is returned many times over

By nieces and nephews and friends
This long list has no end

Such wonderful memories have my sisters and I
Dining at Stouffers and at Northland shop—Oh My

The old phonograph we would crank and play
Dancing around the house all day

This ninety-six-year-old lady was sharp as a wit up on current affairs and really hip

With her short stature, she was easy to spot
White curly hair and smiled a lot

Having health problems and aches and pains
They didn't keep her down, she was really sane

And let's not forget the beloved pet
Cookie's been treasured since they met

We could always count on our Aunt Fran
To keep the family gatherings grand

To her and the world we would like to relay
How much we love her in every way

So strike up the band, sing strong and loud
To celebrate the passing of whom we're all proud

We will miss her dearly, but know she's at rest
Up in heaven with our Lord—He has the *best!*

By Kathy Jean Welton (grand-niece)
History help by Cindy Ann Leinonen (great-grand-niece)
February 28, 1997

There is a saying: con't by Kathy

When someone you love becomes a memory, the memory becomes a "treasure."

We are all lucky to have many treasures of Aunt Fran. I know a few things that we will miss—they are Christmases.

She loved the mad house and all the excitement at Mom and Dad's—there was so much laughter, fun, and always too much food. She was like a little kid waiting for the presents to be opened. We have a tradition of taking family pictures before we can open presents. She would always be an instigator and say, "I think we should be opening presents now." She would always get us laughing.

She could not make that last Christmas with us, so we videotaped the day for her. When she watched the video, she laughed and she cried. She had wanted to be with us so much.

I can remember Christmases from when I was a little girl living in Dearborn. The first thing each Christmas morning, there was Aunt Fran and Uncle Bill knocking on the door. We also had a neighbor that came around each Christmas morning with a bottle of liquor. He got Aunt Fran and Uncle Bill to join right in and have a drink with him to toast the holiday. There are so many fond memories.

Another time we will really miss her is when we have a turkey dinner. Several times a year, it was an unwritten rule that we only had turkey and all the trimmings when Aunt Fran, Mom, and Dad could come and enjoy it with us. I would always cook cranberries or make cranberry relish, not knowing she only wanted the canned cranberry jelly. I finally caught on and learned to open a can of cranberry jelly just for her. At our next turkey dinner, we will miss her dearly.

These are just a few of the wonderful treasures we will keep with us always!

And I am sure each of you have your own treasures of Aunt Fran.

Sage Autumn Crimmins

On This Day in History: Saturday, November 01, 1997

Top News Headlines This Week:

November 2: *Barrymore* closes at Music Box Theater, New York City after 240 performances. November 2: 27th NYC Women Marathon won by Franziska Rochat-Moser of Switzerland 2:28:43. November 2: 28th NYC Marathon won by John Kagwe of Kenya in 2:08:12. November 2: H Abe discovers Asteroid #8120. November 2: Ralphs Senior Golf Classic. November 2: Toray Japan Queens LPGA Cup.

Top Songs for 1997

"I Believe I Can Fly" by R. Kelly
"You Were Meant for Me/Foolish Games" by Jewel
"Can't Nobody Hold Me Down" by Puff Daddy featuring Mase Return of the Mack by Mark Morrison
"Candle in the Wind 1997" by Elton John
"How Do I Live" by Leann Rimes
"I'll Be Missing You" by Puff Daddy/Faith Evans/112
"Un-Break My Heart" by Toni Braxton
"Don't Let Go (Love)" by En Vogue
"Wannabe" by Spice Girls

1997 Prices

Bread:	$0.87/loaf
Milk:	$2.67/gal
Eggs:	$1.47/doz
Car:	$19,260
Gas:	$1.29/gal

House:	$176,200
Stamp:	$0.32/ea
Avg Income:	$56,902/yr
Min Wage:	$5.15/hr
DOW Avg:	8,259

U.S. President: Bill Clinton
U.S. Vice President: Al Gore

Academy Award Winners

Best Picture: *Titanic* directed by James Cameron
Best Actor: Jack Nicholson in *As Good As It* Gets
Best Actress: Helen Hunt in *As Good As It* Gets

People Born on November 1

1929 — Betsy Palmer, E., Chicago, Illinois, actress (*Mr. Roberts, Friday the 13th*)
1935 — Gary J. Player, Johannesburg, South Africa, PGA golfer (British Open 1959, 1968)
1942 — Larry Flynt, magazine publisher (*Hustler*)

On TV in 1997

Union Square
King of the Hill
Hiller and Diller
Diagnosis
Just Shoot Me
Dharma and Greg
Everybody Loves Raymond
Spin City
Suddenly Susan
Veronica's Closet

Hot New Toys in 1997

Tamagotchi
Boggle CD
Water
Giga Pets

Tickle Me Elmo

Top Books in 1997

The Proper Study of Mankind by Isaiah Berlin
The View from Saturday by E. L. Konigsburg

Dear Sage,

One year old! This year has gone so fast it seems. I wish distance wasn't quite so great so we could get to know one another better. But I wanted to let you know that you come from a long line of strong and good women from your mother's side of the family. I don't know your daddy's side. I am sure the same is true also. It makes you believe in immortality and life being a circle.

You know the song "Sunrise, Sunset" from *Fiddler on the Roof?* That is the way Grandpa and I feel. When you are young, you think you will never grow old—then all of a sudden, those years are gone. You turn around and you are old!

I am only going back to the women I have known.

My grandma Manley (Martha Reed), your great-great-great-grandma, came to Big Rapids, Michigan, as a widow with seven children from Canada. She had lost her husband, Henry, in a forest fire. She took in washings and did housework—anything to raise her children. They all turned out well. She lived with us when I was growing up—a wonderful lady. She taught me so many, many things. She died in 1963 at age ninety-three.

My mother, Eva Manley (Tallman, Miller), would be your great-great-grandma, another great lady that went through a lot during her life and made the best of it. She lost her first husband, my father, Ackerson Tallman (he was an electrician for Ford Motor Co.), when she was thirty-eight years old. I was sixteen. He was in World War I and survived a poison gas attack in France, not knowing it would cause Hodgkin's disease later in his life. He was forty-three when he died in 1938.

We survived. I changed my plans for college and got a job with the telephone company when I graduated from high school in January 1939. In the meantime, I met "your great-grandpa, Bill Beeler, and lost my heart. We were married in two years in August 1941. Back to your great-great-grandma (Eva). She worked as a sales clerk at J. L. Hudson Company in Detroit, a famous store that also has a wonderful history. She made a home for us—my sister (Evelyn) and grandma Manley. Then she met and married Merle Miller in 1945. They had a good life together until he died of heart problems in 1960. They had a Dairy Queen in St. Joseph, Michigan. She sold it and came back to Dearborn, Michigan, and lived in an apartment upstairs from my sister and her husband. She was a big part of all our lives, active in her church, Red Cross blood drives, and cancer society. She died in her sleep at age ninety-one in 1991.

I must also tell you about your great-great-grandma Beeler (Marguerette Wirtz, who was my mother-in-law), another terrific lady. She met your great-great-grandfather (Joseph Beeler) when she was fourteen years old. He had just come over from Switzerland with an uncle. He got a job at Kelsey Hayes Wheel Company. Automobiles were just coming in *big* then (1915).

Anyway, Marguerette had made up her mind at fourteen or fifteen that she was going to marry Joseph—and she did in 1917. Your great-grandpa, William (Bill) Beeler, was their first son born in 1919. Over the years, she had four more children. They moved from Jackson to Dearborn, Michigan, in 1931 with a job transfer. History books will tell you about the Great Depression of the 1930s. We lived through it and do remember how tough it was, but as children, we didn't have the worries of enough food on the table like our folks. Grandma and Grandpa, Marguerette and Joseph Beeler, were like second parents to me, especially on losing my dad when I was sixteen. Over the years we became good friends. Grandpa died at age eighty-four in 1976 of prostate cancer. Grandma dies four years later of a rare anemia and heartbreak missing Grandpa. She was eighty years old (1980).

Another great lady and strong woman was your great-great-aunt Frances Tallman Redmond. She was a sister to my father. Born in 1901, she was on her own except for her brothers from the time she was about sixteen. Her father died of heart problems (they did not know and do what they do now) and her mother in the Big Flu epidemic of 1918. She put herself through business school and worked as secretary at Jackson State Prison, then on to Wilson Dairy Company and Sherwin Williams Paint Company in Detroit.

Aunt Fran grew up in the age of the "Flappers." Women were just coming into their own. She had some great stories to tell of "speakeasies," bathtub gin and rum running on the Detroit River during prohibition. She did not like the name she was given at birth—Fanny. When she was in her thirties, she had her name changed to Frances and had to get everyone to stop calling her Fanny. Uncle Bill worked for the Dodge Corporation and they lived on Uncle Bill's salary and used Aunt Fran's wages to invest in the stock market, and they did very well.

As independent as she was, she still considered men a bit superior to women. She also lived with us for a while. Grandma Manley, Aunt Fran, and my mother, Eva, had a great relationship.

She met William Redmond in her late thirties, and they married when they were both in their early forties. Uncle Bill worked for Chrysler Corporation. They lived on Grandpa and my took wages and invested her wages in the stock market. They were also an active part of our lives, all holiday doings, etc. Uncle Bill died of a heart attack while he was taking a nap in 1977. Aunt Fran continued on. In her eighties, she was taking trips to England, Scotland, Greece, and the Holy Lands. Always cheerful and upbeat, a joy to be around, she died at ninety-six of heart failure in 1997.

I guess that brings us up to Great-Grandpa William Joseph Beeler and me, Vivian Louise Tallman Beeler. I graduated in January 1939 at age seventeen. No one would hire me until I turned eighteen. So I got a job as a receptionist in a real estate office for $5.00 a week.

I gave my mother $2.50 and had $2.50 to spend. In those days, it went a lot further, and we were used to pinching pennies. Your great-grandpa came into the office with his mother. They were looking for a larger house. We started talking and found out that we had both graduated from Fordson High—he in 1937. We had not known one another in school. Anyway, he walked me to night school a few nights later, and the story goes on. He was going to Apprentice School at Ford Motor Co. and got a job in the tool room. I did get a job at Michigan Bell when I turned eighteen in September and was a manual telephone operator where you said "number please" and connected wires in different holes. It seems unreal now. We met in the spring of 1939 and were married on August 30, 1941. Great-Grandpa's brother, LeRoy, had met my sister Evelyn during our going out together, and they married a year later.

I got pregnant almost immediately and had a miscarriage at six weeks. We did not have much knowledge of birth control in 1941. That ended my job at the telephone company. I got pregnant again and had Susan Louise on November 30, 1942. We thought we were on top of the world, but World War II was getting closer and closer. Grandpa got several deferments because he was working in the tool room and was married.

On April 13, 1943, we lost Susan very suddenly at four and a half months old. It was probably SIDS. They didn't know a lot about it then, and to this day, I still wonder why. It's like a bad dream now, but I always hate April 13. Life goes on and we were young and in love. I got pregnant again and your great-aunt Carol was born on April 18, 1944. I was staying at Grandpa and Grandma Beeler's because Bill had finally run out of deferments and had to go in the army. He left in March, and we gave up our apartment and I moved into his old bedroom at his folks. Red Cross let him come home to see his new daughter, and then he was sent to an air force base in Texas. In those days, women had to stay in bed for ten days after childbirth. They let me come home from the hospital because my husband was coming home to see me and his new daughter. But Grandpa Joseph Beeler carried me up and down the stairs. What a difference in the way you were born! When Carol was a year old, I took her down to Texas, and we had a room off base with kitchen privileges—one year old and into everything. I am sure your mom will agree. This "lady?" we rented from chewed tobacco, and she had cans and pots all over to spit in. Of course, Carol was fascinated with them, and I ran after her constantly. Even with the war, that was a fun time. We did a lot with other young couples on base in the same boat—no money. We went over to Mexico and saw a bullfight—*ugh!* Carol doesn't remember! She rode a goat and did her swimming in the pool. Anyway, the war ended just before Grandpa was to go overseas. We were very grateful.

His. job was waiting for him at Ford, and we. bought our first house in West Dearborn for $5600.00. Again, we thought we were on top of the world.

In May 1947, your great-aunt Kathy was born. We called her our good luck charm because Grandpa had gone to school and worked so hard. He got into engineering about the. same time and. went from blue-collar tool room to white-collar office.

Life was good to us during those years. In May 1951, your grandma Barbara and great-aunt Alce were born. What fun to have twins! I was twenty-nine and. Had four wonderful daughters. We worked and struggled to make ends meet but what a happy time it was.

Grandpa and I took. up square dancing about that time and got to be really good dancers. Our lives were full. Grandpa was always taking classes and going to school—plus he finished off our attic and made a dormitory for our four girls. Remember in those days, little girls wore dresses every day to school, and there was no perma-press and Grandpa had a clean white shirt for work every day. I did a lot of ironing! I also made a lot of the girls' dresses. I was pretty good at the sewing machine, also cooking and baking. And I loved being a mother and wife. I look back on those days and wonder how I did it all.

We were at a square dance convention in Lansing, Michigan, in November 1964 when I realized I was pregnant again! I was forty-two and thought I was much too old to have another baby. Anyway, Bill Jr. was born in July 1965. A *boy!* Carol was twenty-one, Kathy seventeen, and the twins fourteen. They were all delighted. Billy had five mothers his first year. When they all got married and left home, Grandpa and I were left with a spoiled little boy!

Carol married Edsel Leinonen in 1966. In another year, 1967, Kathy married Jim Welton. Alice married David McCalden in 1968. In the meantime, Grandpa got the job of resident engineer at the Sterling Plant forty miles from our house. He drove it for four years. He got caught in a snowstorm overnight one time. We built a house in Troy. We sold our Dearborn house for $18,000 and put $37,000 into our Troy house and were scared to death. That was big money back then. We cried when we left Dearborn after twenty-one years in that house. Troy was a small town when we moved in 1967. We drove ten miles on two—lane roads to a grocery supermarket.

In thirty-one years there, it is hard to describe all the changes and growth.

To back up a bit, your grandma Barbara Vogt was our last daughter to marry and leave home. She had met your grandpa Ken and was head over heels in love. He was sent overseas in the Vietnam war (the terrible war that nobody wanted or believed in). He proposed to your grandma through his dad, your great-grandpa John Vogt. He sent a diamond and had his dad give it to your grandma Barbara. Exciting and very worrisome times! Grandpa Ken did get home safe and sound, although with some memories he wishes he never had. Anyway, they were married in 1970. Billy was five years old and a ring bearer in their beautiful wedding.

Two years later, your beautiful mother, Krista, came into our lives. She was a lovely baby with lots of dark hair. From pictures we have seen of you, you must take after your daddy with Your blond fuzz. Our family has always been close and full of love. It's kind of hard on Grandpa and I to see our family spread their wings across the country, but that is part of life and to accept the changes that come. The world and technology is changing so fast. I wonder what all you will see and experience growing up in a new century. I am *sure it* will be exciting.

Grandpa and I made a big change in our lives last January when we sold our house we lived in for thirty-one years and moved into Henry Ford Retirement Village. We found we could not keep up our lovely house and yard the way it should be. Age and some health problems made us decide to make the change while we could do it ourselves. We know we made the right decision and we are adjusting to a new lifestyle.

Life is a series of changes. Some are happy and exciting, Some are heartbreaking, But you go on.

I hope, honey, when you get older, you will read this and know how much you are loved and to realize what a wonderful and strong line of women (and men) you come from.

Happy birthday Sage Autumn!

> Love and Best Wishes Always,
> Your Great-grandma Vivian Beeler
> November 1998
>
> $\wedge\wedge$r6

On June 5, 1999, your great-uncle Bill (our son) is getting married to Shannon Pack in Denver, Colorado. This is a very happy occasion for our family. We are all looking forward to traveling to Denver to help celebrate. Hopefully, you and your mom will be coming up from Arizona. We look forward to seeing you again.

Bill's Years as a Rep for Tawas Plating Company

As I told everyone in my story before, Bill retired from Ford Motor Company in February 1984. I wrote about Bill's years as a volunteer for Meadow Brook Hall, now I would like to tell you about him also being a rep for Tawas Plating Company during those same years.

Bill was a person who loved and enjoyed being busy, doing things he thought were worthwhile. I have written about his involvement in church work through the years, also about his helping with the Boy Scouts during the years Billy was in Scouting. I had worried a little about Bill's retirement, wondering if he was going to be bored and how we would handle it. *Ha . . .* I should have known better. Not only did he get involved with Meadow Brook Hall, he also got very involved with Tawas Plating Company and loved every minute of it. Let me start at the beginning.

In the summer of 1984, Gene Jensen, a rep for Tawas Plating Company, called Bill. Bill had known Gene through his work at Ford's. They met for lunch. Gene told Bill that he was getting older and had some health problems. He was diabetic and had lost a foot. He got around fine with an artificial one. But Gene told Bill he would like some help with his work with Tawas. Bill came home and talked it over with me. I could tell he was very interested. That would mean he could keep his fingers in the pie, so to speak, as he would be calling on people he knew at Ford's, plus other car and machine tool companies. Also, that would mean a few more dollars every month as Gene would be sharing his check with Bill. I almost think Bill would have done it for free, but the little extra money was nice. Bill already knew Harold Knight, owner of Tawas Plating Company, and liked him a lot. So of course his answer to Gene was "yes." That was the beginning of almost fourteen years working with and for Tawas. Bill never once regretted saying yes.

The first couple of years, Gene and Bill worked closely together, but Gene was passing more and more onto Bill and phasing himself out. Bill was calling on the Ford people, most of whom he knew from working with them. He was also making a few trips up to Tawas, calling on other companies and meeting different people, taking people to lunch and loving everything about it. He called on Chrysler, Saturn, GM, Machine Tool &

Gear, Prestige Stamping, Metro Stamping, Flint Manufacturing; the list goes on and on. Bill took me on a trip to Kalamazoo in December 1987. We met Harold and Diane Knight at nine in the morning. Diane took me to an art exhibit and a tour of one of the malls. We met the men for lunch at a country club. It was an interesting Day. Bill always tried to include me whenever it was possible. He enjoyed me being with him for the Christmas lunches, etc. In the late 1980s, Harold Knight turned the running of Tawas Plating over to his son-in-law, Kevin Jungquist. Kevin was a very bright young man. Bill admired his knowledge. Over the years that they worked together, they had mutual respect for one another and a great relationship. I got to know Debby and Kevin also and their growing family. They now have two girls aged ten and twelve and a little boy of four. In the early 1990s, Debby and Kevin lost a four-month-old daughter to SIDS. That tragic event brought us closer in some ways. I wrote to Debby and Kevin about losing our first daughter at four months also, probably to SIDS too, although not much was known about SIDS in 1943. We shared their terrible grief.

Gene Jensen died out at his sister's place in California in July 93. Gene had turned most of everything over to Bill several years before that. In going through Bill's notebooks he kept on his business contacts, phone calls, lunches, etc. during his years working for Tawas, I came across so many familiar names. They brought back some nice memories, and I know from the comments people shared that they all liked Bill and respected the work he did. I know he enjoyed working with all of them. He loved calling on and meeting new people and old friends, keeping up to date with business in the car companies. It almost broke his heart when he had to give it up because of health reasons in the fall of 1997. We were getting ready to move into Henry Ford Village.

We made a special trip to Tawas so Bill could say good-bye. He had leather wallets from Orvis for the fellows and a crystal bud vase from Tiffany's for the women as a little remembrance for them. We met at the plant and then went to lunch with Kevin and Debby.

We hear from Kevin and Debby every Christmas. They came down to see me at Bill's funeral. They have kept me on their Christmas list. Kevin thought the world of Bill. It was mutual. I also get a card and note from Diane and Harold Knight. Some people just leave footprints in your heart.

Some of the many familiar names at Tawas Plating were Jack Cuny, Scott Flynn, Jim Waters, Lynnette Norton, Mary Ann.

December 1998

Dear Family and Friends,

Are you ready for an update on us and our family?

This has been a strange and unusual year for Bill and me, leaving our lovely home in Troy after thirty-one years and moving to Henry Ford Village last January. We are *adjusting* to retirement living and it is different. But at this time in our lives, we feel we made the right decision! Life is full of changes and we have to learn to accept them or be very unhappy.

Bill's arthritis is bothering him more and he isn't able to do the things he used to do. I've slowed down also. We do keep busy though. Bill plays Euchre on Monday evenings, pool on Saturday mornings and is involved in a pool tournament right now. We've been taking some classes through adult education to try and learn to use our computer more. We are having a lot of fun with e-mail. Bill still does his needlepoint and is working on another lighthouse right now.

We're both on the Happy Hour Committee and take our turn every five or six weeks. Bill bartends and I'm a hostess and pass out snacks and pick up empty glasses, etc. Happy Hour is on Fridays from three to five. I've also got involved in several committees: (1) Library. You all know how I love my books. (2) Birthday Angels. (I deliver a card and a balloon to a resident on their birthday,) I just have one floor of our building, so it's not a big job. (3) Dinning committee. I take complaints and suggestions to dining services, meeting once a month. It's very interesting! It's a difficult job to feed and satisfy some 1,048 residents. (4) Residents Entertainment Committee. Again once a month meetings to plan programs. Every other Sunday afternoon we have a program from four to five for the residents. It varies from speakers to a variety of music programs. They have had some excellent entertainment here. It takes time and work to contact the different groups and arrange dates, etc. for them to come. It's a fairly large committee and some members know a lot about getting different groups. I'm just new on this and am finding it fascinating. There is always a free will offering and the groups or speakers are paid a modest fee agreed on ahead of time.

And of course, we seem to spend a lot of time sitting in doctor's offices for various problems. Overall though, we are very fortunate. It seems so strange not to plan meals and clean up afterwards. I'm adjusting quite well to that. The food is really quite good. We have to watch and not eat too much. They always have soup, salad bar, different breads and rolls, choice of three entrees, and dessert. We've met a lot of nice people here. We do miss our neighbors in Troy, but keep in touch by meeting for lunches and e-mail.

The nice thing here is you can be as active and social as you want to be. They have all kinds of activities and trips. Bill and I went to the DIA and saw the Angels from the Vatican exhibit. We are going mid-month to see the Rockettes show. We could go somewhere every week if we wanted.

Our apartment is spacious, has lots of windows and light. We overlook a courtyard and gatehouse. Bill misses his garage and basement but is adjusting. My artwork is a bit neglected. I miss my big counter in the kitchen to work on, but I've done some things and have a few for the girls at Christmas. Cindy is a social worker. Besides her job, she is going to Eastern to get her master's degree. Busy, busy . . .

We went to Cincinnati in October for our granddaughter Kelly's wedding reception. She was married in Hawaii on September 20. Her dad had a lovely big family and friends' reception for her and her new husband, Steve Rouff. They seem very happy. Kelly is a flight attendant for Delta. She was able to get some passes so her mom Alice, aunt Barbara, and brother David could be there too. We saw the video and pictures. Beautiful! David is working as a banquet server in Las Vegas at the new Balagia Hotel and doing well.

In November, Barbara and Ken flew their daughter Krista and her daughter Sage, one year old, on November l, home from Payson, Arizona. Our first great-grandchild! What a *joy*! She is a beautiful and happy, healthy, little girl. She is the first baby in the family since Erik, who is twenty-one. Krista works as a floral designer for a florist in Payson and loves it. Daddy David missed them terribly.

Kenny, her brother, is up to his neck literally in Chesapeake Bay. He is working with a contractor for environmental government jobs, running *big* dredging machines and laying pipes underwater. He worked on the Newburg Lake project in Livonia. He just loves his work. He'll be home for Christmas.

Our daughter Kathy is still fighting cancer—good times and bad. Her positive, upbeat attitude and chemo are keeping her here, and we are all trying to adopt her slogan of "one day at a time." Scott is the baker at Milford Bakery and is very creative in his work. He makes some yummy things!

Our son Bill Jr. has been in Denver five years now, and we shipped our much loved black Lab "Katy" to him when we moved. Both Katy and Bill are happy. Plus, he is engaged to a lovely girl, Shannon, who we met a year ago and were hoping something would happen. She fit in our family so well and we all loved her. Anyway, Bill gave her a ring this past February, and we are all delighted! They are planning a big wedding in Denver on June 5, 1999. God willing, we are all planning on being there. Bill is now a Microsoft Certified Systems Engineer. All his schooling is finally starting to pay off. We are happy for them both.

Bill and I are learning from our daughters and son-in-laws on accepting changes and some of life's hard knocks.

Carol is coping with widowhood at fifty-four. Kathy and Jim are coping with her Cancer. Barbara and Ken are learning to accept their only daughter, son, and granddaughter living so far away from them. Alice is always struggling to make ends meet as a single mom. We are so very proud of all of them.

The older we get the more important family and friends become and we count our many, many blessings.

The family from around here were all at Carol's for a lovely Thanksgiving. Kathy and Jim are planning Christmas for all of us at their place.

We wish all of you a wonderful happy, healthy, holiday season. Stay in touch.

Love, Vivian and Bill

Reflections on Our Son's Wedding

Monday, June 7, 1999
Denver, Colorado

First and foremost, we were able to make it out here! With Bill's hospital stays and operations in April and May, things looked very uncertain for a while. Thank you, God, for allowing us to come.

Second, it is so wonderful to see Bill so happy. All of us love Shannon, and she fits in our family so well. We just know it was meant to be. I just wish they were a little closer so we could be together more. Thank you, God, for letting Bill find such a wonderful girl to share his life.

The Wedding

Shannon was such a beautiful bride. Her dress was gorgeous! *But* it was her smile and glow from inside that was so special. Bill seemed very much in control, but his face and eyes as Shannon walked down the aisle toward him told how happy he was and how seriously he was taking his vows. The ceremony was lovely, and the tape they made together to tell their families thank you and how much they loved them had the whole church teary-eyed until the minister pronounced them man and wife and Alice yelled, "Way to go to go, Little Brother." That brought laughter and broke the tension.

The weather for the day was not perfect—a mixture of sunshine and clouds. Perhaps to let them know this is life. It is a mixture of sunshine and shadows, and we learn to roll with it or be very unhappy. Like the minister said, "For better or for worse." Who better to know than Bill's "older parents" who over the years have gone through a lot of joy, love, and sadness. You have to learn to roll with the changes and accept and adjust *and* count your blessings. Our family is our greatest one!

Our hearts ached because our Kathy and Jim could not be there with us because of her illness. Kathy had made all of our arrangements and had us all organized, and it broke our hearts to not have them here. That was one of life's rough punches. Yet they were in our hearts and minds at all times.

We all kept saying, "Kathy would want us to do it this way." When we lit the family candle at the church during the ceremony . . . she was there!

We have never seen Bill smile so much and look pleasant for pictures. They went on all day and evening. It seemed very important to him to have all our family that were here to be together in the pictures. Bill has grown and matured a lot in the past five years. Meeting and falling in love with Shannon was number 1. Getting a "real" job, as he calls it, was number 2. I still can't listen to the tape they made for the wedding ceremony, thanking their families for love and support, without tearing up. We know Bill has always loved us, but for some reason, it has always been hard for him to express emotions. I want to thank you, Shannon, our new daughter for that. I truly believe it is through your love and influence on Bill that he is better able to express himself. What he said on tape means a great deal to his dad and me.

When Bill was born, with me being forty-three and his dad forty-five, we wondered then if we would live to see him graduate from high school., and here we are—older., same age as Shannon's grandma. *But* we made it to his wedding and to see him happy with a wonderful young lady. We are very grateful. Thank you, God.

It was so wonderful to have our family together in Denver—Kenny from California, looking so good and loving his job; Davy from Las Vegas and again looking wonderful, happy and doing well in his job; Kelly and Steve looking like they have the world by the tail (beautiful!); Erik and Cindy, who we do see oftener. Thank goodness, they told us the fun they had with Bill's friends on Wednesday night and the story of R2D2. I'm sure Erik had an education at Bill's bachelor party on Thursday evening. That he is quiet about to his grandma! I want to say thank you to both Cindy and Erik for looking out for Grandma and Grandpa during this trip. I know the others would be the same if time permitted. We couldn't have made this without our family—grandchildren, and Carol, Barbara, Ken, Alice, and Kathy and Jim beforehand, with their advice on the phone and in our hearts.

I keep thinking of different things that this week has brought . . . *memories.* I can't get over how wonderful for Bill that so many of his Michigan boyhood friends could get out here for his wedding and how nice for Bill and me to see them again—Steve Williams as "Best Man," Jim Ku, Scott Siemen, Paul

Harris, Paul and Joel Snyder, Mike and Maria Hess, and Kevin who started it all by moving out here. There are memories of the boys in Scouts . . . marching band . . . theater. How absolutely mind-boggling to think that they are still close, with the distance involved. Also, what a treat to meet his new Colorado friends, of whom we had just heard about—John and Chris Cowperthwaite, Jose and Pam Alvarez and their daughter Paige, whose Godparent is Bill. Chris told me John feels like Bill is a brother to him., and Jose and Pam to ask Bill to be Godparent to their daughter has to speak well for Bill . . .

Bill and I want to compliment Bill and Shannon for the way they planned and handled their wedding. Being so far away, we really could not do very much. Everything seemed to work out well. The rehearsal dinner at the Club House was nice. The food was good, and there seemed to be plenty for everyone. There was a little bit of a frazzle for me with our Cincinnati family getting lost. Thank you, Kevin, for taking me back to the Motel. It gave us a chance to talk and for me to find out how happy you were with Janelle, who you had married just two weeks before. We wish you both every happiness. I forgot an important part. Bill got pinned down and a ball and chain was put on him after the rehearsal. That was something to see. I'm glad no one got hurt! He had to wear it all evening, and it was heavy!

More thoughts and backtracking . . . The Rehearsal at the church was fun. There were lots of laughs, and the most important, a chance to meet Shannon's family. Her parents, Mark and Nancy, are our daughters' ages. How welcoming and warm they were. We can see where Shannon gets her beautiful smile and warm personality. Her grandma, Virginia, who had just lost her husband in March She was very warm and our age. They got married the same day, the same year as Bill and I. It was an amazing coincidence. Shannon's sisters, Ginny and Katie, her brothers, Mark and James along with lots of aunts, uncles, and cousins were also there. To Bill and I, they seem similar to our family—full of love and laughs and of course same heartaches. I think it speaks well as Bill and Shannon have similar family backgrounds. Families are love! To see our Katy and how well cared for and loved she is. Bill and I know it was worth the money to fly her out to Denver to be with Bill and Shannon . . . she is having a wonderful life and all are happy.

The wedding ceremony was beautiful. All of the girls looked so lovely in their lavender sheath dresses and little Paige, as flower girl, did a good job stealing the show for a little while. Again, I repeat, how very happy both Shannon and Bill looked and acted, not acted, but from the heart. What a beautiful view it was from the reception hall, Crystal Rose, up in the mountains. We saw elks, buffalo, and a big mule deer on our way there. The mountains out here literally "take your breath away." We can see how Bill loves it, but at our age, Michigan is the place for us, and we are happy there. The reception hall looked so pretty—the lavender ribbon tied napkins, the hurricane candles on tiles, with rose petals . . . very elegant! The fruit and veggie trays . . . full bar . . . and lots of ice tea . . . a very nice buffet, yummy. Thanks, Bill, for the front row seats when you cut the cake. We enjoyed and had fun. Your wedding cake was so beautiful, and you were right. It also tasted good. I had a sample of each kind, hard to decide which I liked best—chocolate, with mousse, or white with fresh strawberries? You and Shannon did well!

Steve gave a great toast, bringing up Daffy and Popcorn. No Daffy now, but we still have popcorn in the oven most of the time. It is wonderful you have a best friend like that . . . From listening to Shannon's friends and family, I think she is as lucky as you. Sorry to leave early, But we are just so grateful we were there. We heard the garter tossing, which Erik caught, was fun. (I think he's trying to keep up his Dad's tradition.)

Well, it is 3:30 p.m., Denver time now. I'm sure you and Shannon are in Negril at your resort. I have no idea what the time change is there. I know you will enjoy every minute, and it will be over too soon.

We leave in the early morning. It will be nice to get home, but again thank you, God, for letting us come and be a part of Bill and Shannon's wedding!

Love, Mom
Monday, June 7, 1999

Reflections on Surviving a Lower GI or Barium Enema

All of this started on Thursday, September 9. I had a severe pain in my lower left side plus a lot of bloating. We went to see Dr. Demashkieh on Monday, September 13. He suspected kidney stones or diverticulitis. He sent me for abdominal X-ray that day. He saw two white spots showing, which could be stones. He wanted me to set up an appointment for kidney X-ray using dye. I had kidney X-ray on Friday, September 24.

On Thursday September 23, we saw Dr. Attallah for our checkups and for me to get reports of my stress tests and ultrasounds. There was good news. They were fine, *But* Dr. Atallah thought I had inflammation and probably diverticulitis. He put me on Cipro for ten days and I was to make an appointment for lower GI. I was not able to get appointment until Tuesday, October 12. Oh well, it was not something I was anxious to have!

In the meantime, Dr. Atallah was concerned about Bill's elevated liver enzymes. So he wanted him to see Dr. K. Bral and probably have an ERCP. We did see Dr. Bral and he did want an ERCP, which was done on Thursday, October 7. He took biopsies of some kind of blockage in one of the ducts. We would get results on Friday, October 15.

On Monday, October 11, Dr. Kamphampati removed a painful cyst from Bill's right wrist and he had a cast until the 18th.

Monday, October 11, was when I started my instructions for "barium enema day." That was a *fun* day, between Bill's operation on his wrist in the morning and me trying to flush everything out of my body. Mention *citrate* and I start to gag! But I did it and drank enough water to almost float. Then of course I had to sit on the John . . . especially at two in the morning and again at 5:30 a.m. I was *clean*. OK, I was up and wide awake and wanted to get this show on the road. I was too nervous to relax and enjoy the morning paper or anything else. We left for RMC at 8:30 a.m. and made good time; we got there about nine forty. I talked to Judy about her house, trying to ignore why I was there. Besides, I was interested. Judy had always been a big help to us. At 9:55 a.m., Sherri came out to get me. Good on time, we're going to get this over with and a familiar face. Sherri did my abdominal X-ray and kidney X-ray. Nice, then we talked about her puppy that was getting old and paced at night, keeping her awake.

Sherri had me take everything off but socks and put on those lovely Dior gowns. Then she took an X-ray of my abdomen. Then she told me they had goofed and were behind. I had people ahead of me. This was at 10:05 a.m. So I sat. I was freezing, part of it was probably nerves. I tried to look at magazines, but the mind would not concentrate. I was saying to myself, "You can still back out." I forced myself to stay there, getting more nervous by the minute. I kept hearing all those sounds from the X-ray room. Monsoon . . . got to clean up., watch your step . . . the floor is all wet. At 11:40 a.m., I was finally called. There were two nice technicians. If they told me their names, my mind was not recording. They tried to put me at ease. They had me standing in front of a big steel table, talking to me about why I was having this test. Then they started to hand me a drink, like Alka-Selzer; she said it was to make me burp. I said, "I didn't think you had to drink anything with a Barium enema." At the same time Sherri called in, "Mrs. Beeler is here for a Barium enema.". There was a rapid change. The table was down, and I climbed up on it—hard and cold. Then the girls were explaining that they were going to fill me full of barium and then drain it out. They said the doctor would come in and put air in me and take pictures. It looked like a five-gallon plastic container of fluid! I thought, "That all goes in me?" They started the procedure and tried to show me on the screen how it was going in and coating my intestines.

"Vivian, *Vivian*.". They called me and told me I'm supposed to say, "*Here.*" I told them, "I'm trying to imagine I'm not here. I'm on a beach, listening to the sound of the waves and the seagulls." *But* it was not working. I was uncomfortable to put it mildly. Then the doctor came in. I knew the girls introduced him, but again the mind was not recording properly. He was a very cheerful young man, telling me that my colon was like a tire and now it was flat. He injected air to fill it up so he could see what was inside. He said, "I will only put in as much as you can stand." Oh boy, I thought I was uncomfortable with the barium; that's nothing compared to the AIR. That really hurt. I was clenching my teeth and trying not to holler, "Stop!" All the time the doctor was saying, "Oh look, that's your colon. There is some diverticulitis, but let's go on. That looks good, no growths or tumors." He went on and on. They were almost done then. As I complain, I don't think I can take anymore!

The doctor leaves, then there's more *fun*. The girls started rushing around with X-ray plates, and I mean rushing. "Turn on your right side. Hold your breath . . . Breath . . . Turn on your back . . . Hold your breath . . . Breath . . . Now put this pillow under you." I felt like a *beached whale*. This seventy-eight year old body does not turn as easy as it used to. I was flopping around on this hard smooth table, with nothing to grab onto, trying not to get tangled in the hose coming out of my butt and do as they tell me. "Now the tummy., hold., breath. Now the other side." By this time, which side was that? "Hold . . . breath. Almost done."

I forgot to tell you. The girls had told me my job was to keep pinching my cheeks together, to try and hold everything inside. They also told me not to worry if I couldn't. Accidents happen all the time. That what they meant by monsoons. Finally, after what seemed like six hours, they said I was finished and they were going to take the tube out. There was a slight problem. My body didn't want to let go of balloon. After a couple more tugs, then they were trying to help me up. I was light-headed and a little woozy, but didn't say anything. I just wanted to get out of there. They said I did a great job and led me to the bathroom. I *made it!* After sitting on the John for five minutes and trying to get myself collected, I looked at my watch. It was 11:10 a.m. and still Tuesday. I got myself dressed and walked down the hall to meet my husband. He was glad it was over and asked how I was. I said, "Just take me home!"

Sherrie had told me to drink lots of water to flush out the barium, *but* what nobody told me was that I would feel lousy the rest of the day. They tell you can go and eat . . . *ha, ha.* My stomach felt so full and uncomfortable, gas or air rolling around. I was aching and miserable. Food didn't even sound good.

Anyway, today is Wednesday, and things are looking up. I'm a little lame from the struggle and fight with the steel table, but my stomach is starting to feel better and food is starting to look good again. I don't know if that's a good sign. Next I have to get the results.

I thought perhaps if I wrote this down, it would not only help me get it off my mind but maybe in certain ways help the technicians and doctors involved and let them know some of the thoughts and feelings of the patient going through that miserable test. I'm sure most of them have never experienced that test and they really do not realize what the patient is feeling.

Out of Control

P. S. Forgot to mention, even though I was miserable, I do realize how hard the technicians were working. The way they were running with the X-ray plates and trying to get my beached whale body to get in the proper positions, to get the test over with as quickly as possible, they deserve gold stars on their foreheads. I'm sorry I can't remember their names to say "thank you." They certainly earn their paychecks.

December 1999

Dear Family and Friends,

As most of you know, this has been a rough year for Bill and me. He has been in the hospital four times—April, May, and twice in November. He has been just home for a couple of days now, but gaining strength every day. Hopefully the problem is solved (a very diseased gall bladder, causing liver problems). It's puzzling because it did not show on countless tests and X-rays. Anyway . . .

We did have some bright spots. We were able to make it out to Denver in June to attend our son's wedding to Shannon, a lovely young lady who we all love already. We couldn't have picked better ourselves. They were able to come home for a family get-together the Labor Day weekend. In October, the family had a great eightieth birthday party for Bill.

Our Carol is substitute teaching at an elementary school this year and loving it. Our granddaughter Cindy earned her master's degree at Eastern in social work this August. Our grandson Erik graduated from Ferris State in May in criminal justice and is now a Livonia policeman.

Our Kathy and Jim are still working on restoring their 114-year-old home and are completing the kitchen and family room. It is beautiful! Kathy is still fighting her cancer and takes one day at a time. Her attitude is a lesson for all of us. Our grandson Scott is turning out the wonderful breads and goodies at the Milford Baking Company.

Our Barbara and Ken are coping with empty nest syndrome. Their cottage on Russell Island across from Algonac helps. Our granddaughter Krista, husband David, and our first great-granddaughter Sage, who was two in November, live in Sedona, Arizona. Our grandson Kenny works with heavy machinery for environmental projects in San Francisco and loves it.

Our Alice is still in Cincinnati. She just scared us last week with an emergency hysterectomy. Barbara is down there now taking care of her. She is recovering nicely. Our granddaughter Kelly is still flying for Delta. She and her husband, Steve, just built a new home in the Cincinnati suburbs. They moved in a month ago. I hear it is beautiful. Davey is still out in Las Vegas. He is a banquet server at the Bellagio and loves it.

We are all looking forward to Christmas, which will be at Kathy and Jim's this year. For the first time, I can't even remember how long it has been, years and years, I know all of our children, spouses, and grandchildren are coming home for Christmas. Bill and I are very grateful and are counting our blessings. The airlines will be busy. We can hardly wait.

With all that has happened this year, Bill and I know we made the right decision when we moved to Henry Ford Village. The security and safety and help when we have needed it is wonderful. We also have become acquainted with some lovely people, who are becoming friends.

We wish everyone a very *merry Christmas and a happy healthy new year!*

Vivian and Bill

THE NEW CENTURY
2000

March 25, 2000

Dear Dr. Lucas and Ledgerwood,

I've been thinking over what you told us Friday afternoon and it has brought up some questions. Because this is difficult to talk about without tears, I thought maybe I could write it down.

Bill and I have had a lot of good years. It's breaking my heart to see him so sick. We will do whatever you think is best, as we do trust your judgment. You said there were no guaranties that this procedure will do what you want it to do, and we understand that. What we would like to know if it is successful, will it give Bill "quality" life? Or with the Liver infection that has been causing problems for almost a year now will he still be so weak and sick? Also what is the maintenance of that tube? We do flush out the bile duct tube every morning. Also are wondering about His urination and bowels have not been working like they use to. He has had to take quite a bit of laxatives and then sometimes has to resort to enemas. Is everything just wearing out? We have not led "normal" lives for quite awhile now. I not sure how I will manage without him, but we are both in agreement that this is not living. He is so tired of being sick. He has always been a very active person and involved in so many things. He has never been a "complainer," but this is difficult. He's also worried about me. We have a wonderful family and they are very supportive. We have a lot of love. We are fortunate!

I hope you can make some sense out of this. I know my emotions are right on the surface, I'm so tired and worried. We realize Doctors priorities are to save lives and we appreciate that. We know Bill's case has been very puzzling for you. We need your advice as our Doctors and as compassionate human beings.

Thank you for listening to me.

Sincerely, Vivian L. Beeler

P.S. Bill has seen this letter.

Sunrise, sunset, turn around, turn around, and you are old.

Where did all those years go so fast?

I do believe life is a never-ending circle. Our physical life may end, but we go on in our children and grandchildren. Call it our spirits, DNA, genes, or whatever. I know I carry a part of the people before me.

December 27, 1999, through January I and 3, Bill got progressively more tired.

On December 28, skin started to turn yellow, and following days, stool turned gray color.

We talked with Dr. Lucas on Friday December 31, and the doctor called again on Saturday, January 1.

Dr. Lucas advised us to be at Dr. Legerwood's office on ten o'clock, Monday the third.

She took one look and said, "You are visiting us again," and admitted him to Harper.

They did a test on Tuesday the fourth in the afternoon. They used needles, dye, and camera and went into the liver and bile duct. They said it was blocked by small stones or blood vessels. They cleaned it out and put in a port.

With the IVs, Bill was starting to feel some better. They kept him until Friday afternoon, January 7, to make sure he was eating and the bodily functions were working as they should.

Saturday and Sunday were fair days (January 8 and 9}. Sunday was a restless night, and Bill woke with his port aching and hurting. We called the office and Dr. Stotzer called back. There was no inflammation or leakage. Bill had not eaten breakfast. He was very tired and uncomfortable. The doctor told him to take Vicoden and wait and see.

After a couple of hours, Bill did feel better and ate some soup and crackers and half of a pear.

On January 13, we went to see Dr. Lucas. The doctor said he was puzzled why the bile duct was blocked up. "Could it be a blood clot? Anyway, leave port in and come back in two weeks. Have radiologist check things."

He still has days when he is very tired and just does not feel right. Other days are pretty good.

On January 27, we went to see Dr. Lucas. He was advised a chelangiogram. We set up an appointment for Wednesday, February 2, at 8:30 Harper Hospital.

The port and the area around it very uncomfortable for Bill at times.

On February 2, Bill had test, dye, and X-ray, but they did not take the port out. We were told Dr. Lucas had to read the report, which would take two to three days. It was disappointing. Dr. Kline did the test on February 14. We took appointment at Dr. Atallah's. The doctor was surprised at all the weight Bill had lost, but said the blood check was good and heart sounded OK. He said to tell Dr. Lucas. Bill had to be well for his stress tests in April.

Bill is getting progressively weaker and not feeling well.

On March 2 Bill had an appointment with Dr. Lucas. He was also surprised that Bill was feeling like he was. He wanted to set up appointment for another chelangiogram and a CAT scan. That was performed on March 6. Cat scan showed mass. Liver biopsy was scheduled for March 16,

On March 16 we were down at Harper at 7:00 a.m. for biopsy. There was a very bad reaction two hours after biopsy. Bill had uncontrollable shaking and temperature and blood pressure went off the charts. Of course, they contacted Dr. Lucas, and Dr. Baylor from his team came to see him several times and they kept him there. They treated him for a blood infection among other puzzling things.

Bill had an ultrasound on March 22. It showed a blocked vein going from the spleen and intestine into the liver. Bill had quite a bit of pain in his side. They were unsure of the cause. They thought of inserting a tube in his belly going to a vein in his neck, hoping it would direct the fluids filling his abdomen, back into his blood stream. They wanted to wait for the weekend. That was where we were on March 25.

Bill was very tired of being sick. I was on an emotional roller coaster, up one day and down the next, depending on how he was feeling. My gut feeling was that we were losing him. I knew he did not want to go on like this. It was breaking my heart to see him so sick.

Operations & Hospitalization of William J. Beeler

March 16, 1993: Right knee replacement at Crittenton Hospital Rochester, Michigan, by Dr. Jeffery Declare.

September 28, 1993: Left knee replacement at Crittenton Hospital Rochester, Michigan, by Dr. Jeffery DeClare.

February 6, 1996: Turps at Crittenton by Dr. Robert Badalament.

February 4, 1997: Endoscopy by Dr. Al Hadidi at Crittenton.

February 20, 1997:Carpal tunnel on right hand by Dr. R. Kamhbampati.

May 13, 1997: Right hip replacement at Troy Beaumont Hospital by Dr. Lawrence Ulrey.

October 10, 1997: Carpal tunnel on left hand by Dr. Kamhbampati.

April 9, 1999: Collapsed and was rushed to Oakwood Heritage Hospital by Ambulance. Liver Abscess.

May 18, 1999: Turps Repair at Crittenton by Dr. Robert Badalament.

October 7, 1999: ERCP at Crittenton Hospital by Dr. Kambiz Bral.

November 15, 1999: Diseased gall bladder and liver operated on by Dr. Charles Lucas at Harper Hospital.

November 28, 1999: Admitted back at Harper Emergency for dehydration.

January 3, 2000: Admitted back at Harper for jaundice and blocked liver duct. Put in port.

February 2, 2000: Chelangiogram at Harper.

The Detroit News •

Oakland County

PAGE 4D | TUESDAY, APRIL 11, 2000

Doctor eases final journey

Hospice gives patients, families dignity in death

By Mike Martindale
The Detroit News

SOUTHFIELD — William Beeler gazed out his home's window beyond the budding treetops as a bedside oxygen machine hummed nearby.

A few feet away, Dr. John Finn sat with the retired Ford engineer's family, trying to ease their pain.

"Is there anything I can do? Any questions?" Finn gently asked. "Is there anything you would like to tell us, Bill?"

Beeler, slowly turned toward Finn and replied:

"Only that there's nothing to be afraid of."

Such words hit home to Finn, who's counseled more than 6,000 people at the end of life. As executive medical director of Southfield's Hospice of Michigan, he finds modern medicine fails to level with dying patients or their families holding out hope of miracle cures that may not exist.

Dr. Finn's career

Dr. John Finn's medical career started at Wayne State University. Some details:

■ Undergraduate and medical degrees from Wayne State University.

■ Clinical associate professor at the WSU School of Medicine.

■ Founding member, Academy of Hospice Physicians.

■ Received Hospice of Michigan's inaugural Crystal Rose Award April 8 for his groundbreaking work in hospice care.

Hospice takes the view life has its end and there's a time when patients would be better served at home, surrounded by loved ones.

"In many ways I'm working for a company marketing a product which nobody wants to buy," said Finn. "As we get older, more and more people will learn they can experience death at home and dying is a natural and family event.

"But we've also made dying medical," he said. "We've taken a technical approach to our humanity, as if the spiritual and social components don't exist. We over-treat disease, under-treat symptoms, and ignore spirit and soul. We've gone wrong."

But hospice care has received some legitimacy: Medicare, Medicaid and most insurance policies cover hospice equipment and 24-hour nursing advice and visits. It involves doctors, nurses, therapists, home health aides and trained volunteers, willing to carry out household chores.

Finn, who became Michigan's first full-time hospice doctor 14 years ago, said without hospice, Beeler would be in a skilled nursing home bed, declining in uncontrolled pain and then likely end up in an emergency room where he would continue to get acute aggressive medical care before being returned to the nursing home.

Finn described the usual medical model is "to actively treat each and every complication; prolong survival at all costs; and continue that acute care. It never really gets off of it to focus on closing out your life, making peace with your family or making peace with your God.

"The conventional system robs people of certain choices and options hospice can provide: Making the most of your time remaining without the distraction of physicians, consultants, treatments and facilities."

Finn said if people knew the truth of their illnesses and if the hospice concept was explained in a more appealing way, more would utilize it.

Dr. Finn had asked Bill when he was talking to him at the hospital if he could come and interview him when he got home. Bill said "yes."

That is how this article got to be written.

Both Bill and I are firm believers in hospice. I know they helped us a great deal and for the following year.

Twenty-third Psalm

The Lord is my shepherd; I shall not
want. He maketh me to lie down in
green pastures; he leadeth me beside
still waters. He restoreth my soul;
    he leadeth me in the paths of
righteousness for His name's sake.
Yea, though I walk through the valley of the shadow of death, I will
fear no evil; for thou art with me.
Thy rod and thy staff they comfort
me. Thou preparest a table before
me in the presence of mine enemies;
thou anointest my head with oil;
      my cup runneth over.
Surely goodness and mercy shall
follow me all the days of my life;
and I will dwell in the house of
    the Lord forever.

In Memory Of
William Joseph Beeler

Born
October 20, 1919

Entered Into Rest
April 14, 2000

Funeral
Henry Ford Village Chapel
Monday, April 17, 2000
10:30 a.m.

Officiating
Felix A. Lorenz Jr.

Final Resting Place
Oakland Hill Memorial Gardens
Novi, Michigan

April 17, 2000

William Joseph Beeler (Eighty Years Old)

He was born in Jackson, Michigan, and moved to Dearborn, Michigan, at age fourteen, when Dad was transferred to Kelsey Hayes Wheel Plant in Detroit.

Bill was the eldest of three brothers and one sister, who are all here today.

Bill started as an apprentice in the tool and die room at Ford Motor Company in May 1939. He met Vivian at about the same time. They had both graduated from Fordson High School. Bill in 1937 and Vivian in 1939, but had never crossed paths there. Bill went on with classes at Wayne State and different job training seminars and became an engineer on gears, axles, and drive shafts in 1947.

In the meantime between work and school, he and Vivian married in August 41. Then there was Pearl Harbor. With working in the tool room, Bill had several deferments until spring of 1944. Bill served in the army air force for about one and a half years. Just as he was to be sent overseas, the war ended. They had four daughters and lived in Dearborn for twenty-one years. Bill continued to go to school.

Bill had to build his own bathroom in the basement to find an escape from five women. In 1963, Bill was transferred to the Ford Sterling Plant and was resident engineer. He drove it for four years, and in the meantime, Bill Jr. came along as their "bonus caboose." At that time, they decided to build in Troy and lived there for thirty-one happy years.

Bill was always a very active and involved person. He was involved with Boy Scouts with his son for quite a while. He was a member of the Masons, Elks, Ford Alumni, and very active in his church, First St. Paul's Lutheran, in Dearborn and then on the Steering committee for a mission church in Sterling Heights which they joined when they moved to Troy. From about 1952 until 1964 (when Vivian found out she had a bonus on the way), they were very involved in square and round dancing. Bill was president of the club and in charge of the Dearborn area when the National Square Dance Convention was held in Detroit. They also enjoyed hunting, fishing, and golf.

Bill retired from Ford in 1984 after forty-four years. He was a person who had loved his job. After retirement, he joined the Squires Club at Meadow Brook and was active there, doing all kinds of repair jobs, helping with the Christmas Walk and the Concours d'Elegance car show in the summer, loving every minute of it.

During those years, they raised their children and married off their four daughters, whose husbands became their sons too. Then just the previous summer, the girls' "baby brother" who had moved to Denver married a lovely girl. Bill was not feeling very well then, but they were able to make it to the wedding and very grateful for it.

Bill and Vivian also had seven wonderful grandchildren, with the newly-weds expecting in October. They also had 1 great-granddaughter with another due in July.

Forgot to mention, Bill was also a woodworker and loved to build or repair things. Also when he had knee and hip replacements, he took up needlepoint. He made Christmas stockings for all his kids and pillows and pictures that were works of art.

After thirty-one years in Troy, health problems helped Bill and Vivian to make the decision to move to Henry Ford Village. So they went full circle and ended up back in Dearborn.

They both believed life and love are a never-ending circle. They go on through their genes, DNA, etc, in their children and grandchildren. Bill had a lot of faith and was fully aware of what was happening. He was not afraid. He told his wife that they had had a full and beautiful life together and were very fortunate they had as many years as they did. He said, "We did something right because we have a wonderful loving family that always sticks together and is there for one another."

His biggest worry when he was leaving was for his daughter Kathy who was fighting cancer and was very ill right then in Henry Ford Hospital and not able to be there that day. He said, "She needs all of our prayers."

Given to Pastor Felix Lorenz for Bill's Funeral Service; April 17, 2000

June 13, 2000

Dear Family and Friends,

For those of you who were not able to be with us, I wanted to share a bit about Kathy. Kathy preplanned her own funeral six years ago when she was first diagnosed with incurable cancer. She was given two months to two years. She told all of us she was going to beat this disease. She had such a wonderful positive attitude. Even with all the horrible things her treatments caused, she kept saying, "This will pass. Tomorrow will be better, one day at a time." She was an inspiration to our whole family, her friends, and fellow cancer patients. I truly believe and her doctor agrees that her attitude kept her with us. She also put up with some terrible treatments. She was so very talented in so many ways. She and her wonderful husband, Jim, who has earned "sainthood" in our family for his care of her, had so much to live for. It makes you wonder why God needed her now, especially so soon after her dad. I know there has got to be a reason or I would go crazy. Anyway, Kathy had chosen her music and had Erik to play his saxophone. She also requested everything in one day with a dinner afterwards. We were able to follow her wishes. The flowers, people, and tributes to her were overwhelming. She also wanted to be cremated. When we get her ashes, the family around here will meet with Jim and Scott at their place. They have remodeled an old 120-year old farmhouse in Milford and it is beautiful. It's not quite finished yet, but Jim will keep working on it. That is his second love. They have a beautiful wooded area in their back property, and that is where we will scatter her ashes as she wished.

They say God doesn't give you more than you can handle, but today I wonder I'm enclosing her OB notice and a paper she wrote. I thought you might like to see them. Her service was beautiful. Erik opened it with playing "Amazing Grace." The other music was "Nearer My God To Thee," "The Hills Are Alive With the Sound of Music," and "Edelweiss." "The Bend in the Road" was her favorite poem.

Kath's Mom
Vivian

May 25, 1947-August 6, 2000

K—keen, "kid at heart"
A—artistic, architect
T—thankful heart, talented
H—happy, "heart of gold"
Y—"yes" to all she met

Reputation and Character

The circumstances amid which you live determine
Your reputation; the truth you believe
determines your character.
Reputation is what you are supposed to be;
character is what you are.
Reputation is the photograph; character is the face
Reputation comes over one from without, character
grows up within.
Reputation is what you have when you come to
a new community; character is what you have
when you go away.
Your reputation is learned in an hour; your
character does not come to light for a year.
Reputation is made in a moment; character is
built in a lifetime.
Reputation grows like a mushroom; character
grows like a oak.
A single newspaper report gives you your reputation;
A life of toil gives you your character.
Reputation makes you rich or makes you poor;
character makes you happy or makes you
miserable.
Reputation is what men say about you on your
tombstone; character is what angels say about
you before the throne of God.

—William Hersey Davis

Memorial Service
For
Kathy Welton
June 10, 2000

Music prelude by Erick Leinonen on saxophone

Invitation to prayer "Amazing Grace"

Leader: The grace of Our Lord Jesus Christ, the love of God And the fellowship of the Holy Spirit be with you.

All   *And also with you.*

Leader: Father God, we come today as people whose lives have been abruptly changed by the death of one whom we deeply love. This change has brought confusion, anger, loneliness, fear, and doubt. In the midst of these varied emotions, we long for peace and for endurance. We want to feel Your presence.
            May we remember that the reality of Your love is stronger than death and now sustains life on a different plane for this one we love.
            Lord, may the memories of precious moments shared sustain us in this time of grief. May those times of laughter and crying, joy and sorrow, energy and fatigue, conflict and peace which mark our history with this beloved individual be the foundation of hope which sends us into tomorrow.
            Father, place us in Your strong resourceful hands and do those things for us which we cannot do for ourselves. Amen.

Proverbs 31:10-12

Who can find a virtuous wife? For her worth is far above all rubies
The heart of her husband safely trusts her, so he will have so lack
of gain She does him good and not evil all the days of her life.

                                        1 Corinthians 13v: 1-8

All: Chapter 13

> Though I speak with the tongues of men and of angels, but have not love, I have become sounding brass or a clanging cymbal.
> And though I have the gift of prophecy, and understand all mysteries and all knowledge, and though I have all faith, so that I could remove mountains, but have not love, I am nothing.
> And though I bestow all my goods to feed the poor, and though I give my body to be burned, but I have not love, it profits me nothing.
> Love suffers long and is kind; love does not envy, love does not parade itself, it is not puffed up; Does not behave rudely, does not seek its own, is not Provoked, thinks no evil;
> Does not rejoice in iniquity, but rejoices in the truth; Bears all things, believes all things, hopes all things, endures all things. Love never fails.

A Time to Remember

> We come together in *love* and *remembrance*. A link has been broken in the chain that has bound us together, yet stronger bonds of love hold us together. Love is stronger than death. The gift of memory will keep alive the good and true things that we have experienced in the loving times of our life. No one ever dies as long as we remember them.

Family and Friends Sharing Hymn

> Nearer my God to thee

Psalm 23:

> All:
> The Lord is my shepherd; I shall not want. He makes me to lie down in green pastures; he leads me beside the still waters.
> He restores my soul; He leads me in the path of righteousness for His name's sake.
> Yea, though I walk through the valley of the shadow of death, I will fear no evil; for You are with me; Your rod and

Your staff, they comfort me.
You prepare a table before me in the presence of my enemies;
You anoint my head with oil; My cup runs over. Surely goodness
and mercy shall follow me all the days of my life; and I will dwell
in the house of the Lord forever.

Eulogy: Betty Smith, Chaplain, Henry Ford Hospice, Oakland Team

Hymn: The Hills Are Alive With The Sound Of Music

Litany of Remembrance
    In the rising of the sun and its going down,
        We will remember you.
    In the blowing of the wind, and the calm of its stillness,
        We will remember you.
    In the opening of the buds and in the rebirth of spring,
        We will remember you.
    In the blueness of the sky and in the warmth of summer,
        We will remember you.
    In the mid point of the year, and at its beginning and end,
        We will remember you.
    When we are weary and in the need of strength,
        We will remember you.
    When we are lost and sick at heart,
        We will remember you.
    When we have joys and tears to share,
        We will remember you.
    So long as we live, you too shall live, for you will always be a part of us.
        We will continue to remember you.

A mother's love gives us our first glimpse of heaven.

"Love is of God; and every one that loveth is born of God."

1 JOHN 4:7

WELTON, KATHY J.; age 53: of Milford; June 8, 2000; beloved wife of James N.; beloved mother of Scott Welton; beloved daughter of Vivian and the late William Beeler; dear sister of Carol (and the late Edsel) Leinonen, Barbara (Ken) Vogt, Alice Beeler, and William (Shannon) Beeler, Jr.; she also leaves many nieces, nephews and loving friends. Kathy Welton was very active in her community. She served on the Mil-ford Village Zoning Board of Appeals since 1992, and since 1994 belonged to WOCCCA (Western Oakland County Cable Communications Authority) for the Village of Milford. She has had her Builder's License since 1991 and enjoyed hobbies such as sewing, basket weaving, and home renovations. Over the past years Kathy has donated hundreds of animals that she had sewed to the Cancer Society. Funeral from Lynch & Sons (Richardson-Bird Chapel), 404 E. Liberty St. Milford, Saturday, 4 p.m. Friends may visit Saturday 11 a.m. until time of service. Memorials may be made to Henry Ford Hospice. For further information please call at 248-684-6645 or www.legacy.com

Bend in the Road

Sometimes we come to life's crossroads
And view what we think is the end.
But God has a much wider vision
And He knows that it's only a bend—
The road will go on and get smoother
And after we've stopped for a rest.
The path that lies hidden beyond us
Is often the path that is best.
So rest and relax and grow stronger,
Let go and let God share your load,
And have faith in a brighter tomorrow—
You've just come to a bend in the road.
                            —Helen Steiner Rice

In Loving Memory Of

Kathy Jean Welton

Date and Place of Birth
May 25,1947, Detroit, Michigan

Entered Eternal Life
June 8, 2000, Milford, Michigan

Funeral Service
Saturday, June 10, 2000
Five o'clock
Lynch &Sons (Richardson-Bird Chapel)
404 East Liberty Street
Milford, Michigan

Officiating
Betty Smith Chaplain of Henry Tordyfospice-Oakland Team

Lynch & Sons Funeral Directors

November 23, 1999

Thankful? Yes, I am very thankful to be alive on this day.

I am thankful for my wonderful parents who raised me to be the loving, caring person that I am today. They loved and protected me from all the harmful things in this world that was within their power. I am very thankful they are still alive and halfway healthy, being seventy-eight and eighty years old, so I can tell them how much they mean to me. I know they are very upset and feel helpless about my cancer. They would love to give me a cure. I love them for that and for all they have done for me over the last fifty-two years.

I am thankful for my three sisters (Carol, Barbara, and Alice) and brother (Willy), thankful for the fights we had while growing up, for we are the best of friends as adults. They, too, are very upset that they have *no* cure to give to me. Mom, Dad, Carol, and Barbara live in Michigan and have been a tremendous help in getting me to chemo treatments, doctor appointments, and too many tests and scans over the last five and a half years while Jim was at work. I am thankful Carol and Willy are the same blood type as I am and are very generous with sharing when my hemoglobin is too low. Carol gives me extra strength with all her Shaklee vitamins, and Willy gives me an extra boost with a couple of beers in his blood.

I am thankful for my husband, Jim, and son, Scott. They are a major help and support every day. Their love and humor encourage me to get through the next test, the next treatment, the next hospital stay, even the next day. They are my best friends, and I love them dearly. There are no words to say how thankful I am for having Jim and Scott in my life. They are a joy and keep me laughing and loving.

I am thankful for having cancer. I know this sounds weird and I am not a sadist. With having cancer, I have met and made so many new friends that I would never have met otherwise. The medical staff, technicians, chemo nurses, doctors, support groups, social workers, etc. It takes a special calling for these people to deal with all us cancer patients, and I am so thankful for them. They help me get through the many unpleasant days in my life with a smile and/or kind word.

Having cancer has made me appreciate each and every day. I don't take anything for granted. I give thanks for each day that I wake up—watching nature, the deer in the backyard, the chipmunks on the porch, the leaves turning beautiful colors and falling to the ground, the sun shining, the snowflakes falling on my face, sledding and snowball fights, watching the animals at the zoo, and laughing at my three cats doing all kinds of hysterical antics. Life has been wonderful to me.

I am thankful for all the holidays. This year, Alice in Cincinnati with her son Davey from Las Vegas, and Willy in Denver with his wife Shannon will be coming for Christmas. It will be the first Christmas in many years that all five of us siblings will be together during the holidays. I am so excited about this year.

I am thankful to have so many people care about me and my family. This is a wonderful world! I feel blessed to have so much in my life.

Thank you, Lord, for everything!

Written by Kathy J. Welton for
her Thanksgiving Support Group meeting—1999

August 28, 2000

Grief counselors advise that one of the ways to help ease the pain you are going through is to write about it, so here I go again.

Our fifty-ninth wedding anniversary would have been this Wednesday, the thirtieth. It's hard for me to accept that my partner, lover, friend, and soul mate is gone. The hole in my heart is enormous, and it feels like part of me is gone too. I know it is real and my life is going on, but there are times when it hurts so much you really don't quite know what to do.

I miss some of the "little" things so much like, "How you feeling, Hon?" "How's your back . . . knees?. The pat on the butt or shoulder as we passed one another, our good night kiss, and Bill rubbing my back for a minute, splitting a piece of fruit at lunchtime, or splitting a dinner-time dessert . . . and oh, how I miss the company going on our little errands to the stores and perhaps stopping out for lunch! The looking over and sharing a laugh when something was funny on TV . . . I could go on and on.

Then of course the terrible tragedy of losing our daughter, Kathy, just seven weeks after Bill. How does a parent cope with losing a child, regardless of age? It is just not the normal cycle of things. She was so talented and had so much to live for, but I also know realistically that cancer is no respecter of age, talent, or *anything*. Look in the paper and I know there are other families that are grieving also. It brought back memories too of losing our first baby, Susan, to SIDS at four and a half months in 1942. That memory had become like a bad dream of a million years ago, but it is still there.

I am so grateful to my family; all of them keep close tabs on me, and I know they are hurting too. They miss their dad and their sister terribly. But as I am finding out the hard way, life does go on. From talking to the social workers and others who have been so helpful to me, there is no easy solution through grief and there is no escaping it. You have to wade right through the middle of it and everyone is different. We each have to find our own way. I've been reading a lot about grief from a notebook Sandra loaned me. Some of it is very helpful, but it sort of all boils down to each person has to cope with their loss in their own way. People and articles can be helpful, but it is up to us to find our own way. It is the hardest thing I have ever done in my life, and life has not always been kind.

Fall 2000

Bill and I had a marriage based on love, which seemed to grow over the years, and respect for one another's opinions and as a person; our marriage was truly blessed. We grew up together in so many, many ways. We really were very young when we started. Although at that time we didn't think so, I do think that because of growing up during the Depression and both coming from families that valued hard work and commitment, we were older than a lot of the young people of the same age.

Last year at our anniversary, we met the family from around here at Steak and Ale for a lovely dinner and celebration. Kathy had made her luscious strawberry whipped cream angel food cake for our dessert. Bill was feeling better than he had been for a while, and we were planning a family get-together because Bill and his new bride, Shannon, were going to be in town for an unexpected weekend. I keep trying to remember those nice times, but right now they hurt too. I want them back and I know that can never be.

From all the reading I have done, I guess the first year of "firsts" is the most difficult. Somehow God seems to have deserted me at this point in my life. I keep praying, but it isn't a lot of help right now. Hopefully that will change with time also. I do want to believe that Bill and Kathy are together and at peace.

I drove out to the cemetery on Saturday for the first time. The girls had told me not to go alone. But for some reason, something just made me do it on Saturday. Maybe it was Bill kicking me out the door and telling me to go check and see if I liked the headstone I had picked from a picture? I found the grave and headstone without too much trouble and was about to go to the office when the sun glinted on a stone higher up the slope than where I was looking. That was it, so a light from above showed me where it was. I was pleased with the stone—very plain with a Greek key border and the Lutheran Cross at the center. I held up and didn't break apart, but couldn't eat the little lunch I had packed. I stopped at McDonald's across the street and got an ice tea and took my pills, and I also managed to swallow a few grapes. I don't like to take medicine without some sort of food. Anyway, I *made* it and was pleased with myself that I had done it, except my stomach has been hurting since then and I am eating very lightly and carefully. It probably has no connection, but that brings up another worry. I don't want to get sick and be a burden on the family and my doctors are all in Rochester. I've got to do something, but what?

What Would You Want Someone Half Your Age to Learn from Your Example of Successful Aging?

- To always believe in yourself
- To keep an open heart and mind
- Always be willing to learn
- To roll with and accept change
- Take good care of your body
- Moderation in food, drink, exercise
- Keep a sense of humor
- Love and Listen . . . *love* and *listen!*

Successful aging: Depends too on God or fate that your mind and body are still functioning properly. Poor health would definitely change a person's perspective.

You are invited to a Video Baby Shower for Bill and Shannon Beeler:

When: Sunday, September 10, 2000, 3:00 p.m.
Where: Carol Leinonen's 30678 Grandon Livonia, Michigan
Given By: Their Michigan Family

Please be Kind
And
Keep in Mind
We have to Ship
So ...
Don't mean to plead
Or Sound so Grabby
But Money Mails Well!
Then ...
They can Decide
And go for a Ride
To choose whatever
Baby still needs ...
Or
Something Light and Cuddly
That will Fly through the Air
Without getting Wuddly. {excuse me Dr. Seuss}

Knowing this family
Had Fun at their Party
And Pooled their Resources
To Ship
Their Warm Wishes and Love
To all sources, Baby, Mom and Dad ...

Please Pardon the "punny poetry" and Hope to see you there for a Happy Occasion!

Regrets Only ... 734-522-1162 or 313-581-7041

December 7, 2000

Dear Aunt Leona, Linda, and Sandra,

Every time I write this date or see this date, I always think of Grandma Manley's birthday and Pearl Harbor. I bet you do too, Aunt Leona. I've been working on addressing my cards and writing the notes and letters I want to send with them. Since I've been making my own cards, my list keeps growing because everyone who knows I do it seems to want one. It's a compliment in a way, but more work for me . . . oh well.

It's almost 7:00 p.m. and I'm looking out the window and everything is snow covered. It does look pretty, but that means if I want to go anywhere I have to clean off my car, as we don't have garages or carports here. Doggone! I don't go out in the evening though and really don't have to go anywhere tomorrow. Maybe the weather will change.

Tomorrow evening I am supposed to have dinner with Mona and Helen Quinn. Helen is a very nice lady who makes hospital calls, and she met Mona when she was in the hospital. She calls on Mona about once a week just to see how she is doing, and they seem to like one another. Knowing Mona's birthday was on Saturday, she suggested we get together for dinner. I have known Helen for a couple of years. She used to play Euchre with Bill on Monday evenings. Her hospital calls are a volunteer job she says she enjoys doing. Last time I saw Mona she was feeling better and looked better. Sure hope it continues.

Our trip to Colorado was nice, but I don't like the hassle of airports. Having Jim and Carol with me made it more bearable. Sydney was a little doll, and it was fun to hold and love a little baby again. It has been years since I've really held such a little one. Billy is going to make a great daddy. He does everything for the baby, including changing her. Shannon is nursing her, and Sydney is gaining and growing beautifully. She was a very good baby too. I made flank steak pinwheels one evening (a favorite of Bill's). Two other nights Bill cooked for us. They got a steamer as a wedding gift, and he loves to use it. We had steamed shrimp and fresh asparagus one evening and steaks on the grill and fresh broccoli another. He is actually eating *healthy*. He didn't eat many vegetables when he was living at home, except corn. I could see a lot of his dad rubbing off on him, and it really made me feel good. Carol and I shared a queen-size bed in their spare bedroom, and Jim had a nice leather couch downstairs. It was good to see Katy again too. I think she remembered me, but she is getting old and has a bad hip. Bill carries her up the stairs at night part of the time. I was glad to get home too. I guess I'm getting so I feel better in my own little spot. But I'm very glad I did go and see the baby. Bill and Shannon made us feel very welcome, and they seem very happy together. I'm grateful.

I've been making some nut breads, cranberry, date, banana, and putting them in the freezer for now. I also made some chocolate caramel nut cookie bars that are delicious. I got a recipe for chocolate macaroon bar cookies to try also. I'm invited to a Christmas brunch from my Library Committee and also my Birthday Angels Committee on the eighteenth and signed up to bring cookies. I would also like to take a plate to the staff people here that have been so nice to me. So I keep busy. *But* then I read your letters, and I feel like I don't do much of anything in comparison with all the thing you folks are doing—cleaning, sewing, baking, cooking, yard and garden work, knitting, cleaning cars, etc.

How did your doctor appointment go on the fifth, Aunt Leona? Good, I hope. How are the nosebleeds? Sandra, you mentioned you thought you had an upper chest infection along with your allergies? Are you feeling better, I hope? That Christmas story sounds very interesting. I'm anxious to read it. Linda, that must have been a shock to be met by police when you are delivering soup. One of the men in my Support Group (lives in Dearborn) house was broken into just recently. It's scary. That is one thing here I do feel safe. It certainly sounds like all of you enjoy Duchess when she visits you. That's great.

I'm enclosing an article that I wrote that was in our Village paper about starting a watercolor class. The staff here has conned me into trying it. I really don't feel qualified, but they want me to try. Sixteen people have signed up already and I'm scared. The first class will be starting on January 9. Quite a few of them want to know how I make my cards, so I've got another project ahead of me. Wish me luck.

The family around here are going to come to the Village for Christmas Day. We wanted to do something very different from our usual Christmas Day. No one really feels like celebrating, and I came up with the idea of eating here, and no one cooks. I've made reservations for eight in the dining room so we'll see how it works out. It's a buffet and they are having prime ribs and a chicken dish. I've really never been here for a holiday dinner as we usually are at one of the families, but everyone says they are very nice. I'll let you know.

I don't think all these papers are going to fit in my card envelope so I think I'll send it in a bigger envelope.

I hope all of you have a lovely Christmas, I know you have a quiet day because most of your friends are gone, but hopefully it will be nice. I know you will have a nice dinner.

I have really enjoyed hearing all about the farm and all the work involved on it. Like I told you, I don't know anything about living on a farm and I have found it very interesting.

Linda and Sandra, how old are you? Around Carol's age, I think. She is fifty-six. We were wondering the other day. I know your birthday is in January, but I've forgotten the date. I've got a little genealogy chart, but I don't have it on there. I'd appreciate the information, also Norma and Robert's dates.

I think I've talked long enough. With this computer, it saves my fingers from getting so cramped and tired, but my back gets to me after just so long sitting here. Time to change and do something else. In fact I think I'll call it quits for tonight and read.

Take good care of yourselves,
Love and best wishes
Vivian

December 29, 2000

Just a sideline, I'm sitting here at the computer, having just checked my e-mail, and who would have believed back in the 1940s that I at seventy-nine years would be using and enjoying a computer, sending and receiving e-mail.

It's a gray and gloomy day out, and we are supposed to get another thre inches of snow by morning to add to the piles we already have, but they are warning the East Coast to "look out." They expect a huge storm to dump on them.

I was thinking about what I had written yesterday on our life story, telling about how much I enjoyed being a wife and mother. I got to thinking about the book *The Stepford Wives* by Ira Levin published back in the late 1970s or early 1980s. Maybe you have heard jokes about being a Stepford wife? The book was about a town in the East where all the wives were perfect and their husbands were their *kings*. Finally one wife broke out of the mold. Anyway it was interesting.

Our marriage was not like that, even if I did enjoy being a homemaker. Bill always treated me as his equal, his partner and soul mate. You read about these men who through their work and schooling leave their wives behind. It was not so in our case, whether it was because I have always been a reader I'm really not sure, but Bill and I seemed to grow up together. My opinions and ideas were just as important as his.

And as I sit here at the computer, looking out the window on this gloomy, late December day and thinking about our lives together over the years, I think of another point or side of our marriage . . . sex. Every generation seems to think they invented it. No one likes to think that their parents and grandparents had "sex." But how did you get here? Maybe that's another reason our marriage lasted and was so good. Our "sex life" was terrific! That's another area in our lives where we learned and grew up together, and boy, was it *fun!* And, kids, your dad and grandpa was a great lover. While things change with health and age, I still miss the touching and kissing that lasted until the very end. Those of you who were here know this for a fact. I miss him terribly.

Grief

Grief was not a state of mind, but a physical thing, a void, a deadening blanket of unbearable pain, precluding all solace.
—Rosamond Pilcher, *Winter Solstice*

Grief is a tax we pay on our attachments, not on our interests or diversions or entertainments. We grieve for losses only in games we play for keeps .. real love .. real hate .. real attachments broken. Perhaps if we were more willing to leave ourselves open to grief, deregulated., unplanned .. unruly. potentially embarrassing grief .. and bear it's burdens honorably., we'd have less free-floating unattached heart ache to spend on the increasingly, "packaged," bereavement-ops the media serves up .. (Princess Diana—J. F.K. Jr.—. Columbine School Massacre.)
—Thomas Lynch, Tragedy.com and Grief TV

A Rabbi said, "The Aim in Life is to "Grow Your Soul." A Buddhist said, "To Evolve."
They both said on the subject of Immortality "To live like you deserve it."
—Bill Moyer, *On Our Own Terms*

The H-O-W of Recovery

Many artists new to recovery are looking for answers to H-O-W; we can change our lives for the better. The word *how* is sometimes used as an acronym this way:

> H: heart and soul-felt emotional work. Sometimes difficult emotional/spiritual work is required for us to grow beyond our artistically sabotaging expectations, limitations, and fears. We open ourselves to embrace new levels of awareness.

> O: opportunity. We learn to perceive difficulties and obstacles as opportunities to learn ever greater lessons for our growth. Some of us become surprised by how strong we actually become and the lengths to which our art can take us.

> W: willing channels for creative expression. We learn, with time and experience, to become receptive vessels for the mysterious creative process to happen through our souls.

> Today, God, guide me to lessons for H-O-W. Point my steps, please, toward heartfelt opportunities to be a willing channel for my healthful expression. I am grateful you have brought me safely this far in my recovery of myself as a creative person. Thanks for caring. (Linda Coons, *The Artist's Soul: Daily Nourishment to Support Creative Growth*)

> *Perhaps they are not stars in the sky but rather openings where our loved ones shine down to let us know they are happy.*
> —Eskimo legend

ZIGGY

BOOKS
ARE FRIENDS
YOU CAN READ

Sharing Stories

The best things
we can give
our children,
next to good
habits, are
good memories.
— Sydney J. Harris.

Sharing Stories

The best thing a man can do for
his children is to love their mother.
— Fr. Theodore Hesburgh

Community

Friends and pets are not
our whole lives, but they
make our lives whole.

2001

2001: New Year, New Beginnings

And now let us welcome the New Year,
Full of things that have never been.

—Rainer Maria Rilke

Count your blessings. When one door closes, another opens.

We must view change as an opportunity for new adventures and growth.

We must look forward into the future, not dwell on the past.

View the glass as half full, not half empty.

I tell myself all of these things and repeat them again and again. Then why do I still hurt so deeply?

Thomas Lynch says, "Grief is a Tax we pay on attachments." Some days it seems like the tax is too high, and yet I never regret one moment of the years Bill and I had together. Our love over the years . . . simple everyday moments that laid like bricks one atop another, until they formed a foundation so solid nothing could make them fall. Then losing Kathy, seven weeks after Bill, seemed almost more than I could bear, and I wondered if my "foundation" could handle my "grief" without crumbling.

But here it is the beginning of a New Year and here I am somehow coping. Life goes on, and the days go by one at a time. We got through Christmas, which all of us were dreading this year, but by doing something completely different we all made it and the day itself turned out nicely. We had lots of snow, but the roads were dry and the sun was shining. Jim and Scott, Ken and Barbara, Carol, Cindy, and Erik were all here. Alice, Bill, and Shannon called to talk to everyone. The dinner in Great Lakes dining room was very nice, and no one had any cleaning up to do. Of course, as usual we had all kinds of snacks and goodies up there too.

Then, as I was unsure when I would have help again, I asked if they would mind helping me put my Christmas decorations away. Of course, that was taken care of in no time. So now on to the New Year. I have to figure out what and how I am going to handle teaching a watercolor class, and I admit I am scared. Everyone seems to think it will be *good* for me, but right now it seems almost more than I want to handle. I am going to give it a try. Also, I am trying to get back to writing on our life story for the family records. That does bring back a lot of wonderful memories and some ups and downs; of course, that's life, isn't it?

And so one foot in front of the other, one day at a time, I'm trying.

February 14, 2001

The Story Behind My Gold Greek Key Survivor Bracelet

Valentine's Day was always a very special day for Bill and me. Bill had asked me to marry him on Valentine's Day in February 1941. We were married on August 30 that same year.

Every Valentine's Day since then was always special to us. Through all of our years together, we always did or said something that was special for just the two of us; sometimes it was a special dinner out or perhaps one that I made, sometimes flowers or a small gift, sometimes just special words. Bill never forgot that day.

So my first Valentine's Day in 2001 without him really hurt. I was reading the USA paper that day when I saw this ad from Symth Jewelers of this gold bracelet with the Greek key design pictured in it. I really admired it. It was almost like a voice in my head and heart telling me to get it for myself, to call it "my survivor bracelet," for learning to carry on with part of my heart missing. The Greek key design was my symbol of wisdom and knowledge to help me learn to keep going on my own. I ordered it and just loved it. Somehow I have the feeling that Bill made it all happen at that particular time. It is very special to me and I wear it constantly. My family was proud of me for getting it as I was not in the habit of buying expensive jewelry for myself. They agree and think it is a beautiful symbol.

Sunday, February 18, 2001

I'm sitting here at the computer kind of moody and feeling sorry for myself, reflecting on this past week and how difficult it has been—Joe's death and going to the funeral home this past Wednesday, Valentine's Day, and how miserable and rainy it was. It certainly fit the mood, talking with Charlotte and my heart aching because I know what she was going through. Being with the family again yesterday at Susan and Alan's and hearing more about Joe's last days and hospice brought back so many, many memories that are still raw and hurting, thinking on how small the family is becoming . . . Edsel, Evelyn, Wally, Bill, Kathy, and now Joe. Robert and Flora are the only couple left out of the five of us. Carol and Jim were widowed much too young. It all hurts. Charlotte made a remark that is so true. You look around when you are out and everyone is going about their normal lives, laughing, talking, busy. And how can that be when your life has just been torn apart? But as I have found out these past few months, life does go on, and every day you get up and put one foot in front of the other and try and pretend you are going somewhere. Some days you wonder why. What's my reason for going on? At least I have a wonderful family and I know they care about me. That's a big help, but I'm so lonely sometimes, and it seems like the *fun* has gone out of my life. It seems like Sundays are difficult days, and I'm not quite sure why they are different than other days. My heart aches for Char going back to Florida and their empty house; she says she has great neighbors and friends but it's going to be so different.

Well, I think I have sat here and whined enough. The sun is shining although I know it is *cold* out. I'm warm with plenty to eat and a family who cares. I feel fortunate that Bill and I made the decision to move here together before our world fell apart. At least I don't have the responsibility of a house and all it entails, and if something should happen to me I should get care here.

We are having a speaker here this afternoon on Lincoln and with it being President's Day tomorrow it is very appropriate. Weldon Peltz is his name and he was here once before and talked about The Big Bands—very interesting, and I will go and hold an appreciation basket and smile and say thank you to the folks. It does help to stay busy, but I'm still lonely, and I still hurts. It helps to write about it sometimes.

Monday, March 5, 2001, Reprogramming

The March winds are blowing. It is *cold*—twenty degrees with the wind chill in the minus degrees. I had intended to go on some errands to Kinko's and Farmer Jack's *but* decided they were not that important and I was nice and warm in my apartment. This has seemed like an endless winter, perhaps because I feel as if my soul has been frozen with the pain of losing Bill and Kathy. I am hoping with the coming of spring and nicer weather, it will also help to thaw my heart. The support groups I have gone to have been helpful, and I have been reading, reading . . . reading. A book that I am reading now has been helpful, called the *Artist's Soul* by Linda Coons. It is a journal to be read daily, and that is where the idea for reprogramming came from. While she talks about the "artist's soul," she is talking to all of us to be creative in any form. Here is what she has to say." The process of recovery might be envisioned as being similar to the reprogramming of a computer. The computer can put out only the information that is put into it. Similarly, all of us were programmed earlier in our lives to think, feel, and behave in certain ways." That hit me. I have been programmed all my life to be a wife, mother, homemaker, and caregiver. Then my world is turned upside down with the loss of my husband and daughter. I am "lost" in the truest sense of the word. Then I think of Carol losing Edsel at fifty-five and Jim losing Kathy at fifty-three, and somehow they are coping. I think how lucky Bill and I were to have fifty-eight years together. I think also about what a wonderful and loving family I have, and I have to believe that there is a reason God has left me here.

Linda Coons goes on, "In artistic recovery, we can open ourselves to the healthful reprogramming of our souls. We learn the sometimes painful lessons of our limiting programming and thinking. We work through the pain to the reprogramming stage. Then, using positive affirmations, prayer and meditation, journaling, setting limits and respecting boundaries, reading and incorporating recovery information, using the gift of awareness, and other skills and strategies available in recovery, we go on to reprogram ourselves. We educate ourselves to integrate all our gifts, often joyfully, in ways that are unique to us as individuals."

So thinking back to last year at this time and how very sick both Bill and Kathy were I cannot wish them back. Please, God, help me to *reprogram* my soul.

March 28, 2001

I have been having a very rough time the last few days and feel like I'm falling apart. I guess I've hit a "valley." I can't seem to stop thinking about last year at this time. We had just found out that Bill's illness was terminal and the doctors thought hospice was the best answer. Alice was up here as well as Carol and Barbara to help with the decision, and there was none really. That's when we met Dr. John Finn, Director of Hospice of Michigan, very caring person. Bill seemed very accepting, and when Dr. Ledgerwood was talking to him, he looked at me, pointed his finger, and said, "I told you so." Then he told Dr. Finn that there was nothing to be afraid of. We were all grateful when hospice took over and managed his pain. Bill had been watching the clock for his pain shots. There is something very wrong with our medical system that will not allow doctors to control a patient's pain.

Carol came up with the idea of moving in with us so they could bring Dad home to die. Him lying there in that stark hospital room was more than any of us could face. Hospice made all arrangements, and Bill came home on April 1. Hospice showed us how to care for him and they were here every day, and we could call them around the clock. They were absolutely wonderful, but what a heartache to see your partner and soul mate so sick and know there was nothing you could do. It was one of the hardest things I have ever done in my life. Because of Carol, bless her heart, we were able to do it. Also Barbara and Alice were here every day. Kathy was having her own very bad problems, and we were all very worried about her too. Kathy and Jim did make it in one day, but Kathy did not feel well. Then the day before Bill died, Kathy went in Ford Hospital. It was almost too much for one family to cope with. Maybe putting all of this on paper will help me. Writing when things bother me has always seemed to help. I'm not sure about this though.

Robert and Flora made it in from Florida. Bill was in a semi-coma but knew they were here. Joe and Charlotte also made it but just the day before Bill died, and I'm not sure but I think he knew they were here, and now Joe is gone too. Bill Jr. and Shannon made it, and Bill knew they were here. Billy Jr. stayed up all night talking to his dad and holding his hand. Cindy and Erik were here a lot, and Erik had brought "Parker" a couple times when Bill was alert . . . Ken was here quite a bit too. Bill knew he was loved and his family was all here that could be. Because of hospice, Bill was able to die at home with his family around him. Bill died on Friday, April 14, 2000, at about 12:30 p.m. Billy got out the wine, and we all had a "toast" to a wonderful man. I guess I felt numb—relief that his suffering was over but sort of in a *fog*. I know Billy and the girls and I went to the funeral home to make arrangements around 3:00 p.m. I forgot to say hospice was back here almost immediately, and they made all the necessary calls; they had been here earlier in the morning and had been telling us for three days that it would not be long. When we got home from the funeral home, Ken, Erik, and Cindy had taken the bed and medical supplies out of the living room and tried to put the house back in order. I remember on Saturday the girls were going through albums and making picture boards. On Sunday we were at the funeral home from 1:00 p.m. until almost 9:00 p.m. There were so many people and so many flowers. Carol's Card Club brought in all kinds of food and some of Billy's friends did too. It was a long, long day, but it seemed to go by in a hurry. Then on Monday we were at the chapel here at the Village at 10:00 a.m. The service was at 11:00. Felix did a wonderful job. I forgot to mention how much Bill liked Felix and how many times he had gone down to Harper to see him, and Felix also came to visit him at home. Bill had asked Mona to play for his service and had also asked Erik to play his sax. Erik played "Harlem Nocturn." Everyone said what a lovely service it was. Again, I seemed to be running in a fog. The luncheon the Village put on for us in the St Clair dining room was very nice. I tried to follow all of Bill's wishes and I think I did. After the luncheon, all of the immediate family went out to Oakland Hills Memorial Gardens and met in the chapel there for a short service. I can't thank Felix enough for his help. It was cold and windy. My heart seemed to be frozen too.

Now the family was taking turns going out to help Jim with Kathy as she was home from the hospital on hospice also.

April 14, 2001

My Dearest Bill,

It doesn't seem possible that I lost you a year ago today. In some ways it seems like forever and in others like yesterday. I miss you so very much in so many different ways. I feel like part of me is missing, and I have this huge hole in my heart. The pain and heartache some days is almost more than I can stand. But here I am., and I have made it through a whole year. I didn't think it would be possible. Losing you and then losing Kathy seven weeks later is more than one person should have to bear. I have been angry at God and trying to make some sense out of all of this. I am grateful you did not have to go through the pain of losing another child. I know Susan was a lot of years ago, but the memory of that time in our lives still hurts. You and I had talked, and we both knew that we would not have Kathy much longer. But knowing that and having it happen are two different things. I miss talking to her, her enjoyment of all the holidays, her warmth, love, and caring for so many, many things, her peacemaking ability to keep things smooth between the twins and Carol. Since she is gone, they all miss her so much that things have been smooth., and of course, it was never any big issues. They all care about one another and are there for each other. Oh, honey, I miss talking to you about all the little things, and I don't like to make decisions by myself.

You know, honey, in all our years together somehow I just never figured that you would go first. It never entered my mind that I could be a widow until the last year of your life, and then it broke my heart to see you go downhill and go through so many unpleasant tests and operations. You were so brave and kept saying, "I'll feel better soon." You were trying so hard to put up a good front so you wouldn't worry me. Then when Dr. Ledgerwood came in and talked to us and said they really could not do any more and suggested hospice you pointed your finger at me and said, "I told you so." Although we really had never discussed it except for you saying if they did find cancer you were not going to go through what Kathy did. Then when we met Dr. Finn and he asked how you felt about everything, you told him, "There was nothing to be afraid of. I can't imagine being that brave."

Having you home with hospice, with Carol coming over to stay with us to make it possible, was the hardest thing I have ever done in my life. But I am so grateful we were able to do it, and I would do it again in a minute. It brought the whole family closer, and we were all able to find a bit of peace and closure with you being here, and I have to believe it made your dying a bit easier for you. 1 tried my best to do everything you had asked me and have the kind of service you wanted. Felix did a wonderful job, and he used all my notes about your life. Everyone said it was a beautiful service and a wonderful tribute to you. I'm sure you would have approved of the luncheon. The Village did a nice job. Howard and Annette served so well. Howard hugged me and said, "You were his friend." To be very honest, honey, I was running on numbness and nerves. I truthfully don't know how I got through everything. I guess with our wonderful family and the help of God, who I'm sure did give me strength.

Bill, we really did do something right. Our family is wonderful. They have been so good to me and keep close tabs on me, but., they all have lives of their own, and I hope and pray that I will stay well and not have to interrupt or cause problems for them. It's kind of scary living alone. Besides the loneliness, you don't have a partner to discuss things with, and if you don't feel good, you're on your own. I miss the security of putting my knees up against your butt in bed at night., your good night kiss, and you rubbing my back and shoulders a bit The bed is *too* big. I miss . . . I miss . . . I miss our shopping together and stopping out for lunch. It's not fun when you do it alone. I have to *push* myself some days to make myself get out and get going. I miss splitting our fruit at lunchtime . . . grapefruit, oranges, pears, etc. Now I have another piece for another day and it never tastes quite as good. I miss sharing a laugh at a funny episode on TV, although I have not been watching much TV. I don't enjoy it very much, like I did when we watched things together. My books help me escape and have better stories than the ones on TV. I also have done a lot of reading on grief and bereavement and have three self-help daily journal books going. I have spent a lot of money on books, but I know you never minded buying me books; speaking of buying, I bought myself a Greek key gold bracelet. I saw it advertised in the USA paper and really liked it. I call it "my survivor bracelet." I knew you wouldn't mind, and I hope you are proud of me for going on.

The staff here have been wonderful and very helpful. They all thought you were special. I have taken Kristine's grief class and am taking Leslie's mental wellness class right now. They both have been helpful. I also went to grief support group meetings at Hope Lutheran Church in West Dearborn. I'm trying so hard, honey, to learn to live without you. It's *very . . . very . . . difficult.* But I really don't have any choice, so I have to go on and try and find some sort of peace with my life. I have also been trying to keep on with writing our life story, and sometimes I want to ask you questions so badly. So it's going to be more one sided and my memories of the way things happened. The family is happy I'm doing it. I'm writing about the 1950s now—the fun we had getting involved in square dancing, you advancing at Ford's, learning golf, and learning to deal with vendors. Those were good years for us, and they do bring back a lot of happy memories. We were so busy then. I look back and wonder how we did it.

Honey, you would be so proud of Billy. He is a great father, reminds me of you the way he has just taken over and helps Shannon with everything. He takes as much care of Sydney as Shannon and *loves* doing it. Sydney is a beautiful baby. You would just love her; of course, you always loved all of our babies and grandbabies and were so good with them.

Also, Bill just completed another Microsoft test and has one more to go, which he wants to get done by the first of June. Then he is planning on going to Denver University for his master's degree. Can you believe that? Our baby has finally grown up and has plans and goals. We were so worried, as it seemed to take him a long time, much more so than our daughters. I suppose one reason would be that we all spoiled him so much when he was a baby, coming along when the girls were pretty well grown.

Tomorrow is Easter again. Last year I had just lost you and Kathy was so sick in Ford Hospital. I can't wish either of you back as sick as you both were, but honey, you and Kathy are the lucky ones. We are left to feel the pain of learning to live without either one of you, and it is so very hard. Anyway, Barb and Ken are at the cottage. Ken is trying to get the water hooked up this weekend. I am going over to Carol's at 11:45 a.m. and then we will go pick up Aunt Betty (Uncle Eino died a couple of months ago), then will go to the Marriott Hotel at Laurel Park for brunch at 1:30 p.m. Jim, Scott, and Helen will meet us there. Cindy and Erik will be with us. Helen is a question mark. Scott introduced her to Jim, and I guess she is very much in the picture. I don't know how I feel. I want Jim to be happy, he is too young to spend the rest of his life alone, but is this real or just convenient because he is so lonesome? I know he loved Kathy and he took care of her more than a lot of men could have. He earned "sainthood" in our family for his care and love of Kathy So we will see.

Well, honey, I started to talk to you and don't know when to quit, except my back is aching and saying, "Go do something else. I've sat here too long." Oh, Bill, I love you so much I keep telling myself how lucky we were to have had fifty-eight years together, but I wanted more. And I get envious when I see some of the "elderly" men around here and the trouble they have just living. That's when I can't help asking God why did he have to take you.

All my love always,
Vivian

P.S. Forgot to tell you, I'm "teaching" a watercolor class on Tuesday afternoons and everyone coming seems to enjoy it. Sandra got me involved in starting it. I even have a waiting list. Mainly it's women who have painted before and want to get together and paint. We share ideas, and I do help a couple of ladies who have not painted much before. Anne Perry interviewed me for Channel 6 TV, and I am supposed to be on next week.

I'm still involved in all my committees and have to introduce a Mariachi Band next Sunday. I just wrote the PR for the *Pioneer* today. I also made a couple of posters for the volunteer fair that is coming up the end of May—one for the Birthday Angels Committee and one for the Library Committee. I took them over to show Myra and the office. Cheryl and Sister Mary were there. They loved them.

I'm also collecting and sharing a lot of the hospice papers and care booklets with Charlotte, Aunt Betty, and a lady called Marie Pawluk that Sister Mary asked me to share with as she had just recently lost her husband. I know what she is going through too well. So I guess you could say I'm doing a little outreach and trying to help. I hope you are proud of me. I'm trying so hard to keep busy and keep going, and sometimes it is not easy.

July 17, 2001

Memories of J. L. Hudson's

Writing about this grand old store in the year 2001 makes me realize even more what we have lost. Hudson's was a part of our lives, and now even the name will be gone as Hudson's is becoming Marshall Fields. I wonder if this is progress.

Let me give you a bit of history.

In 1881, Joseph L. Hudson, thirty-five years old, opened a haberdashery on Campus Martius in Detroit. Ten years later in 1891, he opened a department store on Gratiot and Farmer, which grew into the wonderful store we knew as Hudson's.

J. L. Hudson Department store reigned over Woodward Avenue and the city like a grand and gracious lady—an arbiter of taste, purveyor of fashion, and epitome of service as much a sentimental phenomenon as a commercial one. It reached its peak during the 1920s and the 1950s. Women wore hats and pearls, and little girls dressed up in Mary Janes and gloves. Christmas did not start until Santa arrived in the Thanksgiving Day parade and entered Hudson's. The twelfth floor was a fairyland of carnival rides, hot dogs, and cotton candy—miles of angel floss and twinkling lights and toys and toys and toys.

The downtown store seemed cool, unhurried, and spacious. Its glass cases of silver, crystal, and bone china were a guide book and finishing school for thousands of Detroiters who were not born to wealth and gracious living. The fourth-floor lounge had stationery and pens available if you decided you wanted to write to someone. You could buy anything at Hudson's. If you bought it at Hudson's, it had to be in good taste. Hudson's would cut your hair, store your furs, shine your shoes and install your storm windows. You didn't even have to bother carrying your purchases home, as they would deliver them the next day in their delivery trucks.

Some of my own personal memories of always feeling that it was a very special place were of taking a bus when I was a young teenager and meeting my mother, who worked at Hudson's for several years, and she taking me to lunch at the cafeteria for employees on the fourteenth floor. It was a very nice place and the food was delicious. We would take the escalator from the top floor all the way down. I loved the mezzanine, the books, and the stamp departments, the elevator attendants and their white gloves, the smells from the bakery department, the huge millinery department, a whole floor of shoes, and all of the latest fashions, taking the girls downtown to shop for new clothes for school every August when the new things came in, my Christmas shopping days with my good friend Phyllis Mitchell. You always felt very special shopping at Hudson's.

I asked the girls what were their memories of me taking them downtown and shopping at Hudson's. Everyone one said they always felt excited and happy. Alice laughed and said she remembered like yesterday Grandma Miller cleaning her, Alice's, fingernails in the back seat when we were on our way downtown so she would look nice. Carol and Barbara both said the lunch, the Ice Cream Clown with the meringue base which they haven't had in years, the BLT's, and now it's the Maurice Salad. They would be excited about getting new clothes and shoes for school, then Carol said she would be excited waiting for them to be delivered the next day. They all remembered always getting dressed up to go shopping. Now look at the people in the malls today. I wonder! Barbara says she remembers very clearly being downtown one evening (probably at Christmastime because Bill was with us), and a "bum" came up and asked her daddy for some money. She says he gave him something.

Then came the shopping centers: Northland Mall in Southfield opened in March 1954 with 136 stores. That was a huge event in our history—a brand-new concept in shopping. They claimed to be the biggest in our nation at that time. Then came Eastland in Harper Woods in 1957, Wonderland in Livonia in 1959, Summit Place in Waterford township in 1962, Macomb in Roseville and Universal in Warren in 1964, Westland in Westland in 1965. Oakland Mall in Troy opened in 1968 a year after we moved to Troy. Somerset Collection also opened in Troy in 1969, Southland in Taylor in 1970, Briarwood in Ann Arbor in 1973, Fairlane Mall in Dearborn and Lakeside in Sterling Heights both in 1976 and on and on, and yes, I did start going to Northland some, but still I liked the downtown Hudson's until Detroit started changing and sadly not for the best.

In 1953, Hudson's logged 153 million in sales. In 1982, sales had dropped to 45 million. It was a sad day for everyone when J. L. Hudson's closed their doors in January 1983 . . . The building sat empty until October 24, 1998, when the whole city watched as it was imploded with 2,728 pounds of plastic explosives. It was a very sad day.

In November 1999, Compuware started building their world headquarters on Campus Martius. A garage serving 1,050 cars is being built where Hudson's stood.

The facts and figures for this little story came mostly from The Detroit Free Press *Detroit Almanac*, a fascinating book filled with information about Detroit.

It's a strange coincidence: I was writing this story today, July 17, 2001, watching the noon news on Channel 4. They showed a live picture from Fairlane Mall in Dearborn. A big crane was changing the name on the Hudson store there to Marshall Fields. It's another sad feeling of loss and old traditions.

Socked By a Memory: Friday, July 27, 2001

I was reading my morning paper, having my breakfast and half watching the *Today Show* on NBC. Katie Couric was talking about Neil Diamond going to be on later in the program for their *Friday Summer Concert* series.

Neil Diamond is an all-time favorite of ours . . . Katie interviewed him a little later. He is sixty now and looks great. He has just recorded a new album called *Three Chord Opera* and is starting a concert tour this fall. I was enjoying listening to him. Then he went on to sing "Sweet Caroline" That was my very favorite. I started crying. It brought back such wonderful memories but hurt also because of what I was missing now and how very lonesome I was.

Bill and I would always dance whenever a band played "Sweet Caroline," and Bill would sing in my ear "Sweet Vivian." One time at a small club, Bill got the singer to dedicate the song to me and sang it using my name. I will never forget that. I had not thought about that for a long time, and this morning it all came flooding back. That broke my tear gate dam, and I was having a difficult time today to shut the flood gates.

It's so strange. I've been going along and thinking I'm doing pretty good. Then something like a program and a song comes along and really socks it to me, and I feel like I'm back almost where I started. I miss Bill so much. I'm trying, but this is a bad day. Tomorrow has got to be better.

It's August, and most people don't look so hot

The final word
By Craig Wilson

I was a child, it was summer, and I was with my grandmother. The only thing I can't remember is where we were, but I know there were lots of folks around.

Maybe down at the beach. Maybe at the county fair.

She leaned over and said five simple words that have stayed with me: "People look better in winter."

I didn't quite know what she meant at the time, but I do now. A coat can hide a multitude of sins.

I doubt if anyone looked that bad in 1959. Even in summer. People took a certain pride in how they looked back then. But I can only imagine what my grandmother, whose handbag always matched her shoes, would say if she came back and looked around this summer of 2001.

For years now, I've wondered what happened to those people who actually contemplated what they were going to wear, looked in the mirror, winked, then headed out the door. Did they all

go the way of the fedora?

This summer, I've been through a dozen airports, two seaside boardwalks and one county fair. All I can report is this: It's not pretty out there.

I could have sworn one man I saw at the Minneapolis airport the other day had just climbed out of bed and wandered into the terminal. Even if he owned a mirror, he didn't stop to look in

By Alejandro Gonzalez for USA TODAY

it before he arrived at the gate in his ripped T-shirt, cutoff jeans and flip-flops.

If you're reading this in an airport, look around. See what I mean?

Did I miss the memo that said everyday was casual Friday, now? Was I absent when the teacher excused us from pulling ourselves together before going out in public? Does anyone care how he or she looks anymore?

I'm not talking about people running out to Home Depot during a Saturday project. I'm not talking about how people look walking the dog through the woods at 6 in the morning. I'll cut them some slack.

I'm talking about people flying cross-country in an outfit you wouldn't wear to take out the garbage.

You only have to spend a day at Disney World to realize that the only "magic" there is seeing how stretch pants can stretch as far as they do.

I was at a nice restaurant celebrating my mother's birthday last month. She was dressed to the nines, as usual. You don't own that many shoes and not

wear the best when you turn 82. I was wearing a blazer. Her friend George had on his classic blue suit.

The man at the next table? He was wearing an old T-shirt and shorts with the ever-expanding elastic band, looking for all the world as if he'd just come in from mowing his lawn, which he probably had.

The good news was, he didn't have on a baseball cap. You know, the ones that never come off. The ones that stay on through dinner, through flights, for eternity.

And what about all those people down at the beach? Talk about not pretty. I'll be the first to admit it's hard to properly cover the body and go in the water at the same time. But couldn't we give it the old college try? The Victorians did it, and I'm beginning to think they might have had the right idea. Seeing less is definitely more.

But there's hope.

Summer is drawing to a close.

Can winter coats be far behind?

E-mail cwilson@usatoday.com

August 30, 2001

My Dearest Bill,

I'm sitting here at the computer on a very warm summer day, just about like the day we got married sixty years ago today. I miss you so much and I'm feeling very sorry for myself today. I'm so doggone lonesome. I went to Westborn fruit market this morning just to get out and do something, and you know how we both liked to have fresh fruit in the house, but, honey, it's not *fun* anymore. We used to have such a good time and enjoy our little errands. Now it's just something to do and take up time.

Carol called last evening and offered to do whatever I wanted to do today, just come over or go out for lunch or dinner. I told her I'd let her know today. But, honey, you know what, I just have to get through this by myself. I don't feel in the mood to go out for dinner. *Sixty years!* I wanted to celebrate it with you. It didn't work out that way, did it? I know I should be grateful for the fifty-eight years we did have and I am. But I wanted more. You and I always enjoyed one another's company even if we didn't talk a lot sometimes. It was just *nice* to be together. This apartment is comfortable and bright and airy, but you are not in it. Some days I can feel you in my heart and close to me, but today I just *hurt!*

I hope you and Kathy are proud of me for surviving like I am doing and keeping busy. But that's all it is. It's busyness; the fun has gone out of things. I got elected to the Library Board last Monday. So that will be another meeting and more responsibility, I suppose. I tried to say *no* but just couldn't do it. Yesterday I wrote my letter to the watercolor students about starting up again in September. I put it in all their cubbyholes. That had been hanging over my head. I finished a tug boat for Barbara and some carousel horses for Sydney. Oh, honey, I wish you could see her. She looks like such a little doll (maybe you can). You always loved babies so much. You would be so proud of Bill, going for his master's, and he is such a good daddy. Honey, we did do something right. Your lessons by the way you lived your life have paid off. It just took him a little longer to grow up. Maybe because we did spoil him so much when he was little?

Well, somehow I will get through today. Maybe I'll have a couple of glasses of wine tonight or something. You know me; I haven't been drinking at all, but maybe my stomach will take it tonight. I've started a new painting, and perhaps I can get involved in that. I'm also reading a good book *The Smoke Jumpers* by Nicholas Evans. He wrote the *Horse Whisperers* which was good. My books, my art, my busyness—all helps, but some days, like today, are just almost unbearable. If you have any influence with God at all, ask him to please help me. I'm trying my best. I'm so lonesome for you, and I miss talking to Kathy too. Carol, Barbara, Alice, and Bill are good, and you know I love them. But today is just a very bad day.

Happy sixtieth anniversary, my dear. My love always, Vivian.

Sunday, September 16, 2001

How do I even begin to write about the events that have taken place this past week? First the terrible terrorist attack on Tuesday, September 11, and the Twin Trade Towers crumbling with thousands of people trapped and losing their lives. Then the Pentagon in Washington, DC, and more lives followed by the plane crash in Pennsylvania. More lives were lost. It was indescribable. The whole nation is in shock, mourning, and disbelief that this could happen in America. Everyone is shaken to their very souls; we know our world will never be the same. I've seen too many bad things. It brought back memories of Pearl Harbor and Kennedy's assassination. This is worse because we don't have a known enemy to fight. The president says we are at war and we will find and destroy the people responsible for this tragedy. But how and when? Our leaders have a very rough road ahead of them.

Then on Wednesday afternoon my own personal world fell apart again. There was a message on my recorder from Alice when I returned from lunch about one o'clock. It said that she had the weekend off and had decided to drive up here. It had been too long since she had seen everyone; she said they would be here about two o'clock. I was looking forward to her and Barb coming; when they came, it was Alice, Barb, Ken, and Carol. I knew immediately that something terrible was wrong. They came to tell me that Barbara had breast cancer and was going in Thursday for more biopsies and to install a port. She had had a needle biopsy on Monday, and it showed cancer 100 percent. We are all terrified, trying in front of one another to be brave, but falling apart inside. I know and I keep telling myself that breast cancer is very different from ovarian cancer. There are a lot more survivors from breast cancer and *it can be cured!*

My heart aches for Barbara; she is so very frightened, with good reason. We have all watched what Kathy's cancer did to her. Carol and Barb were with Kathy for a lot of terrible treatments. It makes me question God and why I should have two daughters suffering from cancer. What have I done wrong? I'm trying to go about my daily life, and nothing I do seems real. I hurt so inside and feel like just giving up and crumbling. The only thing that keeps me going is that I know the family cannot stand anything else to happen right now. I know they are all worried about me. Carol and Alice would like to be basket cases too; they are so upset and worried. Everyone is trying their best to stay *strong!* People keep saying you are strong, just take one day at a time or one moment. That's very hard to do right now. Barbara has a meeting with the oncologists tomorrow morning, September 17, at 8:00 a.m. Maybe we will find out and know more then. This has been hidden and did not show up in her mammograms or an ultrasound. Another worry is how far has it got to.

The Thursday procedure went well, and Barbara said everyone was wonderful to her. She arrived at Troy Beaumont Hospital at 12:30 p.m. and was home shortly after 4:30 p.m. She is very sore but doing all right as she tells me. Barb, Ken, and Alice went out to the Lake to close the cottage for the season. The island friends have been overwhelming in their support. They are the extended family to Barb and Ken. Alice told me that Barbara made a remark whether she would see it next year. How does a mother cope and help her daughter face this and not fall apart herself? I'm praying and praying constantly. I'm wondering if God hears me. I'm hurting so badly and life seems very unfair right now.

One prayer that was answered and I am very grateful was that Shannon was in Fort Meyers, Florida, on a business trip. She had been gone a week and was due to fly home on Tuesday evening.

Of course, with the terrible happenings that took place that day, all air traffic was shut down. Every day she was told a different story, and I don't think anyone really knew what was going on. Thousands of people were stranded all over the world; everything has been affected. Anyway, Shannon did get back to Denver on Saturday afternoon and is with her family, *safe and sound*. That was another worry I had this week, but it had a happy ending for that one. I'm trying so hard to count my blessings. I'm worried about Carol and Alice too. How are they going to handle this? Please, God, help all of us.

MUTTS

GRAND AVENUE

IT'S A DAY THAT CAN'T BE SUMMED UP ON A T-SHIRT.

Reflections on Turning Eighty:
30 September 2001

Strange, I've always thought of eighty as being pretty ancient. How did I get this old? Where did all those years go and so fast?

My body tells me something is going on. It has more aches and creaks and stiff joints, *but* my mind still feels the same inside. Everyone says I don't look like eighty, if eighty has a look. I think one of the secrets of aging is to try and stay young in your heart, to be able to roll with the punches life can give you and to accept the changes. That is a lot easier said than done. Also to always stay open to learning new things and meeting new people, listening to new ideas. Of course, your health has a lot to do with how you cope. My physical health is doing OK, I think, *and* thank goodness, God has left my mental capabilities still functioning on most cylinders. My arthritis is getting worse, but I think that is pretty normal. It's my heart that is broken and bleeding, *but* I put up a good front. Everyone says, "You are so strong." They can't see into my heart, and I guess that's a good thing.

We have lost too many people close to us these last few years: Edsel, who was like a son to us, Aunt Fran, a second mother and friend, Evelyn, my only sister, Wally, Marguerette's husband, then my own Bill, who took part of me with him, Kathy, seven weeks later. No parent should have to go through losing a child. We also lost Joseph, Charlotte's husband and Bill's brother—too many, and each one took a toll in different ways. Now, the news of our Barbara having breast cancer is almost more than I can bear. I know, I know, and I keep telling myself breast cancer is curable! It is a lot different than ovarian cancer, *but* it breaks my heart to see she has to go down such a *rough* road so soon after helping with her sister and watching what our Kathy went through. Life just does not seem very fair sometimes. I'm praying and trying very hard to keep my faith, but sometimes wonder where God is.

The family had a lovely party for me on my birthday. Alice was able to be up here for the weekend, and she took over getting everything ready. We had it at Barb and Ken's as we were not sure how Barb would be feeling. The weather could not have been nicer. It was a gorgeous fall day. We were able to sit out in their backyard and watch the puppies run and play. Carol,

Cindy, Erik, and Eve were there, so were Jim, Scott, Hannah, Barb, Ken, and Alice. Ellie came over too. Alice had made a beautiful black forest whipped cream cake that was a picture and tasted as good as it looked. Scott had brought in his famous bump cake that is always delicious. They had salad and pizza, which is a big treat for me, as we don't get it at the Village. Alice had carved out pumpkins and filled them with dirt and fresh pansies for everyone to take one home. They were so attractive. Kenny called and talked to all while we were there. Kelly had called earlier. Krista had e-mailed me. Davey sent me a birthday card and pictures of his babies (dogs). I talked with Bill and Shannon and got a card, plus a lot of cards from friends both old and new. The staff here has been wonderful to me. I get lots of hugs and I am in all their prayers and their best wishes and prayers for Barbara. It does help. It was kind of an extra emotional day for me, but I held myself together. On Monday, I fell apart for a while but made it with my regular routine. One thing around here is that with so many people not seeing real well, red and swollen eyelids don't show up too much. I guess that's a good thing. I've got such a wonderful family, and I know they love me and care about me, *and* they are worried about me too; this is hard for all of us. But we are in this together and somehow we will make it.

With the terrorist attack happening at the same time, it has been a double burden and heartache for all of us. It's hard to imagine such a terrible thing happening in our own country. It's knocked every one's feelings of safety for a loop. I don't want to see another war, but what is the solution? I do think President Bush is trying his best, and he has good people advising him, but what a terrible job! Pearl Harbor was terrible but different. We had a known enemy, not some evil people that hate America and are hiding in another country. Our country has a conscience. We don't want to kill innocent people. One good thing this has done is made most people realize we are all one color (even if our skin color is different); we are all united in a fight against terrorism. We are all Americans, and we will fight for our country if it is necessary.

I wonder what is in my future and why I am still here. I'm trying to study and take advice from the book *Age-ing To Sage-ing* by Zalman Schachter-Shalomi, trying to learn to be an "elder" and not just an "older." Some days it's difficult. I do try my best to keep busy with my five committees, and I hope I am helping some. I try to enjoy my watercolor class and hope it gives me the inspiration to keep painting. Some days I miss Bill so much I ache inside. And Kathy, I miss her so. Well, I guess that's enough whining. I have to get on with my life and the time I have left.

William "Bill" J. Beeler

My soulmate and best friend . . .

A family leader as the eldest of your siblings . . .
A wonderful Husband . . . Dad . . . Grandpa . . .
You are missed beyond words. BUT .. You taught all of us, with the help of Hospice, not to fear death, but to celebrate LIFE . . . That Love never dies. It lives on in our hearts. You passed on a beautiful legacy of character, courage, and faith that live on in our children and grandchildren . . . Continuing the circle of our family and life. Till we meet again, you are in my heart. Vivian

Sent to Hospice for Memorial Book, October 20, 2001

Tuesday, October 2, 2001

Dear Friends and Family,

I just happened to hear this song on the radio a couple of weeks ago. I was so impressed with the words that I had to pursue it. Probably most of you are already familiar with it. I don't listen to "pop" music very often and I just heard this song sort of by accident. It really "hit" my soul.

To try and make a long story short, I went to Borders across the street and started asking everyone I met. "Do you know of a song called 'I Hope You Dance'?" It took me about six people, and one finally said, "Yes." My girlfriend really likes it. I think it is by Lee Ann Womack. I didn't know the singer or anything before. It turns out there is a little booklet in the inspirational section called "I Hope You Dance" with a small CD in the back with the recorded song. It was for $13.95. I grabbed it and couldn't wait to get home to read it and play the song. I'm going to get that book for my daughters and granddaughters at Christmastime. I think it says something to people of all ages. I am trying very hard to apply it to my life and telling myself, "You cannot sit this life out you have to dance."

I'm enclosing a copy of the words if you have not happened to hear it before. Perhaps you know someone who would also like it as a gift.

Love and best wishes always.

I Hope You Dance

I hope you never lose your sense of wonder
You get your fill to eat but always keep that hunger
May you never take a single breath for granted
God forbid love ever leave you empty handed
I hope you feel small when you stand beside the ocean
When one door closes I hope one more opens
Promise me that you'll give faith a fighting chance
And when you get the choice to sit it out or dance
I hope you dance . . . I hope you dance
I hope you never fear those mountains in the distance
Never settle for the path of least resistance
Livin' might mean takin' chances but they're worth takin'
Lovin' might be a mistake but it's worth the makin'
Don't let some hell-bent heart leave you bitter
When you come close to sellin' out reconsider
Give heavens above more than just a passing glance
And when you get the choice to sit it out or dance
I hope you dance . . . I hope you dance
Time is a wheel in constant motion always rolling us along
Tell me who wants to look back upon their years and wonder
Where those years have gone. I hope you dance . . . I hope you dance

I hope you dance

Sung by Lee Ann Womack
Written by Mark Sanders and Tia Sillers

Saturday, October 20, 2001

Dear Sage,

It's hard for your grandma to realize that you are going to be four years old on November 1, *but* I see by your pictures that you are growing up to be a very pretty little girl. I wish we didn't live so far apart so that we could talk, read, and draw together. I just want you to know that I think of you and your family very, very often and love all of you bunches. I'm wishing you a very happy, happy birthday and a wonderful year to come. Your grandma didn't know what you would like for your birthday, so I am sending your mommy a check. Perhaps Mom and Dad will take you shopping, or they will use it to get something you need or want. Whatever they decide is fine.

Your grandma just got back this week from visiting your uncle Bill, aunt Shannon, and Sydney in. Colorado. Aunt Carol went with me to help, and she broke a bone in her foot the night before. We left, *so* your grandma ended up helping her. Traveling is not easy when you get older like your grandma. I just turned eighty in September, and that doesn't seem possible. I always thought eighty was ancient, and at your age it is. Anyway, honey, we went out there to celebrate my new little granddaughter's first birthday, and it was a lot of fun. You would like Sydney. She is just a few months younger than your brother, Ché. She is a very good baby with a happy disposition. She is walking all over and trying to say words. I was very glad to be able to see her again. I had not seen her since she was three weeks old. Your grandma feels very lucky to have such beautiful grandchildren and great-grandchildren.

I took the pictures of you and Ché along with me and they were so happy to see them. I keep your pictures on my bookcase in my living room, so I see them every day and they make me feel happy. I have a family picture gallery on my bookcases, and they make me feel warm and loved. I talk to your nana and papa nearly every day, and they love you very much too. I will be sending you and your mommy a little booklet, and I want both you and your mommy to read the words and listen to the music, *and* never ever sit this life out. I hope you dance always and always. Happy birthday, sweetheart. Lots of love from Great-grandma Beeler.

Grandma B.

Letter to Sydney on Her First Birthday
from Grandma Beeler

October 20, 2001

My Dearest Sydney,

Your grandma was so very happy to be able to visit you and your mommy and daddy for your very first birthday. I hadn't seen you since you were three weeks old, a little "butter bean" as your daddy called you. You were sweet then, and I was able to rock and hold you. But it was so nice to see what a sweet, happy little girl you are growing into now. It was so much fun to see you walking all over and to see your interest in your books and toys, watching you try to say words. Aunt Carol and I heard you say "pooh" and "book" and try to say "balloon." I know you are going to be talking very soon. Your grandpa Beeler would have loved you so much and been so proud of what a wonderful daddy your daddy is. I know I love you lots and lots, and I am so proud of your daddy and mommy. They are wonderful parents.

Grandpa would have been eighty-two years old today, so it is a bitter-sweet day for me. It also happens to be the "sweetest day," and Grandpa usually got me a card and a couple of yellow roses. I miss that and things we did together. I have wonderful memories, but sometimes I get very lonesome. Then I think of my wonderful family and of being able to be at your birthday party, which was just one week before today. You were such a good little girl and such a sweetie pie. Your grandma keeps looking at the pictures your daddy took, thinking of the nice times of holding you and looking at books with you, playing "Mary Had a Little Lamb" and catching balloons for you to hold. It took a couple of days for you to get to know me, which is very normal, but then you were holding up your arms to me and giving me your wonderful smile. You just melted my heart. I love you so much, honey, it seems strange for me to be this old and have a new granddaughter. But when you add things up, I was forty-three when your daddy was born. He was a big surprise in Grandpa's and my life with his sisters being almost grown-up. Carol was twenty-one, Kathy was eighteen, and the twins Alice and Barbara were fourteen.

Your daddy was a spoiled little boy during his early years as he had five mothers. All his sisters were always at his beck and call. He had a lot of *love,* and they say love does not spoil anyone. Then his sisters got married and left home. That left Grandpa and me with a spoiled little boy. It turned out to be a blessing for us though. I think your daddy kept us young. I was very involved in helping in the schools, as home room mother, helping on field trips, and also working in their libraries. Grandpa got involved in Boy Scouts and thoroughly enjoyed it. Your daddy made some friends in Scouting, who are still his friends to this day, which I think is wonderful. They were in your mommy and daddy's wedding party. We were also involved in Sunday School and your daddy's Catechism classes. Back then, they didn't have the soccer teams like they have now, but it seems like we were always busy. We had some wonderful trips to Florida and staying at the Kon Tiki Motel right on the ocean in Lauderdale-By-The-Sea. Your daddy had a great time swimming both in the pool and the ocean. As he got older, he learned to water ski and went parasailing. We went on trips to all the tourist spots in Florida—Disney World, Cypress Gardens, Busch Gardens, Kitchitee Kippee Springs (sp), Lion Country, Sanibel Island, the Mucky Duck Restaurant on Captiva, and Stone Mountain in Georgia. I think your daddy has some nice memories of those trips.

With Grandpa and I being older parents, we had decided we could not wait for your daddy to grow up before we traveled. So we just took him along. I think it worked out well for all of us. It was enjoyable for Grandpa and I to see all of these things we had never seen or done before *and* it was also fun to see them through the eyes of a young boy growing up. Like I mentioned before, I think your daddy kept us young *but* enough reminiscing. This is about my being there for your birthday party.

It was so nice for me to see your grandma and grandpa Pack and your aunts and uncles on your mommy's side of the family again. Your mommy and daddy have a lot of nice friends and coworkers who came to your party too. I think that there were ten little children also. This Grandma had not been around so many little ones for years. It was fun for me to watch and listen to everything. All of the children were good and had fun. Poor Aunt Carol had to sit in a corner in your daddy's La-Z-Boy chair with her broken foot elevated and just watch. Your aunt Carol loves children, and she would have liked to be in the middle of everything and playing. Your daddy and mommy had a great barbecue for everyone: hamburgers, hot dogs, salads, chips, and of course, our famous Beeler chip dip. Then there was your birthday cake. Your mommy took your shirt off and set the cake in front of you on your high chair tray. Your were so puzzled by everyone standing around looking at you and singing "happy birthday." It took a little while before you even touched your cake. You were a darling to watch. Your mommy actually had to put your hand in the frosting, and then you didn't like the feel of it on your fingers and made faces. Finally you tasted it and found it to be sweet and not so bad, then you really got into it. Your daddy got some great pictures of you with frosting and cake all over you. I was so very glad that I could be there to share in that special day with you. I know at my age and the distance involved you will not be able to know me very well. So I thought by writing letters to you, you will get to know me in that way, *and* you will know how very much I love you.

That same weekend that Aunt Carol and I were there for your birthday party was also the week that your daddy had finals for two of the classes he was taking toward his master's degree. He was staying up half of the night studying. I found out later that he got A's in both classes. See why I am so proud of him. Your daddy also cooked us two delicious dinners: one of steamed shrimp and steamed asparagus, another of grilled filets and steamed broccoli. He is quite a chef. It also warmed my heart to see that not only is he a good daddy, but he is a wonderful husband also. He loves your mommy very much. It startles me a little to see how much of his dad has rubbed off on him and also makes me feel so good. As I told you before, what a wonderful person your grandpa Beeler was!

We also went to Cherry Creek Mall in Denver and had lunch at a Mexican restaurant. You were very good and sat in your high chair and ate bits of food off your tray. Your daddy would take his straw and dribble water in your eager little mouth. It opened like a little bird every time your mama or daddy did that. You entertained Aunt Carol and me royally, and we loved watching you. From the restaurant we went across the street (had to drive, of course) to the "Tattered Cover" bookstore. I had read about it in some of my book review papers and your daddy and mommy wanted me to see it. It was very interesting. We didn't cover too much of it except we had to go to the children's area. What fun to watch you want to pull the books off the shelf to look at them! Then you discovered a big box with blocks in it. It was a deep box, and you leaned over so far you almost stood on your head. You had us all laughing. You were such a happy little girl, a joy to be around. We did find a book about Bear in the Big Blue House and Liking Water that Grandma got for you, as I had seen you watch bear on TV and how much you liked him. I'm so pleased you like books. Your grandma has been a bookworm all her life, and books have helped her through some rough times the last few years. Books can open the world for you and give you a lot of enjoyment. It was a beautiful afternoon, bright sunshine as we went back home. It was time for a rest for everyone.

Aunt Carol and I had to leave to come home the next day, just when you were getting to know us, but that's life. We had a wonderful time out there for your first birthday. And now, Grandma can picture you playing around your house and some of the things you do. I know each day you will do and learn more. Another thing that Grandma loved about being out there was being able to see Katy again. I do think she remembered me, and it was so nice to have her welcome me too. I hated to see how she is getting old, but Grandma and Katy have a lot in common. Our joints just don't want to move and work like they used too. We get *stiff*. Oh well, like the little booklet I gave your mom and you, no matter what, we cannot sit this life out. We have to dance!

Well, sweetie pie, I think Grandma has rambled on long enough. I did want to write to you about how much we enjoyed being out there for your birthday. Your mommy can put this in your baby book and read this to you when you get older. I told your mommy and daddy that I had ordered a bookcase for you, which you should have in about three weeks. I hope it will be useful for all your books over the years.

> Sending bunches and bunches of love to you,
> Grandma B.

The Healing Mass
St. Thomas More Church Troy, Michigan

Saturday, November 3, 2001

What an inspiring and wonderful service on a gorgeous fall day! The sun was shining. The sky was a bright blue and the temperature in the high fifties.

Carol picked me up at 10:00 a.m. as planned and we drove out to the church in Troy. We made good time and arrived there at 9:40 a.m. We did not see anyone who looked familiar, so we sat in the car for ten minutes talking. Alice came out of the church and said they were all inside already. We went in and met a lot of Barb and Ken's island friends who were there for her too. That all started over a month ago when a couple of Barb's friends who belong to St. Thomas More told her about "The Healing Mass" and suggested that she invite her family and friends and come. When you are faced with a serious illness, prayers and church become more important. It's too bad it's like that, but it's human nature. Church and faith were always important to Bill and certainly helped him face death. My faith has always been there, but with what's happened the past few years, I have to admit it has wavered. Carol, Edsel, and their family have been our steady church goers. She told Barbara that she would help hold the church up for her. If the things I write in *Our Story* are to be believed, I have to be honest about things. Anyway . . .

St. Thomas More is a beautiful church. Father Edward Belczak led the service. It's difficult to describe how beautiful and touching it was. The hymns, the choir, the liturgy, the homily all blended together. Father Belczak went to each person who was ill (they had a butterfly name tag pinned to their clothes) and laid his hands on their heads while saying a special prayer. You could just feel the emotion and the power of God. We were all crying, and it's hard for me not to cry in writing this. Ellie, bless her heart, had given us hankies just before the service started. Our Kleenex just didn't do it. Then after Father Belczak had finished with the laying on of hands, he said another prayer and went to each person again, anointing their foreheads and hands with blessed oil, again praying for each of them. I just know God heard him and *listened*. There were about twenty-five of Barb's family and her island friends who were there to support her and Ken. I know the service touched everyone of us. What a tribute to Barbara too that so many of her friends cared enough to be there. It was wonderful. The liturgy, hymns, and service are so close to our Lutheran services. You know, I don't think God cares which church we are in as long as we are praying to him. The service lasted an hour and a half, but it seemed to fly by. We all took communion together also, and that was very special too. I just know and believe that this will help Barb in all kinds of ways.

When the service was over, we were all hugging one another and still trying to control our tears. My tears were for so many things—past memories, but also faith and hope for the future. As Father Belczak said, he was sure all of us had been hurt by life in some way and we were all in need of prayers. How true! I have since heard from other people more about him. They can't praise him enough. Our friend Don Clark who lives here said they had been to two wedding services that Father Belczak had conducted, and he said they had never been to such beautiful services.

But back to Saturday, we all left the church and went to Barb and Ken's. Alice had made sloppy Joes, baked beans, macaroni salad, and of course, one of her *very special cakes*. It was beautiful! Scott had brought in his famous bump cake. Carol had made our famous Beeler dip, chips, pretzels, etc. I had made a Jell-O and an apple crisp. And Barb and Ken's friends had brought all kinds of salads, cheeses, fruits, olives, pickles, and on and on. What a feast and what great company of family and friends! Barbara looked beautiful. She had on a navy outfit and the cutest navy hat with white stripes and white blouse. She said she was feeling pretty good, and she looked like she was. All of us had kind of red eyes and of course no lipstick by that time, but it didn't matter. Alice had worked so hard with all the food and helped Barb get the house ready. It looked wonderful! I'm so proud of all my girls. They have good strong backbones and are *fighters*. Life has not been easy on any of them—Alice struggling as a single mother to make ends meet, Carol losing Edsel at much too young an age and getting on with her life, Barb having both her children move so far away and now having this breast cancer, and of course, they are all still mourning the loss of their dad and sister, Kathy, last year. Life has been rough on all of us the past few years.

What a very special day that was in so many ways! Before I sign off, I have to tell you about Bouy and Sailor. They were Mutt and Jeff, the tall and the short. With all that food on the table, their noses were working overtime. We caught Bouy cruising by the table, just looking, of course. Then her tongue would come out, and before you could say no, a piece of cheese would be gone. She got a lettuce leaf too, which she left on the floor. Then on the next cruise time, Bouy got a good lick of frosting from Alice's beautiful cake. It was funny, really. Bouy's head and nose were exactly table high. Poor little Sailor was standing around with a pleading look in her eyes, saying, "Won't someone help me out? I want some goodies too." Then when a lot of people had gone and the dogs had more room to run, they started a chase round and round, then they would wrestle. *Then* Bouy would nip Sailor's ears and that *hurt!* Yipe! Mom or Dad had to step in and rescue Sailor. Amazing how well they do get along though! I know too that they are very good therapy for Barb. With Alice there now too, she can help watch Bouy when she tries her best to get into mischief. She's still a puppy, not a year old yet.

I wish I could name all of Barb and Ken's friends who were there, but I only know, Ellie, Skippy, Judy, Tim, Midge, Emily, and Jenny. The rest I have met on the island, but when you only see them once in a while it's hard to remember names. I know Barb and Ken know who was there. I think they said there were twenty-eight people who came. Wonderful! A beautiful tribute to a beautiful person and *an absolutely wonderful day!*

Sunday, November 4, 2001

Dear Father Belczak and Members of St. Thomas More,

I had to write to you and say "thank you" from the bottom of my heart for the wonderful service of the healing mass yesterday.

A little background:
My daughter, Barbara Vogt, was diagnosed with breast cancer on September 10. We had just lost my soulmate and her dad a little over a year ago. Seven weeks later, we lost my daughter, Kathy, and Barb's sister to ovarian cancer. She had battled it for six years. Now this. As a mother, it is breaking my heart to watch another daughter go through the ravages of chemo, and there will be surgery. But we are hopeful. Statistics prove there are more survivors from breast cancer than from ovarian cancer. I have two other daughters, Carol and Barb's twin, Alice. I also have a son in Denver, Colorado.

A couple of Barbara's friends are members of St. Thomas More. They had told her about the "healing mass" and suggested she invite her family and friends and come. Our family is Lutheran, but God is God, and I believe we can share our faith and prayers in one another's churches.

I live in Henry Ford Village in Dearborn. Sister Mary Downey works here and has become a good friend and helped me in many ways. I asked her about this mass as I had not heard of it before. She said it was a beautiful, touching ceremony, and she thought it would help all of us.

There were twenty-five of Barb's family and friends who came to support and pray for her yesterday at the service. Barbara is a beautiful person and has touched a lot of lives. This family sticks together and I feel blessed *but* the past few years have been difficult for all of us.

Father, your prayers for all of us, saying that you knew all of us had been hurt in some way, were so true. Your special prayers for the ones who are ill were touching and beautiful. I know God heard and listened.

Father to you and all the committee members who were involved in the service yesterday, I can't thank you enough. You are all angels on earth, and we truly appreciate what you have done for us. It was a very emotional and wonderful service. My tears were for things past and faith and hope for the future.

December 19, 2001

Vivian Beeler
15181 Ford Rd.
Apt. 3 02
Dearborn, MI 48126-4634

Dear Vivian,

I apologize for not getting back to you quicker. I truly enjoyed both your Thanksgiving card and letter, and your Christmas card. I also enjoyed the poem by Robert Green Ingersoll. I will give you an update on the office and my family. First of all, in the office, we have just gone through extensive remodeling. I have been dreading the day I had to clear my office out, but I finally bit the bullet and am just about finished putting my office back together. We have a very fertile office. As you know, Libby Yu-Morse, our nurse practitioner had a baby last December who is now one-year-old and is walking and is a beautiful little girl. Tracy had her second child, a little boy, approximately four-months-ago.

She is doing well. Tracy's identical twin sister Terry is also working in the office and she is as beautiful and wonderful as Tracy.

I am very sorry to hear about your daughter Barb's breast cancer. Debbie from our office just finished surgery, chemo and radiation. She appears to be bouncing back to her old self. Your daughter is in for a lot of hardship; however, it appears that she is in good hands and she will be in my thoughts and prayers.

My father-in-law is doing well now slightly more than two years after his heart transplant. Dr. Atallah was instrumental in helping us meet the right physicians to consider him as a transplant recipient.

Page Two
Re: Beeler, Vivian
December 19, 2001

My personal family is doing well. My wife works in the office two to three days per week. Louis my eldest is in his second year at Ohio University and still pursing a Journalism career. For the past four or five years, he has been writing a fantasy novel. It is approximately 450 single spaced pages and he is working on his last chapter right now as we speak. Peter, my second child is a senior in high school, and may join Louis at Ohio University, but is thinking of going into Telecommunications. My youngest, Grace, is a sophomore and is leaning toward a business degree.

You are right that I need to take better care of myself. I have had a problem throughout my life with my weight going up-and-down. I finally got motivated enough to get back on a diet and hopefully will start to exercise soon.

Again, I wish you the very best. Both you and Bill are in my thoughts and prayers and now I will put Barb in them as well.

May God bless you and your family and hopefully 2002 will be a good year for you all.

Sincerely yours,

Robert A. Badalament, M.D., F.A.C.S,
RAB/TTS/RMD

2002

I don't quite know where to start. Barbara got the lab test back yesterday. Dr. Ruark called her. She had sent twelve nodes to be biopsied. Seven came back with cancer. After all those chemo treatments and the thirty radiations that burned her so badly, you wonder how anything could live. Then there was the mastectomy this past Monday. How much more does my poor daughter have to go through? She has been so brave and kept an upbeat attitude. Alice said she did fall apart yesterday, and I don't blame her. My heart aches so much, and I am so shaky today just from hearing the news. This will mean more chemo. How can I help her and Ken? This is very difficult for him too. I was so in hope that God would listen and the biopsies would be normal.

Today was the day that Susan and Alan were coming with Marguerette to see our apartment and have lunch at Windows cafe. Then we would take them on a tour of the place. They did come, and it was nice to see them. I tried very hard to put up a good front, *but* when we were getting our lunch, I tipped my tray over with a big glass of ice tea on it all down the front of me, embarrassing me no end. I was just too shaky. Fran from the Windows Staff was so nice and had me get another tray and half of the sandwich which I had soaked with tea. I was ready to run crying from the dining room back to my security corner. I didn't. I made it through lunch and then took them on a tour. Now I'm back in my apartment and wondering what I can do to ease Barb and Ken and how I can help. Oh god! Why could you not let it be me? And please tell me, God, how does a mother cope with a second daughter going through all of these horrible things? How do I stay upbeat for them? I'm so scared. I just absolutely cannot lose another daughter. Please, please, God, do not let that happen.

Sometimes when I write about my feelings, it helps me to cope, but I don't seem to be having much success today. I feel like taking pills to space me out or getting drunk to forget the pain. But I know in my heart that neither would help and I would just feel worse afterwards. And I don't want to cause my family any more pain, so somehow or other I have to get through this. When I think about how miserable I am, what must Barb and Ken be going through? And of course, what about Alice and Carol also? It's difficult for all of us. Please, God, help all of us.

Friday, March 15, 2002

Dear Family and Friends,

I just finished a book the other night and was so impressed with it I have to write about it. It touched my heart. It is so full of wisdom for dealing with life. It was written in such a way 1 did not want it to end. I cannot recommend it highly enough. *Run* to get a copy. I guarantee you will have trouble putting it down.

The book is called *Letters For Emily* by Cameron Wright. This is a first novel for him and was inspired by poetry that his grandfather had written. He is married and has four children.

The story is about an older man who has dementia and possibly Alzheimer's. (Why is it people who are my age are always older than I am?)

He knows he does not have long to live and he wants his seven-year-old granddaughter to know him not just as a sick and angry old man but as the person he used to be. So in his lucid moments he writes poetry and letters to her. Don't be misled. This is not a sad story. It is inspiring and uplifting, a page turner. He has a son and a daughter, both married and three grandchildren. The daughter-in-law takes Emily every Friday to visit her grandfather, and they became good friends, thus, *Letters for Emily.* He has not been close to his son and daughter for years. After his death, the family finds three identical beautifully bound books—one for the son, the daughter, and Emily. The books are filled with his poetry. Each poem contains a puzzle, and they have to figure out a password, which they type into his computer. It opens a special letter to Emily. It unlocks the reasons for him being the kind of father he was and lets the son and daughter know him. He usually would start his letters with a story for Emily. The stories tell of his experiences through life with so much wisdom and humor, for example, he tells one story about an old mule. The mule had worked hard for the farmer all his life and now was almost blind. One day the mule fell into an old well. The farmer heard the old mule braying and crying from the bottom of the well. The farmer thought because of all the braying the mule was badly injured too. He thought the kindest thing he could do, as he had no way of getting the mule out, would be to bury the mule in the well. The farmer started to throw dirt and mud on top of the mule. The old mule kept feeling all this dirt and mud coming down on his back. He kept shaking it off and stamping on it until he reached the top of the well, where he climbed out and walked tiredly to his stall in the barn.

The grandpa went on to explain to Emily that when life throws dirt and mud on us, we must shake it off and put one foot in front of the other and go on doing the best that we can.

I could write more, but I want each of you to read this amazing book for yourself. If you do read it, I would love to talk about it with you and get your thoughts on it. I suppose different generations would have different viewpoints on the story. Perhaps because life has seemed to throw a lot of dirt and mud on me the last couple of years, the story touched me so much. A younger friend of mine read this book and was so impressed she recommended it to me. I cannot thank her enough.

Enough said, be good to yourselves,

Love, Vivian

Books

Learning the *write* way

WITH KEYBOARDS replacing face-to-face chitchat for everything from "Hi, Mom" to "Attention, staff," we're writing more than ever. Credit (or blame) technology for the writing boom: Experts predict that by 2005 we'll send 35 billion e-mails worldwide a day — triple the current output.

Sadly, just because we're writing more doesn't mean we're writing better. The informal approach to e-mail often reveals sloppiness when it comes to the fundamentals. We asked legendary wordsmith Jim Bellows, who has edited celebrated writers from Tom Wolfe to Jimmy Breslin, to weigh in on the universal truths of great writing. His new memoir, *The Last Editor* (ANDREWS MCMEEL; $26.95), is in stores, and a documentary of his career will run on PBS next month (check local listings).

His advice:

Be concise. "Remember the old complaint, 'I wrote it long because I didn't have the time to write it short'? Take the time; don't overwrite. Length is not equivalent to importance. Lean prose packs a punch."

Reveal details. "Whether in a newspaper story or an office memo, nothing captures attention like details. I used to tell my reporters and desk people, 'The good writer is a sorcerer at commanding details to serve him.' "

Use plain words. "Writing with clarity isn't as easy as it looks, but it is worth aiming for. Use ordinary language — familiar, everyday words. Remember, you're serving the reader, not yourself. And most important: Make sure it makes sense."

Personalize! "Write with flavor. Not everyone can write with the excitement of [*The Right Stuff* author] Tom Wolfe, but don't be afraid to convey your personality. Don't hide under a wave of jargon and passive verbs. Without style, writing is lifeless." ▣
— Dennis McCafferty

ZIGGY

..IF IT WASN'T FOR LOOKING FORWARD TO THE SUNDAY PAPER MY SATURDAY NIGHTS WOULD HAVE NO EXCITEMENT AT ALL!

www.ziggyzone.com

REFLECTIONS
Seven Things
That Will Destroy Us

Wealth without work; pleasure without conscience; commerce without morality; science without humanity; worship without sacrifice; politics without principle.   Gandhi

Sunday, March 10, 2002

Dear Aunt Leona, Linda, and Sandra,

Received letters from both of you girls yesterday. Wow, do you sound busy with everything you have going on. But like I tell people around here when they say I'm so busy, "It keeps me off the streets and out of trouble."

Sandra, it sure sounds like you are having a lot of problems getting all your test results and things straightened out, plus, your dental problems. I'm sorry you are having so much trouble. It seems like things go in streaks. But 1 know you have been having problems ever since that dog mauling. Hope things will soon be better for you and you will get some answers.

I can't imagine doing all that knitting that you are doing and your sewing projects too. Is knitting relaxing for you? I hope so. You still bake for the farm too, don't you?

Linda, it sounds like the Curtis family really wants you to help them full time. I bet it is fun to see all the new calves and other animals. But also sounds like a lot of hard work. It also sounds like Mrs. Curtis is doing better, which is good to hear. It also sounds like your help is needed with some other families too. You are very busy people. I hope you are able to find the cloth you want for the back of your car quilts.

Aunt Leona, you said in your last letter that your legs just don't work the way you want. Do you use a walker? Or would it help? Are your arms strong enough to use it too? I know, lots of questions. But I see so much around here and what age can do to people, like you have always said, "Old age is not for sissies" It seems like every year I get stiffer in my joints and I do try to exercise.1 use my stationary bike, and I also try to use the stairways instead of the elevator all the time. My checkup was good at the doctor's: cholesterol 155, blood sugar good, liver enzymes good, so for my age, I guess I'm doing OK. I feel fortunate. Like I said, I see a lot around here. Roy has trouble walking any long distance at all. I seem to be doing better walking than he does. He says his legs bother him to walk any distance. Some of these halls are very long. It's quite a hike for him to come over to my place. I have not seen Mona lately. Last time I did she was doing OK.

Love, Vivian

Monday, April 1, 2002

Dear Avis and Ron,

Hope you are both doing well and had a nice Easter. We lucked out on our weather for the day . . . sunshine and in the fifties. I went to church with Carol, Cindy, and Erik, then we met Barb, Ken, Jim, Scott, Hannah, and also Erik's fiancée, Eve, at the Holiday Inn in Livonia for a lovely brunch. It was very nice food and good company. It was a very nice day.

Barb is healing well from her mastectomy of March 4, but not quite as fast as she would like. She has to have four more chemo treatments and is very anxious to get them started and over with. They will be three weeks apart. But the surgeon wants her to heal more first. It's been difficult for me as a mother to watch another daughter go through this. The radiation burned her terribly, *but* we are hoping it *killed* the *cancer*. Barb has what is called IBC breast cancer. That is a very aggressive kind, thus the very aggressive treatments. Barb keeps her sense of humor and a good attitude most of the time. Her husband, Ken, is right there with her all the time and tells her she is beautiful and she is. Alice has her house up for sale and is planning on moving up here to be with Ken and Barb. Ken works brutal hours as service manager at Audette Cadillac. He doesn't like Barb to be alone so much so this was a solution all three came to. Alice will take the summer off and spend it at the cottage with Barb, then she will get a job in the fall. Alice has not had much vacation time since her divorce in 1982, so she is ready for some time off. Being twins, Alice and Barb have always been extra close, so I do think this will work out. Alice's son, David, is in Las Vegas and Kelly, her daughter, is married to Steve and still flies for Delta. I enjoy having Alice closer too and getting to see her often.

There is another change in our family. Cindy, Carol's daughter, twenty-nine, is moving out to Washington State. She received a job offer she could not turn down without taking a chance on it. She is into social work. Her job at Bi-Count Hospital has been very depressing lately, and this opportunity came up. As much as we hate to see her leave, we all encouraged her to "go for it." Social workers are very scarce in that area, and there are a lot around here. Cindy has her master's, plus a few other credits. Carol and Erik are flying out with her on April 15 to help her get settled and also to help her take her two cats, Teagon and Zeke. The hospital that hired her is paying all her moving expenses. I will miss her as she was the granddaughter I did see regularly.

But I wish her the very best, and perhaps she will meet "Mr. Right" out there. She has had no luck here. She dates but has not met the right one.

I stay busy with my committees and art class. I know they are good for me. I liked the colors and samples you sent me of the new pink bathroom, plus the beautiful sunrises and sunsets.

It sounds like Allison is doing very well, and Grandma and Grandpa were very helpful in the car switching around.

I am sending back the letter about your trip to Maine in 1984. I think you should save it for Allison to read later. I found it very interesting, and yes, I do think you had sent some of it before. Bill and I took a trip to east around that same time also, so a lot of the places you mentioned were very familiar. Bill got his fill of lobster with the roadside places. We also had high tea at a place in Acadia National Park. I think it was called Jordan Pond. I'm still working on writing our life story and am up to the late 1980s now. The kids say they are anxious to read it. It's getting so long I think I need an editor.

Bill, Shannon, and Sydney are doing well and hoping to come home maybe in July. I hope it will work out (just for a vacation). I don't think Bill will leave Denver unless it would be for his work. I think that brings you up to date on what's going on around here. I do hope your relations that were not feeling well are doing better. We do (as we age!) have to watch our lifestyle, but I also know it is difficult.

Take good care of yourselves.

Vivian

Monday, April 8, 2002

Dear Nancy,

How are you doing, dear? You have been on my mind so much, especially with Easter coming so soon after losing your husband. Holidays can be very hard to cope with. Nancy, I have to be honest, I don't think you ever get over losing someone you love. You just learn to live with the loss, and it is not easy. Bill will be gone two years this month, and I am still struggling with coping. *But* like Dr. Atallah told me, "You know he loved you and he would want you to get on with your life." I know it's true. Sometimes when I'm feeling sorry for myself, I can feel Bill give me a little kick in the butt and say, "Get going." We were very lucky as we had fifty-eight years together. When I think of you and our daughter Carol losing your husbands at your young ages, my heart aches for you. And my son-in-law Jim also lost our Kathy. Then life doesn't seem fair. *But* it does go on.

I'm doing things I never dreamed I would be doing, like teaching a watercolor class, training people to do volunteer work in our library, using a mike and hosting some of our Sunday entertainment programs. The staff here is wonderful, and they are getting me more and more involved in our Village. I'm working with some of the young people on a mentoring program. And most importantly, I have a great family who love and support me and tell me, "Go for it, Mom."

Nancy, I know you have your work, and I know a lot of the staff there love you (as do some of your patients). I do hope it will help. I'm sending you some booklets and some copies of papers that I received from hospice and the grief support groups I went too. Perhaps some of them will help you in some way. Every individual is different and their grief is different; what helps one may not help another. Take your time; don't try to read too many at once. Just read what appeals to you. I don't need any of them back as I am getting more to replace these. (That's another mission close to my heart, trying to help in some small way the newly widowed.)

Nancy, you are in my heart, thoughts, and prayers.

Vivian Beeler

Saturday April 13, 2002

Dear Aunt Leona, Linda, and Sandra,

Looks like the sun is trying to come out after a rainy morning. At least it is warmer this weekend. Last weekend was so cold. The forsythia bushes are in bloom next to the buildings here and look so pretty. 1 bet you have a lot of early spring flowers in bloom around your place.

I do hope all of you are feeling better. Aunt Leona, you have had a very rough time of it with bronchial pneumonia. I sure hope things are much better now; Sandra, you too. Linda said you were sick also, all of you, in fact. Maybe with the warmer weather it will help. Luckily, I have been pretty good. My right leg is bothering me and has been for quite awhile. I'm not sure if it is the sciatic nerve or what because the pain goes down my leg. I keep hoping it will go away, and some days it is better than others. Aunt Leona, like you said, "This getting old is not for sissies."

Barbara is healing quite well, but is not allowed to lift, and her right arm cannot do the things she is used to doing yet. She gets frustrated as she has always been a hard worker and doesn't like to ask for help. She still has to have four more chemo treatments (three weeks apart). She is anxious to get them over with, but the surgeon wants her to heal more first.

Alice is still waiting for her house to sell, but more people are looking now that it is getting more spring like; she is anxious to get up here to help Barb. They plan on spending a lot of the time at the cottage. Barb can rest and recuperate there.

The movers came and packed up all of Cindy's stuff last Thursday. She is staying at Erik's for the weekend. On Monday, Cindy, Carol, and Erik and the two cats leave for Washington. Cindy's friend who lives out there got an apartment for Cindy. The furniture and her car are supposed to be there on Tuesday. Carol and Erik will help her get settled, and they will feel better knowing and seeing where Cindy is. They will come back home a week from tomorrow. So it seems like a lot of changes in our family. I do think this is a wonderful opportunity for Cindy, and if it doesn't work out, she can always come back home. Cindy is coming and having brunch with me tomorrow. I hate to see her move so far away, but like I said, it is something she has to try.

Bill and Shannon call every weekend, and they are doing fine. Sydney is growing and doing more and more all the time. She is a normal healthy, happy little girl and I'm very grateful.

I keep busy with my committees and my artwork, and of course I still do a lot of reading. Most of my evenings are spent in my nice corner (comfortable chair, footstool, good light) and a good book. I do watch a little TV, but not a lot on that interests me. My books have better stories. I know you like to read too, Aunt Leona. I've always been happy with a good book and a quiet corner.

I'm a little concerned about Roy. He has been having some dizzy spells and light-headedness. He is undergoing some tests right now to see if they can find out the cause. He worries a great deal too, and that doesn't help. He always worried about Evelyn and took care of her. Now he just has himself. He is making some friends and playing cards and dominoes a bit in the evenings, and that's good. He says he is very happy he moved here. He does like it better. Bill and Roy's sister Marguerette is thinking of selling her condo in Brighton and moving here too. I hope so. It would be nice and also better for her, I think. She lost her husband five months before I lost Bill. It will be two years tomorrow. It doesn't seem possible in some ways, *but* life does go on.

It sure doesn't seem fair that your neighbors can get away with burning trash and letting their dogs run loose. It seems like they should be fined or something.

Duchess sure sounds like good company and a smart dog. I'm glad she visits you folks often. It also sounds like there is a lot going on at the Curtis farm—lots of new calves and other animals. I'm sure they are very busy, and you mentioned weddings too.

I haven't seen Mona lately. The last time I did she told me she was becoming more and more a recluse, except for her church work. She has her meal delivered to her apartment every night. I'm not sure that's a good idea, *but* everyone has to do what makes them content.

Take care, Vivian

IBC—Inflammatory Breast Cancer

I am Vivian Beeler. I have been a resident of Henry Ford Village for over four years. I know more about cancer than I would like to. I lost my partner and soul mate to cancer of the bile duct two years ago this month. Seven weeks later, we lost our middle daughter aged fifty-three to ovarian cancer, which she had been fighting for over six years. Now one of my twin daughters, fifty years old, is fighting IBC. She was diagnosed on September 10, 2001. Since then she has had four chemo treatments three weeks apart, a series of thirty radiation treatments, and a mastectomy on March 4. She is healing well but knows she has to face four more chemo treatments, probably starting the end of this month. She is going to be a survivor! While changing gynecologists, her cancer was discovered. Mammograms did not show it.

It's very difficult as a mother to watch another daughter go through the ravages of chemo, radiation, and radical surgery. Our family is all in this together. My daughter Barbara is a beautiful person both inside and out and has a wonderful husband, two grown children, and two beautiful grandchildren in Arizona, also a lot of friends who are helping her through this. In that respect, we are fortunate.

But we are on a soapbox about inflammatory breast cancer because mammograms don't show it and it is misdiagnosed too many times by doctors and technicians.

I have passed out these brochures and talked to the staff here at the Village, and they are interested in somehow letting more people know about this very aggressive cancer. I am eighty years old and consider myself fairly well informed. I did not know about this type of breast cancer until my daughter was diagnosed. All the women 1 have talked to since knew nothing about it either. We all are thinking "lumps."

Cheryl Presley has talked to Anne Perry about this and asked me to see that the medical staff here at the Village know about it. Perhaps there can be a special health segment on Channel 11 about it?

I just know I have to do all in my power to spread the word of this terrible disease so women and men can be aware of this.

Thanks for listening to me.

Lila Lazarus—Health News Person
WD1V Channel 4
550 W. Lafayette
Detroit, MI 48226

Dear Lila,

I'm writing because I need your help on my soapbox. You did such a wonderful job on getting the information on colon cancer out to people. I'm hoping you can help me get information on inflammatory breast cancer out to women and men.

Patricia Ansett, Free Press medical writer, had a big article on the importance of getting mammograms this past Tuesday. Not once was inflammatory breast cancer mentioned. I e-mailed her and am mailing her this same info I am sending you. She was gracious and did answer me. "Perhaps another time." People don't know about IBC. I am eighty years old and consider myself a fairly intelligent person. I did not know of this terrible disease until one of my twin daughters was diagnosed with this on September 10, 2001. Mammograms do not show this type of breast cancer. We have to get the word out on this type of breast cancer.

To give you a little background: My family has had a lot of heartaches the past few years. I lost my partner and soul mate two years ago this month. Seven weeks later, we lost our middle daughter, aged fifty-three, to ovarian cancer. She had been fighting it for six years. Our whole family was involved. I lost my husband to cancer of the bile duct. He went downhill in one year's time. Then Barbara, aged fifty, was diagnosed with this aggressive form of breast cancer. To watch another daughter go through the ravages of chemo and radiation makes my heart just ache. Barb had a mastectomy on March 4 and is healing well, *but* she knows she has to go through four more chemo treatments, three weeks apart, as preventive medicine. So we have learned a great deal about cancer that we really would prefer hadn't been necessary. Barb has a prince of a husband, a grown son and daughter, and two beautiful grandchildren in Arizona. Barb's twin, Alice, and elder sister, Carol, are in this fight with her too. Barb has kept her sense of humor and good attitude. Of course, she has had "down" days. They have wonderful friends who help greatly. All of us are trying to get the word out on this cancer. It is so unknown and so misdiagnosed and hitting more and more young women. Check their web site.

Lila, I feel like you are my friend. I see you nearly every day and admire your dedication to your assignments. I am so in hope this will be something you and your management team will feel is important enough to pursue.

I will do everything in my power to fight for my daughter on this issue. I cannot lose another daughter to cancer. I live at Henry Ford Village in Dearborn and am active in our village life (different committees, etc.). I have got the resident life staff interested in this also. Over the past few years, I have made contacts with so many good people in support groups and hospice programs. In fact, my daughters and I are going to Glida's Club on April 24 to hear Dr. John Finn who is one of the directors of Hospice of Michigan. He was out to visit us at the time my husband was ill. He is a wonderful Doctor and person. There are a lot of *good* people in our world. We seem to hear more about the bad ones.

Barb and Ken are going to be at Comerica Park on Saturday for Race for the Cure.

Thanks for listening to me, Lila. I appreciate your time. I'm giving you Barb and Ken's address along with mine, hoping against hope you can help.

> Sincerely,
> Vivian L. Beeler
> 15181 Ford Rd. #302 Dearborn, MI 48126

#313-581-7041
e-mail: VeeBee248@aol.com

Kenneth and Barbara Vogt
2616 Glen wood
Royal Oak, MI 48073
e-mail: Pybobo@aol.com

P.S. Barb has been having her treatments at The William Beaumont "Rose" Cancer Center in Royal Oak and thinks the doctors and technicians there are great.

Saturday, April 27, 2002

Dr. John Finn
Hospice of Michigan
18831 West 12 Mile Road
Lathrop Village, Mi

Dear Dr. Finn,

It was so nice to see you again last Wednesday evening at Glida's club. I am Vivian Beeler, resident at Henry Ford Village. You said you remembered me and my husband, Bill, who you came to see. You told me he was a wise man. He has been gone two years this month. It will be two years in June since we lost our daughter, Kathy, to ovarian cancer. Now I have one of our twin daughters (fifty years old) fighting IBC. Barbara was diagnosed the day before the terrorist attack last September. She has had four chemo treatments three weeks apart, thirty radiation treatments, and a mastectomy on March 4. The doctors think she is doing well, but she will be starting another series of chemo treatments this Wednesday. Barb keeps a positive attitude. But we are all too familiar with cancer, and it is very difficult as a mother to watch another daughter go through the ravages of chemo, radiation and surgery. I can't help but wonder why. We do not have a family history of cancer. We are all keeping a positive attitude. But I am on an IBC soapbox. People do not know about it. Everyone thinks "lumps." I am eighty years old and I had not heard of it. I am talking and writing to health reporters at TV stations and newspapers and passing out literature. I have the staff here interested in spreading the word. It is so often misdiagnosed.

I am also on a hospice soapbox. You and your hospice team helped me and my family so much. You made it possible for my husband to die at home with all his family around. Our daughter, Kathy, also died at home with the Henry Ford Hospice team. I have a couple of large notebooks filled with wonderful papers that were sent to me by both teams for the year following their deaths. They were and are very helpful. I have made numerous copies and have shared with others who have lost loved ones.

Dr. Finn, I also share your passion for trying to educate doctors on pain management and knowing when to suggest hospice to the family. It wasn't until I wrote a letter to Dr. Charles Lucas and Dr. Anna Ledgerwood and came right out and asked them if I was losing my husband that we got some straight answers from Dr. Ledgerwood. They had more tests scheduled, and Bill was not doing well at all. He was watching the clock for his pain medication and was very miserable. Dr. Ledgerwood came in and talked to all of us. She said she knew in her "gut" that Bill had cancer, even though the biopsies did not show it, and that she really would suggest hospice. She was so kind. I think by that time both Bill and I knew this was it. That's when you were called in, and with your team, you made Bill comfortable.

Dr. Finn, after I wrote that letter and Dr. Ledgerwood came and talked to us, we never saw Dr. Lucas again. Both Bill and I were surprised and hurt as Dr. Lucas was his main doctor. We decided afterwards that Dr. Lucas could not deal with what he considered a "failure" and could not say good-bye. I felt sorry for him as both Bill and I had liked him and had no complaints on his treatments. We saw him pass in the hallway, but he never stopped in again.

The pain of losing your partner and soulmate never goes away, *and* no parent should have to lose children no matter their age, *but* you learn to cope with the help and support of hospice. Take one day at a time, and life goes on. I have a wonderful family that tells me I'm important to them. I'm active on committees here at the Village, have my watercolor painting hobby, and I love to read. A lot of the color and fun have gone out of my world, but I do stay busy and try to give back. The days I feel sorry for myself, I can hear Bill and feel him give me a little kick in the butt and say "get going." He was a wonderful guy, and I count my blessings we had fifty-eight years together. Now, to get my daughter, Barbara, she has been all cleared of cancer! Keep us in your prayers.

Dr. Finn, if there is any way I can help in promoting hospice and getting doctors to realize death and dying are a part of life. To die with dignity is so important, to have a chance for the family to say good-bye. Those two weeks that we had Bill home were the hardest weeks of my life, but I would not change a thing, I'm grateful I had them and would gladly do them again.

Thank you for listening to me. Keep up your good work, and I hope someday in the near future more and more doctors will realize there is a time to let go. I truly believe your hospice teams are angels here on earth.

Sincerely,
Vivian L. Beeler
15181 Ford Rd. #302

Saturday April 27, 2002

Dear Linda and Sandra,

Thank you for keeping me informed. I was terribly sorry to hear your mother is not doing well and went downhill so fast. I was so in hope she could have made her hundredth birthday. But I know bronchial pneumonia and congestive heart failure are almost always fatal to elderly people. I also know she is getting excellent care from both of you. I do wish you had a hospital bed though. It would be easier for you.

Not very much new here. I keep busy with my committees and artwork. I see Roy quite often but have not seen Mona in quite a while. I imagine the farm is very busy right now with the new animals and getting ready to plant.

Sandra, how are you doing? I haven't wanted to say too much in my letters as I didn't know how much your mother knew. I do hope you got those test results, and they were able to help find out what is wrong.

Barbara will probably be starting chemo again this Wednesday. She is scheduled for four treatments three weeks apart. I do hope they will not cause too many bad problems. The doctors feel encouraged they got the cancer but want her to have these treatments as a preventive. We have our fingers crossed. Cindy is out in Washington and has started her new job. So far she likes it and says the people she works with are nice.

I'm thinking of all of you and hoping for the best, whatever that is.

Wednesday, May 29, 2002

Dear Sage,

I thought it has been quite awhile since I last wrote to you, so I just wanted to tell you that Grandma thinks of you often and wanted to tell you so. I saw the video that you and Ché made for your papa's birthday just last week at your nana's. I loved it. You both did a super job singing happy birthday to him. I wanted to reach into the computer and hug both of you. But I will have to do it by mail instead. Sending lots of hugs and kisses to all of you. Oxoxoxooxoxo

I also thought you might like to look at this section of our paper with your mommy and daddy. It has a lot of information about Michigan where your nana and papa and grandma B. live. I thought you might find it fun to look at.

Have you been able to help your mommy and daddy build their pond and waterfall or maybe you have been able to help by playing with Ché? The pictures your mommy sent looked very interesting.

Grandma just finished a picture of a tiger, and I got some copies made at Kinko's so I am sending one to you and Ché. We are having an EXPO tomorrow here at the Village where I live. All the classes and committees have displays in our big dining room. It's to let people know what's available to do and what's going on in the Village. I will be having a big table with paintings from my watercolor class. It will be very colorful and interesting. This is the third year they have had this, and it is always a fun couple of hours. They have music and refreshments.

Your uncle Bill and aunt Shannon are coming on July 12 with your cousin Sydney. I'll enclose a picture of her too. I'm looking forward to seeing them. They are going to be staying out at your nana's and papa's cottage. I wish you could be here too, But that would make the cottage a little bit crowded. I do hope it works out that you will be coming this summer too. Have fun this summer, Sage, and lots of love to all from Grandma B.

Monday, June 3, 2002

Dear Linda and Sandra,

Hope things are settling down for you girls and you are getting into your own lives. It's got to be difficult because 1 know your mom was your boss for so many years.

It is a rainy stormy day today and I understand it's going to last awhile. I don't have to go out and am glad.

I wanted to let you know a couple of things. Roy has been in Garden City Hospital. He might come home today or tomorrow. He went in last Wednesday. He has been having dizzy spells and had one when he was at the doctor's. office. The doctor put him in the hospital for testing. They have been checking the arteries in his neck and back of his skull. He's had MRI, MRA, and quite a few others. I just talked with him a short time ago, and he said he might come home today. He is not feeling too badly. They think one ear is blocked some way, and that is causing a balance problem. He also supposed to see an eye doctor. He says he is on a lot of pills.

The other thing I wanted to let you know is Lois Lenten died. She was my second cousin from Grandma Manley's side, the daughter of Bill and Viola Rosevear. I'm enclosing a notice. I don't know if you remember her or not. She had been in a nursing home for over three years and did not know anybody or anything for quite a long time, so it is a *big* blessing. Her husband Phil is a nice guy and did his best for her. They have two daughters, Carol and Mary Kay. My Carol took me to the funeral home as it was right here in Dearborn. Lois was my age.

I am still having a lot of trouble with my leg. I'm scheduled for an MRI at Oakwood Hospital this Friday at 5:30 p.m. Those appointments are hard to get. This was a cancellation, and 1 grabbed it. I've got to find out what my problem is. It's affecting my walking and is very painful. It's scary because I don't want to lose my independence.

I hope Sandra that you are finding out more about your problems and getting them solved. As far as a get-together this fall, I have no idea right now. There are too many iffy health problems. We'll just have to wait and see. Take care of yourselves,

June 12, 2002

Dear Nora and Ginger,

My heart aches for both of you: Nora, for you losing your dad, and Ginger, for you losing your mother, both at much too young an age. Sometimes life does not seem fair. *But* it does go on, and we have to accept it. Nora, you already know that I lost my dad when I was sixteen also. It's very difficult, and I know the same holds true for losing your mother, Ginger. There is no way to go over, under, or around grief. You have to go through it. Everyone is different and there are no set guidelines.

Ginger, I'm enclosing some copies of leaflets that I had given to Nora earlier. I hope they may help a little, although to be honest not much does at this difficult time. Ginger, I'm so proud of you for completing the scholarship program, and I was pleased to be able to attend the program. Nora, I think you are well on your way to completing it. It is always so nice to go to the dining room and see your lovely smiles. I feel like you are my extended family, and I care about you.

I think you both know that I lost my husband two years ago. Then seven weeks later, I lost a daughter to ovarian cancer. I did not know if I could go on. But with the help of my family, the wonderful staff here at the Village, and you young people in the dining room, life does go on. I don't think you ever "get over" losing someone close to you. You just learn to live with it, *and* it takes time. I think you also know that I have one of my twin daughters fighting breast cancer. I am much too familiar with grief and worry. My daughter "Barb" is going to make it! She is taking preventive chemo treatments right now and has two more to go.

Another reason for writing to you is that I wanted to give you both this little booklet. I'm sure you are both familiar with this song. I came across this booklet by accident last fall and was so impressed with the words that I got books to give to all of my granddaughters. I hope you enjoy them and they inspire you.

"One day at a time. One foot in front of the other. And keep reaching and believing in your dreams."

> My love, prayers, and best wishes to both of you always,
> Mrs. Vivian Beeler

Wednesday, July 3, 2002

Dear Family,

I am so pleased to be writing to you and asking for your help in a *survivor quilt* for Barbara. Jan, one of Barb's island friends, is making her one. It is a *secret* from Barbara. Jan sent me an e-mail with suggestions, and I had copies made to send on to you, along with the squares that Jan sent me. You can get Fabric-Mate pens at any art or craft store *or* do your own thing, as long as it is permanent color.

Barb has a lot of very nice friends who have helped her this past awful year for her. Ken, Carol, Alice, and myself were all with Barbara last Monday when she completed her fourth and *final* chemo treatment! We had a little celebration! The staff at the hospital gave her a certificate and tossed confetti on her. There were lots of tears but of happiness that this hopefully is *over*. It's been a rough year. We also know the next couple of weeks are going to be rough on Barb too. That chemo does such awful things to your body, *but* this is it. She doesn't have to any more.

Anyway, I think the idea of a survivor quilt is wonderful. I understand Jan loves to sew and is very good at it. So let's all help her out and get these squares back to her as soon as possible. You can either mail them back to me or I will put Jan's address at the bottom of this note, whatever. I divided the squares I was given and am sending a couple to practice on and then one to send back. Thanks.

I hope everyone is having a good summer. I'm excited and anxious because Bill, Shannon, and Sydney will be here the twelfth of this month. Then I will see Kenny, Krista, and family and possibly David, Kelly, and Steve the end of the month. Family is what keeps me going.

Lots of love to all, Grandma.
Janice Breyer

1780 Broadstone
Grosse Pointe, MI 48236
Subj: Bobo's quilting friend Janice
Date: 6/26/2002 7:04:18 PM Eastern Daylight Time
From: JBreyer
To: VeeBee248

Vivian,

This is Bobo's friend from Russell Island, Janice. Bobo asked me to make her a survivor quilt, to which I am more than glad to do. I told her to let me "do my thing" and not ask any questions as to how it is going or what I was doing for it. She agreed and so here is my idea and request of you.

I am making the quilt with squares from each of her family and friends. The way this is done is: I will mail you a bunch of muslin squares a certain size along with permanent pens. Your job is to make sure each family member receives a square and writes, draws or sews a memory for Bobo. They can sew something on it, do whatever as long as it is permanent, puffy paint, etc. Maybe a little message to say how much she means to them or a drawing of something . . . they can embellish in anyway. Just make sure they leave me ¼" all the way around to sew them into the quilt.

I hope I have made this clear, but please call me or e-mail me you phone number and I can call you. If you e-mail me your address, I can get these squares into the mail so you can begin to distribute them so we can get them back by the end of July.

I have a friend on the island do her island friends, I have told Olllie . . . But Barb is to know nothing. A big surprise!!!!! I may not get it all done before

Christmas, but it will be worth the wait. Maybe you have seen one before. We made one for my Mom and Dad for their 50th wedding anniversary.

Oh yeah, the can even do photo transfers at Kinko's onto the fabric.

Let's keep in touch and this will be a really exciting project. Remember to tell everyone not to mention it to Barb. Ollie, yes, Barb no. This may be the toughest part of the project.

Please write me back and let me know if you will help me in this mission. I will be up at our cottage from Friday night through next week and coming home July 8th. So I will be without email but we do have a phone.

Stats: Janice Breyer
313-885-5261 Home
810-748-3067 Cottage jbreyer@aol.com e-mail

Hope you don't mind me writing and asking this of you, but I think Bobo will be pleased with it. She is a SURVIVOR!!!!!

Janice

ZIGGY By Tom Wilson

The Detroit News AND Free Press   Sunday, June 16, 2002

FOR BETTER OR FOR WORSE   BY LYNN JOHNSTON

May 2002

Russell Island Foundation
1011 Satterlee Road
Bloomfield Hills, MI 48304

Mr. and Mrs. Ken Vogt
2616 Glenwood
Royal Oak, M9 48073

The Russell Island Foundation would like to invite you to a ceremony honoring the family and friends named on the Russell Island Foundation Memorial plaque.

We will be adding the names of the people honored during the past year. William Beeler and Kathy Welton's names will be included.

The gathering will take place at the Russell island ferry landing on Sunday, May 26, at 10:30 a.m. Please plan on joining us.

A gathering will take place at the dock area/refreshments will be served.

The Board of the Russell Island Foundation

Native American Poem

Don't stand by my grave and weep
For I am not there, I do not sleep.
I am a thousand winds that blow,
I am the diamond's glint on snow.
I am the sunlight on ripened grain,
I am the gentle autumn's rain.
Don't stand by my grave and cry,
I am not there, I did not die.

To Leave a Legacy—An Elder's Imperative
Henry Ford Village
July 2002

Everything before us brought us to this moment.
Standing on the threshold of a brand new day.

- Elder or older"
- Definition of an elder
- Remembering/harvesting/giving away
- Are you "saved?"
- What have you received? What are you open to give "unto the seventh generation?"
- How will the world be better because I have been given the gift of a long life?
- Mentoring

****

An elder is a person who is still growing, still a learner, still with potential and whose life continues to have within it promise for and connection to the future.

An elder is still in pursuit of happiness, joy and pleasure, and her or his great birthright to these remains intact.

Moreover, an elder is a person who deserves respect and honor and whose work it is to synthesize wisdom from life experience and formulate this into a legacy for future generations.

July 5, 2002

Dear Anita and Sister Paula,

I have thoroughly enjoyed taking your workshop on Age-ing to Sage-ing. I am so grateful to Sandra for bringing this to us. I know she has been working for this for quite some time.

I hope I am learning to "harvest" my life experiences. You have given me more and different ideas and ways to look at things that happen in life. I have been writing our life story for our children and grandchildren, trying to include a little genealogy, a little history, what we were doing at that time, and how it affected us. You have opened up new ideas on how to expand and make it more interesting for them. Thank you.

Life has been rough on me the last few years. There have been a lot of losses. I have to believe God has a plan that I must accept and go on. I truly believe life is a circle and goes on with our children and grandchildren. I am very grateful. I have a wonderful family who tell me I am important to them.

It's been a joy meeting both of you and taking this workshop. Keep up the good work.

With sincere thanks, love, and prayers

Vivian Beeler

July 2002

Baptism and Sydney's First Visit to Michigan

My dear darling Sydney,

Grandma wants to write to you about your visit to see your daddy's family and your baptism at Aunt Barb's and Uncle Ken's cottage on Russell Island. At only one and a half years old, it's going to be a little hard for you to remember. I want this to be my gift to you so when you grow up you will have this wonderful time for all of us recorded with this letter and all the pictures your daddy and mommy are taking.

Honey, do you know how much joy it is for me to have a new little granddaughter? All of my other grandchildren are all grown-up, and to have a baby in our family again is absolutely fantastic! Besides that, you are such a sweetie pie, smart, beautiful, and adorable. I know, this is Grandma's opinion, *but* all your aunts, uncles, and cousins think the same thing It is so great to see what a good daddy Grandpa's and my baby has turned out to be. And honey, we just absolutely adore your mommy. She fits in our family like she was born into it. We are so grateful your daddy found her. I think she helped your daddy grow up. Grandpa and I really wondered for a while if he was ever going to. Now I am so proud of him, and I know Grandpa would be too.

Aunt Carol and Erik picked you up from Detroit Metro Airport at 11:45 a.m. on Friday, July 12, 2002. The weather was wonderful in the eighties, a beautiful sunny day. You came to Grandma's home at Henry Ford Village in Dearborn, Michigan. I came down to let you in, and you came right through the doorway into my arms and gave me a kiss. Honey, you melted my heart. You were so sweet. Everything was so strange and new—the hallways, the elevator ride up to my apartment, and my apartment—to you. But you just seemed to take everything in stride and made yourself right at home. Grandma was so very happy to see all of you. You were so busy checking everything out. Erik and Eve came over too and brought Aunt Carol's greyhound "Scooby" and Erik's beagle "Parker." You loved the dogs and were so good with them. You found the picture album Grandma had of "Katy," and that was a favorite with you to carry around. You were growing up with Katy, and she was yours. Grandma had things to make, sandwiches and fruit for lunch, but you were much too busy to eat except for a bit of cheese.

Your mommy and daddy were trying to get unpacked, and they were so tired. They had not had any sleep with having to be at your Denver Airport before five in the morning. You had not had very much either but were still going strong. You were such a happy little girl. It was so much fun to watch you. Grandma and Aunt Carol had not seen you since we were out to your place in Denver for your first birthday last October. Needless to say, you had changed and grown a lot! You sat with me and read books with me a few times, but mainly, you just had to keep moving. You did finally crash when we were getting ready to eat dinner. Grandma had made spaghetti, salad, Jell-O, and rolls for dinner. 1 just knew everyone would be too tired to go out to eat. It really worked out pretty good. I had got your daddy a Bill Knapp's chocolate cake. It was one of his favorites when he lived with Grandpa and I in Michigan. I think he did enjoy it. Erik and Eve left after dinner and Aunt Carol shortly after. It was hard for your mommy and daddy to stay awake, and Grandma was tired also. I had been busy and excited getting ready for your visit. Anyway about 11:00 p.m. we all called it quits. I made your mommy and daddy take my bedroom as Aunt Carol had borrowed a playpen for you to sleep in, and it was in there. We have a comfortable couch, and I told them it would not hurt me for one night. It worked out very well. I think all of you slept pretty good and got rested for your trip to the Lake.

Everyone was up around eight, and your daddy fixed you cinnamon apple oatmeal, and I watched in amazement as you fed yourself. You did such a neat job and did not even have a bib on. You also drank orange juice from a glass with a straw. Such a *big* girl! I forgot to tell you that I watched your mommy give you a bath last night in Grandma's bathtub. You enjoy the water so much. It was lots of fun to watch you. Mommy and Daddy dump containers of water over your head and you just laugh. What a sweetie! Uncle Roy came over to see everyone about 10:30 a.m., and you gave him a kiss and hug also. He was so pleased. Uncle Roy has a little great-granddaughter, Melena, who he sees quite often as they live near him. So, honey, you made his day too.

Then it was time to pack up and go to the cottage to catch the one o'clock ferry. Grandma was sorry to see you go, but knew I would be seeing you out there the very next day. You gave me several kisses and hugs when you left, and like I said before, they melt my heart.

Sunday, July 14, 2002

It's another absolutely gorgeous summer day. Aunt Carol, Erik, Eve, Scooby, and Parker picked me up at 11:00 a.m. to catch the one o'clock ferry to the island. We had brought hamburgers, and Aunt Carol had made a macaroni salad, plus grapes and snack foods. We didn't want Aunt Barb to worry about food and feeding everyone as she was still healing and recuperating from her *last* chemo treatment for her breast cancer. Aunt Alice had made Aunt Kathy's chocolate cherry cake for dessert. One thing about our family is we always have lots of good food when we get together. Your daddy's good friend Steve Williams was at the cottage too, and he grilled the hamburgers. They were delicious.

After we all pigged out and had full tummies, we took the golf carts and rode over to the park on the other side of the island. You were loving it at the cottage. I had seen a little race car swim toy in a catalog and had ordered it for you to play with. It had two holes for your legs to go through and a little steering wheel with a horn. It fit around your body like a big ring. You just loved it, and it worked out so well for you to have in the water. I was so happy I had seen it. Anyway, when we got over to the park Aunt Carol took you in your little boat and your mommy, daddy, Erik, and Steve Williams all were diving and playing off the high dive platform and going down a slide. Uncle Ken, Eve, and I were just watching all the activity. Your mommy had never ever gone off such a high platform before, and we were all proud of her when she did it. You were having such a great time with Aunt Carol. There is a breakwater seawall there, and when boats go by, it sucks all the water out and then it rushes back in. You were just amazing. When the water went out and left you high and dry, you picked up your boat by two handles and ran out to catch the water coming back in. Nobody had showed you. You just did it. You looked absolutely adorable. A lot of people and children at the park were watching you besides Grandma. It was so much fun to see you. You had absolutely no fear of the water. You loved it. Everybody finally got tired and we headed back to the cottage.

Honey, you loved all the dogs, and they loved you. On Sunday you had four dogs to play with: Bouy, Sailor, Scooby, and Parker. They all got along well together too. I sat on the deck and watched all the activity going on around me, enjoying every moment. We did a little more snacking after the park, and then it was time to catch the seven o'clock ferry back to the mainland. Time seems to go by extra fast on the island. You gave me and everyone more hugs and kisses when we left. You were such a sweetheart. Erik drove back home and gave Aunt Carol a rest. We were all tired from all the fresh air and sunshine. I heard that you were sleeping pretty good too, *but* you kept going until you dropped.

Monday, July 15, 2002

It's another beautiful sunny blue sky day. Aunt Carol and Scooby picked me up about 9:40 a.m., and we were on our way to Russell Island and Sydney Marie's baptism. This was a first for Russell Island and quite an event. We stopped at Chicken Shack in Chesterfield Township and picked up our order of chicken and coleslaw. They were very nice, and everything was ready for us at 10:45 a.m. They had opened early to accommodate us. We were on our way again for the noon ferry. We made good time and were there a little early. Uncle Jim and his friend Hannah joined us, and we met Pastor Robert Wagner there too. When the ferry came, we got everything loaded on it and were on our way. Aunt Barb had arranged for five golf carts to meet us. Amazing! When we got to the cottage, you were there with your mommy all dressed up in a lovely white silk dress with little flowers embroidered all over the bodice. You looked like a live Madame Alexander Doll. You were so pretty. (Madame Alexander Dolls are very special collectors' dolls.)

Your baptism took place in front of Aunt Barb and Uncle Ken's cottage under their huge willow tree. It was so beautiful. The sky was blue, the sun was shining, the birds were singing, and the waves were lapping against the shore. The water was a beautiful turquoise blue color. I know God was there, and. Grandpa and Aunt Kathy were looking down and smiling. Sydney, you were surrounded by your Michigan family and friends in a circle of love. The pastor had all of your sponsors, Aunt Carol, Aunt Alice, Aunt Barb (I stood in for Scott, and Steve Williams, stand just behind your daddy and mommy. He gave a short sermon about "planting God's seeds."

He blessed your heart and gave the sign of the Father, the Son, and the Holy Ghost and baptized you. You fussed a little; you were getting tired of Daddy holding you, and you wanted to get down and run. Then when we all held hands and said the Lord's prayer together, you were quiet again. When the short lovely service was over, your daddy let you down, and you were playing in the bowl of baptism water. You made everyone laugh and you dried up the few happy tears from the beautiful service. One of Aunt Barbara's friends gave you a beautiful white rose. Everyone was taking pictures. It was such a wonderful special day for all of us.

Then of course, as is normal in our family, we had another good feast. Aunt Barb's friends had brought salads too to go with the chicken. Aunt Alice had made baked beans and got a water melon. Scotty had sent his famous bump cake with Uncle Jim. Aunt Alice had also made cream puffs to fill with ice cream and top with Sander's hot fudge, which is famous in Michigan. The pastor was able to stay and eat with us, and then one of Aunt Barb's friends who had a boat took him back to the mainland as he had another appointment. Then all of the younger people changed clothes to be back in the water again. You were turning into a little fish and growing gills; you absolutely loved the water and had no fear. You would go right out to your little neck, and if a wave washed over you, you laughed. Needless to say, someone was right there with you at all times. Julia, Danielle, and Nino, children of the family in the cottage behind Aunt Barb and Uncle Ken's, played with you most of the day. They were so good with you, and you loved them. Julia is ten, Danielle is eight, and Nino is four. Your daddy and mommy wanted to take them home with you. I know you will see pictures of them. They played in the sand with you, pushed you around on a little three-wheel bike, chased puppy dogs with you, etc, etc. They are a wonderful family, and their mommy and daddy are good friends with your aunt Barb and uncle Ken. Your mommy and daddy will have to tell you about them.

After two busy days of fresh air and sunshine, Grandma was very tired, so Aunt Carol, Uncle Jim, Hannah, and I packed up to go home on the six o'clock ferry.

I talked to someone at the cottage every day you were there and kept track a bit of what you were doing. Busy, busy, busy . . . *ah,* you were having so much fun and the weather was wonderful—hot and sunny.

On Thursday you came to Rochester Hills to your daddy's friend that he had gone to school with, and all of his old Michigan buddies were there for a get-together. Then on Friday, those same friends came out to the cottage to spend more time together. Quite a few have children now, so you had more to play with. Your mommy and daddy kept telling me what a fantastic time they were having, *but* it was going by too quickly. Vacations and good times always do. On Saturday, you came back to Grandma's at dinnertime. Aunt Carol came over too, and we all went to Rio Bravo for dinner. Grandma saw how much you liked bean burritos. I had heard that you did. In restaurants, it always takes longer than a one and a half year old likes to sit quiet. So Grandma and you went for a walk. You held my hand, and you walked me all around the place. They had one section that no one was in, and it had two huge ceiling fans that you liked to watch. We went back there quite a bit. Grandma loved being with you. You had gotten the prettiest tan while you were at the cottage. Then when everyone was ready, we came back to my place. You loved to push the buttons for the elevator and run in the hallways. Your daddy started to print out pictures for me that he had taken at the cottage, and they were so very good. Your mommy was doing some wash, and we were all talking a mile a minute all the time. You were a very busy little girl, tired, but didn't want to give up. Aunt Carol went home, and your mommy lay down with you. Zonk! You were out. Daddy was still printing pictures. It takes a long time, but they are worth it. You will have a wonderful record of your first trip to Michigan.

Sunday, July 21, 2002

Time goes too quickly. It was time to pack and go home. Aunt Carol came back to have brunch with us in Great Lake's dining room. She wanted to be with you as much as possible too. We took your booster seat, and you were a good little girl. You ate some scrambled eggs and some pancake and apple sauce, I believe. Aunt Carol came back to my apartment for some baggies for our sweet rolls, and you wanted to go with her, which Aunt Carol loved. She said she got stopped in the hallways by a lot of people talking to you and telling her how cute you were, which we already knew!

Time to go. We got to be at the airport at 1:30 p.m. Storms predicted. It is so hard to say good-bye when we don't know when we'll see you again. *But* I loved all of you being here and enjoyed every minute of it. Aunt Carol got all of you inside the airport just in time. She got caught in a very hard rain storm driving back to her place, and the storm delayed your flight too. It was 11:30 p.m., Detroit time, when your mom called to tell me you were home safe and sound. It was a long hard day for all, but I do think the wonderful vacation days and baptism were worth it.

Hope this gives you an idea of your baptism and your first trip to Michigan, honey. It was wonderful for your Michigan family for you to be here. It is a treasured memory for all of us.

My gift to you along with this letter is my little heart and diamond locket that I have worn around my neck for some thirty years. I want to tell you the story of this locket: We are going way back in time. Grandpa and I met one another in the spring of 1939. I was seventeen and had just graduated from Fordson High School in January. Grandpa had also graduated from Fordson High School in June 1937. We did not know one another in school. Grandpa was nineteen when we met. I have told the story of our meeting in my *Story of our Lives*, which you will have a copy of too. Anyway after going together for almost two years, Grandpa proposed to me on Valentine's Day in 1941. He had my diamond engagement ring which he had purchased from Shiffren-Willens Jewelry Store in Dearborn. Remember, back in those days, we were just coming out of a bad depression and most people we knew did not have very much money *and* we were very young.

Grandpa had just been hired by Ford Motor Company when we met. I was so thrilled, and I knew I wanted to spend the rest of my life with him, so of course, I said *yes*. That diamond ring I wore for thirty years on my finger until I had almost worn the band through. By today's standards, that diamond is very small, but it meant a great deal to me and does to this very day. That is the diamond that Grandpa had made into this little heart locket, when for our thirtieth anniversary, he bought me another diamond solitaire to wear on my ring finger. I have worn this locket almost daily since that time in 1971. I want your daddy and mommy to keep this locket for you until you are old enough to understand the sentimental value of it. Honey, I hope it will bring you good luck and you will know how very much Grandma loves you. It is such a joy at my age to have a another wonderful granddaughter, but because of my age, the only way you will really know me is through my writings and my letters to you.

I'm old-fashioned (emphasis on "old"). Most of the mothers of your daddy's friends when he was growing up were in their thirties because your daddy came along as a surprise bonus to us when I was forty-three. I had two decades on them, so I was coming at things from a different perspective. It was hard on both of us. But we made it, I think mainly because Grandpa and I had such a wonderful marriage. Sex is sex, but deep emotional commitment makes a soul mate. Grandpa and I grew up together. We were partners and equals in all things. I hope you are as lucky.

Remember too, honey, all the answers to the big questions are inside of you. You just have to be quiet and listen, which goes way back to the old cliché "Believe in yourself. To thine ownself be true."

Sydney, you are always in my thoughts and prayers. I'll be writing again. Love you always.

Grandma B.

August 19, 2002

Dear Family,

Here I am again. It seems awhile since I have written anything and am sort of wondering where to start again. The summer is almost over, and it seems like time does go by fast. But it also seems like it's more of a struggle to get through each day. This pain in my back, hip, and leg is getting me down. I'm just wearing out like an old car. I've been to several doctors and had two sets of X-rays and an MRI. It all boils down to narrowing of the cartilage between bones and a spur on my right hip. A hip replacement might help some, but then what about the arthritis in my back, knees, feet, and hands? I'm scared of an operation. I remember too clearly what Bill went through. It's a *long* process of recovery, although Bill's was successful. I took care of Bill. What about me? I know the girls would do their best, but this family has had enough. Somehow, I just never thought I would get old. I guess I just figured Bill and I would ride off into the sunset together. Now here I am with these decisions to make by myself. I'm not happy about it. I've had my life, and as long as I was reasonably healthy, I could manage. I don't like the idea of not being independent. I guess I'm feeling sorry for myself.

This constant pain is wearing me down, and if I take too much Darvocet, it makes me a little spacey and no ambition to do anything. I wonder where I am going. I don't enjoy living like this.

There have been some wonderful times this summer being with my family. Bill, Shannon, and Sydney's visit and vacation here was wonderful. Being out at the cottage with everyone and Sydney's baptism was very special. The weather was beautiful. Then a week later, Barb and Alice's families visited, and being together again with family members I hadn't seen in quite awhile. My grown-up grandchildren all seem to be doing well. They all look happy and healthy. I'm so proud of all of them. In that area, I feel very blessed and I am very, very grateful. I seem to live for the family times. I do have a lot of nice friends here at the Village and do try to keep busy with my art and committees, but there is emptiness, loneliness, and a wondering of where am I headed and what's next. I try very hard to just live in today, but sometimes it is just plain scary. I'm not afraid of death. Like I said, I've lived my life. I'm just afraid of the dying process.

History's Mysteries

Whitmore-Bolles at 75

Next month Whitmore-Bolles Elementary School will celebrate the 75th anniversary of its opening.

The school was built in 1927 to alleviate crowded conditions at DuVall (then Southwestern) and Oxford schools. It was the third elementary school built in the district in six years.

In the early 1920s, Laura Whitmore Bolles donated three acres behind the Whitmore family house, about one-third of her estate, for construction of the school.

When she donated the land, Bolles requested that the new school jointly bear the name of her and her husband's settler families, the Whitmore and the Bolles clans.

Dearborn District No. 7 voters approved a bond to purchase land and build an additional elementary school in 1925.

The school board proceeded to buy another six acres adjacent to the land Bolles donated.

The new school was to front Whitmore Street. The original section of the building was two stories high and consisted of 12 classrooms, a gymnasium and an auditorium.

Many early references to the school erroneously spelled the name "Whittemore-Bolles School."

In 1939, Whitmore-Bolles School received a nine-room, two-story addition including eight classrooms and a kitchen.

A decade later, a kindergarten room, another regular classroom and a cafeteria were added to the school.

In the 1950s, Whitmore-Bolles was home to one of three school gardens in the city.

A horticulture unit building was built at the school in 1952-53.

Work on the $33,000 building began in summer 1952 and was completed in late winter 1953. It was first used as classroom space for fifth- and sixth-graders. It was adjacent to the horticulture gardens.

The building had one large classroom, a workroom, a tool room, an office and rooms for equipment. It was to serve the elementary science programs at the school as soon as the overflow of enrollment decreased.

The southwest section of the school property was donated to the city of Dearborn in 1955 for construction of a city swimming pool, but not until after a major squabble.

The city wanted the land for a neighborhood pool. The school district did not want to relinquish its land there. The city threatened to acquire the land through condemnation proceedings.

The school district finally agreed. Work began on the pool in September 1955 and was ready for swimmers the next spring.

The Press & Guide has chosen to honor late Associate Editor Richard Marsh by continuing to run his column.

September 7, 2002

I'm reading a book called *Writing to Heal the Soul.* It's very interesting, and I'm getting quite a few different ideas to add to and continue *Our Story.*

One of the chapters in the book suggests to write out your anger and pain. Just sit down and write without thinking about it ahead of time. OK, here goes.

I'm angry at God and life right now. I feel cornered and don't know where to turn. I'm trying to hang in there, but I'm in so much pain and discomfort I don't know what to do. It seems like our family has been through so much. It just does not seem fair. We lost Edsel, a wonderful son-in-law, husband, and father. Kathy was coping with ovarian cancer. Then we lost Evelyn, Wally, Bill, and Kathy just seven weeks apart. Last year we lost Joe, this year Roy. Also last year, Barbara was diagnosed with IBC and has been through a terrible year. At the same time, we had the terrorist attack on September 11. The whole world seems crazy. The violence all over the world is very scary. Violence in our own neighborhoods has escalated. No one seems to feel the safety and security that we have taken for granted. Our family has pulled together and tried very hard to make the best of everything and to keep a positive outlook. It has not been an easy road for any of us. Now the anniversary of 9/11 is here. That's all the news and TV media are full of. My heart aches for the victims of that terrible day, *but* is it necessary to relive it so much? I am left wondering.

Since last February, I have had pain and discomfort in my right leg, hip, and groin area. It's affecting my back, my life, my everything. It has been progressively getting worse. I have been going to different doctors since last April and coming up with different answers. Hip replacement seems to be the main one. I'm going for an EMG this coming Monday, which is supposed to show whether a pinched nerve might be causing the problem. I'm taking four or five Darvocet a day, and it still is only taking the edge off. Sometimes I just don't know what to do as it hurts so much. It's affecting all of my activities, even my wonderful security corner at night. The pain is so severe my books cannot always take me away to fantasy land and give relief from life's daily stresses. I'm thinking of quitting some of my committees for a while until I find out what's going on. It's painful to walk and do things, *and* that Darvocet is making me lazy. It's painful to paint and do my normal activities. My shower and dressing are very painful. I changed the bed linens yesterday morning and was almost in tears from the pain. Putting on my pants, shoes, and socks is a struggle. Everything is a struggle. It just does not seem fair. Our family has been through so much. Besides the worry and pain for myself, I don't want to put them through more. There are times when I wish I could just go to sleep and not wake up. I know that would be hard on them too, *but* I don't want to live like this.

I've always tried to be an upbeat person and consider my glass half full rather than half empty. I try to keep a cheerful attitude and enjoy all the small daily pleasures of life and the love of my family. I miss Bill so much it is always a dull daily ache. We enjoyed one another so much and in our later years helped one another with the pains of getting *old*. I feel cheated, even though I realize we were lucky to have fifty-eight years together. Carol did not have that or Jim.

Where is this going to end up? It can't go on like this. If a hip replacement would solve the problem, I would take a chance on it. I still feel I can contribute something to life and my family if I feel good, but I can't go on like this. If something happened and I didn't wake up from the operation, that would be OK. I've lived my life and I am not afraid of death, just of the process of dying. I've always tried to live my life by the golden rule and feel like I have been a "good person" trying to give back. I also feel that I have been lucky in a lot of ways and have enjoyed my life. So where is this going to end up?

OK, so I've vented my feelings and emotions at this time. Do I feel better about it? I'm unsure.

Sitting here at the computer looking out the window at a beautiful day with my back and leg aching so much, the two pain pills I've already taken this morning have not kicked in yet, I'm getting desperate. I should go and make copies of some papers for my class, but it's a long way to the copy machine. I'm supposed to have dinner at St. Clair with Helen Kelley tonight. I can't seem to get going or look forward to anything, and that's not like me. I hate it.

Monday—September 16, 2002

By this time all of you know how much I enjoy reading and "words." Here are some "words" I feel that are worth passing on.

> Embracing life as a learning expedition is the first step toward realizing balance. To understand this, it is helpful the difference between living in your comfort zone and in your learning zone . . . Your comfort zone is what your are familiar with, what you know so well the knowledge is almost automatic. Your learning zone is anything that stretches you beyond that, challenging you to learn new skills, new ways of relating. Spending time in our learning zones is essential if we are to grow. And whether we like it or not facing a significant loss throws us smack in the middle of our learning zone. (Joel and Michelle Levy, *Living in Balance*)

Boy, do I relate to that! My whole world and life changed with the loss of Bill and Kathy.

Alice Sebold, author, talks about writing. "I'm fascinated by what we hide from others when we are our public selves, and how in different groupings different layers of ourselves are revealed. It sounds silly but the human animal is fascinating and exploring character fully is one of the most thrilling parts of writing for me."

Think about it. How many different layers do you have?

The love of learning, the sequestered nooks, and all the sweet serenity of books. (Henry Wadsworth Longfellow

I am still learning. (Michaelangelo)

The truly educated never graduate. (Anon)

Happiness consists
in the full employment of our faculties
in some pursuit.
(Harriet Martineau)

Happiness is excitement
that has found a settling down place,
but there is always a little corner
that keeps flapping around.
(E. L. Konigsburg)

All happiness
is a form of innocence.
(Marguerite Yourcenar)

That is happiness;
to be dissolved into something complete
and great.
(Willa Cather)

Happiness depends, as Nature shows,
Less on exterior things
than most suppose.
(William Cowper)

I have sought
for happiness everywhere,
but I have found it nowhere
except in a little corner
with a little book.
(Thomas a Kempis)

There is no duty
we so much underrate as the duty
of being happy."
(Robert Louis Stevenson)

Happiness is a wine
of the rarest vintage,
and seems insipid
to a vulgar taste.
(Logan Pearsall Smith)

Happiness comes
of the capacity
to feel deeply,
to enjoy simply,
to think freely, to risk
life, to be needed.
(Storm Jameson)

Happiness is the meaning and the
purpose of life, the whole aim and end
of human existence.
(Aristotle)

Happiness makes up in height
for what it lacks in length.
(Robert Frost)

Hi Folks,

Thought you might want to hear the latest news on the *stressed out* Vivian Beeler family.

Barb is doing quite well except for some miserable and painful dental work caused by the chemo to her teeth. Alice is still having a problem selling her darling house because of old termite damage to the beams in the basement, which was there when she bought it but not found at that time. Bill Jr., Shannon, and Sydney are fine except getting concerned about Bill finding another job in the computer tech field. His company was taken over by IBM and downsized like all the tech companies today. He has been doing some contract work, hoping it leads to something. Sydney will be two years old this October 12. She is a darling little girl. Got some new pictures, and she is growing so fast. Carol, Erik, Eve, and Cindy are all doing OK I'm very glad to report.

Now it's seems to be my turn to cause more worry in our family. It would be so nice to have a little break from so much stress, *but* you all know I've been having a problem since last February with my right hip and leg. After countless doctor visits and X-rays, MRL EMG, the orthopedic surgeon is 90 percent positive that total hip replacement will take away my pain. So if I pass my cardiac tests which are scheduled with Dr. Atallah who has known me for twenty-three years and he says OK, I'm going for it. I can't live like this. I took my shower and dressed this morning, and I hurt so bad I'm almost in tears. I can't take it much longer. Surgery is scheduled for Tuesday, October 29, at 7:30 a.m. at Oakwood Hospital. I plan on coming through this, but if I don't I've had a good life, no regrets. I sure wish that new technique was available, but I asked about it and the doctor said it's still too experimental. Oh well! If everything goes well, I will be in the hospital for four days and then can come home if I have family members here. Carol, bless her heart, has already made arrangements with Erik to take Scooby and to come over here. There is a possibility that I could go to a rehab center for a week. But these doctors like you to go home, and they send a therapist to right where you live. I'm going for that, I hope. Several people I know here at the Village have had these doctors and are very pleased with results, so cross your fingers for me. Also please don't try and come to the hospital to see me. They keep me busy with therapy there too, and I would rather see you when I feel a bit better at home, OK?

The family around here, Carol, Erik and Eve, Barb and Ken, Jim and Hannah, are taking me to Steak and Ale for my birthday tomorrow early evening. I'm so grateful for my wonderful family. I'm trying hard to count all my blessings.

I thank all of you too for my birthday cards. Enjoyed all of them.

Latest news from the Vivian Beeler family saga to be continued.

Love, Vivian

Tuesday, October 29, 2002
Total Hip Replacement by Dr. Jeffrey Waldrop at Oakwood Hospital

The doctor said it was very successful, but I had very bad arthritis.

Sunday, November 3: I am home with daughter Carol staying with me. the doctor and therapists at the hospital said I was doing well. I would do fine at home with the therapist and the visiting nurse coming to the apartment.

I did therapy three times that week with Bruno. He said I was doing excellent! I did a lot of walking and pushing myself. I sent Carol home on Friday. I was dressing and taking care of myself.

Saturday, November 9: Carol brought dinner in and to check on me. During dinner, I did not feel well—heart racing, hot, a bit lightheaded. Carol called the visiting nurse, who suggested going to ER. She didn't think it had anything to do with surgery. Heart needed to be checked. I went to Oakwood ER about seven. They were very nice and did all kinds of tests—blood work, chest, heart, lung, stomach, X-rays. They put me on monitor with oxygen. They kept me for eight hours. They almost admitted me, but I begged to go home and promised I would slow down and not try to play "Super Woman," just because everyone was praising me and telling me how good I was doing so soon after surgery. Carol stayed the rest of the night and most of Sunday. I was feeling better. I was just completely tired out. Again, I promised I would take it easy and sent Carol home.

I took it much easier the next week. Even the therapist took it easier with me. The visiting nurse was here twice and vitals were OK. I know I just tried to forget I was eighty-one and not "Super Woman." 1 am doing much better now and know I am making good progress. I had post-op doctor visit yesterday, November 20. The doctor took X-rays and checked incision. Inflammation was improving, will be off antibiotics today. The doctor said I was doing very well. I'll see him in a month unless I have problems. Number one rule: Do not bend. I am getting better at dressing with that pick-up stick. I bet it would make a very funny video though. Right foot is still quite swollen and leg painful. The doctor said that would probably last another few weeks and told me to walk, walk. walk. I will graduate from the therapist and visiting nurse this weekend. I am very grateful. I also am blessed with my wonderful family.

Vivian Beeler, November 21, 2002

December 2002: Ken's "The Lady Story"

Our Barbara started to have pain and discomfort in her abdomen on Sunday, December 9. I thought perhaps she had picked up a flu bug of some kind. She was so miserable that Ken stayed home from work on Monday to be with her. She did not want to go to the doctor's. She said she was so tired of doctors and hospitals from all she had been through this past year. Neither Barb nor Ken got any sleep on Monday night. Barb consented to go to the doctor's but could not get an appointment until 1:30 p.m. She did not want to go to BR. the doctor was puzzled and said could be food poisoning or appendix. He sent her for X-rays. It was a long wait, so went to the clinic for them. X-rays did not show enough. The doctor sent her back to the hospital for CAT scan. All of this took hours. Phone calls went back and forth from Ken and Barb to Alice, Carol, and myself, all waiting and anxious. Finally at 2:00 a.m., she got her CAT scan, which showed appendix. There was an emergency operation at 4:00 a.m. None of us were sleeping much that night. We were very worried.

Anyway, when they took Barb into the operating room, Ken was sent to the waiting room for surgery patients. He was so exhausted that he dropped off to sleep. To explain this story, I must tell you that Ken snores. He not only snores loud, he makes all kinds of noises, and he is very conscious of this fact. To hear Ken tell it. He said he halfway woke up and saw this "lady" sitting in the waiting room with him, *but* he was so tired he could not wake up completely. He said he realized the lady was reading and he was also conscious of the fact that he was making all kinds of snoring and loud noises and was very worried about disturbing her. Finally he came to enough consciousness that he recognized it was Carol sitting there with him. He was so glad to see her and to have some "family" there with him. He was also happy to realize it was not some stranger that he was disturbing. It is so helpful to have someone with you when you are waiting and worrying about a loved one. Carol knew that and wanted to be there. Ken said she was an "angel." The doctor came out and said Barb had come through the operation fine. But the appendix had perforated, and there was infection in the abdominal cavity. She would have to stay in the hospital at least five days. It was very serious. He said we should have checked it out sooner *but* . . . After Ken and Carol saw Barb and she got into a room, Carol sent Ken home to take care of the dogs and get some sleep. She spent the day with Barb until Ken got back about 4:00 p.m. Carol said she was glad Ken was not there as Barb was very, very miserable. Carol said she felt so bad for Barb, but there was not a whole lot she could do except feed her ice chips and help her move a bit. Barb did get up to go to the bathroom, which I thought was wonderful with the pain she was in. Alice was on her way up there too. Alice had not been able to leave until the afternoon as Cincinnati had an ice storm and roads were all icy.

Alice arrived at the hospital safe and sound about 8:00 p.m. Alice had called Barb's friends Skippy and Ellie on Tuesday evening, and they had gone over and taken care of the puppy dogs. Ellie spent the night and had a couple of sandwiches made for Ken when he came in from the hospital. Thank goodness for good friends! Carol went home when Ken got back. She called me, had some soup, and was in bed at 6:30 p.m., drained emotionally and physically. It's so hard to see someone you care about in so much misery. Carol's friend Trudy had taken care of Scooby for Carol. Again, thank goodness for good friends. Carol said she was so glad that she was available to go there. Carol picked me up on Friday and took me to the hospital to see Barb. I was so grateful. My heart aches that Barb has to go through more pain and misery. *But* I am also happy that she is going to "get over this"!

So that's the story of "The Lady" and also what happened to Barbara. It's been a rough time for her. Alice stayed from the eleventh until the twentieth, which was a big help for all. I will be so happy when her house sells and she can be up here. I am also grateful that Ken and Barb were able to pick me up on Christmas Day to go out to Jim's in Milford. They left right after dinner as Barb tires very easily and is still very uncomfortable. Hey, it's been eight weeks since my hip operation, and I still get tired very easily and my leg is very uncomfortable at times. It was only two weeks for Barb. I'm grateful they could make it for Christmas.

My greatest wish for the New Year is for my family to have good health and please a little "normal" time without so much stress and worry for everyone.

2003

Fordson High School
celebrates seventy-five years of education in 1939

Barbara O'Brien
Special Writer

March 22, 2003, will mark the 75th anniversary of the dedication of Fordson High School.

Over the next seven months, the current faculty and student body will prepare for a celebration of that event. Revisiting the history of the school and of some of the people who have walked its corridors will be part of that preparation. This series of articles will highlight the decades leading up to the Diamond Jubilee.

The history of the school begins in the 1920s. At that time, the city of Springwells was experiencing a rapid growth in population, thanks to the job opportunities afforded by more than 30 industries housed within its boundaries, Ford Motor Co. being the largest.

As people flocked to the area, the school district experienced an incredible demand for more classrooms. Starting in 1921, the school population doubled each year for five years.

In 1922, the Springwells Township Unit School District, as it was then titled, had a population of 531 students housed in a one-room school (McDonald), two two-room schools (Salina and Roulo), and the first unit of the Miller School. The present Salina School was under construction.

By 1927, the schools included an expanded Miller School, Roulo, Salina, Thayer, William Ford, and Oakman schools. These schools were designed to accommodate thousands of pupils.

Springwells High School students were housed in Miller School. The first graduation class of five people (1925) included the late Honorable George T. Martin, a man who became a benefactor of scholarships to numerous Fordson graduates.

"American Chronicle: Six Decades in American Life" provides demographics of the United States in the 1920s.

The U.S. population was 106,491,000; 52 percent of the population was rural; 35 percent of the households had telephones; 12 percent of high school graduates attended college; life expectancy for males was 53.6 years, for females 54.6 years; the average income was $1,236 per year.

Considering these facts, the vision to the voters of the city of Springwells for the future of their children and their children's children was extraordinary. A bond issue of $2.5 million to be used for the construction of a new Springwells High School passed with almost universal support.

It was the first million-dollar high school built in the United States, the actual cost being $2.2 million dollars. One report estimates that in today's dollars the building would cost at least $220 million dollars. It seems that those citizens started a tradition that continues to be reflected today in community support for the Dearborn Public Schools.

The name of the city of Springwells was changed to Fordson in honor of Henry Ford and his son, Edsel, on Dec. 23, 1925. Consequently, the name of the new high school followed suit and became Fordson High School, according to the research of Richard Marsh, late associate editor of the Press & Guide, published in the *Press & Guide*.

From conversations with early Fordson graduates, a theme emerged. Parents believed that their children would not attend college, so they wished to build a high school with an academic climate. This wish was realized in the design of the architect Everett Lane Williams of the Detroit firm Van Leyen, Schilling and Keough.

Influences included buildings at Yale University, the University of Michigan, and aristocratic halls in England. The beauty of the building, "the school that looks like a college," three times earned Fordson the title of the "Most Beautiful High School in the United States."

If those early visionaries were able to visit the school today, they would find the essential design intact and the exterior of the building very familiar. Changes include the redesign of classroom and office spaces as well as the study halls at either end of the media center.

A mezzanine has been erected in the west end of the media complex. Library tables and chairs that were original to the main room are still in use, many of the chairs displaying the oval metal discs identifying the furniture as property of the school district. The cartoon (study) for a tapestry displayed in Windsor Castle hangs on the west wall of the reading room. The restored Transportation Murals painted by Zoltan Sepeshy, former president of the Cranbrook Academy of Art, look down on current students.

Elaborately carved chairs that were once used by early board members can still be found in the main office of the school, once the offices of the Board of Education and the superintendent. The main lobby displays the busts of ancient philosophers and scholars. Tile work from the world famous Pewabic Pottery is intact, as is the school seal.

New seating replaced the theater seats on the main floor of the auditorium, but original seats can still be found in the balcony.

The beautiful woodwork and decorative plaster-work remain intact in this theater.

The swimming pool no longer has diving boards or a glass roof, but the intricate blue and yellow tile work remains. If time travelers from the '20s were able to visit, they would be gratified to see that the tens of thousands of students who have passed through this school have honored their vision.

The dedication game of the football stadium, Muskegon vs. Fordson, took place on Nov. 17, 1928. It was quite an event, with a fly-over of the stadium. Yellow and blue flowers were dropped from the plane as was the game ball, decorated with blue and gold ribbons, the school colors.

The stadium was something to behold. A reinforced concrete structure, the stadium reflected the same architecture as the school. It included seating for about 50,000 spectators and was state-of-the-art, with steam heated locker and shower rooms, space for concessions, storage rooms, and an electrically heated and lighted press box with its own telephone.

Carved shields between arches represented the coats of arms of each of the schools of the Fordson School System.

According to the pamphlet distributed that day, football was first introduced in the Fordson schools in 1923. The coach had trouble securing the minimum number of players for scrimmages and games.

"Boys in the junior high grades were encouraged to come out and although they were not eligible for varsity competition, they worked out daily, learning the fundamentals " . . ." In the 1927 and 1928 seasons, Fordson won 75 percent of its games. Unfortunately, the dedication game was not one of them!

The mascot, "Tractors," is apparently unique to Fordson High School. Graduates from early classes say that at a basketball game in the '20s, the crowd spontaneously began chanting, "Go

Tractors!" Other sources say that the mascot's name grew out of recognition of Ford produced tractors, and that the football team was exhorted to "plow down the opposition like a tractor."

The weight of evidence appears to rest with the graduates' version.

As the '20s drew to a close, a total of 144 students had graduated from Springwells/Fordson High School. On Jan. 14, 1929, the cities of Fordson and Dearborn merged to form the present city of Dearborn; the school districts remained separate.

The country was reeling from the effects of the Great Depression, but the people of the former city of Fordson continued to rise to the challenge of Webster H. Pearce, state superintendent of education. At the dedication of Fordson High School, he had exhorted the citizens of the community "to support it and make the school a living force in the life of the community." (The Detroit Free Press, March 23, 1928).

And so it was, and so it remains to this day.

(Other sources include the document authored by Yvette Piggush and Cindy Thomack to the State Register of Historical Sites and "The Organization and Development of the Fordson Public School System," available at the McFadden-Ross archives.)

At Fordson, history is in the halls.

School in Dearborn Celebrates
Seventy-five Years Shawn Windsor

Free Press Staff Writer

On Saturday, the celebration for Dearborn Fordson begins, and the sprawling English Tudor-style high school commemorates its 75th anniversary.

But Thursday morning, there is school. So the kids flock to beat the bell.

About 90 percent are Arab-American. These days, expressions are a bit more somber.

Still, plans are made to hit the mall later. Or weekend parties.

Students zip past a statue of Aristotle, past an old Ford tractor.

At the end of the school day, a couple thousand teenagers head for the doors. A few dozen throw on shorts and T-shirts and scurry outside, where a muddy, early-spring field awaits.

They line up under blue skies. And toss a football.

Ten reasons to celebrate Fordson High School's 75th anniversary:

1: Its architecture. Praised as one of the most beautiful schools in the Midwest, the building suggests a 16th-Century English manor house. It cost $2.5 million, an enormous amount in 1928.
2: Its artwork. Six large paintings by Zoltan Sepeshy pay tribute to Henry Ford and transportation.
3: Its statuary. Students share hallways with marble busts of Plato, Socrates, Sophocles, Homer, Apollo and 12 other ancient Greeks, both mythic and real.
4: Its 37,621 graduates. They include UAW President Walter Reuther, longtime Dearborn Mayor Orville Hubbard, community leader

Michael Berry, former U.S. Sen. Robert Griffin and Mike Adray, the late appliance magnate and philanthropist.

5: Its nickname. The Tractors, as in Ford Motor Co.'s Fordson tractors.

6: Its student body. About 90 percent of its 2,100 students have Mideastern surnames, and they include recent immigrants as well as third generation Arab-Americans.

7: Its international reputation.
In 1994, Redbook magazine called Fordson the best high school in Michigan, and the school has been featured on Great Britain's BBC and Canada's CBC.

8: Its football team. The Tractors won the 1993 state Class AA title.

9: Its storied past. Fordson is a registered state historic site.

10: Its show-biz career. Fordson has been the site of several TV commercials and was used for scenes in the 1987 film "The Rosary Murders."
Fordson's 75th anniversary celebration will take place at 10 a.m. Saturday in the school auditorium, on Ford Road, one block west of Schaefer. After the premiere of a video on the school's history, there will be an open house.

Dearborn Fordson High School cost $2.5 million when it was built in 1928. It is a fine example of English Tudor-style architecture.

March 16, 2003

Dear Dr. Barnes,

I personally want to "thank you" for coming to our Village to speak during black history month. I was unable to come to the chapel the day you spoke as I am the leader of our watercolor class that meets at the same time your program was scheduled. 1 felt very fortunate as they taped your speech and I was able to hear you on our in-house Channel 11.

I sat enthralled as I listened to you talk about your grandpa, Ollie G. Barnes the first, and all his accomplishments, your talk of teaching values: education, responsibility, work ethics, spirituality, integrity, and to look inside a person, not just see their physical differences. All of us need that type of reinforcement of our thinking in our world today. You really touched rny heart and made me feel all is not lost in our world. Hearing about Ollie G. Barnes the fourth gives me hope. There is so much violence and so many in our society seem to have lost their moral values; life is scary. Living here at the Village is a wonderful education for all of us, and I know I am learning every day.

I am trying to write our life story for my children and grandchildren; you gave me some ideas of how to pass on some of our ideas in my writings. This is a difficult time of year for me, as just three years ago I lost my partner of fifty-eight years and seven weeks later a daughter to cancer. *But* I am so grateful my husband and I had made the decision together to move into the Village. We had two years that we enjoyed here together. I can honestly say that I do not know of anywhere that I would be happier. The staff here are wonderful! The support and help they give you when you are grieving is beyond duty. They are my friends.

I have been raving about your talk to all of my friends who didn't hear you that day. I was talking to Cheryl Presley and telling her how much I enjoyed it. She suggested that I write and tell you personally. 1 appreciate her idea.

Thank you so very much, Dr. Barnes, for being you and for your inspiring talk. I hope I can hear you again someday.

Sincerely,

Friday April 4, 2003

I am sitting here on a *cold, rainy* afternoon and wondering what life has in store for me. Three years ago at this time, I had Bill home from the hospital with hospice and his days numbered. It hurts to relive that time and I can't help remembering. I have a lot of wonderful memories of our life together, *but* I still miss him so very much. Yes, you accept your fate. You never get over it, *and* Kathy, that pain will never go away.

For over a year now, I have not been pain free, *and* I'm tired of it. I was so much in hope when I had my hip replacement that that would take care of my pain. It did take away that pain. Then the arthritis in my knee and back started in full force. Some of the medications have upset my stomach, so I'm dealing with that problem too. I'm doing everything the doctors suggest. I've been into therapy. I still do leg exercises and elevate my legs for swelling. My right ankle and instep are still swollen from my operation five and a half months ago. I wear surgical support hose and fight to get those on every morning. I'm going right now for a series of three shots, one a week for three weeks, in my right knee. It's something made from chickens (synvisc), an artificial cartilage, to help replace your own that has worn away. I've had two shots and have not noticed any difference yet. The doctor says it could take awhile. I keep hoping, like I said before. I'm so tired of hurting all the time. Even sitting and sleeping, it's there, sometimes worse than others. Sometimes my knee or back wake me at night with the pain. Pain pills don't really take it away, and they also cause other problems. So I'm very careful how I take them. What absolutely scares the very daylights out of me *is losing my independence!* Because already this is affecting my lifestyle. I don't go like I used too. I stop and think. Is this trip necessary? I plan my walking because it hurts and I get so tired. Everything I do is such a big effort. Everyone tells me I look good. I'm trying very hard to put up a good front and also keep myself looking well. I'm trying to keep a good attitude. I truly think that is very important. I thought that by writing some of these things down might help. Whether anyone ever reads this is not important. I think I just need to get it off my chest. But I keep wondering what I will be like in another year. It truly scares me.

Change of subject: This war situation also scares me, not for myself, but for all the young people involved and for their families. I can't help but wonder if President Bush and our military leaders really did the right thing to start this. I'm so afraid it is going to escalate and drag on for a long time. With the technology today, will they use and start chemical and nuclear stuff? My heart aches for all those involved.

Marguerette was here today to look at an apartment in Parkview Terrace, a Hillshire. She had called me and asked me to join her and Susan to look at it. I thought that was very nice. I think she is going to take it. It's in a good location. Again, I'm wondering. Bill and I encouraged Roy to think about moving here, which he did after Bill was gone. I've been encouraging Marguerette and telling her it's a great place. For me it is. *But* will Marguerette think so too? She is very active and has no major health problems. She says she is doing it for her kids because then everything will go back to them and they will not have to worry about selling her condo, etc. Will she be happy here? She is a very independent person. Will she make friends and join in some of the committees? So many questions! I moved in with Bill. We did this major lifestyle change together, *and* it is a major lifestyle change. I can't rave enough about the support and help I received when I lost Bill, *but* we had been so active on committees and doing things that the staff knew both of us and were friends. Will Marguerette? Only time will tell. I feel a little responsible. I also know that Susan and Alan are very happy about it, and that makes me feel good. Alan came over from work and met us for lunch at Windows, which was very nice. I think being with them today and Marguerette making this *big* decision brought back memories for me too. When we moved in here, I was doing quite well. Walking was no big problem. With that spastic angina condition I have had for years, I had learned to pace myself. Life was pretty good; somehow, you just don't think that things are going to change. It's been over five years now. Look at the changes in my life. I'm trying very hard to use Kathy's motto of "one day at a time."

Leinonen Wedding Shower

Honoring Eve Williams

Saturday May 10, 2003

Luncheon: 12:30 p.m.

47609 Pinecreek Driye, Northville,
Michigan Map enclosed—(Aunt Joan's)

Hoping you can join us for this happy occasion.

Please RSVP by May 7

Grandma Vivian Beeler {313} 581-7041

Eve and Erik would appreciate it if
you would share one of your favorite recipes with them.

They are registered at:

Marshall Fields
Bed Bath & Beyond
The Home Depot #2742-160112

Marriage

> How do you account for a long marriage?
> I could say it's a bit like alcoholism . . . one day at a time.
> I never thought of it as an addiction.
> Certainly as a condition. It's also a job that requires attention and work, cooperation and creativity.
> That doesn't sound particularly romantic.
> There's nothing more romantic than going through life, with all its spins, with someone you love, someone who loves and understands you, someone who will be there for the big bouquets, children, grandchildren, a new house, a well-earned promotion, and for the weeds, illness, a burned dinner, a bad day at work.
> There are people who get used to taking care of the bouquets and weeds alone.
> I admire independence. The world would be a stronger place if we were all capable of handling life on our own. But being capable of it doesn't mean being unable to share and depend on someone else. It shouldn't mean being unwilling to. That's the romance.
>
> —Nora Roberts, *Face the Fire*

This was a conversation of a young man asking an older woman how she had such a long marriage. 1 thought it was a very good description.

June 5, 2002

To Erik and Eve on Their Wedding:

There is a lovely little book going around at your wedding showers, asking people to write some of their advices or wishes for both of you. At Eve's first shower at her Aunt Lynn's, my first thought was "*Wow,* that's a subject that will take some thought." Eve's mother told me it would be at her other showers, so I could think about it. Needless to say, I have been thinking. I have decided that there were so many things I would like to say writing about them in the quiet of my own apartment would be the best way for me.

Firstly, let me say that both of you mean the world to me. I have a very happy feeling in my heart that the two of you are meant for each other and will have a wonderful marriage. You both have dreams and goals. My biggest wish for you is that you can have as great a marriage and as long or longer than Grandpa and I had.

Secondly, I really cannot give you advice in the world today. Society and everything is so very different than way back in 1941 when Grandpa and I were married. Hopefully I will finish *Our Story* and you can read about what it was like back then.

But important values are still the same.

Some of the things that worked for us:

- Respect for one another and the other's ideas.
- Best friends, being able to talk about anything to one another.
- Always keeping the lines of communication open.
- Share and help. No woman's work, man's work.
- Encourage and support through good times and bad times.
- When you disagree, compromise.
- Keep God and spirituality in your lives.
- Keep a sense of humor.
- Allow each other some "space" and "alone" time if wanted. While our wedding vows make us "one," we are still individuals.
- Good sex is important and fun, sort of "the icing on the cake," but so many other things enter into it over the years.
- Integrity, trust, kindness, compassion.
- Self-confidence, without it, it's hard to feel empathy and love for others.
- Always say "I love you" and share a kiss when you say good-bye and good night.
- Keep learning and growing.
- Thankfulness. Life has so many things to offer, you should always be thankful for your many blessings.

Looking back and remembering, Grandpa and I did not know all of these things at the time we were married. We were two very young people very much in love. (We thought we were pretty smart and adult at the time.) Thankfully we grew up and learned together. I'm also grateful our love grew over the years and lasted with family and changes. Sometimes marriage can be work; that's where commitment comes in. *But* most of the time it's an adventure and *fun!*

My love, prayer, and best wishes always.

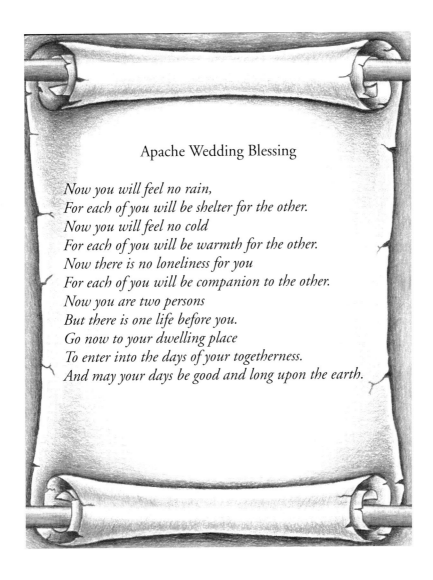

Apache Wedding Blessing

Now you will feel no rain,
For each of you will be shelter for the other.
Now you will feel no cold
For each of you will be warmth for the other.
Now there is no loneliness for you
For each of you will be companion to the other.
Now you are two persons
But there is one life before you.
Go now to your dwelling place
To enter into the days of your togetherness.
And may your days be good and long upon the earth.

Subj: Hugs
Date: 6/30/2003 4:30:10 AM Eastern Daylight Time
From: mishyosvogt@cybertrails.com
To: veebee248@aol.com
File: Image031.zip (693811 bytes) DL Time (49333 bps): < 4 minutes
Sent from the Internet (Details)

Grandma!

Thank you so much for the card and gifts. Thank you for gathering your beautiful prints, I am excited about decorating with them! I really look forward to so many aspects of interior design. I hope to do some exciting things with colors, mats and frames:o).

The Family history is a little more interesting to me than I thought, I ended up laying out and gazing at the lines for more than an hour—the first time. I realized that even though it was just some information on some papers, it some how made me feel a more tangible connection to all of these people, my family.

It was an important realization for me, to see that my family is so much bigger than I normally conceptualize, to see these stranger's names and feel a connection to them, and then to realize that this line goes on forever. It made me see that I am capable of feeling a connection to people that I never thought I could have. And I hope to carry this with me in my daily life. Thank you Grandma

The Kids are doing great, enjoying the Summer.

Sage is doing something crafty almost every single day. Today, she was playing completely self-directed and unbeknownst to her she began dabbling in the art of mosaic, she created little "lists" as she called them—actually list—pads which were very neatly cut stacks of paper, stapled together and the cover embellished with her own personal mosaic design. David and I were so impressed that she hurried off and made two more for each of us.

This energy just comes straight from her heart. So her dad and I just keep encouraging her. Last week David signed her up for a college course! The community college just down the street is offering one week Art courses for little ones. We let her pick what class she wanted to take explaining briefly what the mediums would be, and are you ready? She chose Water Colors, learning techniques of Georgia O'Keefe! She will be starting July 15th.

She has so much heart-drive, which is probably not un usual for a five-year-old, but I get to live with her, and I hope that I can learn enough from her.

Boy, Creativity in our family is abundant, and superb!

Below or attached are some recent (last week) pictures of the kids (the last two are from this spring—see how they grow) enjoying the town's public pool and some of our favorite swimming holes.—There are moments when I am sad that I can't share them with you, but then I remember . . . that I am, because you are always in my heart!

I love you Grandma,
Thanks again,
Krista

Sunday, June 29, 2003

Dear Linda and Sandra,

Here it is the end of June; it doesn't seem possible. I really don't know where the time goes. I get up on Monday morning, and it seems like I just turn around and it's Friday again. I guess that's good because I do seem to keep busy. From the sound of your letters, you girls do also. Your flowers sound very pretty; you sure do have a lot of them. Sounds like your garden is pretty big too. Do the two of you use that much produce? I know you can and freeze some. It's so good that you are able to work at the Curtis Farm, and they seem to help you quite a bit from what you have said in your letters. Between them and Dr. Chalfont, I'm so glad you have friends.

Erik and Eve's wedding was lovely. The weather cooperated, and after a cloudy day, the sun came out. I went to the rehearsal and then the wedding. Eve is a beautiful young woman and made a lovely bride. They seem so happy together. It was a big wedding, about 250 people at their reception. Barb and Ken picked me up and then brought me home about 10:30 p.m. That's late for me to be out anymore. I don't go to bed until 11:30 or twelve o'clock, but I'm reading and in my nightie and robe. They had a wonderful honeymoon in Hawaii. Now they are back and both back to work. Carol is out in Washington with Cindy. She had to have an operation on the twenty-fifth. The muscle at the end of her esophagus going into the stomach was not working right. Acid reflux was damaging her esophagus. She had had a lot of tests, and she knew this when she was home for her brother's wedding. Carol flew out the twenty-third to be there. Cindy is doing OK but can't work for a month and has to be on liquids and gradually add soft foods for about six weeks. It seems like there is always something in this family to keep me worrying about someone. Doggone! Doctors did say this will stop her problem and she will be fine. Somehow they wrapped her stomach around the end of the esophagus and created a new muscle. She has five incisions in her mid-section.

Barbara is staying at the cottage for most of July and August. Bill, Shannon, and Sydney are coming again this summer to see family. They will spend a couple of nights with me and then go to the cottage too. Carol and I will go out there once or twice that week. Then they will be back for another night with me and fly home. They will be here for about ten days. I'm looking forward to seeing them. Sydney is starting to talk a lot at two and a half; she is growing.

Ford Motor Company

100 YEARS

THE ROAD IS OURS
100th Anniversary Celebration

JUNE 12-16, 2003
HENRY FORD II WORLD CENTER
DEARBORN, MICHIGAN

EVENT HOURS

Thursday, June 12	4:00 p.m. – 8:00 p.m.
Friday, June 13	10:00 a.m. – 8:00 p.m.*
Saturday, June 14	10:00 a.m. – 8:00 p.m.*
Sunday, June 15	10:00 a.m. – 8:00 p.m.*
Monday, June 16	10:00 a.m. – 5:00 p.m.

*entertainment until 11:00 p.m.

Mercury Drive
Hubbard Drive
Trail Route
Michigan Avenue
Southfield Freeway
Ford Credit
Ford WHQ
North Entrance
South Entrance

Ford Motor Company
100 YEARS

DIRECTORY

1. Centennial Theatre
2. Rotunda
3. Ford Component Sales
4. Countdown to Kitty Hawk
5. Classic Vehicle Displays
6. SVT Vehicles
7. Ford Racing
8. Ford Division
9. The Ford Collection
10. Food Service
11. 25 Years & Soul Vehicles / 100 Icons That Move The World
12. Lincoln / Mercury
13. Aston Martin / Jaguar / Land Rover
14. Volvo
15. Mazda
16. 100th Anniversary Experience / Model T Journey
17. Employee Resource Groups
18. Future Truck
19. UAW-Ford

TICKETS INCLUDE:

- **Credentials on a commemorative lanyard** for entry all five days

- **A daily assigned parking area with shuttle service** to and from the 100th Anniversary event grounds (one parking pass will be provided for each increment of four paid admissions)

- **Access to all interactive exhibits** from Ford, Lincoln, Mercury, Mazda, Aston Martin, Jaguar, Land Rover and Volvo

- **An opportunity to display your classic car or truck**

- **Access to the Centennial Theatre and Concert Series**

- **Entry to the 100th Anniversary Experience**

- **Admission and free shuttle service** to the Ford Rouge Factory Tour (limited capacity, first-come first-served)

- **Access to the Countdown to Kitty Hawk exhibit** on the grounds of Henry Ford II World Center

- **Discounted admission and free shuttle service to local attractions**, including The Henry Ford (Henry Ford Museum and Greenfield Village), the Henry Ford Estate–Fair Lane, and Edsel & Eleanor Ford House (available to advance ticket purchasers only)

- **Access to Ford Racing Night**

- **Fireworks display** on Friday, June 13

- **100th Anniversary commemorative coin***

- **Discounts on 100th Anniversary merchandise** purchased at THE ROAD IS OURS 100th Anniversary Celebration*

- **Discounts for on-site food and beverages***

*Included with adult and teen paid admission only

www.celebrateford100.com

Celebrate . . . Our Century

FORD MOTOR COMPANY TURNS 100!

Join our history-making celebration, June 12-16, 2003, on the grounds of Henry Ford II World Center in Dearborn, Michigan.

Your visit will be full of exciting, memorable experiences:

- A vast collection of Ford Motor Company cars and trucks representing the past, present and future. Concept cars included!

- Current product displays and interactive exhibits from Ford, Lincoln, Mercury, Mazda, Aston Martin, Jaguar, Land Rover and Volvo.

- Merchandise, food, activities and live entertainment for the entire family.

TICKET INFORMATION

$24.95 gets you a ticket for all five days.

Tickets are $19.95 for Ford Motor Company employees, retirees and their extended families (as defined by A.D and Z Plan eligibility).

Children age 12 and under are **free** when accompanied by a paying adult.

Purchase online at
www.celebrateford100.com

or call our toll-free number:
1-866-410-0367

June 12-16, 2003 • Dearborn, Michigan

www.celebrateford100.com

Toll free: 1-866-410-0367

ACTIVITIES FOR EVERYONE!

A host of activities provide fun for the whole family:

- Make your own CDs with your favorite driving songs in the Mustang Café.

- See the Thunderbird driven by Halle Berry in the Bond film "Die Another Day" (you can "walk the red carpet" and be greeted by celebrity impersonators!).

- Help a team of classic car enthusiasts assemble a Model T and crank it up in less than 20 minutes!

- Practice your golf swing in virtual golf simulators at the Golf Experience.

- Take your kids to visit "Blue," from Nickelodeon's TV show Blue's Clues.

- Watch the action as professional bull riders demonstrate their skill.

- Take in a real Monster Truck Jam, where you can see the Built Ford Tough Blue Thunder Monster Truck.

- Model T Journey – Ride in the car that put the world on wheels – through a specially designed heritage tour to see the people, products and achievements of Ford Motor Company's first 100 years.

Thousands of Ford Motor Company classic cars and trucks will be on display!

Centennial Theatre Concert Series
There will be live performances throughout the five-day event, with special concerts on Friday, Saturday and Sunday evenings:

FRIDAY: Earth, Wind & Fire

SUNDAY: Toby Keith

SATURDAY: Beyoncé Knowles, Friends & Family

Ford Racing Night — The Legends of a Century
This special event kicks off the centennial celebration on Thursday, June 12, starting at 4 p.m. See some of Ford's top NASCAR Winston Cup drivers, get autographs, and attend live question-and-answer sessions.

Ford Motor Company—Hundred Years Memories: May 2003

You asked us to share stories about Ford Motor Company to help celebrate the centennial, so here goes.

I am Vivian L. Beeler, eighty-one years old, widow of William J. Beeler, and living at Henry Ford Retirement Village in Dearborn, Michigan. It seems quite appropriate to live here as Ford Motor Company has always been a part of my life.

I was born in Jackson, Michigan, to Ackerson Tallman, a young veteran who had recently returned from France after fighting in World War I, and Eva Manley. They had met through mutual friends after he returned from the war. They were married in 1919, and I was born in 1921. When I was around a year old, my dad had a opportunity to work for Ford Motor Company at the Rouge plant in Dearborn. We moved from Jackson to Park Street in West Dearborn. Thus began my lifetime of Ford Motor Company being a part of my life. My dad was an electrician at the Rouge plant and worked hourly shift work. My childhood memories are happy ones. I had a sister born a year and a half after we moved to Dearborn, and my maternal grandmother lived with us. Sundays were family get-together times with aunts, uncles, cousins, and friends. A lot of my dad and mother's friends worked at Ford also. One of my favorite uncles, Wilbur Price, worked there too. I wish we had kept better records, so I could remember what he did. Over the years, we moved to Orchard Street in East Dearborn, and I went to Woodward School and then Fordson High School. I grew up during the Depression, and I remember we could not have everything we wanted, and we had to watch how we spent our money. We always had food on the table although maybe not just what we wanted, and we always used up leftovers. I never felt deprived, and looking back, I think it was because we always had love in our family. Another favorite aunt stayed with us off and on. She was my dad's baby sister. They had lost their dad to heart disease in their teens and their mother to the flu epidemic in 1917. She was named Fanny on her birth certificate, which she hated! She legally changed it to Frances when she was old enough. She was Aunt Fran to us. She started working in the business world at sixteen. We always thought of her as kind of a free spirit. She grew up during the flapper and bathtub gin period. She was so good to us. She lived for a while at the Women's Y downtown. It was such a big adventure and treat when she invited my sister and myself to stay with her overnight on a weekend, taking us to a favorite diner and tearoom for dinners. She also taught us hard work ethics too. She was a wonderful treasure all through our lives.

Sadly, we lost my dad in January 1938, when I was just sixteen. He had developed Hodgkin's disease, which was blamed partly due to him being in a poisonous gas attack in France during the war. That changed my plans for going to college and being a teacher. I switched from college courses to business in school. My mother was working at J. L. Hudson's, but it was a difficult period for us. My mother did not drive at that time, and my uncle Wilbur Price gave me a quick course on driving, and I passed my driver's license test. We then had mobility in our blue Ford car. I wish I could remember the year it was made. I remember we were all very proud of it. It was probably a 1935 or 1936 model.

Also in the spring of 1937 or 1938, I remember selling poppies for the veterans on the Gate 4 overpass on Miller Road. I remember my family being a little concerned as there was labor unrest at that time. Now that bridge is recognized by the National Park Service as one of the ten most significant sites in the history of the American labor movement as it was the scene of the 1937 "Battle of the Overpass." The event led to official recognition of the United Auto Workers by Ford in 1941. Now that bridge and that area around the Rouge plant is being readied for tours during the hundred anniversary celebration. I graduated with honors in January 1939 from Fordson High School. I was seventeen years old and no one would hire me. All told me to come back when I was eighteen.1 got a job as a receptionist at Oakman Realty Company for $5.00 a week. I gave my mother $2.50 and I had $2.50. Surprising how far that went in those days. It is laughable now.

But what a lucky break for me! It was while I was working there that I met my future husband, William J. Beeler. He was nineteen-year-old young man who came in with his mother looking for a bigger house to rent in the Dearborn area. They had moved down there from Jackson, Michigan, a few years before. His dad worked for Kelsey Hayes Wheel and had been transferred down to their Detroit plant. Of course, Kelsey Hayes did business with Ford. Bill had just been hired to work in the tool room at Ford and was very excited about it. While his mother talked with the realtors, we got to talking. We found out we had both graduated from Fordson High. I was going to night school there to take more business courses. Bill asked if he could walk me there. In those days, we walked all over. That was the start of our long, wonderful relationship. Bill got into the apprenticeship program for tool and die makers and completed that program. While Bill did not get a college degree, he went to school all his life. Through classes at Ford and also at Wayne State, Bill gradually worked his way up the ladder. He was always very grateful to Ford for giving him the opportunity to do this. In the fall of 1938, I was hired by Michigan Bell and worked as a telephone switchboard operator who said "number please" and connected the parties. My first job was at the Michigan Bell office over the drug store at the corner of Michigan Avenue and Monroe in West Dearborn. We were married in August 1941.

Looking back, we were a couple of young innocents who grew up together and made it work. Of course, we thought we were very grown-up at that time. December 7, 1941, was a Sunday, my grandmother's birthday. I was trying to impress my mother and grandma with my cooking skills and we were eating our dinner when we heard the news of Pearl Harbor. Of course, that changed everyone's life.

Bill was deferred several times because of his job at Ford. He was also a volunteer on a civil service patrol. Our Susan was born in November 1942, a darling little girl. We thought we were on top of the world. Naturally, I did quit my job. In those days, mothers stayed at home with their babies. Then we were awakened from our happy life in April 1943. We lost our Susan to SIDS. In those times, not much was known about it. To this day, there are still questions and I still wonder why. In March 1944, Bill was inducted into the army air force. Our second daughter was born in April of that same year. The Red Cross arranged for Bill to come home to see his new daughter for a few days. They released me from the hospital early to be with my husband. Again, back then you stayed ten days in the hospital when you had a baby. When Bill was inducted, his family graciously invited me to live with them and have the use of Bill's old bedroom while he was in service. It was a large room with lots of room for a crib. My mother-in-law loved babies. Bill was the eldest of five children. They were wonderful to me. I always had a great relationship with my in-laws and am forever grateful. After our daughter Carol was a few months old, I got a part-time job at People's Outfitting Company on Warren Avenue, just a couple of blocks from their house on Neckel. I worked in the office. I made two trips down to see Bill while he was in service. The first I made by myself on the train to Sheppard Field in Texas. My wonderful in-laws took care of our daughter. What an experience! On the second trip, I took our daughter when she was a year old, and we drove down with the wife of one of my husband's buddies. At that time, they were stationed at San Angelo, Texas. This was in the spring and early summer of 1945. Bill was allowed off base, and we rented a room with kitchen privileges from a widowed lady who chewed tobacco. She had "spit cans" all over her house, and I had a toddler who was fascinated by them. I was kept busy chasing her. What fun we had though! All the young married couples were in the same boat, no money, but that didn't stop us from getting together and having good times at the PX and lounge areas. The heat, wind, dust were terrible, but we were young, in love, and having fun together. A group of us made a trip across the border to Villa Acuna in Mexico and saw a bullfight. That was my first and only experience with that. We were all afraid to eat or drink over there. I had taken some things for our daughter. It was an adventure, but one time was enough. All of us were very anxious for the war to be over. I came back to Dearborn in early July as Bill's unit was getting ready for overseas duty. Then thank you, God, the war ended!

In 1944, two other events occurred in our lives, which were important to us. My mother met and married Maro Miller, divorced with three almost grown children. Maro owned a car repair shop. We liked him and got to know his family, whom we also liked and got along with. We were very happy for my mother. The other event was our free-spirited, beloved Aunt Fran, who was like a second mother to us, marrying William Redmond who worked for Dodge Motor Company. Neither one had been married before, and they were in their early forties. Uncle Bill had been the caregiver for his mother, living with her until she died. Aunt Fran was a business professional in accounting for Wilson Dairy and Sherman Williams Paint Company. Both marriages worked out well and were happy ones.

When Bill was discharged in the fall of 1945, he went back to work as Ford Motor Company had kept an opening for him. We were very grateful. With a loan of $500 from Bill's folks, we were able to put a down payment on our first house on Campbell Street just south of Outer Drive in Dearborn. It was $6100 at that time. We lived there for twenty-one great years. In 1947, our daughter Kathy was born. We called her our "lucky baby" as at that same time

Bill became a salaried engineer on gears. Transferred over to the buildings on Rotunda, he worked under a mentor who he said taught him so much—a Mr. Finklestein. As I said, Bill was taking advantage of every class that he could. There were a lot of times that he would come home from work, eat, and go to school. It paid off for us, and that's where I said, "We made it work." It wasn't always easy. Bill was a wonderful husband and father, and he tried very hard to make things better for his family. I loved my role as homemaker, wife, and mother. I learned to be a doggone good cook, seamstress, etc.

In 1951, our twin daughters were born. We were the parents of four beautiful girls, and again we felt on top of the world. Our lives were very full in those years. Bill was a very outgoing person and loved being busy. He was also very handy and could do most anything. He remodeled our attic into a dormitory for our girls and helped with building an addition at the back of our house to accommodate our growing family. He also, in self-defense of living with five females, built and installed a small bathroom in the basement. He also was an active member of our church—St Paul's Lutheran at Beech and Monroe in Dearborn. Although I was a homemaker and was not taking classes, I never felt deprived or left behind. I have always been a bookworm and reader and I learned along with Bill. He always treated me as his equal in every way.

Bill loved learning and his different jobs at Ford Motor Company. He moved in the chassis division from gears to axles and drive shafts. He was what they call now "an old-time loyal dedicated worker." We used to tease him that he had to be the first one there in the morning to let the cat out and the last one at night to make sure the lights were out. We both appreciated the opportunities Ford Motor had given him and he worked hard to "give back " . . .

Our girls still talk about what a wonderful neighborhood they grew up in and what a wonderful childhood they had. Most of our neighbors were young married people, raising their children. Our girls had lots of playmates, and the adults would get together at one another's houses and yards for picnics and parties. Bill and I got into square dancing with our next-door neighbors in the early fifties. We had a ball going around to the different schools in Dearborn and learning from different callers. We did both square and round dancing and really became very good at it. Bill even became the president of the Detroit Area Square and Round Dance Group.

We hosted the Michigan Square and Round Dance Council at the Fort Shelby Hotel in Detroit one year. Square dancing in those years was *big*.

Those were the "golden years," although at the time we did not realize this. Our parents were well and a big part of our lives. Our children were healthy and growing up. We had activities at our church, Whitmore-Boles School, Edison School, and Edsel Ford High School. Bill was doing work that he loved, *and* as I said before, I loved being a homemaker. We took vacations up North by Indian River and also went over to St. Joseph, Michigan, as my mother and step-dad had a franchise in a Dairy Queen over there. Our two older girls remember helping them and loving it. We all loved Lake Michigan. Life was good, and I know we did appreciate that fact, but we were so busy that it is only in looking back when you reach my age now that you know they were some of the very best years in our lives. Of course, during those years we had some times of worry with childhood diseases and the ups and downs of life. Overall, only on looking back can you appreciate those times and memories more. In 1960, my mother was widowed again when Maro died of heart problems. He had been a wonderful "grandpa" to our children, and we missed him greatly. In 1963, we lost Grandma Martha Manley. She was ninety-three and was quite healthy up until the last couple of months. It was another loss that really hurt!

In 1963, our lives changed again. Bill was offered the position of resident engineer at the Ford Sterling Plant. That was thirty-five miles from our house. Back then, we didn't have the roads we have now. It was over an hour and a half commute both ways. It was something that Bill wanted and had worked so hard for. Of course he accepted the position. Earlier, I would drop him off at work and have the car for the day or our eldest daughter who was in high school across the street from where her dad worked would ask to use the car, walk over, and get it. We had to get a second car. We got a green Comet, and everyone was thrilled. Then in the fall of 1964, we were at a square dance convention in Lansing. I had not been feeling well, sick to my stomach, etc. when I realized I *was pregnant!* Carol was twenty and away at Central Michigan University. Kathy was a senior in high school. The twins were thirteen and at Edison. I was forty-three and Bill forty-five. Needless to say, we were shocked. How could this have happened! I was ready to jump off a bridge, cut my throat, anything. We had "our family." Now we know it was another one of the best things to happen in our lives. We had a *son!* And now have a wonderful daughter-in-law and a beautiful two-and-a-half-year-old granddaughter. But think back in 1964—writing to your daughter in college to tell her that her mother is pregnant and telling all of our family. *Shock!* But I truly believe our son kept us "young." I was active in the schools, swim lessons at the Y, etc. Bill became active in the Boy Scouts along with our son. It was another learning and growing experience. But getting ahead of my story . . .

Back to 1965 when Bill Jr. was born. He had five mothers and was quite a spoilt little boy. In our small house, his crib was in the middle of the girls "dormitory." They had to quietly sneak up the stairs at bedtime because of course babies went to bed earlier than teenagers.

Bill also was finding the long commute tiring and in bad weather was caught a few times and ended up staying overnight—not good. We decided it was time for another change. We looked and looked at properties and subdivisions in the Troy, Sterling Heights area. We decided on Emerald Lakes Subdivision in Troy, just about six miles from the Ford Sterling Plant. We built a house—$37,000.00 at that time, and we worried if we could afford it. It was another learning experience but *fun!* But I cried when we left Dearborn.

At the same time we were looking at properties and buildings and getting ready to move, our daughter Carol was planning her wedding. She had met and fallen in love with Edsel Leinonen. We liked him a lot and were happy for both of them. Edsel had just served two years in the military and was going to Wayne State for his degree. He had just been hired by, you guessed it, Ford Motor Company. His dad, Matt, worked at the assembly plant and his elder brother John also worked at Ford. Edsel ended up being an analyst in traffic control in the Ford building at Rotunda and Southfield. He worked with E & L Transport and also scheduled the railroad transport. Our Ford family was growing.

Carol graduated from Central with a teaching degree in June 1966, and she and Edsel were married on June 18, 1966. We were very proud of her and happy for both of them. They had a beautiful wedding at St. Paul's with their reception at Roma Hall. How many mothers of the bride carry a one-year-old son down the aisle? Bill and I were learning how expensive college and weddings were, plus building a house.

We moved to Troy in January 1967 with three daughters, a son, and a beagle "Corky." Our daughter Kathy had graduated from Edsel Ford just before Bill Jr. was born in 1965. That was a trip. There I was very, very pregnant, wondering how I was going to manage the bleachers for the graduation. We solved it by bringing a lawn chair, and I sat over on the side lines. Our Kathy took a few classes at community college but was not really interested in going on to college. She loved the business world. She worked first for a small private company and then got a nice job at National Bank in Detroit. She was very good in finances and math. She was dating a young man James Welton, who was going to Western Michigan. Jim's dad, Nelson, worked for Ford in engine engineering at the "Tripoli Building" by twin ponds in Dearborn. They were married in December 1967 at Faith Lutheran Church in Sterling Heights with a family and friends' reception at our home. It was very lovely and their choice. When Jim graduated, he was hired by Ford Motor Company and worked in welding processing—fixtures, hoods, doors, decks, first at the Rouge office building, then in later years at Wixom. More Ford family for us; of course everyone drove Ford cars!

Going back a couple of years, our twins were very angry at us for moving and taking them away from their friends and not allowing them to go to Edsel Ford where their elder sisters had graduated. We could see their side of it but also felt we had no choice. Also we were excited by a new home, a four-bedroom colonial. We were the sixteenth family in the neighborhood, across the street from Walker Lake. We chose a lot across the street from the lake as I was worried about living on the lake with a one-and-a-half-year-old. Ha! He learned to swim like a fish and spent a lot of time with boys around his age who lived across the street from us. Our subdivision was built where there were old gravel pits which were made into lakes. Today there are over six hundred homes in that area; it is beautiful. When we moved to Troy in 1967, Rochester Road was just a little two-lane highway. We drove ten miles to get to a big supermarket. Now Troy is a *big* city. Our twin daughters caused us some worries and heartaches with their rebellion, skipping school, etc. But they were cute girls and "identical twins," which made them popular. It wasn't too long before they made friends and adjusted to a degree.

Alice was going with a young college student, David McCalden, in her senior year of high school and became pregnant. David was a nice young man from a very similar family background as ours. They were so young, but they declared their undying love for one another and wanted to be married.

Both families met and agreed to this. So there was another wedding in our family on November 8, 1968, at Faith Lutheran Church. David did have to give up college for a while. Bill was instrumental in getting David a job on the assembly line at the Ford Sterling plant. Now we had three son-in-laws working for Ford Motor Company. David was ambitious and a hard worker and took advantage of classes to advance himself. A few years later, he had an opportunity for an advancement at the Ford Batavia plant in Ohio, and they moved down there. Alice and David divorced later, but David is still working at the Batavia plant and met his second wife there. Bill and I have two beautiful grandchildren from Alice and David's marriage.

Back at the "ranch." There we are in our four-bedroom, much larger home, and our girls were all getting married and leaving. Our other twin daughter Barbara was still with us. Again, she was not interested in college. She started as a switchboard operator at Audette Pontiac in the Troy Motor Mall on Maple Road while on a co-op program at high school. While there, she met her husband-to-be, Kenneth Vogt, who was working in the service department.

And heavens, his dad worked for General Motors Company! "Traitors" in our Ford family! We had so many laughs about that in all of our family parties and get-togethers. To this day, Ken is still working for Audette Cadillac. Ken was in the service and was sent over to Vietnam for over a year in the payroll department. Barb moved on, after graduation from Troy High School, to work for Schmidt and Smith, a rep company. They liked her and were very good to her. Again, she did not want college; she loved the jobs she was doing in the business world. All of our girls were dedicated, hard workers. We were very proud of all of them. Barb and Ken were married soon after he returned from Vietnam on June 27, 1970. They were married in the Methodist Church on Adams Road, with a reception at a hall. I've forgotten the name of it which was on Utica Road in Sterling Heights. It was another very lovely wedding. At this wedding Billy was five years old and a ring bearer in the wedding party. Barb said Ken had very bad nightmares for a long time with the things he had seen and been through in Vietnam. The veterans of that war have never received the recognition that they deserve. Of course, that's just my opinion.

Now here we are, Bill and I, alone in a big house with a spoilt five-year-old son. Bill Jr. (Billy) missed the attention of his sisters being at home with him. We all survived, but here we are with a GM car in our driveway along with all the Ford cars when Barb and Ken were over. Strange! Billy started Troy Union School, and I became active as a volunteer at the school. I was also taking him for swim lessons at the Y in Royal Oak with the three boys across the street from us. We also had our church activities. Bill had been on the Steering Committee at St. Paul's Church in Dearborn to start a mission church in the north area. From that came Faith Lutheran Church in Sterling Heights. Those were busy years too. Kathy and Jim had our first grandson, Scott, in 1968.Alice and David had Kelly in 1969 and David Jr. in 1971. Barb and Ken had Krista in 1972 and Kenny Jr. in 1975. Carol and Edsel had Cindy in 1973 and Erik in 1977. They were seven beautiful healthy grandchildren growing up with their "Uncle Billy" who was just three years older than Scott. He was just "Billy" to them. Only when they were older did they jokingly call him "uncle." Over those years, Bill's three brothers and one sister were married and starting their families also. Our parents were growing older with health problems. We lost Bill's dad in 1976 from heart and prostate problems. That hit all of us very hard. Then we lost our uncle Bill to heart problems. Bill's mother seemed to go downhill from that time until we lost her also in 1980. We were learning that life could hand you some very rough knocks. Bill as the eldest sibling in his family was always looked up to, to take over and make family decisions and take care of family business. His brothers and sister trusted him. He always lived up to their trust. Over all these years, we have always had a great family relationship, for which all of us are grateful. I also had a few health problems—gall bladder operation in 1972 and spastic angina problems with two heart catheterizations in 1975 and 1981 so that I was in the hospital for a few times. I had a periodontal surgery and a kidney cath when my potassium was mixed up. Then just last year, I had a hip replacement. But here I am at eighty-one, living and experiencing Ford's hundredth anniversary, and Bill at eighty, who was always my "rock of Gibraltar," is gone. Life is very strange at times, but you have to learn to roll with the changes or go completely crazy.

In the 1970s, when most people our age were traveling after raising their families, Bill and I were raising a son and loving it. As I mentioned before, he kept us young. Instead of traveling around to see the world, we planned two—and three-week trips in the summers when school was out to Lauderdale-by-the-Sea and stayed at the Kon Tiki Motel right on the ocean. Barb and Ken had gone there (compliments of Joe Schmidt) for their honeymoon and told us how very nice it was. We did that for eight or nine years while Billy was growing up. The three of us loved it. We took day trips around to do sightseeing and of course saw most of the Florida attractions: Disney World, Busch Gardens, Cypress Gardens, etc. Billy got in all the swimming he loved, both ocean and pool. Every year we met nice people and relaxed and enjoyed our vacations.

In February 1982, Bill and I had our first "alone" vacation. We took a two-week Caribbean cruise on the *Nordic Prince.* It was a fortieth anniversary present for us. Our families had a wonderful party for us on our anniversary in August 1981. We both loved the cruise so much we really didn't want to get off the ship. We had trusted our sixteen-year-old son to stay alone for the first time with his sisters checking on him. It worked out well!

Again, I backtrack. In 1978, I was getting a little bored. I wasn't as active in the schools and had time on my hands. I answered an ad for Christmas help at Dalton's bookstore in Oakland Mall. I did not tell anyone I was going to do that. I've always been a bookworm and loved books and been around them for as long as I can remember. I did it as a dare to myself. They hired me immediately! What an ego boost for me! I only worked three days a week, six hours a day, which was perfect for me. I was home shortly after our son came home from school; again, that was what I wanted. I loved that little job. I was a cashier most of the time, but I also learned a lot about the book and publishing business. I've always said that I would have almost paid them to let me work there. I was there for eight years until arthritis in my knees got so bad it was painful to do the bending needed for restocking and reaching under the tables, etc. I was sixty-five, and it was time for a change.

During those years, our son graduated from Athens High School in June 1983. We celebrated with a big family get-together and picnic in our backyard. That summer we lost our beloved Dalmatian, "Daffy," who was sixteen years old and had grown up with our son and grandchildren. That too was hard on all of us. Animals do become a part of your family. In September 1983, we took Bill Jr. up to Lake Superior State to start college. After some forty-three years, Bill and I were alone in our house. It was a very strange feeling, *but* we enjoyed it!

In February 1984, Bill retired from Ford Motor Company after forty-five years with the company. He felt it was the right time, but as he had always liked his job so well, it was a little difficult to say good-bye. His fellow workers had a wonderful retirement party for Bill at The Monte Carlo Club on Van Dyke Road in Utica. I'm not sure if it's still there or not. A lot of his coworkers, family, and friends were there. Our daughters and son had worked out a little skit that they did for everyone, telling what growing up with their dad had been like. It got a lot of laughs. Some of his coworkers did a little "roast" too. Everyone seemed to have a good time. There are more wonderful memories.

But now what? I was a little concerned and wondering what Bill was going to do and how this retirement would affect him. I still had my little job at Dalton's, which Bill encouraged me to keep as he knew I loved it. I should have known better and not been worried at all as it wasn't very long and Bill was busier than ever. Bill was invited to join "The Squires," a men's group that did volunteer work at Meadow Brook Hall in Rochester. He loved it whether he was repairing and regluing stair treads, painting at Knoll Cottage, or dressed up and helping the Docents show visitors through the mansion. He helped in the Christmas walk every year and the Classic Concours every August. He was a volunteer for fourteen years and was very well liked. The Squires invited their wives to a lot of nice events too. Bill was also asked by Gene Jenson, who was a rep that worked for Tawas Plating Company, to help him out as Gene was having some health problems. Gene had been one of the reps who had called on Bill when he was working at Ford. Bill was familiar with Tawas Plating Company and had met Harold Knight, its owner. He liked their work. Bill decided to give it a try. Again, he loved the work, *and* he was back to calling on the people he knew at Ford Motor Company and other companies too—keeping his fingers in the automotive pie, so to speak. Gene in a few years turned everything over to Bill as he moved out to California for his health. Bill kept that rep job too until we moved to Henry Ford Village in 1998, plus Bill had always enjoyed woodworking as a hobby. He had different equipment in our basement and garage. He was always making bookcases for my book collections, end tables for the girls, a big cart to lug things for Barb and Ken at their cottage, and frames for my paintings when I got into artwork. He also made a lot of easy-to-carry very handy footstools that I did paintings on for all of our families. Ha! And I had worried about him keeping busy and being happy when he retired from Ford! That old saying" when one door closes, another opens" certainly seemed to apply.

Meanwhile, it took us a couple of years to wake up to the fact that our son going to Lake Superior State kept changing his majors and was really not getting anywhere, *except* learning to make beer, party, ski, snowboard, rock climb, etc. So it was time for some serious talking. We were not going to continue to pay for that. It ended up that our son came back home to live; he got a job at Eddie Bauers at Lakeside Mall and transferred to Walsh College at the Troy Campus. It took a few years, but he did earn his degree in business administration. *Whew*!

Also while Bill Jr. was living at home again, he talked us into getting another dog. In 1991, we got an eight-week-old female black Lab puppy from a breeder in Flint. We named her "Katy;" of course we all fell in love with her.

During those years when I quit my job in 1986 at the bookstore, I started taking art classes through adult education at Niles School on Square Lake Road in Troy, about a mile from our house. I started out with "drawing on the right side of the brain" and went on to a colored pencil class, both taught by Joan Cox. I found out that I had a little talent and I loved it. From there, I continued with watercolor classes taught by both Joan Cox and Jo Chiapelli. They were both excellent teachers and I learned so much. My family liked my work and were very proud of what I was doing. It was back then that I started making our Christmas cards from one of my paintings. Now it's a tradition. I do wonder how long I can keep it up. Every year it seems to be more work. Of course, my card list keeps growing too, as more and more people want my cards. That is a terrific ego boost for me though, and I'm grateful. This past year I sent 120 cards. That's a lot of gluing and addressing. Some people have told me that they keep every one of my cards, and quite a few have told me they frame them. It's comments like those that keep me going. Also, it's so nice to go to my families' homes and see my paintings on their walls. It's another boost for my ego.

During those years after Bill retired, we traveled more and had some beautiful trips. We had a three-week trip where we went East and covered a lot of history—Liberty Bell, Independence Hall, Boston, Paul Revere's Ride, Boston Tea Party. We visited New York and got caught in a hurricane going to Hartford, Connecticut. Bill had his fill of lobsters in Maine. We had tea at Waldon Pond in Acadia National Park and enjoyed the spectacular fall colors driving through Vermont, etc. We went on another trip for six weeks and drove all over the southern route to California and back the northern route. We saw so many things and so many national parks. I wrote a whole notebook about it, plus made two big picture albums of things we had seen and enjoyed. It was a fantastic trip, and we both enjoyed every minute of it. Except in San Diego, Bill had Montasuma's revenge. Thank goodness it did not last long. Everything else was fabulous. Another time we went to New Orleans, and that area of the south was wonderful. That year we had two spring seasons—one down south and one when we got home. Fun! It was during that trip that we visited Bill's brother Joseph, who had worked for Detroit Edison. He had retired and built a lovely home in Leesburg, Florida. It was a beautiful place. We came home through Ashville, North Carolina, and visited the Rockefeller Estate. Bill was so interested in the manor homes of the wealthy people after learning so much about Meadow Brook Hall and the Dodge Estate. We both liked Meadow Brook so much better.

In June 1990, we lost my mother. We had just celebrated her ninety-first birthday and Mother's Day with her. She died in her sleep. It was a shock, but what a blessing. She had not been really well since she had had the shingles a few years ago. It's quite a mortality check when you lose your last parent and realize you are now the oldest in the next generation.

In March 1993, Bill had his first knee replacement by Dr. Jeffery Declare at Crittenton Hospital in Rochester. He had been having problems for quite awhile, but he put off doing anything until it was necessary because of the pain. It was successful as Bill was very faithful with his therapy. That same year in August, Bill Jr., who was not having any luck getting the type of job he wanted in our area, decided to move out to Denver, Colorado. He had a good friend from high school who had moved out there and was buying a condo. Bill Jr. had been out there to visit him, as they were both skiers who changed over to snowboarders. They loved the area. His friend convinced Bill Jr. to move out there, share expenses with the condo, and look for work. Bill Jr. loaded his Explorer and followed. "Go West, young Man, go West." There were more changes in our lives.

In September of that same year, Bill had his other knee done by the same doctor. Again, it was successful. But just because I'm not going into details here does not say it is an easy thing to go through. Remember, Bill was still doing his volunteer work while keeping up with his rep job and still doing woodworking, needlepoint, etc. We also, with Kathy and Jim pushing us, got a computer. They got and installed it for us, and Kathy was giving her dad lessons. They thought, and they were right, that with their dad's operations and not being able to be as physically active, a computer would also help him stay busy. We both loved the e-mail part of it. Bill enjoyed some of the card games, and I learned to do my writing on it. As you can see, I'm still doing it. But, oh, how I need my Kathy back to give me more lessons. I didn't pay enough attention back then. Of course, I need her back too just to fill the hole in my heart. During those same years, Bill took up needlepoint too. He said, "If your mother and Aunt Fran can do it, I can too." He bought a small kit of a Cardinal from Frank's and taught himself. He liked it, so he decided to take lessons at Jacobson's Birmingham store. He did beautiful work and learned a lot of different stitches, using different threads. All of our family have pieces of his work and beautiful Christmas stockings.

Looking back though, I can see that's when our lives started to slide downhill with more health and family problems. In July 1994, our daughter Kathy was diagnosed with incurable cancer. They could not find the original source and treated her for ovarian cancer. That shook our world. It's very difficult to put into words what a parent feels when one of your children receives that kind of diagnosis. Your heart aches beyond comprehension. Kathy and Jim had such a great marriage and were still working on their remodeling of the old farmhouse they had bought in Milford years before. Kathy was so active with helping Jim with their projects. She had got her builder's license. She was on the Zoning Board and the Cable Board in the city of Milford. She was a beautiful seamstress. She could do anything she put her mind to. She was *loved*. She put up a fight for six years and went through some terrible treatments. She amazed her doctors and everyone. We had a wonderful Christmas Day at Kathy and Jim's in 1999. She wanted everyone to come there and was doing very well. Grandchildren from all over came home, also Bill Jr. and his wife Shannon from Colorado. Our family was together for a holiday none of us still here will ever forget. It was bittersweet for me. I had a "gut" feeling things were going to change. Right after Christmas that year, Bill's sister, Marguerette, lost her husband to lung cancer. We were able to make it to the funeral, but Bill was "yellow" with jaundice and back in the hospital a few days later. We lost Bill in April

2000 and seven weeks later our Kathy. Mere words cannot describe the heartache.

Again, I have to backtrack. During the middle and late 1990s, we were having to hire out more and more work as neither Bill nor I were not able to do what we had always done—window washing, gutters cleaned out, yard work, and just general housekeeping, etc. That's when we started thinking about moving to a retirement home. Henry Ford Village opened in 1993. We were not ready then, but kept our eyes and ears open. In February 1996, Bill had a Turps operation for prostate cancer by Dr. Robert Badalament. It was successful but took its toll on Bill's health and energy.

In January 1997, we lost our son-in-law Edsel to suicide. It's hard to even write about the pain of that. Edsel was such a loving and caring person. He was "son" to Bill and me. He had a good marriage and two children of whom he was very proud. Cindy had graduated from Central Michigan and was working in the social work field. Erik was in the criminal justice program at Ferris State. *But* Edsel had diabetes and had had a small stroke the summer before. He had not really been his "old" self since then. All of us truly believe that he had another stroke and could not face life and the fact that he might be an invalid, especially after just having taken care of his mother and watching her slow death with dementia. Edsel was also looking at early retirement as he had almost thirty years with Ford. We also think that was affecting him too. No one really knows. All we know is the fact that it was not our Edsel that we knew and loved. Something drastic happened to him that caused him to do that.

Then one month later in February, we lost out wonderful Aunt Fran. She was ninety-six. Up until two weeks before she died, she was doing quite well. We could all rationalize her death, but it still was a big loss in our lives.

In the spring of 1997, Bill had his right hip replaced by Dr. Lawrence Ulrey at Troy Beaumont Hospital. It was again successful, but took a toll on both of us. Bill during that same spring and fall also had Carpal Tunnel operations on first his right hand and then his left. We were calling him "the bionic man." That summer we decided that *now* was the time to make our move. We visited Henry Ford Village and liked what we saw. Bill knew several people he had worked with over the years who lived there and liked it. Quite a few were Ford retirees. We did visit some other places, but there was nothing compared to the Village. Our family was delighted with our decision as they had been concerned about all of our increasing health problems. All of them helped us in all different ways to get ready and move. Our son-in-law Jim was our organizer and getting things sorted. Everyone helped with a garage and estate sale. It was a difficult decision as we both hated the idea of leaving our beautiful home and neighborhood. We also knew it was a very wise one. We were learning that we had to accept change in our lives and to bend with it.

We were a little surprised though that it took awhile for our house to sell. The real estate people explained that it really was the wrong time of year for a big family house to go on the market (September). They told us that families looking for homes make their decisions by September as their children are back in school already. Anyway a couple with college-aged children did buy it in December and were thrilled with it. We moved to Henry Ford Village on January 21, 1998. It was a very wise decision. We both felt like we had come "full circle" to be back in Dearborn again. A few days before we moved, Barb and Ken took our beloved Lab "Katy" to the airport, and she was shipped out to Bill Jr. in Colorado. It was difficult to give her up, but we knew we could not handle her in a third-floor apartment. It would not be fair to her either. We were both happy there and loved our corner apartment with all the windows and light. Bill got involved immediately. He started helping at Happy Hours on Fridays as bartender. We were getting acquainted and joined a "lunch bunch" which went to different restaurants on the third Wednesday of the month. Our group has changed a lot over the years, as we have lost a lot of original members, but I am still going with them. I also got involved in the Birthday Angel Committee, Library Committee, and then the Entertainment Committee; Bill was playing pool with a group of different men and playing in their tournaments. Our lives were busy and full. Just before the first Christmas we were there in 1998, we lost my sister, Evelyn, who had had a lot of different health problems. That left Bill's brother Roy by himself. Of course, our Kathy's treatments and her ups and downs were a major worry for us. Then in April 1999, Bill was not feeling well. He collapsed and was rushed to Oakwood Heritage Hospital for treatment. He was treated for what they thought was a liver abscess. He also had a Turps repair operation in May. Our lives were a series of doctor visits.

That same spring, our son was planning his wedding with Shannon for June 7. Bill Jr. had brought her to Troy for the family to meet her in the summer of 1997, *but* he also told us it wasn't serious. Ha! All of us really liked Shannon and thought she was a very good influence on Bill and hoped something would come of it. We were all happy about them getting married. Bill Jr. had told us that if we couldn't make it out there, he was not getting married. I'm not quite sure I believe that, but I do know it was important to him, for us, to be there. We did make it, and it was a beautiful wedding. I wrote about it another time, and it is in my papers. Our Kathy and Jim did not make it. They had planned to, but she was not up to it at the last minute and was in the hospital for more treatments. It was a *big* disappointment for all of us. Carol, Alice, Barbara, and Ken were there along with Erik, Cindy, Kelly, Steve, Davey, and Kenny. It was a beautiful time, even though we were all worried about Kathy, and Bill was not up to doing a lot. Bill Jr. was very happy to have most of his family there. All of us loved Shannon and were happy for both of them.

That summer, there were a lot of doctor's appointments for Bill. His liver enzymes were high and the doctors did not like that. There were a lot of different tests. It was hard on both of us. In my heart and soul, I knew something was not right and I was scared both for Bill and our Kathy, and selfishly me.

On November 15, 1999, Bill was operated upon for diseased gall bladder by Dr. Charles Lucas at Harper Hospital. They said they did not find any *cancer*. We were elated! Carol, Erik, Cindy, Barb, Ken, Jim, Kathy, and Scott brought Thanksgiving dinner to our apartment that Thanksgiving. It was a nice family day, but Bill was not able to eat very much and was admitted back into the hospital for dehydration on November 28 and on January 3, for jaundice and blocked liver duct. They put in a port. That same time, our Kathy had a stroke that affected her speech and she was in therapy. Life was getting hard to handle with my constant worry about Kathy and Bill. In February, Bill went for a chelangiogram at Harper. Still they did not come up with why he was having so much trouble and not recuperating like he should have.

Valentine's Day that year was a good one. Bill had an appointment to see Dr. Atallah and got a good checkup on his heart along with encouraging words. Valentine's Day had always been a very special day for us since that was the day Bill had asked me to marry him way back in 1941. We went to Main Street Restaurant in Rochester for a lovely lunch. We even split a Turtle Sundae to celebrate, but things did not get better. On March 16, Bill was back at Harper for a liver biopsy test when he had a very bad reaction and was kept in the hospital. On March 27, I wrote a letter to Dr. Lucas and his partner Dr. Anna Ledgerwood, with Bill's complete knowledge, asking them to please tell us the truth about what was going on. Dr. Ledgerwood came in and talked to both of us, and she said she was sure it was cancer of the bile duct and there was nothing more they could do. She suggested hospice. Bill looked at me and said, "I told you so." *We* had both known it but did not want to acknowledge the fact. Bill had been watching the clock for his pain meds as he was in a lot of *pain*. Dr. Lucas did not see Bill again. We heard he had wanted to try more unpleasant tests and treatments and did not agree that it was cancer. We suspect he just could not acknowledge what was happening. Who knows? But it hurt as both Bill and I had liked him. Carol, Barbara, and Alice were all with Bill and me when we met Dr. John Finn from hospice. He was so understanding and helpful. Bill told him, "There is nothing to be afraid of."

Because Carol, bless her heart, put her own life on hold, we were able to bring Bill home with the help of the wonderful hospice program on April 1. Carol moved in with me and helped me care for Bill. Barbara was here almost every day. Alice came too and Jim and Kathy one day, and the next day Kathy was back in the hospital. Bill and Shannon came. Bill's brothers, Joe and Char, Roy, and sister Margurette, Robert and Flora came too. Ken, Erik, and Cindy were here a lot too. Bill kept up his good spirits, telling me he loved me, demanding orange juice when we weren't fast enough, wriggling his toes at us when we had thought he was sleeping. Hospice kept him free from pain, and we were so very grateful. He was slipping into a coma, but he knew when Billy got here, and Billy sat up with him the whole night just talking to him and holding his hand. We lost him at noon on Friday, April 14. The whole family was around him. He was surrounded by love. That was one of the hardest things I have ever done in my life, but I would do it again in a minute. If death is a part of life, then this is the way to go—at home, with all your family around you. I can't tell you how grateful we are to the hospice program for allowing families to do this.

The next few days are sort of a blur. I know we went to Howe Peterson Funeral Home and made arrangements and also made arrangements with the Village to have the service in the chapel and catering here for a luncheon afterwards. Everyone told me it worked out well, and I remember more than I think I do. Thank goodness for my wonderful family! Our Kathy was in Henry Ford Hospital through all of this, and of course, Jim was with her as he should be. The Reverend Felix Lorenz whom Bill had met through hymn singing and who had called on Bill in the hospital and here at home gave the service. He was so helpful and has been ever since. Mona played the organ, and Erik played "Harlem Nocturne" on his sax. The Village put on a very nice luncheon, but I couldn't tell you what we had to eat. Then the immediate family went to the cemetery for the burial service. I remember the sun was shining, but there was a very cold wind. I was cold inside and out.

Then Kathy came home from the hospital also with hospice. Kathy did not give up; she kept saying she was going to beat it (cancer). But we lost her on June 8, seven weeks after her dad. It was a very difficult time for all of us. It's hard to write about as it brings back so many memories. Time does have a way of dulling the pain and loss, *but* I don't think you ever get over it. You just learn to adjust and try your best to live with it "one day at a time." Then was another blow to our family. At the very same time that our country was hit with that terrible September 11 attack, our Barbara was diagnosed with inflammatory breast cancer. The following year was "brutal" for her. First she had chemo, then radiation, then mastectomy, then more chemo. As I am writing this, our Barbara is cancer free, and we are so very grateful. Barb's husband Ken and her sisters were with her every step of the way. Cancer is not easy on anyone. It's a long hard road for everyone. There is so much of it around today. I wonder what we as a society are doing wrong. I can't rave enough about the staff here at the Village. I can't think of a better place to be when you lose your partner and a daughter and then have another daughter ill. The help and support they provide at times like that is exceptional. I consider so many of them my "friends." I get nice hugs when we pass in the hallways. Sandra and Myra gently pushed me into starting a watercolor class, and I have found it has helped me too. Then there are Leslie's mental wellness classes, Kristine's grief support classes, Cheryl Price's cancer support group, Sister Mary, lunches, talks, "Age-ing to Sage-ing" classes, Cheryl Presley's and Kelly's friendship. Diane and Shannon at the front desk, the service people, the security people, too numerous to name, Dr. Merritt and staff, I could go on and on. I find I am doing things I never thought I could do, for instance, introducing groups using the microphone for the Sunday Entertainment Committee, being on the nominating committee for the Resident's Council, helping at the Annual Expo and Art Fair, leading a class in water color, plus my regular committees. I also made it through hip replacement surgery on November 29, 2002, with Carol again putting her life on hold and moving in to care for me.

Now here I am three years after losing Bill and our Kathy, which surprises even me. I didn't think I could go on with such large holes in my heart. The arthritis in my knees and lower back is getting worse, and to be honest, it is "scary" what old age does to your body. They are celebrating the Ford Motor Company's hundredth anniversary. I'm eighty-one and they are hundred. My whole life has revolved around them, the automotive world, and my family. Now living at Henry Ford Village, it brings it even closer. We have Henry Ford's Memorial Garden across from the gatehouse at the entranceway. We celebrate his birthday every year in July. The grounds and Village have displays for the anniversary. They have some of my mementos, one of Bill's badges, a salaried pass, deck of cards picturing the Sterling Plant, seventy-fifth anniversary magnet, Henry Ford stamped envelope, along with other people's mementos, in a locked glass case in our rotunda area. There are lots of great pictures What a wonderful display! I have been reading most of the articles in the newspapers (and saving the ones that appealed to me), listening to programs on TV about the Ford legacy, hearing Douglas Brinkley on his new book *Wheels* about Ford Motor Company on the CNN Bookspan channel. Very interesting! Then the following week his dad, David Brinkley, died, a man who so many of us felt that we knew from listening to him over the years. I made a special trip over to Fairlane to pick up my ticket for the Centennial. I wanted to have it, along with the commemorative coin. Our weather this spring has not been the most cooperative, and on the first day of the celebration it was pouring rain. The Model T's that had traveled cross country for this event arrived in a pouring rainstorm. Friday night's program and fireworks show was postponed until Sunday because of wet grounds. Then the sun came out, and the rest of the celebration had beautiful weather. I heard a lot of good reports about it. I did not try to go as I was leery about all the walking involved and also the heat. I can't do the simple things I never even thought about before.

I did thoroughly enjoy reading about it and listening to the special programs, *and* I had a front row seat for the fireworks show on Sunday evening. They were *spectacular!* I felt like they were right in my backyard.

They were so very beautiful, and it was a twenty-five minute show. I don't even remember the last time I have been that close to a fireworks display. I watched them in awe and in comfort in my nightie and robe from my dining room window.

I couldn't help but think about how much Bill would have enjoyed all of this. He would have been right there to take in everything. He also would have been so pleased that Ford Motor Company was back with the Ford family in charge. He had met Henry Ford back in his tool room days, also over the years Henry Ford II. He cared about the company and felt a part of it. He did not like Jacques Nassar being in charge and the changes he was making. He would be so happy about Bill Jr. taking over. I also feel like Ford is still a part of my life. They give me a pension every month. I drive one of their Crown Vic, which I love. I'm grateful. I wish them the very best in this next hundred years.

June 20, 2003

THE FAMILY CIRCUS

"Grandma remembers things I never heard of."

6-24

roit News, 615 W. Lafayette Blvd., Detroit, MI 48226.

It was this little article that got me started to write Memories 100 years & me

History

Help us celebrate Ford's 100th

The Detroit News invites you to help us honor Ford Motor Co.'s centennial. Tell us your tales about this icon of American industry and the family that helped make Detroit into Motown. Maybe you worked on the assembly line or toiled in an office at Ford headquarters. Perhaps you grew up in the shadow of the Rouge plant or toured the famous factory as a child. To share your stories, as well as photos, documents — any Ford memorabilia — write to us at Ford 100, The Detroit News, 615 W. Lafayette Blvd., Detroit, MI 48226; e-mail fordmemories@detnews.com or visit our Web site at www.detnews.com/history.

— Compiled from Detroit News staff and wire reports

The Ford Model T

A Short History of Ford's Innovation

Henry Ford did not invent the automobile or the assembly line. He did, however, change the world by using an assembly line technique to produce cars which could be afforded by everyone. From 1909 to 1927, the Ford Motor Company built more than fifteen million Model T cars. Without a doubt, Henry Ford transformed die economic and social fabric of die twentieth century.

While Henry Ford and his team were planning for his new car, he attended a race in Florida where he examined the wreckage of a French race car. He observed that it was made from a different type of steel and the car parts were lighter than those he had previously seen. He learned that this new steel was a vanadium alloy and that it had almost three times the tensile strength of the alloys used by contemporary American auto makers. No one in America knew how to make vanadium steel, so Ford financed and set up a steel mill. As a result, the only cars in the world to utilize vanadium steel over the next five years would be French luxury cars and the Ford Model T. Ford's use of vanadium steel explains why so many Model T Fords have survived today.

Ford is often quoted as saying, "I will build a motorcar for the great multitude." At the time, it was a revolutionary business model to lower a product's cost and the company's profit margin in exchange for increased sales volume. Up until this point in time, the automobile had been a status symbol and cars were painstakingly built by hand for the wealthy. By the end of 1913, Ford's application of the moving assembly line had improved the speed of chassis assembly from twelve hours and eight minutes to one hour and thirty-three minutes. In 1914, Ford produced 308,162 cars, which was more than all 299 other auto manufacturers combined. By the time the last Model T was built in 1927, the company was producing an automobile every twenty-four seconds.

In 1906, Ford secretly set up a place to build his cars in a building on Piquette Avenue in Detroit. Ford spent nearly two years designing the Model T, building on knowledge gained from the production of earlier cars, like his Ford Model N.

Henry's car changed the world forever. In 1909, for $825, a Model T customer could buy a reliable automobile that was fairly easy to drive. Ford sold over ten thousand Model T cars in the first year of production, a new record for any automobile model.

Ford applied the moving assembly line concept to his production facility late in 1913. His staff constantly monitored production and relentlessly analyzed the statistical measures to optimize worker productivity. Over the years, Model T Fords came in many different models, all built with the essentially same engine and chassis: the Model T Roadster, coupe, coupelet, runabout, roadster torpedo, town car, touring, and the four door and two door sedans.

No one really knows if Henry Ford ever said that the buying public could have Model T Fords "in any color, so long as it's black," but it is commonly attributed to him. While this saying is true for the model years after 1913, earlier cars were available in green, red, blue, and gray. In fact, in the first year, Model T Fords were not available in black at all.

The switch to black cars was likely due to Ford's optimization of the assembly line and to reduce the time lost in waiting for the various paints to dry. In 1926, in an attempt to boost sales, colors other than black were once again offered.

The first production Model T Ford (1909 model year) was assembled at the Piquette Avenue Plant in Detroit on October 1, 1908. Over the next nineteen years, relatively few changes were made to the basic design. By

1926, the design was so antiquated that the cars could not compete with more modern designs from companies like Chevrolet. The year 1927 was the last year for Henry's lady, the "Universal Car."

Ford women pulled strings.

Henry's Wife, Clara, and Edsel's Wife, Eleanor, Used Clout
Anita Lienert, Special to *The Detroit News*

> Clara Bryant Ford, the wife of auto pioneer Henry Ford, was so wrapped up in her home and garden that the plain-spoken Michigan farmer's daughter said she used a seed catalog for a pillow.

> Her daughter-in-law, the more glamorous Eleanor Clay Ford, wife of son Edsel, was the niece of department store owner J.L. Hudson and a Grosse Pointe matron known for her signature pearl chokers and her love of modern art and French furniture.

> The pair emerged from the shadows of domestic and society life at crucial moments in the history of Ford Motor Co. From the board room to the assembly line, their influence would be felt for generations.

> Contemporary female descendants of Henry Ford—hampered by decades of unfulfilled potential—are still struggling to have a similar impact on the workings of the global automaker.

> It was Clara, known as "Callie," who, in 1941, begged her virulently anti-union husband to sign what she called called a "peace agreement" between organized labor and management.

> "I felt her vision and judgment were better than mine," Ford said later, according to the book "The Fords: An American Epic," by Peter Collier and David Horowitz. "I'm glad I did see it her way. Don't ever discredit the power of a woman."

In September 1945, Eleanor, by then Edsel Ford's widow, joined forces with Clara in a move that would literally save the then faltering family business.

The two typically deferential women gave the now senile elder Ford an ultimatum: Make Eleanor's son, 28-year-old Henry II, president of the company or Eleanor would sell her 41.6 percent share of the family stock. Henry Ford complied.

There is little hard evidence of one last sign of Clara's influence, but its truth doesn't seem far-fetched.

Clara loved the color blue and planted acres of blue scilla at her Fair Lane home. It is said that Henry ordered that his company's blue oval logo—which exists to this day—match Clara's favorite shade.

He Said It

Here are a few notable quotes from Henry Ford himself:

- Nothing is particularly hard if you divide it into small jobs.
- Anyone who stops learning is old, whether at twenty or eighty. Anyone who keeps learning stays young. The greatest thing in life is to keep your mind young.
- If money is your hope for independence you will never have it. The only real security that a man will have in this world is a reserve of knowledge, experience, and ability.
- My best friend is the one who brings out the best in me.
- Obstacles are those frightful things you see when you take your eyes off your goal.
- A bore is someone who opens his mouth and puts his feats in it.
- You can do anything if you have enthusiasm. Enthusiasm is the yeast that makes your hopes rise to the stars.
- The best we can do it size up the chances, calculate the risks involved, estimate our ability to deal with them, and then make our plans with confidence.
- A market is never saturated with a good product, but it is very quickly saturated with a bad one.

- Coming together is a beginning, staying together is progress, and working together is success.

Henry Ford Big Wheels Turning

Lee Iacocca

The only time I ever met Henry Ford, he looked at me and probably wondered, "Who is this little s.o.b. fresh out of college?" He wasn't real big on college graduates, and I was one of 50 in the Ford training course in September 1946, working in a huge drafting room at the enormous River Rouge plant near Detroit. One day there was a big commotion at one end of the floor and in walked Henry Ford with Charles Lindbergh. They walked down my aisle asking men what they were doing. I was working on a mechanical drawing of a clutch spring (which drove me out of engineering forever), and I was worried that they'd ask me a question because I didn't know what the hell I was doing—I'd been there only 30 days. I was just awestruck by the fact that there was Colonel Lindbergh with my new boss coming to shake my hand.

The boss was a genius. He was an eccentric. He was no prince in his social attitudes and his politics. But Henry Ford's mark in history is almost unbelievable. In 1905, when there were 50 startup companies a year trying to get into the auto business, his backers at the new Ford Motor Co. were insisting that the best way to maximize profits was to build a car for the rich.

But Ford was from modest, agrarian Michigan roots. And he thought that the guys who made the cars ought to be able to afford one themselves so that they too could go for a spin on a Sunday afternoon. In typical fashion, instead of listening to his backers, Ford eventually bought them out.

And that proved to be only the first smart move in a crusade that would make him the father of 20th century American industry. When the black Model T rolled out in 1908, it was hailed as America's Everyman car—elegant in its simplicity and a dream machine not just for engineers but for marketing men as well.

Ford instituted industrial mass production, but what really mattered to him was mass consumption. He figured that if he paid his factory workers a real living wage and produced more cars in less time for less money, everyone would buy them.

Almost half a century before Ray Kroc sold a single McDonald's hamburger, Ford invented the dealer-franchise system to sell and service cars. In the same way that all politics is local, he knew that business had to be local. Ford's "road men" became a familiar part of the American landscape. By 1912 there were 7,000 Ford dealers across the country.

In much the same fashion, he worked on making sure that an automotive infrastructure developed along with the cars. Just like horses, cars had to be fed—so Ford pushed for gas stations everywhere. And as his tin lizzies bounced over the rutted tracks of the horse age, he campaigned for better roads, which eventually led to an interstate-highway system that is still the envy of the world.

His vision would help create a middle class in the U.S., one marked by urbanization, rising wages and some free time in which to spend them. When Ford left the family farm at age 16 and walked eight miles to his first job in a Detroit machine shop, only 2 out of 8 Americans lived in the cities, By World War II that figure would double, and the affordable Model T was one reason for it. People flocked to Detroit for jobs, and if they worked in one of Henry's factories, they could afford one of his cars—it's a virtuous circle, and he was the ringmaster. By the time production ceased for the Model T in 1927, more that 15 million cars had been sold—or half the world's output.

Nobody was more of an inspiration to Ford than the great inventor Thomas Alva Edison. At the turn of the century Edison had blessed Ford's pursuit of an efficient, gas powered car during a chance meeting at Detroit's Edison Illuminating Co., where Ford was chief engineer. (Ford has already worked for the company of Edison's fierce rival, George Westinghouse.)

After the Model T's enormous success, the two visionaries from rural Michigan became friend and business partners. Ford asked Edison to develop an electric storage battery for the car and funded the effort with $1.5 million. Ironically, despite all his other great inventions, Edison never perfected the storage battery. Yet Ford immortalized his mentor's inventive genius by building the Edison Institute in Dearborn.

Ford's great strength was the manufacturing process—not invention. Long before he started a car company, he was an inveterate tinkerer, known for picking up loose scraps of metal and wire and turning them in to machines.

He'd been putting cars together since 1891. Although by no means the first popular automobile, the Model T showed the world just how innovative Ford was at combining technology and markets.

The company's assembly line alone threw America's Industrial Revolution into overdrive. Instead of having workers put together the entire car, Ford's cronies, who were great tool—and diemakers from Scotland, organized teams that added parts to each Model T as it moved down a line. By the time Ford's sprawling Highland Park plant was humming along in 1914, the world's first automatic conveyor belt could churn out a car every 93 minutes.

The same year, Henry Ford shocked the world with what probably stands as his greatest contribution ever: the $5-a-day minimum-wage scheme. The average wage in the auto industry then was $2.34 for a 9-hr. shift. Ford not only doubled that, he also shaved an hour off the workday. In those years it was unthinkable that a guy could be paid that much for doing something that didn't involve an awful lot of training or education. The Wall Street Journal called the plan "an economic crime," and critics everywhere heaped "Fordism" with equal scorn. But as the wage increased later to a daily $ 10, it proved a critical component of Ford's quest to make the automobile accessible to all. The critics were too stupid to comprehend that because Ford had lowered his costs per car, the higher wages didn't matter—except for making it feasible for more people to buy cars.

When Ford stumbled, it was because he wanted to do everything his way. By the late 1920s the company had become so vertically integrated that it was completely self-sufficient. Ford controlled rubber plantations in Brazil, a fleet of ships, a railroad, 16 coal mines, and thousands of acres of timberland and iron-ore mines in Michigan and Minnesota. All this was combined at the gigantic River Rouge plant, a sprawling city of a place where more than 100,000 men worked.

The problem was that for too long they worked on only one model. Although people told him to diversify, Henry Ford had developed tunnel vision He basically started saying "to hell with the customer," who can have any color as long as it's black. He didn't bring out a new design until the Model A in '27, and by then GM was gaining.

In a sense Henry Ford became a prisoner of his own success. He turned on some of his best and brightest when they launched design changes or plans he had not approved. On one level you have to admire his paternalism. He was so worried that his workers would go crazy with their five bucks a day that he set up a "Sociological Department" to make sure that they didn't blow the money on booze and vice. He banned smoking because he thought, correctly as it turned out, that tobacco was unhealthy. "I want the whole organization dominated by a just, generous and humane policy," he said.

Naturally, Ford, and only Ford, determined that policy. He was violently opposed to labor organizers, whom he saw as "the worst thing that ever struck the earth," and entirely unnecessary—who, after all, know more about taking care of his people than he? Only when he was faced with a general strike in 1941 did he finally agree to let the United Auto Workers organize a plant. By then Alfred P. Sloan had combined various car companies into a powerful General Motors, with a variety of models and prices to suit all tastes. He had also made labor peace. That left Ford in the dust, its management in turmoil, And if World War II hadn't turned the company's manufacturing prowess to the business of making B-24 bombers and jeeps, it is entirely possible that the 1932 V-8 engine might have been Ford's last innovation.

In the prewar years there was no intelligent management at Ford. When I arrived at the end of the war, the company was a monolithic dictatorship. Its balance sheet was still being kept on the back of an envelope, and the guys in purchasing had to weigh the invoices to count them. College kids, managers, anyone with book learning was viewed with some kind of suspicion. Ford had done so many screwy things—from terrorizing his own lieutenants to canonizing Adolf Hitler—that the company's image was as low as it could go.

It was Henry Ford II who rescued the legacy. He played down his grandfather's antics, and he made amends with the Jewish business community that Henry Ford had alienated so much with the racist attacks that are now a matter of historical record. Henry II encourage the "whiz kids" like Robert Mc-Namara and Arjay Miller to modernize management, which put the company back on track. Ford was the first company to get a car out after the war, and it was the only company that had a real base overseas. In fact, one of the reasons that Ford is so competitive today is that from the very beginning, Henry Ford went anywhere there was a road—and usually a river. He took the company to 33 countries at his peak. These days the automobile business is going more global every day, and in that, as he was about so many things, Ford was prescient.

Henry Ford died in his bed at his Fair Lane mansion seven months after I met him, during a black out caused by a storm in the spring of 1947. He was 83. The fact is, there probably couldn't be a Henry Ford in today's world. Business is too collegial. One hundred years ago, business was done by virtual dictators—men laden with riches and so much power they could take over a country if they wanted to. That's not acceptable anymore. But if it hadn't been for Henry Ford's drive to create a mass market for cars, America wouldn't have a middle class today.

?

Edsel B. Ford
Condensed from several articles in 1989, by Edsel owner Ron Osborn
Drawings by Harry Bradley

I have prepared a short story on the life of Edsel Ford. As most of us know, Edsel died in May, 1943, so it seemed fitting to honor the man on the 46th anniversary of his death, whose car and club are named after him.

The story deals with his youth, his fascination with car design and development, his Presidency of Ford Motor Company and his untimely death at age 49. Let me say that finding articles on Edsel Ford was no easy task. Edsel lived in the shadow of his father so much that very little is known about him even today. Even as President of Ford, he made very few major decisions. It was usually Henry that made the final decisions for the Company. However, Edsel enjoyed cars; especially car design. It was his hobby as well as his specialty. Edsel had other hobbies, like photography, fast boats, painting and sports, but cars remained his lifelong favorite.

During his early childhood, Edsel and his father worked side by side on cars. Later on, Edsel became more fascinated by the shapes of automobiles than by their inner workings. As a teenager, he built several speedsters, mostly T-based. Edsel was indulging in a common pastime of the day, one shared by quite a few young men with money, the difference being that Edsel had an unlimited supply of parts. This love of styling and building cars would come in very handy as time went on.

I found a statement by Edsel which was dated in 1922—"Father makes the most popular car in the world. I would like to make the best car in the world—Lincoln." In the late '20s, it was Edsel who guided the styling of the Model A, and gave it the mini-Lincoln look. At the time Henry was too busy straightening out the innards to worry about the A's outlines. He didn't care what the car looked like as long as it did what he wanted it to do, and it was painted black (*REMEMBER?*).

Edsel regularly had cars built for his personal use. Two of his personal favorites were his 1932 and 1934 speedsters. The 1932 was a V-8 Boat-tail speedster, and was built with the help of stylist-designer E.T. Gregorie.

The '32 was a beautiful car with quite a number of radical features for its time. All aluminum body, pantalooned fenders, bullet headlights, no running boards, split windshield and V'd grille shell.

Two years later in 1934, Edsel again called on Gregorie to build him another speedster. It again had an aluminum body, but this model was lower than the '32, and the headlights were mounted at the axle height. There were twin-windscreens, no doors, and the overall effect was that of a pure racing car. Edsel has no intention of producing any of these cars in quantity, and for the most part he kept them out of his father's sight. Seems Edsel kept his speedsters inside a gardener's shed at his home.

Edsel became the guiding light behind Ford's styling section, and as mentioned before, the Lincoln became Edsel's crowning achievement. But he also saw the Zephyr and most other pre-war Fords through their various stages of body design. As one can see, these were very happy times for Edsel. Unfortunately, there would be fewer of these happier times, as the pressures of running the Ford Motor Company, an overly-demanding father, and America's entry into the Second World War would begin to take its toll on Edsel.

After Edsel's death, both speedsters were sold. Where the '32 went is unknown, but the '34 ended up in Florida, and as of 1970, belonged to Earl Pallasch of Deland, Florida.(It was photographed in Amelia Island, Florida in January 1999, and is still in good condition.)

Edsel was twenty-five years of age when he became President of Ford, but the appointment was no more than a cruel hoax. Foxy old Henry had redesigned the Presidency and was making noises about organizing a rival firm to build a better and cheaper car than the Model "T." Henry had no intention of relinquishing control of the Ford Motor Company, nor did he plan to organize another company. He was simply diluting and very effectively the value of Ford's stock, preparing to buy out the small minority stockholders and assume total control. Edsel was being manipulated, and he would be manipulated, harassed, tormented and humiliated all the remaining days of his life.

Once, when all the Ford brass, including Henry, were attending a luncheon, Henry rose from the table and yelled at Edsel to "shut up," and stormed out of the room. Apparently Henry had overheard Edsel remarking that there was some merit in placing hydraulic braking systems on all Ford products, which were being done on virtually all of Ford's competitors. It didn't pay to criticize Ford cars—not in Henry's presence at least—and this included Edsel. One side note on the subject; Edsel's brother-in-law and closest confidant, Ernest Kanzler, had learned that in 1926. Kanzler, a second Vice President at Ford, composed a six-page letter in January of that year, pointing out that Chevrolet sales were rapidly gaining, while Ford's were in sharp decline. Kanzler, while delicately refraining from direct criticism of Henry's beloved Model "T," called for a more competitive six cylinder car. "With every additional car our competitors sell, they get stronger and we get weaker."

It backfired, and Henry was furious. Thereafter, Ernest Kanzler found himself ignored, ridiculed, and victimized in every conceivable way. Ultimately, while Edsel was out of the country, Henry had Kanzler fired.

On one occasion, Edsel had contracted for the construction of a new office building. It seems both Accounting and especially the Sales department had long since outgrown their quarters. Henry was out of town at the time that the plans were made and the contracts let. (One suspects that this may not have been coincidental!) Upon his return, the elder Ford took note of the excavation that was underway and demanded to know what was going on. Edsel, doubtless with a mixture of pride and dread, described the new building which would supply Company with badly needed office space. Henry wanted to know for whom? This should have been Edsel's cue to pitch for the needs of the Sales department—something Henry could understand. Instead, however, the younger Ford mentioned first the accountants. Without waiting to hear another word, Henry turned and marched out of Edsel's office.

The next morning, when the accountants reported for work, they found their offices stripped. No desks, chairs, files or telephones. Even the carpeting was gone, and they were out of a job. Henry had abolished the Accounting department with which he had never had any patience with anyway, and overnight had seen to the removal of its furniture and equipment. He then informed Edsel that there was now plenty of room for the Sales staff. People wondered then, and still wonder, why Edsel put up with such treatment. A few reasons I found were:

☛ Some said it was out of love for his father.

☛ Edsel had three sons. Perhaps he was simply hanging on until the day that they could take over.

☛ Doubtless there was the factor of family loyalty. For Edsel to have left the Company would almost certainly have depressed the value of Ford stock, all of which was held by family members.

☛ Others, more cynical, pointed out that Edsel derived a very handsome income from the Ford Motor Company.

☛ Most importantly, from all the evidence, Edsel Ford was simply not a combative individual. Confrontation and conflict were totally foreign to his nature.

In any event, Edsel mostly kept his torment to himself. Only rarely did he reveal his inner emotions to anyone—some perhaps to his wife Eleanor, and to Ernest Kanzler before he was fired by Henry.

Frustration and suppressed rage make a poor recipe for good health and long life. Not surprisingly, Edsel fell victim to ulcers. In time, the ulcers led to something far worse. Early in 1942, he underwent abdominal surgery. Ten months later, he was hospitalized again, this time for something called Undulant Fever. (My medical book describes this as a persistent form of Brucellosis transmitted to humans from lower domestic animals, or by their by-products, and characterized by a recurrent fever, sweating and pain in the joints.) As part of a bland diet, Edsel had been drinking milk from his father's dairy, and of course old Henry would not permit the testing of his herd, much less the pasteurization of the milk. But the doctors found something far worse than undulant fever, as bad as that was. Edsel's ulcers had become cancerous, and his condition was deemed inoperable. He was sent home to die.

Henry Ford refused to admit the truth about his son's condition. "It was all due to Edsel's high flying lifestyle," he said. "If Edsel would stop smoking or eat a proper diet, or go see other doctors, his health would improve." But early in the morning of May 26th, 1943, death came for Edsel Ford. As I mentioned earlier, he was only 49. This story might have had a different ending if Edsel had been able to stand up to his stubborn father, demanding that he be allowed to run the Company without interference. But Edsel was Edsel, putting the feelings of others before his own.

Edsel did make an impact during his short life, though:

- On his community. For years Edsel Ford was one of the largest donors to the Detroit Community Fund.

- On the Arts. A talented landscape artist in his own right, Edsel served for many years as President of the Detroit Arts Commission.

- On the product line. It was Edsel who influenced his father to take over the bankrupt Lincoln Motor Company, saving one great car from the fate of so many others during the '30s.

- On his family. Edsel was the kind of parent who always was there, sharing the joys and problems of his children. Edsel's final irony was the fact that the car that was intended by his family to do him honor turned out to be a dismal flop.

- And, yes, on his father. In the end, it was Edsel who persuaded the old man to replace the Model "T," to mechanize his windshield wipers, to adopt—finally—hydraulic brakes, to engage in some semblance of long range planning and to make peace with organized labor.

One has to wonder whether Henry Ford ever comprehended what he had done to his only son. It seems unlikely. Certainly he never even began to understand this complex gifted man, nor did he ever really try. Nevertheless, he was grief stricken at Edsel's death. Less than four years after Edsel's death, the old man himself was gone.

In conclusion, I think a statement made in 1970 by Mr. Henry Edmunds, Director of the Ford Archives, pretty well sums things up when he said:

Edsel was responsible for many good things in the Company's history—insistence on verve and dash in product styling, on a reliable and safer product, on fair and courteous relationships with dealers and the public. He possessed an unquenchable sense of fitness, an insistence on doing the right thing. A single instance among many would be his little-known achievement in making Ford Overseas a strong segment in the Ford marketing empire. He did all the essential things that Henry refused to do, and consequently held the Company together during several crisis periods in the 1930s. In true retrospect, he seems less a tragic figure than popularly supposed. Without him, the Company might never have attained the solid image it was today.

Thursday, June 2, 2005

JOSEPHINE FORD

Car dynasty's prankster was

By SHAWN WINDSOR
FREE PRESS STAFF WRITER

The sometime socialite never passed up a chance to pull a prank. She was a member of the Ford dynasty, a benefactor who passed on millions to the arts and charity, and the most private of Henry Ford's four grandchildren.

But Josephine Ford was also known to have engaged in food fights and was particularly fond of flipping pats of butter to the ceiling, according to Ford family biographers.

If she were sitting next to a grandchild at a dinner, say, she would ask him what was in his spaghetti and when he leaned over to look, she would push his face into the plate.

Biographers wrote in "The Fords, An American Epic" that "she was something of a madcap."

Josephine Ford died Wednesday at Henry Ford Hospital of natural causes. She was 81.

"Throughout her life, my aunt embodied the spirit of giving and

| 1923-2005

serious about philanthropy

family loyalty," Bill Ford, chairman and chief executive, wrote in a company-wide e-mail Wednesday. "Her love for Ford Motor Co. was unsurpassed and all of us will mourn her passing."

With Josephine Ford's death, the only surviving grandchild of Henry Ford is William Clay Ford Sr., 80, the owner of the Detroit

Lions who stepped down as a director of the company last month after almost 57 years on the board.

Even those who chronicled the Ford family knew little of Josephine. Her public profile was minimal, and she never held a formal

Please see FORD , Page 2B

Josephine Ford as remembered by Bill Ford: "Throughout her life, my aunt embodied the spirit of giving."

FORD I Prankster was serious in philanthropy

From Page 1B role within Ford Motor Co.

"She never expressed an interest in working for the company," said Dave Lewis, a professor of business history at the University of Michigan.

She was content to lead the life that she did, Lewis said, and was a credit to the Ford family.

She was best known for giving tens of millions of dollars to the College for Creative Studies in Detroit, the Henry Ford Health System and the Detroit Institute of Arts.

Said DIA Director Graham W.J. Beal: "You reach for the superlatives and you can't be overstating it; she was an unparalleled patron. Always, she gave."

She gave every year to the annual fund. She donated fantastic works of art, including Vincent Van Gogh's "The Postman," valued at $40 million.

She also gave more than $10 million to the Henry Ford Health System, whose Josephine Cancer Center is one of the largest such centers in Michigan. She gave more than that to the College of Creative Studies—$25 million.

Josephine Ford was born in 1923 to Edsel and Eleanor Ford. She was the third of Henry and Clara's four grandchildren, and their only granddaughter. She married Walter Buhl Ford II, who came from another Ford family, and they raised four children, Walter Buhl Ford III, Eleanor Clay Ford, Josephine Clay Ford and Alfred Brush Ford.

"She was lucky to have married him," Lewis said. "There were many fortune seekers swirling around her."

Her husband was a partner in the design firm of Ford & Earl. He died of cancer in 1991.

Josephine Ford became one of Ford Motor Co.'s largest shareholders, having acquired more than 13 million shares of Class B stock, or 18 percent, by the time of her death.

She used money to donate and left the business to her brothers.

She once said, "What else is there for a girl who wasn't competitive to do but try to escape all that Ford stuff?"

Because of who she married, wrote family biographers Peter Collier and David Horowitz, she didn't escape the family name. She was by profession an interior designer, and her gentle and unassertive husband made space for her, which insulated her from family pressures.

Collier and Horowitz wrote that Josephine Ford "had not made much of a success of her own life, metamorphosing from a slender beauty into a large woman with an alcohol problem who seemed at times a professional eccentric. Her relationship with the company was largely ceremonial and she regarded it all as something of a mystery."

She got along with everybody in the family, trying to keep them together. Outside the family, she kept a small circle of friends.

And then there were her dogs.

Wherever she went she took them with her, according to the authors.

"Like maybe after a Thanksgiving dinner," said her son, Buhl, "she might bring 15 dogs into the room and they'd be jumping all over the furniture . . . She loves dogs and keeps on buying them."

"My mother brought a great deal of joy to all of us—not only family members, but members of the communities in which she was involved," said another son, Alfred Ford. "We'll always remember her as a fun person to be with. We'll miss her."

The funeral will be Monday at 4 p.m. at Christ Church Grosse Pointe, 61 Grosse Pointe Blvd., Grosse Pointe Farms,

Contact shawn windsor at 313-222-6487or wijidsor@freepress. com.

Ford Family Tree

Shown are the descendants of William Ford (1826-1905) and
wife Mary Litogot (1839-76):

First Generation

Henry Ford
1863-1947, m. Clara Jane Bryant

Second Generation

Edsel Bryant Ford
1893-1943, m. Eleanor Clay

Third Generation

August 10, 2003

Dear Linda and Sandra,

Here it is almost the middle of August. Another week and the state fair will be starting. The kids are already talking about school starting. It seems the older I get, the faster the time goes. I'm hanging in and learning more about how to pace myself to do the things I want to do. I just can't walk and do the things I used to, and sometimes it makes me angry at my body. But that doesn't do any good. So I just have to accept and be grateful I'm still able to do what I can. Mona was in the care center again and now is back in Oakwood Hospital, but I can't seem to find out what is wrong. I'm going to talk to a social worker again this week and see if I can get some info. Last I heard it was her heart.

Sandra, I hope you are feeling better and getting stronger. It is very nice of the Curtis family to arrange jobs that you can do. It sure sounds like they had a lot of calves born this spring and early summer. I have had California and Florida strawberries but did not have any Michigan ones this year. I have been enjoying Washington State cherries though. They have been delicious.

We had a very nice time while Bill, Shannon, and Sydney were here in July. Sydney is growing so fast and seems so smart for a two-and-half-year-old. She was a joy to be around. She loves books and sat on my lap while I read to her which I loved. I was also out at Barb and Ken's cottage a couple of days with them, and it was fun to watch her swim and play. Bill and Shannon are good parents and make her mind well. She is a very happy, good-natured child. I sure wish they didn't live so far away. But that's life.

Linda, you mentioned you were never allowed to have friends when you were growing up. I couldn't help but wonder why. Norma and Robert had friends when they were growing up as I remember. Everyone should have friends I think. We need them. I still am friends with a few of my old neighbors from Troy, and I have made friends here. I would be lost without them.

I took part in our Annual Art Fair here last Friday. I had a big table to display quite a few of my pictures and cards. I also dressed up in a purple and white striped top and white slacks with a *red hat* with purple ribbons and a *red* feather boa around my shoulders. I was doing a takeoff on that poem by Jenny Joseph: "When I'm an Old Women I'm Going To Wear Purple With a Red Hat that doesn't go." I had a copy of that poem on my table. Everyone got a big laugh when they saw me. I just felt like doing something different. Carol came over and helped me as we had to take everything over to the care center for the fair. They had a lot of craft and art displays, a white elephant sale, musical entertainment, cotton candy, pop corn, ice cream bars, etc. It was a fun afternoon. Boy, was I tired that evening! But I did it!

They try very hard to have different things around here to keep the residents interested. We just had our annual election of new officers for the Resident Council, and I was on the Nominating Committee for that. I found it very interesting. I'm working on my Christmas card design for this year and am carrying out that theme of red hat and purple idea. I'm using a snowman or maybe woman.

Barbara is in town for a few days and is coming and having lunch with me tomorrow. She usually stays at the cottage in July and August. She is going back out Tuesday.

Today we are having a concert pianist for our Sunday Entertainment Program, so I will be going over to help with that at 3:30 p.m. We don't usually have entertainment in the summer. But this guy was in town, and we got him for a reasonable price so are putting on an extra program. He was here last year and everyone liked him.

That's about it from around here. I hope you are both well. I know you both keep very, very busy. Hope the rest of the summer goes well for you. Take care,

Vivian

The Blackout of August 2003

Monday, August 18, 2003

Wow! What an experience! I'm still a bit shaky and light-headed from nerves, tension, and heat, *but* I survived. They are selling T-shirts with that saying on them. We have never had an experience like this before, never had so many power plants across the country gone out all at once—New York, Pennsylvania, Ontario, Canada, parts of Michigan, and parts of Ohio. Of course, it had to happen on the hottest days of summer when we were in the high eighty and ninety degrees. Now everyone is scrambling to find out the cause. No electricity, no water—that was hard.

Our power went out just as I was thinking about getting ready to go down for dinner on Thursday, August 14 at 4:11 p.m. We had no storms in the area, so everyone was wondering what was going on. I walked downstairs and rumors were flying There were reports of how widespread the power outage was and that it was a terrorist attack. Then our water supply was not working. Phones were out. Cell phones were not working either. Staff here were flying around. It was a little frightening. I had dinner with Margaret Green, and we were able to have a hot dinner. The dining staff were advising people to eat early as they didn't know how long they could keep the food hot. They also started setting up the tables on the turnover with plastic and paper goods. I walked slowly back up the stairs to my apartment and rummaged in Bill's dresser drawer and found a little transistor radio. Of course, it didn't work, but I rummaged in another drawer where Bill had kept extra batteries and found a battery for it, and then I felt in touch with the world again. It was an eerie feeling not to know what was going on. Reports were coming in that power stations were down from the Eastern Seaboard and were widespread. *But* it was no terrorist attack! I walked downstairs again to let some of the people know. I had the radio with me. By that time, some other people had got their old radios out and staff was going around reassuring people. Phones were still not working. Of course, this had to happen on the hottest days we had that summer. Temperatures were in the high eighties. Elderly people and there was no air conditioning, and some were on oxygen while some in wheelchairs and unable to get up or go downstairs . . . not good.

Thursday night was not a good night for me. I didn't like not being able to contact my family. I was wondering how all of them were faring, and I knew they would be wondering about me. I was too hot to be comfortable and a little panicky, almost like I didn't have enough air. And they started to warn us not to drink the water if we did have water. My water did come back on, but I had no way to boil it. I left the radio on all night as company and slept off and on. I said a prayer to Bill that I had found his radio and he had left me a battery for it in his supply of batteries. I felt like he was trying to look after me.

I can't rave enough about the staff here at the Village. They must have got in touch with everyone who worked here somehow. We had people coming around Thursday night checking to see if we were OK, and they did that at least three times on Friday, offering to bring us water and food if we could not get downstairs and asking if they could help in anyway. They asked us not to use candles unless they were contained and whether we had flashlights. Thank goodness I had that oil lamp too, which helped a little. It's very hard to read by flashlight, so mainly I just listened to the radio. Everyone who knows me knows how much my being able to read means to me. I'm lost without it *and* also not being able to contact my family. I felt more alone than I have ever felt in my life. I knew I was safe and as I said the staff were wonderful, but I did not like that feeling. Everything was so *dark . . . eerie!*

On Friday morning, I worked as quick as I could to get orange juice out of fridge to take pills and had half of a banana. I washed, got dressed, and walked downstairs to see what was going on. I saw staff there who I thought must have spent the night. Everybody looked hot and tired, but they were smiling and trying to cheer everyone up. Windows Cafe staff were handing out water, bagels or Danish, and fruit for breakfast. They had a huge fan in the front lobby doorway, and I cooled off a little there. Everyone was trying to help everyone else, which was nice to see. They put together box lunches of sandwiches, fruit, and a bottle of water for lunch and for our supper. They worked so hard. They had to make a lot of deliveries to people who could not get downstairs. I think they had sons and daughters of employees helping in too. You could eat in Windows Cafe or Great Lakes if you wanted, but I brought mine back upstairs. I knew Margaret could not get up and down the stairways, and Marguerette was at Susan's when this happened. That's a funny side story too. Susan and

Alan hid Marguerette's car keys so she could not come back here. Good for them! They had lots of bottled water and a generator, so they made out there quite well. They did not have any water though, and that part was bad. Marguerette was going over there on Sunday to stay with their dog "Chance" for the week as they were going up north. They kept trying to call here to find out what was going on, but of course like everyone else, they had no luck getting through.

A little after 11:00 p.m. on Friday night, our *power* came back on. *Oh, what a blessing!* We had had storms on Friday afternoon too. The fans were working but no cool air. The outside air was a bit cooler it seemed after dark. I was sitting around in just my nightie, trying to ration my ice water. That bothered me a lot not being able to drink as much ice water and ice tea as I wanted. They gave us bottled water but were limiting everyone to one bottle at a time. I know it was enough to live on, but I like my ice cold water and tea. I've never been a pop person. It just makes me more thirsty.

So when we had our power again, I was boiling water. It was such a relief to have lights again too. We certainly do take our electricity for granted and are very spoilt. What a wake-up call! I do know that I am going to have bottled water and batteries on hand if this should happen again. The fans in my apartment cooling unit were blowing, but there was no cool air coming through. I found out after a wonderful shower when I got dressed and went downstairs on Saturday morning that there was a flood over where the pumps for our units were. They were working hard, but they estimated that they would be fixed by Sunday. Oh boy, my apartment was ninety degrees. I was very miserable, but again staff was around to check and see if we had a puddle of water under our refrigerators. They did not want anyone to slip and fall. I lucked out on that. There was no water puddle.

My phone did not stop ringing on Saturday morning. It was so wonderful to talk to my family. They had all been trying to get me and I knew that, but I still had felt that alone feeling. Carol's power didn't come on until early Saturday morning. Traffic had been grid-locked around the area as traffic lights were not working and no gas could be pumped at the stations. People were driving around looking for water, ice, gas, etc. It was crazy. It seemed very nice to be able to watch some of this on TV.

Windows was serving a free lunch to everyone, but the lines were very long. I had crackers, cheese, and fruit in my apartment. I was so sticky and warm. I kept boiling water and making ice all day. I was so hot I was getting sick to my stomach, so I went down to the lobby about 3:00 p.m. and stayed until after dinner. They did have a hot dinner for us, but I wasn't very hungry. I don't even remember what it was. Marguerette did come home on Saturday morning after they had talked with me and found out that power was back on. She wanted a shower too, as Susan and Alan still did not have water. We had dinner together, and she invited me to her place as her building had air. But I stuck it out; after the sun went down, there did seem to be a slight breeze, so I sat around in my nightie again. At least we did have lights and ice, so I could have all the liquid I wanted. Bill and Shannon said that there were amazing reports of what had happened on their TV stations. Alice also said the TV reports were crazy. One very good thing was that there was very little rioting or looting in any of the cities affected. People were generally trying very hard to help one another.

I managed to sleep off and on Saturday night and did get my sticky head washed on Sunday morning. Our air came back on about 11:00 a.m. on Sunday. What a blessing! I did meet Marguerette for brunch, but again I was not very hungry. On Sunday afternoon I just read the papers, checked my e-mail, and basically did nothing. I was beat. I talked to the girls again and Jim called. They had been up in Bay City for the Tall Ship Festival so had missed all of this as Bay City was not affected. Lucky them!

On Monday I had planned on going to Westborn Market for fresh fruit, etc., but still I was so tired with no energy that I stayed in. I did write a thank-you letter to the staff. They had worked so hard they deserved a lot of thank yous. But, of course, I know they did not please everyone. I also started to write this to put with *Our Story* that I'm trying to write. Now it is Tuesday, August 19, and things are trying to get back to normal. I did go out to Westborn this morning and also stopped at CVS and Farmer Jack's. The stores still do not have all the shelves stocked. There was a tremendous amount of food lost, I understand. Westborn Market had a lot more fruit than Farmer Jack's; I'm very glad I went there first. I do like my fresh fruit.

Carol went out to stay at the cottage with Barb for this week, and of course, she took Scooby with her. I just talked with them, and they are having a great time. Now to get myself straightened around and back to "normal."

But what is "normal"? This morning there was news of a suicide bombing of the UN building in Baghdad, killing twenty people and injuring many more. Another suicide bombing in Jerusalem of a bus killed a lot of people. It is so sad, and in our own area, a father killed his four children. I guess we just have to take each day and show our love for our families and each other and enjoy what we can.

Monday, August 18, 2003

Dear Larry and *all* the Staff of Henry Ford Village, also volunteers,

Thank you, thank you for the care and concern everyone showed for us and worked so hard to make sure all of us were doing OK during this past emergency. There really are not words to describe how reassuring it was to have people knocking on our doors three and four times a day or evening to find out if we needed water or food or if we were able to make it downstairs.

I know it was not an easy task and it took enormous planning and effort on everyone's part. It was an eerie feeling to be so cut off from our families with the phones not working and water and power gone. All the staff here made it easier for all of us. The ninety degree temperatures in our apartments were hard on us, and all of you knew it. The water you were able to get us was a lifesaver. Never again am I going to be caught without a backup of bottled water. I'm not a pop drinker. I had to ration myself Friday and Saturday. I was hot and unhappy, but that was my fault for not having an extra supply in my place. Now I'm boiling water like crazy, making ice cubes, and enjoying large glasses of ice tea and ice water *and* appreciating every swallow.

I spent several hours in Great Lake's lobby on Saturday afternoon and appreciated the cool air Isn't electricity *wonderful?!* The young people in the dining room did such a great job, trying so hard to take care of a bunch of crabby, hot, old people. It was late Sunday morning when Chapel Court got cool air again. But I know everyone was doing their best. It's been a rough few days, physically draining for all of us. I know a lot of the staff did not get much rest or sleep. I wish I could name all of you who gave me hugs and kind words. A lot of you know me and know I consider you my friends. I feel so lucky to be living here at the Village. I'm so fortunate too because my phone rang constantly when power was restored. Every one of my family called, and all said they knew in their hearts that I was all right because I was living here. All of them want to thank you also.

Now here we are on Monday morning, almost back to normal. Still boiling water, but we can handle that. Computers are working again. *POWER!* We are spoilt. Let's all appreciate what we have and one another. Again thank you. My heartfelt love, prayers, and best wishes to all.

Vivian Beeler

The Detroit News

Founded August 23, 1873

E-mail: hpayne@detnews.com

HMMM...

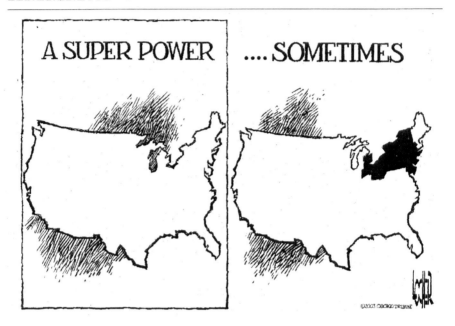

Why point the finger at deregulation?

Deregulation has been fingered as a culprit, but the transmission and distribution system has not been deregulated—in fact, regulation of this sector has *increased* throughout the 1990s.

What deregulation occurred in the 1990s occurred exclusively in the generation and retail sales sector . . . not in the transmission and distribution end of the business.
—Peter Van Doren, Cato Institute, on the Blackout of 2003
iT'S THE GRID

We're a superpower with a Third World grid. We need a new grid.
—Bill Richardson, governor of New Mexico, a former U.S. energy secretary, on CNN

FOR THE RECORD

If people think there is a bullet-proof electrical system, they are mistaken.

    —Carl R. Danner, a power expert and director at LECG, an economic and financial consulting firm, in the *Los Angeles Times*

A MATTER OF WORDS

I'd like to thank Fox for all the publicity . . . when I read "intoxicated or deranged" and "shrill and unstable" in their complaint, I thought for a moment I was a Fox commentator.

    —Al Franken, left-wing political satirist, in the Washington Post, on being sued by Fox News for trademark infringement for using the words "fair and balanced" in the title of his forthcoming book *Lies and the Lying Liars Who Tell Them: A Fair and Balanced Look at the Right*

LIGHTER LOAD

While the savings per piece might be small, when you consider the fact that we issued boarding passes for 57 million customers in 2002, it adds up.

    —Mary Stanik, Northwest Airlines spokeswoman, explaining the carrier's switch to lighter-weight paper for tickets and boarding passes

Compiled from *Free Press* news services

He who laughs last...

Sunday, August 24, 2003

Here I go off on a tangent again, but perhaps by writing some of these things down, the people who are reading this now will get to know me a little better, and that really is the purpose of *Our Story.*—to get to know and realize that we were flesh and blood people with the same feelings, emotions, etc., of whoever is reading this now.

Read these words the other day and they impressed me:

> We all tend to edit our memories to suit our visions of who we are, of what we've experienced and endured to become our present day selves." (Written by Alan Lightman and reviewed by Linda Castellitto, *Reunion*)

> Then on the morning of the blackout, August 14, 2003, my horoscope for the day in the *Detroit Free Press* said this:

> Libra: It's one thing to know your purpose in life but another thing to put it into words on paper. Fiddle with this concept today.

Interesting . . . then in the afternoon we lost our power and water. Doesn't everyone wonder once in a while what their purpose in life is, especially when you reach my age and wonder if there is a purpose left in your life? My girls tell me I'm important to them, and while Billy does not say it, he shows it by his actions and phone calls. He is in a bit of denial that I am as old as I am. I suppose it's difficult for him being born later in our lives to really realize it. I do so appreciate their phone calls every week and also talking to Sydney and Shannon along with Bill. It means a lot to me.

Well, I think that is enough philosophy for today. I better go and get involved in one of my books or check the book channel on TV and listen to someone else. I did make another blueberry pecan cake today, just because I had the ingredients in my apartment and felt like baking. Sometimes I just have to bake something. I used to be such a good cook and baker and loved doing it. At times, I miss it terribly. But then when I do make something, I'm so tired afterwards. My back just won't take standing and fixing and mixing things anymore. I'll probably freeze the cake. It does freeze well and I use it when someone is over or pass it out to some friends around here. It is a *good* cake.

I read the cutest story called "Eat Cake" by Jeanne Ray. The heroine in the story relieved her stress by baking cakes. In the story, it became a big business for her. I don't plan to go that far. Ha! Talk to you later.

Mud Puddles Dandelions

When I look at a patch of dandelions,
I see a bunch of weeds that are going to take over my yard.
My kids see flowers for Mom and blowing white fluff you can wish on.
When I look at an old drunk and he smiles at me,
I see a smelly, dirty person who probably wants money and I look away.
My kids see someone smiling at them and they smile back.
When I hear music I love,
I know I can't carry a tune and don't have much rhythm so I sit self-consciously and listen.
My kids feel the beat and move to it.
They sing out the words.
If they don't know them, they make up their own.
When I feel wind on my face,
I brace myself against it.
I feel it messing up my hair and pulling me back when I walk.
My kids close their eyes, spread their arms and fly with it, until they fall to the ground laughing.
When I pray,
I say thees and thous and grant me this, give me that.
My kids say, "Hi, God!
Thanks for my toys and my friends.
Please keep the bad dreams away tonight.
Sorry, I don't want to go to heaven yet.
I would miss my mommy and daddy."
When I see a mud puddle
I step around it.
I see my muddy shoes and dirty carpets.
My kids sit in it.
They see dams to build, rivers to cross, and worms to play with.
I wonder if we are given kids to teach or to learn from?
No wonder God loves the little children!

Enjoy the little things in life, for one day you may look back and realize they were the big things.
My wish to you mud puddles and dandelions and may God bless this day and all days for you.
"Love doesn't make the world go round.
Love is what makes the ride worthwhile."

Sunday September 14, 2003

Dear Linda and Sandra,

Not a lot of news since I wrote to you last month except for the blackout. I'm enclosing a copy of what I wrote about it if you are interested in reading it. I'll put it in with all the things I write to include in *Our Story* I am writing for the family.

You girls sure do keep busy, and that's good. I'm not able to do all the things I used to do, but I do manage to keep myself busy. My watercolor class has started up again. I take July and August off. I'm still on my committees. Carol did take me out to Barb and Ken's cottage again the first week of September. Kenny Jr. was here from California for a week with his folks. Ken had that week off also. It was a beautiful day and nice to see Kenny. He is doing very well and loves his job in the San Francisco Bay area. He has learned to run big machines to repair and maintain the bridges, buoys, and everything connected with the Bay area. He loves it. He has a steady girlfriend but is not married yet. He is twenty-seven.

I had some home-grown tomatoes from Barbara's plants, and there sure is nothing like them for taste. They feed us well here, but we don't get the home-grown stuff. I have bought a few ears of corn at a fruit market I like.

I was able to get a few Red Haven peaches in that same market. They were delicious.

I guess that rain that they have said we are going to get is really going to get here. It is getting very cloudy and dark for this time of day. Cindy has met a young man she is getting serious about. She is bringing him to Michigan in October to meet the family. He sounds nice, so we will wait and see. Cindy is thirty now, so I hope she can find someone. Life and society are so different now than when I was growing up or even raising my family.

I haven't heard anything about Mona, so no news there. Bill Jr. will be in Melbourne, Florida, for the next few weeks for training in his new job with the Dictaphone company. There will be twenty new employees from all over the country there for training. It should be interesting for him. They are staying at a Quality Inn and being shuttle-bused to training centers. It's right on the beach, so Bill is hoping to get some surfboarding in. He figures if he can snowboard he can surf. Shannon and Sydney will be alone for a while but very happy he got this job. He had been off work for a year when IBM downsized. Alice is also starting a new job, still waitressing, but in a smaller restaurant closer to where she lives. She had to give up the other job. It was a large Mexican restaurant and they had very heavy pottery dishes. The trays were very heavy to carry, and Alice's back has been giving her trouble. This is a new restaurant and Alice has known the owners for twenty years. We are all hoping it will work out for everyone.

Carol has been called several times already to sub for a teacher and she loves it. Barb is doing well and is quilting like crazy. She just loves it and has finished several quilts. She made me a beautiful one and gave it to me as an early birthday present. She machine quilts, all different patterns, and puts them together with their backing, but she sends them out to be quilted together. She made Kenny a quilt with all kinds of surfing material and one for Krista with hippie material. I've been to the fabric stores a few times with her, and I'm amazed at all the different fabrics they have now. It's a wonderful hobby for her now, and I'm so proud of the beautiful work she is doing.

I imagine from your letters that the farm is really busy now with fall things. It sounds interesting and a lot of hard work.

It has started to rain, so I had to go and close some windows I had left open. We do need rain though, so I hope it will last long enough to do some good. I forgot to mention the doctor has me going for physical therapy again to see if it will help my back and knees. This arthritis is getting worse and is painful, doggone it. Oh well, take care of yourselves.

Saturday, September 27, 2003

My Dearest Sydney,

You will soon be *three years old!* It doesn't seem possible. It ·seems almost like yesterday when Grandma and Aunt Carol came out to see you when you were born, and now you are turning three. Happy . . . happy birthday, honey.

Grandma is sitting here at her computer, looking out her· window on a cool breezy day with a mixture of sun and clouds. It definitely looks like *fall*. It makes me think of the times when your·daddy was growing up and we made trips to Big Red Apple Orchard up near Romeo. There you could ride a hay wagon out into the orchard and pick your own apples. Of course, we always had to have cider and donuts while we were there. We also always had to buy popcorn there. They grew the best popcorn. It always popped up so well. That was before microwave popcorn became so popular. You will have to ask your daddy if he remembers going there. He always liked to get up on the ladders as high as he could to pick the apples. He liked to try and scare Grandma. All of us looked forward to it every fall. It was a fun family time. Grandpa loved apple pie and apple crisp, and we always tried to get Northern Spy apples for me to make them. Grandma still makes apple crisp once in a while when we have a family get-together.

Grandma was so happy to see you and your mommy and daddy when you were here this past July. Sydney, you were such a loving, happy little girl, I could tell your momma and daddy were wonderful parents. It was so much fun when you sat on my lap and we read to one another. I would read for a while and then you would tell me that you were going to read. You repeated a lot of the words back to·me and kept turning the pages. I was amazed at how well you did for your age. Then I loved watching you at Aunt Barb and Uncle Ken's cottage on Russell Island. Aunt Carol·brought me out twice, and we had such nice days together. You were like a little fish in the water—no fear whatsoever. You reminded me of your daddy when he was growing up . . . a little daredevil!

It was also fun to watch you play with Kathy and Tony's children—Julia, Danielle, and Nino. You had such a good time with them and the·dogs, Bouy, Sailor, and Aunt Carol's Scooby. You were on the go every minute of the day. You were a joy to watch. All of your cousins from your daddy's side of the family are all grown-up already. With us having your daddy later in our lives, our other grandchildren are adults. Having you come along· when Grandma is in her eighties is a very special blessing for her. Knowing that I will not be around when you are grown-up makes me want to write to you. You can read these letters and stories and know that I loved you very much and valued our time together. I love talking to you on the phone too, and hearing you laugh and play in the background when I am talking to your momma and daddy is always a treat.

Grandma combined your birthday and Christmas presents this year because the doll cradle, high chair, doll, and blankets all go together. I hope you will have a lot of enjoyment playing with them. Aunt Carol is making some padding and blankets for your cradle, and you will get those when she finishes them. She offered to help me out with them. I used to do a lot of sewing, but now it is difficult for me to get out· my machine or I'm just getting more lazy. Aunt Carol offered, and I took her up on it. She loves doing things for you anyway 'cause she loves you lots too. I wish we could be there for your birthday, but it's not possible this year. We did make it out there for your first birthday and really had a good time. You have grown and changed so much since then, but that's the way it should be. Have a wonderful birthday, sweetie pie. I'm so happy you have your mommy's side of the family out there to help you celebrate.

Thursday October 30, 2003

Dear Rosly,

Here it is Halloween time again. The time certainly does seem to go by fast. It's a beautiful fall day out today. I went out on some errands this morning just to enjoy the nice weather. I know we will be having a change soon. The outlook for tomorrow's weather is good also. I'm always happy when it is nice for the children to go trick or treating. Do the children celebrate Halloween in your area? The Resident Life Staff here have a little party for the residents in the afternoon, and they encourage people to dress up in costumes if they want to. I have a purple and red outfit, a red hat with fluffy ribbons, and a red feather boa to wear if I don't lose my nerve. But my family is encouraging me, and I probably will. I have a red and purple tote bag I will carry candy in to pass out. I'm probably getting a little crazy in my old age, but anything to keep a sense of humor and get some laughs. We have had a lot of deaths lately. Of course what can we expect in a retirement home? But it still hurts the people left behind.

Rosly, I want to thank you for my birthday gift and card. You always remember, and I do appreciate that. That hot roll warmer is lovely and so different from what we have here. I gave it to Carol to use as she entertains more than I do now. She was thrilled with it. I will see it when I go to her house for dinners.

Everyone in my family is doing well right now, and I am very grateful. My granddaughter Cindy (Carol's daughter) is our social worker out in Washington State. She was home a couple of weeks ago for a friend's wedding and brought along a friend whom she met at the hospital she works at. She brought him home to meet the family as they were talking of getting married. We all liked him very much, and he gave Cindy an engagement ring while they were here. We are very happy for them. They plan on being married back here next October 16. Her brother Erik and Eve were married this past June and are very happy also. Erik is our policeman in Livonia, Michigan, and doing well. Eve is going to Wayne State University for her master's in audiology.

It was just a year ago that I had my hip replacement. That pain is better, but it seems like I traded it for my knees and back to act up. It's arthritis wearing on my joints, and most everyone our age have these same type of problems. I have to pace myself, and I can't do the things I used to or walk as much. It's kind of discouraging at times. I try to keep a good attitude as there are a lot of people worse off than I am. I still have my watercolor class and I am on most of my committees. I want to keep going as long as I can.

Bill Jr., Shannon, and their little daughter Sydney came for a visit this July, and it was so great to see them. Sydney is growing so fast and is a darling little girl. Children seem to learn so fast these days and be so smart. She was a delight. I'm enclosing a picture of her this summer. She turned three on October 12.

Rosly, we ate dinner with some people whose grandparents were Swiss and had a nice conversation with them. Have you ever heard of the R. J. Hirt Company here in Detroit? They have been into business of cheese and nuts for years and years. This couple were telling me that they (the Hirts) came from Switzerland. (They knew them.) Bill and I had been in their store years ago, but we didn't know their background. We got talking about Leckelie (sp) cookies and how good they were. Would you be kind enough to send me the address for them? I don't know that the Hirt Company carries them and I don't get down there anymore.

I do hope things are going well for all of you. I know your brothers were having problems. This getting old is not any fun. We just have to enjoy what we can each day and be grateful. Take care of yourself.

Tuesday, November 11, 2003

Dear Cindy and Joe,

Thank you, Cindy, for trusting me enough to tell me what's going on in your life. No, your mother has not told me about Joe moving in with you, so we both know that she is unhappy about the situation. *But* that doesn't mean that she loves you any less. I know all she wants is for you to be happy and successful in your life. She is so proud of both you and Erik with good reasons.

Let me see if I can explain from my point of view. I can't speak for your mom, but with her being my daughter, I suppose some of her thoughts come from growing up with Grandpa and me. Remember I'm eighty-two. There are two generations between us. In my generation, living together before marriage was an unheard of sin, and having a baby out of wedlock was always a very hush-hush deal. This is way back in the dark ages of the 1930s and 1940s. The whole world and society have changed so much since then, and before that . . . Remember, my mother and our beloved aunt Fran were just reaching their very early twenties when the flapper era was coming into being. Women were bobbing their hair and shortening their skirts. Heavens to be! It was shocking to their parents. I can remember Aunt Fran telling tales about going to parties with bathtub gin and speakeasies. She was much more adventurous than my mother. Then when your mother was a teenager along came the Beatles and Elvis. That took us as parents at that time by surprise and concern. They caused quite a revolution at that time. Now looking back, how tame they were compared to Britney Spears and Christine Aguilera! And the things you see on TV today, I don't feel that I have ever been a prude, but it does bother me about some of the role models our young people have today. I'm not sure about all those tight clothes and bare skin on young teenagers when their hormones are just starting to rage. It kind of seems like they don't realize they are asking for trouble. I admit I worry about raising children in today's world. There is so much casual sex, plus violence in today's society. But I have also learned over the years that every generation has worried. I have also learned over the years to do the best you can, except change and roll with it. It has not always been easy. Grandpa and I were very lucky. We both came from loving families, and being married so young, we both still lived at home with our parents—in my case, my mother and grandmother (I lost my dad when I was sixteen). Being very honest with you, Cindy, it was very difficult to keep our hands off each other, but somehow we managed.

Rochester Urology, P.C.
Robert A. Badalament, M.D., F.A.C.S.

December 13, 2003

Ms. Vivian Beeler
15181 Ford Road
Apt. 302
Dearborn, MI 48126

Dear Vivian:

Thank you so much for keeping me up to date and the beautiful Christmas card, as well as the psalm which I have passed around to the girls in the office (I hope they do not start wearing purple just yet).

Please excuse the informality of the dictated note. My wife handles most of the Christmas cards and I figured I better just send you the note now or it may get lost in the shuffle.

I know you are enjoying your grandson, Sidney, and I hope and pray that your daughter is doing well with her bout of breast cancer. There are a lot of similarities between breast and prostate cancers. A lot of times the researchers for prostate try to see what is going on in the breast area, and vice versa, since both of them are hormone sensitive cancers.

As far as my family, Louis will get his broadcast journalism degree at the end of this school year, and he is looking at graduate programs right now. My second boy, Peter, is in telecommunications at Ohio University with Louis, and is a sophomore. He plans to be an animator. I am glad both boys are doing what they want to, but I hope that they are not two starving artists. My daughter, Grace, is a high school senior and would like to play field nockey on a college level, and has several schools interested in recruiting her. My wife and I are hanging in there, a year older and wiser. Thank goodness, the health of our family has been holding out and everybody is doing well.

My best wishes for the upcoming New Year. May God bless you and your family, and don't let that arthritis get you down. See a good rheumatologist, perhaps he can help you.

All my love,
Bob Badalament

Christmas 2003

My Christmas this year was made very special for me by my family. This is our fourth Christmas without Bill and Kathy and six years since we lost Edsel and our world seemed to start falling apart. It doesn't seem possible, but it's just proof that life does go on, even when living is painful. Christmas always brings back memories, and you can't help but remember what things used to be like. There is always sadness mixed in with the happiness and joy of the season. Holidays are difficult for a lot of people. With all the holly jolly starting right after Halloween, it makes a long emotional season and it takes its toll, especially when age is creeping up on you and you are very concerned your body is falling apart. Your big fear is becoming a burden on your family.

There has always been a lot of love in our family, but let me tell you how very special they made me feel this year.

Cindy and her fiancé Joe Rivet got in late Saturday, December 20, from Longview, Washington. They were going to church on Sunday and then Cindy was having quite a few of her good friends over for dinner and the afternoon. I was invited to join them, but as I was just getting over a sinus cold and not feeling my best, I decided to stay home as I knew Monday would be a big day.

Carol had invited me to go with Cindy, Joe, Erik, Eve, and her out for a lovely dinner and then down to The Masonic Temple to see the musical comedy *The Producers* by Mel Brooks. It was a special Christmas present to all of us, and it turned out to be very special indeed. We went to Paisano's, a great Italian Restaurant, and all enjoyed a delicious dinner. While at dinner, I gave Eve one of the gold rings promoting strong women in our family. Bill and I had started that tradition as we had given all our granddaughters one several years ago. I wear one also. They know when they wear it that they are loved. We gave all our grandsons a Sterling silver pocket cross angel with a saying on the back that said "Angels shall guard thee" to help keep them safe. I gave one to Joe as he was joining our family. Erik pulled his out of his wallet to show me that he carries his all the time. Cindy also had her ring on. It made me happy to carry on the tradition. Then we moved on to the theater for the play. It was absolutely hilarious. I can't remember when I have laughed so long and so hard that my stomach hurt. It was two and a half hours that seemed to go by like ten minutes. I didn't even think once about how much my back was aching it was so funny. It had been so long since I had been out to dinner and a play. It brought back wonderful memories because Bill and I used to do that quite often. It was wonderful, and I'm running out of adjectives. I can't thank Carol enough for thinking of doing that. There were three generations of us in our little group, and everyone of us enjoyed it. That says something about how good it was. Plus the company I was in was great; they all made me feel special and loved. What a wonderful present! I got home at about 11:00 p.m. but was so wired up because of the evening that I wrote to Susan and Alan about the play on an e-mail because they are going to see it the coming week. Then I read for a while. It took quite awhile to settle down before I could go to bed. Oh, I forgot to mention. They had predicted rain for Monday evening. It was cloudy, but it did not rain until after eleven o'clock when we got home. Luck! That was on Monday. Tuesday was a halfway restful day. I cooked shrimp to take to Carol's on Christmas. Then . . .

Barbara and Ken had invited me to spend Christmas Eve afternoon with them and have a grilled steak dinner. It was another treat. Barb said I wasn't to think about driving. She was picking me up. We also had some snow flurries on Tuesday, enough to cover my car. How nice not to have to clean it off and to be waited on. The roads were just wet, but there were lots and lots of traffic with last minute shoppers. Barb was here about 2:30 p.m., and when we got to their place, Ken had just been home a few minutes from his work. There was fire in the fireplace, so nice and cozy and Christmas all through the house, no matter where you looked. They took me on a tour of the bedrooms upstairs, which they have been redoing. There were fresh paint and new carpets. The beds were covered with quilts that Barbara had made. They were just beautiful. My favorite one is called Sunshine and Blue Water. And it looks like it—bright yellow walls, beautiful blue and yellow quilt, white painted furniture, sandy-colored new carpet . . . lovely. Ken's bedroom had all the moose borders and decorations and his special rag quilt and new kind of oatmeal carpeting. It was great! The downstairs had all the nautical things put away and was newly decorated in kind of old-fashioned Victorian. It was so different than before and looked lovely. No matter where you looked you saw something new and interesting. I also noticed my paintings all over the place and Dad's needlepoint pictures and pillows around. What a warm feeling! There were quilt racks around with beautiful quilts on them. I had seen the big bedroom downstairs this summer when Barb redid it in "shabby chic," and I had painted the cabbage rose picture for her. It was lovely with all the pinks and purples and white wicker furniture. Her quilts were so wonderful on all the beds. I'm just so amazed that she has made so many in less than a year. (Just a side note if other people are reading this and wondering why Ken's bedroom is upstairs and Barbs down, Ken snores so very, very *loud*. He not only wakes himself up, he wakes everyone else too. This is their way of solving this problem, and everyone in our family knows this. We have all heard Ken at one time or another.) We also know of their love for one another, even more noticeable in these last two years of "hell" for Barb. It is so wonderful to see her happy and feeling good and looking forward to enjoying the holidays. I am so very grateful.

Back to my lovely Christmas Eve . . . I forgot to mention my greeting by Bouy and Sailor when we arrived there. Sailor was barking and wagging her tail and Bouy was moaning with her rag baby in her mouth. Both were trying to get to me as they know Grandma always brings "treats." I do miss having a dog. They are such great company. Then Barb made me sit and brought out a Christmas stocking filled with all kinds of goodies—candies, notepads, candles, Seabiscuit Video, special tin ship filled with yummy caramels, sunflower dishtowel and dish cloth, magnetic grocery list. What fun! I don't even remember the last time I had a Christmas stocking. Then there was a package from Sailor with a teddy bear wearing a foou fou red hat and a purple scarf. Such a darling! Then there was a package from Bouy with a teddy bear wearing a hat with ear flaps like the one Dad used to wear when he was hosing the skating rink in our backyard or shoveling snow. I used to hate it on him but knew it kept him warm. How clever! It brought back so many nice memories. Barb said the minute she saw it she could see Daddy in the backyard at the skating rink. This was back in Campbell before we moved to Troy.

Meantime Barb had us snacking on pita crisps with pine nut hummus, which was very good. We also had show and tell while she showed me all her quilts she had made and which I had not seen. She had received five from "Magic Linda" the quilter that afternoon. They were just gorgeous, each prettier than the other. They were beautiful materials with wonderful stitching on them from her special quilter. They were very special. She also surprised me by showing me a rag quilt she was giving to Carol on Christmas with Carol's colors and all different kinds of material with daisies on them. She had really hunted for them. Daisies are Carol's favorite flowers. Barb said she didn't tell me about it as she was afraid I might leak the secret! I knew Carol would be thrilled. Then she brought out a package from Alice to me. That brought tears, of course. It was a lovely rag quilt that Barb had taught Alice to make when she was down for that weekend a couple of months ago. It was made from all kinds of doggie prints, doggies, bones, paw prints, etc. It was so nice. I knew she had made Davey one and was working on one for Kelly and Steve, but I had no idea she was making one for me. There was a lot of love stitched into it, and I deeply appreciate it.

Ken grilled great strip steaks on the grill to go with baked potatoes, a beautiful tossed salad, and a layered ribbon Jell-O salad—another yummy dinner. We just don't get that kind of food here at the Village, and I can understand why. Ken brought me home about seven o'clock which was getting my witching hour. What a wonderful Christmas Eve! And then I had a very nice talk with Alice later in the evening. I also made an apple crisp that evening. After all those years and years of cooking and baking and especially for the holidays, I just had to do something. The girls had told me not to, to save my back, *but* it aches all the time anyway, so why not do something useful?

There was a little more snow overnight, so we did have a white Christmas! Barbara called and said they were picking me up. That was another nice present for me. I didn't have to make a couple of trips to the car and clean off the snow. They were here about 11:15 p.m., and we had a pretty drive through Hines Park. The trees looked so beautiful with the fresh snow on them. The young people were already there, and we were also welcomed by Scooby, Parker, and Bella. I had treats in my pocket for them. It was fun to be around the family dogs. Jim, Hannah, and Scotty arrived shortly thereafter too. Carol's house looked so Christmassy and nice, and again, I saw paintings of mine and Dad's Christmas needlepoint pictures and stocking. Everyone had made and brought all kinds of goodies and snacks to nibble on while we talked, laughed, and caught up on what everyone had been doing. It does seem in our family, and I'm sure it's true in a lot of other ones, that we have lots and lots of food at all of our gatherings—shrimp. veggies, breads with dips, deviled eggs. Hannah had found a recipe for a veggie dip that I used to make in one of Kathy's cookbooks and she brought it. It did taste like I used to make. It was a treat.

Then following family traditions, it was family picture taking time of all the families in front of the Christmas tree. There were tears and laughs as we so missed the ones who were not with us anymore. I know they are there in our hearts *but* . . .

Then we were on to presents exchange time. The last two years 1 had said, "Let's not do the presents anymore as everyone was hurting from the recession and we were all grown-ups now and it was just nice to be together."

With Barbara feeling well again, she and Carol had got together and said, "Let's do it again, but keep it small." They did not tell me. They told me later that I had "given" with the framed pictures that I had given to them. Carol forgot to tell Cindy also (she was upset) in all the confusion and with Carol being sick with a cold just before Christmas. Anyway, it did bring back some more fun and laughter in our Christmas.

I forgot to also mention that Cindy had come down with a nasty double ear infection on Tuesday. She and Carol were having a mother and daughter day and shopping for bridal dresses when this happened. They ended up at an Urgent Care Center, and Cindy had to cancel all plans for Tuesday evening and Wednesday. It goes to show that you just never know from one day to the next—the best-laid plans, etc.

Carol was so surprised and pleased with her daisy quilt from Barbara. There were more tears and laughter. We were all so grateful to see Barbara feeling good and happy again. I got a lovely book from Eve and Erik called *Why I Love Grandma*. It Ws delightful. Scott gave me a small teddy bear with a red hat, a purple scarf, and a red hat pin, so now I have a mother and daughter red hat bears. They are darlings. I got a pretty yellow-flowered teapot, candies, and jellies. Like I said when I started this, my family made me feel very special and loved this Christmas. Not that they don't all the time, but it seemed special this year. Plus we were all so excited and happy for Cindy and Joe that they had found one another and seemed so happy.

Now for the funny story that will go down in our history book of family funny things that happen. Poor Eve will never live this down, but it is so funny we have to tell it. Besides, I think Eve knows that we love her dearly, and this could have happened to anyone.

Cindy had made a nine-by-thirteen Pyrex casserole of cheesy potatoes for our dinner. Barb had brought a beautiful layered Jell-O salad also in a nine by thirteen casserole. They were both covered with foil. Someone told Eve to put the potatoes in the oven while we were exchanging gifts. I think you know the rest. After a while, someone said that maybe we should check and see if the potatoes were hot. That's when it was discovered that the Jell-O salad was in the oven and the potatoes were still *cold*. Everyone was laughing so hard about "the baked Jell-O" which went down the drain. Dinner was delayed until the potatoes were hot. Eve felt terrible but couldn't help laughing also. She felt badly as she knew those layered salads take a lot of time. Ken and I were very happy that we had had some on Christmas Eve. It was delicious! I'm sure Eve will never put another foil-covered casserole in the oven again without checking under the foil! I'm sure Barbara will never make another one of those salads without thinking about it also . . . memories . . .

Anyway, we had a delicious ham dinner, just a little later than planned. Erik had to eat as he had to leave to go to work by three o'clock. He made it. The Livonia Police Department is very good to their officers. If things are quiet, they are allowed to come home and be with their families for the holidays, as long as they keep their radios on and stay in the city of Livonia. Erik was back within the hour, and I was able to see him in his uniform and have my picture taken with him. That was nice for me. Scott had brought a pumpkin pie and a Santa cake that was a darling. We had cookies, candy, apple crisp . . . wow! There was too much as usual. Of course, everything was topped with real whipped cream.

Joe gave me a lovely card with a note telling me how much my giving him that angel pocket cross meant to him. I appreciated it. I do think he is going to fit in our family very well. Like I said, it is so nice to see Cindy so happy.

I was getting pretty tired out by that time. Barb and Ken had left a little later. Carol had said she would bring me home, so when I mentioned that I better get home, Jim offered to bring me home. I appreciated it, and it saved Carol a trip. Jim and Scott brought all my goodies up to my apartment for me and saw me safely inside. I got some more nice hugs.

It didn't take me long to get my nightie and robe on, and I just sort of "marinated" the rest of the evening. Ken told me that Kenny had given him that word when Ken had said he was just going to "veg out." He told his dad, "Just marinate.". It seems to fit.

I talked with Shannon, Sydney, and Bill in the evening. They wanted to hear all about my Christmas and told me they had had a good one. I had talked to Alice on Christmas Eve, and Krista called on Christmas night. I'm exhausted but feeling very blessed.

January 4, 2004, Sunday
(Added P.S. to My Christmas Letter)

I had a lovely surprise visit by Kenny and Gina from San Francisco. They had come in on Friday as Kenny was standing up in a wedding of one of his best friends he had gone to school with. That was rehearsal night. Saturday was the wedding. I knew it was a quick and busy weekend for them, so I did not expect to see them. I had seen them in late summer when they were here for a vacation at the cottage. Anyway, I received a phone call from Kenny on Saturday saying they were all coming down and have brunch with me on Sunday. What an unexpected pleasure! I called Carol to let her know and see if she could join us. It was so nice. Kenny and Gina both looked so good and seemed very happy together. They also had brought me a beautiful "big" Asian spice candle and plate with flowers and leaves imbedded in it. Candles today are so unusual and beautiful plus they smell so good. Barb and Ken were both just beaming; they were so happy to have them home. Everyone said the wedding was wonderful and talking about how handsome Kenny was in his tux. I do have good-looking grandsons! Carol had made it over also, and it was so nice to all be together again. It was a nice visit with lots of hugs and love. As I said before, I feel very blessed with my family.

None of us know what tomorrow has in store for us. Our family has been through some very rough years together. In some ways, it has made us stronger. I think it has also made us all realize that we have to enjoy and hold on to all the good things that come our way, live in the present and be grateful for each day and one another.

P.P.S. I received a lovely note and thank you card from Eve, telling me how much she appreciated her ring and being included in a tradition that started before she knew Erik. Again, what a great family!

Mom-Grandma & Great Grandma

2004

Henry Ford Village Computer Club

Of Dearborn, Michigan

| Volume 2 Number 7 | Seventeenth HFVCC Newsletter | Tuesday, January 18, 2004 |

We have been awarded an honorable mention in the 2004 Newsletter Contest at the APCUG 2005 Annual Conference in Las Vegas

New Feature Introduced In our Newsletter: Cartoons by Ken Nash

Our Newest Contributor, **Ken Nash**, Cartoonist, Graphic artist,

www.nashken.com

See page 5

Many Thanks To All Who Contribute To Our Newsletter.

Some Are Remarkable Residents:

- John Machetta
- Jean Andrews
- Ginny Knutson
- Mary McMahon
- Caryl Kerber
- Ruth Eis
- Vivian Beeler

Some are Great Guests:

- Joan Martin
- Ken Nash

And Some Are Respected Relations:

- Erin Kay and Mark Minckiewicz
- Lauren Rodriquez (Motion Graphic Artist In Residence, par excellence)

From Grateful, Indebted, Elderly Editors:

- Gene Fette
- Marie Minck

A Happy, Hale and Hopeful Year in MMV

Next HFVCC Meeting on 2/15/2005

Our Quarterly Newsletter on 4/19/2005

he Henry Ford Village Computer Club

- Meetings on the 3rd Tuesdays 10:30-11:45 a.m. in the Mackinac Room
- Two computers in the Library
- Eights Computers in the Computer Lab in the lower level
- Two game computers in the Recreation Room in the lower level
- Classes held in the Computer Lab on Mondays and Thursdays

omments, articles and suggestions are welcome
Contact: Marie Minck,   editor, 313-624-8386 CC303
Gene Fette,   co-editor, 313-582-4710 PT616

Many thanks to the *Benson Ford Research Center* of *The Ford* for their permission to use photographs from their collection.

Watercolor map of the American Hemisphere designed by *Vivian Beeler*

The masthead and cap images designed by *Alternate Visions, Northville, MI*

To the Family of Esther Virginia Matheson,

Virginia was my friend for almost six years, and I got to meet and know quite a few of you through our friendship. I knew she was very loved by all of you through our friendship. I thought that by writing to you folks about our friendship and our lives together here at the Village it might help all of us have a closure.

I did so enjoy our friendship, and I have missed her greatly since she has been ill. Let me start at the beginning.

My husband, Bill, and I moved into the Village in January 1998. We met your mother shortly after she moved in, in the spring of that same year. She was eating with a very nice lady who lived near her; her name was Marie Holmburg. Bill and I had been eating at different tables and starting to get acquainted. We had met Margaret Green, whose company we enjoyed, She was eating with Stella Osborn and Bernice Hyde. Margaret lived just down the hall from your mother. You have probably heard stories about how Stella latched onto Margaret because years ago they had worked at Crowleys together. They really did not know each other well at that time. Stella was having trouble with her eyesight, and Margaret being such a "softie" was helping her fill out her menu, checking her mail, and kind of waiting on her. Stella could be demanding at times, and we all tried to help Margaret. Stella could also be nice company and despite all her health problems was not a complainer. She has been gone a little over a year now, I believe. She was one of the lucky ones here. She was here one day and gone the next.

You have probably also heard stories about Bernice. She was a Scottish lady who had taken over three or four businesses of her husband's when he died. Her son who was sixteen at that time had asked his mother to keep the businesses for him so he could run them when he finished his schooling. Bernice was a very sharp, intelligent lady and could be delightful company. She could also be "imperialistic" at times. She was used to everyone doing as she said and having instant service. She could be very loud about it and did embarrass the rest of us at times. She wanted *hot* water for her tea, and if it was not hot, everyone in the dining room knew about it. She was still driving to her place of business here in Dearborn and signing checks when she was in her late eighties. She was quite a lady—interesting. Then she had a stroke and had to go over for assisted living and is now gone. Bernice also had a wonderful family who were here frequently and also took her to their places. We met several of them. Living in a place like this is kind of hard to explain. We are all getting older and worried about what life has in store for us. We talk about it together. None of us are afraid of death. It was the process of dying that frightened us. Again, none of us wanted to be a burden on our families, *but* that's something we have no choice in.

Back to meeting and becoming friends with your mother. It just sort of happened that Bill and I, Margaret and Stella, Bernice, Marie, and your mother all started to sit together every evening. It was an interesting table. People started to tease Bill about his "harem." He didn't mind. Bill was a person who had always pitched in and helped where he could. He was the eldest of five and had helped in later years with first his parents then my mother and aunt. I forget just when Marie left us for assisted living, and then because she did not have any children, a niece moved her to a place closer to her and we lost track of her. Everyone liked Bill. In the spring of 2000, I lost my Bill after a fairly short illness (cancer) and seven weeks later our middle daughter to ovarian cancer. I was a wreck. Your mother and Margaret helped me cope with their friendship, and so did the wonderful staff here. Also, as Nedra knows as we have talked a lot over the last few months, I am blessed with a wonderful family too.

Anyway, then we were down to five—Bernice, Stella, Margaret, your mother, and myself. We kept eating together. Sometimes for a change, your mother, Margaret, and myself would tell Stella we had other plans or company coming, and the three of us would meet and have our dinner together at Windows. It got to be quite a steady Tuesday evening ritual, and we all looked forward to it. We did have to concoct stories though, as Stella could be very nosy about Margaret's comings and goings. I think Bernice was in assisted living then. Margaret is such a sweetheart soul that your mother and I made up stories for her. Perhaps you've heard about that. We talked about what was going on in our families, our children's lives, our grandchildren, some of their joys, and sometimes some problems—nothing really that was too personal, but things that were interesting to all of us. In that way, we really got to know and care about one another. I remember hearing about

Beth going to veterinary school and how proud your grandmother was when you graduated and started in that practice. I remember Beth joined us for dinner a few times and how enjoyable that was. Vicky's wedding . . . how special that was and what a good time she had! How she worried when Chris's husband went on trips to the Middle East and was so happy when he returned safely!

There were stories of growing up in Homer, Michigan, and her father being a doctor—meeting your dad, your dad singing in the Don Large Chorus for WJR, the wonderful Christmas parties they had, going back to school for her teaching degree, teaching in the Detroit schools and the changes in the later years.

She showed us the wonderful Matheson cookbook that I believe Nedra's daughter worked on and put together. She talked about Laurie and her four children so far away in Washington State, Little Joe and his boundless imagination, her grandson, and family in Midland with the four little children, including triplets, her granddaughter in Indiana. She talked about Denny and Carol's move to Arizona. She hated to see them move so far away, *but* at the same time she said that they should do what makes them happy. She proudly showed us pictures of their beautiful home in Arizona. She was very worried about Carol's battle with breast cancer; that brought us even closer, as I also had a daughter fighting breast cancer. Thank God both are doing fine now! She told us about the times spent at Nedra and Dan's home, the leg of lamb dinners, even wonderful hamburgers from their grill. (Those were a treat for all of us as we didn't get them here.) How beautifully Nedra decorated her home for the holidays! I could go on and on. She was so very proud of all of you. Your mother in turn knew a lot about our families; we enjoyed sharing with each other.

I know when your mother first moved in here that she was a little unhappy. She missed Florida. Change is difficult at any age, especially when you get older. I do think that she adjusted very well though and was content after she got more into life here at the Village. I know she loved the ceramic class, and she made some lovely things. She gave Margaret and me each a small candy dish and also a tea caddy that she made. We were delighted with them. She also got into some bridge groups and enjoyed playing with those ladies. I'm not a card player, so we did not share that.

One Sunday, your mother and I took the van to Dearborn Inn and had a lovely dinner. She also went with me to the funeral home when Stella passed away. I am on the Sunday Afternoon Entertainment Committee, and she and Margaret would come over to the chapel or to Windows for the programs and we would sit together. She met some of my family when they came to visit me. I truly believe we were all interconnected in some way. Some people touch your life and you become closer to them than others. Your mother was one of those people for me. My heart has been heavy these last months for all of you. These up and down illnesses was the last thing your mother wanted.

Sometimes life can really throw you some curves that hurt. We have to believe that there is a reason.

I think I have rambled on long enough, but as I told Nedra on the phone last evening, writing this has been running through my mind ever since I got the news of your mother's death. I do think it is a blessing, and I know she is in a better place. Your mother will be another person to live on in my heart. I feel a relief and a closure in writing down these thoughts. I hope they will help all of you in some small way by letting you know that your mother and grandmother was a very special lady and touched a lot of lives in a wonderful way. Take care and best wishes always,

Vivian Beeler.

Sunday, March 28, 2004

Dear Linda and Sandra,

Hope you girls have a nice Easter. I will be with my family, and we are going to an Easter brunch at a holiday inn. We have been doing that for quite a few years now, and we all enjoy it. I'm hoping I will be able to eat and enjoy it also. I think I told you that I have been having digestive problems and have been very uncomfortable. I have had colonoscopy, endoscopy, CAT scan, stomach X-rays, upper GI, and lower bowel tests. I'm so tired of going to the doctor's and not getting too many answers. It sounds sort of like what you girls have been going through also, especially you, Sandra. All my tests have showed a very large hiatal hernia, and a couple of doctors have suggested surgery. But not all agree. I've put myself on a very bland diet and very small portions, but so far there's been not too much help. I don't have any energy, and it's interfering with my life. I'm disgusted with this thing of getting old.

Sandra, I hope they have found out what your balance problem is. That's got to be very miserable also. Linda, I hope you are getting better from that car accident and from hurting your shoulder and back. You girls are too young to have all these problems. Maybe with spring coming, we will all feel better.

Cindy started work here at the Village on March 18. So far she likes her job very much and says everyone is very nice to her. Her office is over in RG, and she does quite a bit of work with Alzheimer's patients. She does a lot of evaluations. Joe Rivet, her fiancé, arrived here also and started his new job at Henry Ford Health System on March 22. He also likes his new job. His son, Corbin, is here for a month with him. Carol has become an instant Grandma and is babysitting for them right now. Corbin is a delightful little boy. He is three and a half years old. That makes three great-grandchildren for me with Sage and Ché. Carol says Corbin is well behaved and easy to take care of. They have been over here several times. They will all be here next Saturday morning for a "bunny breakfast" and Easter egg hunt that the Village has for little ones of residents. I have never had anyone to invite before, so it should be fun.

Alice sold her house to a young cook at the restaurant where she worked and moved up here on March 26. She has been off work because of back problems for a while. The doctors have told her that she has to get out of the waitressing business and not carry those heavy trays anymore; she loved what she did, but it's time for a change. Workman's comp has been helping with her doctor visits and PT. She is to continue PT up here for a while. It was a big decision for her, but we are all happy she is back here in Michigan. Barb and Ken have a large enough house, and she and Barb are very close anyway. They always have been. Barb has taught Alice some of her quilting techniques, and both girls are very enthused about making them. Alice will get some kind of a job after she rests a bit and her back is feeling better. So there are quite a few changes in our family. I'm very happy to have more of my family back here so I will see them oftener. It will make our Easter and holiday get-togethers bigger. I like that.

I think I have filled you in on what's going on in my family. I still have my watercolor class. I missed a couple of weeks because of doctor appointments or tests. But I keep going. I'm still on my other committees, but it's getting harder for me to keep up. Walking for too long is a problem. The MRI showed what could be a small cyst pressing on the nerves in my lower back. I really have to pace myself. Oh well!

I do hope Dr. Chalfont is feeling better. He has had a long siege of it. It sounds like the Curtis family really knows how to work together to get things done. They do have a lot of new calves born every year. I'm sure they are very interesting to see. I suppose everyone is really getting busy now with April almost here. I do hope both of you girls will be well enough to help if they need you. They sound like very nice people.

Take care of yourselves, and as I said before, I wish you a nice Easter and good health this spring.

Vivian

Sunday April 4, 2004

Dear Avis,

I enjoyed your card with update and what's going on in your life. Thanks. Sorry it's taken me so long to get back to you. I too have been having some health problems. I've been X-rayed, scoped, CAT scanned and had an MRI, etc. from one end to the other. All they could find was that my hiatal hernia has gotten larger. It seems to be causing me a lot of digestive problems; plus the MRI showed narrowing of channels in the lower back with possibly a small cyst pressing on the nerves, causing back pain when I walk too far or do too much. It's just so much fun getting *old,* isn't it? I'm grateful. It could have been worse, but March was full of doctor appointments and tests. Enough!

Happy changes in my family! Cindy, Carol's daughter and our social worker, has moved back to Michigan and was hired here at the Village. They were delighted to get her with her experience, and so far she likes it here very much. She works mainly over in the care center right now, so I don't see her too often. But she met Mr. Right out in Washington, and he moved back here also and got a job at Henry Ford Health Center downtown in his field. He does auditing in the office. So far he is happy with his job also. He was married briefly before and has a darling three-and-a-half-year-old little boy "Corbin." We all like Joe and Corbin, and they fit in our family very well. He does have to share custody with his ex-wife, and that is a big expense of flying Corbin back and forth. Cindy loves being an "instant mother," and Carol loves being "grandma." She is taking care of him while he is here for this month. He goes back to Washington on April 17. They will have him again in the summer for eight weeks. Kids seem to adjust with these different times than when we were growing up. Cindy and Joe have a big wedding planned for October 16. Cindy is thirty-one and seems very happy. They were all here yesterday for a Village "Bunny Breakfast" and Easter egg hunt. It was lots of fun for me because this is the first time I have had a little one to invite.

Then Alice sold her house to a young cook at the restaurant she worked at. She has been having lots of back problems from carrying those heavy trays, and the doctors told her she had to give up that kind of work; she has been having therapy, etc. Workman's comp has paid for it. She moved in with

Barb and Ken on March 26. We are all very happy to have her back here. She was down the other day for lunch with me and came today for our brunch. It is so nice for me to have another daughter close by. Eventually she will look for another type of job up here. Next week she is earning some money doing dog-sitting for some friends while they are gone for four days. Barb and Ken are using a lot of her things at their cottage and discarding some older stuff out there. Alice and Barb have always been very close, and I'm sure it will work out. She is very conscious of giving Barb and Ken their alone time. Barb taught Alice quilting, and they are both addicted and doing beautiful work. Barb is also making some "BoBo's Besty Travel Bags" for breast prosthesis. She came up with the idea because she needed something, and one of the stores, Susan's Special Needs, is very interested in selling them. Also the Sharing and Caring Group at Beaumont Hospital is interested. Barb is checking into getting a copyright or trademark and is meeting with a lawyer tomorrow. We are hoping it will take off. The rest of the family is doing well. We will be getting together for Easter at the holiday inn we have gone to for several years. They have a lovely brunch that everyone enjoys, and no one has any work. I'm grateful for my family and feel blessed to have such a caring one.

Sounds like you also are blessed with a caring one. Your new living arrangements sound very nice. I wish you all kinds of good luck. We have to learn to accept changes and roll with them, don't we? We've got to keep a positive outlook and a good attitude. Nobody likes whiny old ladies.

My very best to all of you. Have a nice Easter.

Saturday, May 8, 2004

Dear Linda and Sandra,

Hoping that you have almost all of your repairs, siding, eves, and electrical work finished now. It does sound like you have had a lot of major repairs to be done. With all of those things accomplished, your house should be nice and cozy now. It seems like when you own a house, there is always something that has to be done. *And* everything always costs money.

It sounds like the Curtis family really define the word "family," the way they all work together and help one another with everything. It's too bad that there are not more families like them. I hope Mrs. Curtis is feeling better and walking better. Age sure can play tricks on your body as I'm finding out the hard way. All of my tests I have had have come back negative, but I am still having digestive problems and am very careful about what I eat. The doctors are puzzled but say it does happen. I keep a record of what I eat and when. But it doesn't seem to make any difference. I don't know whether any particular food causes my discomfort. So I'm just trying to make the best of it. Lots of people are worse off than I am.

I imagine the farm is really busy right now with lots of new animals arriving. I do hope that you are feeling better, Sandra, and have got some answers to your problems. I know both of you want to help out at the farm if you can. Also I hope that Dr. Chalfont is coming along and doing much better since his heart operation. Dogs sure know when their masters are not well, and it does affect them too. Hope Duchess is better now too.

It is so nice for me to have Alice living up here now. I have seen her quite a few times. Barbara and Alice came and picked me up last Monday and took me out for Mother's Day early. Barb and Ken are at their cottage this weekend and Alice is working. Alice got a job helping in a plant and greenhouse operation that sets up for the summer on Woodward Ave. not far from where she lives. It's the kind of work she loves and is very good at. Her yard and flowers were always fantastic. She also landscaped and did other people's yards with flowers as a sideline to her waitressing.

It's Sunday late afternoon and I just got back home from being with my family for Mother's Day brunch at the holiday inn we have been going to for several years. They have a very nice brunch there, and everyone enjoys it. We all were together for a few hours, and no one had any work, which was nice. It's turned out to be a nice day weather wise. They have been predicting storms all day, but so far we have not had any. It is hot and muggy out though. I drove over to Carol's at noon and then went with her. We stopped at a neighbor's of Carol's on the way home and got to pick a bouquet of lilacs. We used to have two lilac bushes in our yard in Troy, and I miss that smell every spring. Carol tries to get me a bouquet every year. I just need one nice smell and I'm satisfied. There are some things that you never get over missing when you live in an apartment. But I know this is the best place for me at this stage in my life.

On May 20 we have our annual expo here at the Village, and I have to set up a table with a display from my watercolor class. It is a colorful table with all the different pictures displayed. Every club or class and group here in the Village has a display. There are over 120 different groups. This is all volunteer work. It is to show everyone all the different things that are available for people to do here. It is always very festive and nice. They have nice refreshments—fruit trays, crackers and cheese trays, sweet breads, punch or lemonade. It lasts from 10:00 a.m. to 12:30 p.m. It is quite a bit of work to get ready for it as I make a big tri-fold poster board with the smaller paintings on it, and it stands up in the middle of the table. The marketing department wants us to put up our displays again the following week when they have a marketing luncheon for the people who are thinking of moving here. They want them to see what is available to do here; this is the first year they have asked us to do that.

Cindy likes her job here, but I don't see her as she is over at the care center most of the time. She told me today that eventually she will be over here in the independent living section. Then I will probably see her more. It is so nice to have here back in this area though and is able to be with us for family get-togethers.

Bill, Shannon, and Sydney are planning on coming here for vacation in August this summer. I am happy about that. I know Sydney has grown a lot. She will be four in October. Carol has been teaching a lot, and she loves that. That's about all the news from here. As I said before, I do hope both of you are doing well and things are going along well for you.

Dave Barry

Wisdom Can Be Found in Odd Places

A Commencement Address to the College Class of 2004

This is your big day—the day when you jam four years' worth of un-laundered underwear into a Hefty bag and leave college, prepared by your professors to go out into the real World.

The first thing you'll notice is that your professors did not go out there with you. They're not stupid; that's why they're professors. They've figured out that college is a carefree place where the most serious real problem is finding a legal parking space.

So your professors are going to Stay in college until they die. Even then, they'll go right on teaching classes. This is called "tenure."

But you, the members of the Class of 2004, have committed the grave tactical blunder of acquiring enough credits to graduate.

So now you're leaving college and embarking upon the greatest adventure—and the biggest challenge—of your young lives: moving back in with your parents.

Decades ago, when I graduated from college, my friends and I would rather have undergone a vasectomy with a fondue fork than move back in with our parents.

But times have changed, and today many graduates don't want to go straight from college into a harsh and unforgiving world fraught with unbearable hardships, such as no free high-speed Internet.

And so many of you will return home, hand your Hefty bag to Mom for processing, and move back into your old room, which is filled with your childhood memories, not to mention the faint aroma of gerbil doots.

Is this a bad thing? Does the fact that you, a grown adult, are moving back in with your parents' mean that you're a sponging loser?

Yes. You are SpongeBob LoserPants.

No! Sorry! I mean: No. It's fine! Your parents don't mind! They're thrilled to have you back home! Even from way up here on the podium, I can hear their teeth grinding with joy.

Besides, it's only temporary, right? In time you'll get tired of living with your parents, with their constant nagging about how you need to find a job, or at least help with the housework, and could you put gas in Dad's car when you borrow it, and can you explain the Mystery Thong that Dad found in the backseat cup holder, and "My god is that a tattoo?" and could you not play that music so loud at night, or could you at least play some decent music, we're not "squares" you know, we like good rock "n" roll, we like the Mamas and the Papas, the Beatles—though not the later Beatles—but this music today, you can't even call it music, it sounds like angry men clubbing a yak to death with electric guitars, and "How could you get a tattoo there?" and there are 15 Starbucks—no wait, now it's 16 Starbucks—within walking distance of this house and surely one of them would be happy to hire somebody with a degree in anthropology, and here's an article I found in Women's Day about tattoo removal that you might want to . . .

"Don't you walk away, when I'm talking to you!" ..

Yes, graduates, as much as you love your Mom and Dad, you're realistic enough to understand, deep down inside, that they are the two most annoying human beings on the planet.

And so the time will come—I give it six weeks—when you realize that you can no longer continue living-with them. And so you will summon your courage, take a deep breath, and ask them to move out.

It's only fair! They've had the house practically to themselves for years! Now it's your turn! Let them go work at Starbucks.

Of course, eventually, you, the. Class of 2004, will want to have a career. You may think you'll never find your dream job, but trust me: If you set your goals high, and you never, ever give up, I guarantee you that one day, you will find yourself working for a huge impersonal corporation run by morons.

Everybody does!

It's not so bad: You get a little cubicle where you sit all day doing some tedious corporate thing that has absolutely nothing to do with anything you learned in college.

For diversion you'll speculate with your fellow cubicle dwellers on how your corporation manages to survive under a management team with the combined IQ of a kielbasa.

On your break, you'll go buy a mocha latte from Dad. You'll settle into a comfortable routine and before you know it, you'll have kids of your own. And one day, you'll send them off to college.

When that happens, Class of 2004, change the locks.

Dave Barry's column appears most Sundays in "The Way We Live." Write to him at c/o Detroit Free Press, 600 WFort, Detroit MI 48226.

Memorial Day Weekend:
May 30, 2004—Reflections, Thoughts

It's been quite awhile since I have sat down at my computer to write about anything that's going on in my life at this point. There are several reasons for that, I think. My health seems to be going downhill with this aging process, and I am very unhappy about that. There have been lots of doctor appointments and lots of different tests since the first of the year. None of them have shown any *big* problems. But I know my body is not doing as well as I would like. I'm still having a lot of stomach and digestive problems. It's sometimes worse than others, and I can't figure out why. I keep track of what food I eat and when, to no avail. My right leg and knee are really getting very painful at times along with my back aching. There are times when I have a great deal of pain just walking around my apartment. There are times when I'm walking somewhere and I have to sit down or I feel like I will fall down. That's scary! I ache and hurt even sitting with my legs up at times and in bed lying down, and that's scary also! What's going on? I wish I could find out. It's not enjoyable to live like this. Sitting here at the computer my back starts aching, and I'm sitting so I don't know how much I will write. It has also affected my artwork. I want to paint and get going on something, and my back and leg pain make me sit down. Not fun! I try to put on a good front for everyone, myself included. Sometimes it's difficult!

What I really wanted to write about was watching the dedication of the World War II Memorial in Washington yesterday. I thought it was beautifully done. It brought back so many memories of that time in our lives. It also was a very emotional program to watch for our generation. Tom Brokaw called us "the greatest generation" and wrote a book about us. He was one of the speakers at the dedication. Along with the commander in chief, Kelly (at that time), Tom Hanks, the actor who was instrumental in getting that monument started with his movies *Band of Brothers* and *Saving Private Ryan,* was also there, and so were past presidents, Bush and Clinton, President George Bush, and veteran and senator Bob Dole. They all gave short and moving speeches.

There were sixteen million men and women who served in World War II; four million are alive today, but they are dying at the rate of a thousand a day. The memorial honors all, not just the veterans, but all the people whose lives were interrupted and burdened with uncertainty, sacrifice, rationing wonder how long and when. All of us had lived through the Depression. We never took a dollar for granted or spent it without thinking. We were a join-up generation. How can we help? In World War II everyone was involved, from grandparents on down. Women joined the workforce and the armed services. Those of us left at home saved tin foil, grease from cooking, and string, all turned in to be recycled, and helped in some small way. People knitted socks and gloves. Children saved any gum wrappers and pieces of string. Our meat was rationed and so was gasoline for our cars. There were blue stars in our windows for our husbands, sons, or daughters serving in the armed forces. Then way too many gold stars replaced the blue for the young people who would never come home again. We wrote letters, sent care packages, and waited anxiously for the mail. Communications were a lot different back then. The war was not on television. We did not even know what TV was. It was a Buck Rogers, Star Trek thing at that time. We listened around our radios for all the news programs.

Young men at that time had no choice; when your draft number came up, you went, or they came to get you. In that war, we knew what we were fighting for, *and* we knew who the enemy was. Today's war is so different and our country is so divided.

Back to the memorial dedication: In 1993 people started talking and realizing that there was no memorial to all the veterans of World War II. It took until 2001 to get it started. There was a great deal of political bickering, and art critics could not agree on a design. Finally Architect Friedrich St. Florian was chosen with his design. Tom Hanks and Senator Bob Dole were very instrumental in raising money so that it was mainly paid for through donations. Even school children sent in donations. It opened in April of this year. Here is an article from the Detroit News, dated May 30, 2004, written by Lisa Hoffman from Scripps Howard News Service: Washington

> From the sculpted gold stars aligned on a wall to the bronze eagles grasping victory laurels from above, the nation's new World War Two memorial is a study in symbols.

Architect Friedrich St. Florian adorned the 7.4 acre plaza with an array of elements that pay homage to the troops who fought and perished, the sacrifice of those who toiled on the home front and the contributions of America's allies in the war that historians say was the defining event of the 20th century for the country.

"We have built a very powerful memorial that really is commensurate with the enormity of the event," St. Florian said when the structure was opened to the public in April.

Here's a look at the symbolic elements that make up the $172 million memorial:

Two 43-foot arches stand at the north and south ends of the plaza. They represent the two major theaters of war, the Atlantic and Pacific. Each arch contains four bronze columns upon which are perched four 2,600-pound American eagles lifting a wreath, which commemorates the U.S. and allied victory on that front.

Fifty-six pillars, which extend in semi-circles from either arch, are inscribed to honor the U.S. states and territories at the time of the war. Each 17-foot-high, granite pillar carries two sculpted bronze wreaths. An oak wreath represents America's industrial strength, and a wreath of wheat symbolizes the nations agricultural heart. Each pillar is open at the center to signify the loss of lives. The pillars are connected by twisted bronze ropes that represent the extraordinary unity of America during the war.

Lining the ceremonial entrance to the memorial on its east side will be 24 bas-relief panels that depict the country's mobilization of its abundant resources . . . Agricultural, industrial. Military and human. {Because of delays, only 18 were placed for Saturday's dedication.}

One set of 12 sculpted panels, created by sculptor Ray Kaskey, represent the Atlantic front. There are figures depicting paratroopers, the Normandy invasion on D-Day, medics in the field, the air war, tanks in combat, the Battle of the Bulge, Russians meeting Americans at the Elbe, women in the military,

"Rosie the Riveter" and aircraft construction, enlistment, the lend-lease program and the Battle of the Atlantic.

Twelve Pacific front panels include figures engaged in shipbuilding, agriculture, submarine warfare, jungle warfare, the Navy in action, embarkation, field burial, war bond drives, Pearl Harbor, amphibious landings, the liberation of Europe and V-J Day.

The Freedom wall, a curved, 9-foot-high structure, is studded with 4,000 gold stars, each commemorating 100 of the more than 400,000 soldiers, sailors, airmen, and other troops who gave their lives. During the war, the gold star symbolized the family sacrifice—families placed them in their windows to signify the loss of a loved one.

Waterfalls on each side of the Freedom Wall, semi-circular fountains next to the base of the arches and the historic Rainbow Pool that forms the center of the plaza, symbolize the overseas nature of the war. The water elements also represent the continuity of life and the perpetual connection of the present to the past.

These are some of the things that impressed me and that I can remember from the speeches. The memorial is on the mall between the Washington Monument (who was described as the father of our country) and the Lincoln Memorial (who was described as the preserver of our country) Sixteen million men and women served in World War II. Four million are still alive today but are dying at the rate of one thousand a day. Kind of scary facts. Soon there won't be any of our generation left. We will just be in history books. I guess that is part of the reason that I have been trying to write *Our Story* because I want my grandchildren and great-grandchildren to know that we were "real," honest-to-goodness human beings, that we had feelings and emotions just as they do today.

The GI Bill was in a sense a memorial and a tribute to our service men and women of World War II. So many took advantage of the education it provided. Some became rich, famous, and powerful and have been our leaders in our country. It took awhile for those who survived to adjust back into civilian life, and they did not talk about their experiences in active service. They felt an obligation to those who didn't make it back. Democracy is not free; it is very costly. Our veterans paid a high price.

There were a thousand invited guests. The veterans came slowly, some walking with canes, some in wheelchairs, and the lucky ones who were still able to walk on their own. Remember, it was my generation I am talking about. I'm sitting here in front of my TV and I'm eighty-two. All of these veterans are in their late seventies and eighties. They all looked so proud to be there and represent their comrades. It was very moving, and I had the box of Kleenex handy. The speakers—Tom Brokaw, Tom Hanks, Senator McGovern, Senator Bob Dole, President Bush—gave short and excellent speeches, honoring the veterans who were there and their fallen comrades. They also mentioned our leaders during those difficult times who are all gone now—President Roosevelt, Prime Minister Churchill, General Eisenhower. They also talked about Bob Hope who would have been 101 years old on this day, his untiring work entertaining the troops in all parts of the world.

It brought back so many memories for me and how it affected our personal lives. I was just a twenty-year-old new bride when Pearl Harbor was attacked. My new husband, twenty-two years old, was so proud to be on the apprentice program in the tool room at the Henry Ford Rouge plant.

Here it is June 14, Flag Day. It's taken me awhile to get back to writing. We had the sixtieth anniversary of D-Day with week-long ceremonies. The actual day was June 6, 1944. On June 5, this year, President Reagan died. He was ninety-three years old and had been suffering from Alzheimer's for the past ten years. According to all the news sources, Reagan had planned his own funeral right after he was diagnosed with Alzheimer's. It went on for a whole week full of ceremonies and processions. I felt very sorry for his wife, Nancy. She looked very tired with good reason. Anyway, I have been inundated with history, reliving so many memories and things that have happened in our family during those years. Plus, these past two weeks I have been very concerned about Barbara who has had pneumonia. Needless to say, it has been a little stressful! I do want to write more on what I originally started to share with you a little of what our lives were like during those times that you will just read about in your history books. I told you when I started *Our Story* that I wanted it to be a little genealogy, a little history, and our own personal story.

Back to the World War II memorial and my memories ...

Historians who write about that era say that World War II was a pivotal point that changed our world more than any other time. Our industries and manufacturing, engineering leaped ahead with automobiles, planes, trains, super highways, television, and on and on. It changed our social structure. Women were not just wives and mothers anymore. They joined the workforce, and they brought up their daughters to realize that they could do anything they wanted. Before World War II, women worked, but their jobs were limited it seems to teachers, nurses, and secretaries with a few exceptions. Interesting! The world found out what we had known all along. Women are every bit as smart as men and smarter in a lot of ways! Another sideline that happened at that time was that women started to wear slacks. Before that time, you were not a lady if you wore trousers. I never had a pair of slacks until after we got our first house on Campbell in Dearborn when Bill got out of service, and that was in 1945. All of our neighbor ladies were wearing slacks. It took me a little while to get used to the idea. The girls still remember my housedresses and aprons. Now at eighty-two, 1 don't want to wear dresses anymore. Slacks are much more comfortable for me.

Carol and Cindy just came in. I knew something was very wrong. Carol had been with Barb, Ken, and Alice at the doctor's for a consultation. Barbara's cancer is back. It has showed up in her lungs as pneumonia. So again ...

Our world falls apart. We have all been worried about that happening but have tried very hard to look on the bright side of things. My heart is aching for her and our family. She has to go through some more very unpleasant tests and procedures to determine the type of treatment she can have. Barb has come right out and told us that she will not have any more chemo or radiation. There is a new drug out called "Herceptin" that is supposed to be very good for this type of cancer. Please, God, let it be our miracle drug.

Heart of the City

By Mark Tatulli

Tomb of the Unknown Soldier

Here are some interesting facts about the Tomb of the Unknown Soldier and the Sentinels of the Third United States Infantry Regiment, "Old Guard."

1. How many steps does the guard take during his walk across the tombs and why?
   Twenty-one steps. It alludes to the twenty-one gun salute, which is the highest honor given to any military or foreign dignitary.
2. How long does he hesitate after his about-face to begin his return walk and why?
   Twenty-one seconds for the same reason as answer number one.
3. Why are his gloves wet?
   His gloves are moistened to prevent him losing his grip on the rifle.
4. Does he carry his rifle on the same shoulder all the time, and if not, why not?
   No, he carries the rifle on the shoulder away from the tomb. After his march across the path, he executes an about-face and moves the rifle to the outside shoulder.

5. How often are the guards changed?
   Guards are changed every thirty minutes, twenty-four hours a day, 365 days a year.
6. What are the physical traits of the guard limited to?

For a person to apply for guard duty at the tomb, he must be between 5′10″ and 6′2″ tall and his waist size cannot exceed 30.″

Other requirements of the guard are as follows:

After *two years*, the guard is given a wreath pin that is worn on their lapels signifying they served as guard of the tomb. There are only four hundred presently worn. The guard must obey these rules for the rest of their lives or give up the wreath pin.

The shoes are specially made with very thick soles to keep the heat and cold from their feet. There are metal heel plates that extend to the top of the shoe in order to make the loud click as they come to a halt. There are no wrinkles, folds, or lint on the uniform. Guards dress for duty in front of a full-length mirror.

The first *six months* of duty, a guard cannot talk to anyone or watch TV. *All* off-duty time is spent studying the 175 notable people laid to rest in Arlington National Cemetery. A guard must memorize who they are and where they are interred. Among the notables are: President Taft, Joe E. Louis (the boxer), and Medal of Honor winner Audie Murphy (the most decorated soldier of WW II) of Hollywood fame. Every guard spends *five hours a day* getting his uniforms ready for guard duty.

The Sentinels Creed:

> My dedication to this sacred duty is total and wholehearted. In the responsibility bestowed on me never will I falter. And with dignity and perseverance my standard will remain perfection. Through the years of diligence and praise and the discomfort of the elements, I will walk my tour in humble reverence to the best of my ability. It is he who commands the respect I protect. His bravery that made us so proud. Surrounded by well meaning

crowds by day, alone in the thoughtful peace of night, this soldier will in honored glory rest under my eternal vigilance.

More Interesting Facts About the Tomb of the Unknowns Itself:

The marble for the Tomb of the Unknowns was furnished by the Vermont Marble Company of Danby, Vermont. The marble is the finest and whitest of American marble, quarried from the Yule Marble Quarry located near Marble, Colorado, and is called Yule Marble. The marble for the Lincoln memorial and other famous buildings was also quarried there.

The tomb consists of seven pieces of rectangular marble: four pieces in sub base, weight—15 tons; one piece in base or plinth, weight—16 tons; one piece in die, weight—36 tons; one piece in cap, weight—12 tons.

Carved on the east side (the front of the tomb, which faces Washington, DC) is a composite of the three figures, commemorative of the spirit of the Allies of World War I.

In the center of the panel stands Victory (female). On the right side, a male figure symbolizes Valor. On the left side stands Peace, with her palm branched to reward the devotion and sacrifice that went with courage to make the cause of righteousness triumphant.

The north and south sides are divided into three panels by Doric pilasters. In each panel is an inverted wreath. On the west, or rear, panel (facing the amphitheater) is inscribed the following:

HERE RESTS IN HONORED GLORY AN AMERICAN SOLDIER KNOWN BUT TO GOD

The first Tomb of the Unknown Soldiers was a sub base and a base or plinth. It was slightly smaller than the present base. This was torn away when the present tomb was started in August 27, 1931. The tomb was completed and the area opened to the public at 9:15 a.m. on April 9, 1932, without any ceremony.

Cost of the Tomb—$48,000; Sculptor—Thomas Hudson Jones; Architect—Lorimer Rich; Contractors—Hagerman & Harris, New York City; Inscription—Author Unknown.

Interesting Commentary:

The Third Infantry Regiment at Fort Myer has the responsibility for providing ceremonial units and honor guards for state occasions, White House social functions, public celebrations and interments at Arlington National Cemetery, and standing a very formal sentry watch at the Tomb of the Unknowns.

The public is familiar with the precision of what is called "walking post" at the tombs. There are roped-off galleries where visitors can form to observe the troopers and their measured step and almost mechanically silent rifle shoulder changes. They are relieved in a very formal drill that has to be seen to be believed.

Some people think that when the cemetery is closed to the public in the evening this show stops. First, to the men who are dedicated to this work, it is no show. It is a "charge of honor." The formality and precision continues uninterrupted all night. During the nighttime, the drill of relief and the measured step of the on-duty sentry remain unchanged from the daylight hours. To these men, these special men, the continuity of this post is the key to the honor and respect shown to these honored dead, symbolic of all Americans unaccounted and for Americans dead in combat. The steady rhythmic step in rain, sleet, snow, hail, heat, cold must be uninterrupted. Uninterrupted is the important part of the honor shown.

Recently, while you were sleeping, the teeth of hurricane Isabel came through this area and tore hell out of everything. We had thousands of trees down, power outages, traffic signals out, roads filled with downed limbs and "gear adrift" debris. We had flooding, and the place looked like it had been the impact area of an offshore bombardment.

The regimental commander of the U.S. Third Infantry sent word to the nighttime Sentry Detail to secure the post and seek shelter from the high winds to ensure their personal safety.

They disobeyed the order!

During winds that turned over vehicles and turned debris into projectiles, the measured step continued. One fellow said, "I've got buddies getting shot at in Iraq who would kick my butt if word got to them that we let them down. I sure as hell have no intention of spending my Army career being known as the damned idiot who couldn't stand a little breeze and shirked his duty." Then he said something in response to a female reporter's question regarding silly, purposeless personal risk. "I wouldn't expect you to understand. It's an enlisted man's thing." God bless the rascal! In a time in our nation's history when spin and total BS. seem to have become the accepted coin-of-the-realm, there beat hearts—the enlisted hearts we all knew and were so damn proud to be a part of—that fully understand that devotion to duty is not a part-time occupation. While we slept, we were represented by some damn fine men who fully understood their post orders and proudly went about their assigned responsibilities unseen, unrecognized, and in the finest tradition of the American Enlisted Man. Folks, there's hope. The spirit that George S. Patton, Arleigh Burke, and Jimmy Doolittle left us survives.

On the ABC evening news, it was reported recently that, because of the dangers from Hurricane Isabel approaching Washington, DC, the military members assigned the duty of guarding the Tomb of the Unknown Soldiers were given permission to suspend the assignment. They refused. "No way, sir!"

Soaked to the skin, marching in the pelting rain of a tropical storm, they said that guarding the tomb was not just an assignment—it was the highest honor that can be afforded to a service person. The tomb has been patrolled continuously 24/7 since 1930.

We are very, very proud of our soldiers in uniform!

The Meaning of the Poppies—May 15

If you happen through a shopping mall or a public square this May, you might see veterans selling crepe-paper flowers to raise money for soldiers and military families weakened by war. The flowers are poppies, and it is worth recalling their meaning on this Memorial Day, fifty years after the start of the Korean War.

The image of poppies will tease the memory of many Americans, who, as school children, learned by heart John McCrae's First World War poem "In Flanders Field." Flanders was the site of very bloody fighting in that famously bloody war, but Colonel McCrae, speaking as if dead, chose to suggest the carnage subtly:

> *In Flanders fields the poppies blow, Between the crosses, row on row*
> *that mark our place; and in the sky the larks, still bravely singing,*
> *fly, scarce heard amid the guns below.*

It is natural that the scarlet poppies of Flanders would come to symbolize a rebirth and remembrance of those lost in battle. They grew amid the muck of war in soil watered by the blood of the dead. But to the classically schooled soldiers who fought World War I, the poppy also summoned the image of the blood-red flowers of ancient lore.

In these tales, young men—Adonis, Hyacinthus—were killed, and the red anemone or crimson hyacinth grew where they fell. As the mythologist Edith Hamilton suggested, these stories probably "give a hint of black deeds that were done in the far-distant past . . . when it might happen, if the fields around the village were not fruitful, that one of the villagers would be killed and his—or her—blood sprinkled over the barren land."

The poppy, then, also recalled the fact that young soldiers are sent to risk death and to die in a sacrificial defense of their community. Such an offering is a hard thing to ask, and it is harder still if those killed are forgotten or if their death serves vanity, not life.

It has been fifty years since North Korea invaded South Korea and began the Korean War, which lasted for three deadly years. Four million Koreans were killed, and the United States, which at the war's peak defended South Korea with as many as half a million soldiers, lost 55,000 troops—nearly as many as in the twelve-year Vietnam War.

U.S. involvement in Korea was unpopular with many Americans, partly because it seemed far from U.S. interests. Yet the fact remains that American soldiers in Korea fought a tyrannical communist government believed to be part of a larger threat to American freedom. The grim and brutal battles they won checked that force and left South Korea, decades later, independent and increasingly free and wealthy. Whatever one's view of this "Forgotten War," their actions created something real, not vain.

These Americans kept faith with us. We keep faith by remembering, not forgetting. The veterans' poppies call us to do so—and call us to ensure that those who die in every America war are likewise remembered and not asked to die in vain.

Sunday, June 13, 2004

Dear Kim and Brad,

I was so pleased that I was able to attend your beautiful wedding. You both looked so happy. Kim, you were just glowing! Your dress and veil were so very lovely, and you looked so beautiful in them. I also loved the color and style of your attendants' dresses. Andrea looked beautiful too. I was so happy to meet your mother also, and again, she looked lovely. There are not enough different adjectives to describe everything. I thought it was a fantastic wedding, and everything seemed to go very smoothly. I'm sure the rest of your day went well also. The weather came through at the last minute, and I was so pleased for all of you. Brad, we have never met, but I have heard nice things about you. Knowing Kim, I'm sure you are a super nice guy. You and your attendants looked great too.

I wanted to send my congratulations and best wishes to both of you for a long and happy marriage. I'm enclosing a copy of a letter I wrote to my grandson and his new wife when they were married last June. They just celebrated their first anniversary and are very happy and doing well. As "Grandma," I feel with the years I have lived and things I have experienced over the years, just maybe I could give some ideas to make a marriage work. As I said in my letter to Erik and Eve: Kim, if you and Brad can have as long and happy a marriage as I had with my husband, that would be my wish for you.

I'm thinking of both of you today, probably on your way to Tahiti, hoping you both have a wonderful time. I'll be anxious to see pictures when you get back to the real world again.

My love, prayers, and best wishes always.

Sunday, June 13, 2004

Dear Mr. and Mrs. Mato,

Thank you for inviting me to Kim's wedding. I was so happy I was able to attend. It was absolutely beautiful in every way. I think a great deal of your daughter. She is a lovely young lady. It has been wonderful to get to know her over the past few years. I knew Andrea also, but she left the Village before I knew her well. You would be very proud of Kim to see how she interacts with the people in our generation. She has made a lot of friends here. We have a lot of nice young people that work here, and of course, it's the same as other places. There are some people that you become closer to than others. I had a grandson who got married last June 5 and have a granddaughter who is getting married this coming October. So Kim and I had a lot of wedding plans to talk about. Also it's been a joy to see Kim grow, with college, her internship here, her engagement, etc.

It was very nice to meet you, Pam, and you looked beautiful also. I loved the colors of the bridal party. That's the first time I had been to Divine Child Church, and I was very impressed with how lovely it was.

I hope Kim and Brad have a wonderful time in Tahiti and a long and happy marriage. I also hope that you folks can have as great a relationship with your new son-in-law as we had with our three. Over the years, they have become sons to me, and that's a wonderful feeling. I'm very grateful that I had fifty-eight years with my husband and that I have a wonderful family that cares about me. I know Kim has a great family also. I believe families are our center and help us handle every aspect of life.

My best wishes to all of you always.

You Are Invited To A

BRIDAL SHOWER

FOR: Cindy Leinonen and Joe Rivet

When: Saturday—August 14, 2004
Where: Family Buggy Restaurant,
11502 Plymouth Road
South-east corner at Middlebelt Road,
734-427-8360

Time: 12:00 p.m. to 2:30

Given by her family

Hope you can join us for this happy occasion.
Cindy and Joe would also appreciate if
you would share one of your favorite recipes with them.

RSVP: By Monday—August 9
Carol: 734-522-1162
Vivian: 313-581-7041

When You Marry Him

When you marry him, love him.
After you marry him, study him.
If he is sad, cheer him.
When he is talkative, listen to him.
When he is quarrelsome, ignore him,
If he is jealous, cure him.
If he cares naught for pleasure, Coax him.
If he favors society, accompany him.
When he deserves it, kiss him.
Let him think how well you
Understand him.
But never let him know that
You manage him . . .

Aunt Barb and I found these verses on antique samplers, and we bought them. Both of us thought they were very appropriate. We were at the United Methodist Church in West Dearborn for their quilt show and craft sale on October 29, 2004.

When You Marry Her

When you marry her, love her.
After you marry her, study her,
When she is blue, cheer her.
When she is talkative,
By all means listen to her.
If she dresses well, compliment her.
When she is cross, humor her.
If she does you a favor, kiss her.
When she is jealous, cure her.
If dinner is cold, eat it, not her.
When she looks pretty, tell her so.
Let her feel how well you
Understand her.
But never let her know she
Isn't the boss.

These verses might have been written years ago, but the message is still worthwhile.

Grandma's Reflections:
Cindy and Joe's Wedding, 16 2004

Sitting here at my computer on a gray, misty, chilly afternoon on October 21, 2004, I am fighting a cold and feeling a little lonesome and sorry for myself, as yesterday was Bill's eighty-fifth birthday. It's funny how even after four years of being alone, those dates on a calendar can *hurt!* It's something I have come to realize that you never "get over it." You just learn to live with it. Some days and times are more difficult than others.

What I really want to write about is my granddaughter Cindy Leinonen and Joseph Rivet's wonderful wedding on October 16, 2004. I'd also like to share some of the things I learned and heard that brought them to this beautiful day, and also to share with whoever may read this, how very grateful I am to and for everyone in my special family. That also includes people in my extended family. Everyone of you have a special place in my heart, and without you I could not keep going.

Cindy had decided to spread her wings as she felt like things were not going exactly the way she had dreamed of. She was doing fine, but in my opinion, I think she was a little bored and also a bit burned out with her jobs around here in social work. She had this opportunity to take this job out in Washington State. It was a big ego boost, as they wanted her enough to pay all her moving expenses out there. It was also more pay than she was getting here. Washington State does not have social workers available with master's degrees like we do in this area. Cindy loved the area and did well in her work out there. Being the type of person she is, she made friends too. Also, one of her best friends, Leslie, who Cindy had gone to school with back here, lived just an hour away. They did a lot of things together, *but* Cindy missed her family! She felt left out when holidays rolled around and special occasions came along. Air fares are expensive and getting time off work not always easy to do. Her brother Erik was getting married to Eve on June 7, 2003. She wanted to be here. Dress fittings were difficult as well as lots of other things. Her aunt Barb was fighting inflammatory breast cancer. I had to have a hip replacement. Aunt Betty's health was going downhill. Also, Cindy herself was having very bad heartburn problems and the doctors wanted to operate. Cindy wanted her mama and her family. It did work out, as things usually do.

Cindy made it here for her brother's beautiful wedding to Eve. Of course, time at home always goes by too fast. Then at the end of June 2003, Cindy had her operation at the hospital she worked at. Carol was able to fly out there to take care of her, and Cindy was very grateful. At that same time, a young man named Joe Rivet who worked at the same hospital as Cindy in the accounting department called Carol to see how Cindy was doing. He also sent her flowers. Cindy had met Joe and knew who he was, but they had never dated or been close. Joe had been married before and had a little boy Corbin who was about two and a half at that time. He shared custody with his ex-wife. Things changed from that time on. Of course, I didn't know all the details, but from what I have heard, Cindy fell in love with both Joe and Corbin. *And,* also what I have seen and heard, that love was returned a thousand times over. Cindy was thirty and was beginning to wonder if she would ever meet Mr. Right. Cindy brought Joe and Corbin home in October 2003 to meet the family, and everything fell into place. Joe and Corbin fit in our family, and we were all very happy for them. Joe had been in touch with Carol through e-mails and phone calls and had a ring for Cindy to surprise her. They planned their wedding for October 2004. They were here at Christmastime in 2003 and made a lot of the arrangements then.

Early in 2004, Cindy began sending resumes to places back here. She really wanted to move back here to be close to her family. Joe also seemed to want a change and was very willing to move to Michigan. The only setback was the custody of Corbin. Joe and Cindy would loved to have full custody of Corbin, but Heather, Corbin's mother, wanted him also. That is very understandable, I think. Anyway, I don't know all the details, but it did get worked out. Divorce is hard on everyone, especially young children. Children have two different families and lifestyles, and you can't help but wonder how it will affect them. One thing I do see though is, Corbin seems to know he is loved by a lot of people and doesn't seem to be to affected by the going back and forth. We can just hope that it will continue.

In March of this year, Cindy was hired by Kelly Trudell, head of Resident Life, and Leslie Dubin, Head Social Worker, here at the Village. Needless to say Carol and I were delighted. The Village and Leslie had tried to hire Cindy four years ago but the pay was not enough, and of course that is important. Needless to say, Cindy did have to take a pay cut from her Washington job but felt it was worth it to move back home. I have known

Leslie since Bill and I moved in here almost seven years ago. She has always been there for me and has helped me through some very rough times. I consider Leslie a very good friend and one of my extended granddaughters. Kelly also is a treasure. The staff here at the Village is wonderful in my opinion. So many of them have become my good friends over the years, and as I said before, they help me keep going—Myra, Sandra, Sister Mary, Cheryl Presley, Cheryl Price. They too are my extended family and have a place in my heart.

Back to Cindy and Joe. After Cindy knew she had a job waiting for her here at the Village, she needed to find a place to live. Cindy's very best friend from elementary school days, Jim Woukila, took care of that problem for them and found them a nice apartment in Livonia. I forgot to tell you that Joe had been sending his resumes around the Detroit area also. He was hired by the Henry Ford Hospital in the accounting department at almost the same time that Cindy was hired here at the Village. It certainly looked like that was meant to be. Of course, they had to move across the country and start new jobs, getting the courts to let them bring Corbin, etc. Needless to say, it was a little stressful on everyone. But again it all worked out. Cindy drove across the country with her two cats, Zeke and Teagan. I guess that was quite a trip. The cats were not too happy. A week later, Joe drove the same route with Corbin, who I heard was much better than the cats. Remember, this is just my version, and some of the dates and times may not be totally right. Cindy started her job on March 18, 2004. Two days after her thirty-first birthday, Joe started his job a week later and Carol became "Grandma Carol" and took care of Corbin. They get along beautifully, and Carol loves being a grandma. Sadly though, they do have to take Corbin back to his mother after a few weeks and wait until it is their time to have him again. Corbin was here for eight weeks this summer and got to meet Sydney when Bill and Shannon were here on vacation the first two weeks in August. Sydney and Corbin's birthdays are not quite a month apart and both turned four this fall. They got along wonderfully and were so much fun to watch together.

We were also able to have a family shower for Cindy and Joe on August 1, 2004, just before Shannon and Bill had to go back to Colorado. We had it at The Family Buggy Restaurant on Plymouth and Middlebelt in Livonia. It was very lovely. It was fun to get the family together for happy times, and Cindy and Joe got a lot of nice gifts. Cindy had never met Sydney before.

With her being in Washington State and Bill and Shannon in Colorado, their vacation times here had never been together. After meeting Sydney and watching her, Cindy talked to Bill and Shannon about their feelings on letting Sydney be a flower girl in their wedding. Sydney is a very outgoing little girl and very loveable to everyone. (In fact, Bill and Shannon have to keep a close eye on her) Corbin is shy, very lovable also, but first he has to get to know you. Corbin of course was going to be in the wedding party. Cindy and Joe thought that by asking Sydney to be a flower girl and walking with Corbin, as the two of them got along so well together, would be a help to Corbin. Besides, Sydney was a darling little girl and would be an asset in their wedding. They had not planned on having a flower girl before. Bill and Shannon agreed, and it really worked out just great. I told Cindy that I thought Corbin and Sydney would steal the show, and they almost did as they were so adorable together coming down the aisle. Carol told me after the wedding that it's a good thing Sydney was there as Corbin got very shy when he saw all the people in the church and without Sydney to hold his hand he might not have walked down the aisle. They couldn't steal the show from Cindy and Joe though as the two of them were just glowing with happiness, but I am getting ahead of my story.

It was a busy summer for everyone with Cindy and Joe adjusting to their new jobs and doing all the wedding planning with Carol. Cindy and Joe had asked me if I would consider making the design for the covers of their wedding programs, and they gave me a few ideas of fall themes. I told them I would try but no promises. I fooled around and came up with an idea of a fall tree, and they loved it. I felt honored. I went ahead then and got Kinko's to color print them. Then I folded them and tied them with gold cording. I had the original framed for them. That was my wedding gift to them. They seemed very happy, and that warmed my heart. Cindy and Joe also invited me to go to taste the wedding cake with them and Carol. That was a fun thing to do. I also went with Cindy and Carol one evening for a fitting of Cindy's wedding dress. I enjoyed that also. Weddings are so much more complicated now than when Grandpa and I got married. Of course, Carol and Barbara both had big weddings, but I don't remember that we had to do quite so many things. That was back in 1966 and 1970. It was kind of a nice coincidence though. Burton Manor where Cindy and Joe had their reception used to be Roma Hall where Carol and Edsel had their wedding reception.

Finally, the month of October arrived. Corbin flew here with Joe's Mother, Edna, on Saturday, October 9. On Sunday, the tenth, Cindy and Joe had a belated birthday party at Carol's for Corbin who had turned four on September 23. It served two purposes, one to celebrate Corbin's birthday and for being back here and for the family to meet Edna, Joe's mother. Erik, Eve, Cindy's good friend Jim, and friend Carol, with her son Lucas, two and a half years old, all were there.

It was a beautiful fall day, and I drove over to Carol's through Hines Parkway. Some of the trees were turning color and were beautiful. I had to sort of meet and greet and eat and run. I was hosting "The Livingston Lamplighters" for our Sunday afternoon entertainment program, and I had to be back there at 3:00 p.m. I had made the arrangements for the group to be here quite a few months back, so I felt obligated to be here, especially as so many of our committee members had been having health problems. We had sixteen men here who sang "Barbershop Harmony," and they were absolutely fantastic! The residents loved them. Not only was their music beautiful, their rapport with the audience was wonderful. My announcing them went well. I don't know why I get so uptight about doing it. Everyone says I come across very clearly and do a good job. Anyway ...

On the Wednesday before the wedding, October 13, I got a call from Scott. He had just got home from the hospital where they had done an emergency appendectomy on Tuesday evening. *Wow,* this family! You just never know, *but* he was doing fine! In fact when he called me, he sounded just great. He was still hyped on the drugs. I heard that evening and the next day were a different story. He was able to be there at the wedding, and we were very grateful. He didn't do any dancing though!

The wedding weekend was there! Our weather during September and the first part of October had been beautiful with sunshine and blue skies—perfect fall weather. Of course, it changed. There were rain, winds, and gray skies starting Thursday. You know what though? It didn't make any difference to that wonderful weekend. Cindy and Joe were so happy. Most of my family were able to be here, and everyone was doing well that we had our own special sunshine inside all of us.

Erik and Eve picked me up a little after 5:00 p.m. on Friday the fifteenth. Erik had a cold that he was trying to fight off. Eve had just had mid-terms and thought she had done OK, but those tests are always stressful. We stopped at Baker's Square to pick up pies we had ordered for the rehearsal dinner and then went on to Faith Lutheran Church for the rehearsal. Right after we got there, Bill, Shannon, and Sydney came in. They had just got in from Denver and drove right from the airport to the church. Sydney ran right to me and gave me a great big hug with lots of smiles. She melted my heart. She is such a darling little girl. We are so lucky. It was so good to see them again. I met Leslie Vannier, again, after not seeing her for several years with her being out in Washington. She is a very good friend of Cindy's. I also met her fiancé Eric, who had flown here with her. Jim Wuokila, Cindy's very best friend, who we have known for years, was there. I met Reverend Elizabeth Meharg who had also flown in from Washington to be a part of their service. Andrew VanBergen came in from Chicago to sing at their wedding. He had also sung at Erik and Eve's wedding. He has a wonderful voice. He is the son of Carol and Edsel's old and dear friends, Sue and Ken VanBergen. They all met right after they were married back in 1966 and have remained close friends all these years. Now that's *special!* Just a side note, Andrew is a pediatric heart surgeon. Rehearsal went well, and Sydney and Corbin renewed their friendship almost like they had just seen one another yesterday. It was nice. After the rehearsal, we all went back to Carol's for a rehearsal party cook-out, which because of the weather had to be inside. It didn't matter. Erik still managed to grill hamburgers for all, with the grill pulled up near the door wall. Also, with all the snacks and other food available along with Carol's great macaroni salad and lemon and chocolate silk pie for dessert, everyone was soon full with delicious food and great company.

Erik's good friends from Ferris State, Jeremy and Angie, had also joined us. One of the nicest things that happened and which I will never forget about that evening was Jim W. making a toast to Cindy and Joe. He got everyone's attention and then said, "I will never forget when I first met Cindy's grandma which was about twenty-one years ago." (Jim must have been about ten or eleven at that time.) "She was sitting on the arm of a chair in this family room and holding hands with a gentleman, and she leaned over to give him a kiss. I thought, 'Oh, Cindy's grandma has a boyfriend.' Then I found out that was Cindy's grandpa, and they had been married for years and years. He has been gone for around four years now and is still missed. I had never seen two older people so much in love. My wish for Cindy and Joe is that they will have the same kind of marriage." By this time I was all choked up and in tears, so I may not have his exact words right, but I think this was the main part of what he said. I was so surprised that he had remembered something like that back when he was so young and was so impressed that he had never forgotten it. You never know what actions or words of ours will be remembered. Jim has always been very special to both Grandpa and myself. We saw him so often at family doings at Carol and Edsel's that we always considered him an extended grandson. I will treasure his words the rest of my days.

By this time it was getting late, so Bill, Shannon, and Sydney brought me home, and they started to get settled in. I was so very happy to have them here. Then there was a knock on the door, and there were Barb and Alice. What a lovely surprise! They wanted to see "Little Butterbean" and Bill and Shannon too. Barb had also brought me a new wall hanging for my bedroom door. It was made to look like pears cut in half and was so pretty. Barb just gets better and better at this quilting hobby.

What a lovely evening! It started with Erik and Eve picking me up. It seems like being with and sharing things with all of "my family" is what makes my life worthwhile and enjoyable. To all be together for such a happy occasion is just wonderful! Needless to say, none of us got a lot of sleep that night, but it was nice because no one had to hurry to be anywhere or be ready until the middle of Saturday afternoon. Cindy had asked us to be at the church around 3:00 p.m. It was nice not to have to rush. Everyone took their time getting ready. Bill made a trip to White Castle for food for their lunch as he had to have his "White Castle Fix" when he comes to Michigan. I had got a hamburger at Windows for my lunch. Everyone looked so nice when we left for the church about 2:30 p.m. Bill looked really sharp in his suit and tie. I had not seen him dressed up for years. Shannon decided to dress Sydney at the church so that her "princess dress" would not get all wrinkled in the car seat. Shannon looked lovely in a pretty black dress with a little bit of beading, and I was teasing her about her high heels. When I was her age, I wore high heels too. Now at eighty-three, I'm in a navy pant suit with a lacey white blouse and my navy "ortho" shoes. Cindy had told me that she wanted me to be comfortable, so I was.

It was still raining off and on but not too bad. Cindy was just getting into her dress when we got there. She looked so beautiful. Eve and Leslie looked lovely in their taupe color dresses. But Erik had given Eve his cold, and she was kind of miserable and trying to hide it. Carol looked radiant in her navy blue dress with beading. Boy, I've got a good looking family. Shannon got Sydney dressed in her beautiful ivory full-skirted long dress and her hair fixed with a beautiful ribbon, and she did look like her favorite Disney princesses. The photographer came and started taking lots of pictures. Edna, Joe's mother, also looked lovely in her champagne-colored dress. Corbin was adorable in his tux. I went down to see the groom and Erik to see how they were holding up. They also looked great. Bill made a trip to 7-Eleven to get bottled water for everyone, which was greatly appreciated. Barbara and Alice came in to see us and Kelly, who I hadn't seen in two years. Before we knew it, it was time to "get the show on the road."

Mark escorted Joe's mother down the aisle, and then Andrew escorted me. A lot of people had made it to the church for the ceremony, which was very nice. The procession started with the minister, Robert Carr, and the groom walking down the aisle together. Reverend Elizabeth was already up in the front. Next came Jim and Leslie, who went and stood on the bride's side, then Erik and Eve who stood on the groom's side.

With Joe not having many people from his side who were able to be there, that was a bit different and worked out very nicely. Next came Corbin and Sydney. They were adorable. There were lots of oohs and aahs from everyone there. Corbin had his head down as he was very shy; Sydney had a big smile on her face, holding his hand while walking down the aisle. Corbin went to stand by his daddy, and Sydney who was supposed to stay back went right along also, and Erik took her hand and she stood beside him beautifully all through the ceremony. Carol and Cindy came down the aisle together, and again there were some oohs and a few teary eyes. They were both just glowing and looked so beautiful. Carol gave Cindy away to Joe and the minister and then came and sat beside me. Joe was looking at Cindy as if she was the most wonderful thing that had ever happened to him. Shannon, Bill, Barb, Ken, and Alice sat right behind us. In fact, Alice came up and sat on the other side of me after Carol joined me, which made me happy.

The ceremony was very nice. Cindy is going to give me a copy of the Reverend Elizabeth's sermonette for Joe and Cindy to include in this writing. One thing that I had never seen before and I thought was very nice and also very appropriate was called "Blending of the Sands." In this ritual action, an alternative to the lighting of a Unity Candle, the union of Cindy and Joe was symbolized as they poured two different colors of sand into one container. Since there was also a child who will share in this new family, a third container of sand representing Corbin was also included in this ritual action. As the tiny grains of sands, once blended, can never be separated and poured again into individual containers, so we pray will the union of Joe, Cindy, and Corbin be inseparable. Corbin was very much into this pouring of his little container of colored sand into the one blending all of them. It was very special. At the time they were doing this, Andrew was singing the beautiful song "I will be here" by Steven Chapman. It was lovely and the words very meaningful. I have enclosed a copy of the words in this writing also.

The ceremony was soon over, and Mr. and Mrs. Joe Rivet walked back down the aisle together. They looked radiant!

The wedding party stayed behind for lots of pictures up by the altar. The rest of the people went on to Burton Manor for the reception. The bar was open as well as a table with snack foods, cheese, crackers, veggies, etc. It was very nice. Corbin and Sydney were very good and played together while all the pictures were being taken while also doing their part when they were asked to be in them. It was fun to watch everything. Then it was time for us to also go to Burton Manor. Bill and Shannon were very proud of their daughter with good reason. We were all sitting at the front No. 1 table with Carol, the Reverend Elizabeth, and Joe's mother, Edna. Barb, Ken, Alice, Jim, Scott, Hannah, Kelly, and Steve were at a table right next to us. Joe and Cindy had put little place cards with fall leaves on the border (which they had asked to do) to match the wedding program into small picture frames with names and the assigned table numbers on them. They made nice keepsakes for the guests to take home. Shortly after we got to the hall, the wedding party arrived, and the nice DJ announced them as they came in. Cindy and Joe went immediately to the dance floor and did a special dance for everyone and then moved on to the head table. They looked very nice and did an excellent job. There were a lot of cameras flashing. Then dinner was served, which consisted of very nice salad with rolls, then a hot plate of both roast beef and chicken, red skinned potatoes, and green beans. Everything was delicious.

Cindy and Joe had requested for no banging spoons against cups or glasses for them to kiss. If you wanted them to kiss, they had to sing a song, either individually or the entire table. That was fun, interesting, and different. The DJ went around with the mike for people to use. Several tables sang songs for them, and our Sydney stood up on a chair, took the mike, and sang "I love you, You love me. We are a happy family" to the bride and groom, looking like as if this was something she did every day. She was adorable. I was a proud grandma, needless to say. I am very proud of all my grandchildren. In their own ways, they are all special to me, and this includes the ones I received by marriage and by friendship. I feel very, very lucky and grateful. It was a very nice feeling to have one granddaughter getting married and another one four years old being a part of her wedding. It was special! I was so happy that I was able to be a part of this happy occasion and to have so many of my family there—my kids, Carol, Jim, Barbara, Ken, Alice, Bill, and Shannon; my grandkids, the bride and groom, Cindy and Joe, Erik, Eve, Scotty, Kelly, Steve, and Sydney, as well as Jim W., Leslie, and Dave Dubin. It's a scary feeling for me to realize that I am the oldest member left in both my family and Bill's family. I know I was the oldest person there at the wedding. *Wow!* I read a saying the other day that I think is most appropriate and true. "Family faces are magic mirrors. Looking at people who belong to us, we see the past, present, and future."

I was so proud of Carol too. It was a beautiful wedding, and everything went along so smoothly. I know it was a lot of work on Carol's part; of course she had help and input from Cindy and Joe, and she loved doing it for them, but Edsel was missed. He would have loved it.

The time went by quickly. Everyone seemed to be having a good time—dancing and talking to friends and family. Carol, Cindy, and Joe had arranged a wedding cake piñata for the children, and they had a lot of fun with that. Corbin, Sydney, Ian and Andrew (Ang and Paul's children), Laura, Shawn, Austin, Mark Leinonen's daughter Elizabeth, Michelle, and Denny's Meleana, plus I'm sure some children I didn't know, all had a ball. Ian and Andrew are always so good about sharing their candy and toys with the younger children. It was so nice to see. Also, "the chicken dance" came up again, and adults and children had more fun with that. The grandchildren still remind me of learning that dance from Bill and me when we had come back from our wonderful cruise in 1981. The servers at Burton Manor were very good. They served the wedding cake and also their good cannolis to everyone. I heard later that they also served their famous pizza at eleven o'clock. We had left around 10:30 p.m. I remember that they did that way back in 1966 when Carol and Edsel were married. I think I have already told you that at that time it was called "Roma Hall " . . ."

As I mentioned we had left around 10:30 p.m. We were all tired out—Bill, Shannon, and Sydney because of the Colorado time change and not a lot of sleep and me as I was not used to those kind of hours anymore. We all agreed however that we thought the whole evening was a very big success! When we got back here, we all got ready for bed and comfortable, but we did stay up talking and just enjoying being together. Shannon also had to pack up again as they had to get up at 5:00 a.m. to be ready to leave for the airport by six. We were all wishing they could have stayed longer but were so grateful that they were able to come. Sydney was so good and so loveable. It was a very short night for all, and it was hard to say good-bye, but again, I'm grateful for the time we had together.

I heard from Carol, Cindy, and Joe later that right after 11:00 p.m. everyone pretty much left. They packed up all the wedding presents and took them to Carol's. Grandma Edna and Corbin went back to Cindy and Joe's apartment and Cindy and Joe to a hotel for their very short honeymoon. I understand that they had Sunday together and went to the Fisher Theater Sunday evening to see the play "Thoroughly Modern Millie," then went back home. On Monday, all of them went over to Carol's to open presents, which was a fun time. I had also been invited, but I thought it best that I stayed home and rested. On Tuesday, they had made arrangements to go on The Rouge Factory Tour and had invited me to go with them. It was another misty rainy day, but we all enjoyed the tour. I thought it was very worthwhile and was so happy they had included me. It seemed strange to be in the same area where Grandpa had started his career with Ford Motor Company, as an apprentice in the tool room, and where I had occasionally picked him up from work, also, to see that famous bridge again where I had sold poppies for the veterans the same May (not on the same day, thank goodness) that they had that fight that is in your history books between the union and Ford Motor Co. It was so many, many years ago. I did have to swallow my pride a bit and use a wheelchair as I just could not walk that far. After the tour, we went to Big Boy for a late lunch and I enjoyed a Slim Jim, which I had not had for a very long time. It was another day of being with my family, and that I appreciate so very much. Cindy and Joe both had to go back to work on Wednesday. With Corbin being here, they did not want to miss their time with him, so they delayed their honeymoon. I understand they had a cruise booked for February. Corbin and Grandma Edna went back to Washington State on November 2, Election Day.

These "reflections" have taken me much more time to write than I had originally planned. Also, they have gotten longer. That's one thing that I never know. When I sit down to write about something I'm never sure just what is going to come out. I sit here and whatever comes out on the paper is written from my thoughts and feelings of that day. Here it is November 4, another rainy misty day. I have written about these "reflections" off and on when the mood would hit me. I do hope that whoever reads these will realize that these are written from my heart and memories. Perhaps some of the details are not quite correct, but I don't think that in the long run it will matter. It has been a beautiful time for Cindy and Joe and for the people who love them. I do wish them the very best of everything and again a marriage similar to what Bill and I had.

P.S. We had an important presidential election during this time also, and our country has been very divided. Now we have George W. Bush elected again. I have been very unhappy about him getting us into the war in Iraq. But I'm not sure whether John Kerry could do much about that either. We knew that neither man could keep all of their campaign promises. Now that Bush has been elected again, I do hope that the Senate and Congress will get together and try and heal the division in our country. I have never been either a strong Democrat or Republican. I have always tried to vote for the issues and the man. But I have always voted. It is a privilege and an honor to be an American. God bless our country and help our leaders. While I realize this postscript has nothing to do with Cindy and Joe's wedding, it is history at this time in our lives, *and* as I mentioned before, when I sit down to write, I never know exactly what is going to come out.

Henry Ford Village

October 22, 2004

Ms. Vivian Beeler
CC302

Dear Viv,

On behalf of Henry Ford Village, I would like to thank you for your of our 5' Annual Gala to benefit our Benevolent Fund through your donation of a beautiful framed pansy print to our Silent Auction. (As you know, a "Beeler Original" is always a coveted item!) The Auction generated a lot of interest and excitement at the Gala and raised an additional $3,560 for the Benevolent Fund. In all, $308,000 was raised to continue the important work of the Benevolent Fund and your donation is an important part of our success.

Since the Benevolent Fund began providing financial support for residents in 2000, it has distributed over $611,000 for resident care. Benevolent care continues to be a growing need at Henry Ford Village and your contribution will enable us to continue to provide financial support for residents who have depleted their assets due to a prolonged illness.

Henry Ford Village's commitment to our residents is to provide them with a "home for life." As a result of your kindness and generosity, they will be able to remain at Henry Ford Village surrounded by those who know and love them.

Thank you so much for your participation in our Benevolent Fund Gala and for supporting our mission in such a special way. you are so special to me and to everyone who know you: thank you for being a blessing in a blessing in my life xo

With Love and Gratitude,
Cheryl Presley
Community Relations Manager

Hear Ye! Hear Ye!

Annual Family Christmas Party

When: Sunday, December 5, 2004
Where: Henry Ford Village, 15181 Ford Road at Greenfield.
        Apt. Chapel Court 302 . . . Vivian Beeler
Time: 2:00 p.m. until?

Hosted by: Marguerette and Vivian

Also including: The Residents and their families

Village Christmas Party from 2:30 to 4:30 . . . Crafts for children . . . Pictures with Santa. Punch and Snacks . . . Also for those of you who have not been here before . . . To see where Marguerette and I live.

Please bring a appetizer or cookies to share. My oven, fridge, and microwave will be available to use if needed.

RSVP only if unable to make it: 313-582—0417 M. Wagner. 313-581-7041 V. Beeler.

I take full responsibility for this wild idea of our Christmas Party for this year! I know it will be crowded. BUT . . . We're FAMILY! Thought the children would enjoy having something to do, as I saw what a good time Ian and Andrew had last year. The Village is beautiful at this time of year. There will always be a family member here in my apt. so, we can leave it open for everyone to come and go as they want.

LET'S GIVE IT A TRY . . . COME ON . . . HUMOR ME. I'm the MATRIARCH: (now that's scary)

Webster's Dictionary.
1. A woman who rules her family or tribe. (?) Ha!
2. A woman of great age and dignity. (age, yes), (?)
   Love to all, Vivian, Mom, Grandma, Aunt
   Hope to see all of you at the Party!

Henry Ford Village

Cordially Invites You to
"Come and Celebrate The Joys of the Season"
At
The Residents Holiday Extravaganza!

Sunday, December 5, 2004
2:30 p.m.-4:30 p.m.

Great Lakes Clubhouse
&
Renaissance Gardens

The Festivities will Include:
Live Music
Children's Crafts
A Visit from Santa
The Holiday Boutique
Delectable Refreshments
A Complimentary Professional Family Photo
(photo packages are available)

My Holidays: 2004

January 4, 2004

I haven't written anything on the computer in quite a long time, except for answering my e-mails, and that technology I really do enjoy! I thought I would write about how with the wonderful help of my family the holidays are bearable and parts of them enjoyable! Since Bill and Kathy have been gone, life has not been that good to me. My own health has gone downhill since I hit eighty, and life seems to be getting more and more difficult. I try very hard to keep a good attitude, but some days it's *tough!* This pain that I have in my back and leg just does not let up. It is with me all the time. Darvocet eases it a bit or I feel it does 'cause it relaxes me a little. It has other bad side effects, and I don't want to be a zombie, so I am very careful how I use it, mainly in the late afternoon and evening. I hate this complaining, but doggone, life is not very much fun anymore. I have to plan all my activities and then can only do so much. Everything is such a big effort, and I wonder where this is all going. Death does not frighten me, but this process of dying does. Then too we have just had one of the most historic disasters that has ever happened in our world. One hundred and fifty thousand dead from an earthquake below sea level and a tsunami tidal wave. Whole villages wiped out. This took place over in Sri Lanka, India, Thailand, and Indonesia. It caused so much death and destruction, and now they are worried about disease among the survivors. It is not even comprehensible, and here I am complaining. It makes me stop and think.

Sorry, I did not mean to get off on this tangent and bore you. I've told you before, I never know what is going to come out when I sit down to write. Anyway, my holidays started very early this year. On November 17, Barbara and Alice came down to help clean out my computer room and to get me organized. I had come up with the wild idea of having the family Christmas party here at my apartment, combining it with our Annual Residents Christmas Party that they put on for us. With all the activities for children and picture taking with Santa Claus, I thought it would be fun to try it. Also it would be a break for give Susan, Alan, and Carol from having it at their houses. Sandra, Michele, and Cathy Jo wanted to host it if Marguerette and I could get a room here. They were all taken. That's when I got this other idea. Being the "matriarch" of the Beeler family now (scary thought), I sent out invitations asking everyone to humor me and give it a try.

So that meant I had to get busy and get my place cleaned up. My computer room has been used as my garage, my basement, and my attic. When I didn't know what to do with something in it went. It badly needed some help. Barb and Alice tore into it and really organized me. They brought down storage shelves and put them against the wall and in the closet. They sorted things out for Treasure Sale shop and for trash. It was amazing. I had a room again! It was a very rainy day, and they were so busy that we just went down to Windows and got a quick sandwich there and then back to work. We got so involved that I forgot my Entertainment Committee Meeting and missed it. But it was worth it. Here it is January and I still am enjoying my nice computer room. I don't even feel like I have to close the door if anyone stops in. They did a fantastic job.

On November 18, Carol came over and she helped me get all my Christmas decorations up from the storage units and put them around. She even got the tree decorated while I was resting. I'm getting to be a good watcher, but it does bother me when I want to be doing also. This is the first time in my life that I have decorated for Christmas before Thanksgiving. *But*, hey, I took advantage of when the girls could help me, and I am very grateful to all of them. I just can't do those things on my own anymore, which is hard to admit. Now my place looked like Christmas and was ready for the family party. I'm looking forward to it.

On Thanksgiving Day, Erik and Eve picked me up. We had had a little snowfall the night before. We did not have much in Dearborn, but the closer we got to Milford the more we saw. It was so beautiful, like a Winter fairyland. The sun was shining and the trees were so beautiful. It was *cold* so the snow stayed on the trees. Jim's house looked beautiful. Jim and Hannah had a very good Thanksgiving turkey dinner with all the trimmings. Our new family member, Joe, Cindy's husband, loves to bake and cook, and he had brought a peach cobbler to have along with Scotty's pumpkin pie. It was yummy. We all told him he could stay in the family. We ate early as Erik had to go to work, but Eve stayed and came home with Carol and me. The landscape and trees were just gorgeous going home, but the closer we got back to the Dearborn area, the less snow we had. It was almost like two different countries. Of course, they had sent turkey and Scotty's rolls home with me so I could have a couple of good turkey sandwiches later. It was a very nice day. Barb and Ken had gone up to the cabin for the weekend and Alice had to go to work, so we missed them, but we knew they were all doing well. Ken had not been up to the cabin since Barb was diagnosed with breast cancer, and to have the weekend with her up there was very good for both of them. They had asked me earlier if I would mind if they went. I said, "Of course not, I'm happy you have the opportunity to go." Ken usually has to work on the Friday after Thanksgiving, but he was able to get that one off. As I said, it was good therapy for both of them. We also found out on Thanksgiving that Erik had made as a detective! I know he has been aiming for that position. He starts first of February. We are all happy for them. Erik will work on weekdays and have weekends and holidays off. I am so proud of all my grandchildren. They are all hard workers and strive to get ahead. Of course I'm talking about my seven grown-up ones. Sydney is only four, but from what we can see she will be right up there also.

Our family Christmas party was a success! It was a little crowded at times, but it was all family. The weather cooperated also as we had a beautiful sunny day. Angela and Paul were not able to come at the last minute as Paul's dad was ill and they were having a family weekend. Ian and Andrew enjoyed the activities along with Meleana. The grown-ups seemed to enjoy seeing where Marguerette and I lived and how beautifully we had decorated the Village for the holidays. We had loads of food of all kinds, which is normal for any of the Beeler parties, starting way back with Mom and Pop Beeler when those family parties first started the first Sunday in December. *Traditions!* It's so nice to keep them going.

I had been working on my Christmas cards for what seemed like months now—with coming up with the design, taking it to Kinko's to reduce and copy, then all the gluing on the blank cards. This year I came up with an angel. Then after I got the cards made, I decided to put glitter on the angel's wings. It was more work and time and my back ached, *and* I have no one to blame but myself! Plus, my list keeps growing and growing. Had to go back to Kinko's for more copies. It ended up I sent out almost 140 cards. I made a mistake several years ago of sending cards to all my doctors and the staff here at the Village. The staff has increased in size and I can't ignore anyone. Plus every year I know more people here who touch my life in some way. It is an ego boost for me when I meet people and they tell me how much they enjoy getting my cards, but it is getting to the point that I'm swamped by all the work involved. I'm not sure what to do about it. I've got to think about this.

There is always a lot going on around here in December. They have a lot of school and church choirs come in for programs. The Sunday Entertainment Committee, of which I'm a member, has Pete Waldmeir the newspaper columnist come for the Goodfellows with all donations going to that fund. We also had Lance Luce, the theater organist, come for music along with Pete's talk about the Goodfellows. People were very generous, and we collected almost $1,200. The Detroit News Paper matched this fund, so it was well worth the while. The Goodfellows do a lot of good for the people of Detroit and have for years and years.

We had our Christmas tea on December 13 with the combined committees of Birthday Angels, Library, Movies, and Bulletin Board. It was very nice. On Sunday, the nineteenth, Cindy and Joe had invited me to go with them and Corbin, and also Carol, to see *The Polar Express* with Tom Hanks at the Imax Theater at Greenfield Village. It was a delightful movie in 3D. You felt like you were right in the movie yourself. Cindy had got tickets ahead of time as every showing was pretty much sold out. They picked me up about 5:30 p.m. and dropped me off right at the door to the theater. It had turned out to be a bitter cold day, plus windy. Brrrr! We had very good seats and all enjoyed the movie. Tom Hanks did a great job.

They were going to get a bite to eat after the movie and asked me to go with them, but with it being so cold I opted to go right home to my nice warm apartment. It was nice to be included though. It was a nice and a different evening for me.

On Christmas Eve afternoon Ken and Kenny (in from San Francisco for a week) picked me up around 3:00 p.m. We had about a six-inch snowfall on the twenty-third. They shoveled my car and parking area out for me. I was very grateful. Kenny looked just great and said he was very happy with his job, life, and Gina. It was so nice to hear. We went back to their place. It looked beautiful—the lights and decorations outside with the fresh snowfall. It was a winter wonderland. The inside was all Christmassy no matter where you looked. There was fire in the fireplace, plus, the smell of a pot roast cooking for our dinner. Also, I was greeted with wagging tails and begging eyes by three puppy dogs: Bouy, Sailor, and Sadie. I did take treats for them which they appreciated. Barb looked so good, and for the first time in years Alice was with us. What a treat! Alice was doing the cooking and had made a wonderful dinner of tender pot roast, mashed potatoes and gravy, carrots, onions, fresh green beans. It was so yummy! They try hard here, but no way did it compare to a good home-cooked dinner. Then she had a chocolate pudding pie with *real* whipped cream. We were stuffed. She sent a pie plate home with me with all the goodies in it for me to microwave later. I had it on Sunday evening and it was excellent. Again, after our dinner we all sat around the fireplace in the family room with all the puppy dogs. It was so cozy and pleasant, so very wonderful to be with family on Christmas Eve. Since Bill has been gone, the holidays are just something that are difficult to get through; being with my family helps in so many ways. This is the second year that Barb has fixed a stocking for me. As I said, I have not had a stocking for years. I have filled a lot and thoroughly enjoyed doing that, but I have not received one. She finds all kinds of neat goodies and nice surprises to put in it, plus always a new toothbrush, a *big* orange, and candies. Again, these are traditions. This year I also got a lump of coal in the cutest little tin from the puppies. That was good for lots of laughs! Alice and Barb had also found some of my favorite old-fashioned Carmallows and Sanders honeycomb chips. What a nice surprise! it was lots of fun.

Ken and Kenny brought me home about 8:30 p.m. Kenny drove down their side streets to let me see all the luminaries and Christmas decorations which were so pretty. I enjoyed that also. Barb had planned on going to church, but she was pretty beat. Those treatments really take a lot out of her. While they are helping (for which we are all so grateful), they are brutal to go through. Her energy level is very low and she has been going overboard doing things with Kenny being home this year to make everything perfect for Christmas. She and Alice had even made rag quilt covers in Christmas fabrics for the puppies to lay on for the couches. It was a beautiful afternoon and evening for me.

Christmas Day . . . another wonderful family day! The weather was still very cold and snowy, but Barb and family picked me up to go over to Carol's for the afternoon. We drove through Hines Parkway and it was beautiful. It seems so great to have Alice here to enjoy the holidays with us too. It's been way too many years. Cindy, Joe, Corbin, Jim, Scotty, and

Hannah were already at Carol's. Carol had the toy soldiers that her daddy had made a lot of years ago out in her front yard, and they looked so *good!* I think he made those in around 1987 for our front door area on Sandshores. It was right about that time that I started taking art classes in adult education at Niles School in Troy. Drawing the toy soldiers was the very first Christmas card that I made to send out. I used colored pencils and markers for them. I didn't have any idea at that time what I was getting myself into. Ha! Kathy and Jim had them on their porch in Milford for several years when Bill and I moved here to the Village from Troy. Jim passed them on to Carol this year, and she was thrilled to have them. It is nice they are staying in the family. Carol's house also looked beautiful, and she had Christmas decorations all through her house too. What a treat for me to go to my families' houses and see how they had decorated, also to see Bill's and my artwork on their walls. Kenny got to meet Eve and Joe and catch up with Cindy and Erik, which was nice. I love having my grandkids around. Kenny had already met Corbin when he was at the cottage this summer, and Carol and I were out there too.

Of course, again we had lots of food. For years at Christmas, we started out having snacks and appetizers when everyone arrived. Everyone brings something, and it is always interesting and delicious. I had cooked shrimp, which was an easy out for me. I forgot to say that I had also made a batch of Aunt Mae's sour cream cookies. I divide the dough into half and put nuts in just part of it. I took the plain ones to Barb, Ken, and Alice on Christmas Eve and took the ones with nuts to Carol's on Christmas. They all love those cookies, but baking is getting to be a effort for me as much as I like to do it. I also made our chocolate cherry cake that everyone likes for Christmas Day. So I did do a little bit. We had hot dips and spreads, veggies, etc. After everyone enjoys all the goodies, we always take family pictures in front of the Christmas tree. Then it's present time. I had suggested a couple of years ago that we cut down on gift giving. My budget just wasn't able to handle buying things for everyone as much as I would like to. We tried it and found out that Christmas just didn't seem the same. (Of course, we were all trying to cope with the loss of too many people we loved—Edsel, Bill, Kathy, plus the grandchildren's jobs taking them away from this area.) Anyway, last year we had a small gift exchange, which made the day more festive. This year the family that was together at Thanksgiving time came up with the idea of each one buying a $20 unisex gift and playing a game. They decided to start with the oldest—ha, me! Then the next one could either draw from the pile or take the opened gift from another person. It really was quite a bit of fun. One gift of trivial pursuit really got "grabbed" from the young people. Barb and Ken had been at the cabin, and they had already been making quilts to give to the young people. Alice had been in on the quilt making. So they did not participate in the game this year with good reason. Cindy, Joe, Erik, Eve, and Scotty were absolutely thrilled with getting a homemade quilt from their aunts. So that was a *big* hit with them.

I had accumulated quite a few matted and framed pictures, several from years back, that no one had spoken for, so I gave each family a picture this year. Most of them were flowers, but I did have a deer and fawn (just the heads) and also some seals. I gave the deer to Scott and the seals to Kenny, pink magnolia to Erik and Eve, pink lilies to Jim and Hannah, yellow and orange tulips to Carol, yellow green tulips to Barb, gerber daisies to Alice, and fall Leaves to Cindy and Joe. Everyone seemed happy with my choices as I told them they could change or switch if they wanted, but no one wanted to. It was a nice feeling. Of course, Corbin got presents as the gift game was only for the adults. He was very much into *Star Wars* this year. One of my biggest reasons for being grateful for my family is the laughter and fun everyone seems to have when we are all together. Every single one seems to enjoy being together. After the gift exchange and visiting, then it was time to eat again. Carol had got a lovely spiral sliced baked ham and made cheesy potatoes and an applesauce raspberry Jell-O salad. The girls had brought green bean casserole, baked beans, and on and on.

With everyone's tummies full again, we usually wait awhile for dessert. Again, there were lots of choices: Scotty's famous Bumpy Cake, my chocolate cherry cake, Carol's wonderful grasshopper pie. Certain foods seem to have become *traditional*, and everyone look forward to them during the holidays. I'm sure it's the same in most families.

Barb, Ken, Kenny, and Alice left soon after we had dinner as Barb was wiped out from all the Christmas buildup and activities. She was going through so much with those "Herceptin" treatments every Monday and the terrible headaches they gave her. She puts on a very good "show," and she looks good, but you can see the stress in her eyes, especially when she gets tired. I am just so very grateful that we have all been able to be together for this holiday and everyone has been relatively well and able to enjoy everything. We were very lucky this year too to have Joe and Corbin, our newest family members; also Kenny and Alice were here with us too. Cindy and Joe offered me a ride home if I was up to staying awhile longer. My family is good to me and seem to enjoy my company. I figured I was good for another hour or so, as I had had a quiet morning. I took advantage of their nice offer. It is just so wonderful for me to be with my family; when I would get home these last few years, it has been just me and no one to talk to and hash over the day. I miss that so very much. But I have to count all the blessings I do have. I do know all my family cares about me. When I don't see them, I get phone calls or e-mails. It's the only thing that makes life worthwhile anymore. They tell me I'm important to them, and they need to know I'm there to call and talk to, which reminds me I had nice phone calls from Sydney, Bill, and Shannon. They do call me every week. There were also calls from Krista and cards and notes from Kelley and David.

I hate being a widow. I miss Bill so much; life just isn't fun anymore without him. But again, I have to think how very lucky I was to have all those years together. Carol was widowed much too soon, and I'm so very proud of the way she is handling her life. I know she is still hurting. Alice has been on her own and struggling for so many years. Life has not been easy for her. Now Barb and Ken are facing this terrible cancer together and coping. Bill and Shannon seem to be doing OK, and I know they love their little "Butter Bean." Sydney is such a darling four-year-old. All my grown-up grandchildren seem to be doing well and all are very hard workers. It makes me feel very proud of all of them. So again I say to myself, "Stop feeling sorry for yourself. You have a great many things to be thankful for!"

The last week of the year was a quiet one for me, and that was just fine. I did get out on a few errands to CVS and the grocery, Office Max for new ink cartridges, Michaels and Westborn, not all in one day of course. I do one or two errands at a time, and that's all my back and legs will take. *But,* again, I'm grateful I can still do them. The weather was quite mild and cooperated for getting out without shoveling snow. I painted some and finished my "Snow Ladies." I took them to Kinko's for copies, and so the days go by.

2005

On New Year's Eve, Betty and Don Clark invited me up to their apartment to watch a movie with them. It was one of Carol Burnett and Alan Alda in *Four Seasons*—light and funny, very enjoyable. I took some of Cindy and Joe's wedding and Christmas pictures to show them of our family. It was a nice break in the weekend. They are a lovely caring couple and very good friends to me, *and* so I start 2005 with worries and wondering what this New Year will bring, *but* I'm hoping for the best.

January 23, 2005

It took me all this time to write this, just sitting down and writing when the mood hit. I finished "My Holidays: 2004" yesterday during a very snowy day. It started during the night and snowed all day. It was very windy and *bitterly* cold, not a day to be out unless you had too. We got twelve inches officially. Today the sun is shining brightly, but it is still very cold. This morning it was two degrees. The East Coast is getting clobbered and airports are getting affected all over. There were also play-offs for the Super Bowl with The Atlanta Falcons playing The Philadelphia Eagles in Philadelphia in the NFC. It showed them trying to blow the snow off all the seats and getting the stadium ready, plus it's also bitterly cold there. It's not somewhere that I would like to be. The AFC is playing in Pittsburgh, not any better. There it's The Pittsburgh Steelers against the New England Patriots.

Also in our news headlines today is Detroit's Mayor Kwame Kilpatrick and a fuss about his cutting back on public services, both staff and cars, and he has a new 2005 Lincoln Navigator for his wife and family. Plus there are also allegations about his nightclubbing in Washington, DC, while there for the inauguration of George W. Bush. He does make the headlines. How much is true I have no idea, but can't help wondering. Speaking of the inauguration, that was something I am deeply angry about. There was over forty million dollars spent on all pomp and circumstance, balls, parades, etc. They said it was all donated money, but we know it was donated by those big corporations that will be demanding pay backs from the government. Plus over twenty-one million was spent on all the security people they had to have, for which we pay the bills. At the same time, our economy is very bad, schools don't have enough teachers and supplies, and our young people are being killed and wounded over in Iraq, fighting a losing war without proper equipment, and Bush justifies spending this kind of money. I'm unhappy with him and his attitude.

The tsunami disaster is still in the news. The death toll is almost up to 200,000. It's beyond belief. They have been having all kinds of benefits, concerts, and drives of all kinds to raise money for those poor people.

Then back on the home front in my own little world, Carol and I had a delicious dinner at Red Lobster one evening, and she helped me get all my Christmas decorations put away. She insisted that evening was one of my Christmas presents. I'm very grateful.

Just a week ago, Cindy picked me up, and we met Carol, Eve, Erik, Joe, and Eve's parents at Ruby Tuesdays for another good dinner to celebrate Erik's twenty-eighth birthday. Erik and Eve brought me home after we had gone back to Carol's to finish the evening with ice cream and a delicious lemon birthday cake that Eve had made. She, too, is a good baker. It's so nice to be included in these happy occasions.

The next evening Barb and Ken came down and took me to Andiamo's in Dearborn for a very elegant and delicious dinner with them. They had told me when they went up North for Thanksgiving that they were going to take me out for dinner some evening for not having Thanksgiving with me. I had told them that it was not necessary. I was just so happy for them that they were able to get away for a few days. I forgot all about it. But they hadn't and we had another lovely evening. Like I have said, anytime I'm with family, I'm happy.

On another note, Dr. Merritt sent me for an EMG test at Oakwood Hospital to see if it would show a reason for my constant pain in my back and leg. I went for that on January 20. I used the transportation from the Village. I knew the girls were all busy, and Barb had too much of hospitals and doctors. Alice's car heater was out and our weather has been very cold. So I just did it. I would have driven, but I wasn't sure how I would feel after the test, so I decided to try the village transportation, and it worked out just fine. I had a very nice doctor, and while the test is not pleasant with sort of electric shocks and small needles poking in your legs, it is bearable. The doctor told me I was a very good patient. I told him I tried not to holler too loudly. I also asked him if he could tell me anything about the test. He said, "Yes, you have a pinched nerve in your lower lumbar region, SI, that's causing your pain." It is crazy to say, *but* I was happy to hear that. I was starting to think that I was a mental case and imagining this constant pain. Now at least, I knew what was causing it. The doctor said therapy might help, but there was not a lot they could do—disintigration of my spine, etc. Old age is fun!

I'm due to start therapy this Tuesday. So we shall see. I will go back to Dr. Merritt on February 5. I'm painting. I try to keep one going to work on when I feel like it. I have finished some calla lilies that I'm very happy with and am working with some new Dr. Martin's liquid watercolor paints now on a poinsettia picture. I'm experimenting, sitting here at the computer when I feel like it, reading my books. I just got the new John Grisham's book called *The Broker*. I'm also going to my committee meetings and helping with our Sunday programs, and so my life goes on.

P.S. Monday, January 24, 2005

Just to keep you informed, Philadelphia Eagles won the NFC title over the Atlanta Falcons 27 to 10 and The New England Patriots won the AFC title beating the Pittsburgh Steelers 41 to 27. They will be playing in the Super Bowl in Jacksonville, Florida, on February 6. Ha! I'm not such a big football fan, but to let you know I do read the front pages and try to keep up with what's going on around me.

All the weather guys are calling this past weekend "the big blizzard of 2005." It really did cause a lot of problems for travelers all over with airports shut down, etc. Boston over got two feet of snow. I guess we have to feel lucky with just one foot. They say it was the biggest storm in some fourteen years.

On a sad note, I feel like I have lost a friend. Johnny Carson died yesterday of emphysema. He was seventy-nine. We used to watch him so much in the thirty years he was host for *The Tonight Show*. Bill always watched the eleven o'clock news and then Johnny's monolog. I didn't always watch the news as I didn't like to hear all the bad stuff before I went to bed. I usually had my nose in a book, but I would come and watch Johnny's monolog with Bill. Then depending on who his guests were, we watched a bit or went to bed. In thirty years of watching, those people become your friends—Ed McMahon, Doc Severinsen. *The Today Show* this morning was a tribute to Johnny Carson, a celebration of his life. It was really well done, I thought. Tony Bennett sang a song that they said was Johnny's favorite: "I'll be seeing you." That kind of broke me up. I've lost too many people the last few years. It is one of my favorite songs also. I'm wondering too, how long we'll have Tony Bennett, another contemporary? Life!

My First New Car At Eighty-three Years Old!

Sunday, March 6, 2005

This has all happened so fast, it's hard for me to believe. Looking out in the parking lot while I'm writing this on my computer, I'm looking at a beautiful new Ford 500 that belongs to me (at least for two years). It's color is called Merlot, a shiny dark red. It's loaded with sun roof, moon roof, lots of bells and whistles inside that I will have to learn about!

Let me tell you how this all came about.

I have been very happy with our '98 Crown Vic that Bill and I got the summer after we moved here to the Village. With the way my body has been acting and kind of falling apart, I figured that the Crown Vic would last me as long as I would be able to drive. I was very comfortable in it, and it drove easily, *but* I did have to put new brakes on it last fall to the tune of about $800. The battery went dead twice on me and I got a new battery. Then twice the last couple of months, the front tire was very low. They checked it and the last time they said the cap valve was leaking, but I should think about maybe getting new tires. I can't tell you how upsetting it was for me to go out to go somewhere and have something wrong with the car. Bill always took such good care of our cars. I never worried about them. I just got in and drove, so . . .

Two weeks ago today, Billy made his usual weekend call to me. I was complaining about what had happened with the latest tire problem and asking him what he thought about me getting new tires. He said, "Mom, I think you should see about leasing a new car. You have a nice car to turn in, and I don't think the payments would be that much a month for you, plus then you would have reliable transportation." He really got me thinking. The next three days my mind just went round and round. I talked to Carol and Barb, and they both thought I should look into it. On Wednesday, the twenty-third of February, I called John Hillman at Bill Brown's Ford Dealership where we had purchased our '98 Crown Vic. Bill had liked John Hillman, also Carol and her family have dealt with him for years. I talked to him and made an appointment to come in and see him the following day at 10:00 a.m. I could hardly believe that in the next hour and a half, I looked at new cars, got my '98 Crown Vic appraised, and started the paper work to get this new Ford 500. Nothing was signed as I said I wanted to talk to family first, *but* if everything worked out like we thought, I would pick up a new car on Monday, February 28, at noon. Carol was teaching, but she called the dealership while I was still talking to John and made arrangements to meet me at the Family Buggy for her lunch hour and to hear about what I was doing. The Family Buggy Restaurant and Bill Brown's Dealership are only about a half mile apart and very close to where Carol lives and the school she teaches at. She was very proud of me and what I was doing by myself. We had a nice and quick lunch as she had to get back to school. It was nice to talk to her as I was all wound up! I did go on to Meijer's which is in that neighborhood too but came home worn out. No sooner had I got in the door than Billy was on the phone. He was very concerned that I was not going to get ripped off—you know "little old lady" and "unscrupulous car salesman." He had left messages on Carol's recorder and had called Barb to see if she knew where I was. It was funny but nice the way he was looking out for his mom. He talked with Carol later that day and thought I should get more for the Crown Vic. She called John Hillman, and they did come up with another two hundred dollars! The appraiser had said $4800.00. I got $5,000.00.

I had to call AAA Insurance and get that taken care of to be transferred on Monday, the twenty-eighth. I also talked with Dick Newton at Financial Services to see what he thought about me doing this. He thought I could handle it OK. All this time, my mind was going in circles and wondering if I was really doing the right thing. It was quite a weekend for me. I cleaned out Crown Vic as much as I could. Snow was predicted for Monday, and I was worried about that too.

I had a follow-up visit at Dr. Merritt's at 10 on Monday morning and my blood pressure was high. I told her what was going on and why it was probably high, but I had to go back in a week to have it checked just to be safe. Then I was on my way to Carol's as she had offered to go with me to pick up the car and see what I was getting. I had to sign a million papers, but I finally got the car. It was beautiful. Carol liked it also. John gave me a little lesson in where everything was and how to drive it. It felt comfortable to me and I was not worried about being able to learn, with the shift on the console. I did turn the wipers on a couple of times and have since also, but it doesn't do anything except wipe the windows and I'm learning OK. It drives very easily, and I feel confident and safe that I can handle it all right. I lucked out also because the snow they kept predicting did not come until later. Carol had me drive around a big square mile to get the feel of the car, and then we pulled into Daly's for a late lunch hamburger. I dropped Carol off at her home, and she said I did fine driving. I didn't scare her at all! I stopped at Kinko's to get my panda picture copied. Rebecca who had been helping me there and doing a great job was at the dentist, so I left them to pick up the next day. By this time, we were getting some mixed rain and sleet, but I was home safe and sound with a new car! Billy was on the phone again soon after I got in the door. It really pleased me that he was so interested and trying his best to look out for me even from Denver.

We did get that snow—a good six inches. *And it was cold!* Needless to say, I did not go out on Tuesday. About noon on Wednesday, I couldn't stand it any longer. I had to go out and drive my new car! First though, I had to clean all that snow off, and it was heavy and took quite awhile. I probably should not have done it cause I really was tired and hurting But I went to Farmer Jacks and got some nice fruit, etc. I loved the way it felt driving my car. I'm hoping I did the right thing and sort of feel like I did. The family seems to think so, and that's nice.

I'm still talking with the insurance company to try and get monthly payments down. I changed from $50 deductible to $500, which the family also advised. I'm waiting for some nice weather so I can go to Rochester and try out my car besides doing just little errands around here. I'm going to have to wait a bit though; according to the weather guys, more snow is on the way for Tuesday and dropping temperatures. Of course, it still is winter in Michigan. It does seem like this has been a long and very cold and snowy winter. More like what we had when I was growing up. The last few years have spoiled us with the milder winters.

Now I just hope and pray that my body will behave and not fall apart on me anymore so that I can enjoy getting out and driving my new car!

Friday, March 18, 2005

Dear Hildegard and Roger,

Here we have snow on the ground again this morning. It doesn't really seem like Easter is almost here. This certainly has been a very long, cold, snowy winter. I received this letter from Rosly yesterday so I know Easter is very close.

Hope this winter has been good to you folks health wise and you have been able to enjoy your bowling leagues. Our Barbara is still getting her Herceptin treatments every Monday and has her ups and downs. She keeps a very good attitude, and we are all hoping for the best. I'm coping with a pinched nerve in the S1 area of my lower back. Walking is more and more painful. But I'm also fighting to keep going.

The big news for me is that I leased a new Ford 500 and picked it up on February 28. This all came about very fast. I had gone out twice in the last couple of months and found a tire almost flat. It was difficult for me. Bill had spoiled me by always taking care of our cars. I was still driving our '98 Crown Vic and had expected it to last me as long as I was able to drive. I had got new brakes and spent $800 last fall on it. I was complaining to my son about probably having to buy new tires, etc. He said, "Mom, I think you should look into leasing and then you would have reliable transportation." I talked to the rest of the family, and they agreed with him that it was a good idea. So at eighty-three, I went out by myself and picked out a new car. I went to a salesman at Bill Brown's, with whom Carol and family have dealt with for years and from whom Bill and I got our '98 Crown Vic; this all happened in a week's time. It's beautiful in a metallic dark red called "Merlot." I love driving it, but I haven't gone very far. I was waiting for the weather to get a little better. I keep hoping I did the right thing, but the family thinks so. Bill Jr. was calling sisters and dealership to make sure his *mom,* "little old lady," didn't get ripped off by an unscrupulous car salesman. It was kind of funny and nice.

Please take your time with this letter. There is no hurry. I do hope this finds both of you well. Have a wonderful Easter and thanks for doing this for me.

Thursday, March 24, 2005

Dear Rosly,

I was so happy to receive your Easter greetings and nice letter. But I'm very sorry to hear that you had lost your brother Max. In another way, I am relieved for him. He is in a better place and not in any more pain. I truly believe that death can be our friend. It is the ones that are left behind that grieve the loss of someone they loved that it is difficult for.

I enjoyed reading about happiness by Bertold Brecht. I agree with a lot of what he is saying. We have to find happiness within ourselves and live in the present. "Yesterday is past. Tomorrow is a mystery. Today is a present. Enjoy!" I have always tried to think of my glass as "half full" rather than half empty. I do think our attitude makes a big difference in our lives. I have always liked the saying, "Our attitude is the crayon that colors our world." In getting to know you, Rosly, through our letters to one another, it sounds like you are a very positive person. Always trying to make the best of any situation that life throws your way. I truly admire you for that. I also agree with the idea that we have to keep learning and keep busy.

It was nice to hear that Alexander is doing well in his schooling. I'm also very glad to hear that Michael is spending his military time in Switzerland. I am so saddened and unhappy about so many of our young people being killed and wounded over in Iraq. I really disagree with our president on our being there. I don't think we belong in Iraq and they don't want us there. I'm wondering if it will ever end. My heart goes out to all the families with their young people involved in this tragedy.

It sounds like Anneleis had a very difficult time with the flu. I am happy to hear that she is doing much better. My daughter Alice had a very bad case of the flu also, but she was not in the hospital. It took her a long time to get her strength back. It affected a lot of people this winter. We have also had a very cold snowy winter, and it is not over. We had a two-inch snowfall again yesterday, but it is melting today as the temperature is going up to forty degrees. Everyone around here is very anxious for spring and to see the green grass and beautiful flowers again. It doesn't seem possible that it is Easter week already. I realize that it is early this year. Our weather people say that we are going to have a warm-up this coming week and could get up in the middle-forties. That will be a nice change for us. We know that spring will return as it does every year, but sometimes it seems a long time in coming.

It was nice that Rosemarie was able to visit and be with Anneleis while she was in the hospital. I'm also glad that Udo and the children did not have it that badly. I send my prayers to Walter and Frieda; they have been in ill health for a long time.

Barbara and Ken are in Arizona to spend Easter with their daughter Krista, her husband, David and their two grandchildren, Sage (six) and Ché (four). They have been planning this trip for months. Their son Kenny and his girlfriend who live in the San Francisco, California area, are also flying there for the weekend. It will be the first time since Krista and Kenny were teenagers that they will all be together for the Easter weekend. Arizona is about a four-hour plane flight from Michigan. I have been so anxious for them that things would work out for them to go. Barbara's energy level was very low from her treatments, but she was determined to make it. She keeps a very positive attitude, but cancer is such a terrible disease, and it does take a toll on your body. They are there safe and sound and very happy to be together, but Sage came down with the chicken pox just before they arrived so was not feeling very well. Sage was so happy to have her "Nana" and "Papa" there to visit her though.

The rest of the family who live around here will be at Carol's for Easter dinner. The newly-weds Cindy and Joe have Corbin with them for the Easter holidays, so they are very happy about that. Carol and Corbin came over and had lunch with me yesterday, which was nice. Carol is babysitting for Cindy and Joe while Corbin is here. Carol loves children and says Corbin is very easy to care for. Carol has been very busy with her sub-teaching this year and has enjoyed that also. Bill Jr., Shannon, and little Sydney are all doing well and planning on coming to Michigan again this summer. We all look forward to their vacation time visit with us.

Rosly, you did not mention how you were doing, and I hope that means you are doing well. You did not say anything about any more fainting spells and I was very happy to hear that. Aging does take a toll on our bodies. I am having more difficulty with walking. It is becoming painful. I have found out through tests that I have a pinched nerve in my lower spine area that is causing my problems. I have been into therapy, but there is not much that can be done. I am trying to make the best of it and keep going. Again, we go back to creating our own happiness and keeping a positive attitude.

I know my Easter wishes are not going to reach you until Easter is over with, but I still can hope you had a nice holiday. Plus, I know spring is just now starting to show us it is coming back, so I can wish you and your family a very happy spring.

The snow has melted again, so I went out on some errands this morning. It seemed good to get out in the fresh air again, even though I still had to wear my winter coat. I was able to get some wonderful strawberries that are grown in Florida. They are such a nice treat this time of the year.

I am never able to answer your letter right away as I send it by mail to a friend who worked with Bill to translate for me. They are very nice and willing to do this for me. Roger married a German girl when he was over there during World War II. I have never met them in person, but Roger thought a lot of Bill and offered to continue to help me with your letters. We correspond through the mail also.

I am happy that you enjoy my cards. I try to keep a painting of something going all the time. I have a table by my dinette windows that I can leave my things out on. That makes it easy for me to just go and paint a little when I feel like it. I really enjoy doing flowers. I think perhaps it is because they are so lovely and cheerful. They help you to think nice thoughts.

My very best wishes for a healthy and happy summer for you and your family.

Your USA cousin, Vivian

Yippee! Yahoo! Hurray!

You are invited to a Wedding Reception
for Kenneth G. Vogt Jr. and Gina Risso!

It will be held at Ken & BoBo's Cottage on
Russell Island, Algonac Michigan.

The celebration will take place Saturday, July 23rd, 2005,
from 4:00 p.m. to 8:30 p.m.

Cocktails 4:00 p.m. and Dinner at 5:30 p.m.

We are hoping you can join us for this special adults—only occasion.

KenJoe and Gina are getting married

July 2nd, 2005 in San Francisco, California.
They will be arriving in Michigan on July 21st.

We are so blessed to have Gina become part of our family, and
we are very excited to have this wedding party for the newly weds!
My brother Bill Jr., Shannon, and Butter Bean will be coming in
from Denver to share in this exciting family celebration!

Please RSVP as soon as possible due to the
act that this wedding reception is going to be held on the island.
The caterers need a response
AS SOON AS POSSIBLE . . .
Thank you!

Call (248) 549-2327 or the cottage at (810) 748-9462
KenJo and Gina will be residing at:
27 Woodward Avenue Sausalito,
California 94965
after their Michigan visit!

September 4, 2005

Julia Ruggiro,

In the world, heroes surround us every day. They come in all shapes and sizes, but all seem to carry the same traits. Heroes, to me, are courageous people who live life to the fullest and not worry so much about themselves, but other people.

I have many heroes, but one special person who has deeply inspired me to become a better person is Bobo. Bobo is a grandmother, friend, and so much more to me, but just a few years ago, she was diagnosed with breast cancer. During that time, she showed so much strength and courage and ended up fighting it off. A few years passed, and this summer she was diagnosed with cancer once again. This time though it spread throughout her whole entire body. Every time I see her, she acts like nothing is wrong, and never worries about a thing. When someone is sick, she puts away all the pain she has and cares for that person. She is an extraordinary person inside and out. Bobo deeply appreciates anything and everything people do for her. One time she put away all her pain for me was when I was in the hospital last summer. She offered to help my family and me with anything we could need. Bobo has always made me feel good about myself and is truly one of my heroes. Bobo is a hero to me, and I deeply appreciate and care for her.

Julia turned this paper in for a school assignment and gave us a copy of it. It is a beautiful tribute to my daughter.

Sunday, September 11, 2005

Four years ago today, terrorists attacked the twin towers in New York, the Pentagon in Washington, and plane Flight 93 that was probably on its way to crash into the White House when they (the terrorists) were overtaken by brave passengers and crashed in a field in Pennsylvania. Two weeks ago today, Hurricane Katrina hit the Gulf Coast destroying New Orleans and cities along the coast of Mississippi, Alabama. They are calling it one of the worst natural disasters our country has ever known. Plus we are in the middle of a war in Iraq that is going nowhere, killing and wounding our young people—another Vietnam. In my own opinion we should never started this. It was Bush and his ego that got us in this mess with Iraq.

Today is a beautiful sunny day, with temperatures in the eighties and low humidity, perfect for doing most anything, *and* a lot of people are suffering with the memory of the loss of loved ones and also the poor hurricane victims with the loss of everything they owned. I can't even comprehend and imagine that.

It's ironic for me. The newspapers and TV newscasts are full of programs for remembering and honoring all the people who were lost four years ago. They are also still full of the hurricane disaster—who to blame for the slow response and how best to help. That coastline and cities will never be quite the same again.

The irony for me is that at the same time of the terrorist attack, our family was hit with the news that Barbara was diagnosed with stage 4 inflammatory breast cancer. She had to start chemo, radiation, and then mastectomy immediately. We were all still trying to come to terms with losing Bill and our Kathy. These last four years have been very difficult for all of us. Our Barbara, especially, has been through "hell" and has kept up a wonderful attitude! Then at the same time as Hurricane Katrina was wrecking the Gulf Coast of our country, Barb found out through more bone scans and MRIs of her brain that the cancer had spread through all parts of her body, and they told her that the prognosis was just a few months. Barbara said she had known since she was first diagnosed that she didn't have a lot of time. I think we had all known this but hoped and prayed for a miracle. Now I'm going to lose another daughter. I would give anything in this world to be able to trade places with her. My heart is breaking, and I can't help but wonder *why*. This will be daughter number three for me. Is any mother or parent supposed to go through this? *And* how do I handle it? Losing our Susan at four and a half months to SIDS, way back in 1943, has diminished to a bad dream with our being lucky and having four more daughters and a son. I kind of always felt that God gave us twins to make up for losing Susan. *But* losing another daughter brings back the pain that Bill and I went through way back then.

As I have written over and over again, these last four years have been another emotional roller coaster. When Barbara was doing well, then all of us were doing pretty good. And of course there have been some happy times. A lot of them I have written about over these past four years. Bill Jr., Shannon, and Sydney's visits have been a joy. So was Erik and Eve's wedding showers and wedding. Ditto for Cindy and Joe's. Meeting Joe and his little son Corbin was also a joy. I was so happy for Cindy. Our family holiday get-togethers, our family times at Barb and Ken's cottage in the summer, birthday celebrations, just simple meetings for lunches, etc. I loved every one of them and kept trying very hard to count all my many blessings. But again life without Bill is like the color has gone out of my world. Alice sold her little home and moved up here to be with her twin. I had mixed emotions. As it turned out, a month after Alice moved up here Barb's cancer reared its ugly head again in April 2004. She has been on Herceptin and different treatments continuously since then. This past summer has been another "hell" for her. Bill and Shannon had a hard time coming face to face with it while they were here. Kenny and Gina were married on July 2, 2005, in San Francisco. Barb and Ken had a wonderful wedding reception for them on July 23 at the cottage with all of us and their island "family" there. Barb put on a good show and handled it well. Alice was her "worker and carried out Barb's plans." Both Barb and Ken told Alice that without her it would not have happened or at least been as lovely as it was. Kenny and Gina seem very happy and are expecting in January.

At almost the same time, Erik and Eve took me out for dinner and told me their happy news. They are expecting in February. Our family circle is growing.

I was so happy when Alice moved back up here as I kept hoping I would see her more. *But* as all best laid plans go things have not worked out like we had hoped, with Barb's increasing dependence on Alice (through no fault of her own, it's that damn cancer). Alice has been Barb's right arm. I've told Alice that this is the reason she is up here now. Barb and Ken do need her.

Since I turned eighty, my health has seemed to go *south*—first, hip replacement, endoscope, colonoscopy, continuing back pain, MRI's, then back surgery. Thank goodness for Carol, my reliable daughter. She has always put her life on hold whenever I have needed her. But I worry about her too with all her arthritis, especially in her thumb joints and her shoulder. I also know that Alice and Barb feel badly that this *cancer* has taken over. My heart aches so much it's a wonder it just doesn't break and give up. I'll have to be honest and say that there are times when I wish it would. I'm not sure how much more heartache I can take.

I'm back to seeing Dr. Keller again, but there is really nothing she can do. Nobody knows what to say. There are no words that really help at a time like this. Just knowing people care and a hug sometimes helps a little. I am also seeing Dr. Reeder who has taken Dr. Merritt's place here at our Medical Center. He seems nice. It's hard to go to new doctors and start from the beginning again. Dr. Reeder did take blood tests and found out that I'm anemic and hemoglobin down to eight. That does account for some of my terrible tiredness. I just finished that stool testing for bleeding, which I really don't think I have. She wants me to take iron. I hate that because of the side effects. We'll see. I'll go back and see her again this Thursday.

Sister Mary came up for a little visit last Thursday, which was very nice. She is so special. The staff here are wonderful. Myra gave me a hug in the hallway and told me that they were all going to be paying me visits and I would not be alone during this time. But much as I love them, they are my extended family. No one can take this pain away. 1 pray, but I don't seem to get any relief. If there is a God, I sure have a lot of questions for him.

Thursday, September 15, 2005

Myra just left after a little visit to check on me and see how I was doing. The staff here are great and they do help with their care and concern. *But* Carol picked me up yesterday, and we went into Royal Oak to see Barb and Alice and to have lunch together. Our plans were that if Barb felt strong enough she wanted to go to National Coney Island for Sanders Hot Fudge Cream Puff. We did make it. We had some hugs, tears, and laughs together, and everyone ate and enjoyed their cream puff. It is just breaking everyone's hearts to see how Barb is going downhill and is so terribly weak. She is blaming it on the radiation treatments, and we know that is one of their big side effects. But we wonder. She has lost so much weight. I noticed the difference in just a week and half since I had seen her. She's so thin and gaunt looking. It breaks my heart. I hope and pray she will be strong enough to go up North to the cabin when their family get here next week. Barb has her heart set on going even if it's just for a few days. She wants a festive thanksgiving dinner with them all together. All the planning and organizing is falling on Alice, and I'm worried about her too. She says she is fine and can handle it. This is taking a terrible toll on her as she takes care of Barb and helps her 24/7. Carol and I left there with our hearts very heavy. I did not sleep well last night. I can't imagine what is going through Barb's mind. She has so much to live for. Life is not fair!

I saw Dr. Reeder this morning for a follow-up appointment, and I do not have any bleeding from that test I took. That's good. She still wants me to take the iron pills to build up my blood and perhaps help with some of this tiredness. She said also that she wishes she could help with heartache, but again there are no magic pills for that. I have a follow-up in three weeks.

Cindy and Joe have invited me over to have dinner at their place with Carol, Erik, and Eve on the twenty-fourth. Erik and Eve have just found out that they are going to have a little daughter. They are so excited and have invited me to go out for dinner with them this Monday. They want to show me their ultrasound pictures. Carol is having her family and Jim, Scott, and Hannah over to her place for a pizza party on the thirtieth to celebrate my birthday. (I wanted to skip it, but they won't hear of that.) I'm so grateful to my family. They are all trying their best to help me get through this. It's hard for all of them too. Ken is devastated. I'm not sure how he will get through this either. There are too many worries and no answers.

The Voices of Henry Ford Village

Volume 13 Fall 2005
By the Residents of
Henry Ford Village
Radio Memories by Betty Bunts

NATIONAL BROADCASTING COMPANY, INC.

MERCHANDISE MART

CHICAGO, ILL.

Remember the Golden Days of radio back in the early thirties when radio was king? Then, Chicago was the center of radio dramas, both daytime and nighttime, at the NBC network studios located in the Merchandise Mart.

I have memories of those days because of a small, red autograph album with the signatures of some of the popular actors and announcers of that time. My father was a writer for NBC. He kept the autograph book on his desk and as the actors who worked there, or celebrities who toured the studios came by, they signed the book.

Echoing that period are the names: Amos and Andy, Fibber Magee and Molly, Lum and Abner, Vic and Sade and Don Ameche. Two from other fields were the aviatrix Amelia Earhart, and silent film star Francis X. Bushman.

As a writer, my father had plays produced on the First Nighter, Grand Hotel, The Irene Rich Show, and the National Farm and Home Hour.

Turn a page of the album and time is turned back to the era when families gathered around the radio and listened to news, music, comedy, drama, and adventure coming magically through the air. Long ago days. Radio days.

*   *   *

Thank you to Vivian Beeler for this beautiful fall art.

Henry Ford Village Computer Club
Dearborn Michigan

| Volume 3 Number 3 | Twentieth HFVCC Newsletter | Tuesday, October 18, 2005 |

Surf the

Internet Part One:

With Joan Martin

Monday,

October 10, 2005

6:30-8:30 P. M.

Resident

Computer Lab

Cost $10

Next HFV Computer Club Meeting:
Mackinac Room 10:30-11:45 AM
Tuesday, October 18, 2005
Next Quarterly HFVCC Newsletter:
January, 2006

N O T I C E :
Gene Freeman will be replacing Marie Minck
As editor of the HFV Computer
Club Newsletter
As of January 2006
Long may he reign!
Best wishes, Gene.

Vivian Beeler, our resident artist,
helps us to celebrate the fall season.
as we take time out to extend our
support to all those displaced by
Katrina and Rita.

Monday, October 10, 2005

Dear Rosly,

I write to you with deeply saddened heart. We are losing our Barbara. The doctors have said it will only be a few months. The cancer has spread all through her body and into her brain. She has not had a good summer as they have tried a lot of different treatments that have not done any good. She has lost a lot of weight and is very frail and weak. She keeps a remarkable attitude through all of this, and we are so proud of her. But the heartache of losing another daughter is almost more than I can bear.

We have had some good times over the summer months, and I have tried to cherish those. Barbara and Ken's son Kenny Jr. was married out in California on July 2, 2005. They have been living together for five years, and we have all met Gina and liked her and hoped they would marry. They are expecting a baby in January, so that decided things for them. Everyone is happy about it. They were here for two weeks the end of July. As miserable as Barb was, with Alice following Barbara's planning, plus a lot of their island friends helping, they had a big wedding reception for Kenny and Gina at their cottage on July 23. The weather was beautiful, and Barbara put on a great front. The party was a big success! Bill Jr., Shannon, and Sydney had just arrived here on the twenty-second for their two-week visit, so they were able to be there also. It is a beautiful memory for me to cherish. Also I was glad to see Sydney, Bill, and Shannon again. Sydney is growing so fast and seems to be such a smart little girl. She is very outgoing and very loveable. I'm sending a couple of pictures that were taken at her daycare school with the children dressing up in different hats.

It was very difficult for Bill and Shannon to see Barb so sick this summer. The whole family is devastated by this. We try to make the best of it and just take one day at a time. We have to believe God has a reason and a plan, but it is very hard to see right now. Carol has been taking me in to see Barbara quite often. She is still at home with a home care nurse coming every other day. Alice is still working sometimes at her landscape and plant job, but she is Barb's main caregiver. Krista, her husband David, and children Sage (seven) and Ché (five) were here for almost two weeks, and Krista stayed on for another ten days. Ken's bosses at his job have been very good, letting Ken have a lot of extra time off too. When there are other people with Barb, then Alice goes to her job. Krista is Barb and Ken's daughter in case you have forgotten. They live in Arizona. Krista is a very lovely young woman and an excellent mother too.

Sunday, October 30, 2005

We lost our Barbara on October 15. Funeral notices are added and also an article that was in our daily newspaper. Oh Rosly, the past few weeks have been very difficult for all of us. My heart is breaking, and I can't help but wonder why I'm still here at eighty-four and I've lost two beautiful daughters who had so much to live for and were so talented and giving. I have to believe that there is a reason for this or I would go crazy. *And* I am so very grateful that Barb is out of her pain and suffering. This past summer has been very bad for her. That cancer just ate her alive; it is such a terrible disease.

Her funeral service was standing room only. She had so many friends and people that loved her.

Rosly, I do live in a wonderful place. The staff here and the friends I have made over the years have been wonderful to me. I'm also enclosing a letter I wrote to try and express my thanks to everyone. They did publish it in our Village paper, which was quite an honor for me. I have never seen a letter like that in our paper before.

My heart is so heavy I don't feel up to writing to you like I should. I hope you will excuse me, and I will try and write more later on. I loved the scarves you knitted and sent to me and Sydney. They are very much in style right now and are lovely. Thank you so much for your thoughtfulness. I also appreciated the papers. There have been so many disasters all over our world it makes you wonder what is going on. There is so much tragedy for so many people. I was sorry to hear about Max and Frieda but can't help but feel that they are out of their suffering and in a better place. I am concerned about your fainting spells also and hope and pray that the doctors can find an answer for you. That has to be very frightening.

Another piece of *good* news though is that Erik and Eve (Carol's son and our young detective), who were married two years ago, are expecting a little girl in February. We are all happy about that. Kenny and Gina's baby will be born in January, so that will make me a great-grandma of five: Sage and Ché, Krista and David's children; Corbin, Cindy and Joe's little boy; and two new ones. Life does go on. Bill Jr., Shannon, and Sydney will be here at Thanksgiving time. They were heartbroken that they couldn't be here for Barb's funeral, but Bill Jr. had started a new job and also had finals on his college course he was taking. They did see her this summer, and that was what counted. Thanks for understanding my heartache right now. I know you do, Rosly.

From: Higgins, Lori (lhiggins@freepress.com)
To: veebee248@sbcglobal.net;
Date: Mon, August 1,2011, 11:21:25AM
Cc:
Subject: RE: Using obituary?

Hi Vivian, I just forwarded your email to Jody Williams, who handles reprint issues for the Free Press. She's on vacation until Aug 8 so you may not hear back from her until then I doubt it will be a problem but she's the person who makes these decisions. Thanks.

Lori Higgins, Education Reporter
Detroit Free Press
615 W. Lafayette
Detroit, Ml 48226
313-222-6651 (office)
248-219-6895 (ceil)
www.freep.com
Follow me on Twitter: @ Lori A Higgins

From: Vivian Beeler [mailto:veebee248@sbcglobal.net]
Sent: Monday, August 01, 2011 11:15 AM
To: Higgins, Lori
Subject: Using obituary?

Dear Lori,

I am Vivian Beeler 89 years old and Mother of the late Barbara Vogt. I am writing "Our Story" for my family and plan an having it printed by a self publishing company May t use the OB article you wrote about my daughter in it? You wrote the article in October 21, 2005. I don't plan on selling the book {?} as I am writing just for all my 8 grandchildren and 11 great-grandchildren and any other family members that want to read it.

I hope you are still at the Free Press and you will get this or someone will answer me. You did such a wonderful article on my daughter I really would like to include it.

Thank You and hoping to hear from you very soon.
Vivian Beeler 313 581 7041 or e-mail

Safely Home

I am home in Heaven, dear ones;
Oh, so happy and so bright!
There is perfect joy and beauty
In this everlasting light.
All the pain and grief is over,
Every restless tossing passed;
I am now at peace forever,
Safely home in Heaven at last.
Did you wonder I so calmly
Trod the valley of the shade?
Oh! but Jesus' love illumined
Every dark and fearful glade.
And He came Himself to meet me
In that way so hard to tread;
And with Jesus' arm to lean on,
Could I have one doubt or dread?

Then you must not grieve so sorely,
For I love you dearly still,
Try to look beyond earth's shadows
Pray to trust our Father's Will.
There is work still waiting for you,
So you must not idly stand;
Do it now, while life remaineth—
You shall rest is Jesus' land.
When that work is all completed
He will gently call you Home;
Oh, the rapture of that meeting,
Oh, the joy to see you come!

In Loving Memory of

BARBARA "BO-BO" VOGT

Date of Birth
May 20, 1951

Date of Death
October 15, 2005

Services at
A. J. Desmond & Sons Funeral Home
Vasu, Rodgers & Connell Chapel
32515 Woodward Avenue
Royal Oak, Michigan

Date of Service
Thursday, October 20, 2005
11:00 A.M.

Officiating
The Reverend Edward Belczak

Barbara S. Vogt

Born in Detroit, Michigan on May 20, 1951

Departed on Oct. 15, 2005 and resided in Royal Oak, MI.

Visitation: Wednesday Oct. 19, 2005

Services: Thursday Oct. 20, 2005

Please click on the links above for locations, times, maps, and directions.

(SIGN GUESTBOOK)   (VIEW GUESTBOOK)

Barbara was a resident of Royal Oak for 30 years.

Barbara was a volunteer for Sharing and Caring at Beaumont Hospital. Formerly she was an office administrator for Absolute Document Destruction of Rochester Hills, MI

She loved spending the summer on Russell Island and hanging out at the cottage. She also enjoyed gardening, collecting rocks, quilting and driving her little boat "Misty Harbour". Barbara was also a dog lover.

Beloved wife of Kenneth (married 35 years). Mother of Krista Ann Vogt-Crimmins (David) and Kenneth Vogt, Jr. (Gina Risso). Nana of Sage Vogt-Crimmins and Ché Vogt-Crimmins and soon to arrive child of Kenneth & Gina. Daughter of Vivian and the late William J. Beeler. Sister of Alice "Ollie" Beeler (her twin), Carol Leinonen and William "Billy" Beeler (Shannon) and the late Kathy "KiKi" Welton.

Funeral service Thursday 1 am at A. J. Desmond & Sons Funeral Home, 32515 Woodward Ave., Royal Oak.

Family will receive friends Wednesday 2:00-8:00 p.m.

In lieu of flowers family suggests memorial tributes to Sharing & Caring, c/o William Beaumont Hospital—or Russell Island Foundation—or The Michigan Humane Society

VIEW OBITUARY AND SHARE MEMORIES AT
www.DesmondFuneralHome.COM

From the Heart of Vivian Beeler

I would like to express my thanks and deep appreciation to all my HFV family and friends for all of your outpouring of support, prayers, cards, hugs in the loss of my daughter, Barbara Vogt, to Inflammatory Breast Cancer. She was fifty-four. She was an identical twin to my daughter Alice.

As most of you know, Bill and I moved into HFV almost eight years ago. It was one of the wisest decisions we had ever made. During our marriage we had been blessed with four beautiful daughters, and when I was forty-three, we had a surprise bonus caboose son. Bill and I had two great years here before I lost him in April 2000. Seven weeks later, we lost our middle daughter Kathy to ovarian cancer. She was fifty-three and had fought it for six years. The support I received from the staff and the friends we had made at that time helped me cope with my pain. Kristine Anderson had a grief support group then that was very helpful. Myra and Sandra gently pushed me into starting my little watercolor class. That has been great therapy for me, and perhaps I have been able to help a few other people also. The other committees I have been on have kept me busy and also helped—Birthday Angels, Sunday Entertainment, Mentoring, Dining Services, and also the library at that time. We have some wonderful people living here.

So many on the Staff here have become my good friends, and over the years other people here have touched my heart with their friendship and caring.

Our Barbara was diagnosed with stage 4 inflammatory breast cancer in September 2001, just before the terrorist attack on September 11, 2001. So our family had a personal disaster at that same time.

Mammograms don't show inflammatory breast cancer, so we have been on a soapbox to tell all young women. You don't have to have a lump. IBC is hard for doctors to diagnose. So check carefully for any changes.

Even with my heart breaking from my losses (parents should not have to bury their children), I can't rave enough about the staff here at the Village. That includes all the departments, Resident Life, Medical Center, Security, Maintenance, Housekeeping, Dining Services, my young friends there too, Barb keeping all the plants so beautiful around here, etc. I have been overwhelmed by all their caring. A lot of them had met my Barb. She had such a vibrant, outgoing personality. She drew people to her like a magnet. She had so much to live for, and as a heartbroken mother I can't help but ask why. I have to believe there is a reason and she isn't in any more pain. Thanks again from the bottom of my heart and thanks for listening to me.

Vivian, 2005

Detroit Free Press www.freep.com
Barbora Vogt: Battled Breast Cancer With Courage
By Lori Higgins
Free Press Staff Writer

October 20, 2005

Courage? Barbara Vogt had it.

She had it in 2001 when, shortly after being diagnosed with inflammatory breast cancer, she stopped her husband as they left a doctor's appointment and declared, "Mister, I've got my gloves on now. Let's fight."

She had it a year ago, when she walked into a funeral home with her twin sister, told the director she wanted to make funeral arrangements, and when she was asked for whom, she said, "For myself."

And she had it recently, when, her health deteriorating, she planned an early Thanksgiving celebration, bringing in her daughter from Arizona and her son from California.

That dinner was in late September. On Saturday, Mrs. Vogt died at her home in Royal Oak. She was 54.

"I can't say enough about her. I'm one of the luckiest guys in the world," Kenneth Vogt, her husband of 35 years, said Tuesday. "I loved her so much. God, we had fun together."

Several things defined Mrs. Vogt. She was a quilter. She collected rocks. She loved dogs. And she loved to travel. She especially loved spending time at the family's cottage on Russell Island, near Algonac.

After her diagnosis with breast cancer, she became tireless in her quest to educate people about the disease and to raise money for a cure. She volunteered with Sharing and Caring, a support group at the Rose Cancer Center at Beaumont Hospital, where she was treated.

And, though she worked various jobs, ranging from day care provider to office administrator, Mrs. Vogt was mostly a nurturer ~ to her children, her husband, her family and friends, and even to strangers with breast cancer whom she met online. To them, she gave advice. And, for many, she made quilts.

"She knew she was helping others. It gave her great comfort to do that," Kenneth Vogt said.

"She was very generous. Very outgoing. And she just gave of herself."

The two met Aug. 12, 1968, the day Kenneth Vogt received his draft orders. She was a switchboard operator at an auto dealership in Troy. He was a dispatcher in the service department.

By February 1969, when he was in Vietnam, he knew she was the one. And so, he bought a diamond ring, shipped it home and asked his father to propose to her—by proxy.

There were many beautiful moments in their relationship, including one a year ago while they were at the beach. Mrs. Vogt, who was fond of collecting rocks, picked up one shaped like a heart.

"She said, 'Mister, I'm giving you my heart.' That rock to this moment sits on my nightstand next to my bed," her husband said.

Mister was her nickname for him. He called her Pye, though he can no longer remember where the name came from.

At her funeral today, Mrs. Vogt's casket is to be draped with a quilt. Not one she made, but one that inspired her.

Her good friend Jan Breyer sent swatches of fabric to Mrs. Vogt's friends soon after she was diagnosed with cancer. The friends were asked to write encouraging messages. They did, and Breyer sewed the swatches together.

That was what started Mrs. Vogt's passion for quilts. Since 2001, she had made about 60.

In addition to her husband, Mrs. Vogt is survived by a daughter, Krista Ann Vogt-Crimmins; a son, Kenneth; her mother, Vivian Beeler; two sisters; a brother, and two grandchildren.

The funeral service will be at 11 a.m. today at the A.J. Desmond & Sons Funeral Home, 32515 Woodward Ave., Royal Oak.

Contact LORIHIGGINS at 248-351-3694 or higgins@freepress.com.
Copyright © 2005 Detroit Free Press Inc.

August 29, 2005

My dear darling daughter,

How do I even begin to talk to you and tell you how my heart is breaking and I'm being torn apart? *And* don't you dare feel guilty! This is not your doing or your wishes. I can't even imagine what you must be going through. Honey, I have to tell you again and again how very proud I am of you and the way you have handled all this terrible *crap* these last four years! You have shown so much strength and courage you have taught all of us lessons, *but* I'm selfish. I can't understand why God needs you now. I want you and need you here to take care of me while I cope with this aging process. This brings back the pain of losing Susan all those years ago, and of course, we all still miss our Kathy. Life is just not fair! I would give anything in the world if it could be me. I'm ready and I've lived my life with a wonderful husband and partner, who I still miss every day. *But again* don't you feel guilty. I don't know the reason God wants you now, and I don't understand it. They say we have to have faith, and that is a reason for everything, but right now I'm having trouble seeing it.

Honey, I have to be honest and tell you that I have lived with this fear of losing you since you were first diagnosed with stage 4 inflammatory breast cancer. I knew then it was bad and your time with us was limited. Of course, I kept hoping for miracles but really have not seen any. My heart aches for everything you have been through to fight this damn disease. You are a fighter! I'm so very, very *proud* of you, *and* honey, you know that saying about leaving "footprints on people's hearts." You have left so many "footprints" on so many, many different people's hearts, people you don't even realize you have helped with your smile and words of encouragement that you will never ever be forgotten—the sharing and caring friends you have made, all of your island family, your courage, encouragement, and joking in the middle of some awful treatments with all the people you met in all the different departments of Beaumont, doctors, technicians, nurses, and patients, your friends in all the quilt shops, and of course our own family. Honey, the list goes on and on—the hundreds of quilts you have made, your little purses, your bowls, wall hangings, your giving "gifts" to all, all the while going through "hell" with those awful treatments. Your smiles and jokes to all even in the midst of terrible pain and discomfort, trying to make everyone feel better *and* succeeding!

All of you girls are proving to me that you are your daddy's daughters. I'm hoping I had a bit to do with it too. Yesterday, when you were talking to us and telling us your plans you reminded me so much of Daddy and the way he faced death. But, honey, Daddy was eighty years old, and while I was devastated, I could accept it. I don't want to lose you. Parents should not have to lose their children. There should be a law against it. I'm having a rough time accepting the fact that I have to lose you too. I'm trying very hard to follow my little routine and take all my meds, plus some nerve pills with the doctor's permission. I know the last thing this family needs is for me to fall apart right now, but honey, it is so tempting. I wish I could take your hand and go with you. But I guess God doesn't want me right now, and I will try to hang in there for the rest of the family, but I can't help but wonder at times what good I am. My physical body is wearing out, and I not sure how much more heartache my heart can take. I keep trying to count my blessings and think about all the *good* memories we have had as a family. I keep trying also to pray and ask God to help me cope and be there for my family, but right now I'm angry at God and can't help ask *why*.

Mainly, honey, I just thought writing to you might help both of us—me to vent some of my feelings and also to let you know again how *proud* I am of you. Also I want you to know if I can do *anything* to help you besides tell you how much you mean to me and how much I love you. Please let me know.

Tomorrow Daddy and I would have been married sixty-four years, and I can't help but think about that date. We did have fifty-eight wonderful years together, and my heart aches that none of my daughters will have that privilege. Again, life is not *fair!*

August 30, 10:25 a.m.

My dear, I thought this letter was finished, and I was going to mail it to you this morning. Then I talked to you last evening and got your news. Honey, I didn't think it could get much worse. I was wrong. Again, I can't imagine what you must be feeling and going through to hear news like that. It is just not *fucking fair!* You know I have never talked like that in my life, but I am so angry that you have to face this terrible ugliness and more pain both physical and mental. I didn't think my heart could hurt anymore. I was wrong. *But* don't you dare feel guilty. You *did not plan this.* I haven't talked to anyone this morning so I don't know what you have decided, but again you don't have much of a choice. Again. it's not fair that one person has to face what you are facing, and I don't understand anything right now. All I know is that I love you and have ever since you started to grow in my tummy, and I can't bear the thought of losing you except I don't want you in any more pain. That tears me apart. *My* dear, just know that you are always in my heart, thoughts, and prayers. Give my love to Ken and Alice too as I know how much they are hurting also. It's strange how a mother's heart can expand to include all of her children, and Ken is my son too, always has been since you married him. And he is your prince, which reminds me, Jim called last evening and he is devastated too and understands in his own way what all of you are going through. He loves you too, Barb.

Enough! Honey, you know me. When I get writing I don't know when to stop, and now I'm repeating myself, but I can't say I *love you* enough.

Mama

Page 1 of 1
Subj: Janice
Date: 10/20/2005 6:38:01 p.m. Eastern Daylight Time
From: J Breyer
To: VeeBee248

Dearest Mom Vivian,

I know we are all exhausted and drained from the past couple of days, with today being the climax. It went off just like she planned, the music, Father Belczak and all her loved ones around her.

Thank you so much for the offer to go to Carol's for lunch, but I had work to do. You know, one minute I would be fine and then burst out in tears. We will all miss her so, but I know in my heart she is all around us. It was probably nice just to be family and hold each other.

When is KenJoe and Gina going back? I really didn't get a chance to talk to long to anyone. I know Ollie is going to Cincinnati for a couple of days and she needs that too. She must be exhausted. Ken will have Krista and the puppies. Ken is going to need us all.

I think about how the room was filled today . . . how she touched so many . . . what a beautiful woman. So very strong.

I didn't know about the article in the paper today, until Skippy came up to me and asked if I saw it. I didn't get to read it until just an hour ago when Tom brought it home. I could hardly read it, for the tears just streaming down. Did the paper call Ken and interview him? I am going to have it framed and put it up at the Island.

I will miss her so very much. Those 2 to 3 phone calls a day, quilt fabric shopping and tell each other about each stitch we planned. I don't know if you know this but, she is the only person who ever made *me* a quilt. Two years ago when I had surgery, she made me a "healing quilt." We all have her love she gave us, along with those cherished "stitched" gifts she enjoyed making. Oh my . . .

Let's be pen pals with each other, like she was with us. I've gotten so I don't even sign on but maybe twice a week now, since she stopped writing. I will miss all those great e-mails with pictures and jokes.

Take care my dear and I will keep you in my prayers . . . Love, Janice

Subj: Re: Detroit Free Press article
Date: 10/21/2005 11:47:18 a.m. Eastern Daylight Time
From: cdevlin@DNPS.COM
To: VeeBee248@aol.com
Sent from the Internet (Details)

Thank you for your prayers and kind response. We do have many similarities, I am from a family of 5 (all girls), I have three children and four grandchildren. So I can only imagine the pain you have suffered in your lifetime. The circle of life is children outlive their parents. In my position of helping people with our death notices I see this chain often broken. It hurts my heart. I will keep you and your family in my prayers. You have been blessed in other ways and I hope those wonderful moments give you the strength to enjoy your life. I am sure you have much love and support from your family and friends. I wish you all the best!

Carolyn

Carolyn Devlin Detroit
Newspaper, LP
New Media

From: VeeBee248@aol.com [mailto:VeeBee248@aol.com]
Sent: Friday, October 21, 2005 10:29 a.m.
To: Devlin, Carolyn
Subject: Re: Detroit Free Press article

Carolyn, thank you my dear for your personal note. I will include your sister in my prayers. You know exactly how my Alice feels, {like she has lost half of her}. Cancer of any kind is such a terrible disease . . . How do they pick who to write about in the paper? It was a beautiful article and Barb was a beautiful person. I've got some questions, like why I'm still here and God needed my daughter Kathy five years ago, {ovarian cancer} and now my Barb. I'm eighty-four and have had a good life, a wonderful husband and partner for fifty-eight years and now I've lost another beautiful child. I've been so blessed with a wonderful family, five children, eight grandchildren three greatgrandchildren and two more on the way. Parents should not have to lose their children. It's not the right circle of life and the pain is almost unbearable . . . Thanks for listening and my love and prayers to your sister, they have made some wonderful strides is helping to cure this disease. I have a dear friend here at Henry Ford Village where I live that had the same type of cancer as your sister four years ago and she is doing just fine.

My Love, prayers and best wishes to all of you. as a side note. I love my morning Free Press . . .

Subj: Re: Janice
Date: 10/21/2005 4:34:32 p.m. Eastern Daylight Time
From: J Breyer
To: VeeBee248

Dear Mom Vivian,

I cannot even imagine how Ken feels, he is so lost without his Pye. I have felt numb all day. Had to do an exhibit and pack the car for another one for Sunday.

I'm just going through the motions today.

Just called Ken to let him know I was thinking about him and the kids, Ollie too. By the way, did Ollie go to Cincinnati? I will try her cell later. He was distraught and so very sad. I said "Ken you wouldn't want her to come back . . . with the pain." We have to let her go and be in great peace with the Lord. Of course, it is only words right now . . . he loved her so much! She always said "He loves me too much." But they were the greatest couple I know and I don't think you can ever love someone too much. Oh how empty he feels now without her. He talked about how she is all around him . . . she made that house their home with all the things she cherished. We called them "chuch-kees" (polish for stuff), Mister called them "Chuckies."

I know it is very hard on you too, losing Barb. Please, call me any time to talk, it makes me feel good too. I will give you my cell and home number. Remember, any time. Tom loved her too.

I need your phone number and address. I would really appreciate it, if I could call you and we could talk. We will keep in touch. Talk later,

Cell: 313-570-7518 Home: 313-885-5261

Love and prayers,
Janice

From the heart of Vivian Beeler:

I would like to express my thanks and deep appreciation to all my HFV family and friends. For all of your outpouring of support, prayers, cards, hugs, in the loss of my daughter, Barbara Vogt to IBC Breast Cancer. She was 54. She was an identical twin to my daughter Alice.

As most of you know Bill and I moved into HFV almost 8 years ago. It was one of the wisest decisions we had ever made. During our marriage we had been blessed with four beautiful daughters, then when I was 43 we had a surprise bonus caboose son. Bill and I had two great years here before I lost him in April of 2000. Seven weeks later we lost our middle daughter Kathy to Ovarian Cancer. She was 53 and had fought it for 6 years. The support

I received from the staff and the friends we had made at that time helped me cope with my pain. Kristine Anderson had a Grief Support Group then that was very helpful. Myra and Sandra gently pushed me into starting my little Watercolor Class. That has been great therapy for me and perhaps I have been able to help a few other people also. The other committees I have been on have kept me busy and also helped—Birthday Angels, Sunday Entertainment, Mentoring, Dinning Services, twice, and also Library at that time. We have some wonderful people living here.

So many on the Staff here have become my good friends and over the years other people here have touched my heart with their friendship and caring. Our Barbara was diagnosed with Stage 4 IBC breast cancer in September of 2001, just before the terrorist attack September 11, 2001. So our family had a personal disaster at that same time. Mammograms don't show inflammatory breast cancer so we have been on a soapbox to tell all young women . . . You don't have to have a lump. IBC is hard for Doctors to diagnose. So check carefully for any changes.

Even with my heart breaking from my losses, [parents should not have to bury their children],I can't rave enough about the Staff here at the Village. That includes all the departments, Resident Life, Medical Center, Security, Maintenance, Housekeeping, Dinning Services, my young friends there too, Barb keeping all the plants so beautiful around here, etc. I have been overwhelmed by all their caring. A lot of them had met my Barb. She had such a vibrant, outgoing personality she drew people to her like a magnet. She had so much to live for and as a heartbroken Mother I can't help but ask why? I have to believe there is a reason and she isn't in any more pain. Thanks again from the bottom of my heart and thanks for listening to me.

Winter 2005 Issue
Volume 11
Henry Ford Village Retirement Community
Voices of Henry Ford Village
Wisdom By Doris DeDeckere

When you pick up a pen to write something, do you realize that a man once said, "The pen is mightier than the sword." We all have things we want others to read . . . but do we? In receiving a ridiculous and rather unbearable letter, I wrote off steamy reply and mailed it the same day.

(Advice: Hold a letter like that for two of three days and read over. Would you still send it? Or would you consider giving both your brain and your pen forty lashes and write it over in a more sensitive manner? I not only strained a relationship, I Darn near severed it. An improper response, a nasty reply to a credit card company, the phone company, any merchant, relative, or friend can alter the responding result in a manner you properly won't rejoice over. The following was written by Omar Khayyam and I've never forgotten it:

Words
The moving finger writes, and having writ, moves on; and neither piety nor wit can cancel half a line nor tears wash out of it.

When you put a pen to paper, think as you write . . . or save it for two or three days and read it over. "Dear Sir or Madam" will go over better than "than "Dear Jerk" Just a little philosophy from a now most friendly writer.

Thank you to resident artist Vivian Beeler for this happy illustration!

December 7, 2005

Dear Dr. Susan Reeder,

I had a follow-up appointment at Dr. Taylor's yesterday, and we were talking about the Village. She mentioned that she would really like to get over here to visit and see the place for herself. She said she had passed it numerous times and is getting more and more patients from here. I said I would love to have her come and have lunch with me and see what we have here. She said that she would love to. She also said she would like to meet you and asked me if I would try to set it up. She gave me her card with her secretary's phone number to get in touch with. She also said that Wednesday is the best day for her as she does not operate or see patients. Would you be interested and could this be worked out with you too? You could invite anyone else you wanted her to meet and perhaps take her to the medical center after lunch. I thought I would try to invite Cheryl and Myra if they were available. This would be my treat. It would be nice if she could see the Village at Christmastime, but I know that is pushing it with your busy schedules. Hoping to hear from you about this. No. 581-7041

Sincerely,
Vivian Beeler

P.S. Thanks for the report that my iron is back in the normal range.

2006

March 1, 2006

Dear Sage and Ché,

I bet you two are happy to have your mama back home after her visit to see your new cousin, Maeyana. Uncle Kenny and Aunt Gina sent grandma pictures of her, and she is such a beautiful baby. I feel very, very lucky because now I have five great-grandchildren. I have both of you, Cindy and Joe's son Corbin, and Erik and Eve's new little daughter Madilyn. I have got to see and hold Madilyn because they don't live too far from me like you do. I wish Grandma could have magic wings so she could fly and pop in to see you every once in a while. But I have to be satisfied with your pictures and talking to you on the phone. I have your pictures on my bookcase in my living room, so I look at them every day. I love both of you so much.

I am sending you our Erickson Paper that has an article about me in it. I thought you might like it for one of your albums or scrapbooks. I'm also sending our daily paper about Punch-key Day here in our area. I was talking to your mama about it on the phone so thought all of you would like to see what it's like. The day before Ash Wednesday and the starting of Lent is called Fat Tuesday. It all started when some of the people decided to give up all fats, sweets, and goodies for Lent, which is six weeks before Easter. So on that Tuesday they used up all their fats, eggs, and sugars and made great big jelly donuts called Paczki in Polish and pronounced Poonch-key. It is a very big deal in the Detroit area, and everyone eats Poonch-keys on that day. They also have a great big Mardi-gras Party in the New Orleans area, pictures of which they showed on TV, and you might have seen some of them. It is kind of a fun day around here.

Grandma is also sending you a few pictures of your new cousin Madilyn Louise, whom they are already calling Maddylou part of the time. I know your mama will have lots of pictures of your new cousin Maeyana. I think they are both very pretty names, and Grandma is happy because both babies and their parents are healthy and doing fine. Grandma is also very happy and excited to hear about your mama having twin babies growing in her tummy. You are going to have little brothers or sisters or one of each. Won't that be fun? I hear you are already thinking of names for them. Good for you! I just know your nana is in heaven watching over all of us and helping to plan things.

Grandma is so happy to hear that you both like school and you are learning all kinds of new and interesting things. Both of you are going to be such a big help to your mama and daddy when your new little sisters or brothers arrive. I talk to your papa and your aunt Alice very often, and they keep me up to date on things. Also I love it when your mama calls me. I love all of you so much and carry all of you in my heart. Stay well and take care. I'll write again or talk to you soon. Love you tons.

Free Press Newspaper,

You asked us to write on our best Mother's Day gift ever received.

How do you define "best"? When you have a loving and fairly large family, there are so many different things over the years—from the homemade cards, plaster hand prints, macaroni pins, and necklaces to the grown-up get-togethers. It's difficult to pick the "best." I would say they are "memorable memories" of love, sharing, and caring over the years.

Mother's Day in 1993 stands out in my mind because we did something different and a little special. My husband, Bill, was a member of the Squires Club and volunteer at Meadow Brook Hall. That is the estate of Maltida Dodge and Alfred Wilson in Rochester, Michigan. He had made arrangements for us to have Mother's Day brunch there. Three of our four daughters, their husbands, and five of our seven grandchildren, at that time, plus our son were able to join us.

We all enjoyed a lovely brunch in the elegant dining room at the hall. The weather cooperated. It was a gorgeous spring day. After brunch, Bill took the family on a tour of the mansion and gave his family a history lesson of how it came to be. He loved his volunteer work at the hall and was an excellent docent.

We walked around the grounds outside and through the wooded area to Knoll Cottage, the play house, that the Wilsons had built for their daughters, Frances and Barbara. The trees were so beautiful, and there were wildflowers all over in the wooded area.

Looking back, that day was a special gift. A perfect day!

Vivian Beeler CC 302 #581-7041

June 9, 2006

Dear Dianne and Harold,

I'm hanging in there, but I have to be honest, losing Barbara has been very hard to accept. I can't help but ask God why. I've lost three daughters now, and that's more than any parent should have to take. Our first baby, little Susan, was a SIDS victim at four and a half months, similar to Debby and Kevin's baby. In fact, that's how I first got acquainted with Debby. I wrote to her after we had heard what had happened. As we all know, life does go on, and we have to believe there is a reason. Ken, Barb's husband, has been having a terrible time, and so is Alice, Barb's twin. I've been trying to hold them both up. Ken and I have always had a good relationship, and I'm "Mom" to him. He lost his own mother to cancer right after they were married. Alice (she has been divorced for years) left her life in the Cincinnati area and came up here to be with her twin through these last two years. She has since moved back to that area as she has a daughter and son-in-law close by and a lot of friends there also. There really is a twin thing. I've seen it all their lives, so I do understand in my own way how Alice feels that half of her is gone. They always were very close, and Alice was a wonderful caregiver. Barbara did need her here. *But* the last six months of Barb's life were very hard. I miss her laughter; she was always so full of life and joy, and even during some of the worse times, she would have us all laughing. She had so much to live for—a wonderful husband, a daughter, son-in-law with two children in Arizona, aged eight and five, and a son for whom we had a wedding reception on Russell Island in August. Russell Island is just across from Algonac.

Barb and Ken have had a cottage there for twenty-nine years. Krista and Kenny grew up there in the summers. You take a ferry to the island; there are no cars. Bill and I used to call it "Lug Island" because you had to lug everything over on the ferry and down to their cottage. They do have a beautiful spot almost at the head of the Island with an empty beach lot next door. They look right across the river to Algonac. That was Barbara's paradise. She just loved it out there. We had a lot family doings out there over the years. The whole island was small enough that it was like one big family and everyone helped each other. Barbara was a *big* part of it. Some of their closest friends keep in touch with me, and they say that already the island is not the same. Ken had a very hard time going out there to check on it and take care of getting it ready for the summer. Kenny Jr., his wife Gina, and my new great granddaughter Maeyana Pye will be here sometime this summer, and they want to go there. Pye was an affectionate name that Ken had for Barb and doesn't even remember how it started, but Kenny wanted to use it in his daughter's name. They live in the San Francisco area, so I haven't met her yet. I have seen lots of pictures, and she is a little doll. She was born on February 7, 2006. Then on another happy note, our daughter Carol's son Erik who is our detective on the Livonia Police Force, and his wife Eve had Madilyn Louise on February 11, 2006. So I have two new great grandchildren, and I feel blessed because they are both normal, healthy, beautiful little girls. That makes five for me. I saw Madilyn when she was just fourteen hours old. What a joy that was! I do get to see Maddy quite often and am grateful. It's been a long time since I have held and cuddled a baby. Now, of course, she is responding to everyone with smiles, gurgles, and coos. What a little doll! I'm also happy to say that both daddies are so proud of their daughters, and they have pitched in from the beginning and do everything for them except breastfeed!

Our Carol keeps very busy with her sub-teaching in the elementary school close to her, plus her church work and babysitting. She just *loves* being a grandma. She already has been having a taste of it even before Madilyn. When her daughter Cindy (our social worker) married Joe almost two years ago, he already had a little boy Corbin from a brief marriage that didn't work. Corbin is five now. The hard part there is sharing custody as Corbin's mother lives in Washington State. They would like to have full custody. Joe is flying to get Corbin this week for an eight-week stay. For a joint custody child, he is remarkably well adjusted and a darling little boy. Cindy met Joe when she was working out in Washington State for two years. She got too homesick and felt she was missing too many family doings, and Joe was very willing to make a change and come to Michigan. He is into auditing and working for The Henry Ford Health System and doing well. Carol, Cindy, Joe, Erik, and Eve are my support system here. They are wonderful to me. That did bother Alice about moving back to the Cincinnati area, but it was really best for her.

Bill Jr., Shannon, and my darling granddaughter Sydney (aged five) call every weekend and some e-mails in between. They are all doing well, and Sydney takes Suzuki piano lessons, swim classes, gymnastics, soccer, etc. of course not all of them at the same time. She is doing very well on the piano. She gave the family here a recital down in our chapel last year when they were here at Thanksgiving time. It amazed me and everyone else too. They are coming for a short visit the end of July, and she wants to give us another recital. She is also getting like a little fish in the water—*no* fear, which is not always good. They really have to watch her. They loved to spend time at the cottage with Barbara and Carol, and I would go out there. Now they aren't sure they want to go back. Billy and Barb always had a closeness as she was the last one to get married and leave home. Plus Barb and Shannon became buddies. This has been hard on all of us. Just saw *Race for the Cure* on TV news today which brought tears. Barb and Ken were part of that three years ago. Even last year, she had registered but couldn't make it. When you see all the people that are affected by this terrible disease it is heartbreaking. They just have to find a cure. I wish they would bring our young people home from Iraq and spend the money on research for some of these terrible diseases.

I really did not plan to write so much about Barbara and family, but when I sit down to write sometimes I just don't know what is going to come pouring out. I hope I'm not boring you. You did ask me about my life at Henry Ford Village, and I haven't even mentioned that yet but will now.

I can't think of a better place for me to be at my age eighty-four, and in my circumstances. I just am so very grateful that Bill and I made the decision together to move here. It was a very wise decision. We had two *good* years here before I lost him and our Kathy just seven weeks later. The support from the staff and friends we had made in those two years helped me get through that time. They have a wonderful staff here, and so many of them have become my personal friends also. A lot of them are like extended adult grandchildren and children to me.

It doesn't seem possible it was eight years in January that we moved here from Troy. We bought a corner two-bedroom, two-bath apartment. I love all the light. I have what is called a cook's table, stainless steel, from Williams Sonoma that fits under one of my dinette windows, which I use for my art table. When I'm working on something, I can just leave things out, which is much easier than having to put things away every time I paint. It crowds our dinette a bit but is well worth giving up the space. The master bedroom is quite large with a walk-through closet into the bathroom with a glass door shower. The other bathroom has a tub. With all my arthritis, tub baths are out for me. I love my shower. I have room in my bedroom too for a nice reading chair and ottoman, with a drop down chain lamp with lots of light. The apartment has a walk-through kitchen with regular stove and fridge and quite a few cupboards. The living room is nice size too with big picture windows that overlook the courtyard and gatehouse and over to that garden of which I'm enclosing a postcard. I think I have one of the nicest views of the whole complex. Our second bedroom is where we put the computer and also more bookcases. My art books, magazines, and art supplies are starting to overflow. Now I call this room my basement, garage, and attic. Whenever I don't know what to do with something it goes in there. When Bill, Shannon, and Sydney come to visit I have a queen size air mattress for the living room floor, and Sydney sleeps with me. I love that, even with dolls, books, and stuffed toys. She is such a happy child and so smart. It seems to me that children today grow up so fast and really are smarter. I guess with all the media exposure and computers, plus pre-schools, it all adds up.

We have seven buildings in this complex. Six of the buildings are for independent living like my apartment, with all kinds of floor plans. One building is where they have the assisted living apartments for the residents that need some help in managing their daily living. They serve three meals a day over there. It also has the care center there for residents who need nursing care. They have a rehab section there too. The third floor there is for patients with Alzheimer's and dementia.

In the independent living, one meal a day is included in our monthly rent. Most people choose dinner, but you can also buy your breakfast and lunch at our Windows Cafe. They also use Windows for people who want to carry out their dinner back to their apartment. We have two large dining rooms—The Great Lakes, where the server takes your order and serves your dinner to you, and the St. Clair Dining Room, which is a buffet. Both dining rooms have nice salad bars, plus you have three or four entrees to choose from. Then you can always get baked fish or chicken. The meals are really pretty good. They try very hard to please everyone, but with twelve hundred people there are always some that you can't satisfy. The only thing I have to say about the food is that it's kind of like eating at the same restaurant every night. It's nice to have a change. So when my family comes over, we go out to eat.

I seem to keep very busy. I still have my little watercolor class on Tuesday afternoons, which I enjoy. The attendance varies with doctor appointments, etc. I have between three to seven people there every week. I do take July and August off for a little break. I'm also on our Sunday Afternoon Entertainment Program. We try and have different programs every other Sunday from September through June. Sundays are long days for some people, especially for those who don't have families nearby. We ask for a $3.00 donation as we have to pay the artists who come. Most of our programs are musicals with a speaker once in a while with favorites like The Detroit Edison Glee Club, Bob Milne, ragtime pianist, Lance Luce, organist, Barbershop Quartets, all kinds of different musical groups or people. Last week we had a woman singer and pianist who sang and played a lot of Broadway show tunes and songs we danced to when we were younger. We have groups of young people from the performing arts schools that are excellent—Mariachi bands, The Red Garter Band. (They are getting older and hard to get now.) We try to vary the programs and try to keep the price range within $500.00.

I'm also on our Birthday Angels committee. The staff gives birthday cards and a balloon to each resident on their birthdays. Our committee members all have a floor assigned to them and we deliver the cards and balloons hopefully before noon for the birthday person. I have the fourth floor of our building. We pick them up in the crafts room on this side of the complex. Some months I have six or seven, some months two or three. It varies, not a difficult job. I'm also on the mentoring committee. We keep our eyes open in the dining rooms and watch to see that the young servers are not having problems with some of the residents or whether they just want to talk to us. I have made a lot of young friends by doing this. Living where I do, we have a lot of Arabic students and also black. They are a very nice group of young girls and boys. A lot of them are working toward our scholarship program. They have to complete five hundred hours of service in their last two years of high school or the last year of high school and the first year of college or tech school to earn the scholarship. Then they get $1,000.00 a year paid directly to their school. We had thirty-seven young people this year who completed those requirements. They have car washes and bake sales to help earn the money too. Every spring we have a scholarship drive here for the residents to contribute to that fund. I think we got close to $100,000 this year. The students really seem to appreciate it. I'm on the Newcomers Committee too; we are assigned a newcomer who moves in, and we call them to ask if they have any questions or perhaps would like to have dinner with us some evening—just little things to make them feel welcome.

I think at last count there was 129 groups, clubs, and different activities. If you can't find something out of all of those that interests you, it's kind of a shame. You can stay in your apartment, watch TV, and grow *old!* We have all kinds of arts and crafts, choirs, any kind of card games, scrabble, wood and hobby shop, support groups, Bible study groups, exercise classes, fitness trainer with exercise room and latest equipment, a beautiful library, the list goes on and on. I forgot, we also have the computer lab, ping pong, shuffle board, etc. We also have a lot of volunteers who teach English to the foreign born and also people who read for the ones with low vision. Whatever you like to do, you can probably find it here. *Oh,* Harold, I know you love to plant and take care of flowers. Residents can also have a garden spot. Gee, I sound like a salesman for this place, don't I? Besides if you and Dianne ever plan on anything like this, you would go where you would be closer to your family. Bill and I did enjoy the time we had together here, and I'm grateful as I said.

I do have a lot of arthritis and back problems. My warranties are running out, and I think I need a good lube job. Ha! I had a back operation a year ago. I had a cyst between two of my lower vertebraes, which was pushing on my sciatic nerve. That was very painful, and it was difficult to walk. The operation was a success in that it took away the terrible pain shooting down my leg, but she couldn't get all of it (for good reasons), and it is still causing constant back pain. I can't walk any distance, so I have been taking a water aerobics class since February, twice a week for an hour. We do have a lovely pool and hot tub right here. The pool is only four feet deep but feels good, and I can do the exercises in the water. It is painful for me to dress and undress and it quite a hike over to the pool area, *but* I'm doing it. I know I need the exercise. Sorry to say it has not helped the back pain and I have to take some pain meds, but I know all the rest of my body benefits from it. My whole life has changed completely with losses and physical problems, but again you have to keep believing there is a reason. We just don't know it. I've got a lot of questions. There is a saying, "Your attitude is the crayon that colors your world." I try very hard to live by that. I think that's one reason I love to paint flowers because they are so bright and happy.

I can't believe I have written this much. I do hope that I have not bored you folks silly. I certainly have given you an update and then some on me, my family, and life at Henry Ford Village. I didn't tell you though of all the special events that go on here during the year—volunteers brunch in May to thank all the volunteers, our big annual expo that was on May 25. All groups have displays to show the residents what is available to them and what is going on around here. My class watercolor table was very colorful. Dining services always go all out for these affairs with beautiful fresh fruit, cheese and cracker, tea, breads, etc. Dining services also plans theme special dinners for each dining room about every four to six weeks. They are fun. The Arts and Craft Fair is coming up on August 4. I will probably have some of my artwork on display. We can sell things then if we want, but I never sell my work. You just donate 10 percent to our Benevolent Fund. That's the fund they have for when people's money runs out due to long illnesses, They continue to care for you until your time runs out. That is part of the Erickson management promise when you move in here.

I have written this over a three-day period, and now my printer is acting up. I have to call for service in the morning.

Hope you enjoy the cards I'm sending to show something different from a Christmas theme. My very best wishes to all of you, and I do hope I haven't scared you off and you will keep in touch.

As ever, Vivian

June 14, 2006

Hi, I just got my printer going again. They have a young man here whom we can call for computer service, but he is very busy as he is the supervisor of pre-maintenance also. He told me yesterday that they are doing computer service on Tuesdays and Thursday now. He was just a very young man when Bill and I moved in here, so I've kind of watched him grow up. He was married a few years ago, and they have a thirteen-month-old little boy,

Matthew. He is so proud of him. I love to listen to these proud daddies. Anyway, perhaps I can get this printed out and sent to you folks now.

I did have a delightful day on Monday. Alice made a special trip up here with one of her close friends because she said she needed a "mama hug" and sister hug too. They got here about 1:30 p.m. Eve came over so Maddy could meet her aunt Alice. Maddy gets sweeter every time I see her. We had the nicest visit. Then Eve and Maddy left, and the four of us went for an early dinner as the girls were hungry. We tried a new Longhorn restaurant in a new shopping plaza they are building not far from me. We all enjoyed our dinner with lots of laughter and a few tears. Then the girls took me over into a World Marketplace. I had never been in one, and it was fascinating to just look at everything. They also have a beautiful new Barnes and Noble bookstore there. It was just delightful to be out with my daughters. Alice's friend Chris is one of my adopted daughters. I was worn out, and Carol had to get home to her greyhound, "Scooby" and Alice and Chris had to get on the road for home. It had been six months since Carol and I had seen Alice, and it did us all good. They got back home safe and sound about 1:00 a.m. as I had Alice call me so I could sleep better.

Tomorrow I have my swim class, and then two of Barb's closest friends who called are coming to take me to lunch and then shop around our treasure sale downstairs. It's sort of like a flea market.

Jackson

August 12, 2006

Dear Linda and Sandra,

It certainly sounds like you girls have been very busy with doctors, physical problems, and insurances, plus all the things you have been doing to help at the Curtis farm and your own place. I hope you are both feeling better and getting everything straightened out.

It's been rather a hard summer for all of my family. Barbara loved their cottage so much up by Algonac that's it's been difficult not to have her here to enjoy it this year. Ken is still having a very rough time, and so is Alice. I think being an identical twin does make you feel like half of you is missing. Ken goes out on Saturdays to keep up the yard and see that the cottage is OK, but he hasn't been able to stay overnight. Kenny Jr. and Gina are coming with Maeyana over the Labor Day weekend. We are all hoping that will help. I'll finally get to see my great-granddaughter. Her pictures are darling. She and Maddy just turned six months old. I do see Maddy quite often, and it has been a joy to watch her grow and develop. It's been a long time since I have been around a baby. She is a little sweetie. Both babies look about the same size and from what I hear are doing almost the same identical things. We are hoping it will work out so we can see them together. Kenny and Gina will only be here for five days, so we will have to wait and see.

The weather is certainly beautiful this weekend. I wish it could stay this way. I don't do to well in that ninety-degree weather. I just stay inside if possible. I wish I could tell you that my back was feeling better, but I still have a lot of pain and have to pace myself. It gets very discouraging at times because I was always a person who liked to keep busy. I'm still on my committees, still do my water aerobics class twice a week, and have my watercolor class on Tuesdays, but everything is such a big effort. Oh well, I'm glad I'm still able to get around and take care of myself.

We had a very nice weekend the end of July. Bill, Shannon, and Sydney were here for three full days. It was so good to see them. Carol brought Corbin over on Friday, and we all had a nice day together, staying around here and taking the children to the swimming pool. I even went in with them, and they got a big kick out of Grandma in the pool with them. On Saturday, Billy had his reunion with his Michigan buddies, and he arranged with Carol to come to. It was out at his friend Joel's house on a lake in Milford. He's been wanting me to come for several years, but their get-together is too long for me to handle. So this year he arranged with Carol, and then she brought me home when I got tired. It worked out well, but it was that real *hot* weekend, so even by the water it was *hot*. But at least I got to see all the boys who were in school, band and Boy Scouts with Bill. I had watched them all grow up. Most of them are married now with children, so it was really nice to see them. Carol brought me home after about two hours around four. I couldn't take the heat any longer. Their house was air conditioned, but everyone was outside by the water or in it. It didn't make sense to sit in there alone.

On Sunday, after all got showered and dressed, Alice came up from Ohio, which was wonderful. I had not seen her since early spring. Carol came over, and we all went and had brunch in our dining room. Then the rest of the family around here came over—Erik, Eve, Maddy, Cindy, Joe, Corbin, Ken, Jim, Hannah, and Scott, also one of Bill's friends with his wife and two girls aged nine and thirteen. I had a *full* apartment, but it was so nice. We went over to the chapel, and Sydney gave us a piano recital on the grand piano they have there. She played six songs and did very well using both hands and all from memory. She has been taking Suzuki piano lessons for almost two years now. We were all very proud of her. She is a very outgoing and happy child, nice to be around, and a very pretty little girl. That's a proud grandma talking. Then all the children and parents who wanted to went over to the swimming pool and had a lot of fun. Erik and Eve even took Maddy in the pool with them. They have swim diapers now, which makes it OK for babies to go in a public pool. Nothing can leak out. There were several other families there too, as like I said it was that very hot weekend. After the swimming, we ordered pizzas, and I had veggies and dips and chips and dip. Scott had brought a huge Bumpy Cake like Sanders used to make—chocolate with chocolate fudge frosting and bumps of marshmallow crème across it, so everyone had plenty to eat and all enjoyed. Carol and Alice stayed after everyone had left and spent the rest of evening just talking and enjoying one another's company. I had to get up at 3:00 a.m., and Carol was here at four to take them to the airport. So none of us had much sleep that night. I was sure tired but enjoyed every minute of it. It just went by too fast. They arrived home about 10:30 a.m. our time safe and sound . . . 8:30 a.m. Denver time. It still amazes me.

Krista and twin babies are doing fine. She has followed the doctor's orders and stayed on bed rest, which has been difficult for her. She has always been a hard worker. *But* it has kept the babies inside to grow properly, for which we are all very grateful. The doctor says everything is fine, and if she starts any contractions now they will all be OK. Her actual due date is first week in September. She says she is very, very large and very uncomfortable. I can remember that feeling. Also the babies have been very active, which is a good sign. Krista says Sage and Ché have been a big help to her, but they are anxious to see their new sisters.

I think that kind of fills you in on my summer. It doesn't seem possible that it is the middle of August already. When Alice came up here to see her brother and family, she went out to the cottage for a few days. She cleaned it from top to bottom and weeded all of Barb's flower beds. She said she had promised Barb that she would do it. Ken appreciated what she did. She came back to my place on Friday, August 4, to help me with our annual art fair. I'll try and send you a picture. I could not have participated in it if I hadn't have help with setting up the display and taking it down, so it worked out very well for me. Carol has been busy all summer with babysitting Corbin and little Maddy. Cindy is taking Corbin back to Washington tomorrow. That's so hard for them, but Corbin seems to be a well-adjusted little boy. This terrorist business and flying is scary, but it's probably safer right now with all the restrictions and security. It seems like our whole world is going crazy. I don't like listening to the news.

As I said before, I hope this letter finds both of you feeling a lot better and being able to help on the farm more.

October 25, 2006

Dear Cousin Rosly,

It was so very nice to receive your nice birthday letter and lovely watercolor card with the very beautiful sheer table cloth. I always look forward to your letter at that time. Rosly, I have misplaced or lost the information of when your birthday is. I feel badly because I have not sent you a card at that special time of the year for you. Would you please let me know in your next letter?

I am so very sorry to hear of all the terrible pain and problems Anneleis has had with her back. I can relate; although my back problem is different and not as serious, I do have constant pain. I am on a pain patch and a few pain pills too, but they only take the edge off. I tried a stronger dosage but did not like the way it made me feel, so I went back to the lower dosage. Mine is due to arthritis, the inflammation, and a little cyst and spur pushing on nerves in my back. It affects me if I walk very far at one time. I do have to pace myself. But I am eighty-five, and you and I both know that age is not kind to our bodies. We just have to accept God's will and try our best to live with it. I know how you worry as a mother. It doesn't matter how old our children get, they are still our children. I do hope Anneleis is feeling better with more time. Please tell her I will keep her in my prayers. It's nice to hear that Rosemarie is doing fine. It certainly sounds like Walter has a strong spirit to keep going like he does. I admire him. Rosly, you mentioned your dizziness, but did not say much about it. How are you managing with it? Can you still get around and go places? I certainly hope so.

It certainly is nice to hear that the grandchildren are doing well. I know that is a blessing for you.

We had a very *hot* summer, and it seemed to go by very fast. The flowers around our buildings, courtyard, Ford birthplace garden, and the entranceway have just been outstanding this year. They have been so beautiful they almost take your breath away. Everyone was talking about them, all the residents and the people who came to visit. They just pulled all the annuals out this past week. Even though September and October have been chilly, cloudy, and rainy, the flowers still looked good. Our fall weather has not been very nice this year. We are still hoping we will have some Indian summer weather and sunshine before November gets here.

I don't know if you pay any attention to our baseball teams in Switzerland, but everyone here in our area is all excited because our Detroit Tigers Baseball Team made the world series this year. They are playing the St. Louis Cardinals. They have each won one game apiece. The team to win the best of seven games (four) is the world Champion. It's been nineteen years since our Tigers have been in the series, so this whole area has got Tiger fever. I'm not a big sports fan, but I try to keep track of our home teams so I don't feel stupid when my grandchildren talk about them. It does seem nice to see everyone so happy about something with this horrible war in Iraq still going on. I think our president made a huge mistake in getting us involved in it. We are losing so many of our wonderful young people and so many families are suffering. My heart aches for them.

Yes, Rosly, I have two more great-granddaughters born on August 18, 2006. Krista had to have a c-section as one of the babies was breech. Also, they wanted to come much too early, and the doctor put her on bed rest for the last two months. It was difficult with two other children, but Sage was eight and Ché was six, so they were able to help quite a bit. It was difficult for Krista because she has always been a hard worker and was busy all the time. She didn't want to take any chances with the babies though. She had the c-section two weeks early, and the babies are normal healthy little girls. We feel blessed, and we do feel like Barbara had a hand in planning this for her daughter.

Sedona Sue weighed 5 lb. 8 oz., and Simone Louise weighed 6 lb. 6 oz. Krista was very large. I told her she took after me as my twins weighed 6 lb. 6 oz.—Alice and Barb (6 lb. 8 oz.).

Ken had a very rough time going out to their cottage this year. That was Barbara's paradise. She just loved it out there. It is a beautiful spot right on the St. Clair River at the mouth of Lake Huron. He went out only on Saturdays to cut the grass and keep the place up. He could not bear to stay overnight. Kenny Jr., Gina, and little Maeyana came to visit from California over Labor Day weekend, and stayed on for a few days. They came down here twice so I could see and play with Maeyana. She is a beautiful little baby and was almost crawling when they were here. I had Carol and her family over on one afternoon. Kenny and Gina wanted to see their cousins and Erik and Eve's baby Madilyn. They were born just four days apart. That was a fun time. We put both babies (six months old) on a blanket in the middle of my living room floor. All the adults sat around and just watched them. It was better than any movie or show. They were just fascinated with one another.

Monday, October 2, 2006

Dear Linda and Sandra,

It doesn't sound like you girls have had a very good summer with all the physical problems you both have been having. Plus, it seems like you are having lots of bad luck with your car too. I'm sorry. I'm sure it is a scary thing to have your mammogram test come back unusual and then for them still not know what's wrong after a biopsy. I sure hope you have the results now and also hope that they turned out well. Let me know. I'm hoping it is just a benign cyst or some little thing like that. That can be very common but scary until you find out exactly what's wrong.

I have two more new great-granddaughters. Krista had her twins on August 18, the day you had your surgery. She had to have a c-section as one of the babies was breech. Both babies and mama are doing fine. Sedona Sue weighed 5 lb. 8 oz. and Simone Louise weighed 6 lb. 6 oz., both eighteen inches long. The doctor thinks they are identical from the afterbirth, etc. although Sedona has darker hair than Simone. Of course, they lose most of that baby hair anyway. They are beautiful healthy babies, and that's what is important.

Carol had all the family from around here over to her place on Saturday to celebrate my eighty-fifth birthday. Ken picked me up and brought me home later, which was very nice. It was a miserable rainy day. Carol had me pick out the menu, and I picked spaghetti, salad, rolls, Angel food cake with fresh strawberries, and vanilla ice cream. It was very good. I hadn't had homemade spaghetti for a long time. The sauce they use here is not like I used to make, and Carol uses my recipe. I was hungry for it. Plus, that's an easy dish to feed a group, and I didn't want Carol to work too hard. She is so busy all the time anyway. Everyone enjoyed the dinner. I got to play with Maddy again, and that's always fun. She is getting heavier and likes to keep moving, so I can't hold her too long, but she's fun to watch too. She's almost ready to crawl and got two bottom teeth that are almost through the surface. She chews on everything. It was so much fun to see her and Maeyana together when Kenny and Gina were here. Maeyana is a beautiful baby too. Kenny called me on my birthday and said that Maeyana is crawling all over now. They have to really watch her. I went from three great grandchildren to seven this past year. Wow—Sage, Ché, Corbin, Maeyana, Madilyn, Sedona, and Simone!

Wednesday, October 4, 2006

Dear Susan,

I feel like I know you as I have heard so many nice things about how you helped my daughter, Barbara Vogt—BoBo. She thought so much of you and considered you one of her good friends. I also think we might have met at the funeral home. It just doesn't seem possible that it has been almost a year and will be October 15.

It's been a rough year for my family, her twin Alice, and her husband, Ken, to cope with her loss. I so miss her laughter. No matter how sick she was, she was always cracking jokes and making everyone laugh. She helped so many, many people all through her illness was also on a soapbox to spread the word about inflammatory breast cancer.

I had been planning on sending you a card and bookmark, just to say "hello and how are you doing?" and to tell you some of the things that have been happening in Barbara's family. Then the Twist section in Sunday's paper was full of cancer stories and also of your store. *But,* Susan, I read it from cover to cover, and nowhere in it did it mention inflammatory breast cancer. It made me very upset. You know and I know that while it is not as prevalent as finding a lump in your breast, it does affect a lot of young women. The cancer foundations, walks, etc. never mention it. We both know Barb was on a soapbox to inform people, and I have passed out a lot of pamphlets too. Ken said he found more in a drawer, and I asked him for some more. Somehow we have to get the word out so it can be diagnosed *sooner!* I plan on writing to the writers who put that cancer section of the paper together. I wrote to Lila Lazarus when she was on Channel 4; she did answer and said she had to talk about what they told her to, but she said she was keeping the information.

Elizabeth Edwards has a new book out called *Saving Graces.* The reviews say it really is more about they losing their son Wade in a car accident at sixteen than about her fight with her breast cancer. One of the quotes they used that she describes really hits the nail on the head for me. "She says people should know that even though you put on a stiff upper lip, inside you are crumbling." After losing two daughters to cancer, this sure makes sense to me. I can't help but wonder why I'm still here at eighty-five. I've lived my life and both my girls had so much to live for. Life just doesn't make sense. But it does go on, and we have to make the best of it, one day at a time . . .

Speaking of life going on, I don't know if you have heard or not, but I would like to pass on some family news. Barb and Ken's son, Kenny, and his wife Gina, who live in the San Francisco area, had a baby girl, Maeyana Pye, on February 7, 2006, Weighing 9 lb. 2 oz. She is a beautiful healthy baby and is starting to crawl all over now at seven months. Then shortly after we lost Barb, their daughter Krista got pregnant, very unexpectedly, as Krista and David already had Sage, who will be nine on November 1, and Ché who was six in July. This was not a planned pregnancy, and all of us were wondering if Barbara had something to do with this, as Krista had *twin* girls on August 18. Krista had to be on bed rest the last two months as they wanted to come early. That was a difficult and worrisome time. *But* everything worked out fine. Krista had a c-section on the eighteenth and had two beautiful and healthy baby girls. Sedona Sue weighed 5 lb. 8 oz. and Simone Louise weighed 6 lb. 6 oz. The doctor thinks they are identical from the afterbirth. This has really bonded Krista and me and brought back so many memories that I thought I had forgotten. Alice weighed 6 lb. 6 oz. and Barbara weighed 6 lb. 8 oz. Both Krista and I were huge! Krista is doing fine and is one busy young mother. She is nursing both babies too. Krista says Sage is a *big* help and another little mother. Both children are thrilled to have new sisters. Also in our family news, Carol's (Barb's elder sister) son Erik and his wife Eve had a beautiful, healthy little girl last February 11, just four days after Kenny and Gina. Madilyn is also doing fine, and I do get to see and play with her quite often as they live in Livonia. That makes four great-granddaughters for me in this past year, plus the three I have already, which makes seven for me, so as I said before, life does go on but is so bittersweet as we know how much Barb would love to be here to love and enjoy them. There is such a big hole in all of our hearts.

Ken has had a very difficult time going out to their cottage this summer. He goes out either on Saturday or Sunday and takes care of the place but just can't bring himself to stay overnight. You know how much Barb loved the cottage. That was her paradise. Kenny and Gina were here for six days over Labor Day weekend, so me and "Papa" got to see Maeyana. They were down here for lunch and the afternoon the day after they got in. Then they came again the next day late afternoon, and the rest of the family around here came over for a get-together. We really enjoyed watching Maeyana and Madilyn play together. They were fascinated with one another. All the adults sat around and oohed and aahed. It was better than a movie. They are both such beautiful babies and doing everything they should for their age. Both very proud daddies sat next to one another and compared their daughters. Susan, I do feel blessed with my family. They are so good to me and tell me that I'm important to them, but I would have traded with either daughter if I could have. Ken, Kenny, Gina, and Maeyana did go out to the cottage for three days and two nights, and Ken managed with them there. Alice was supposed to have come up, but it just didn't work out. It was disappointing for all.

My son Bill Jr., Shannon, and my darling granddaughter Sydney were here for a long weekend in July too, and we had another family get-together, but you can't help feeling those holes. Bill and Shannon couldn't face going to the cottage this year either.

When I told Alice that I was writing to you, she wanted me to be sure and tell you hello from her. She moved back to the Cincinnati area last December 2. She meant to stop in and see you but time got away from her, but she thinks the world of you also. She wants me to give you her phone number. She just has a cell phone. She is waitressing again and has Sundays and Mondays off. She starts at either three or four in the afternoon the rest of week. Her number is 513-600-9192, address is 4302 Batavia Meadows Dr. # 39, Batavia, Ohio 45103.

I hope I haven't bored you with rattling on and on. When I get started writing, I never know where and how I'm going to end up. I also hope all the family stuff makes sense to you, but knowing Barb like you did, I think it will.

I'm still trying to keep up with my committees and have my little art class on Tuesday afternoons, but my arthritis in my back is getting worse and not much can be done about it, so everything is an effort. *But* I am going to write some more letters and see if someone will listen and get more information out on inflammatory breast cancer. It's something I feel very strongly about and will do all I can to make people more aware of it.

I do hope things are going well for you, and while I don't know the ladies in your shop, I want them to have a bookmark also. This is the first painting that I have done that was long enough to make bookmarks and then they happened by a happy accident. I have given out almost a hundred now, and everyone tells me they make them feel good. It's an ego boost for me and makes the work worthwhile. Take care.

October 6, 2006

Laura Varon Brown, Elaine Lok
Cathy Payne,
Patricia Montemurri,
Cary Waldman,

Dear Twist Editor and Writers:

Please, Please listen to me. I read The Twist section of last Sunday's paper from cover to cover and not once did anyone mention IBC Breast Cancer. In fact I have not read or heard anything about it in any of the cancer articles or TV programs about it. I'm very upset and angry because we have to get the word out about it. YOU DON'T HAVE TO HAVE A LUMP TO HAVE BREAST CANCER! If you just type in IBC BREAST CANCER on the web you will come up with tons of information about it. BUT . . . Not many people know about it and we are losing too many of our young women to it. Granted, it is not as prevalent as finding a lump but by the time the Drs. make the correct diagnoses it is already in advanced stages . . . I know from personal heartache . . . October 15th will be the 1 year anniversary of losing my beautiful daughter Barbara to IBC Breast Cancer . . . Let me tell you our story:

I am 85 years old and live at Henry Ford Village in Dearborn in the Independent Living Apartments. My husband and I had 58 years of a great marriage together. We had 5 children. Four daughters, including a set of identical twin girls. Then when our oldest daughter was in college and the others teenagers, I had a surprise pregnancy and we had a bonus caboose boy. We have 8 grandchildren, 7 adult young people and one darling 6 year old girl, whose Daddy is our bonus son. My husband was an engineer at Ford Motor company for 45 years and I was lucky enough to be a homemaker. We have always been a close family that cared about each other for which I feel blessed. In 1994 our middle daughter Kathy at 47 was diagnosed with an unknown source tumor which Drs. said was terminal. She was treated for ovarian cancer and fought it for 6 years, surprising Drs. We learned a lot about cancer during those years and what a fighter our daughter was. She had a wonderful husband who took care of her wonderfully. I can't thank him enough and we are still close. They had one son who was an adult at the time and was also there for his Mother.

In January 1998 my husband and I moved to Henry Ford Village from our home in Troy as we just could not take care of a big home and yard the way it should be. My husband had already had both knees replaced and one hip. We were calling him the bionic man. He was strict with his therapy and recovered fine. He had always been healthy, but he was a fighter too, not a complainer . . . It was a very smart move for us and we enjoyed our new lifestyle, outside of our worry about our daughter Kathy. She went through some terrible treatments, Chemo, Draining her lungs, in and out of hospital, lost her hair three times, but she kept fighting and saying. "One day at a time" Tomorrow will be better" . . . She was such a talented young woman. Kathy and her husband were remodeling a 114 year old farmhouse in Milford. Kathy had her builder's license, was on the Zoning Board and Cable board in the City of Milford. She was also a beautiful seamstress. While she was fighting for her life she made hundreds of stuffed animals and dressed them in darling outfits that she also made. All the family got some of those special stuffed animals, and she gave a lot them to the children's cancer center at Henry Ford Hospital. She wrote a beautiful letter to her support group at Thanksgiving time, telling how cancer had touched her life and brought in so many friends that she would have never met. Kathy and her husband were active members of Gilda's Club. We went to a lot of functions there with them. Met some wonderful people and learned a great deal. As a side note, Jim has gone ahead and finished their house and it is beautiful. It was on the Milford Historic Home Tour this past September.

Then in the summer of 1999 my husband became ill. He had already been diagnosed with prostate cancer in 1996 which after a "Turps" operation, was under control with hormone treatments, It was not the cause of his illness. A diseased gallbladder which they removed in November and said NO CANCER. BUT . . . He just kept going downhill. I lost him in April of 2000. Drs finally said they thought it was cancer of the bile duct? Seven weeks later we lost our Kathy. With the support of my family and the wonderful staff and friends I had made here at the Village I kept going but it was a terrible year for me and my family. Since my husband's first knee replacement in 1993, myself and my family have been on an emotions roller coaster with a lot of heartache. In 1997 our oldest daughter Carol lost her husband at 55 to diabetes and a stroke. Very suddenly. Edsel was like a son to us and they too had a wonderful marriage.

September 10th, 2001 our Barbara was diagnosed with IBC Breast Cancer. Our world fell apart again. September 11th we all know what happened on that date . . . Double whammy for all of us. Barb had been going to Drs. all summer trying to find out why her breast was so sore and inflamed. She was treated for an infection and a virus. She had had her mammogram and had another one, but of course IBC DOES NOT SHOW UP ON MAMMOGRAMS . . . Finally one of her Drs. took biopsies and discovered the cancer. It had progressed to Stage 4 by that time. That's why we have to get the information out to young women. We have a Cancer Support group here at the Village. They had never heard of IBC breast cancer. My family have been on a soapbox passing out pamphlets, talking and telling people about it. No one we talk to has ever heard of it. Barbara was another fighter like her sister Kathy and went through "hell" with the chemos, surgery, and radiation which burned her chest so badly she had trouble getting comfortable bras. That's where she and Susan of Susan's Special Needs became such good friends. Barb was very active in Beaumont's Sharing and Caring program, helping with their golf outings, luncheons, anything to help raise money for research, etc . . . Again, we were so proud of her. No matter how sick she was she never lost her sense of humor. She would have everyone in the chemo room laughing. They loved Bobo . . . [her nick name.] When she got into quilting she made a quilt at the request of Dr. Pass, head Dr. of oncology at that time at Royal Oak Beaumont, to hang in her office. I believe she has since moved to New York. Barb was one of our twins. Her and her twin, Alice traded places on the examining table for a Drs. checkup one day. Pulled open her paper jacket and said see I'm all healed . . . Had the Dr. just cracking up. That's my girls! Barbara also had a wonderful husband who was with her every step of the way too. Their adult son and daughter and family sadly did not live close by. Kenny in California and Krista, David, and 2 grandchildren Sage and Ché in Arizona. They were here as much as possible. Like I said before, we have always been a close family. Barbara was a secretary for a Shredding Company in Rochester but had to quit her job as her treatments made her to sick to work on a regular basis. They kept her job for her and wanted her whenever . . . but it was too much . . . They are still good friends with her husband Ken. After a year of hell, Barb had a pretty good year and we were all so encouraged and hoping she was going to beat the odds. Barb and Ken have had a cottage on Russell Island across from Algonac for about 30 years now . . . It is a beautiful spot. That was Barb's paradise. She couldn't wait for summer to spend her time out there. There are no cars on the Island, you have to take a ferry across. My husband and I used to call it "Lug Island" as you had to lug everything over . . . Even drinking water. But they loved it and their children grew up there. They love it too. The Island is like one big family and Bobo was a huge part of it. They had a golf cart Survivor Parade the first summer she was feeling good again. One of her dear friends sent all of her family and friends muslin squares and asked everyone to put a design on them and sign them, and send them back to Jan. It was amazing the different and original squares she got back. She made Barb a beautiful Survivors' Quilt . . . It so touched Barb that she asked Jan to give her lessons. She became addicted and in two years time she made over 80 quilts. She sewed all the time. She gave quilts and wall hangings to all her close friends and family. I have a lot of her things that I treasure. This was a daughter that I had to almost sit on to teach to sew a button or hem . . . She made several breast cancer quilts with beautiful pink fabrics for Caring and Sharing to auction off at their money raisers. I believe Susan of Susan's Special Needs has one too. Barb used the machine to sew the patterns together and through the internet met a wonderful lady she called "Magic Linda." She sent her quilts to her and she machine quilted them following the patterns on the materials. They were just breathtaking . . . She spent hundreds of dollars on machines, materials, etc. Her husband never complained because it made her happy that she was accomplishing something . . . *AND* . . . she made so many people *HAPPY!* Barb told me when she was creating a pattern and making it come out well, that it kept her mind from going in dark places . . .

Looking back and writing to you has made me realize even more how many people both my daughters touched, helped and left footprints in their hearts. I have always been very proud of them but even more so now. Except . . . No parent should have to lose their children no matter what age. It's just not the right circle of things. My heart goes out to "Maddie" and her Dad, who you have had several articles about in the paper lately. Also going to the treatment rooms with my daughters and seeing all the young people that cancer affects is heartbreaking.

Elizabeth Edwards in her new book "Saving Graces" was quoted by one of her reviewers and to me it says it all . . . She said, "People do not realize how raw the pain is when you lose a child. You may put on a stiff upper lip but inside you are crumbling." I so agree. It hurts all the time and the pain does not go away.

Both Barb's husband Ken and her twin Alice have had a very rough year. Both call me often and say it helps to talk to me because I understand their pain. I do, and I try to help them but I'll be honest, it's draining on me too. Perhaps that's one of the reason's I'm still here if I can help? Alice gave up her life to be here to take care of her twin. Alice lives in the Cincinnati area. She has been divorced for years, also has 2 adult children and both girls were like second mothers to each other's children. They were always very close. Last Spring and Summer were terrible for Barb, and Alice gave her wonderful care, which Barbara really appreciated. But . . . again it took a lot of courage and strength on Alice's part to do it. Barb had terrible radiation burns on her buttocks from radiation to try and help with the pain in her legs. Alice was dressings those several times a day, plus coping with the pain her twin was in. Barb had said before that she would want hospice but the cancer was eating away at her brain too and she kept saying no to hospice until two days before she died. Then Alice was at the end of her rope and got the Dr. to order it. Alice would not change a thing because she knows Barb wanted her there but now she feels guilty because she thinks she could have done more. She is reliving last year all over again. Plus she feels like half of her is gone, literally. That's where I'm trying to help with my talks to her . . . This is getting way to long, but still have a few things to tell you . . .

Barb and Ken's son Kenny and his wife Gina had a baby girl Maeyana Pye Vogt, February 7, 2006, weighed 9 lbs 2ozs. Barb knew they were expecting and was very happy about it. Maeyana is a beautiful healthy 7 month old baby now, This is proud great-grandma talking. Then shortly after Krista lost her Mother she unexpectedly became pregnant. Krista and David had not planned any more children as they had a girl and boy and were happy with 2 children. Then another pregnancy! *AND* . . . TWIN GIRLS . . . We are all wondering if Barb had a hand in this? Or perhaps that's what we want to believe . . . Krista delivered healthy twin girls by c-section August 18, Sedona Sue weighed 5 lbs 8 ozs and Simone Louise weighed 6 lbs 6 ozs. All are doing well. Dr. thinks they are identical from afterbirth, etc . . . This makes 4 new great-granddaughters for me this year. Barb's older sister Carol's son and his wife had their first baby Madilyn Louise, 7lbs 6 ozs February 11th. Four days after her cousin Maeyana. They are all absolutely beautiful babies and I do feel blessed about that. Life does go on but . . .

I'm trying hard to be a "Elder" rather than an "Older." but it's getting more difficult. I also had a hip replacement in the fall of 2002 and back surgery for a cyst pushing on nerves in the spring of 2005. I'm still on several committees here and lead my little Water Color Class, but my good friend "Arthur" {arthritis} is taking over and getting more aggressive, doggone it, and I have to really push myself. I am so very tired of coping with all this pain and heartache. But, if I can help to get more information out on IBC Breast Cancer and save a few lives it will give my life more purpose.

Just remembered too that Lore Higgins, one of your writers, interviewed Ken wrote a nice OB article about Barbara last October that was in the paper.

Back to ORIGINAL subject . . . Will someone please look into IBC Breast Cancer and get more information about it into the papers along with all of the regular kind with lumps . . .

I do hope I have not bored all of you but I had to write this and try my very best to do something about this terrible disease. All Kinds . . .

Sincerely,

Vivian L. Beeler
15181 Ford Rd. #302
Dearborn, MI 48126

E-mail at *veebee248(a)sbcglobal,net*

Phone #313-581-7041

Inflammatory Breast Cancer Rare, Aggressive

By Judy Fortin
CNN

Atlanta, Georgia: Sandra Mahncke thought she was coming down with the flu in late April, but instead of a quick recovery, she has spent the last five months in a race for her life.

She started feeling bad at work. "I had body aches and felt like I had a fever," says Sandra, "by the time I got home and changed my clothes I noticed that my left breast was very inflamed and bright red."

Those are classic symptoms of inflammatory breast cancer or IBC. According to the National Cancer Institute, IBC is "a rare but very aggressive type of breast cancer." It accounts for 1 to 5 percent of all breast cancer cases in the United States.(Watch Health Minute on inflammatory breast cancer—1:16?)

As with many other cases of IBC, Sandra's wasn't diagnosed right away. Her gynecologist thought she might have mastitis, a fairly common breast infection. When the redness and swelling didn't clear up after one course of antibiotics, the doctor ordered a mammogram. That's when Sandra first knew something was wrong. "Obviously, I was kind of shell-shocked and in disbelief," recalls Sandra. A breast surgeon broke the news that Sandra's biopsy tested positive for cancer. Sandra says, "It's very frightening and because it's an uncommon disease and we haven't heard a lot of stories from other people."

In spite of its name, Inflammatory breast cancer isn't caused by an inflammation or infection. Experts say IBC occurs when cancer cells block the lymph vessels in the skin of the breast. Surgical Oncologist Sheryl Gabram of the Winship Cancer Institute at Emory University in Atlanta, Georgia, says IBC "presents itself like an infection with redness and swelling, but unlike traditional breast cancer, there usually isn't a mass." There can also be ridging on the breast and an inverted nipple. A mammogram might reveal thickening skin. (Watch more on symptoms, treatment—6:31?)

Dr. Gabram says the best way to make the diagnosis is by looking at a woman's breast and obtaining a biopsy. While there are no specific risk factors, experts believe it is more common among African American women and those with a higher body mass index. Typically, IBC is diagnosed in younger women. Sandra is a forty-eight-year-old mother of three teenage boys.

"Twenty years ago, women did not live beyond two years with this disease," says Dr. Gabram. Now, the National Cancer Institute puts the five-year survival rate between 25 and 50 percent. Part of the reason is early diagnosis, the other is aggressive treatment.

"Starting with chemotherapy first, to get control of the disease in the breast as well as throughout the body, followed by surgery and then radiation therapy can definitely decrease the local recurrence as well as increase survival," states Dr. Gabram.

Sandra is halfway through her chemotherapy sessions. She'll have a mastectomy in a couple of weeks. Her husband, Peter, is by her side as she's hooked up to an IV drip and administered chemo. Her doctors don't think the cancer has spread, but Dr. Gabram says IBC can be tricky and is more likely to metastasize than other cancers.

Despite her health crisis, Sandra believes she's lucky, and she's been told her prognosis is good. She advises other women not to wait and make an appointment with their doctor immediately if they notice any unusual changes in their breasts.

She says "it's a totally different world. You really have to shift gears and look at everything in a totally different way . . . it's definitely not easy. Having the support of doctors and nurses, friends and family makes a world of difference."

Judy Fortin is a correspondent with CNN's Medical Unit. Her Health Minute features appear Monday through Friday between 1:00 and 6:00 p.m. on CNN Headline News.

Find this article at:
http://www.cnn.com/2006/Health/10/06/IBC/index.html
Check the box to include the list of links referenced in the article.

ABC News

Pain, Itching Part of Rare Breast Cancer
IBC's Nontraditional Symptoms Make It Hard to Detect

October 11, 2006—Most women associate breast cancer with a lump, but there are other ways that the disease can manifest itself.

Millions of people didn't know about a rare form of cancer called Inflammatory Breast Cancer—IBC—until Michelle Esteban from ABC's Seattle affiliate KOMO-TV shined a light on the difficulties of diagnosis.

"It's just so sad." she said. "Every woman that I've interviewed who has been diagnosed with Inflammatory Breast Cancer never heard of it until she got it."

Pain, Warmth, Itching
After running the story in May, KOMO's Web site was flooded with an overwhelming 14 million hits, the most in its history.

Viewers e-mailed their friends and family, urging them to watch the report and learn more about the little-known form of breast cancer that shows itself with untraditional symptoms.

"There is no tumor. But there often is a red rash. There can be itching. The breast can swell . . . It can be hot to the touch. There can be stabbing pain," Esteban said.

The redness and warmth are caused by cancer cells blocking the lymph vessels in the skin. The skin of the breast may also appear pink, reddish-purple, or bruised and appear pitted, like the skin of an orange.

Other symptoms include heaviness, burning, aching, increase in breast size, and tenderness.

These symptoms usually develop quickly, over a period of days or weeks. Swollen lymph nodes may also be present.

Because it lacks the typical telltale sign of a lump, mammograms and self-breast exams rarely detect this very aggressive form of cancer.

IBC catches victims off guard and in many cases, is a silent killer.

"If I had heard of it prior, I probably would have been more suspect that something was wrong rather than just young and dumb," said IBC victim Kristine Turck.

How to Protect Yourself
Dr. Susan Manzi talked with ABC News' Diane Sawyer about IBC and discussed what women could do to protect themselves from nontraditional breast cancers.

Manzi emphasized that IBC is very rare, accounting for between 1 and 5 percent of all breast cancer cases in the United States. But she urged women to be aware of changes in their bodies.

"Not all breast cancers are painless lumps, and not all of them can be detected by mammograms." Manzi said.

A diagnosis is not a death sentence. Treatment is usually chemotherapy, followed by surgery and/or radiation.

Manzi said that while the medical community knows about IBC. women must be their own advocates.

"Again, these symptoms are ones, which come on quickly," she said. "So if you have them and they are not going away, this is something you should ask your doctor about, keeping in mind that inflammatory breast cancer is rare."

Copyright © 2006 ABC News Internet Ventures

TRADITIONS!
THE BEELER FAMILY CHRISTMAS PARTY

Started way back by MOM and POP—Grandma and Grandpa Marguerette and Joseph Beeler . . .

Who added: William Joseph, LeRoy Henry, Joseph Jr., Marguerette Esther, and Robert Franklin . . . AND . . . They added Vivian Louise, Evelyn Frances, IdaCharlotte, Walter P., and Flora Marie . . .

Look where it's gone now. WOW! Let's do our part to keep the Tradition going. Come and join in . . .

WHEN: Sunday, December 17, 2006
WHERE: Carol Leinonen's at 30678 Grandon, Livonia, MI
TIME: 2:00 p.m. until . . .

Please bring finger food to share: Appetizers, Snacks (hot or cold, Oven and Micro available), Veggies, Fruit, Dips, Cookies or Sweets . . . Take your pick . . .

Sure Hope to see you there. With Love to all, The Matriarch, {ugh}, Mom, Grandma, Great-Grandma, Aunt . . . Vivian

RSVP: If you are unable to come. Carol's phone # 734-522-1162

December 15, 2006

Dear Diane, Harold, and Family,

I think of you folks so often and hope everything is going along fine, both in your personal lives and in Tawas Plating. This news from the automotive companies is discouraging and kind of scary. I do hope Tawas Plating is hanging in there and doing OK.

It doesn't seem possible that it is Christmastime again. Sometimes I wonder where the time goes. It seems like I get up on Monday mornings, and before I turn around it is Friday. I guess that's a good thing though. I do seem to have gotten myself into an overload with my Christmas cards this year. I have always enjoyed it before, but this year it has been a real chore. To be honest, I'm getting very tired of my partridge in the pear tree. It seems like I have been working on them for months, gluing and putting them together. I brought this on myself though. When we moved in here, I started giving cards to the staff (so many of them are my good friends), and over the eight years I have been here, the staff has grown. Plus, every year I have made more friends here. Now everyone looks forward to getting a "Vivian" card. I have to admit it is an ego boost, and I get a lot of nice thank-yous. I'm thinking though that this will be the last year, as this constant pain in my back from inflammation and little spurs and cysts pressing on the sciatic nerve is really getting me down. I try very hard to keep a good attitude, but everything I do is such a big effort and I have to really push to get things done. I'm still on my committees and have my little watercolor class, but walking is painful also. I really don't like what age does to our bodies. I take the water aerobics class twice a week to try and get exercise. The water feels good and I know it is good for me, but it doesn't do a thing for the back pain, doggone it. I also know the emotional depression hasn't helped me either. Barb's husband Ken and her twin Alice are still having a very bad time. They both call me a lot, and I try to help them (they say I do), but it drags me down too. I would never tell them that. Life can be difficult. I do know that I live in a very good place. I'm so very glad that Bill and I made the decision together to move here. It was a wise one.

Bill Jr., Shannon, and Sydney (who was six in October) were here for a visit this summer. That was a joy. Sydney is such a happy, beautiful little girl. She is taking Suzuki piano lessons and is doing very well. She gave the family who lives around here a concert on the grand piano in our chapel. She played six songs from memory, with no music, using both hands. We were all impressed. Plus, she has had swimming lessons and swims like a little fish and also plays soccer (her daddy was her team coach), and she is learning to ski and loves it too. She is anxious to use a snowboard like her daddy. She is doing well in her first full days of school this year. Can you tell I'm a very proud grandma? Having seven grown-up grandchildren and then having a little one again is a delight. Just wish Colorado wasn't quite so far away. They want me to come out to visit, but I can't handle the airports and travel. I'm much better right here in my comfortable apartment. My grandson Kenny Jr., wife Gina, and little Maeyana were here also to visit from California. It was another wonderful time. I got Carol and my grandchildren here—Cindy, Joe, Erik, Eve, and Madilyn—to come over one day at the same time as Ken, Kenny, and family. We had a ball watching the two babies together. They were fascinated with one another. Maeyana was born on February 7 and Madilyn on February 11 this year. We put them on a blanket in the middle of my living room floor and sat around and watched them. It was better than any show. Both proud daddies Kenny and Erik sat next to one another and compared their daughters. Both are beautiful normal babies. What a blessing! Then on August 18, my granddaughter Krista and her husband David in Arizona had twin girls, also normal and healthy—Sedona Sue, 5 lb. 8 oz., and Simone Louise, 6 lb. 6 oz. Krista and David already had Sage (nine) and Ché (six). They had not planned any more children, but Krista became pregnant shortly after her mother's death. We wonder if Barbara had a finger in that.

Two more blessings . . . Ken is going out there for the holidays, and Kenny, Gina and Maeyana will also be there. I think it will be very good for all of them to be together. Ken is concerned about leaving me at Christmastime, but I encouraged him to go. He is taking Carol and me out for a holiday dinner together tomorrow night (sixteenth). I will be at Carol's Christmas day with the rest of the family around here—my grandchildren Cindy, Joe, and Corbin. Corbin is Joe's little boy from an earlier brief marriage that didn't work out. Cindy loves him like her own, and they wish they could have him all the time, but have to share custody. He is here now for the Christmas holidays. He is a delightful little six-year-old and seems to be very well adjusted even though he has two homes. He's one of my seven great-grandchildren. Erik, Eve, Maeyana, Scott, my son-in-law Jim and his wife, Hannah, of about a year will also be there; Jim deserves to be happy, and he was so lonesome without Kathy. They will be there too. I'm Mom to both Jim and Ken; they don't have any family of their own. We are their family, and I'm grateful we have such a great relationship. I know I could call either one if I needed help, and that's a nice feeling. They are all so good to me. I get to see and play with little Madilyn quite a bit and thoroughly enjoy it. It's been a long time since I was around a baby, and it's fun to watch their growing process. Both Maeyana and Madilyn are crawling all over now and pulling themselves up to things. Both are very happy babies as they are surrounded by love. I also talk to Krista quite often. She is one busy young mother. With her having twins, it has brought the two of us even closer.

I do seem to rattle on when I start writing. I hope I haven't bored you too much. This was supposed to be a short Christmas note.

Dear Debby and Kevin,

This is a copy of the letter I sent to your folks. I told them I was sending a copy to you. I also sent some pictures of my new great-granddaughters, Sydney, Bill Jr.'s daughter, and Corbin in the pool with us and the Village art fair. I asked them to share the pictures.

I love your Christmas letters telling about what your girls and Jared are doing along with you folks. You certainly are a busy family, but it seems like all young families are today. Amanda and Ali sound like delightful young ladies and involved in so many *good* activities. They grow so fast, don't they? Kevin and Debby, these are your golden years! Enjoy every minute. I keep thinking of that song from *Fiddler on the Roof*: "Sunrise . . . Sunset . . . turn around and it's gone." That's the way I feel. How many community plays have you folks and the girls been in this year? I thought it was so neat the year you were all in the same play.

Kevin, I'm sure it's a big challenge to keep the business running the right way with this economy today. I'm sure it takes more hours than you would like. Hang in there. It seems like things just have to get better. You were another son to Bill, and he was very proud of you. Since I had my hip replacement, I use Bill's La-Z-Boy chair a lot. Never liked it before, now it's the most comfortable place for me. When I'm in it, I like to feel like Bill's arms are around me, and it gives me a sense of peace.

I'm sure you will have delightful holidays. I think of you often and wish all of you the best always.

Love Vivian

December 18, 2006

Dear Betty and Earl,

I certainly hope this finds you both doing OK. I totally dislike what aging does to our bodies. I wonder how you folks do it to pack up every six months and change places. Wouldn't it be easier just to stay in Florida all the time? I know Earl can't handle the cold weather, so Michigan is out as a year round place, even though our winters have been a bit milder the last few years. Charlotte seems to love it where she is year round in Leesburg, and I know you have told me Earl has a sister there. I am so grateful that Bill and I made the decision together to move here. It has been a very wise one for me. I still am able to drive, but we do have everything here that we need, so in bad weather I just stay in.

Everyone who have been Dearbornites felt very badly about losing Mayor Guido. You just have to say the word "cancer" to me and it makes me shake. It is such a horrible disease and takes way too many young people, including Bill and our daughters. I still miss them all terribly. But life goes on. I am grateful for my family that I have left. They are all so good to me, and I deeply appreciate it. Carol is having Christmas this year for all the family who are still around here. The holidays are hard though, and I will be grateful when they are over. On the bright side though, I have four new great-granddaughters this year, and they are all beautiful, normal healthy babies! What a blessing! Kenny Jr. and Gina had Maeyana Pye Vogt out in California born on February 11, 2006. Erik and Eve Leinonen had Madilyn Louise on February 11, 2006. Krista and David Vogt-Crimmins had twins on August 18, 2006, Sedona Sue and Simone Louise, born in Arizona. Krista got pregnant shortly after she lost her mother. They had not planned on more children as they already had Sage (nine) and Ché

(six). We do wonder if Barb had her fingers in that. Anyway Krista is one busy young woman. Ken, Gina, and Maeyana, plus Papa Ken, will be there for Christmas. I am so glad they will all be together. I think it will be good for all of them. The rest of this letter is a part of a copy I sent to some other friends that I don't see very often and like news from me at Christmas. So hope it all makes sense to you. I wrote the next part of the letter on the fifteenth.

It doesn't seem possible that it is Christmastime again. Sometimes I wonder where the time goes. It seems like I get up on Monday mornings, and before I turn around it is Friday. I guess that's a good thing though. I do seem to have gotten myself into an overload with my Christmas cards this year. I have always enjoyed it before, but this year it has been a real chore. To be honest, I'm getting very tired of my partridge in the pear tree. It seems like I have been working on them for months, gluing and putting them together. I brought this on myself though. When we moved in here, I started giving cards to the staff (so many of them are my good friends), and over the almost nine years I have been here, the staff has grown. Plus, every year I have made more friends here. Now everyone looks forward to getting a "Vivian" card. I have to admit it is an ego boost and I get a lot of nice thank-yous. I'm thinking though that this will be the last year, as this constant pain in my back from inflammation and little spurs and cysts pressing on the sciatic nerve is really getting me down. I try very hard to keep a good attitude, but everything I do is such a big effort and I have to really push to get things done. I'm still on my committees and have my little watercolor class, but walking is painful also. I really don't like what age does to our bodies. I take the water aerobics class twice a week to try and get exercise. The water feels good and I know it is good for me, but it doesn't do a thing for the back pain, doggone it. I also know the emotional depression hasn't helped me either. Barb's husband Ken and her twin Alice are still having a very bad time. They both call me a lot and I try to help them (they say I do), but it drags me down too. I would never tell them that. Life can be difficult. I do know that I live in a very good place. I'm so very glad that Bill and I made the decision together to move here. It was a wise one.

Bill Jr., Shannon, and Sydney (who was six in October) were here for a visit this summer. That was a joy. Sydney is such a happy, beautiful little girl. She is taking Suzuki piano lessons and is doing very well. She gave the family who lives around here a concert on the grand piano in our chapel. She played six songs from memory, with no music, using both hands. We were all impressed. Plus, she has had swimming lessons and swims like a little fish, also plays soccer (her daddy was her team coach), and she is learning to ski and loves it too. She is anxious to use a snowboard like her daddy. She is doing well in her first full days of school this year. Can you tell I'm a very proud grandma? Having seven grown-up grandchildren and then having a little one again is a delight. Just wish Colorado wasn't quite so far away. They want me to come out to visit, but I can't handle the airports and travel. I'm much better right here in my comfortable apartment. My grandson Kenny Jr., wife Gina, and little Maeyana were here to also visit from California. It was another wonderful time. I got Carol and my grandchildren here—Cindy, Joe, Erik, Eve, and Madilyn—to come over one day at the same time as Ken, Kenny, and family. We had a ball watching the two babies together. They were fascinated with one another. Maeyana was born on February 7 and Madilyn on February 11 this year. We put them on a blanket in the middle of my living room floor and sat around and watched them. It was better than any show. Both proud daddies Kenny and Erik sat next to one another and compared their daughters. Both are beautiful normal babies. What a blessing! Then on August 18, my granddaughter Krista and her husband David in Arizona had twin girls, who were also normal and healthy, Sedona Sue, 5 lb. 8 oz., and Simone Louise, 6 lb. 6 oz. Krista and David already had Sage (nine) and Ché (six). They had not planned any more children, but Krista became pregnant shortly after her mother's death. We wonder if Barbara had a finger in that.

Two more blessings . . . Ken is going out there for the holidays and Kenny, Gina, and Maeyana will also be there. I think it will be very good for all of them to be together. Ken is concerned about leaving me at Christmastime, but I encouraged him to go. He is taking Carol and I out for a holiday dinner together tomorrow night (sixteenth). I will be at Carol's Christmas day with the rest of the family around here—my grandchildren Cindy, Joe, and Corbin. Corbin is Joe's little boy from an earlier brief marriage that didn't work out. Cindy loves him like her own, and they wish they could have him all the time, but have to share custody. He is here now for the Christmas holidays. He is a delightful little six-year-old and seems to be very well adjusted even though he has two homes. He's one of my seven great-grandchildren. Erik, Eve, Madilyn, Scott, my son-in-law Jim, and his wife, Hannah, of about a year will also be here. Jim deserves to be happy and he was so lonesome without Kathy. They will be there too. I'm Mom to both Jim and Ken. They don't have any family of their own. We are their family, and I'm grateful we have such a great relationship. I know I could call either one if I needed help, and that's a nice feeling. They are all so good to me. I get to see and play with little Madilyn quite a bit and thoroughly enjoy it. It's been a long time since I was around a baby, and it's fun to watch their growing process. Both Maeyana and Madilyn are crawling all over now and pulling themselves up to things. Both are very happy babies as they are surrounded by love. I also talk to Krista quite often. She is one busy young mother. With her having twins, it has brought the two of us even closer.

I do seem to rattle on when I start writing. I hope I haven't bored you too much. This was supposed to be a short Christmas note. Sending some pictures of Sydney and my great-grandchildren. Hope you enjoy them.

Since I had my hip replacement and back operation, I use Bill's La-Z-Boy chair a lot. Never liked it before, now it's the most comfortable place for me. When I'm in it, I like to feel like Bill's arms are around me, and it gives me a sense of peace.

I'm hope you will have delightful holidays. I think of you often and wish both of you the best always.

Love Vivian

2007

February 7, 2007

Happy, happy first birthday to my great-granddaughter, Maeyana Pye Vogt!

Honey, it doesn't seem possible that a year has gone by since you were born. I remember the call I got from your very proud daddy the day you were born. I was so happy to hear that you were a beautiful, healthy little baby and that you were a beautiful, healthy little baby and that you and your mama were doing just fine. I just couldn't help but feel sad that your Nana Vogt was not here to welcome you too. She would have been so very happy. But, Maeyana, I just have to believe that she is watching over you, surrounding you with her love and keeping you safe.

Your daddy and mama kept me informed of how you were doing with phone calls and sending me pictures. Then this late summer you came to Michigan for a visit, and I got to meet you in person. What a thrill for Grandma! You were such a beautiful little girl, and I got to hold you, love you, and watch you sit on my living room floor and play. You were almost ready to crawl and such a happy baby. I got to see you and your mama and daddy, plus Papa Vogt, for two days while you were here. The second day your Aunt Carol and your cousins Erik and Eve came over with their baby Madilyn, who was born just four days after you. What a joy for Grandma to hold both of you and watch you play together! I felt blessed that I was here to share in this exciting time. Watching my very proud grandsons and my granddaughters, Gina and Eve, with their new daughters made me realize even more that life does go on and the family circle expands with each new birth. The love and joy that you bring helps in some small way to ease the hurt from our losses. I know your nana Vogt lives on through you. I saw some expressions on your face that reminded me of her.

Also, honey, I want you to remember what the book I'm sending you says: You are a *very special person!* There is no one else in the world like you.

Grandma loves you very much, honey, and I know you will have a wonderful birthday because you are surrounded by *love!*

Sending lots and lots of love to you and your mama and daddy.

Great-grandma Vivian Beeler

February 11, 2007

A very happy first birthday to Madilyn Louise Leinonen!

Dear Maddy, Great-grandma Vivian remembers so clearly the night you were born. It doesn't seem possible that a whole year has gone by already. I remember how very proud your daddy was when he called to let me know you had entered our world and to tell me that both you and your mother were doing fine. He also told me how beautiful and perfect you were. The whole family was so happy that you were finally here to join us.

A little later that morning, your aunt Cindy called me and asked if I would like to go to the hospital to see you. I was thrilled that they had thought of me and how much I would love to see you in person. In the early afternoon, your aunt Cindy and uncle Joe came and picked me up to go to the hospital. Maddy, I got to hold and love you when you were just fourteen hours old. I can't describe in words how much good it did me to see and hold you. You were such a little doll. You were my fourth great-grandchild and the very *first* one that I got to hold when you were brand new. I felt very blessed. Your momma and daddy were so happy, plus all the rest of your family. We had been waiting to see and cuddle you with lots of love in our hearts.

It has been such a joy to me, Maddy, to watch you grow this year. Again, you are my first great-grandchild who lives in the same area that I do. So I have been able to be a part of your life at all our family gatherings, and also your baptism which was a very special day. You also have been over to visit me when your cousin Sydney, aunt Shannon, and uncle Bill were here from Colorado this summer. You went swimming in my pool here and had a good time, Then you were here again when your cousin Maeyana and her parents, also your cousins, Kenny and Gina, were here from California to see me and our family. Maeyana was born just four days ahead of you, so you were the same age. But it was the first time that we had met Maeyana, besides seeing pictures of her. She was a little sweetie too. We got a lot of cute pictures of the two of you playing together and also of me holding both of you. What a joy! The two of you were just fascinated with one another, both almost ready to crawl. We put the two of you down on a blanket in the middle of Grandma's living room, and we all sat in a circle around the two of you and had so much fun watching you. It was better than any movie or show.

We had several get-togethers when your cousin Corbin was here too. Corbin took such good care of you and loved playing with you. I was always invited to the family get-togethers and I felt very loved too. Each time I saw you, you were doing something new and different. So interesting! It had been so long since I had been around a little one, and I was enjoying every time I saw you. You have been such a *happy* baby with big blue eyes and such a winning smile. You have everyone wrapped around your little fingers, and no one minds a bit.

Maddy, you helped make our Christmas better this year, along with Corbin. It was fun to watch you open your presents and have lots of fun with the paper and boxes. Watching you in your little jump seat at Grandma Carol's was fun too. You bounced so hard and with so much energy that we thought you were going to fly right out of it. You were also getting more vocal and letting us know that *you were there!*

Maddy, Great-grandma wishes the very best for you always. When you get older and are looking back at the time you were born, I want you to realize how much joy and love you brought to Grandma's heart and how much fun I was having watching you grow. I am looking forward to sharing in your first birthday. Remember too, honey, like the book *The Night You Were Born* says, "You are very *special!*," no one else is like you. In today's world, you can do and be anything you wish. It just takes determination. Always follow your heart, your dreams, and the golden rule.

My love, prayers, and best wishes always,
Great-grandma Vivian L. Beeler

Francis X. Kotcher, Jr. C.P.A., P.C. February 16, 2007
Certified Public Accountant
6281 Emerald lakes Drive
Troy, Michigan 48085-1333

Dear Frank,

Here I am again. It seems like every year rolls by faster. I do know though, with every year that passes, that Bill and I made a very wise decision when we decided to move to Henry Ford Village. It doesn't seem possible but I've been here nine years last month. I don't know of anywhere that I would be happier at my age and with the health problems I have from ageing. I truthfully never believed I would still be around this long. Life is strange. On a happy note, I had four new great-granddaughters born in 2006. All beautiful, healthy babies. That gives me a total of seven, with two boys among the girls. Trouble is I only get to see one on a regular basis. The others are in California and Arizona. I'm blessed though, as my grandchildren call me often and share lots of pictures and news of the babies. I'm very grateful as they tell me that I'm a "cool" Grandma, and very important in their lives.

I'm still on most of my committees and have my little Water Color Class. Enclosing a Erickson paper with an article about me again. I have to pace myself and some days are very difficult . . . BUT . . . I just try to take one day at a time . . . I hope this has been a good year for you and your family.

Income stays the same but all my expenses keep going up so I'm trying to watch closely how I spend my money. I feel so sorry for all the people in the Automotive field. It is so different than it used to be. Downright scary. Also my heart aches for all the young people that we are losing in that Iraq War. It seems like such a terrible waste of young lives to me. I want them HOME.

I still am good friends with Jean and Dar Darovich who lived next door to us on Sandshores, so I hear about our old neighborhood. We loved our 31 years there . . . OK . . . Business . . .

I hope I have included everything you need for my taxes this year. Feel free to call Dick Newton's office if you have any questions they can help you with. Richard P. Newton, 33133 Schoolcraft Road, Livonia, MI 48150. (734) 427-2030. Fax (734) 427-30

There I go . . . talking too much and ran out of space. Thank you, Frank. Sincerely,

Vivian Beeler
15181 Ford Rd.# 302
Dearborn, MI 48126
(313) 581-7041
Email: veebee248@sbcglobal.net

May 29, 2007

To: Myra McInerney, Loretta Nelson, and Velda Hahn (Captain of CC)

Dear Myra, Loretta, and Velda,

After a lot of thought I am going to resign from The Birthday Angel Committee. The constant pain in my back caused from stenosis, arthritis and a spur pushing on my sciatic nerve has made walking painful for me. I have really enjoyed being on this committee for the nine years I have lived here and hate to give it up. BUT Life changes and we have to change with it, (or go crazy) . . . I already have a replacement for the 4th floor of Chapel Court which is my floor assignment. Dorothy Henderson of CC 218 would very much like to have it as her floor. She is already a committee member and delivers in another Building. She would like to be transferred to Chapel Court. Hope this will work out for all.

I have made so many good friends on this committee but hopefully will continue to see most of them.

So, I'm not going to say "good-bye," as I plan to see all of you in the hallways and dining room.

Sincerely, Vivian Beeler—CC 302, 581-7041

P.S. Velda, You have been an inspiration for me. With your low vision handicap and other health problems you have just kept on going with a *GREAT* attitude! I thought if you could do it, I could too but this pain got the best of me. I admire you and am so glad you consider me one of your friends. It's meeting and knowing people like you that make this such a wonderful place to live . . .

June 2007

Dear Sydney

Grandma is sending you these articles from our paper about things in Michigan. You can have your daddy tell you about that big bridge as he crossed it a lot of times when he went to school in Lake Superior State.

The other article about the beaches in Michigan I thought was interesting and they are beautiful. Grandma has seen quite a few of them. I hope that someday you will have time on your vacation to Michigan to go and spend some time by Lake Michigan. Your uncle Steve doesn't live far from the lake. I think your mama and daddy told me that you did go over to the beach one day from Uncle Steve's.

I hope you are having fun with your soccer games and judo lessons. Are you learning to play golf with your mama and daddy? I hear you got your own set of golf clubs. That's pretty special. Grandma is getting anxious to see you on August 1. Won't be to long now.

Sending lots and lots of love, hugs, and kisses to my wonderful granddaughter Sydney.

June 18, 2007

Dear Julie's elder *sister*, Susan, and Family,

I was so shocked and saddened by the news that Julie was gone *and cancer* had claimed another talented beautiful young woman. I just want to scream against the unfairness of life and that terrible, terrible disease. I can't help but ask God why. Why can't he take some of us who have lived our lives and would so gladly change places with our loved ones and who have so much to live for? Parents should not have to bury their children. It just is not the right circle of life. It's a hurt that you never get over, and it actually seems to grow with time.

All you have to do is look in the paper and every day in the OB column you see where cancer has claimed more young people and other families are going through what you have. It is heartbreaking. *We have to find a cure!* Plus my heart breaks for all the families who have young people in Iraq. They live in fear every day, and so many of their loved ones don't make it home, or if they do sometimes, their minds or bodies are broken. I want them all home. I have never believed we should be there.

Susan, I remember a time when Julie was traveling a lot for her job. She called Bill and I as she was in Troy. She came over, and we went out for dinner together and had such an enjoyable time. While catching up on family and reminiscing about things, we remembered as you girls were growing up *and* of course, Aunt Fran. She was a second mother to me, and she has always had a big place in my heart. All of us, blood relatives and spouses, *loved* Aunt Fran and Uncle Bill. That love was returned in so many ways. We were all their "children."

I am so very sorry that I can't be there to share in Julie's memorial service and to see everyone. Age is not being kind to my body and walking is painful. The warranties are running out on my back and the sciatic nerve is affected. I don't think I could handle that ride to Jackson very well. I have an appointment to see the doctors at The Pain Management Clinic the twenty-seventh of this month. That again brings up the same question to me. *Why?* I'm ready. Leave the young people.

All of you are in my thoughts and prayers.

Susan, Carol told me that your mother didn't even know Julie was gone? That was another shock for me. I had no idea that Jean was affected like that. The last time I had talked to her she seemed fine on the phone. I had wondered why I had not heard from her in so long, but blamed myself too for not calling or getting in touch. I have been fighting depression and constant back pain, and I just haven't done all the things that I should have. I haven't called Bud or Barb either and am feeling badly about that too. Life just seems difficult. I've been trying to keep Ken's and Alice's heads above water too. They both seem to rely on me and call me often. They both are still having a very bad time. There definitely is a special bond between identical twins and even twins who are different. I just recently found a support group called The Twinless Twin and am hoping to get some books to help Alice.

Carol and her family are my "rock of Gibraltar." They are so good to me. Bill and Shannon stay in close touch, but being so far away it makes it difficult for them. *But* talking to Sydney and them every week does help, and they will be here again this summer.

Hoping things go as well as they can this weekend. Keep in touch.

I'm not sure if you have my latest e-mail address: veebee248@.sbcglobal.net

I will be sending a memorial for Julie when I get an envelope to a cancer group, or I do have Leader Dogs for the Blind here. Did you or Julie have a special one?

Friday, July 11, 2008

Dear Barb and Family,

I was shocked when Carol called me and told me about Bud. I know we have not been in touch lately but had no idea this could happen. Carol did not have all the details.

I am very sorry. There really are no words that can help at this difficult time. Just to let you know that other people care and are thinking of you.

I am so sorry too that I cannot make it up to Jackson. Age is taking its toll on me. I have been having a lot of lower back and sciatic nerve problems. In fact, I just went to another back specialist last Tuesday. I have to go for another MRI this coming Tuesday. Carol offered to bring me to Jackson for Bud's service, but I don't think I could handle that ride. I feel badly about not being there, but I hope you folks will understand. I'm very grateful that I can still take care of myself and that Carol and her family are so good to me. Bill Jr. and family will be here for a week from Colorado the end of the month, so I'm looking forward to that.

I think of my mother, aunt Fran, and aunt Elma so often and how they all handled getting older so well. *But* we all come from good genes, and we do the best we can.

> My love, prayers, and best wishes to all of you.
> Vivian

P.S. I know Leader Dogs was a favorite charity of Bud's, so I am sending a donation in his memory to them.

Tuesday, August 1, 2007

Dear Ken,

I am so glad that you came on Sunday, but I could see from your face that you were getting more and more unhappy with the noise, confusion, and laughter. Ken, I felt your pain too. Family get-togethers are very bittersweet for me. I am so grateful to have my family around me, but I also see and feel those huge empty holes where the people we loved so much are not there with us, *and* it *hurts!* But again life goes on, and we have to cope.

Your life did not change a lot after Edsel died while Carol's world was turned upside down (as yours is now). I know you missed him and it hurt that he was gone, but your own life did not change a lot. I also know you felt bad for Carol, but you and I did not really understand what she went through until we both had to walk in those shoes. Edsel was like a son to Bill and me, and losing him was such a heartache, but again our lives went on, except at that same time we were worrying about our Kathy and what she was going through. Then that horrible spring and summer of losing both Bill and Kathy, I didn't want to live. Somehow with the help of my family, my doctors, the help and support I received from the staff here at the Village I kept on going. Maybe that's why people keep telling me I'm a strong woman. You know from our conversations that it's not easy for me and sometimes are worse than others. You also know that I would have gladly changed places with any of my loved ones, but again I didn't have that choice. Carol, Barbara, and Alice all kept telling me they needed me, and they stressed the fact to me that Edsel, Bill, and Kathy would be the first people to tell me to keep going . . . living and laughing! When we were together, we would all rub our rings together and say, "We are women, we are family, we will stick together, we are strong, and we will keep laughing!" We would remind one another of that when we talked on the telephone. Bill and I got those rings for our daughters and granddaughters because that was what they symbolized. "Our family is a continuing circle. We love, respect, and support one another in all things, at all times, and we are strong women."

The world will never forget September 11, 2001. We will never forget that time because that's when our own personal family world fell apart again with Barbara's diagnosis. I'll never forget September 12 when you, Barb, Carol, and Alice knocked on my door and came to tell me. My heart fell when I saw all of you because I knew something was terribly wrong. We all knew from the beginning that the outcome was not good with the cancer already being in stage four, but our hearts and brains did not want to accept that. So all of us rode an emotional roller coaster for four years hoping against hope.

And talk about strong women, look what Kathy and Barbara went through. They both kept smiles on their faces and said, "Tomorrow will be better!" They were both unbelievable with their wonderful attitudes and by keeping everyone around them *laughing!* Laughter was very important to Barbara, Ken. Laughter is medicine and healing. Laughter does not mean that you don't miss that person and you are not hurting. *But* you have to laugh through your tears. "Mister," you know Barbara would be the first person to tell you that.

Ken, you and I have a very special relationship. It means a lot to me. You, too, are like a son to me and I love you very much. I'm very worried about you, and I'm not alone. The rest of the family noticed how unhappy you were, and they are worried too. They love you and want to help you in any way they can. Carol, Alice, Bill, and Shannon all talked to me after everyone had left Sunday. They all are still raw and hurting from the loss of Barb, and all of them missed her terribly on Sunday. They also know Barb would tell them to keep moving and enjoy each moment. Love my grandchildren for me. Give them extra love for me. Remember I am a part of them. Also, I will always be near you in your hearts.

Anyway, I thought and thought about what I could do or how I could help you, so I just decided to pour out some of my feelings and thoughts of what's in my heart to you on paper. I hope you will understand, and in some small way maybe it will help you a little bit. I certainly don't want you to feel angry. Barbara loved light, sunshine, laughter, and you, "her *prince*." She would be very unhappy with you for not letting in some sunshine and light into your heart, cottage, and home. Open things up, Ken. Try and open her bedroom door and let the light in and enjoy her beautiful things. Carol told me the other evening that the day Edsel died and you two stopped there on your way from the airport, Barbara said something to her that made her laugh. That was our Barbara. She loved laughter and making people laugh. Laughter was medicine to her and laughter helped her cope with bad things. Ken, when we talk you tell me that you are fixing up the house the way your "Pye" would want it. When you clean up the house and yard, you tell me you are doing it for Pye, and I'm proud of the way you are taking care of things, *but* Ken, somehow, someway, you are going to have to go a big step forward and try to open everything up . . . doors, drapes, curtains. I know my daughter too, Ken, and she hated darkness. She loved the light, sunshine, and things being *open*. She would want you to open her bedroom door to let the light in and hopefully someday to be able to look at all her beautiful things in there and enjoy looking at them.

Guess what? I was finishing up this letter to you, and you called me on your way back to work from taking care of Bouy. I didn't get this finished yesterday, so I was working on it when I got your phone call. I was so happy to hear what you said about Sunday because I was really worried about you when you left here. To hear you say that you were glad you came made me feel better. Thanks, dear. We are starting to read one another quite well.

I do hope Ken that I have not upset you in any way as that's the last thing I want to do. I'm just trying to figure out ways to help you. There is no time line on grief. Everyone is different. For me, I can accept Bill's death because of our age, etc. I don't like it but understand it. Regarding Edsel and my daughters, I try every day to get over my anger of losing them and that terrible disease that takes so many young people. I'm trying very hard to just take one day at a time and try to enjoy the moment and the good things when my family that I have left are around me. I was so glad to hear you say you were going out to Arizona in October to see your new little granddaughters, plus Sage, Ché, and Maeyana. They all need Papa's love. Also pleased to hear you sound a little excited about maybe going camping a couple of days with Kenny.

I love you very much, Ken. Please take what I said in this letter as trying to help you cope and a few suggestions with love behind them.

Thursday, August 30, 2007

Dear Krista, Kenny, and families,

I wanted to write to both of you to tell you about last Sunday, the twenty-sixth, when your mother's wishes were finally carried out. I hope in my trying to tell you about the day and how beautiful it was all of you will have a sense of peace. It's hard to explain how much lighter my heart feels to have your mother's spirit, soul, call it what you will, free and in her "paradise."

I wish with all my heart that you, Alice, Bill, and Shannon could have been there too, but at this point in time, it's almost impossible. It was an absolutely gorgeous day! A perfect "Pye" day as your dad called it—bright blue sky with a few white puffy clouds, the sun sparkling on the water, temperature in the middle eighties, with a slight breeze blowing.

Your aunt Carol picked me up right after 12 noon. We took I-94 all the way to 23 Mile Road and around to Algonac. We made great time with no road tie-ups, which was unusual. We were there in plenty of time for the two o'clock ferry. We had never seen so many people waiting for the ferry. Turns out there was a wedding reception on the other side of the island,

and they were all going to that. They showed us the name, but we didn't recognize it, and your dad didn't know anything about it either. Anyway, we did manage to get on the first ferry trip, as Bud had to make two trips to get everyone over. Thanks to your aunt Carol. She kind of maneuvered us in the right area to get on.

Your dad was waiting for us with the golf cart. The little roads to your cottage are so beautiful. Bouy was happy to see us, and I had brought a couple of dog cookies for her. She was a good girl and sat for them very nicely. We walked through the cottage and out the front door. Your dad told us things were messy and not to look around, as if we cared. He seemed anxious for us to just get outside. Carol and I were just reliving some wonderful memories. The yard looked good. Your dad has been doing a great job in keeping it up. Of course, the flower beds were not like they were when your mom and Alice took care of them. But, like we told your dad as he was apologizing about them, there is no way that he could do everything and keep them as they were. The beds of Black Eyed Susans were beautiful. Plus, your dad had put a couple of those big flags along the breakwater. The three of us and Bouy just sat on the deck for a while, not much conversation. We were just reliving some of the happy times we had had there. Listening to the waves rolling in and watching the boats on the river, none of us felt like talking much.

Your dad went in the cottage and brought out your mother's ashes. There was a boat with two fishermen right in front of your cottage at that time, and your dad said, "Let's wait until they leave." That made sense to both Carol and me. When they left, your dad looked at us and said, "I don't know how to do this."

I said, "There is no right or wrong way to do it. We just do it." I had told him earlier that your mom had requested that she wanted her ashes sprinkled in all her flower beds and around her big tree in your front yard. Your dad started sprinkling her ashes from the bag in her rock garden.

He made a remark, "I wish the kids could have been here."

Carol and I both said, "Yes, and Alice and Bill and Shannon too." Then I asked him if I could do around the big tree, and he passed the bag to me. I was pouring them out into my hand, sprinkling them, and saying to myself, "My darling daughter, you are free now in your paradise." On the way to the flower bed at the front of the breakwater, I took Bouy's paw and stuck it in the bag and then rubbed her paw at the edge of the garden. Bouy wasn't real happy about that. She gave a little squeal, but she was your mom's pride and joy too. Your dad thanked me for thinking of that. Your dad had given Bouy's leash to Carol and asked her if she would bring Bouy along with us. Then it was Carol's turn, and she put her hand in the bag and took out a handful to sprinkle on another flower bed.

Then back to your dad, and he started doing as Carol and I had. As he sprinkled, he kept repeating, "I love you, Pye." It's not an easy task, and we were all thinking our own thoughts. We kept sharing, and we covered all the areas your mom wanted us too. Your dad asked me, "What about putting some on all those rocks on the back side of her garden by the beach?"

I said, "Yes, thanks for thinking of that. We all know how much she loved her rocks." When we were finished, the three of us just stood and hugged one another. Bouy was right there with us too. It was an emotional time for all of us.

But as we stood in our hug, your dad said, "Thank you so much, Mom, for waking me up." Of course, that brought more tears. I really can't describe the feeling of peace I got through that we had carried out your mother's wishes. It was like a *huge* weight was lifted off my heart. Both Carol and I told your Dad that we could *feel* Barb's spirit all around us and she was so happy to be *free!* We weren't just saying that, we both just could! On Tuesday evening, I watched an absolutely gorgeous sunset from my apartment Windows, and it felt to me that my daughter was smiling at me and saying thank you. Her spirit feels alive in my heart again, and that gives me some peace, which isn't to say that I don't miss her like crazy. But then I still miss Edsel, Grandpa, and Kathy too. I don't think you ever get over losses like that. You just learn to cope the best you can.

Back to Sunday . . . The three of us sat on the deck again, and your dad got me a glass of ice water. Then he got very antsy and kept asking me what time it was. He asked if he could take us down to the ferry loading area and then come back and close up the cottage and bring the other golf cart and Bouy as he was coming home on the four o'clock ferry also.

We said of course. He drove the golf cart right up to the deck, and we got on. As we rode to the ferry, I said my silent good-byes to Russell Island. I found out later that Carol did the same things. We both have beautiful memories of happy times there. Carol was telling me later about how much she had enjoyed it when Barb had her come out and stay with her in the late summer or early fall. Carol said they had such fun together. Once or twice, Judy was out there too, and Carol said it was great. She and Judy got along great.

Anyway, I also said my good-byes to the ferry and of being on the water with the boat rocking in the Sunday boat traffic waves. I love that feeling. It is getting harder and harder for me to get on and off the ferry. My body just doesn't cooperate the way I would like it too. Oh well, I'm glad I can do what I can. Your dad gave both Carol and me big, long hugs and thanked us again for coming. He was very anxious to get home. All in all, I thought your dad did very well. He held himself together, and you both would have been very proud of him. He called me again Monday evening and said he couldn't thank me enough. He said he had one big regret, and when I asked what it was, he said he wished we would have done it the year before. I told him to please not stress over that. That was *past* and we had carried out her wishes now. That was what was important. He also told me that he wrote to your mother on Sunday evening, and I told him that was a good thing. Writing or journaling seems to help him, which is good. I know it does me and has all my life. I had taken a picture of Alice and your mom together and had it in my pocket, as I wanted Alice there. I also had touched your pictures before I left for the island and again after I got home, so I felt you there too. I know you all wanted to be, and you were, in our hearts. That's why I'm writing to you in detail about the day, We felt your love and spirits there with us. I wanted to share some of our thoughts and feelings so you could feel like you were there too. I hope this will help in some small way.

Your Aunt Carol and I were both hungry as we hadn't had much since breakfast. I had a bite at 11:30 a.m., but Carol rushed home from church to let Scooby out and get over to pick me up. Your dad had told me that he did not want the day to be a celebration of any kind, and Carol and I of course went along. I was just so happy with what he was doing. But your mother had told us that when we spread her ashes in her paradise she wanted everyone to *celebrate* her life. You know how your mom always had everyone laughing. Even when she was so sick, she would find something funny to make us laugh. I so admired her for that. So Carol and I stopped at "The Tin Fish" on the way home. We toasted your mom with ice tea and lemonade and enjoyed a lovely shrimp dinner at a table looking out on beautiful Anchor Bay. We both knew she would have wanted us too. It was the first time we had been there and we thought it was *great*. We found out from Alice later that that was a favorite place of your mom's. I can see why. Usually when we were on our way home from the island, we would have eaten at the cottage and had dogs in the car, etc. Just a side note: We both had to use the restroom, and Carol went first after we had ordered our drinks. Then I went. As we were eating our salads, we both started to speak at once, and what we both wanted to tell one another was "that neither one of us wanted to wash our hands," but your mom was "free" in her paradise and in our hearts. It's strange the thoughts and feelings that hit you out of the blue.

Carol got me home about seven o'clock. We were both physically and emotionally tired out but with very good feelings about the day.

I'm so grateful that your dad and I have good communications with one another. I had wondered when I sent him that letter if he would speak to me again. I'm so grateful that it worked out the way it did. Like he told me, "he just was not thinking." Your dad and both of you and your families are very important to me. I love you all so much. I do hope that by sharing my thoughts and feelings on last Sunday that you will feel a part of it too. You were there!

October 7, 2007

My dear Sydney,

It doesn't seem possible to Grandma that you are going to be seven years old next Friday. *Wow!* You are growing up so fast.

I was thinking about you all weekend and hoping you were having a good time at your uncle's wedding. I will be anxious to see pictures of you all dressed up in your beautiful dress. I bet you looked like a little princess.

I got the birthday card you made for me, and I just loved it. I'm putting it on my fridge so I can look at it every day. Thank you very much, Sydney. You are doing so well in your writing and drawing. I'm very proud of you.

I didn't know what to get you for your birthday this year, so am just sending money. You can talk with Mama and Daddy about how to use it, OK? Anyway, I wish you a *very happy birthday!* You can call me and tell me all about it. I'll be thinking of you and sending all kinds of good wishes and tons and tons of *love! I love you to the moon and back!* Have a great day, sweetie.

November, 2007

Ms. Vivian Beeler
15181 Ford Rd Apt #302
Dearborn, Ml 48126-4634

Dear Friend:

"It's time to get off the sidelines and get in the game."

Those are the words of Neal Shine, the former Detroit Free Press publisher and architect of the newspaper's Children First campaign. Neal, whom we loved and who loved Detroit and its people, passed away last April. Yet, his inspiration lives on through the Gift of Reading program.

Since its creation in 1987, the Detroit Free Press has distributed more than 650,000 books to needy, at-risk Michigan children and has supported literacy programs all around the state. We provide these books to children during the holidays, and in some cases a Gift of Reading book might be their only holiday gift.

Thank you for your past contribution to the program. Because the needs of some children persist, we would like to ask for your help once again.

Your tax-deductible donation can help make this holiday season a memorable one for the children who need reading help the most. Please make your check or money order payable to "Gift of Reading" and send it to P.O. Box 640703, Detroit, Ml 48264-0703.

Young children need to discover the pleasures of reading, and that books just aren't for school or homework. Your contribution will help a youngster learn that reading can become a life-long habit that frees the mind to explore life's possibilities.

Thank you for caring, and please accept our wishes for a happy holiday season.

Sincerely,
Debora Scola
Secretary
Detroit Free Press Charities

The Gift of Reading * Detroit Free Press Charities *
615 W. Lafayette Blvd., Detroit, Ml 48226
Detroit Free Press Charities, Inc.

Saturday, December 15, 2007

Dear Friends in charge of "The Gift of Reading"

I had the article by Dan Shine laying on my table where I write my checks, when I received the letter from Debora Scola about the Gift of Reading program. I loved the article by Dan as I was a big fan of his Dad's. Although we had never met and Neal did not know me, I still felt like we were friends from reading his columns for so many years. I still miss them . . . I think I have sent my little bit every year since Neal started this charity. I wish it could be a lot more. I have been a bookworm all my life and I'm 86 now. Books have helped me through some very rough times the last 10 years. But way before that opening a new book was like opening the best present in the world. You never knew where they were going to take you . . . Up, Up an Away, opening the doors to the world and to the magic of the printed word. I am so very grateful my eyes are still OK. I would be absolutely lost without my books and being able to read them. My 5 children all grew up watching how much enjoyment I got from my books. Of course I read to them before they were even born. All of my nieces and nephews call me their "Book" Aunt, as I always gave books or Gift Certificates for books for their presents.

I started taking Water Color lessons at Adult Education in Troy about 1988. Found out I had a little talent and just loved doing it. I have been making my own Christmas Cards since then. Hope you enjoy it . . . I had two wonderful teachers, Jo Chiapelli and Joan Cox at the Niles Education School in Troy.

Ten years ago we lost a wonderful son-in-law to diabetes and a stroke. My husband and I made a wise decision and moved to Henry Ford Village in January 1998 from our 4 bedroom colonial in Troy. We had 2 great years here when I lost my soul mate and partner to cancer. We had 58 wonderful years together. Seven weeks later I lost our middle daughter to Ovarian Cancer. 2000 was not a good year. The Staff and friends and family helped me get through . . . Then at the same time we lost the Twin Towers to Terrorists, one of my twin daughters was diagnosed with Stage Four IBC Breast Cancer. Double, double whammy . . . she was a fighter like her sister before her and she fought it for 4 years. We lost her in 2005. both girls were so talented, had wonderful husbands, grown children, and so much to live for. I would have traded places with either one if I could have. I have to believe god has a reason or I would be completely bonkers . . . Books and my water color painting have helped keep me sane.

Over the years I have written to different writers at the Free Press about things that they wrote about. Most of them complimentary and also the last 2 years because I am on a Soapbox about IBC Breast Cancer. Too few women know about it. You DO NOT HAVE TO HAVE A LUMP! If I can help just one family from going through what my family has gone through it would be worth so much to me.

As 1 said, I'm widowed now and on a fixed income so have to watch my spending, but had to tell you how much I believe in this charity. Children are our future. Reading and education are the only way this world will ever have any peace.

I also had to tell you about Inflammatory Breast Cancer just in case anyone there can spread this information on to more people.

I do want to tell you too that I have a wonderful family, {what's left}, and they care about me. I am very grateful. I have 7 grown grandchildren and one 7 year old, who is a joy. Born to our {Bonus Caboose} son. 8 Great grandchildren and another one due in May. I am still Mom to my two son-in-laws. When I start to write I have a tendency to rattle on . . . Thank you for listening to me . . .

Vivian L. Beeler
15181 Ford Rd. #302
Dearborn, MI 48126
veebee248@sbcglobal.net

YAHOO! MAIL Print—Close Window

Happy New Year, Mrs. Beeler!

Thank you so very much for your contribution to the Gift of Reading. Your gift helps make it possible for us to provide books for more than 15,000 children every year. And as you know, reading is a true gift, a blessing to be treasured. I'm proud and honored to be involved in a program started by Neal Shine, the kindest and most loving man I've ever known. He would have been moved by your letter. I'll share it with his family.

Thank you also for sharing your talent with me . . . what a beautiful picture! And after reading the pamphlet on IBC, I think I shall always remember the warning.

Best wishes to you, Vivian. God bless you and your family.

Deb Scola
Debora Scola
Community Affairs Director
Detroit Media Partnership
615 W. Lafayette Blvd., Detroit, Ml 48226
313-222-6895 | cell 313-815-3788 | dscola@dnps.com

Sunday, December 09, 2007

Dear Rosly and Family,

I can hardly believe that Christmastime is here again. The time just seems to fly by, which in one respect is very good. It is a beautiful and blessed time of year. I received your lovely Christmas card yesterday and suddenly realized that I had not answered your very nice birthday letter to me. Rosly, I hope you will except my apology. I really don't know where the time has gone. I never thanked you for that beautiful and useful purple wrap that you sent to me. I feel badly about that. I'm sure you wondered if I had gotten it. It was not good manners on my part to not let you know. Please forgive me. I will try very hard not to let that happen again.

You had a lot of good advice in your letter to me. I loved that Tibetan wisdom you sent to me. I love words and the way they are put together. They can advise, help, and make music in our minds. Thank you.

I also agree with what you said about our "golden years" being after World War II. We both can be so grateful that we have had such good lives, and I know I have a lot to be thankful for. As you said this aging business is difficult, but we have to be thankful for each day and just do the very best we can.

Carol had the family at her house for Thanksgiving, and Jim is going to have Christmas. Again, I count my blessings. Also, I can report to you that Ken and Alice are doing a little better, which makes my heart happy. Alice is getting into the health care field, and she loves it as she gets so much satisfaction from being able to help people. It all started when her doctor's wife, Gretchen, who has known Alice for years, asked her if she would be interested in helping out her elderly parents. They want to stay in their own home but cannot manage like they did before. You and I know a little about that, don't we? Toni, the wife is 88, and Bruce the husband is 91. Toni was in the hospital for a while with a bad infection in her shoulder. So Alice would go over to their house and help Bruce get dressed and take him to the hospital to see Toni, plus do any other errands and see that he ate. When Toni came home, she still goes over early. Does their housekeeping and fixes home cooked meals for them about three times a week. Does any errands for them and took Toni to rehab, doctor and dentist appointments, etc. They have all become very fond of one another. Bruce has a lot of trouble in standing and walking, but Toni is very independent, and Alice says that she keeps things picked up and does as much as she can. They have three daughters. Gretchen lives near them but works at the schools in administration. Tina is in Florida and has been up to see her folks a few times and will be here for Christmas. Heidi lives in Texas and also has been up here. They all like Alice very much and are grateful to her. Alice still works at the restaurant on Saturday nights and is going to help them on Christmas Eve and New Year's Eve. Doing this has really helped Alice and given her a reason for living. Gretchen has told

Alice also that she knows a lot of people that would like her service, but she said, "My folks come first!"

Rest of my families are doing fine, and I'm going to be a great-grandma again in May. Erik and Eve are having another little one. Madilyn is twenty-two months old now, so it will be nice spacing. They are happy about it.

We are under a winter storm watch today—snow, freezing rain, sleet, a bit of everything which makes driving treacherous. Like you mentioned in your letter, there have been so many catastrophes all over the world, it does make you wonder what is going on.

Like you said too, Rosly, that everyone our age has their cross to bear. Age is not kind to most people. So we just have to be grateful for what we can do. I know I have to pace myself, do a bit and then rest my back. I get discouraged sometimes, and then I look around me and I count my blessings. I have a family who loves me, a wonderful place to live with a lot of lovely friends, and I feel very lucky because as you said, "I have had a good life with a lot of happiness in it."

Thank you for all the kind words about my paintings. I still love to do it but can't do it as much as I would like to, as it bothers my back. I'll just keep doing what I can.

Sending lots of good wishes and blessings to you and your family for this Christmas season and a wonderful year ahead.

2008

January 2, 2008

Dear Gretchen,

I can't even begin to tell you how very grateful I am for you giving my daughter Alice the opportunity to take on another job and ease out of the restaurant business! Plus, she loves what she is doing and is getting a great feeling of satisfaction out of doing something so worthwhile. She misses her family and her twin so much, and this has given her a reason to live. I was very worried about her state of mind and the depression she had sunk into. I can hear the difference in her voice, and she was excited about Christmas this year. She told me that there are certain things that your dad does that reminds her of her daddy. She loves your folks, Gretchen, and would do anything she could to help them. Then all of your family have been so nice to her. She feels needed, and we both know how important that is. Her dad and I tried so many times to get her out of the restaurant business over the years, but she loved it—making sure people had an enjoyable dinner out, and she was good at it.

I'm sure she has told you that I'm eighty-six, and age is not kind to our bodies. My husband and I did make a very wise decision in 1998 when we moved here to Henry Ford Village. We had two good years here before I lost him in 2000. Then seven weeks later, we lost our middle daughter Kathy to ovarian cancer. She had fought it for six years. It was a terrible time for all of us. That's when the staff here at the Village gently pushed me into starting a watercolor Class. It has helped a little. There is always something going on here at the village. We have seven buildings of independent living—an assisted living one and nursing care one, so we are pretty well covered. We have a 125 different clubs and activities, so if you want to stay in your apartment and be bored it's your privilege. The staff is wonderful here, and so many of them have become my good friends. I'm Grandma to a lot of them. I imagine Alice has told you that I've had to give up some of my committee work as with stenosis, arthritis, and sciatic nerve acting up, walking is getting more and more painful. I'm so tired of constant pain. I had one back operation which helped for a short time. Been to Pain Management Clinic for a series of three shots in my back. It didn't help. Doggone it! So I try to pace myself and put a smile on my face when I leave my apartment. Nobody likes to be around whiny old ladies.

My eldest daughter, Carol, who is a sub teacher, is my "rock of Gibraltar." She is always available when I need her. But I try not to "need" her too often. I miss Barbara so much in so many ways. She was always there for me too. I know I could count on Alice if she lived up here too. The girls had become my friends, and we had so much fun together. I wished so many times it could have been me. I would have traded places in a minute with either of my girls. Our "Bonus Caboose Son" is out in Denver, and while I hear from them regularly, they are a long way away. Traveling is just too much for me anymore. My family keeps telling me I am important to them, that they need me to talk to, but I wonder. Both Kathy and Barb's husbands are "sons" to me and I'm their mom, so I am very lucky and grateful. My grown-up grandchildren keep in touch and so does *my* little Sydney (aged seven) in Denver. Plus, I have seven great-grandchildren and another little one due in May, all beautiful, normal healthy babies.

I hope I haven't bored you too much. I start to write and I just rattle on and on. My whole purpose in writing to you was to "thank you" for giving my daughter a new change and chance on life.

She was upset this morning and called me as the roads were bad with the snow you got and she couldn't get out to meet your folks at Perkins. But I was glad to hear they stayed in too. Hopefully she got over there a little later when the roads would be better. We've had several snowfalls here too. I just go out when the roads are dry and no ice. I don't want or need to *fall*.

Tell your husband thanks for me too for all the help he has given Alice over the years. I do worry about her not having any insurance, and I know he has helped her a great deal over the years.

I also know your folks are in very capable and *caring* hands. I'm very proud of what a hard worker my daughter is.

Take care and stay well. Best wishes always,

February 27, 2008

Dear Rosly,

I understand exactly what you are saying when you say that every year they go by faster and every year we seem to slow down more and not get all the things accomplished that we would like too. You don't have to apologize to me for not writing sooner. It seems to take me longer and longer to write letters nowadays. I am just very grateful when I do hear from you, and please don't ever worry about how long it might take you. Rosly, you can see I'm the same way. Age does so many strange things to our bodies, and this slowing-down process we just have to accept and do the best we can. Like you said, sometimes I am just too tired to write even though I am thinking about you often. I am on pain medication for the stenosis, arthritis, and sciatic nerve back pain, and I know that slows me down too. When a person is dealing with health problems, we just have to do the best we can. I am grateful I am still able to take care of myself.

It certainly sounds like you have a *big* project going on your house. Hopefully your big window is in by this time. I wish you the very best of luck on your other alterations and hope they will go smoothly for you. It does sound like a big job and a lot of changes.

I'm surprised that Basel does not have senior living homes. They are becoming more and more prevalent around here with people living so much longer. They are not all nursing homes. They are apartments for people who just can't take care of their homes anymore. They also have dining rooms if you want to eat your meals in them, plus transportation for doctors and shopping. Henry Ford Village where I live happens to have three levels of care here: independent living where I am, then assisted living where you need help with showers, dressing and perhaps medications, and then nursing care. So I am very lucky. Assisted living and the nursing care will be available to me if I ever need it. I hope and pray not, but we never know from one day to the next.

It doesn't seem possible Easter will be here on March 23. We have had a very snowy and cold winter. Everyone is looking forward to spring and warmer weather.

It is nice that you see Alexander once a week. I'm sure he appreciates you feeding him and doing his laundry for him. I know what you are saying when you said you want to do it as long as you are able. It makes us feel good when we are able to help in some small way.

I'm so sorry to hear about Udo. I do hope and pray that he is doing better now. That is a huge worry for everyone.

I also hope that Rosemarie has found a job. Michigan is still in very bad economy, and jobs are very scarce for everyone. So many people are laid off from the automotive business and looking for work. I don't ever remember seeing the economy this bad. It's scary for everyone.

It's nice that you and Walter keep in touch, but I can understand it with being twins. There is a special bond there besides being brother and sister. I saw it all my life with Alice and Barbara.

The Resident Life Staff here at the Village talked me into having a watercolor show and sale last Tuesday on the nineteenth. Two others in my class joined in too, so there were three of us. I had taken my original paintings to Kinko's (a copy store) and had prints made from them, also the reduced <<<IMAGE>>> for my cards I make. I matted and framed a lot of the prints, and they came out quite well. Sandra and Myra from our staff helped set up for the show. We had it in one of the meeting rooms. It was very colorful with all the paintings from the three of us. They also had containers of ice water and lemonade and plates of crackers and cheese. I have never sold my paintings as someone in my family has always wanted them. With these being just prints of my originals, I was willing to see if they would sell. I sold fourteen at $50.00 a piece, which I thought was pretty good. We did not have as much traffic as we had hoped as there were a lot of things going on that day. Anyway they want me to have another show in a few months on this side of the complex. We were on the other side for this show. There are seven buildings in the Village, so it is quite a large complex. Carol came over to help me, and also Marguerette helped a lot too. We had to load them all up in carts to get over there, set up, and then take down and repack to bring back. We were all tired that evening.

Now that that is over with, maybe I can get back to painting some again. But there again I'm slowing down a lot. Oh well!

All of my family are doing well, and I'm very grateful. They all keep in touch with me too, for which I am also grateful. I think I told you that Eve, Erik's wife, is having another baby in the end of May. They found out that it is a little boy. They are going to call him William Edsel and are excited. Little Madilyn was two on February 1l. That will make eight great-grandchildren for me. Life does go on.

Rosly, I hope that you and all your family will have a blessed Easter, also that your spring will bring you warmer and nice weather to enjoy. Sending all of you my love, prayers, and best wishes always,

Monday, February 4, 2008

Dear Dory,

You have no idea how much you are missed at our table at dinnertime. You were always so upbeat and usually had some interesting or unusual little thing to tell us about that you had heard on TV. It's going to be another long six weeks or so while you are at RG. Then do you have any reprieve before you have to have your second operation?

Maureen says she has been going to see you every day. I'm not quite sure how you feel about that as you said you did not want visitors until you felt better. She told us that you had your first therapy today and that she was hurting for you. I'm not sure if you wanted company for that. Ethel said she was there on Sunday when she and Gayle went. She said they didn't stay long and that your daughter was coming too. She said she thought Maureen might leave when they came, but she didn't. She also wonders how you feel about the daily visits. Maybe we have it all wrong and you enjoy it. Hope so because you sure don't need any more frustrations at this point.

I helped with our Sunday program yesterday. It was excellent. It was a group of young ladies from The Detroit School of Performing Arts, tenth through twelfth grade. They were all dressed in long black dresses with a string of pearls around their neck. They looked lovely. *And wow*, their voices were just beautiful, sent chills up and down your spine. We have had the young men's group from that school here three times, and they were *great* too. I didn't realize they also had a young ladies group until this year. The residents loved both groups, so I will try to have both of them back. It's too bad that the newspapers never write and show pictures of these talented young black people. Not all are into drugs and guns. They make you feel good.

I had a busy day today. I went to my exercise class, got back for lunch, and Aurica came for my monthly cleaning at 1:00 p.m. Dr. Reeder had wanted me to see Dr. Marinescu as my ankles and legs have been swelling so. I've been on lasix, which helps a little but not enough. Anyway I had an appointment at two to see him. He talked to me a bit and then did an ultrasound on my heart. He said my heart muscles show some weakening and set up a stress test for me on Thursday afternoon at 3:00 p.m. I'm going to try the Erickson Advantage transportation for it. His office is over by Cherry Hill and Outer Drive. It's not far, but weather is so uncertain. First impression of him was good. When we lived in Troy, I had a stress test every year. It's been two years since my last one, so really I am overdue. Dr. Marinescu knows Dr. Atallah the cardiologist I went to see in Troy. That made me feel pretty good too.

Tomorrow I have a ten o'clock appointment with Dr. Reeder for another check of my potassium and the swelling. Then I'm starting up my watercolor class again at 1:00 p.m. On Wednesday is that Erickson Advantage luncheon. I so wish you could go with me.

Carol was over on Saturday and had dinner with us. She brought me lots of pictures of my great-grandchildren out in Denver, which I really was happy to get. My little twins are a year and a half old now. Both are darling but look entirely different. Simone has white blonde hair and blue eyes while Sedona is of smaller build with brown hair and brown eyes. Kenny and Gina were there from California with their little daughter Maeyana who will be two the seventh of this month. I've got some beautiful great-grandchildren, and I'm so grateful as they are all normal and healthy. It was quite a little family reunion. They had wanted me to come, but I'm just not up to traveling. I think I told you about my granddaughter Krista moving to Denver with her four children, and my son Bill and wife Shannon taking her under their wing. Alice was not able to go at the last minute as she got that twenty-four-hour stomach virus and was throwing up all night before she was supposed to fly out. It was disappointing for her, but she is going to go a little later. She got it from Toni the woman she helps. It's going around. My son-in-law Ken went too. He was so pleased to have Carol's company to fly with, and Carol said it was nice to have a man take care of things. Good for both of them. Everyone was well while they were together. Ken was a little overwhelmed at times with all the babies and children running around but was also glad to see all his family.

I got to get to bed, Dory, so I can face another day. I hope I don't bore you with all this family stuff, but it's something to write to you about and we've talked enough that I think you can figure out who I'm talking about. If not, I'll answer questions later.

Think of you so often, my dear, and keep hoping that the pain and discomfort is not too bad. It has to be rough though. I know you are not a complainer, but my shoulder is here if you want to call. Sending lots and lots of love and healing wishes.

My dearest Sydney,

I talked with your mama today, and she told me about your grandma Ginny being so sick that the angels will soon be coming to get her to take her to heaven. *And,* honey, it's OK to be sad because you are going to miss her. Heaven is a place that none of us fully understand, but we just know and believe that when a person we love dies their spirit and soul go to heaven. We know then that they are not sick or in pain anymore, and honey, they get to see and be with all the people that they have loved and who have gone to heaven before them, and that makes them happy. Sydney, I am eighty-six years old and have lived a long and full life like your grandma Ginny, but even living so many years, I cannot fully explain heaven to you. It is a place that we have to accept with faith and just know that when God sends his angels for the people we love they are going to be well and happy. Faith and believing also means that we know that they live on in our hearts and souls, and they are still with us in spirit. There is an Eskimo legend that I like to believe. It goes like this: "Perhaps they are not stars in the sky but peepholes that our loved ones are looking down at us and smiling." I also like to believe, Sydney, that they are watching over us from heaven and they can hear us when we talk to them from our hearts. Honey, I am going to copy a couple of poems and send them to you for you to read with your mama and daddy. I think they are very good and have helped me understand death and dying a little bit better.

God saw you were getting tired
And a cure was not to be,
So he put his arms around you
And whispered "Come to me."
A golden heart stopped beating,
Hard working hands now rest.
God broke our hearts
To prove to us
He only takes the best.

Afterglow

I'd like the memory of me
To be a happy one,
I'd like to leave an afterglow of smiles when life is done.
I'd like to leave an echo whispering softly down the ways,
of happy times and laughing times and bright and sunny days.
I'd like the tears of those who
Grieve to dry before the sun,
Of happy memories that I leave
When life is done.

Honey, save this letter and read it again when you are a little older because death and dying are difficult for people of any age to understand. When we lose a person we loved, it makes us very sad and that's OK. But we also have to realize that that person is not sick anymore and is at peace. Like I told you earlier in this letter, they live on in our hearts, and we have to be happy for them that they are not in any more pain. Your grandma Ginny lived a long and full life, and these last couple of years have been hard for her and her family to see her sick. In her case, death can be a friend and a blessing. It's OK to miss her, but she would want you to be happy for her too. There is another great poem in the Bible in the Book of Ecclesiastes called "Time to live and a time to die," and now is your grandma's time to die. Life goes round in a circle, honey. At seven years old, it is hard to figure out. It's still hard for me sometimes at eighty-six years. We just have to believe and have faith. I hope what I have written to you will help you understand a little bit, Sydney. I love you so much, honey, and I know your grandma Ginny did too and always will.

Grandma B. is thinking about all of you and sending lots and lots of love.

I love you to the moon and back, honey.

Friday, May 16, 2008

Dear Barbara and Bob, Bill and Marie,

I never did send you folks a card at the time Margaret passed away. I've been going to write to you about our friendship and knowing one another for about ten years, and now it's been several weeks already. Time just seems to have a way of flying by. I was so glad that I was able to make it over to the funeral home and see you. Margaret meant a lot to me and was a good friend. The one bad thing about living here is you make friends and then you lose them, and it hurts, even when you know it is a blessing.

I'm not exactly sure how our friendship started, but I think when my husband Bill and I moved in here in January 1998 and started to eat in Great Lakes dining room, your mother came over to me and said that I looked so familiar to her, plus my voice sounded familiar. She wanted to know if I had worked at Crowley's. I said, "No, but I used to shop there." Anyway, we hit it off and started eating together. My Bill was used to looking after older women as he had helped me with my mother and my aunt, plus we had had four daughters, so he was used to females. Margaret thought he was such a nice gentleman as he would always ask if he could get her anything and held her chair if it was convenient. We were eating with Bernice Hyde, the Scottish lady, and Stella had latched on to your mother at that time. Then a Virginia Mathison joined us, and I've forgotten the names of others. I'm the only one left now. It's scary, *but* I was a little younger back then. I'll be eighty-seven in September. *Wow!*

Over the years, I heard stories about your mother growing up on a farm in Iowa, which were very interesting—butchering their own meat, their schoolhouse, and the tornados that were quite common. Then she told me about being active in the Eastern Star and the Masonic doings, parties, and dances. Her husband didn't want her to work, but after you kids left she got a job at Crowley's and enjoyed it. She was so proud of both of you and her grandchildren and great-grandchildren. She talked about making waffles for you, Bill, when you would come over for lunch here *and* the one time she set off the alarm and was so embarrassed. She belonged to that stitch and sew group when she first moved in here, and she showed us the beautiful afghans she made with the embroidery on top. She was always so enthusiastic about my artwork; she always made me feel good. We truly enjoyed one another's company. Of course over those same years, she heard lots about my family too. She had met both Kathy and Barbara, the daughters that I lost to cancer, and felt very heartsick for me. She still remembered Carol too the last time that she saw her. We used to discuss about cooking holiday meals for our families and how much we enjoyed doing it while we could. We both missed being able to do it anymore as we both liked to cook and bake. In the later years though, I used to cheat a little by using frozen pie crusts or box cake mixes, but your mother made everything from scratch. I'm not a big fan of cheesecake, but your mother years ago made a pineapple cheesecake that was out of this world. It was yummy. She brought it down and shared one evening.

I just heard last evening that Helen Morrow is doing much better and is coming back to her own apartment today. She might be joining us for dinner tonight.

Margaret left footprints in my heart, and I'm so glad I had the privilege of her friendship. I'm also glad I got to know her family. We always told one another how lucky we were because we both had families that cared about us. You do see some sad stories around here. Truly I don't know where I would be happier in my circumstances now than here. The staff is wonderful and so are my friends. I'm hoping God will be good and take me before I have to go to RG. I'm not afraid of death. It's the process of dying that scares most of us at our age. Like your mother, I've had a good life and a wonderful marriage. The last years have been hard. *But* life goes on. I had a lovely Mother's Day with my family. We went to the Marriott Brunch out by Laurel Park. I had lots of phone calls from my families out of state, flowers, and cards. I'm very grateful.

I'm sure this was a difficult Mother's Day for you folks, but I do feel that Margaret is at peace.

All of you take care, and I send my love and best wishes to all,
Vivian Beeler
H.F.V. cc302

POINT LOOKOUT RESORT AND CONFERENCE CENTER

ARTWORK CONTEST RULES AND GUIDELINES

1. All Erickson residents are eligible to participate.
2. Artwork MUST BE TURNED into the Office of Myra McInerney, Lead Community Resources Coordinator, by 4:00 p.m. on Thursday, June 5, 2008.
3. TO BE ELIGIBLE FOR JUDGING, ALL WORKS MUST HAVE BEEN COMPLETED WITHIN RECENT YEARS.
4. Artwork eligible for display and judging will include the following categories:

CATEGORY	MEDIUM
Painting I	Acrylics, Oils
Painting II	Watercolor
Photography	Photography

5. Artwork must depict attractions, monuments, landscape, sports, themes local to the Resident's community (ex: a Greenspring resident in the Washington, DC, area may take pictures of the cherry blossoms by the Jefferson Monument while a Henry Ford Village resident paints an antique Ford Mustang)
6. Three pieces from each campus will be chosen on Friday, June 6, 2008, and then sent to Point Lookout in Northport, ME for judging. Each resident participant will be rewarded a gift certificate.
7. Three pieces among all of the campus submissions will be chosen as the grand prize winners. GRAND PRIZE WINNERS WILL WIN A TRIP TO MAINE TO ATTEND THE GRAND OPENING CEREMONIES ON JULY 8TH AND 9TH!

Important Dates to Remember for the Contest:

> - Thursday, June 5, 2008—Turn artwork into the Office of Myra McInerney, Lead Community Resources Coordinator, by 4:00 pm
> - Monday, June 16, 2008—Point Lookout judges select the Grand Prize Winners
> - Tuesday/Wednesday, July 8-9, 2008—Point Lookout Grand Opening Ceremonies
>   www.visitpointlookout.com

Henry Ford Village

15101 Ford Road
Dearborn, MI 48126
313-584-1000
June 10, 2008
Vivian Beeler
CC302
Henry Ford Village

Dear Vivian:

On behalf of Henry Ford Village Community Resources I'd like to congratulate you for being one of the winners whose painting was selected for the Pointe Lookout grand opening. It is now in the mail and will be on permanent display at Erickson's new, beautiful Pointe Lookout Conference Center in Maine. It will be entered into the competition for the grand opening of Pointe Lookout. Let's hope you win there, as well!

Enclosed is a gift card for use at the Village Market as a token of appreciation from Erickson. I would like to add my thanks and appreciation to you for giving your beautiful painting to Pointe Lookout. It represents the Village beautifully!

Sincerely,
Myra R. McInerney
Community Resources Coordinator
Cc: Deena Gibson
67 Atlantic Highway www.visitpointlookout.com
P.O. Box 119
Northport, ME 04849
P: 800-515-3611
F:207-789-5968

Point Lookout

Resort and Conference Center
July 25, 2008

Dear Ms. Beeler,

We would like to sincerely thank you for participating in our recent resident artwork contest here at Point Lookout. All of the submissions we received were of the most professional quality and we are so happy to have them decorating our halls as a reminder of the impressive talent of so many Erickson residents.

We would especially like to thank you for making such a meaningful impact on our Grand Opening on July 10. During the open house, over 500 guests and John Erickson himself viewed an exhibit of the resident artwork on display in the Veranda of Ginley Hall. All of the artwork was and will continue to be greatly enjoyed and praised by our staff, visitors and guests.

Again, thank you for being part of our Grand Opening and Point Lookout. The artwork will serve as an enduring legacy of Erickson residents and the experiences they will find at Point Lookout.

If you would like additional information or have any questions about Point Lookout, please call us at 1-800-515-3611.

Thanks and Best Wishes,
Mark Blair
Point Lookout, Director
And the Team at Point Lookout

August 2008

There are so many days that I get up in the morning and wonder why I am still here. I'm so tired of constant pain and of not feeling good. Everything is such a big effort, and I have to push myself to do even small things. Then I have a day like last Friday. I saw Virginia Foote in the hallway, and she mentioned again how much she enjoyed my cards that I had sent her when she had her knee operation. She said she had framed one. A short time later, I ran into Cheryl Presley. We hugged as usual. Then she started telling me how much she admired me as a mentor and that she hoped as she aged she could accept bad things that happen in our lives and show everyone that life does go on and that one can get some enjoyment in living. She told me that I proved that even though we have tragedy in our lives we don't have to turn into a bitter, unpleasant "old" person. She brought tears to my eyes with her compliments. She also told me that Kelly said she wanted to be like me when she got "old." Kelly has told me that herself. That's a *big* compliment too. I feel grateful to the staff here at the Village. So many of them have become my special friends, and I truly love them as my extended family. Maybe that is my purpose in life now—to do my painting and make my cards and send them to people who need a little cheering up or to let them know they are not alone.

It's getting more difficult for me to do my painting and make my cards. My back hurts so badly at times. *but* painting does keep me busy and gives me a sense of accomplishment when my painting turns out well. I tell myself, "What if it does take me twice as long as it used to? What's my hurry?" I don't know. Life is difficult. I keep telling myself that God has a reason for all that has happened to me and to please give me the strength and courage to carry on.

I am rambling and talking to myself on a beautiful August afternoon, 2008

September 19, 2008

Dear Hildegard and Roger,

Did your summer go by as fast as mine did? It doesn't seem possible. I guess it's true what they say, that the older you get the faster time goes. Rosly never forgets when my birthday is coming up, which is very nice of her. Another hard to believe fact is that I will be eighty-seven on the thirtieth of this month. *Wow!* But my body tells me that's true. I had another MRI this summer on my back. The doctor said he could try an X-stop operation, but it would only do a little and there could be other complications. I said *no.* I just have to take my pain meds and pace myself and live with it. Bill Jr., Shannon, and Sydney (who will be eight on October 12) were here for a week the end of July. That was so nice. We had a lot of family get-togethers while they were here. Alice got up here from the Cincinnati area at that time too. My family are all doing fine, which I am grateful for, and the ones around here include me in everything. Again, I'm grateful, but I do have to refuse some doings. I'm still going to my arthritis exercise classes three times a week, and I know they are good for me. Plus, my watercolor class started again after Labor Day. I'm also still on our Entertainment Committee, and we started up again in September too, so I do keep busy. I just have to sit more than I used too. Oh well!

Sure hope you folks have had a good summer and have been able to carry out all your activities and are getting into your fall activities now. It will be nice to hear how things are going for you.

As ever, Vivian

Monday, September 29, 2008

My dear Sydney,

Grandma finally got to the UPS store to mail your unicorn picture to you. I hope you like the matting and pretty blue frame you picked out for it. When I went to pick up the picture (after they framed it), I saw these Hannah Montana posters. I know you like her, so I got one for you and one for Sage. I hope you can give it to Sage when you see her.

I'm sending this package of Cherry Bites to your daddy just 'cause I know he likes them, and I thought it would be a little surprise for him. Tell him when he chews them he is supposed to think of his mom.

Tomorrow is Grandma's eighty-seventh birthday. *Wow!* And then on October 12, you will be eight years old. You told me that you were going to have a sleepover with your best friends for your birthday. I'm sure you will have a lot of fun. Grandma will be thinking of you. Aunt Carol had Uncle Ken, Uncle Jim, Hannah, Scott, Cindy, Joe, Erik, Eve, Maddy, Will, and me over to her house yesterday to celebrate my birthday. It was very nice. I wish you and your folks could have been there too. *But* I have to be happy with phone calls.

Take care, honey. I *love you to the moon and back!*

October 16, 2008

Dear Avis,

Thank you for the lovely birthday greetings and nice newsy letter. I have been wondering about you. I never worry about cards being late. I'm just happy to hear from friends.

Avis, I was totally shocked when Carol told me that you had lost Donna. My heart aches for you. Parents should not have to lose their children. I know too well that it happens, *but* that does not make it *fair!* Yesterday was three years since we lost Barbara and it's been eight years for Kathy. The hurt just never goes away. Oh, you adjust and life goes on. People don't like to be around complainers. It makes them too uncomfortable, so you put a smile on your face when you leave your apartment and do the best you can. I like this saying: "Attitude is the crayon that colors your world." I try to pick bright crayons.

I'm sure that having your life turned upside down and inside out at our ages is very difficult to say the least. It does sound like you are in a nice place and have some family around, which is a blessing. I was happy to hear that Allison is coming to visit you at Thanksgiving time. Granddaughters can be very special. You mentioned getting a doctor, and also health insurance has been a nightmare. I can well imagine. Ford turned us over with $1,800.00, and we had to sign up for another insurance plan—big headache. That was last year. Thank goodness, with HFV being a part of the Erickson Corporation they have come up with what they call "The Erickson Advantage," which I joined last year. It's pretty good, but nothing like what we were used too. I have to go to their doctors and the co-pay is higher. Right now I'm in what they call the donut hole. I have to pay for all of my medications until the first of the year, then they pick up again. That hurts . . . big time, *but* I try to count my blessings because I'm a lot better off than some folks without health Insurance. This economy in our world today is downright scary. Erik, Carol's son, and Eve are moving to Chicago because Erik got a job he wanted there, while this area offered nothing right now. They are just going to rent out their house and will be renting in Chicago. I hate to see them go, as I saw them quite regularly, *but* you have to do what's best for your family. They have two beautiful children. Madilyn will be three in February and little Will is five months old. It's been so much fun to watch them grow. Erik says they will be home for the major holidays, but it won't be the same. Again, this is one of life's curves that I have to roll with or be terribly unhappy. Avis, I thought, *foolishly*, that when you got up to be our age, life would be easier, not so complicated, etc. *Ha!* My warranties are running out in my back so that I can't travel anymore or just don't want to. I'm quite content to stay right here. Like you, I like myself and get along well with me. I'm fortunate I can still enjoy my books and I still paint a little. I use the computer for writing and e-mails and still have my little watercolor class. It's therapy for all of us, and I am on our Sunday Afternoon Entertainment Committee. These things all keep me busy and the days go by *fast*. Forgot, I take an arthritis exercise class three times a week too. Our young instructor is getting married on October 25 and going to Australia for his honeymoon. He asked me to take over the class while he is gone. *Wow!* I said I would try as I know the routine quite well. It won't be the same, but the main purpose is to keep the people coming to exercise and not get out of the habit, which makes sense.

We had some rain and wind last evening and it took some of our leaves down. The weather has been beautiful, but I know we are in for a change very soon. Carol and I drove out to South Lyons last Sunday. Erik and Eve had invited us and Eve's family for brunch. It was kind of a last family get-together for right now, and the color in the trees was beautiful as it was a picture-perfect day. I had driven over to Carol's and then went with her. I still drive to Carol's and grocery stores. Medical Center is right here, another blessing. With our independent living apartments we just get one meal a day. You can choose breakfast, lunch, or dinner. Most people take dinner unless you have other plans with family, etc. They also have transportation to doctor's and grocery stores and once a week to a different shopping center. I think Erickson has a place or maybe two in that area.

Are you in an area that you can see all the beautiful fall colors? Hope so. That is quite a deal to come full circle like you have done. I do hope it works out well for you. Knowing you the little I did, I know you make yourself adjust and like me like your own company when you are alone. We are blessed when we have family that cares about us too.

Got to go rest my back. It tells me what I can and can't do. It could be worse so I'm lucky. Take care, Avis, and keep in touch.

As ever, Vivian

Memories

You opened a flood gate when you asked for stories about The Book Cadillac. I feel like a history book; so much has happened during my lifetime along with The Book Cadillac. I am an eighty-seven-year-old widow, and I spent my wedding night at The Book back on August 30, 1941.

It was such a very special night, and to stay at The Book meant a lot to us. We were two very young people, nineteen and twenty-one, who thought they were very grown-up and had the world by the tail. I had met my future husband two years before in the spring of 1939 when I was working as a receptionist at a real estate office on Oakman Blvd. in Dearborn. I was earning $5.00 a week. My future husband came in with his mother as they were looking for a house in the Dearborn area. His dad had been transferred from The Kelsey Hayes Wheel Company in Jackson to the one here in Detroit. I was living with my mother, grandmother, and sister in a house on Orchard in Dearborn. I had lost my father in January 1938. He was a World War I veteran and had survived a poison gas attack in France in 1918 before the war ended. After some time in a veterans hospital, he was given a clean bill of health and discharged. His death at forty-three because of Hodgkin's disease was blamed on the poison gas. It's a long story, but what I'm trying to show is that neither my future husband nor myself had much money. We grew up during the Depression, but as children and young people, we did not even realize that we were poor. Both our fathers had hourly jobs (my father worked for Ford Motor Company as an electrician), not always forty hours a week though. We had food on the table and were taught to clean our plates. We both had loving families, aunts, uncles, and cousins. Family get-togethers were an important part of our lives. The world is so different today, families scattered all over the country. One thing I have learned in my lifetime is "things change. You have to accept the changes or be very unhappy." Attitude is the crayon that colors your world. Anyway . . .

After meeting in the real estate office, Bill started walking me to night school at Fordson High, from which we had both graduated, but we did not know one another in school. I had wanted to go to college and be a teacher, but with the death of my father, there was a change of plans. I had to work, thus I had to do night school for business courses. My mother had got a job selling sportswear at the J. L. Hudson Company. Money was very scarce. When I turned eighteen, I was hired by the Bell Telephone Company and I was a "number please operator" in their office on Michigan and Monroe in West Dearborn. I loved it. Bill had also been hired as an apprentice in the tool room of Ford Motor Company. We were falling more and more in love and thought we were on top of the world. We went dancing at the Graystone and Walled Lake Ballrooms. We heard and loved all the big bands of that era. A movie and ice cream were big treats. My Bill proposed on Valentine's Day, February 14, 1941, and gave me a small diamond solitaire which I proudly wore for thirty years. On our thirtieth anniversary, I received another diamond solitaire, a bit larger this time. I had worn the first ring nearly through, so Bill wanted to get me another one. The first one was made into a locket, which I also wore for years. I have given it to my eight-year-old granddaughter to have as a remembrance from me.

Planning our wedding was such fun and so different than the weddings today. We had a church wedding with about 125 people. I wore a moiré taffeta bridal dress with a sweetheart neckline, long sleeves with a flared skirt, and a small train. I also had a waist-length bridal veil with a small pearl tiara. I felt very elegant, and it cost me a total of $125.00.1 got the dress at Hudson's bridal shop with my mother's employee discount. My sister and a cousin were my maid of honor and bridesmaid. Their dresses were long pretty dresses that they had worn to their proms—one peach and one pastel blue. All the fellows wore dark tuxes, and I thought they looked so sharp and my husband so handsome. After the wedding ceremony and pictures, everyone went back to my mother's for punch and wedding cake. It was a lot different from most of the weddings today.

A little side note: Moiré taffeta was being promoted for fall weddings. Of course, I wanted to be in style. The temperature on that late August day was up to almost ninety degrees. I was very, very warm and uncomfortable in that taffeta dress, something we laughed about over the years.

My husband's dad was born in Switzerland and came to America in 1914. He was so proud to be an American citizen, but of course he grew up making beer and wine. My mother and grandmother were of the school that alcohol was wrong. I can remember that my dad had a bottle in the back of the cupboard for medicinal purposes. Ha! It seemed to come out when his brother and some friends came over. My grandmother never said a word; she thought the world of my dad. Anyway, back to the wedding reception . . .

After the punch and cake at my house, my husband's folks invited those who wanted to, to come over to their place for sandwiches and beer. Of course, the new bride and groom made an appearance too. I had changed into a brown silk suit that my grandmother had made for me for my "going-away outfit." I felt special and very grown-up.

We said good night to all and headed off as a newly married couple. When we got to "The Book" and registered, I felt like everyone was looking at us, and I wanted to pull out our marriage license. It was such an elegant place, and it did make us feel very special. It was a wonderful night. Thank you for giving me the chance to reminisce. We grew up together and were always going to school and learning. We had respect for one another and the other's ideas. My Bill climbed the ladder at Ford Motor with schooling at Wayne State and hard work. I was a homemaker and loved it. We had five daughters and a bonus caboose son when I was forty-three. There are so many stories over the years—Pearl Harbor, my Bill's Air Force Service, losing our first daughter to SIDs, Korea, Vietnam, Desert Storm, Iraq, building our first house in 1967 for $37,000 and moving to Troy for thirty years, then full circle and back to Dearborn to live at Henry Ford Village in January 1998. Then I lost my husband to cancer in 2000 and seven weeks later lost our middle daughter to ovarian cancer. On September 11, 2001, my daughter Barbara was diagnosed with Stage 4 inflammatory breast cancer which she fought for four years. We lost her in 2005. Life has given me some hard knocks. Parents should not have to bury children. Enough! Up until the bad things started to happen, we had a truly blessed marriage and partnership that lasted fifty-eight years. Our love just kept growing from our magical night at The Book.

I have been so happy to see the articles in the paper about the Book's renovation and the pictures on TV of how lovely it looks again.

I warned you that you had opened my memories flood gate. I know this is much too long. But it's fun to write about anyway.

October 22, 2008
Vivian L. Beeler
15181 Ford. Rd. #302
Dearborn, Michigan 48126
313-581-7041

October 9, 2008

Dear Rosly,

I received your very nice letter, birthday wishes, and beautiful handkerchiefs several weeks ago. It is always so nice to hear from you, and you never forget my birthday. Thank you so much, Rosly. Carol had the family who lives in this area to her home to celebrate my birthday on Sunday the twenty-eighth. I am very grateful for my family and enjoy being with them. Marguerette had a delicious birthday cake and decorated our table in the dining room here at the Village on my birthday. That was a nice surprise, and our table companions were in on it. I got lots of cards and good wishes from the residents and staff.

I totally agree with you. Our world is in a terrible mess. It is getting very scary. For the first time since I've been voting, I am unsure of who to vote for in our coming presidential election. I don't want four more years of Bush, and I'm afraid that's McCain's policy, and I have some questions about Obama. I like what he is saying he wants to do, but I am a little worried about his ties to the Muslin world. Plus, our whole world is in such an economic mess it's scary. Also there is so much violence in our world today. Where has our respect for one another gone? I wish we could solve this, but hopefully it will all work out.

My heart goes out to Anneleis. It's got to be so hard to have to look for a job at her age and with the economy the way it is. Erik and Eve, Carol's son and daughter-in-law, my grandson, are moving to Chicago this month. Erik got a job there that he wanted. Our area here in Michigan did not offer him anything that he wanted and could make a good living at. Chicago is about a five-hour drive from us, not really far but not easy for Grandma Carol to babysit Madilyn of two and a half years and little Will of five months. Carol just loved taking care of the children a couple of days a week, and she will miss it. I'll miss seeing them quite often also.

They are just going to rent their house here with the housing market—so awful—and will be renting a place in Chicago. Eve is a doctor in audiology, so she will not have any problem getting a job there. Anything to do with health care is booming. My daughter Alice (Barbara's twin) has been taking care of an elderly couple for a year now. Her doctor just told her recently that he had three patients who could use her help full time if and when she needs more work. Her doctor and his wife are the couple who got her into this caregiving and out of the restaurant business. She is taking care of her doctor's wife's parents. They just love her. They have three daughters: one in the Cincinnati, Ohio, area where they live, one in Texas, and one in Florida. The daughters who live away come to see their parents quite often, but the parents want Alice to be there also when they are here. They really like the way Alice helps them. They love her cooking too. She is an excellent cook. Would Anneleis be interested in anything like that type of work? Just a crazy suggestion . . .

My son, Bill, his wife Shannon, and Sydney were here the end of July for a week. It was so nice to see them. Sydney has grown so much and is getting tall. She will be eight the twelfth of this month. She still takes piano lessons and plays well. She also takes judo classes and loves them. Bill says his daughter is going to know how to protect herself from anyone. Isn't it terrible though that we even have to think about things like that? She loves to read, and that pleases me so much as I have always enjoyed my books and reading. My books along with my painting have helped keep me sane these last eleven years when bad things started to happen in our family. I try very hard to count my blessings every day because the family that I do have left cares about me and says I am important to them. I see so many people here who don't have families, or if they do, they don't get along. I think that is so very sad.

Erik and Eve are having a brunch at their house this coming Sunday the twelfth. Erik called from Chicago to invite me. Carol will pick me up. They live about an hour's drive from here. They have invited Eve's family and Erik's family to kind of have a get-together before they move. Erik did tell me that they will be back for all the important holidays—Thanksgiving and Christmas. That will be nice to look forward to. I just hope the weather will cooperate with good road conditions.

We are having delightful weather this weekend—sunny skies and temperatures between sixty-five and seventy degrees Fahrenheit during the daytime hours. It is cooler overnight. I hope we will have some more of what we call Indian summer weather. Leaves are turning and will be falling soon. It is a beautiful time of year. I do like the fall weather.

Roger said to be sure and say "hello" and give best wishes from both of them. He is so good about translating your letters for me. He said Hildegard had a knee replacement this early summer, so it cut down on their playing golf, but she was doing much better now, and they would be bowling again this winter.

Walter sounds like a remarkable man to still be living alone with all the pain that he has. I am so grateful that I can still take care of myself too. Some days are difficult, but I want to keep going. I am glad I live here at the Village and can get help if I need it. I do have housekeeping once a month to do the more difficult cleaning that I can't seem to manage anymore. Between times, I keep it up myself, and of course I do have my dinner available every evening if I want. I usually do take advantage of that as it is included in our monthly bill. Plus, I enjoy the sociability of the friends I have made here. I'm sorry to hear that you are still having trouble with dizziness. That has to be very hard and limits you in things that you can do. Just getting to know you through our letters, I know that you are the type of person that does not give up easily. We just never do know what age is going to do to our bodies, do we? So we do the best we can. We come from good genes and solid working people before us. We want to set good examples also.

Rosly, I never know what to send you. You always send me such lovely things—handkerchiefs, scarf's, stoles, etc. Carol suggested that you might like some of my cards to use, so I am sending a packet of them for you to use and hopefully enjoy.

I do hope that Anneleis will have already found a job or will find one soon. I'm glad to hear that your grandchildren are all doing well and that you see Rosemarie often. I don't think you mentioned if all your renovation work was finished. Sure hope so.

Take care, Rosly. It doesn't seem possible, but the holidays will be here before we know it. It does seem like every year goes faster, doesn't it? Let's hope the world news is better by the holidays.

Sending my love, prayers, and best wishes always to you and your family,
Vivian

To April and Matt on your wedding,

At the bridal showers of my grandchildren, there was a lovely little book being passed around for the people there to write their advice or best wishes to the bride and groom. My first thought was "*wow*, that's a subject that will take some thought." So I decided to come home and think about what I would say. I decided, in the quiet of my own apartment, to write each of them a letter with some of my thoughts. April and Matt, while I don't know you as well as I know my grandchildren, I feel like you could be my grandchildren also, so I'm sending this letter on to you.

Firstly, I care about both of you. I have a happy feeling in my heart that the two of you were meant for each other and will have a wonderful marriage. You both have dreams and goals. My biggest wish |for you is that you can have as great a marriage and as long or longer than Grandpa and I had—fifty-eight years.

Secondly, I really can't give you advice in our world today. Society and everything is so different than back in 1941 when Grandpa and I were married. Hopefully I will finish *Our Story*, and you can read about what it was like back then. (I've been writing our life story for our grandchildren and am almost finished.)

Things change *but important values are still the same!*
Some of the things that worked for us are the following:

Respect for one another and the others ideas.
Best friends, being able to talk to one another about anything.
Always keeping the lines of communication open.

Share and help—no women's work, man's work.
Encourage and support through good times and bad times.
When you disagree, compromise.
Keep God and spirituality in your lives.
Keep a sense of humor.
Allow each other some "space" and "alone" time if wanted.
While wedding vows make us *one*, we are still individuals.

- Good sex is important and fun, sort of the "icing on the cake."
- But so many other things enter into it over the years: integrity, trust, kindness, compassion.
- Self-confidence: without it, it's hard to feel empathy and love for others.
- Always say "I love you" and share a kiss when you say good-bye or good-night.
- Always keep learning and growing.
- As a wife and husband too, always have time for "date nights" or special time together, because I can tell you from experience life goes by *fast!* Like that song: "Sunrise . . . sunset," your children will grow and leave because you as parents were "The wind beneath their wings." That's as it should be. *But* then you are two again. That can be another adventure in this journey they call *life*.
- Thankfulness: Life has so many things to offer. You should always be thankful and count your blessings.
- Looking back and remembering.

Grandpa and I did not know all of these things at the time we were married. We were two very young people very much in love. (We thought we were pretty adult and smart at the time.) Thankfully we grew up and learned together. I'm also very grateful that our love grew over the years and lasted with family and changes.

Marriage can work! That's where commitment comes in.
Most of the time, it's an *adventure and fun!*

Friday, December 05, 2008

Dear Hildegard and Roger,

It doesn't seem possible Christmas is less than three weeks away. Every year seems to go by faster. I hope you folks are doing well and will have nice holidays and a healthy and good 2009.

They have been putting up the Christmas decorations all of this past week, and our Village is looking beautiful. They do a marvelous job around here. They are having their annual Christmas party for the residents and their families on the fourteenth. They always have a Santa Claus for the children and take family pictures. There are also Christmas Crafts for the different age groups, little make and take projects that the kids enjoy with lots of snack goodies to munch on and hot chocolate too. It is always very nice.

My family that's around here went out to Milford to Jim and Hannah for Thanksgiving. Then I was back at Carol's for Friday turkey dinner too. Erik and Eve and their two little ones were at her folks for Thanksgiving Day, so Carol had us back to her place on Friday so we could see them too. I had two nice family days *and* lots of turkey.

On Christmas Day, we will all be at Carol's. I'm very fortunate that my family cares about me and I'm always included in all family doings. I don't do any late-night doings anymore and don't miss them either. I'm very content to be in my own space at night. Not much new to write about since my birthday letter from Rosly the end of September. I don't think I told you though that my grandson and his wife, Eve, with Madilyn who is "almost three" and little William who is "six months" moved to Chicago this fall. They had bought a nice house out in South Lyons about two years ago, but Erik had a chance to get a better job that he liked in Chicago. So they rented their house in S. Lyons and rented a house in Chicago for right now to see how things go. Eve has her doctorate in audiology, so she can get a job almost anywhere. With their two little children, she just wants part-time, which she was able to get. They were my only great-grandchildren that I saw quite regularly. Doggone, now I will just see them at holiday time. Last Friday at Carol's, I had such a good time holding and playing with little Will. He is such a happy baby, smiling, cooing, and talking to you. It won't be long until he is crawling, then he won't want to sit on anyone's lap. He'll want to *go*. He kind of swims now when you put him on his tummy on the floor. It's fun to watch. Maddy is a very busy little girl and constantly on the go. I wish I had just a little of their energy.

There is no hurry on translating this letter as I won't be writing much until the first of the year. Thanks again to both of you for doing this for me. Stay well.

Vivian

Friday, December 05, 2008

Hi Sydney.

Did you have a good week? Hope so. I loved the e-mail you sent to me. Thanks, honey.

I saw these Peppermint Pigs in a catalog and read the story behind them. I thought, "What a neat idea." So I ordered one for our family here to use after our Christmas dinner, and I ordered one for you folks. We can all use all the good luck we can get, right? Read the story about it and have fun with it on Christmas Day, OK?

I also sent you an ornament to hang on your Christmas tree. Hope you will like it. Grandma doesn't get out to shop like I used to, so I look through catalogs and order things from them. It doesn't seem possible Christmas is less than three weeks away. It's coming fast. What are hoping that Santa will bring you this year? I think with the economy so bad this year, there will be a lot of children that Santa is not going to bring very much to. So maybe we can help him and share a few of our things. Grandma always shares with a program called "Gift of Reading." I send them a check along with a lot of other people, and they make sure that all boys and girls get a new book for Christmas. You know how much we like our books, so I want everyone to have books. I have a feeling you will agree with me on that. We have to "give" as well as "receive," right? You have always been generous in sharing your things, Sydney, and that makes Grandma happy.

I'm working on addressing my Christmas cards, so I better get back at that job this afternoon. I'm enclosing some cartoons and calendar pages on which I liked the sayings. Hope you will like them too.

Lots and lots of love to you and your mama and daddy. Have a good weekend. It will be over with when you get this, but that's all right. Take care, honey. Love you to the moon and back.

Grandma

December, 2008

Dear Dr. Bob,

Sure hope you and your family are doing OK. I had put your Christmas card from last year aside to write a note in it, and it got lost in the shuffle of my things. I came across it when I was doing cards this year. I apologize. I'm sending both this year.

When I last heard from you, you were recovering from a gall bladder operation and were telling me how much you appreciated your wife taking care of you, that it had even brought you closer. You knew I would appreciate that because of my care of Bill, and you saw how much we cared about each other. Love for one another in a good marriage seems to grow even as our lives change, *and* isn't that wonderful?

Is your eldest son still perusing a journalism career? He must be almost through college, unless he is going on for another degree. Perhaps you folks have two in college now. Boy, that hurts the finances, but it's so very important in today's world. Whatever, I do hope all of you are doing fine. In this scary world today, it's sad to say but in your field you will never run out of patients. One thing I can say is that they are getting a terrific and knowledgeable doctor and one that cares about them as a person. That makes such a difference in a doctor-patient relationship. Over these last twenty years or so, I have had all kinds. My internist here at Henry Ford Village is very nice along with a great staff, so I feel fortunate. Dr. Bob, this was a very wise move that Bill and I made when we moved here. I don't know of anywhere I would be more content, especially when life throws you the curves that mine has had. I have made a lot of friends here, and a lot of the people on the Staff have become my *good* friends too. It doesn't seem possible but I will be here eleven years next month. We moved down here on January 18, 1998. Where do the years go? I keep thinking of that song from *Fiddler On the Roof:* "Sunrise, sunset."

I do keep busy even though I don't like what age is doing to my body. I have constant back pain from arthritis, stenosis, and just plain degeneration. I'm on Fentynal pain patches, but they only take the edge off. I did have one back operation in 2005 to relieve a cyst that was pushing on the nerves. It helped for a while but I had another MRI this summer, and this specialist suggested that an X-spot operation might relieve some but with no guarantees. I didn't go for that. I'm fortunate because I have a family that cares about me and as I mentioned lots of friends also. I'm also "Grandma" to a lot of our young servers in the dining rooms, and that's nice too, I still have my little watercolor class and I'm still on our Sunday Entertainment Committee. I started over a year ago to go to an arthritis exercise class three times a week. It's led by a young man Matt, who came in as our new fitness director. I sort of became Grandma to him and his fiancée in April. They were married on October 25 of this year. Lovely young couple! Anyway, he asked for volunteers to lead the class while they were on their honeymoon to Australia as they would be gone almost a month. No one volunteered, so Matt asked me if I would do it. Dr. Bob, I've never been one to lead. I'm a good follower or behind the scenes worker, but I'm finding myself doing things now that I would not think I could in my younger years. I couldn't say "no" to Matt, so I did do it, and everyone said I did a good job. Now Matt is going to be gone to a class this coming Wednesday, and I will be leading the class again. I said "I thought my job was over," and Matt said he didn't want me to forget how to do it, so looks like I will be called on when he can't make it. He's got a lot of different classes going here: swimming, balance, tai chi, personal help. Matt is twenty-eight and has a wonderful personality. He will go far I think. Everyone likes him. Oh, he started up a Wii bowling night too.

I've had Christmas cards from Tracy with pictures of her children every year and love to get them. I had a new great-grandson born last May twentieth, William Edsel, named after his great-grandpa and his grandpa. I'm been able to watch him grow and be with him to play. He is so sweet and such a happy baby. He joins his big sister Madilyn, who will be three in February.

That makes eight great grandchildren for me. Wow! I count my blessings because they are all normal healthy children. Selfishly, I wish they were closer to me as they are scattered all over our country, but I get pictures. My son, Bill Jr., wife Shannon, and my granddaughter Sydney who turned eight in October have been here for a visit every summer, which I love. They live in Lakewood, Colorado. Sydney takes piano, judo, swimming, soccer, skiing, not all at the same time, of course. She loves to read, which pleases me a lot as I've always been a bookworm. We talk every weekend.

I've rattled on way too long, I hope I haven't bored you too much. I miss seeing you. Let's hope 2009 will be a better year for everyone.

Vivian

Saturday, December 6, 2008, 12:01 PM
Saturday 12/6/08
From' "HKnight107@aol.com" <HKnight107@aol.com>
To: veebee248@sbcglobal.net

Dear Vivian:

Dianne and I are still in Michigan, and today we are working on the Christmas Tree. We still have all the family to our house for Christmas Eve and Christmas Day. Our little ones are growing fast. Amanda is in her second year at The University of Michigan, Ann Arbor. Where does the time go?

After Christmas we are planning to leave for Florida until Mother's Day. Dianne is ready to leave with all this snow and cold.

I think of you each day as I read my bible and take out the book mark you made for me. I just love it.

Dianne and I hope that you are doing well, and close to your family. We do think and talk about you often.

God Bless!

Harold & Dianne
Harold J. Knight, CPA
PO Box 552
East Tawas, Michigan 48730-0552
Telephone 989-362-2980 Fax 989-362-2980 hknightl

at&t YAHOO! MAIL Class c

Saturday, December 6, 2008 12:56 PM
Hello
From: "HKnight107@aol.com" <HKnight107@aol.com>
To: veebee248@sbcglobal.net

Dear Vivian:

What a nice note and full of good news. I wanted to respond about Tawas Plating Company and Tawas Powder Coating Company. My two son in laws, Kevin and Brian, manage the businesses and my only involvement is to be in the background if they need to talk with me. Our daughter, Lynette, stills does all the accounting and we have coffee together each week day and discuss everything. I have tried to teach my children to ask God each day to give them wisdom, and guidance in all things. I truly believe that God has watched over us and our businesses are still holding their own. These are unprecedented times and it takes all of our skills to keep all our costs under control. But for now we are thankful for what we have. Our employees are also very helpful to watch things with us. If the auto industry survives, we will survive also. I also have always told my children to never be in debt, unless it was absolutely necessary. Again we are thankful that our businesses owe nothing. That makes the pain a lot easier.

If Bill was here I am certain he would not believe this has happened. I just pray that our new government leaders will be able to guide us through this depression.

I will be watching the mail each day for your Christmas Card and it will be displayed along with all the ones you have given to us over the past years.

You are so special!

Love,
Harold & Dianne
Harold J. Knight, CPA
PO Box 552
East Tawas, Michigan 48730-0552
Telephone 989-362-2980 Fax 989-362-2980 hknight107@aol.com

Wednesday, December 17, 2008 9:07 AM
RE: Bonnie
From: "Kelly Moran" <kelly.moran@erickson.com>
To: veebe248@sbcglobal.net

Hi Vivian,

Yesterday was just so emotional that I never got a chance to call you. I am so sorry for that. I intended to come up and see you this morning. We don't really know what happened. We think she had a heart attack and just died. This was so unexpected. The family is doing ok and just trying to recover from the shock. Bonnie was such a wonderful woman and someone that we all loved dearly. She was a true grandma to all of our children and so often helped us through the years. When my mom and dad were so sick she was always there and just offered us the love she so freely gave to so many.

My brother-in-law Kevin is doing ok and handling things. The funeral is this Friday here at HFV (10 am) with a luncheon following. I know this is a loss but in every situation there is a silver lining. Bonnie did miss Mike and another Christmas without him was very hard. We are all looking at it like God called her home and Mike met her with a hug and a kiss. Death is hard but the belief that she didn't suffer was a gift is something we are all grateful for. I too am sorry for YOU and the loss of your friend. Plainly . . . it stinks! I love you so much!

Kelly

From: Vivian Beeler [mailto:veebee248@sbcglobal.net]
Sent: Tuesday, December 16, 2008, 8:51 PM
To: Kelly Moran
Subject: Bonnie

Oh Kelly, What happened? I know she wasn't feeling very well and the oncology Dr. had her on some pills that made her sleepy. I missed her at class today. I knew something was wrong because she is always there. sometimes it was just her and I. we were the two regulars. Then, I go over to St. Clair for dinner on Tuesday evenings to eat with Helen Quinn and Jean Wagner and my sister-in-law, Marguerette. When we sat down Helen said I'm so sorry about Bonnie. She knew we were friends. then Marguerette spoke up too and they both said at the same time that she had passed away. It took my breath away. My heart aches for her family and I'm going to miss her like crazy. We had become quite close since Mike died.

Then I worried my table companions because I didn't eat my dinner. But, I tried to reassure them, when something bad happens my stomach just forms a knot and I can't eat until I get my emotions under control.

I'm grateful for Bonnie's sake that she wasn't ill for a long time and she is happy now to be with Mike again, but it hurts, and I keep thinking of her family especially at this time of year, that includes you too Honey. Life . . . we never know what going to hit us next. love you dear . . .

Grandma Vivian

2009

January 10, 2009

Dear Rosly and Family,

Another holiday season over with and the beginning of another New Year, 2009. Let's hope and pray it will start a turnaround of all the bad things that are happening in our world today. Our new president has a huge job to do, and we all hope he is going to make a difference. It seems like the whole country is getting ready for his inauguration, January 20, and looking forward with hope to Obama taking over. It's been a long time since we have had hope. Politics and politicians can be so downright dirty sometimes. It's hard to know what to believe.

I always appreciate your Christmas letter, and I also am enjoying using that beautiful engagement calendar book that you sent me. Rosly, you always send me the most thoughtful and lovely gifts—hankies, scarves, shawls, and they are different from what we can buy here in the States. I can never think of anything that you might like that would be different for you. That's why I sent you a packet of my watercolor cards, knowing that they would be unusual for you. It's amazing to me that you have around fifty now and have kept them all. That is quite an honor for me. Wish you would give me some ideas of what you might like. I really think that USA merchandise is sold all over the world, but I could be wrong.

Our snow and cold weather started early for us this season. We have had a lot of snow before the holidays, and that is a little unusual. I'm hoping it doesn't foretell that we are going to have a long and snowy winter season. I am still driving short distances, but I find I am unable to clean the snow off my car when there is any amount on it. So I have to stay in, which really is no problem. We have a little Village store that carries all the necessary groceries—milk, breads, eggs, canned fruits and vegetables, all kinds of snack foods, ice creams, etc. Of course, we do get our one meal a day here too, which is included in our monthly fee. I do not do a lot of cooking anymore. Most of the people in the independent living apartments (I am one of them) go to the dining rooms in the early evenings for their dinner. We go not only for the meal but for a nice social hour also. In the assisted living section and the nursing care section, they are given three meals a day. I am very grateful that I am still able to take care of myself, even if it does take me longer to do things. I can understand that with your dizziness you are glad to have

Rosemarie close to you. Our daughters have become our friends as we age and are a very important part of our lives. Carol is the only daughter that I have close to me now. Alice is about a five-hour drive away, and Bill Jr. and family are out in Colorado, a long way away. I do talk to them often.

I am sure that it is a joy for you to see Berenice and Alexander often. I'm sure also that it gives you a great deal of satisfaction to be able to help them out. I'm also glad to hear that they are both doing well. I certainly can appreciate Anneleis taking classes to help her get back into the job market as a medical secretary. There are so many older people today going back to school or taking special classes to get back in the job market. Our world has changed so much since we were young.

I received a lovely Christmas card from Anneleis and Udo. Tell them that I do appreciate their greetings.

I do have some family news that is nice. Charlotte who was married to Bill's brother Joseph is moving up to live in Henry Ford Village, where I am and so is Marguerette. Joseph died the year after Bill in 2001. They had a lovely home in Leesburg, Florida, which Charlotte kept up by herself. She finally decided that it was too much trouble for her, so she decided to move up here. Both her daughter and son live in this area. It took quite awhile for her house to sell with our economy, but it finally did. She closes on it on January 23. She will be moving up here right after the closing. Her daughter, Cathy Jo, picked out her apartment for her and is seeing to the fixing up of it. She is so excited that her mother is moving here. Cathy is a very nice young woman, and it will be nice to see her more too. So three sister-in-laws will be living in the same complex, but all in different buildings. It should be very interesting. We have always gotten along well together, but of course we have never been this close to one another. We are all independent people, and I know it will work out very well. Both Marguerette and I are hoping that Charlotte will be happy here as it is because of us that she is moving here.

Also in the line of family news, my grandson Kenny, Barbara and Ken's son, who lives in California now called me last Sunday to tell me that I was going to be a great-grandma again. That will make it number nine for me. This new little one will join her mama and daddy and Maeyana, who will be three in February. They are very happy about it and are expecting the new baby in July. My son-in-law Ken was out to California to spend the Christmas holidays with them. He is still having a very rough time with the loss of Barbara. I do believe that women are stronger and able to cope with things better than men or most men. It certainly is not easy though.

My grandson Erik, Carol's son, is very happy with his job in Chicago. His wife Eve is working part-time at an ear clinic, and she is happy there also. They both take the "El" or train to work. Chicago has much better commuter transportation than we have in this area. Here everyone has to drive to get to their jobs. The four of them were here for the Christmas holidays. It does help to have little children around at Christmastime.

We had another snowfall yesterday and got about another eight inches. So far, this is a very snowy winter. It's also supposed to go down to almost zero temperature for the next week. Brrrr . . . it's a good time to stay in. The ski resorts are happy with the snow and doing pretty good. I do have a dermatologist appointment tomorrow but have made arrangements to have our transportation here take me with the weather being so uncertain. Another nice thing about living here is that we do have transportation services for doctor appointments.

I hope Walter is doing better since his eye operation. That has to be very painful for his eyelashes to grow inside like they do. Hopefully the operation helped. I think that we all come from strong stock from our parents and ancestors as it seems that we keep going no matter what life throws at us. We do have to thank God for that.

Rosly, I do like your motto that you want to adopt. It is good advice. This is the way Roger translated it:

> How many wonderful hours has God now presented me, How many good years, how much love and how much help can I in little things see without waste where I alone stay. Then can one only be surprised over God and over the wonders that he does. Simply only surprises.

Thank you too for the good wishes and candle burning at Christmastime for me and my family. I am wishing the same good wishes to you and your family.

Vivian

January 2009

Dear Sage and Ché,

Grandma is so sorry you did not get your Christmas checks at Christmastime. Somehow they got lost in the mail. I've talked with both my post office here and also the Denver one. They have checked all over, but they can't find it. I had Christmas cards for everyone in it with a special check of your own for the two of you. I had put all five cards in a brown envelope so they would all get there at the same time. Ha! It didn't work. Anyway, I'm going to try again. I want you to have your Christmas money from Grandma.

Sage, I did look at Target and Kohl's for Hannah Montana clothing, but they were out of most everything and I wasn't sure of your size you wear now either. I thought it would be best if you picked out what you want anyway. Ché, I don't know your sizes on clothes either.

I'm so sorry I can't come to Denver to see all of you, but Grandma's body is just getting old and doesn't want to work like it used too. Hopefully, I can see everyone this summer when the family plans to get together for Scotty's fortieth birthday party. I hear all kinds of nice things about all of you from your uncle Bill, aunt Shannon, and Sydney. I am so happy that you are getting to know one another. I also heard that you are back in school, and Grandma is wondering how you like your new school. Sometime when you have time, maybe you can write me a short note and tell me. I love to hear from you.

Your aunt Ollie and aunt Carol are so excited to be going out there and to see everyone. I hear Simone and Sedona are darling and doing all kinds of neat things now. I'm asking everyone to take lots of pictures of all of you together so I can see how much everyone is growing.

I love you guys so much and hope when you finally do get your Christmas money you will have fun spending it. Also have fun with all the family there for the January twenty-fifth weekend. I bet Maeyana has changed and grown too. It will be fun to see her. Take care and stay healthy and lots and lots of *love* to all!

June 17, 2009

Dear Betty, Jim, and Myra,

I've really enjoyed being a member of The Sunday Entertainment Committee. The end of this season will make it officially eleven years. The time has come to hand in my resignation. I'm tired.

The residents here don't realize how lucky they are. *Congratulations* to you, Betty and Jim. Because of the *great* job the two of you are doing, the people here continue to have wonderful entertainment every other Sunday.

I was so afraid, after losing Bob Phelps so suddenly, that the committee was going to fall apart. Instead, because of the two of you, the committee is running beautifully! How Bob did all of it by himself, I'll never know. He let all of us be lazy. The two of you took over and assigned everyone a job, besides just showing up on Sunday programs and a few other things. It is a much more balanced committee now, although I know the two of you still do a lot more.

I've seen a lot of changes over these eleven years, here at the Village and in my own personal world. Losing my husband of fifty-eight years and two daughters to cancer sure flipped my world upside down. Staying active and busy has helped me survive, but again, the time has come for me to slow down. It's nice to know I'm leaving with the committee in such good hands. Myra, thank you for the love, support, and help you have given me over these years. Remember, way back you taught me how to use a mike?

Thanks for listening to me, and I'll see you at the Sunday programs as a paying resident. I will miss the camaraderie and jokes.

Sincerely,

Tuesday, June 30, 2009

Dear Hildegard and Roger,

Where does the time go? 2009 is half over. It doesn't seem possible. Hope you folks are doing OK and able to play golf and keep up with your summer activities. I do keep busy with classes here at the Village and my painting for which I am very grateful. It just takes me longer to do everything now which before I just did and took for granted. Age sure can slow you down, but I try to keep a good attitude and count my many blessings.

I usually hear from Rosly around Easter time but did not this year. I wondered if she was doing OK. I hope so, as I know she has had some health problems too. I'm sure this letter will answer that question. Please take your time translating as I will be here. My traveling days are over, and I really don't mind as I am very comfortable here. Bill Jr. and family will be coming for the last week of July, and I am really looking forward to seeing them. Sydney will be nine this coming October and is quite a grown-up young lady now. I do talk to them almost every weekend, which I enjoy. My family cares about me and I am truly grateful for that. I will be going over to my daughter Carol's for a small family get-together on July 4.

Roger, did you ever believe the automotive companies could be going through what they are going through? My son-in-law Ken who has been service manager for Audette Cadillac for thirty-four years is going to be out of a job as they are one of the dealers that are closing. He is sixty-one and says he is tired. Work has been very stressful the past couple of years, a lot different than it used to be. As of now, he does not plan on looking for any other job. I'm concerned about him though as he still has not moved on a lot from losing our Barbara. I feel he needs something to do with his time. Hopefully it will work out. I have to think positive.

I'm always glad to hear from Rosly as then I can check up on you folks too. Take care.

Tuesday, July 14, 2009

Dear Linda and Sandra,

Thanks for your letter, Sandra. I have been wondering about you girls and if you were finally back in your house. It sounds like you have had one thing after another go wrong and not very reliable people to help you. It's too bad there are so many crooked people out there in our world today. I certainly hope things will soon settle down for both of you. It has to be very stressful to live like that, and that does not help your health any. Stress can cause all kinds of things to go wrong in our bodies as I'm sure you know.

Not a lot of news from here. I keep busy, but I am getting slower and slower. Everything takes me twice as long to do, it seems. I'm just very grateful that I am able to take care of myself. I go to an arthritis exercise class two or three times a week, and I think it helps to keep me moving. The stenosis and arthritis in my back is very painful, so I can't walk very far at a time, but at least I can still walk. So I guess for being eighty-seven going on eight-eight, I'm doing pretty good. I'm still able to drive but don't go any long distances anymore.

Bill Jr., Shannon, and Sydney are coming for a week on July 24, and I am really looking forward to seeing them. Sydney is eight and a half now. She is growing so fast and a very smart little girl. She gets along well in school and loves to read, which makes me happy. Carol and families are doing fine. Corbin is here for the summer, so Cindy and Joe are happy too.

I have a new great-grandson, which makes it number nine for me. Wow! So Robert isn't the only one having new babies. Kenny and Gina out in California had little Kenjo on July 10. He weighed 8 lb. 15 oz., and Kenny said he didn't even look like a newborn because he was so big. Both Mother and baby are doing fine. Maeyana was three last February, and she is thrilled with her new brother. I'm waiting for pictures to see him. Kenny is Barbara and Ken's son in case you have forgotten.

Alice is still working for that same elderly couple and is doing OK. She sent me pictures of the garden she makes every year, and it is beautiful. The owners of the apartment complex she lives in let her put in whatever she wants across the back of their property, and I can see why. It really makes their property more beautiful. She calls it BoBo's Garden and says Barbara sprinkles it with angel dust, and that is why it grows so well. It is wonderful therapy for Alice, and I'm so happy that the apartment managers have let her do this. She has enlarged it again this year, and it is getting quite large, but she enjoys it and works in it every chance she gets. The apartment property backs up to the woods, so the garden has a good background. Alice has hauled rocks and logs and really created a lovely area with her colorful perennials and annuals. Her doctor's wife hired her to plant flower beds for their new home. It's the doctor's wife's parents that Alice takes care of. She sent me pictures of the flower beds, and they were lovely too. The doctor and his wife were very pleased. Their neighbors called them and commented about how beautiful they were. That made Alice feel good.

The weather has been pretty nice this last week, not too hot. I don't do well in real hot weather, so I like it when it doesn't go over eighty. I hope your air conditioner is working for you when it does get hot.

I have not had any raspberries lately but have had some very good peaches. I love all the fresh fruit we have in the summer. I try to eat lots of vegetables and fruit too. I know what you are saying about the large portions that restaurants give. I can't eat that much food at one setting. When we go out, I most always bring part of my meal home. Here at the Village, we can order small portions which is very good. The St. Clair Dining Room over on the other side of the complex (where Mona lived) is a buffet style, so you can take just what you want. That's good too.

I'm still painting some, but again I've slowed down, and like I said before, everything takes me longer. I did a lighthouse a short time ago, which came out quite nice. I'll send you a card that shows it. I like the sky. It seems like a happy picture.

Good luck with all your dentists and eye doctor's appointments. I hope your car will hold out for you. Take care.

Saturday, July 18, 2009

My dear Sage and Ché bear,

Grandma has to apologize to both of you for taking so long to "thank you" for that lovely bracelet you made for me. It is very nice, and I will treasure it always.

Sage, I also appreciate your note and flower picture you did for me. I want to thank you also for sending me a copy of the story you wrote. I really enjoyed reading about Jessica and the singing contest and was happy she was able to participate in the contest. It sounds like you know you have to study and work hard to get to do fun things. That's so important, honey, and it pleases me that you realize it. Aunt Carol told me how glad she was to see all of you and how much she loved you and being with all of you. She thought your mom, Krista, was doing a great job parenting all of you.

Sunday, July 19,

I just got back to my apartment a short time ago. Your papa picked me up about ten fifteen this morning, and we went to a lovely restaurant for Sunday brunch. We met your aunt Carol, Cindy, Joe, and Corbin there. It was on a golf course "Fox Hills" out near Plymouth. It was a beautiful setting and it was a beautiful day. Cindy and Joe had planned this as a kind of spur of the moment. Joe had said, "Why do we need a special occasion to get together? Why don't we just get together every once in a while?" Sounded good to all of us, so we went and really enjoyed the delicious food and being together. Your papa and I talked about your new cousin, Little "Kenjo." We are so happy for your uncle Kenny, aunt Gina, and Maeyana. I'm waiting for pictures to see what my new great-grandson looks like. Little Kenjo makes t nine great-grandchildren for me. I feel very lucky. I hear you two were staying with your daddy for a while. I hope you are having a very good summer vacation.

I'm getting excited as your uncle Bill, aunt Shannon, and Sydney will be coming to Michigan this next Thursday for a week. It will be so nice to see them again. It's too bad we all live so far apart, but that is the way most families have to live in today's world. People have to go where the jobs are.

We just have to be satisfied with letters and phone calls to one another most of the time.

Family Visit: Vacation, July 23 to August 1, 2009

What a *great* vacation it was this year! Everyone was well, and everything on everyone's agenda was pretty much accomplished.

It was so great to see them. Bill and Shannon looked great, and Sydney is growing so fast and turning into a beautiful young lady. She is a *joy!* Carol picked them up from the airport about 9:15 p.m. on Thursday, July 23. Of course, they made a stop at White Castle for Bill to have his Michigan sliders. I even ate one when they got here about 10:30 p.m. Carol stayed awhile, and we just talked and enjoyed being together. Carol left as she was going to Chicago on Friday morning with Cindy and Corbin. Joe was there as he had been teaching there all week. They all stayed with Erik and Eve and family. It was a mini family reunion for them, and they all had a good time too. They came home on Monday.

In the meantime, back at the ranch, we had kind of a lazy Friday morning, and Sydney slept in and caught up a little on the time change. At lunchtime, we went over to the new Coney Island Leo's Family Restaurant across the street from me that I had been wanting to try. It worked out well. Then we went on to Best Buy, and Bill helped me pick out a small TV for my dinette area. I found one backed by Best Buy, Dynex, for $159.00. We came back, and Bill installed it for me. What nice pictures, so clear, and many more channels! The other one was full of snow, and I could only get channels 4 and 7 since they had gone digital. It's so nice to have Bill here for anything that has to do with all this new technology. Plus, he likes to spend my money . . . or his inheritance.

Sydney and I tried out her new drawing books with the ink pads that I had here for her. It was fun drawing with her. I had bought a locket for Sydney for her birthday in October, but I asked Bill and Shannon about giving it to her now so it would be personal. They said "sure," so we had an early birthday gift giving. It was a Sterling silver necklace with three stars. One star had a diamond chip, and on the back it said, "You are my Shining Star." I also gave her an October little angel figurine that she had seen in our Village store when they were here for Steve's son to be baptized. She was pleased. Hopefully, she will enjoy the necklace more as she gets older and is into jewelry. Then I had to put my legs up and rest for a while as we were leaving for Birmingham about four o'clock.

Paul and Dawn Shiner's daughter Alexandria was Mrs. Potts in the musical Beauty and the Beast. Knowing Bill and family would be in town, they had asked them about going to see the play and their daughter. Friday was the last performance. I was invited to go along also. The four of us went to Max and Erma's for dinner before the play. It was very nice. It had been a lot of years since I had been at Max and Erma's. Then we went on to Seaholm High School for the play at 7:00 p.m. It was a delightful play, very professional, by Daydream Productions. Alli has a wonderful voice and was excellent as Mrs. Potts. Costumes were spectacular. We all enjoyed the play very much. It was nice for me to see Paul and Dawn again. It doesn't seem possible that they have a daughter starting college this Fall. It doesn't seem that many years ago Bill's friends were over at our house on Sandshores. They were all in school together—scouts, band, etc. It's so nice, I think, that they have all stayed good friends through the years and they always have several get-togethers when Bill and Shannon are in Michigan. Anyway, it was almost eleven when we got home. Needless to say, I was beat, but had thoroughly enjoyed every minute of the day and evening. I'm not used to being out in the evenings anymore. All of us called it bedtime after talking just a little while.

On Saturday, I was up about eight and tried to be very quiet so the others could sleep. I got ready for my 10:30 a.m. hair appointment. Bill and Shannon were up, taking showers, etc. when I left for my appointment. We were expecting Steve Williams and family to be there about lunchtime, and they were—Steve, Julie, Megan, Nicole, and new baby son, "Wylie." He was so cute and such a happy baby. I got some pictures with me holding him. I loved playing with him. They grow so fast, and Wylie will be crawling pretty soon. Then the holding times are over, as they have too many things to explore and do. If you are lucky, you get to hold them when they get tired or sleepy. It was nice to see all of them again, and of course, this was the first time that I had met Wylie. We decided to eat lunch down at Windows as that would be the easiest for all as they would be getting ready to go out to Milford for their annual reunion with Bill's Michigan friends. Joel and Melissa have a home right on a lake, so it makes a great spot for a get-together. Weather cooperated too, so children were in the water most of the day and a good time was had by all from the reports I got. I'll have to be honest too. I enjoyed the peace and quiet of the afternoon and evening. I love them so much, but this aging has a lot of drawbacks. I get tired just from confusion and out of my little routine. It makes me angry but no sense n fighting it. It just is, and I hear this from my friends, my age too. The family returned about 11:30 p.m., and everyone was soon in bed.

It's Sunday, July 26. I am looking forward to another day with my family. Alice was on her way up here to see Bill and family and me. She got here in time for all of us to go down for Sunday brunch in Great Lakes dining room. Alice looks good, and it was so nice to see her also. She brought different quilts she had made for baby blankets. They were all darlings and so cuddly and soft. She had made two for Wylie, Steve and Julie's little boy. I heard later that they really loved them.

Brunch worked out well, and we all got our tummies full again. In the afternoon, Sydney played the piano in the lobby of Great Lakes for Grandma and Aunt Alice, plus everyone in the lobby. She had quite a nice audience. She is doing very well. It's amazing to watch her fingers. She is so outgoing and seems to love to play for an audience. She just lights up with her beautiful smile when people clap and tell her how nice it was to hear her. We had a nice visit together, and Alice and Shannon went through some old picture albums and sorted out their own family pictures and took with them. We left about 5:30 p.m. to go to Kiernan's Steak House for dinner. Bill said that is a must when they come to Michigan. It is a lovely place and the food is excellent. I think we all had filets, which are my favorite on the menu, plus their baked potatoes which are so yummy and a nice fresh salad. Billy treated all of us, which was very nice. Back to my place and then there was more talking and enjoying one another's company. Alice had brought her dog "Sadie" with her, and she was so well behaved and very protective of Alice. When Alice made her bed for the night on the floor by the front door, she made Sadie's bed right in the corner by hers. Sadie did not move from that corner until Alice did. It was comical and also touching.

On Monday, everyone was moving rather slowly, but there was no hurry for anything and it was nice. Bill, Shannon, and Sydney got packed up and left about 11:00 a.m. to meet their friends on the Ausable River for two nights of camping. On Tuesday, they were renting canoes and kayaks and spending the day on the river. We had a little rain here, but they said the weather cooperated up North and they were dry. I also heard later what a good time they had with their friends—Mike, Maria Hess, and family and Steve, Julie Williams and girls (Wylie was home with Grandma and Grandpa). Shannon had never been camping before, and she enjoyed it. But Sydney told me she was glad to get home to my place with nice bathrooms.

Back to Monday. Alice and I got ready and went to Applebee's for a nice lunch, and then we spent quite a bit of time in JoAnn's. Alice was showing me all the different fleece material and the no pilling kind that she used for baby blankets. It was fun to look around at all those different things with her. We were both amazed at how large scrap booking has become. It was nice to have the time alone with Alice, and we talked and talked. We got back to my place a little after 3:00 p.m., and Alice packed up to make the trip home. She left about four o'clock. Needless to say, I was tired, *but* it was a good tiredness from being with my family. I did do a few loads of easy wash—towels, etc. Other than that I just read and took it easy. It was the same on Tuesday and Wednesday. Bill and family got stuck in a traffic tie-up on I-75, so they were a little later than planned on getting back here. Anyway, they got back about 6:30 p.m. safe and sound. All wanted showers before they even ate. They ordered Jet's Pizza. I had already eaten some, but I did eat a slice of Jet's. It was very good. It was a nice evening. We just talked, and I heard all about the camping trip, canoeing and kayaking. Everyone made their own Hobo dinners that they had learned in Boy Scout camping the first evening and all enjoyed. They were new experiences for Shannon and Sydney. The canoeing and river trip on Tuesday was fun for everyone. Sydney was telling me about being in a kayak by herself. Her daddy did say he had a rope on the kayak. (Thank goodness!).

Carol called us on Wednesday evening with some very happy news. She said she wanted us to know before Corbin could say something at the zoo. Cindy is eight and a half weeks *pregnant!* Cindy hadn't wanted to say anything quite this early, but because of all her doctor appointments and everything going on they had to tell Corbin as he wondered what was going on. Smart little kid! *But* the doctor said things are going fine. The measurements are right and the baby's heartbeat is strong. They are so excited and happy. I just hope and pray they can have a nice healthy baby and that Cindy will be OK too. Because Cindy is diabetic and a little older, they are checking her frequently. After losing so much money in trying to adopt from China, Vietnam, and then Guatemala over the last four or so years and the terrible disappointment when all the governments canceled the adoptions, they wanted a baby so badly they decided to try on their own, even though doctors had warned them it could be risky. We have to believe things will be all right! All of us are excited and happy for them. Cindy is ten and a half weeks now.

It's Thursday, July 30: A beautiful day, and the weather is cooperating with us. I'm so glad about that. I have wanted to go to the zoo for years, ever since they had built the polar bear exhibit with the water tunnel that you walk through. When I had mentioned going if they had time, Bill had said, "Sure we can do that." The Denver Zoo does not have a polar bear exhibit, so they wanted to see that also. We left here about 10:30 a.m., and Carol and Corbin met us there. In fact, we saw them in the parking garage as we were parking. I missed having my handicap permit. I got to see about replacing it. When we got through the main gates, Bill and Shannon went to get a wheelchair for me. I knew that was the only way I would be able to see the zoo. It's difficult to give up your independence, but was very grateful that my family wanted to take me. There was no way I could have walked all day like they did. The polar bears put on a show for us and swam around and over our heads a couple of times. I was fascinated! It's such a huge animal and so graceful in the water. We were very lucky, I understand, as the polar bears do not always come out and swim and show themselves to the people. We stayed quite awhile watching this one bear. I was also fascinated by the penguin exhibit, the way they waddled around and looked so important. They are so sleek in the water and swim so fast. Wow! It was feeding time, and I was amazed at how polite they were. It seemed like they took their turns coming up to the young lady who was feeding them fish. Those two exhibits were the two that I had wanted to see the most, so I was very happy and satisfied. We stopped at the Artie North Food Court and had some lunch. I had a hot dog, some had hamburgers, and Corbin had a nacho. The rest of the zoo was just gravy for me—monkeys, gorillas, rhinos, elegant giraffes, anteaters, groundhogs, camels. peacocks, tigers, and lions.

Bill got tickets and we went through the special touring dinosaur exhibit that has been there at our zoo since this summer. That was quite something to see too. Those animals were built life size. Their eyes, mouths, and bodies moved. They made noises and a couple of them spat at you. Corbin got spit on and thought "it was cool." It was something pretty special to see as the dinosaurs were set in forest and water settings and they really looked quite *real!* I think the adults enjoyed the exhibit almost as much as the children. We were back around 3:30 p.m. and resting awhile before dinner. Carol had gone back to her place with Corbin. She came back to my place after Corbin was picked up as Bill had invited her to go to dinner with us. We went to "Benihana" about 6:30 p.m. That is another restaurant that Bill likes to go to when they come to Michigan. It amazes me the way Sydney knows how to order from these nice restaurants, and she eats very well too. She told the waitress that she wanted a "Ramune" when the waitress was taking our drink orders. Sydney had to tell me what it was as I had no idea. It turns out it is a nostalgic Japanese children's drink in strawberry or lemon-lime, similar to a U.S. soda pop. Sydney also asked her dad if they were going to order "Edamame." Again she had to explain what it was to me. It turns out it is something like Sugar Snap Peas. They are served hot in two glasses, one filled with the peas and an empty one to put the pods in. It amazed me how fast Sydney ate them. They tasted like peas to me. They are an appetizer in Japan. They were a vegetable to me. Nice way to get your veggies. We all ordered fried rice and combinations of chicken, steak, and shrimp. It is fun to watch the show the chef puts on, and the vegetables really taste very good the way they are grilled. Bill and Shannon are both pros with the chopsticks. Carol and I stuck to our forks. We all enjoyed our dinners and left the restaurant very satisfied with good food and excellent company! Carol stayed for a while, and the four of them played a new game that Paul Shiner had got for Bill. I was just too tired. I enjoyed sitting in my La-Z-Boy with my legs elevated, listening to their talk, laughter and just watching them together. Sydney is so smart and growing up so fast. I love her laugh. Midnight got here too fast, and Carol took off for home to get some sleep before our day together the next day. We all called it night-night.

It was Friday, July 31, our last full day together. Boo-hoo . . . all nice things come to an end, and we just have to appreciate what we do have. It had been a wonderful vacation time together as everyone had been well and felt good. After the morning showers, we got ready for the 11:05 a.m. 3D showing of *Harry Potter and the Half Blood Prince* at the Henry Ford Imax Theater. Carol and Corbin were here at 10:30 a.m., and we all got in her van and took off for our Harry Potter adventure. It was the first time for me. I have not read any of the books or seen any of the movies, so I am way behind the times. I will say it was interesting and something to see. This modern technology is truly amazing! Sydney and Corbin really enjoyed it. It was a two and a half hour movie, so it was about 1:35 p.m. when we got out of the theater. Carol was having us all over to her place in the night for a spaghetti dinner, so she took Sydney and Corbin to Big Boy for lunch, and Bill and Shannon brought me home to elevate my legs and rest for a while. They wanted to go and see Scott at Bi-County Hospital on the East side. It's sad. I haven't said anything because it's heartbreaking and we all feel helpless. I'll try to make a long story short.

Scott has had HIV1 for quite awhile. They didn't tell me because they didn't want to add to my worries and heartache. As long as Scott took his medicine and took care of himself, he was doing OK. But because all of this, also being upset with Nick and not having enough money to pay his bills, Scott started drinking again, not eating or doing anything but watching TV, drinking, and smoking. How he got the money for liquor and cigarettes we don't know for sure. We do know he used food money for a lot of it. Anyway, Scott has Aids. He has lost his short-term memory. Tests show his brain has shrunk. He has also lost control of his bodily functions and doesn't realize when he has to go to the bathroom so is wearing diapers. From what Jim has told us, Scott will never be able to live by himself again. My first and eldest grandchild, forty-one years old, and really nothing to live for! It was another heartbreak for me. How many do I have to endure? I'm almost glad that Kathy is not here. She would be devastated. I can't tell you how much I admire Jim. He has been bending over backwards to try and help Scott in all kinds of ways. *And* I only know the half of it as I know they are trying to make it as easy as possible for me. Jim is working with Social Security and all kinds of government agencies to find out what is best for Scott. Jim and Hannah cannot take care of him. It would be a 24/7 job and not fair to either one of them. Jim took such excellent care of Kathy the six years that she was fighting ovarian cancer and now this with Scott. It sure makes you wonder about life. It isn't fair. As of right now, Scott is in a group home in Redford. Jim says he really likes the people who own the place and also the guy who is in charge and will be taking care of Scott. I do hope it will work out.

So that's the story, and it's hard even to write about it. That explains why Bill and Shannon wanted to go and see Scott. They invited me to go with them, but with the movie and then going to Carol's later, I knew I had to get some rest. I hate what age does to our bodies, but I try and make the best of it. I did go with Carol to see Scott on Sunday, August 2, the day after Bill and Shannon left for home. He looked better than I had thought he would be from what Billy had told me, but not our Scotty. Bill said his eyes looked kind of vacant and so depressed with nothing to live for. *And that's true!* Ever since Scott got involved with Nick, he lost all his good friends (and he had a lot of them), and he said he has no one to hang out with or talk to. For some reason we don't know of, Nick seemed to be able to walk all over Scott, and he didn't stand up for himself. Who knows? Both Bill and Shannon were shook up from their visit to see Scott.

Bill and Shannon got back to my place a little after five o'clock and told me about their visit. We left for Carol's shortly after. The weather was very nice, and we were able to sit outside on Carol's deck. Cindy and Joe were there, and Sydney and Corbin had been having a good time playing together. Everyone enjoyed Charlie and Scooby too. Ken got there just as we were getting ready to eat, so that worked out well too—good spaghetti, salad, and breads and brownies and ice cream for dessert. It was very nice. I love just sitting and listening when my family are together. I don't hear everything they say, another aging process, but it's still enjoyable. I treasure family times more and more. Jim and Hannah were supposed to come also, but Jim called later, and Carol put him on speaker phone (with his permission), and he tried to bring everyone up to date about Scott. They have been going to meet people and had so many phone conversations with government agencies. Jim says he is getting a whole new education. Plus, Hannah had an infection in her mouth and had not been able to eat except soft foods and liquids, and they had been going to the dentist often too. It never rains but it pours as that old saying goes.

We left about 10:00 p.m. to come back to my place. Bill and Shannon started packing everything so they wouldn't have too much to do on Saturday. Vacation time sure flies by, but to be honest, all time seems to go by fast. I'm very grateful that I never have time to be bored.

Last night I got to sleep with my Sydney. She swims like a fish in bed. Every now and then I feel a leg or arm or "Fluffy" (her stuffed doggy) moved around, even her head sometimes. I like it and I will miss it.

It was Saturday, August 1, and we were up and around. It was so nice that their flight was not until the middle of afternoon and we could all have lunch together (not getting up in the middle of the night for an early morning flight like they have had before). Carol came over about 10:30 a.m., and we set out to try a Mexican restaurant that I had heard was good. It was Mexican Fiesta on Ford Road and Telegraph. The parking lot was empty, and Shannon went and looked in the front doors, but saw no one. Just as she was getting back in car, a man came to the doorway and motioned for us to come in. Both Bill and Shannon said it was a good Mexican place. The ones we had been to before when they have been here they didn't think too much of them. Carol and I are not any judges of that type of food, so we just go with the flow. Billy had me get the Super Tostada, which was very good but twice the size I could eat, and they said that doesn't carry-out to well. Chips get all soggy, etc. I did enjoy it though. They had some mixed plates of some kind, and Sydney had a bean burrito. I forget what Carol had. Bill treated us all again. It was very nice. We came back to my place after Bill got the car vacuumed and washed. They also stopped at Target and picked up a case of water for me. We just sat and talked until they had to leave for the airport shortly after 2:00 p.m. I'm so proud of myself . . . no tears! I held them in until they left, wondering when I would see them again. *But* it was a *beautiful* time together with lots of nice memories of being able to share the sad things, while being together.

Tuesday, December 22, 2009: Early Morning

Dear Billie,

You have been on my mind so much lately. I know the holidays and in fact any special day—birthdays, anniversaries, Valentine's Day—are so very difficult when you have lost your partner of so many, many years. You look around, and everyone is so busy and seems happy. Christmas Carols are playing, and you wonder how they can be so carefree when pain and heartache is tearing you apart. I know how I feel, and the holidays and the others are still "bittersweet" for me. I love being with my family, and they all care a great deal about me. We are a close family, always have been and had so much fun and good times together. Now when we get together, our gatherings are smaller, and there are all those *empty* spots and it just hurts so much. Plus, you know that your children and grandchildren feel it too, even if it is not talked about at that time. They hurt too. It's not an easy road to travel. You can't help but wonder sometimes what God has planned for you and pray he will give you the strength to cope.

I admire you, Billie. You put a smile on your face when you join us and are trying so hard to not spoil other people's enjoyment of the moment. Then sometimes out of the blue something will just sock you in your very gut and you can't stop the tears. *And*, Billie, that's OK. It's sometimes healing, and all of your good friends understand because we have been through it and all we want to do is help you cope in any way we can. Billie, you and I have also lost children. No parent should have to endure that agony. It is not the right circle of life. The holes in your heart from their loss are indescribable, and it never heals. I'm sure when I mention something about my little granddaughter Sydney (aged nine) out in Denver it hits you about your Sidney. I'm sorry. Then we are getting older and age is not kind to our bodies, so we are fighting the pain of health problems too. Once in a while, you can't help but feel that life isn't fair. I know you love your family and they love you, but no one can take the place of your partner. It seems like your whole world just turns completely upside down and all the color and joy are gone. Life is not fun anymore when you can't share it with your partner, especially when you have been married all your life it seems, have grown together, and always had a partner to do things with. So before this turns into a book, I just want you to know how much I appreciate your friendship, getting to know you better, and your hiking over to the care center to see me. I love you, dear, and I look for your lights also and feel better when I see them on. You can call me anytime.

I know you said you would be with your family this Christmas. I'm thinking and wishing the best for all of you, Carla, Robert, and I'm sorry I've forgotten Robert's wife name. Will your grandsons be there? I hope so. The more around you who love you helps. Families are so scattered in today's world. I know mine is, with my son and family in the Denver area, my daughter Alice in the Cincinnati area. She is the one who lost her identical twin when we lost our Barb in 2005. She sold her home in Ohio and moved up here to care for her twin the last two years of Barb's life. Barb's husband Ken is service manager at Audette Cadillac and works long hours. We all appreciated the care she gave her twin. There is a closeness there that is really indescribable, and she has had a very rough time. Again after being a waitress all her life, she is in the health care business and taking care of her doctor's wife's parents, trying to rebuild her life with her daughter and husband Steve nearby. She also has a son working out in Las Vegas. She was married very young and divorced after ten years. It's another story. We talk nearly every day on the phone. She has her own apartment and has landscaped the back area of the complex for free because she enjoys beauty and flowers and gardening so much. It's therapy for her. Management is happy as it is *beautiful.* I have pictures I'll show you some day. Thank goodness for our eldest daughter, who is my friend as well as my daughter and my "rock." She lives in Livonia. My two son-in-laws who lost their wives (my Kathy and Barbara) are still *my sons!* They are so good to me, and I know I can call either of them at any time and they would do their best to help me. Barbara's husband Ken lives in Royal Oak, and he is picking me up on Christmas morning and taking me out to Milford to my other "son" Jim for Christmas. Jim did marry again because he could not stand to be alone, with my blessing. He is too young to spend the rest of his life by himself. I wish Ken would too, but that's another story. Jim took such wonderful care of our daughter, He did things for her that most men cannot handle. He is almost a saint to me for that.

Carol will be there. Sadly, she was widowed ten years ago. Her husband had diabetes and a stroke and didn't make it at fifty-five. Carol has made a life for herself. She's been an elementary school teacher and one that the kids always love. She makes them mind, but they also learn and have fun doing it. I'm very proud of her. She has a married son who has two children, Maddy aged three and Will eighteen months. They will be there too, and so will be her married daughter Cindy, who is pregnant but at high risk. That's another long story for another day. Her husband Joe will be there, as also Scott, Kathy and Jim's grown-up son. So it will be a nice gathering. After being in "Outer Space" for three weeks, I am looking forward to seeing my family. Plus I know I will have lots of phone calls from my grandchildren all over the country.

And of course I will receive call from my family in Denver. I feel blessed with the love I receive, but again nothing can take the place of your best friend and partner. Hang in there, kiddo. We live in a wonderful place, and God must have some work he wants us to do yet. After coming out of that operation and still having my mental capabilities, I feel humbled, grateful, and want to pay forward.

Love you, Billie, and I hope I have helped in some small way. My love, prayers, and best wishes to all your family. God bless.

P.S. I just write from my heart, and I never quite know what I'm going to say until it's on the paper.

From: Kelly Moran (kelly.moran@erickson.com)
To: Vivian Beeler
Date: Tue, December 29, 2009, 10:22:01 AM
Subject: RE: The Greatest Chrustmas Gift of all!

Vivian,

I am still getting caught up on email and just read this! I am so relieved and pleased that you are HOME and doing ok! I will continue to pray though . . . rehab and therapy can be a pain! Cindy sounds like she is doing well and that is so wonderful to hear! I can't wait to hear about her shower! What a lucky woman to have a grandma like you!

Do you need anything? Want anything? Is there anything that I can do to help! Stay tough! I think your purpose is to offer love to so many . . . during these tough times we need to be reminded of what is important and YOU are a shining example of what is important!

Love you!

From: Vivian Beeler [mailto:veebee248@sbcglobal.net]
Sent: Monday, December 21, 2009, 12:20 PM

To: Kelly Moran
Subject: The Greatest Chrustmas Gift of all!

I'm HOME And loving every minute! I'm so humbled, grateful and blessed with coming through that torture at 88 and waking up with my mental facilities still intact! God did not want me yet evidently, so It must mean I have some work to do. Painting? Helping and being an inspiration to other people having a terrible time? Whatever? I want to pay it forward! I will get through the pain of therapy by gritting my teeth and letting the tears roll. I'm the only one who can do it! I'm a STUBBORN OLD LADY and

I will do it! Kelly my dear, I can't even begin to Thank You and Pat for your help in getting me home. I've been so worried about Carol recouperating herself from that arthoscopic knee surgery and running after me and trying to help her son with his children when he goes to Chicago Tuesdays and Wednesdays to finish his term at the college there. He is working on his Master's Degree and will continue up here, His wife Eve is working full time to support the family and Erik is Mr. Mom since his job in Chicago fell through. Of course we are all DELIGHTED to have them back. They have a lovely home in South Lyons and had rented it for the year they were in Chicago. They are using my car while I'm not able to drive, they had cut down to one car in Chicago because of the El. I'm so glad I could help them.

Cindy had to quit her job with being pregnant as she is HI Risk with diabetes, plebitis [sp] and a few other problems After 3 adoption fiascos and thousands of dollars lost, she wants a baby so very badly. Keep her in your prayers. So far the baby is Heathy and normal and already weighs 3 and one half lbs. at just over 6 months. Carol and I are very worried about her but of course don't let her know. she has good Drs. and they are watching her carefully. Carol and I are having a Family shower for her Jan. 10th in the private dinning room here at Great Lakes. Looking forward to it. Again, I love you so much along with Eileen and you have helped me more than you know. I also had a chance to get to know your Dad a little better over in RG. He stopped in my room several times and we talked abit. He added me to his prayer list. I can see where you girls get your golden hearts from.

Jennie over at RG is another person I got to know a little better. What a lovely person she is too. Kelly the Staff here at the Village has helped me so much, I love living here and getting to know and love everyone of you! It will be 12 years in January since Bill and I moved in. I have never been sorry a day. You can share this with anyone you care too because most of you know me anyway. OH, after a horrible time on my first Friday at RG. at 4 in the afternoon until 4:30 when I got help, the next day coming out of the dinning room I almost bumped into Peter Crane and his Father-in-law. Lovely man. He asked if they could walk with me and see my room as he was showing his Father-in-law the place. I said of course, when we got to my room he asked me if I would be completely honest with him and tell him how things were over there. I told him what had happened to me on

Friday afternoon, both he and his father were SHOCKED and said that should never ever happen. He would look into it. Then he thanked me for being so honest with him because he knew it was embarrassing for me to tell someone I barely knew this story. Perhaps you have already heard it. Anyway I felt like God had put him in my path that day. I think he is going to be a great director {Boss}. Sadly my Back problems are still with me and will be the rest of my life so it's killing me now, I've got so many stories to tell you more good than bad. I could write a book. I start Therapy at 2:30 this afternoon so will rest until then. I'll be wiped out the rest of the day but my good friend Dory Neiland has been an Angel to me and see about my mail and food. Love all you guys. God Bless,

Vivian

Hi folks,

Hope your holiday was nice. I had one of the *best* Christmases I have had since losing our Barb. Ken picked me up shortly after 10:00 a.m. It was *pouring* rain, He had brought me the groceries I had called and asked him if he would get a couple of days before. He did a great job and got everything I wanted. I had little gifts for the great-grandchildren and Cindy and Joe's little one. Boy, is Cindy getting big! It's all in front. From the back you can't really tell. She said it is getting very active and she has to pee a lot, plus hard to find comfort in sleeping, but she is so *happy.*

I think I told you I had made our traditional fruit Jell-O. So Ken made two trips down to the car before he came back for me. He also took that old walker out of my living room. I was happy about that, so I used my new Lincoln walker. Ken had got a Cadillac so it would be easier for me to get in and out of. It was my first ride in a car since my surgery. I loved it, even in the pouring rain! At least it wasn't *ice.* We missed our turn to Milford because of the foggy weather and rain. You really could not see the road and signs very well so we were the last ones to get to Jim and Hannah's. Carol had picked up Scott and brought him there too. It worked out well. I have to give Hannah credit. Their house was beautifully decorated, and the ham dinner with all kinds of side dishes was very good. It was very nice. It was fun to watch little Will eat. He's so serious about his food. He's like, "Don't bother me. I'm concentrating on getting this food in my mouth as fast as I can." He uses his fingers a lot but feeds himself very well. Maddy had made me a pretty little bracelet from a jewelry craft kit she got at Christmas—little crystal beads and my three initials as charms hanging on it. It's a darling. She calls me Great-grandma, all one word. She's growing so fast. They are beautiful children. I'm feeling very lucky.

We played our little game after dinner. Erik and Eve took the children home for their naps as Will was getting cranky and needed his nap. Besides they were struggling right now moving back and Erik not working and going to school. They weren't able to play the game. It worked out for the best. In the game, they put all the presents in a pile in the middle of the floor, and everyone draws a number. We all buy a $25.00 gift. No more than that. Then No. 1 picks a gift and opens it. The next one can take from the pile or take No. 1s gift, and on and on that way. Not being able to get out shopping or asking anyone to get something for me, I put $25.00 cash inside a roll of toilet paper. That was the hit of the party. That gift got passed around and taken so many times I lost count. I think Joe ended up with it. They were all nice gifts—gift certificates to restaurants and Home Depot, nice chocolates, and nuts, etc. I got a $25.00 GC to Barnes and Noble. I was happy. Then we had dessert—pumpkin pie. chocolate cake, and my fruit Jell-O with of course real whipped cream.

Yummy! I was beat, and everyone was getting ready to leave. Ken stopped at a CVS on the home and got a few items for me that I needed from the Drup Store, and they were open. We got back to my place close to 5:00 p.m. Ken got me upstairs and brought all my goodies up and took off for home and Bouy. It was still pouring rain. I think we broke a record for the wettest Christmas since they started to keep records. I talked to Kenny and Alice and heard about your steaks. UPS bring me meat, I eat it . . . sorry . . . That really was funny but expensive for you.

I got your Christmas card today and I love it. Wow! Sydney is growing so fast she looks almost like a teenager already. Beautiful! Thanks. Carol and Ken are coming and having early dinner with me on New Year's Eve Day. They are having prime rib as one of the entrees, then duck and a salmon. It is always very festive and extra nice. The hours are eleven to two. Then the help gets to go home after clean up and do their own thing which is fine with me. I have been so tired. I just rested last evening and after my Saturday hair appointment got a few things at Windows and stayed up here the rest of the day. I talked with Carol, Alice, and my friend Dory, who has been so good to me and helped me so much I asked her to join us next Thursday too. I am going to call Charlotte and Marguerette, and if they are not busy, I will ask to join us too. I know Char will. The other one is debatable. I think I told you Susan stopped in to see me specially and brought me a beautifully wrapped present. When I opened it last night, it was a $75 GC from Barnes and Noble. Nice! I had given them a quite large Southwest picture last year and wouldn't let them pay anything. I know Jean was waiting. She said it was for my courage and my operation as she figured I would have enough flowers. I do have with all that Jim and Hannah sent me, as well as Ian and Andrew.

My back is killing me. I got to head for my chair. Love you guys so much and wish all of you the best always.

Mom and Grandma

2010

Memorial Day 2010
Part of my family. Carol-daughter, Ken-Son-in-law,
Grandchildren & Grear Grandkids

My 10 Great Grand Children

New Year's Day, January 1, 2010

Dear Hildegard and Roger,

Wishing you folks a healthy and happy 2010!

Hoping your Christmas holidays were all good ones. I had a beautiful Christmas after almost a month in outer space somewhere. At least it seemed like that. My knee surgery was a success the doctor told us. But I had some age-related complications and was kept in the hospital a full week instead of coming home on Friday as I had planned. Also when I was discharged from the hospital, I had to go over to the rehab section of our care center here at the Village and was there for a week and a half. Our plans we make don't always work out. I did finally get back to my apartment on Thursday, December 17. What a wonderful feeling! I was so grateful and humbled by my experiences. I felt that God did not want me yet, and my mind seemed to be intact, so that means I still have some work to do. Not exactly sure just what that is yet, but I will figure it out so I can "pay it forward."

My knee surgery was a lot harder than my hip seven years ago. Of course I am seven years older too. The therapy is very painful, learning to bend and use that knee again. *But* I'm a stubborn old lady, and I made up my mind I will do it! I want to walk right again. The pain that I had in my knee is gone. It is just the pain of the surgery, and that will get better with therapy and time. I'm grateful. I still have my back pain from stenosis and arthritis, but I will probably always have that so I just need to pace myself and learn to live with it. I have therapy three times a week. I did at the hospital and rehab center too. Every day I can feel a little improvement, and again I'm grateful. I had a lot of good care and met so many different doctors, nurses, and aides. Most of them were doing their very best to help me. I have a lot of thank-you notes to write, but that is something I want to do. They deserve some praise, and on the lower level, I want their supervisors to know how kind and good they were,

Enough about me. I received Rosly's Christmas letter when I was over in the care center. I'm just now starting to check my e-mail and use my computer again. I can only do a little at a time, but it seems good to be back. Glad you folks can still bowl and keep up with the activities you enjoy. Thank you for your card and nice compliments. I truly appreciate them.

Best wishes always.
Vivian

February 7, 2010

Dear Rosemarie and Family,

I was so sorry to hear about your mother's illness. We just never know from one day to the next what will happen to us. I feel badly that I haven't written to you sooner, but I have been battling some health problems myself. My knee operation took me a lot longer to recover than I had planned on. Being eighty-eight didn't help any. I had several smaller problems in my recuperation period and had to go over to our rehab care center for a while. Then when I did get back to my apartment I got a cellulite infection in my incision as well as Bronchitis. Needless to say, I did not bounce back like I had hoped to. Like I said, we just never know what life has in store for us. I am feeling some better now, but my back is causing me problems as I have arthritis and stenosis in it. I just have no energy to do much of anything.

My problems sound very minor compared to your mother's, and I am grateful for that. Our very cold and damp winter weather has not helped any either, but here it is—February already. Time has a way of flying by somehow. My daughter Carol has been coping with arthritis in her knees also and has had that arthroscopic surgery on her left knee, but it did not help her a lot, sad to say. We didn't pass on very good genes, I guess, as she has been bothered with arthritis in her hands and body for a long time. She did have both her thumb joints operated on several years ago, and it did help her some, which was very good. She loves taking care of her grandchildren aged four and twenty months. Her daughter Cindy is due to have a baby on March 6, but it is High-risk pregnancy so they may take the baby a little early. We are all hoping for the best. Cindy and her husband Joe want this baby very badly.

I am very glad that I live where I do. It doesn't seem possible that I have been here twelve years this month. I have a lot of friends here both residents and staff and it helps a great deal. They take very good care of us here. Of course, I am still able to be in the independent living section, Thank goodness.

I really don't have very much to write about as I have not been doing a lot of my normal activities. I hope this finds all of you well and your mother doing the best she can. I do hope she is not in a lot of pain. Give her my love and best wishes and let her know she is in my prayers every day.

Your USA cousin, Vivian

Summer 2011: Looking back over this journal or book, before I send it to the printers to be put together, I realized I had not written anything during the year of 2010. I can't just skip a year, especially when some good things happened, along with all my doctor appointments and my body warranties wearing out.

Thank goodness I had jotted a lot of notes on my calendar and engagement calendar book, so using those and my memory, I'll tell you about my life in 2010. As you already know, I was recovering from my left knee operation and going to therapy three times a week all through January. Therapy did help, and my knee was doing quite well. I was pleased because those therapy sessions were not pleasant. They hurt! It's the only way to get walking again, and I was determined to do that. I did have my first bout with cellulite infection around the incision and was put on antibiotics.

On March 3, 2010, Evan Joseph Rivet was born, weighing in at 8 lb. 1 oz. Corbin is now a big brother. Cindy ended up having to have a caesarean operation. Mother and baby are doing well. I'm very grateful. Carol took me to the hospital to meet Evan, my tenth great-grandchild. What a sweetie! Our family is blessed to have beautiful babies. They are such little miracles and such a joy to hold when they are brand new to this world of ours.

On March 26, the Village had their Bunny Breakfast with the Easter Bunny and the egg hunt afterwards. I was lucky this year as Erik, Eve, Madilyn, and Will were able to come along with Grandma Carol and Aunt Alice. Alice had come up on Friday to see me as we had not seen one another all winter. I had a lovely two days with Alice on Friday and Friday evening and then the grandchildren and both Carol and Alice on Saturday.

On Friday, Alice took me to JoAnn's Craft Store. It had been quite awhile since I had been in a JoAnn's or Michaels's, so I really enjoyed it. We also got a few things at Meijer's, and by then I was worn out, so I went back home to rest. We went out and had a nice dinner together, but I truly can't remember where we went, and it really does not matter. The main thing is that we enjoyed being together and talked, talked, talked. Maddy and Will were so good at the Bunny Breakfast, and they ate quite well. In fact, we all enjoyed the food. Dining service does a very nice job to make things look extra special and good for the Easter Bunny Breakfast. It was so much fun to watch the children when they saw the big Easter Bunny. He was going around to every table, and his helper had a basket full of candies for the children to pick from. Maddy was much more interested in hugging the Easter Bunny than the candy right then. Erik and Eve got pictures. Will was a little bit shy. He didn't quite know how to deal with that big white rabbit. He was content just to watch his sister and the other children. He wasn't quite two years old yet. After the breakfast, we went back over to the Great Lakes dining room, and the staff had divided the room up in sections according to age groups. They used the cards room for the babies, up to two years of age. It was amazing how fast the little ones caught on to finding the plastic eggs filled with candy and little prizes. Grandma Carol and Eve were helping Will find his, and Aunt Alice was helping Maddy so they both ended up well supplied. Alice told me later how much fun she had because she is not around little ones that often. I'm glad she was there to participate. On our way over to Great Lakes, Maddy and Will were sitting on my walker, and I pushed as it rolled easily. They got our picture coming down the hallway on the TV camera Tom Radke was operating. They ran the tape later on channel 11, which is our in-house TV channel. I got a copy for Erik and Eve to have as it was cute and showed a lot of different things. After it was over, we came back to my apartment for a little while, but by that time, the children were pretty tired so it was time to go home with their candy and prizes. Maybe Evan can join them in a year or two, but he isn't even a month old yet. Cindy and Joe did bring Corbin several years ago when he was four or five. Corbin was so shy that he didn't get much candy. That was the year that Ian and Andrew came too, and they shared all their candy with Corbin, The nice thing about that was that no one had told them to or even suggested it. That was a fun day for all of us.

April was not a good month for me. On the ninth, my upper side front tooth just broke off at the gum line. It really left a big hole and hurt my vanity! I saw Dr. Watson, and he said I had to go to the oral surgeon and have the root removed before he could make a tooth for me. On April 23, I had an appointment with Dr. Miller, and he removed the root with no problems. I was very grateful. I've had enough pain lately. I did have quite a few dental appointments and Dr. Watson did make an artificial false tooth to cover that big hole. It made me feel better about smiling, etc. Eventually I did get a permanent tooth and was pleased. Of course, all of this cost money, $2,000 plus $200 for root removal. Dental work is not cheap.

On April 21, I broke my second toe on the left foot. I came around the comer barefooted and rammed it into the leg of my kitchen stool. I was in pain, pain, pain and so mad at myself for my carelessness. I checked with Dr. Kompus our podiatrist here at the Village, and he sent me for an X-ray. Of course, it was broken. Dr. Kompus taped my second and third toe together and gave me a flat boot to wear. I've had so much fun this month. Ha!

Mother's Day on May 9 was a very quiet day as the family had decided to go to Fox Hills Golf Course for their lovely buffet brunch, but not until May 16. The Brunch is just as lovely, but it is not nearly as crowded and also a little cheaper. It worked out very well, and everyone enjoyed being together and the lovely food.

On May 20 was our Annual Expo here at the Village. That is where all the different groups have displays of what they do and what is available to all the residents. We have about 125 different activities going on here, from Bingo and Bunko to woodworking and watercolor painting and everything in between. If you want to stay in your apartment and become a couch potato, that's your choice. Most people get out and into some group that appeals to them, meet people, and make friends. We have a monthly activity planner that tells you when all the different classes or groups are meeting. It's amazing to see every year the colorful displays that people come up with and it's interesting to walk around and see what all is available. It's your own fault if you complain about boredom. There is always volunteer work if that is what you would like to do too.

It's a big job getting my watercolor class display put together and set up but worth it I think for the nice comments we receive. The painting tables with oil and pastel seem to be the most colorful ones along with the watercolor one. The Village furnishes a refreshment table: cheese and crackers, assorted fresh fruit, tea breads, lemonade, plus a lot of door prizes They have Great Lakes dining room decorated so nicely with balloons and colorful signs. When it is over at 12:30 p.m., I am beat. Someone usually helps me pack up to get home. Then I just let things set until I rest for a while. This year with the expo being on the twentieth, Erik and Eve were celebrating Will's second birthday with a little family party at Carol's. Susan picked me up and gave me a ride over to Carol's, which was doggone nice of her. It saved someone in my family from making a trip over to get me. She is so thoughtful and caring. It was a very busy day but enjoyable.

On May 18, I started a new "memory" class that the Village offered. It was led by Matthew Hawn, Kelly Moran, and Jerry K. It was held twice a week for eight weeks in classroom 2. I found it very interesting. We did have quite a bit of reading homework. In class, we did quite a few little memory puzzles and games: word lists were given and we were asked to make a story connecting the words, and that made it easier to remember them. Connecting a person's face and name together in some way made it easier to remember. We learned lots of little tricks to try and help our memory. There were no marks given for the class, and no one was embarrassed if something was hard for you to do. You could find something else that you had no trouble with. Everyone's brain works differently. Most of the people attending thought it was a worthwhile class to take.

On May 27, Kenny, Gina, Maeyana, Kenjo, Krista, Larry, Sage, Ché, Simone, Sedona, and Briana (Larry's daughter) flew in from California and Colorado. They had been planning this for several months. Both Ken and I had been eagerly waiting to see them. I wanted to meet my great-grandchildren whom I had never met and also to see their parents and Sage and Ché again. I had heard a lot of good things about Larry and his daughter Briana, so I was anxious to meet them too. They had been planning a family get-together for Saturday, May 29. Everyone was meeting at Ken's around lunchtime. The weather was perfect for that time of year, in the mid-seventies and bright sunshine all day. Carol picked me up about 11:30 a.m. and we got there around noon. Erik, Eve, Maddy, and Will were already there. Cindy, Joe, and Evan arrived shortly thereafter. I got lots of *hugs* from both my grandchildren and great-grandchildren, which I loved! The children were not a bit shy. They had all seen my picture, and their parents had told them about me, which was great. It was a wonderful family day, and I enjoyed every minute of it. There were lots of food as usual—pizza, salad, fresh fruit, cookies. It was very good. Gina took lots of pictures, and after their vacation, she made a book for all of us to have a copy of. It is fantastic! That was a lovely bonus surprise. I just sat and watched the children play, and it got warm enough that they ran through the hose. Even little Will and Kenjo had a pail of water to play with. Will kept trying to sit in his. It was funny. Kenjo is not quite walking yet, almost though, and he has his own way of getting around. He won't be a year old until July. Little Evan is not quite three months, so he didn't have a pail of water. Carol had brought a bunch of outdoor toys for the children—bubbles, sidewalk chalk, paddle balls, coloring books and crayons, and play dough. The children were very pleased with all their goodies. I forgot to mention that with all the commotion and activity Bouy took it all in stride and was excellent with all the little ones. Carol and I were the last ones to leave about 6:00 p.m. I think I was beat by that time but loved every minute of it. Cindy and Joe had left earlier as Joe had to study. Erik and Eve stayed longer, but they too had plans for the evening. I'm so grateful that the cousins could be together at least for a little while. Kenny and Krista both told me that they would see me very soon when we left. I did not do anything that evening or even all day on Sunday. My body needed the rest, I think.

I got a call on Monday morning that they would all be down later that afternoon if it was OK with me. Of course, it was OK with me. I was delighted! The gang got there around 4:30 p.m. The kids got the toy box out, and Briana asked if she could draw at my art table and if I had paper she could use. Of course I did. She can draw very well; she likes to draw these modern girls' heads. They look good. Larry lived up to all the nice things I had heard about him. I really like him, and to see Krista so happy makes me feel really good inside. Ken and Kenny decided to get Boston Market dinners for everyone, so they took orders and went to pick them up. We have a Boston Market very close to the Village on Ford Road. The young people took care of seeing that all the little ones got what they wanted, and they waited on me too. There are not too many advantages of getting old, but I think this is one of them. I had not had a Boston Market dinner in several years, and it tasted very good to me. After everyone was finished eating, they cleaned things up and bundled up the trash and took it home with them so I would not have to worry about it. Oh, Barbara, I wish you could be here. Your children and grandchildren are so wonderful. You would just love them to pieces. Hopefully you know what's going on down here as you are always with us in our thoughts and hearts. It was another lovely day.

On Tuesday and Wednesday, Ken and all the kids went out to the cottage. I heard from everyone they had a wonderful time. The weather had cooperated and stayed warm for this time of year. They were planning on coming back here for the day on Friday. Alice was coming up to see them also. On Thursday, I got a little ambitious and took the bus to the Dearborn Farm Market and bought ground beef and stuff to make spaghetti sauce, also things to make a salad and garlic bread, plus grapes, ice cream, and cookies for dessert. On Thursday evening, I made a big pot of spaghetti sauce. I had not forgotten how, thank goodness. I had always cooked and served good dinners all of my adult life, and I wanted to do something for this visit to help out. I don't like this feeling of not being able to pitch in and help. So making something so simple as spaghetti sauce made me feel better.

On Friday, June 4, Alice got up here about 11:00 a.m. and the gang about 11:30 a.m. What an absolutely beautiful day! We were together, and the weather was sunny and warm. It was nice to see Alice with the children. She is Grandma Ollie to all of them. They are all so outgoing and loveable. We went down to Windows for lunch, and that worked out well. All the children are good eaters. Quite a few of my friends stopped by to say hello and meet my family. Jenny, one of the Windows staff, made little bracelets for all the little ones. All of the staff here are so nice and will go out of their way to do something nice for the residents. After lunch was over, we decided to go outside so the children could run around and play ball or whatever. Gina had her camera again and took a lot of different pictures. One set was of the children lying on the ground and shaking their heads so their hair was flying all over. They came out very nice and unusual. She got one of "Papa" Ken with Simone sitting on his shoulders, peeking through the leaves on one of the trees. She is a darling. She does get some unusual shots that are not posed in any way. Little Kenjo was being pushed in his stroller, and they were hoping he would take a little nap. He did not get too much sleep, but he did get a little rest.

Briana had stayed upstairs to draw and had drawn several different girls' heads when we got back. She is good at them. Everyone wanted to go swimming when we came back upstairs, which we had planned on. Everyone changed into swimsuits, and away we went to the pool. Friday afternoon we had the pool to ourselves, which was nice as there were eleven who went swimming. Ken and I were the only ones who didn't. We were content to just watch. Children and grown-ups had a ball playing together. There is no shallow end. I think it is all of four feet as it was made for an exercise pool for adults. All the little ones had to wait their turn with an adult to hold them. Sage and Ché could manage by themselves and of course Briana too. After about an hour and a half of pool time, we went back upstairs to change into dry clothes. Then Alice, Krista, and Larry got the dinner put together. They made salad, fixed bread, cooked spaghetti, etc. They fed all the little ones first and then the grown-ups ate. We had fruit, cookies, and ice cream for dessert. Everyone said it was good, which in turn made me feel good too. They stayed for a short time after dinner, but everyone was getting tired so it was time to head for Royal Oak and beds.

It was such a beautiful day with a lot of nice memories. I did get time here and there to talk with Krista, Annie, and Kenny. I feel very special that all of them spent three different days with me when they only had a week. It is difficult to say good-bye when you don't know when you might see them again. It is so doggone expensive for families to fly. I'm very grateful that they stay in touch with phone calls and e-mails; that helps.

Fall 2010

During the summer, Dr. Reeder had sent me to see a neurologist, Dr. Daniel Singer. He was a nice young doctor, and I remember him so well because I was taking that memory class, which I had also mentioned to him during our conversation. One of the exercises that we were to practice that week was that when we met a new person, in order to remember their name, we had to take a mental picture of them with a little camera we have in our brain in our head and repeat their name back when we were introduced. I mentioned this exercise to Dr. Singer, and he put a silly look on his face and said to me, "Do I have to take my shirt off?"

I laughed and said, "No."

He did another crazy pose and said "Will this do for your picture?" I laughed again and said that would be just great and pretended to take a picture. Also we were to try and think of a song with their name so we wouldn't forget it. I came up with the song "Danny Boy" with Daniel Singer. I have only seen Dr. Singer once, but I have not forgotten him. I think it was because you don't usually expect a doctor to act silly for you. Anyway, back to business, Dr. Singer did recommend that I go to see the doctors at the Dearborn Management Pain Clinic and see if they could help me.

I did start going to them in June and went through a series of epidural shots in my back similar to what I had had at the Heritage Pain Clinic several years ago. I also went through some testing shots for a neuron-stimulation device, which made me feel worse. All of these took time of course, and I went to the pain clinic quite often during the summer and fall of 2011. I was getting discouraged as nothing seemed to be helping with the pain that never let up. Then I was had Carol to take me and used a lot of her time. I felt badly as she was busy with Corbin; in fact, he went with us a couple of times. To top it all off, I had another bout of cellulites, and Dr. Marinescu sent me to Oakwood Hospital on October 26, 2010. I got good care, but with my back pain, I did not get much of any kind of sleep. They did let me come home on Friday afternoon the twenty-ninth. I was there for four days but four days too long. They warned me that I might have recurring bouts with that. Aging and poor circulation has a lot to do with it. That was something else to keep an eye out for. Ken had come down to see me when I got the news I could go home, so I called Carol, and Ken helped me get home and had the things I needed. He is very good to me too. I am so very grateful for my family.

Thanksgiving was out at Jim and Hannah's this year, but we didn't get together until Saturday for our Thanksgiving. We waited so Erik, Eve, and family could be with us. Hannah did a great job on the dinner, and the table looked so festive and pretty all decorated for Thanksgiving and fall. It was nice of them to change their plans to still have it.

I also had decided to give the little ones their Christmas presents from me. They get so much at Christmastime, I thought why not split it up a little as my gift had nothing to do with Santa Claus. I had got those stuffed animal night lights for them. Will and Evan got a turtle and Maddy got a ladybug. They seemed very happy with them. In the dark in their rooms at night, they show the constellations of the stars on the ceiling.

I had taken my bowl of fruit Jell-O and came home with turkey and rolls for a couple of very good sandwiches.

It seems like I have been working on Christmas cards all year as I had the poinsettia design done the first of the year and had it printed early. Of course, then it's a matter of cutting the prints out and gluing them on my blank cards. I do a bit at a time and then have to rest my back. Frustrating! I'm on so much pain meds too that I think it is making me lazy. Somehow I'll get them done. I always seem too, and I complain about the work every year. A part of that is my own doing as I started sending to my friends on the staff and then couldn't ignore the rest of staff even if I didn't have a close association with them. Every year my list kept getting longer and longer, plus every year I seemed to make a few more friends. I really don't like to say how many I send out, but I know everyone is curious. I sent out 211 this year. I did two designs, one of a poinsettia and one of a mother polar bear and two cubs. I sent out mostly poinsettias while I sent polar bears to the children.

On Christmas Day, some of the family came to the Village for their holiday buffet, which is always lovely. Again because Erik and Eve wanted their children to have Santa Claus come to their own place, Carol was having Christmas dinner at her place on Sunday the twenty-sixth. Jim, Hannah, Scott, and Carol were here, and it worked out just fine. Everyone enjoyed the food, and we just sat around and talked for a while. Cindy and Joe had decided to let Corbin stay home too and play with all his new Christmas toys. Ken was out in Colorado with Krista and family, Bill, Shannon, and Sydney. Things change with the years and people get separated by distance, and we have to accept the changes or be very unhappy. I try to adjust to whatever is going to be and enjoy the family I am with. I get a lot of phone calls too from people who can't be there, which is always nice. Jim and Hannah had made plans for that Sunday after Christmas, so they said they would not be there at Carol's.

Carol had a nice dinner, and it was nice to be with the young people and watch the children play. Corbin is very good with all the little ones, and they just love him.

This brings us up to the end of another year. Each one seems to go faster than the one before it. I'll leave you with this thought by Abraham Lincoln: "The best thing about the future is that it comes only one day at a time."

November 1, 2010

Dear Dr. Mitchell Sheer and wife,

I can't thank you enough for the good care you gave me while I was in the hospital. I so appreciate you treating me as a person and someone with mental capabilities still fairly intact. You have a *great* bedside manner! As I told you in the hospital, you are going to be a wonderful doctor. I wanted your wife to know this too. I have two grandsons about your age who are happily married, and they each have two little ones now. They are working so hard on their schooling and doing well—one is teaching in Chicago and one in Sausalito, using heavy machinery and in environmental work. I am so grateful as they both think I am a "cool grandma" and they keep in touch with me. There is a lot of love in our family, and my family cares about me. I am *lucky!* You remind me of them in certain ways, and I mean that as a compliment.

Over the years I have run into doctors who just treat you as another number or problem and really don't take time to explain things to you as they think you wouldn't understand anyway. None of your team gave me that impression. I felt that I was in very good hands with all of you.

It is so wonderful to be home and in my own comfortable La-Z-Boy that fits my body. I pile three pillows under my legs and also have the La-Z-Boy tilted back. My legs are starting to look like my normal legs and I have ankles again. I am also getting some *sleep*. I think I had about three hours there in the hospital with this sciatica problem. I am going to have to go and talk to the back surgeon about that. That old saying is sure true that "old age is not for sissies." All the warranties are running out. Death does not frighten me; the process of dying does.

All of my friends are so happy to have me back here too. There certainly is "no place like home." I meant what I said in the hospital that if you would like to bring your wife and see Henry Ford Village, I would be more than happy to show you around. We have quite a place here with seven buildings all connected by hallways, our own medical center, bank, Village store, chapel, plus, independent living, where I am, assisted living, and our rehab and care center. We have PT and OP departments too. All in all, we are pretty self-contained. We have over 125 groups and activities, so you can certainly find something you like to do among all of those. I will be here thirteen years in January. I had two good years with my husband of fifty-eight years before I lost him in a year to cancer of the bile duct, and I told you I had lost two beautiful daughters to ovarian cancer and inflammatory breast cancer. Sometimes life is not kind. This is a wonderful place to live though in times like that. The staff here are so wonderful, and I have made a lot of personal friends with a lot of them, plus the resident friends you make. I taught a little watercolor class, and hopefully I can get my back straightened around and open it up again. I call myself a "hobby artist." I have not had art training. I took it up as something to do at adult education in Troy in my late sixties. I found out I had a bit of talent and just loved it. I use patterns and anything I find helpful. I had two excellent teachers when I started out and got a lot of books and magazines that teach me too. *My* painting has been a lifesaver for me these past ten years; it has helped keep me sane. I'm sending two cards, one for you and your wife—she sounds so nice—and one for the team, OK?

Well, I have rattled on long enough, I think. I like to write, and when I start, I just write from my heart, and it just keeps coming. I got to go get my legs up again. I hope I haven't bored you too much. I wish both you and your wife the best of everything always and thank you again.

November 7, 2010

My dear Helen,

Ninety years old! What a blessing for our world. You are a very special lady! I remember when I first met you about twelve and a half years ago. Bill introduced us and told me that he played Euchre with you on Monday nights with Jean Wagner and Joe Schmidt. He really enjoyed his Monday night Euchre games. Don't you wonder sometimes where those years have gone? Then Jean, Evelyn, and I all lost our husbands within a short time of one another. You got us together and started our Tuesday night dinners together, which are still going on, with changes during those years.

I admire you so much, Helen, for all the good work you do for the Village and your friends. I feel privileged to be one of your friends. I am so very sorry that I missed your special birthday party. I have never received such a beautiful invitation. It was just *lovely!* I know your daughters put on a lovely party for you, and I missed out on a very special evening. I have been having a rough time getting rid of this cellulite infection, and I have no idea where it came from. I didn't know anything about it until I got it and then found out how serious it could be. It scared me. If the infection gets down into the bone, you can lose your leg. So, needless to say, I am following doctor's orders. They have been keeping very good track of me and the infection, and it does seem to be going away and I am very grateful. I'll see the doctor again on Monday. Then Tuesday I go to a back specialist to see if he can help me with this sciatica that I have. I hope so. I want to get back to doing my regular things. I am only about ten months behind you in age and have things I would like to do yet. But I am leaving it all in God's hands.

I enjoyed seeing you and your daughter, even if it was only for a couple of minutes, and that birthday cake was so yummy! Thank you for thinking of me, but that's like you. You are a very special friend, who I am so grateful God put in my life. I wish you the best always,

Vivian

Sunday, December 5, 2010

Hi, Kathy and Family,

Another year has rolled around. *Wow!* They go by so fast it seems. It doesn't seem possible that I have lived here for thirteen years in January. How did Carly and Kevin get so grown-up? That doesn't seem possible to me either. I hope things are going well with all of you and your business is surviving this terrible economy. It's time for a turnaround! I keep in touch with Jean Darovich, who lived next door to us, and she keeps me updated on Karen and family a bit. I hear Marie is pregnant and Karen and Kurt will be grandparents. They will love it. Maybe she has already had the baby. I'll have to ask Jean, or Karen will tell me on her Christmas card as we still exchange cards at Christmas.

This year has not been kind to me physically. I was recovering from my knee replacement and had a couple of dental problems that took a lot of appointments and money. Then my sciatic nerve kicked in, and I've been doctoring with that since last April. That's on top of my spine disintegrating from arthritis. I'm still going to the pain clinic for that. I think I'm going to become a regular druggie, and I don't care!

On the bright side, my family is doing well, and I have ten beautiful, normal healthy great-grandchildren now. They are scattered all over the country, but I hear from their parents and get pictures. I do get to see my newest one, Evan, He was born last March to Cindy and Joe, Cindy is Carol's daughter, and they live in Livonia. He is so cute. I saw a lot of them as Barbara's children Kenny and Krista came last spring to see me from California and Colorado. Krista has four and Kenny has two. That was a joy. We had such a good time together. They just came down here in three different days, which I thought was wonderful as they were only here for a week. One day we all went to the swimming pool, and the children and parents had a ball. I just watched. I had gotten ambitious to make a big pot of spaghetti sauce. So Alice and the girls took over, made a salad, cooked the spaghetti, and got dinner on the table. We ate in shifts to have enough room. They did all the cleaning up too. It worked out very nice. We had ice cream and cookies for dessert.

Bill Jr., Shannon, and Sydney were here for a little over a week in July, and that was another treat. We had a family party here on the last Sunday they were here, and Sydney gave us a piano recital on the grand piano in the chapel. She is doing very well and turned ten in October. It doesn't seem possible. She is a lovely young lady inside and out. I'm so proud of Bill and Shannon and their parenting. I saw Steve Williams and his family when Bill was here as they are still good buddies. Did you know that Steve and Julie had a little boy last Christmastime? Wylie is so cute—lots of dark hair, takes after Julie as Steve is still blond. I saw his daughters Megan and Nicole too, and they are getting very grown-up. Nice girls!

Those are the good times, and I am so grateful that I do have a family that cares about me. We will be having two Christmases this year. On Christmas Day, the family around here—Jim, Hannah, Scott, Carol, Cindy, Joe, Corbin, and Evan—will be here for the holiday dinner they have. Their holiday dinners are always a lovely buffet with lots of goodies. Then on Sunday, Carol is having us at her house as Erik, Eve, and children will be in from Chicago. Jim and Hannah will be involved with her family on that day. Again, I just find a comfortable chair and watch and do my share of eating, of course. My La-Z-Boy is a godsend. I elevate my legs with pillows after I tilt the chair back, and I am most comfortable that way. I even sleep in my chair as it's painful to lie in bed with this sciatica. Oh, I had a bout of cellulitis and ended up in the hospital for four days and was not happy. I don't want that again. You didn't say what your problems have been. You just said something like an involvement for a couple of weeks in November.

I think that brings you up to date on me and my family, maybe too much. Oh well, at eighty-nine I guess I can get away with most anything. *Ha*! I've been getting my hair done twice a week as my scalp gets itchy. They finally know how I like it. Give Kim my love and best wishes. I hope she is doing OK. Her daughter must be quite grown-up now too.

Take care and stay in touch. I love hearing about your family and you and Martin.

Love,
Vivian

2011

Dear Pat,

What a darling card! And how true! I do think about all of you often. It brings back nice memories of our get-togethers of the four cousins and our family get-togethers also, all with our super Aunt Fran. What a wonderful lady! I think she was a second mother to all of us. How things change over the years, and the older you get, you lose more and more of your loved ones. We have to learn to accept and roll with the changes or be very unhappy people. It's difficult, but everyone goes through it, and if you are a close and loving family like we have all been, it hurts.

I really appreciate you writing me back so soon with the info about your mother. I really did not know that she had Alzheimer's. Did that start before you lost your dad? I wasn't able to come to his funeral (health reasons), so I missed catching up on any information. I felt badly about it. Isn't it strange that both Jean and your mother are affected? It is such a sad disease for the person and for the family. Does your mother still know you? We have a special floor in our care center here for diseases like that. It's strange to me as I am the eldest of the four cousins, and while my warranties are all running out and my body is falling apart, my mind is still working fairly well. I'm very grateful for that. I never expected to live this long as I have had slight heart problems since I was in my forties and here I am. I will be ninety next September. I have chronic back pain from sciatica, stenosis, and arthritis, so I have no desire to break any age records. I'm lucky too because my family still care about me and are very good to me. I hear from my grandchildren who are out in California, Colorado, and Las Vegas, and they were all here to see me last spring, which was wonderful. I met several great-grandchildren of whom I had only seen pictures, and that was a joy. I have ten great-grandchildren now, and they are all normal healthy beautiful children. What a blessing! Carol lives the closest to me in Livonia and she is my rock. My son-in-laws, Jim and Ken, who lost Kathy and Barbara are my sons too and stay in close touch. Jim married again as he could not stand to live alone, but his wife goes along with all our family doings. I don't think Ken will ever marry again, but who knows? I certainly want them to be happy as they were both so wonderful to their wives. My son, Bill Jr., is still in Colorado and he's doing well. They come every summer to see me. My little granddaughter Sydney is ten already. Where do the years go? I'm glad you get to share Sally's grandchildren with her. They are such a miracle. How exciting that you folks are going to have one of your own soon. I'm happy for you.

Do you have any contact with your aunt Jean and Susan and Bob? I have not heard anything from them in quite awhile. I didn't get a Christmas card this year, which rather surprised me. I wonder about them too.

I was so happy when I heard that Sally and Bob have your folks home, and you can all get together there as you have always done. Nice to hear that everyone is doing OK.

Alice is still having a rough time from losing her twin but is hanging in there. She is down in the Cincinnati area. We don't see her as much as I would like, but we talk on the phone a lot.

I think I have bought you up to date on my family, and again, I really appreciate your writing to me. I really don't want to lose touch with you folks.

Sure hope the rest of the winter goes OK for everyone, and hopefully we will keep in touch.

Give my love and best wishes to all the family. God bless.

February 25, 2011

Postmaster of Dearborn
3800 Greenfield Road
Dearborn, Michigan 48121

Dear Sir,

A group of us here at Henry Ford Village were talking about what wonderful postal service we received from our Post Lady, Marianne Chochorowski, Route 26026. She is fast, efficient and friendly. She is the best we have ever had here. We all appreciate her excellent work. We also thought it was time that we let her boss know what a terrific job that she does for all of us as it is not an easy job.

Here are just a few names of the group that were talking, I know if we had passed a paper around for people to sign and join us in our "Thank You" we would have had hundreds more, just from CB 1 section. We just didn't take the time.

You have a true "gem" in Marianne and all of us "Thank" her from the bottom of our hearts.

Sincerely, Ralph and Gerri Bloom, Ethel Krepps, Colleen McSeveny, Billie Lange, Pat Carey, Doris Nieland, Rose Slessor, Johanna Kirkhart, Florence Goulin, Vivian Beeler

August, 2011

Eleventh Great-grandchild, Audrey Vivian Rivet:
August 10, 2011

Picture is of sister's in-laws—Charlotte, Me, Marguerette, and Robert—Brother-in-law. Both Marguerette and Charlotte live here at Henry Ford Village too.

It's hard to know where to start as so many things have been going on. First Cindy was due to have a cesarean for the baby on Friday, August 12. She went to the doctor for her checkup on Wednesday and they kept her. Little Audrey Vivian Rivet was born at 2:15 p.m. on Wednesday, August 10, 2011, weighing in at 7 pounds 13 ounces, 20 inches long with lots of dark hair and beautiful! Mother and baby are doing fine. I am very grateful as I did worry about them with Cindy's problems and high-risk pregnancy. Nothing is easy for Cindy though as she did develop an allergy from the latex or rubber in the bandages and had an itchy red rash that went all over her body. She was miserable. Evan also had a hand and mouth virus that could be catching, so there were no hospital visitors except Grandma Carol. Cindy had to be so careful of the medicines she took for allergies as she was nursing the baby, so the rash took longer to clear up, but finally it did. Carol did take me over to see Audrey Vivian on Tuesday, August 16. Audrey had just eaten and was sleeping, so I got to cuddle and hold her for almost an hour, and then we had to leave. She was so sweet and tiny. You forget how tiny they are—little miracles, with perfect ears, eyes, noses, fingers, and toes. I love the smell of new babies and the little squeaks and sounds they make when they are sleeping. Audrey does have lots of dark hair like her grandma Carol did when she was born. Our family circle is expanding, and I am grateful I am here to see some of it happening. Corbin is a big help with Evan. He plays with him a lot and keeps him occupied. Plus, he can lift him up for Cindy to dress and change or just to cuddle. Cindy is not allowed to lift anything yet over the baby's weight because of her cesarean. Corbin left last Sunday, the twenty-sixth, to go back to Washington. That is difficult for everyone. Corbin seems to be a very well-adjusted little boy leading two different lifestyles. He reads a lot and if I am in pain doesn't let me do a lot of things I would like to. Hopefully I will get help soon. We went back to my place, and the family insisted I sit and put my feet up and rest so I would be ready to go to Kiernan's for dinner. Ken came down at 5:00 p.m. to join us. It seemed so strange not to have Carol with us too, as she always has been before. She was busy taking care of the boys with Cindy in the hospital with Audrey. Cindy did come home on Saturday; that's when that rash really kicked in on her good.

We had a lovely dinner as usual. That's one of the favorite places to go when they come to visit. I had my 6 oz filet with salad and a wonderful baked potato, plus a glass of Riesling. I wanted to also mention how well Sydney looked for ways to help me. She would wait for me to slide out of the car. I had my cane with me, and she would get on my other side and hold my arm or have me put my arm on her shoulder to help me walk. No one had told her to do that outside of a general remark of "help Grandma." That gave me a nice warm feeling too. We came back to my place and I got my robe on, and all of us just relaxed and talked and talked again. Ken left about ten o'clock for home and Buoy. A *great day* altogether!

On Saturday, I had my usual hair appointment with Leila at 11:00 a.m. Sydney had said she wanted to go with me. She did get up and take her shower and was ready to go when I was. I love taking her with me and introducing her to people. Some she remembers meeting before when she has been here. When we got back upstairs, it was lunchtime, and we did go to Miller's for hamburgers. It was very good as usual. Back to my place, and they got ready and left for Joel's out in Milford for their annual "Toddfest." It was very *hot* with storms predicted for late afternoon. We did have storms go through with lots of wind, thunder, and lightning. Bill and Shannon said that everyone who wanted to swim got to swim before the storms came and o also use Joel's boat. His place is right on the lake and his backyard goes down to a nice beach. Carol took me out there a few years ago, so I could see everyone and see where Joel and Melissa lived. I had watched most of them grow up, marry, and start families, so it was very enjoyable for me. I do remember that it was a very hot day and I don't do too well when the temperatures get near ninety degrees, so we did not stay long. Sadly Joel and Melissa got divorced this year. Melissa told Joel that he wasn't making enough time for her and she didn't want to be married. They have two darling little girls, Aspen and Vivienne. It's very difficult for them, but it seems to be happening more and more these days. I think it is so great that all of them have remained such good friends and plan their vacation times around when Bill and Shannon come to Michigan to see me. Anyway, they had a good time with all their friends and got back here doing very well in his schoolwork, so that is all good. He will be back at Thanksgiving time. Evan misses him terribly and doesn't understand why Corbin is gone. Carol has been going over to help Cindy more with Corbin gone and Joe back to work. Little Audrey is a night owl just like Evan was, so sleep is a luxury for Cindy.

Bill, Shannon, and Sydney got here on the eleventh about 5:30 p.m. What a joy it was to see them! They all looked so good to me, and Sydney is getting taller and looking older. She is a beautiful young lady and so loving. Bill and Shannon are doing a great job parenting. Sydney is spoiled, in a way, with material things, but she has rules too that she has to follow and jobs to do to earn her allowance every week. She has a beautiful smile and is very outgoing. My friends here at the Village thought she was just delightful. Of course, this proud grandma was not going to disagree with them either. On Thursday evening being tired of traveling and the time change, they just ordered Jet's pizzas to eat. It tasted yummy to me. I was so happy to have them here. We just talked and talked. I gave them my bedroom again this year. As I've written before, I am much more comfortable sleeping in my La-Z-Boy.

Friday was kind of a nice lazy morning, then we were going to Miller's Bar for their special hamburgers. Bill and Shannon had rented a Ford Navigator. There was lots of room which worked out well. On the way to Miller's as we passed Chelio's restaurant, Bill said, "I've always wanted to try that place." So there was a minor change of plans. Anyone familiar with hockey or the Red Wings knows Chelio. He has a restaurant in Chicago too as that's where he grew up. We were all a little disappointed with the food, but it was an interesting place to see with all the Red Wings and hockey stuff. Bill said he was glad to see it and could say he had been there, but he does not plan to go back. After lunch, we went to The Wine Merchant store also in West Dearborn. They used to have a store in Troy and perhaps still do. There were several brothers, and they each ran their own wine store. They are well known in the area for having all kinds of different beers and wines and unusual things for parties. It's a fun store to look around in. Bill and Shannon got what they wanted for their Toddfest at Joel Snyder's in Milford on Saturday. We also stopped at Westborn Market, and I got some beautiful cherries. They were very protective of me and kept asking how I was doing. They hadn't planned on the wine store with me, but I asked them to go as I had not been there in years and remembered how interesting it was to walk through. Bill and I used to stop in there once in a while. I miss doing things like that. This is chronic around midnight. I sat dozing in my chair. Sydney went right to bed, but the three of us talked for another hour or so. I had had a very quiet afternoon and evening so felt rested.

On Sunday morning, they were up ahead of me to get ready for their trip to Silver Lake over by Lake Michigan. They had all made reservations at a resort there by the sand dunes. By they, I'm talking about Bill's Michigan friends who had been at "Toddfest" on Saturday. Every year they make plans to go somewhere for a few days together. They have been to "Kalahari" in Ohio, Cedar Point and Water Park, Animal Safari, all in Ohio too, also canoeing on the Au Sable River and camping out. That was the only one that I heard any complaints about. Some did not like camping out. I think I would go along with that. I like my modern conveniences. I had four days of quiet again and was very happy to see them on Wednesday evening when they got back here. They ordered pizzas again, but I had already eaten my dinner as I knew they were going to be late. We sat up talking again, and I heard all the nice and fun things they had done. The weather had been perfect for them, and I was happy about that. We have had a very hot summer. July broke all kinds of records for ninety-degree weather, and August was continuing. But it was nice for people by lakes.

On Thursday I had an 11:00 a.m. hair appointment for my birthday party on Friday evening. Sydney wanted her nails done, so she went with me again. Everyone loves to have her come and visit me. When we got back, Carol was here. It was the first that she had seen Bill, Shannon, and Sydney helping Cindy and Joe with their new little daughter. That's a first for their visits. We all went to lunch at Chili's, and then they brought Sydney and me back here, and they took off to get things for my party. Sydney and I had a nice afternoon together. We walked down and got my mail and said hello to a few more people. I rested, and Sydney read for a while and then watched the Disney Chanel on TV. They got back about 5:00 p.m., laughing, happy, and tired out. I asked what they done, and they told me that I could wait and find out at my party! I'm nosy and want to know what's going on, but it sounds like I'm just going to have to wait, doggone it. At least they told me that they had had a fun afternoon together. When they got ready, we went to Mongolian barbecue restaurant in West Dearborn for dinner. Bill took good care of me and helped me get my dinner before he got his. It's an interesting place, and the food is good. Sydney just stuck with steak and pasta noodles. We were then back at my place and just talked again. Shannon and Carol got together at my computer and were printing out family pictures that I had on it on a DVD. They spent almost three hours on that project and said it was fun. They had found out that the Edison room had this big movie screen where they showed movies in there. They asked and got permission to use it as they had come up with this idea of the CD with family pictures playing on it. It was close to midnight when Carol left for home to try and get a little sleep.

Friday, August 19, 2011—party day! What a day and an evening that I will never forget! Everyone except Sydney was up and taking turns with the shower. Alice and CC got here before noon. It was so good to see them, and it seemed like a long time since I had seen Alice. She looked good to me, *and* she had got her hair cut short again. She looks more like my Alice. I was so happy that she had finally done that. I think it makes her look younger. We decided to all go over to Leo's across the street. Alice and Carol both love those yero sandwiches, and we also got ompa saganaki, that Greek melted cheese with warm pita bread. It is so good. I just had a small Greek salad with my ompa. The rest seemed happy with what they ordered. We were back at my place as they wanted to see if the Edison room was ready to decorate, and they said it was. I had strict instructions to put my feet up and *rest!* I had asked to go and watch them decorate and got big *no's* from everyone. I was getting very antsy! And I have to admit nosy too, I guess.

Sydney came running back a couple of times, but she just said things were looking nice. Ken came about 2:30 p.m., and I called Bill's cell phone so someone could let him in over there. I heard later that he went with Bill to pick up some things from Westborn Market, and that helped Bill. They all got back here a little after four to freshen up and change clothes. I had already gotten ready. I wore that grey slub silk suit—Alfred Dunner of course. I wore a white sweater under the jacket with pink roses embroidered around the neckline with some sparkles in them. It was the outfit I had bought at the outlet store in Howell when Carol took me out there this spring. I had just worn it once before on Mother's Day when the family took me out for brunch at Fox Hills. They had told me that I could go over at five to see everything. I had warned them too that a lot of the people here came early to things. Sure enough, there were a couple of people waiting. I was so awestruck with how festive and beautiful the room looked that I don't even remember who was there early. They had a beautiful sunflower in the middle of the tables, chocolate candy bars with my name on them, and yellow napkins with my name in purple. I understand that Julie, Steve's wife, did the design for the balloons, candy bars and napkins. It was lovely, simple, and elegant. It made the tables look so nice. Then there were ninety plus yellow balloons saying, "Happy Ninetieth Birthday Vivian." They had hanging up everywhere. My birthday cake was a work of *art*. It had my yellows and oranges, peach and greens—all the designs were in pastel colors. It was gorgeous! Also it tasted as good as it looked we found out later—cherry nut and chocolate, two of my favorites. The cake was on a raised platform and got a lot of oohs and aahs. They had coffee and tea service, lemonade, pop, wine, or beer. They had fruit trays, cheese trays, veggie trays, all with dips and crackers with the cheese. They all came from Westborn Market, and again they were works of art.

The family told everyone as they came in to sit anywhere they wanted and to help themselves to the snacks because it would be a little while before dinner was served. Most of us who live here have got in the habit of eating dinner earlier than we used to in our homes. I was trying very hard to greet everyone as they came in, but I missed some when they came in a group. I felt very honored with so many of my friends and family there. I hadn't seen some of my nieces and nephews for a long time. That was special too. Some of the children I hadn't seen since they were babies, and now they are almost teenagers. Time does go by fast. Robert flew up from Florida. What a nice surprise! Flora was on a trip with her sister, which had been in the planning stages a couple of years. I just wish I would have had more time to talk to Robert. It seemed like I was talking to someone all the time though, and that evening went by much too fast. The caterers showed up with the dinner, and it looked delicious. There was chicken, meatballs, mosacholli, green beans, tossed salad and dressings, rolls that were different and very good. There was a lot of food, and people were invited to go back for seconds and some did. Everyone said it was very good. My stomach played its usual tune when I'm excited on either happy or sad occasions; it just knots up on me, and I can't eat. I had nibbled on some fruit and cheese, so I was fine. Alice and CC got in their restaurant mode and were serving drinks, mostly coffee and tea to the older people, and it did help. I was grateful for that too, and they are so good at that, making people feel special. I forgot to mention too that the DVD of family pictures over the years was playing on the big screen on the stage. There was no sound, but we didn't need that. It was fun to watch and just repeated over and over again, so it was running all the time.

Carol had made picture boards too, which were great! We had a lot of nice comments on those. That took a lot of her time too with everything else that was going on. The girls all worked together to serve the cake while Carol did the cutting. Susan pitched in and helped during the evening too. It was nice. No one seemed to be in a big hurry to get home; they sat and talked and had another cup of coffee. I got to talk a few minutes with Jean and Dar. I was so happy to see them. They were leaving on a trip to Portugal and Spain on September 2 and were looking forward to that. They both looked good to me. So many of Bill's Michigan friends came too—Joel and Paul Snyder, Mike and Maria Hess with Ava and Drake, Steve and Julie Williams with Megan, Nicole and Wylie, They all made me feel so good. Paul and Dawn Shiner had a family fiftieth wedding anniversary that same evening and felt badly they couldn't make it to my party. Those things happen, and they sent their good wishes with the others. It's so much fun to see all of them and their children as I have known most of the boys since Troy Elementary, Smith Middle School, or Athens High School—Boy Scouts, band, drama, fun. I met Aspen and Vivienne, Joel's little girls. Vivienne had drawn me a picture because our names were the same except spelled differently. She was only about five. I thought that was so sweet and special. I got several nice hugs from both the girls. It was nice to see Ava again, Mike and Maria's little girl. She is just a little older than Sydney, and they have been best friends since they were about three years old. They only see one another once a year when Sydney comes to Michigan, but they carry on every year as if there had been no separation. It's nice to see. I should say the same for the adults too. I do think that there a lot of e-mails back and forth over the year. I think it says a lot of good things about all of them. They haven't let life or distance interrupt their friendship. I know it makes me feel good.

Mike, Maria, Ava and Drake came back to my apartment for a little while after the party. That was nice too. When everyone left after telling me and different family members what a lovely party it was, I was sent home to get my robe on and *rest!* Boy! My kids are getting bossy. The family stayed and divided food as there was a lot left over. Joel and Paul got some for their canoe trip that they had postponed one day so they could make it to my party. Jim, Ken, Alice, and Carol took some too. Then they had to clean up the place and leave it in decent shape. They had ordered the beverage service from our caterers here at the Village, and they were telling me later how helpful they were. Also Steve, manager of St. Clair Dining Room, loaned them tongs for the fruit, cheese, and veggie trays. One of the women from catering got them the platform for the cake and covered it with white cloth so that the cake was displayed better. I know the table looked very festive and pretty with all the flowers and birthday decorations. When everyone got back to my apartment, they just sort of collapsed, and we all discussed the party. Mike, Maria, and the children came by for a little while too. The children went off in my bedroom to do their own thing. It was a wonderful evening!

Outside of the evening going by too fast for me, I thought it could not have been better. How I am going to thank everyone to let them know how special they made me feel and how grateful I am will be a challenge.

Saturday was a very lazy day for me. I was moving slower than usual. It was a nice day though as my family were still here. Carol came over, and Alice and CC were still here along with Bill, Shannon, and Sydney. Bill went after Tubby sandwiches for our lunch, and we all enjoyed. They have Subways out in Denver area but no Tubbys. Bill claims Tubbys are better. So once a year we have a Tubby sandwich. I don't have either one that often that I can compare. I had their original, and it tasted good. Ken came down shortly after lunch and brought Bouy. All of us enjoyed seeing her, and Bouy was very good. Again we just sat around and talked. Alice and CC left for home after lunch; as I said before, it was so good to see them. Alice called about 8:00 p.m. and said they were home safe and sound. It's always good to hear. We were all getting ready to go to Benihanna's for dinner when I decided not to go. I was still full from my Tubbys and so tired that the thought of all that food and sitting there for a couple of hours just threw me. I convinced the family that I was better off just staying home. Carol had brought Corbin with her as he needed a change from the new baby and doctors because of Cindy's rash. Carol said he really loved Benihanna's with the show the chef put on. It was his first time there. It is a fun place and the food is excellent, but I was very happy with my decision.

Later I had a piece of chicken from the party and a good roll and fresh fruit. That tasted good to me.

When the family got back, we sat and talked again. I had already got my robe on. We never seem to run out of things to talk about. Corbin was joining in playing with Sydney and was much more outgoing. It takes him a little while to warm up. He has always been very shy. He told Grandma Carol that he had a very good time, which was nice to hear. In fact, when Carol had first suggested going home, Corbin had asked if they could stay a little longer. It made me feel good too. It was another enjoyable day. I hate to think about them having to leave the next day.

On Sunday, August 21, Shannon and Bill were up fairly early as they had to get packed, We decided to have brunch downstairs at 11:00 a.m. I called the ladies I eat with and told them our plans and told them that if they would like to join us it would be at 11:00 am. They all showed up. They think my family is wonderful, and you already know how much I love them. Carol came for brunch too and to also be with them one last time for this year's visit. I'm so glad she could make it. I enjoy her company anytime and am so grateful that she lives close by. The ladies really had a ball eating with us as we always have a lot of laughs when we are together.

All good things have to have an ending, doggone. Bill, Shannon, and Sydney left for the airport about 1:30 p.m. It seems like every year it gets harder to say good-bye, until next time. I'm proud of myself though; I did not cry. I almost did and had to swallow extra hard. Carol left shortly after they did as she had things to do. She knew she would be helping Cindy as Joe had to go back to work. Corbin just has one more week. I spent the rest of the afternoon just kind of putzing around as I was restless and just couldn't seem to settle down until my back was screaming. I'd rest a bit and then do something else. Finally in the evening, I did settle in and watched something on TV. I cannot tell you now what I watched and it really does not matter. The weather was nice all the time they were here, which was another plus in a wonderful ten days. They were more *beautiful memories!*

I can't think of a better way to wrap up *Our Story* than on a happy note with my telling you about my wonderful ninetieth birthday party. I want to get this put together and printed while I am still able.

Life is a journey, and it is not always predictable. You think you have everything figured out, and you come to a bump, bend, or fork in the road. Looking back, I have no major regrets, and I certainly have never been bored. Losing our son-in-law and our daughters is something I will never get over. The most important thing is I have *loved* and been *loved!* What life has in store for me these last remaining years I have no idea. I just hope and pray I can handle it with dignity and courage.

I hope you will enjoy reading this, and some of my ramblings will help explain who I am.

In rereading this, I noticed that I repeated quite a few things and phrases, but I decided to leave it as I had written at that time. Remember, this was written over a ten-year period—bits and pieces here and there when the mood hit me to write. Then in the more recent years I used more letters as they told what was going on in my life at that time.

Vivian and her Girls

Favorite Family Recipes

Aunt Mae Weatherbee's Sour Cream Cookies

This recipe was given to me when I was a new bride in 1941. These have been a family favorite for a lot of years.

2 cups sugar
1/2 cup soft butter
Cream well together. Add three well-beaten eggs.
1/2 teaspoon salt
1 teaspoon soda
1 teaspoon baking powder
1 teaspoon vanilla
1 teaspoon lemon juice (can add grated lemon rind if desired)
1 cup sour cream

Alternately add sour cream and flour enough to handle well

Varies with type of sour cream and weather.

Usually 2 1/2 to 3 cups of flour

I find if I chill the dough after mixing, it is not quite so sticky as you do not want to use an over amount of flour. Makes a soft cake like cookie. Drop from spoon (small rounds) on greased cookie sheet. Bake ten to twelve minutes at 350 to 375 degree oven.

If you like pecans, they are excellent chopped and added to *cookie dough*.

Kathy's Chocolate Cherry Cake

1 box chocolate cake mix
1 can cherry filling
2 eggs
1 teaspoon almond flavoring (optional)
Mix together well. Spread in greased and floured jelly roll pan. Bake at 350 degrees for about twenty-five minutes.

Icing

1 cup sugar
5 tablespoons margarine
1/3 cup milk

Bring to boil. Boil one minute. Add 6 oz chocolate chips (1 cup). Stir until melted. Pour over cake—work fast as it turns fudgy and is hard to spread. Enjoy!

Grandma's Apple Crisp

For a large thirteen-by-nine-inch glass baking dish, melt 3 tablespoons of butter in bottom of pan. Peel and thinly slice eight to ten baking apples in bowl (be generous). Stir in about one cup of sugar. Use your judgment, depends on how tart the apples are. Also stir in one and a half to two teaspoons of cinnamon.

Put in baking pan (13" × 9"). Cover with Streusel topping (recipe below).

Streusel Topping

1/2 Cup Flour
1 Cup Oatmeal
1 Cup Brown sugar
1 Cup Chopped Nutmeats, Walnuts, or Pecans (your favorite)

Mix well. Pour on 1 stick (8oz) melted butter and again mix well. Pat on and cover apples. Bake for about one hour to one hour fifteen minutes at 350 degrees in oven. Cover pan for first half hour with foil. Then remove (so topping does not get too brown). Also, put tray or foil under to avoid chance of apple juice running over. Serve at warm or room temperature with sweetened whipped cream.

Serves 10 to 12

Pork Chops in Spanish Rice

Lightly brown four to six pork chops in small amount of cooking oil. Transfer from pan into a nine-by-thirteen-inch baking dish. In same fry pan, ·cook four to five slices diced ·bacon and one small chopped onion until bacon is crisp. Add one package of rice—a Roni Spanish rice—and brown as directed on package. Add tomatoes as directed and cook as directed on package. If desired, put one slice of raw onion on each chop. Spoon Spanish rice over pork chops. Cover with foil. Bake in 350-degree oven for about forty to fifty minutes. Remove foil for the last fifteen minutes. Serve and enjoy.

Tuna Fish Biscuits—Family Favorite

Depending on how many you plan on serving, follow recipe for Bisquick Biscuits—one batch or double recipe.

Pat or roll biscuit dough into a rectangle about half inch thick. Pat on tuna mixture, leaving about one-inch around edges. Roll up, starting with long side, into a jellyroll, seam on bottom. Cut into slices about one and a half inches thick. Lay on a greased baking pan. Bake at 375 to 400 degree in oven until golden brown. Serve with a sauce made from cream of celery soup. *Yum!*

Tuna Mixture

> One to two large cans of tuna, again depending on many you are serving. Drain and mix with finely chopped celery and onion. Use your own judgment on how much you like. Mix with just enough mayonnaise to hold together to pat on biscuit dough.

Sauce

Thin cream of celery soup with milk until desired, sort of like a gravy.
Heat and serve hot to spoon over tuna rolls.

Vivian

Flank Steak Pinwheels

Take one flank steak, rolled as tight as you can jellyroll fashion and freeze.
Slice thin while still half frozen and roll in Italian bread crumbs or plain
bread crumbs, then add Italian seasoning. Add egg, with small amount of
water. Beat with fork, and add salt and pepper to taste. Dip steak pinwheels
in bread crumbs, then egg, and then crumbs again. Amount depends on
how many you are doing at a time.

I made them and put on a wax paper-covered tray until ready to fry. Use
good cooking oil and a bit of butter if desired. Just enough to cover bottom
of fry pan. Fry until nicely browned, turn and do other side. May have to
add bit of oil. Keep warm in oven until all are cooked.

These can be baked in oven with a light dusting of cooking spray, but don't
have quite the flavor.

This recipe was given to me from an Italian square dance friend, Mickey
Bevak, in the 1950s. He had made them for one of our pot luck get-togethers.
Everyone loved them, and I have made them countless times since. I know
we have to watch our fried food intake, but good for a special treat. *Enjoy!*

Chicken Delectable: Serves 6

6 boneless, skinless chicken breasts
1 package dry onion soup mix
1/2 to 3/4 lb. sliced fresh mushrooms
1 can cream of mushroom soup
Lemon juice
1/2 cup light dry sherry
Butter
Salt
Pepper
Paprika

Place chicken breasts in flat baking dish. Sprinkle with salt, pepper, paprika, and package of dry onion soup mix. Sauté mushrooms in a little butter and lemon juice and sprinkle over chicken.

Mix sherry with cream of mushroom soup and pour over casserole. Cover tightly with foil and bake in 350-degree oven for about an hour and ten minutes. Remove foil the last fifteen minutes.

Strawberry Angel Food Whipped Cream Cake

    1 Angel food cake, sliced horizontally into three layers
    1 large package frozen sliced sweetened strawberries (drain juice)

Sprinkle one to two teaspoons plain gelatin over juice. Heat to dissolve gelatin, then cool and add strawberries. Chill. Add two cups heavy cream, whipped until stiff and sweetened to taste. Fold in thickened strawberries. Frost between layers, top, and sides of cake. Decorate with fresh strawberries if desired. Refrigerate until serving and *enjoy!*

This was a cake I used to make years ago, then Kathy took over and made for a lot of family birthday celebrations because it was so delicious. If you are going to be serving it very shortly after making and frosting it, you can skip the gelatin process. It just holds it up for a longer time period.

Cherry Dump Cake

    1 can (20 ounces) crushed pineapple, undrained
    1 can (21 ounces)} cherry pie filling
    1 package plain yellow cake mix
    12 tbs. (1 ½) sticks butter, melted
    1/2 cup frozen coconut thawed (optional)
    1 cup chopped pecans

Place rack in center of oven and preheat to 350 F. Spoon pineapple evenly over the bottom of ungreased thirteen-by-nine-inch pan. Cover the pineapple with the cherry pie filling. Pour the dry cake mix evenly over the fruit mixture so it reaches all the sides of the pan. Drizzle the entire pan with the melted butter. Sprinkle the coconut and pecans evenly over the top of the cake. Bake until the cake is a deep brown and toothpick inserted in center comes out clean (Fifty-five to sixty minutes). Serve warm with scoop of ice cream or whipped cream, just as good cold. Best to use a glass pan if you want to store leftover cake in fridge. Fruit will discolor a metal pan. If you are going to eat it all right away, it doesn't matter. Might lower oven temperature to 325 F for glass pan.

You can vary the flavor of this dump cake by using different pie fillings, such as peach or apple.

—Anne Byrn, *The Cake Doctor Cookbook*

Daughter—Carol—Me—Son—Bill
Lake Michigan in background April 2011

Edwards Brothers Malloy
Thorofare, NJ USA
July 5, 2012